German
Pocket Dictionary

German – English
Englisch – Deutsch

Berlitz Publishing
New York · Munich · Singapore

Original edition edited by the
Langenscheidt editorial staff

Project management: Heike Pleisteiner
Lexicographical work: Howard Atkinson,
Martin Fellermayer, Stuart Fortey, Heike Pleisteiner,
Robin Sawers, Karin Weindl

Inset cover photo: © Punchstock/MedioImages

This dictionary uses the standardised German spelling
system as of 2004.

This dictionary has been created with the help of dictionary databases owned by HarperCollins Publishers Ltd.

Neither the presence nor the absence of a designation
indicating that any entered word constitutes a trademark should be regarded as affecting the legal status
thereof.

07
08
09
10
11

© 2006 Berlitz Publishing/APA Publications GmbH & Co.
Verlag KG, Singapore Branch, Singapore

7.
6.
5.

Trademark Reg. U.S. Patent Office and other countries.
Marca Registrada.
Used under license from
Berlitz Investment Corporation.

Printed in Germany
ISBN 978-981-246-870-3 (vinyl edition)
ISBN 978-981-246-874-1 (UK paperback edition)

6

| *(check/ cheque)* | typical object of the equivalent German expression (in this case, 'cash a *check/cheque*') placed within brackets and *italicised* |
| einlösen | German equivalent of the English word in standard script |

Are all the entries structured in this way?

Every entry more or less follows the simple structure outlined above. The clear differentiation between various forms and meanings will lead you to the correct translation. In addition, the *italicised* information in brackets can denote a subject or object of the given word, or else it can indicate the general context in which the word is used:

> break up **1.** *vi* aufbrechen; (*meeting, organisation*) sich auflösen; (*marriage*) in die Brüche gehen (...) break down *vi* (*car*) eine Panne haben; (*machine*) versagen; (*person*) zusammenbrechen

What is the purpose of the information in *italics*?

Information in *italics*, with or without brackets, often provides a more precise indication of the different meanings of a word. This information might refer to synonyms (words with a similar meaning), possible subjects and objects, etc. and is included in order to indicate which translation should be used in any given context.

Italics are also used to provide grammatical information, as well as to clarify the meaning and use of a word for which there is no direct translation:

> Mehlspeise *f sweet dish made from flour, eggs and milk*

> Einwohnermeldeamt *nt registration office for residents*

What can I find under each entry?

Look at the following entry:

> cash 1. *n* Bargeld *nt*; *in ~* bar; *~*
> *on delivery* per Nachnahme
> 2. *vt* (*check/cheque*) einlösen

This example will serve to illustrate the main elements, which are itemised and explained below:

cash	the **word** itself in **bold print**
1.	Arabic numeral to differentiate between different parts of speech
n	part of speech (in this case, noun) in *italics*
Bargeld	German equivalent of the English word in standard script
nt	gender of the German equivalent (in this case, neuter) in *italics*
;	semi-colon used to separate the translation from the typical usages which follow
in ~	the expression *in cash* in **bold italics**
~	the swung dash as part of the expression stands for the main word **cash**
bar	German equivalent of the English expression in standard script
~ on delivery	the expression *cash on delivery* in **bold italics**
per Nachnahme	German equivalent of the English expression in standard script
2.	Arabic numeral to differentiate between different parts of speech
vt	part of speech (in this case, transitive verb) in *italics*

How to use this dictionary

Where do I find what I am looking for?

The **Universal German Dictionary** contains over 36,000 references, which are listed **in alphabetical order**. The only exceptions to this strict rule are **phrasal verbs**, which are entered directly under the simple verb form. This means, to take an example, that **keep back, keep off, keep out, keep to** and **keep up** are all entered directly under **keep**. The entry for the word **keeper** follows the phrasal verbs, although strictly speaking it ought to come alphabetically between **keep back** and **keep off**.

The letters **ä, ö** and **ü** are treated on the same basis as **a, o** and **u**. Thus the entry for **träumen**, for example, comes between **Traum** and **traumhaft**.

For the **pronunciation** of German words, see the notes on pages 9–14.

How do I find what I am looking for?

The structure of the individual entries is the same for both sections of the dictionary.

Each entry is structured using Arabic numerals (1, 2, 3 etc.). These can differentiate between different **parts of speech** (noun, adjective, adverb, verb, etc.):

> **search 1.** *n* Suche *f (for* nach); *do a ~ for* IT suchen nach; *in ~ of* auf der Suche nach **2.** *vi* suchen *(for* nach) **3.** *vt* durchsuchen

They can also differentiate between the different **meanings** of a word:

> **Druck 1.** *m* (*-(e)s, Drücke*) PHYS pressure; *fig* (*strain*) stress; *jdn unter ~ setzen* put sb under pressure **2.** *m* (*-(e)s, -e*) TYPO printing; (*product, typeface*) print

Contents

Translations of verbs are often followed by the prepositions which they take in *italics*. Equivalents are then given in standard script and the cases they take in *italics*.

> **inform** *vt* informieren (*of,
> about über + acc*); **keep sb
> ~ed** jdn auf dem Laufenden
> halten

For further information on the use of *italics*, you should refer to the **List of Abbreviations** on pages 15–16.

What is the purpose of cross-references?

Cross-references are always indicated by the → symbol. They usually refer you to another word of similar meaning or to an alternative spelling of the given word. When you look up the cross-referenced word, you will then find the translation(s) and other relevant information:

> **Januar** *m* (*-(s), -e*) January; →
> **Juni**
>
> **Juni** *m* (*-(s), -s*) June; **im ~** in
> June; **am 4. ~** on 4(th) June,
> on June 4(th) ; **Anfang/
> Mitte/Ende ~** at the be-
> ginning/in the middle/at
> the end of June; **letzten/
> nächsten ~** last/next June
>
> **homeopathic** *adj* (*US*) → **ho-
> moeopathic**
>
> **homoeopathic** *adj* homöo-
> pathisch

What is the purpose of the context indicators?

These help you to differentiate between the various meanings of a word and the contexts in which they are used:

> **dressing** *n* GASTR Dressing *nt*,
> Soße *f*; MED Verband *m*

The most common of these indicators are written in SMALL CAPITAL LETTERS and can be found in the **List of Abbreviations** on pages 15–16. Less common indicators are not abbreviated and are given in *italics*.

> **knight** *n* Ritter *m*; (*in chess*)
> Pferd *nt*, Springer *m*

How is the register of a word indicated?

This dictionary provides information on the following types of register: *fig* (figurative), *pej* (pejorative or derogatory), *fam* (familiar or informal) and *vulg* (vulgar). As far as possible, translations of words with such indicators have been chosen to reflect the same register. In other words, a vulgar German word or expression will be translated by a suitably vulgar English word or expression, and so on. These indicators can be found in the **List of Abbreviations** on pages 15–16.

What type of grammatical information can I find in this dictionary?

A list of the **Irregular German Verbs** contained in this dictionary can be found in the appendix on pages 596–599. Irregular verb forms are given in italics immediately after the verb and are also listed as separate entries:

> **schwimmen** (*schwamm, ge-*
> *schwommen*) *vi* swim
>
> **schwamm** *imperf of* **schwim-**
> **men**
>
> **geschwommen** *pp* *of*
> **schwimmen**

Irregular **plural forms**, as well as the **genitive forms**, are given after the relevant nouns:

> **Haus** *nt* (*-es, Häuser*) house;
> **nach** ~**e** home; **zu** ~**e** at
> home

The **List of Abbreviations** on pages 15–16 contains all the indicators for grammatical information used in this dictionary.

What can I find in the appendices?

In addition to the **Irregular German Verbs** mentioned above (pp. 596–599), the appendices also include chapters on **Numbers** (pp. 600–602), **European currency** (p. 603), the **States of Germany, Austria and Switzerland** (pp. 604–605), **Temperatures** (p. 606) and **Weights and measures** (pp. 607–608).

Notes on the pronunciation of German words

The rules governing the pronunciation of German words tend to be more straightforward than their English equivalents – and there are fewer exceptions. This means that you can apply these rules consistently without any great fear of being incorrect.

In order to help you understand the basic rules, we have divided our guidelines into the following sections: **consonants**, **vowels**, **stress**.

We have concentrated on those German sounds which follow different rules from their English equivalents and on those which do not exist in English at all.

Consonants

Silent consonants

The only silent consonant in German is **h**, which is silent or not depending on its position in a word. It is pronounced at the beginning of a word (as in **Held** *hero*) or between two vowels (as in the name **Johannes**). It is silent when it comes between a vowel and a consonant (as in **Fehler** *mistake*) and when it comes at the end of a word (as in **froh** *happy*).

When **h** is used in combination with other consonants (such as in **sch** and **ch**), different rules apply (see under **combinations of consonants**).

Single and double consonants

Most German single and double consonants are pronounced in the same way as their English equivalents.
The rules and examples below show **only** cases in which they are pronounced differently or (in the case of **ß**) do not exist in English at all.

conso- nant	rule	example
b	often pronounced **p** (as in the English hal**b** poet) at the end of a word,	
	sometimes at the end of a syllable	**Ab**stieg
c	pronounced **ts** (as in the English bits)	**C**D
	pronounced **k** (as in the English kite) in words of foreign derivation (most cases)	**C**annabis, **C**ola
d	often pronounced **t** (as in the English taxi) at the end of a word,	Lan**d**
	sometimes at the end of a syllable	un**d** so weiter
g	often pronounced **k** (as in the English kite) at the end of a word,	Zu**g**
	sometimes at the end of a consonant; pronounced **ch** (as in the Scottish loch*) if the word ends in -ig	Flu**g**zeug lusti**g**
h	see **silent consonants** (above)	
j	usually pronounced **y** (as in the English young)	**J**oghurt
q	pronounced **kv** in combination with the vowel **u**	**Qu**iz
r	rolled at the back of the mouth (similarly to the Scottish **r** sound)	**r**und
s	pronounced **z** (as in the English zebra) when it comes between two vowels	le**s**en

ß	pronounced **s** (as in the English six) never occurs at the beginning of a word	**Fußball**
t	pronounced **ts** (as in the English bits) when followed by the letters -ion	**Intuition**
v	mostly pronounced **f** (as in the English fork)	**verstehen**
	pronounced **v** (as in the English vote) in words of Greek or Latin derivation	**Veto**
w	pronounced **v** (as in the English vote)	**wo, Wunder**
z	pronounced **ts** (as in the English bits)	**Zunge**
*	This sound does not commonly exist in English. It can best be described by comparing it to the sound made at the beginning of the word *human* in the phrase '**a h**uman being'.	

Double consonants within one syllable always make the preceding vowel short (**Krabbe, paddeln, kommen, gewinnen, muss, fett**).

Combinations of consonants

In German, certain combinations of consonants (if they are pronounced as part of the same syllable) produce a sound which is not found in English. The most difficult for English native speakers is the following sound:

ch This combination produces a guttural sound which can best be described by comparing it to the sound made at the beginning of the word *human* in the English phrase '**a h**uman being'. However, the sound can be pronounced in two slightly different basic ways, depending on the vowel sound which precedes it: in a word such as **lachen** (*to laugh*), it is produced at the back of the throat (as in Scottish lo**ch***), whereas in **ich** (*I*) it is produced at the front of the mouth and sounds a little more like the English **sh** (as in fish).

The following consonant combinations also produce sounds different from their English equivalents:

chs	pronounced **ks** (as in the English kicks)	**Lachs, wachsen**
ng	always pronounced as in the English singer, never as in finger	**Hunger**
sch	always pronounced **sh** (as in the English shoe)	**Frosch, Schiff, verschwinden**
sp	at the beginning of a word or syllable, pronounced **shp** (as in the English phrase cash prize)	**Sport, verspätet**
st	at the beginning of a word or syllable, pronounced **sht** (as in the English phrase fish tank)	**Stein, verstehen**
th	always pronounced **t** (as in the English taxi)	**Thunfisch**
tsch	pronounced **ch** (as in the English chicken)	**Quatsch**
tz	pronounced **ts** (as in the English bits)	**Katze**

Vowels

Long and short vowel sounds

German vowel sounds can be long or short. Certain sounds (such as those produced by the letters **ä**, **ö** and **ü**) have no direct equivalent in English – in these cases we have given an approximation of the sound.

letter (-s)	vowel sound produced	example
a	short (close to the English fan)	**Hammer**
a, ah, aa	long (close to the English marmalade)	**Vater, Bahn, Aal**
ä	short (close to the English set)	**ändern**

ä, äh	long (close to the English b**ear**)	**Käfig, ähnlich**
e	short (as in the English w**e**t)	**endlich**
e, ee, eh	long (close to the English g**ay**, but with no concluding **y** sound)	**edel, Fee, Fehler**
i	short (as in the English **i**gloo)	**in, Kinn**
i, ie	long (as in the English f**ee**l)	**Kino, tief**
o	short (as in the English h**o**p)	**kommen**
o, oo, oh	long (close to the English f**o**ld)	**los, Moos, Kohl**
oh	long (close to the English m**ore**)	**Ohr**
ö	short (close to the English fl**i**rt, but shorter)	**können**
ö	long (close to the English fl**i**rt)	**Löwe**
u	short (as in the English f**u**ll)	**Mutter, unter**
u, uh	long (as in the English p**oo**l)	**tun, Kuh**
ü	short*	**dünn**
ü, üh	long (close to the English t**u**ne, but with a raised tongue)	**über, fühlen**

* There is really no English equivalent to this sound. The word **dünn**, for example can best be produced by pronouncing the English word **din** with pursed lips.

Diphthongs

A diphthong is in effect the combination of two vowel sounds. There are relatively few of these in German.

ei, ai	as in the English m**y**	**fein, Haifisch**
au	as in the English n**ow**	**August**
eu, äu	as in the English t**oy**	**neun, äußerst**

Stress

Most German words are stressed on the first syllable. The only major exception to this rule concerns words beginning with prefixes such as **be-**, **ent-** and **ver-**, which are usually stressed on the subsequent syllable (**be<u>a</u>ntworten**, **Ent<u>t</u>äuschung**, **ver<u>m</u>uten**).

Additionally, some words of foreign (especially Latin) derivation are stressed on the final syllable (**Caf<u>é</u>**, **Elef<u>ant</u>**, **Sold<u>at</u>**, **Stati<u>on</u>**).

Abbreviations

a.	also		*(Imperfekt)*
abbr	abbreviation	*impers*	impersonal
acc	accusative	*in cpds*	in compounds
acr	acronym	*indef*	indefinite
adj	adjective	*interj*	interjection
adv	adverb	*inv*	invariable
AGR	agriculture	*irr*	irregular
ANAT	anatomy	IT	IT, computing
art	article	*jdm*	jemandem
ART	fine arts	*jdn*	jemanden
ASTR	astronomy,	*jds*	jemandes
	astrology	*jmd*	jemand
AUTO	automobiles,	LAW	law
	traffic	LING	linguistics
AVIAT	aviation	*m*	masculine
BIO	biology	MATH	mathematics
BOT	botany	MED	medicine
Brit	British	METEO	meteorology
CHEM	chemistry	MIL	military
COMM	commerce	MUS	music
conj	conjunction	*n*	noun
contr	contraction	NAUT	nautical
dat	dative	*nom*	nominative
ELEC	electricity	*npl*	plural noun
esp	especially	*nsing*	singular noun
etw	etwas	*nt*	neuter
f	feminine	*num*	numeral
fam	familiar, informal	*or*	or
fig	figurative	*pej*	pejorative
FILM	film, cinema	PHOT	photography
FIN	finance	PHYS	physics
GASTR	gastronomy,	*pl*	plural
	cooking	POL	politics
gen	genitive	*pp*	past participle
hist	historically	*pref*	prefix
HIST	history	*prep*	preposition
imperf	past tense	*pron*	pronoun

pt	past tense	THEAT	theater/theatre
®	registered trade-mark	TV	television
		TYPO	typography, printing
RADIO	radio		
RAIL	railways	*US*	North American
REL	religion	*vaux*	auxiliary verb
sb	somebody	*vi*	intransitive verb
Scot	Scottish	*vr*	reflexive verb
sg	singular	*vt*	transitive verb
SPORT	sports	*vulg*	vulgar
sth	something	ZOOL	zoology
TECH	technology	~	swung dash
TEL	telecommuni-cations	→	refer to

A

à *prep + acc* at ... each; *4 Tickets à 8 Euro* 4 tickets at 8 euros each

A *abbr* = *Autobahn*; ≈ M (*Brit*), ≈ I (*US*)

Aal *m* (-(e)s, -e) eel

ab 1. *prep + dat* from; *von jetzt ~* from now on; *Berlin ~ 16:30 Uhr* departs Berlin 16.30; *~ Seite 17* from page 17; *~ 18* from the age of 18 **2.** *adv* off; *links ~* to the left; *~ und zu* (*or an*) now and then (*or* again); *der Knopf ist ~* the button has come off

abbauen *vt* (*tent*) take down; (*in number, degree*) reduce

abbeißen *irr vt* bite off

abbestellen *vt* cancel

abbiegen *irr vi* turn off; (*road*) bend; *nach links/rechts ~* turn left/right; **Abbiegespur** *f* filter lane

Abbildung *f* illustration

abblasen *irr vt fig* call off

abblenden *vt, vi* AUTO (*die Scheinwerfer*) ~ dip (*Brit*) (*or* dim (*US*)) one's headlights; **Abblendlicht** *nt* dipped (*Brit*) (*or* dimmed (*US*)) headlights *pl*

abbrechen *irr vt* break off;

(*building*) pull down; (*end*) stop; (*computer program*) abort

abbremsen *vt* brake, slow down

abbringen *irr vt jdn von einer Idee ~* talk sb out of an idea; *jdn vom Thema ~* get sb away from the subject; *davon lasse ich mich nicht ~* nothing will make me change my mind about it

abbuchen *vt* to debit (*von* to)

abdanken *vi* resign

abdrehen 1. *vt* (*gas, water*) turn off; (*light*) switch off **2.** *vi* (*ship, plane*) change course

Abend *m* (-s, -e) evening; *am ~* in the evening; *zu ~ essen* have dinner; *heute/morgen/gestern ~* this/tomorrow/yesterday evening; *guten ~!* good evening; Abendbrot *nt* supper; Abendessen *nt* dinner; Abendgarderobe *f* evening dress (*or* gown); Abendkasse *f* box office; Abendkleid *nt* evening dress (*or* gown); Abendkurs *m* evening class; Abendmahl *nt das ~* (Holy) Communion; **abends** *adv* in the evening; **montags ~** on Monday evenings

Abenteuer *nt* (-s, -) adventure; **Abenteuerurlaub** *m* adventure holiday

aber *conj* but; *(nevertheless)* however; **oder ~** alternatively; **~ ja!** (but) of course; **das ist ~ nett von Ihnen** that's really nice of you

abergläubisch *adj* superstitious

abfahren *irr vi* leave *(or depart) (nach* for); *(skier)* ski down; **Abfahrt** *f* departure; *(from motorway)* exit; *(in skiing)* descent; *(piste)* run; **Abfahrtslauf** *m (in skiing)* downhill; **Abfahrtszeit** *f* departure time

Abfall *m* waste; *(household)* rubbish *(Brit)*, garbage *(US)*; **Abfalleimer** *m* rubbish bin *(Brit)*, garbage can *(US)*

abfällig *adj* disparaging; **~ von jdm sprechen** make disparaging remarks about sb

abfärben *vi (in the wash)* run; *fig* rub off

abfertigen *vt (parcel)* prepare for dispatch; *(at the border)* clear; **Abfertigungsschalter** *m (at airport)* check-in desk

abfinden *irr* 1. *vt* pay off 2. *vr* **sich mit etw ~** come to terms with sth; **Abfindung** *f (money)* compensation; *(for*

employee) redundancy payment

abfliegen *irr vi (plane)* take off; *(passenger also)* fly off; **Abflug** *m* departure; *(becoming airborne)* takeoff; **Abflughalle** *f* departure lounge; **Abflugzeit** *f* departure time

Abfluss *m* drain; *(of washbasin)* plughole *(Brit)*; **Abflussrohr** *nt* waste pipe; *(outside)* drainpipe

abfragen *vt* test; IT call up

abführen 1. *vi* MED have a laxative effect 2. *vt (tax, charges)* pay; **jdn ~ lassen** take sb into custody; **Abführmittel** *nt* laxative

Abgabe *f* handing in; *(of ball)* pass; *(charge)* tax; *(of statement)* making; **abgabenfrei** *adj* tax-free; **abgabenpflichtig** *adj* liable to tax

Abgase *pl* AUTO exhaust fumes *pl*; **Abgas(sonder-)untersuchung** *f* exhaust emission test

abgeben *irr* 1. *vt (luggage, key)* leave *(bei* with); *(homework etc)* hand in; *(heat)* give off; *(statement, judgment)* make 2. *vr* **sich mit jdm ~** associate with sb; **sich mit etw ~** bother with sth

abgebildet *adj* **wie oben ~** as shown above

abgehen *irr vi (letters)* go; *(button etc)* come off; *(amount)* be taken off;

(*road*) branch off; ***von der Schule ~*** leave school; ***sie geht mir ab*** I really miss her; ***was geht denn hier ab?*** *fam* what's going on here?

abgehetzt *adj* exhausted, shattered

abgelaufen *adj* (*passport*) expired; (*time, period*) up; **die Milch ist ~** the milk is past its sell-by date

abgelegen *adj* remote

abgemacht *interj* OK, it's a deal, that's settled, then

abgeneigt *adj* **einer Sache** *dat* **~ sein** be averse to sth; **ich wäre nicht ~, das zu tun** I wouldn't mind doing that

Abgeordnete(r) *mf* Member of Parliament

abgepackt *adj* prepacked

abgerissen *adj* **der Knopf ist ~** the button has come off

abgesehen *adj* **es auf jdn/ etw ~ haben** be after sb/sth; **~ von** apart from

abgespannt *adj* (*person*) exhausted, worn out

abgestanden *adj* stale; (*beer*) flat

abgestorben *adj* (*plant*) dead; (*fingers*) numb

abgestumpft *adj* (*person*) insensitive

abgetragen *adj* (*clothes*) worn

abgewöhnen *vt* **jdm etw ~** cure sb of sth; **sich etw ~**

give sth up

abhaken *vt* tick off; **das (Thema) ist schon abgehakt** that's been dealt with

abhalten *irr vt* (*meeting*) hold; **jdn von etw ~** keep sb away from sth; (*prevent*) keep sb from sth

abhanden *adj* **~ kommen** get lost

Abhang *m* slope

abhängen 1. *vt* (*picture*) take down; (*trailer*) uncouple; (*pursuer*) shake off **2.** *irr vi* **von jdm/etw ~** depend on sb/sth; **das hängt davon ab, ob ...** it depends (on) whether ...; **abhängig** *adj* dependent (*von* on)

abhauen *irr* **1.** *vt* (*branch, arm etc*) cut off **2.** *vi fam* clear off; **hau ab!** get lost!, beat it!

abheben *irr* **1.** *vt* (*money*) withdraw; (*receiver, playing card*) pick up **2.** *vi* (*plane*) take off; (*rocket*) lift off; (*in card game*) cut

abholen *vt* collect; (*at station etc*) meet; (*with car*) pick up; **Abholmarkt** *m* cash and carry

abhorchen *vt* MED listen to

abhören *vt* (*vocabulary*) test; (*phone call*) tap; (*tape etc*) listen to

Abitur *nt* (*-s, -e*) German school-leaving examination, ≈ A-levels (*Brit*), ≈ High School Diploma (*US*)

abkaufen *vt* **jdm etw ~** buy sth

from sb; *das kauf ich dir nicht ab! fam* I don't believe you

abklingen *irr vi* (*pain*) ease; (*effect*) wear off

abkommen *irr vi* get away; *von der Straße* ~ leave the road; *von einem Plan* ~ give up a plan; *vom Thema* ~ stray from the point

Abkommen *nt* (-s, -) agreement

abkoppeln *vt* (*trailer*) unhitch

abkratzen 1. *vt* scrape off **2.** *vi fam* (*die*) kick the bucket, croak

abkühlen *vi, vr, vt* cool down

abkürzen *vt* (*word*) abbreviate; *den Weg* ~ take a short cut; **Abkürzung** *f* (*of word*) abbreviation; (*path*) short cut

abladen *irr vt* unload

Ablage *f* (*for documents*) tray; (*for whole office*) filing system

Ablauf *m* drain; (*of events*) course; (*of deadline*) expiry; **ablaufen** *irr vi* (*liquid*) drain away; (*events*) happen; (*deadline, passport*) expire

ablegen *vt* put down; (*clothes*) take off; (*habit*) get out of; (*exam*) take, sit; (*documents*) file away **2.** *vi* (*ship*) cast off

ablehnen 1. *vt* reject; (*invitation*) decline; (*be against*) disapprove of; (*applicant*) turn down **2.** *vi* decline

ablenken *vt* distract; *jdn von der Arbeit* ~ distract sb from their work; *vom Thema* ~ change the subject; **Ablenkung** *f* distraction

ablesen *vt* (*text, speech*) read; *das Gas/den Strom* ~ read the gas/electricity meter

abliefern *vt* deliver

abmachen *vt* take off; (*date, price etc*) agree; **Abmachung** *f* agreement

abmelden 1. *vt* (*newspaper*) cancel; (*car*) take off the road **2.** *vr* give notice of one's departure; (*from hotel*) check out; (*member*) cancel one's membership

abmessen *irr vt* measure

abnehmen *irr* **1.** *vt* take off, remove; (*receiver*) pick up; (*driving licence*) take away; (*money*) get (*jdm* out of sb); (*purchase, fam:* believe) buy (*jdm* from sb) **2.** *vi* decrease; (*slim*) lose weight; TEL pick up the phone; *fünf Kilo* ~ lose five kilos

Abneigung *f* dislike (*gegen* of); (*stronger*) aversion (*gegen* to)

abnutzen *vt, vr* wear out

Abonnement *nt* (-s, -s) subscription; **Abonnent(in)** *m(f)* subscriber; **abonnieren** *vt* subscribe to

abraten *irr vi jdm von etw* ~ advise sb against sth

abräumen *vt* *den Tisch* ~ clear the table; *das Ge-*

schirr ~ clear away the dishes; (*prize etc*) walk off with

Abrechnung *f* settlement; (*invoice*) bill

abregen *vr fam* calm (*or* cool) down; *reg dich ab!* take it easy

Abreise *f* departure; **abreisen** *vi* leave (*nach* for)

abreißen *irr* **1.** *vt* (*house*) pull down; (*sheet of paper*) tear off; *den Kontakt nicht ~ lassen* stay in touch **2.** *vi* (*button etc*) come off

abrunden *vt* **eine Zahl nach oben/unten ~** round a number up/down

abrupt *adj* abrupt

ABS *nt abbr* = ***Antiblockiersystem***, AUTO ABS

Abs. *abbr* = ***Absender***; from

absagen *vt* cancel, call off; (*invitation*) turn down **2.** *vi* decline; *ich muss leider ~* I'm afraid I can't come

Absatz *m* COMM sales *pl*; (*in text*) paragraph; (*of shoe*) heel

abschaffen *vt* abolish, do away with

abschalten *vt*, *vi a. fig* switch off

abschätzen *vt* estimate; (*situation*) assess; *jdn ~* size sb up

abscheulich *adj* disgusting

abschicken *vt* send off

abschieben *irr vt* (*asylum seeker etc*) deport

Abschied *m* (-(*e*)*s*, -*e*) parting;

~ **nehmen** say good-bye (*von jdm* to sb); **Abschiedsfeier** *f* farewell party

Abschlagszahlung *f* interim payment

Abschleppdienst *m* AUTO breakdown service; **abschleppen** *vt* tow; **Abschleppseil** *nt* towrope; **Abschleppwagen** *m* breakdown truck (*Brit*), tow truck (*US*)

abschließen *irr vt* (*door*) lock; (*bring to an end*) conclude, finish; (*agreement, deal*) conclude; **Abschluss** *m* close, conclusion; (*of agreement, deal*) conclusion

abschmecken *vt* (*sample*) taste; (*with salt etc*) season

abschminken *vt* **1.** *vr* take one's make-up off **2.** *vt fam* **sich** *dat etw ~* get sth out of one's mind

abschnallen *vr* undo one's seatbelt

abschneiden *irr vt* **1.** *vt* cut of **2.** *vi gut/schlecht ~* do well/badly

Abschnitt *m* (*of book, text*) section; (*of cheque, ticket*) stub

abschrauben *vt* unscrew

abschrecken *vt* deter, put off

abschreiben *irr vt* copy (*bei, von* from, off); (*give up on*) write off; COMM deduct

abschüssig *adj* steep

abschwächen *vt* lessen; (*statement, criticism*) tone

down

abschwellen irr vi (inflammation) go down; (noise) die down

absehbar adj foreseeable; **in ~er Zeit** in the foreseeable future; **absehen** irr **1.** vt (end, consequences) foresee **2.** vi **von etw ~** refrain from sth

abseits 1. adv out of the way; SPORT offside **2.** prep + gen away from; **Abseits** nt SPORT offside; **Abseitsfalle** f SPORT offside trap

absenden irr vt send off; (letter etc) post; **Absender(in)** m(f) (-s, -) sender

absetzen 1. vt (glass, spectacles etc) put down; (passenger) drop (off); COMM sell; FIN deduct; (cancel) drop **2.** vr (leave) clear off; (mud etc) be deposited

Absicht f intention; **mit ~** on purpose; **absichtlich** adj intentional, deliberate

absolut adj absolute

abspecken vi fam lose weight

abspeichern vt IT save

absperren vt block (or close) off; (door) lock; **Absperrung** f blocking (or closing) off; (obstacle) barricade

abspielen 1. vt (CD etc) play **2.** vr happen

abspringen irr vi jump down / off; (participant) drop out (von di)

abspülen vt rinse; (dishes)

wash (up)

Abstand m distance; (time gap) interval; **~ halten** keep one's distance

abstauben vt, vi dust; fam (steal) pinch

Abstecher m (-s, -) detour

absteigen irr vi (from bicycle etc) get off, dismount; (at hotel) stay (in + dat at)

abstellen vt (bag, tray etc) put down; (car) park; (light, machine etc) turn (or switch) off; (bad practice etc) stop; **Abstellraum** m store room

Abstieg m (-(e)s, -e) (from mountain) descent; SPORT relegation

abstimmen 1. vi vote **2.** vt (aims, dates) fit in (auf + acc with); **Dinge aufeinander ~** coordinate things **3.** vr come to an agreement (or arrangement)

abstoßend adj repulsive

abstrakt adj abstract

abstreiten irr vt deny

Abstrich m MED smear; **~e machen** cut back (an + dat on); (expect less) lower one's sights

Absturz m fall; AVIAT, IT crash; **abstürzen** vi fall; AVIAT, IT crash

absurd adj absurd

Abszess m (-es, -e) abscess

abtauen vt, vi thaw; (fridge) defrost

Abtei f (-, -en) abbey

Abteil nt (-(e)s, -e) compartment

Abteilung f (in firm, department store) department; (in hospital) section

abtreiben irr **1.** vt (child) abort **2.** vi be driven off course; MED carry out an abortion; (pregnant woman) have an abortion; **Abtreibung** f abortion

abtrocknen vt dry

abwarten 1. vt wait for; **das bleibt abzuwarten** that remains to be seen **2.** vi wait

abwärts adv down

Abwasch m (-(e)s) washing-up; **abwaschen** irr vt (dirt) wash off; (dishes) wash (up)

Abwasser nt (-s, Abwässer) sewage

abwechseln vr alternate; **sich mit jdm ~** take turns with sb; **abwechselnd** adv alternately; **Abwechslung** f change; **zur ~** for a change

abweisen irr vt turn away; (application) turn down; **abweisend** adj unfriendly

abwesend adj absent; **Abwesenheit** f absence

abwiegen irr vt weigh (out)

abwischen vt (face, table etc) wipe; (dirt) wipe off

abzählen vt count; (money) count out

Abzeichen nt badge

abzeichnen 1. vt draw, copy; (document) initial **2.** vr stand out; fig (be imminent) loom

abziehen irr **1.** vt take off;

(bed) strip; (key) take out; (number, amount) take away, subtract **2.** vi go away

Abzug m (photo) print; (opening) vent; (of troops) withdrawal; (of amount) deduction; **nach ~ der Kosten** charges deducted; **abzüglich** prep + gen minus; **~ 20% Rabatt** less 20% discount

abzweigen 1. vi branch off **2.** vt set aside; **Abzweigung** f junction

Accessoires pl accessories pl

ach interj oh; **~ so!** oh, I see; **~ was!** (surprised) really?; (annoyed) don't talk nonsense

Achse f (-, -n) axis; AUTO axle

Achsel f (-, -n) shoulder; armpit

acht num eight; **heute in ~ Tagen** in a week's (time), a week from today

Acht f(-) **sich in ~ nehmen** be careful (vor + dat of), watch out (vor + dat for); **~ geben** take care (auf + acc of); **etw außer ~ lassen** disregard sth

achte(r, s) adj eighth; → **dritte**; **Achtel** nt (-s, -) (fraction) eighth; (liquid measure) eighth of a litre; (glass of wine) ≈ small glass

achten 1. vt respect **2.** vi pay attention (auf + acc to)

Achterbahn f big dipper, roller coaster

achthundert num eight hundred; **achtmal** adv eight

times

Achtung 1. f attention; (esteem) respect **2.** interj look out

achtzehn num eighteen; **achtzehnte(r, s)** adj eighteenth; → **dritte**; **achtzig** num eighty; **in den ~er Jahren** in the eighties; **achtzigste(r, s)** adj eightieth

Acker m (-s, Äcker) field

Action f (-, -s) fam action; **Actionfilm** m action film

Adapter m (-s, -) adapter

addieren vt add (up)

Adel m (-s) nobility; **adelig** adj noble

Ader f (-, -n) vein

Adjektiv nt adjective

Adler m (-s, -) eagle

adoptieren vt adopt; **Adoption** f adoption; **Adoptiveltern** pl adoptive parents pl; **Adoptivkind** nt adopted child

Adrenalin nt (-s) adrenalin

Adressbuch nt directory; (personal) address book; **Adresse** f (-, -n) address; **adressieren** vt address (an + acc to)

Advent m (-s, -e) Advent; **Adventskranz** m Advent wreath

Adverb nt adverb

Aerobic nt (-s) aerobics sg

Affäre f (-, -n) affair

Affe m (-n, -n) monkey

Afghanistan nt (-s) Afghanistan

Afrika nt (-s) Africa; **Afrikaner(in)** m(f) (-s, -) African; **afrikanisch** adj African

After m (-s, -) anus

Aftershave nt (-(s), -s) aftershave

AG f (-, -s) abbr = **Aktiengesellschaft**; plc (Brit), corp. (US)

Agent(in) m(f) agent; **Agentur** f agency

aggressiv adj aggressive

Ägypten nt (-s) Egypt

ah interj ah, ooh

äh interj er, um; (disgusted) ugh

aha interj I see, aha

ähneln 1. vi + dat be like, resemble **2.** vr be alike (or similar)

ahnen vt suspect; **du ahnst es nicht!** would you believe it?

ähnlich adj similar (dat to); **jdm ~ sehen** look like sb; **Ähnlichkeit** f similarity

Ahnung f idea; (vague) suspicion; **keine ~** no idea; **ahnungslos** adj unsuspecting

Ahorn m (-s, -e) maple

Aids nt (-) Aids; **aidskrank** adj suffering from Aids; **aidspositiv** adj tested positive for Aids; **Aidstest** m Aids test

Airbag m (-s, -s) AUTO airbag; **Airbus** m airbus

Akademie f (-, -n) academy; **Akademiker(in)** m(f) (-s, -) (university) graduate

akklimatisieren vr acclimatize oneself

Akkordeon nt (-s, -s) accordion

Akku m (-s, -s) (storage) battery

Akkusativ m accusative (case)

Akne f (-, -) acne

Akrobat(in) m(f) (-s, -en) acrobat

Akt m (-(e)s, -e) act; ART nude

Akte f (-, -n) file; *etw zu den ~n legen* a. fig file sth away; **Aktenkoffer** m briefcase

Aktie f (-, -n) share; **Aktiengesellschaft** f public limited company (Brit), corporation (US)

Aktion f campaign; (military, police) operation

Aktionär(in) m(f) (-s, -e) shareholder

aktiv adj active

aktualisieren vt update; **aktuell** adj (subject) topical; (modern) up-to-date; (problem) current; *nicht mehr ~* no longer relevant

Akupunktur f acupuncture

akustisch adj acoustic; **Akustik** f acoustics sg

akut adj acute

AKW nt (-s, -s) abbr = **Atomkraftwerk**; nuclear power station

Akzent m (-(e)s, -e) accent; (emphasis) stress; *mit starkem schottischen ~* with a strong Scottish accent

akzeptieren vt accept

Alarm m (-(e)s, -e) alarm; **Alarmanlage** f alarm system; **alarmieren** vt alarm; *die Polizei ~* call the police

Albanien nt (-s) Albania

Albatros m (-ses, -se) albatross

albern adj silly

Albtraum m nightmare

Album nt (-s, Alben) album

Algen pl algae pl, seaweed sg

Algerien nt (-s) Algeria

Alibi nt (-s, -s) alibi

Alimente pl maintenance sg

Alkohol m (-s, -e) alcohol; **alkoholfrei** adj non-alcoholic; *~es Getränk* soft drink; **Alkoholiker(in)** m(f) (-s, -) alcoholic; **alkoholisch** adj alcoholic

All nt (-s) universe

alle(r, s) 1. pron all; *~ Passagiere* all passengers; *wir ~* all of us; *them; ~ beide* both of us/you/them; *vier Jahre* every four years; *~ 100 Meter* every 100 metres; → *alles* 2. adv fam finished

Allee f (-, -n) avenue

allein adj, adv alone; (unaided) on one's own, by oneself; *nicht ~* not only; *~ erziehende Mutter* single mother; *~ stehend* single, unmarried; **Alleinerziehende(r)** mf single mother/father/parent

allerbeste(r, s) adj very best

allerdings adv admittedly; (definitely) certainly, sure

(US)

allererste(r, s) adj very first; **zu allererst** first of all

Allergie f allergy; **Allergiker(in)** m(f) (-s, -) allergy sufferer; **allergisch** adj allergic (gegen to)

allerhand adj inv fam all sorts of; **das ist doch ...!** (reproaching) that's the limit; **...!** (praising) that's pretty good

Allerheiligen nt (-) All Saints' Day

allerhöchste(r, s) adj very highest; **allerhöchstens** adv at the very most; **allerletzte(r, s)** adj very last; **allerwenigste(r, s)** adj very least

alles pron everything; **~ in allem** all in all; → **alle**

Alleskleber m (-s, -) all-purpose glue

allgemein adj general; **im Allgemeinen** in general

Alligator m (-s, -en) alligator

alljährlich adj annual

allmählich 1. adj gradual **2.** adv gradually

Allradantrieb m all-wheel drive

Alltag m everyday life; **alltäglich** adj everyday; (average) ordinary; (life, walk etc) daily

allzu adv all too

Allzweckreiniger m (-s, -) multi-purpose cleaner

Alpen pl **die ~** the Alps pl

Alphabet nt (-(e)s, -e) alpha-

bet; **alphabetisch** adj alphabetical

Alptraum m → **Albtraum**

als conj (comparison) than; (time) when; **das Zimmer ist größer ~ das andere** this room is bigger than the other; **das Essen war billiger ~ ich erwartet hatte** the meal was cheaper than I expected (it to be); **~ Kind** as a child; **nichts ~ (Ärger)** nothing but (trouble); **anders ~** different from; **erst ~** only when; **~ ob** as if

also 1. conj so, therefore **2.** adv, interj so; **~ gut** (or **schön**)! okay then

alt adj old; **wie ~ sind Sie?** how old are you?; **28 Jahre ~** 28 years old; **vier Jahre älter** four years older

Altar m (-(e)s, Altäre) altar

Alter nt (-s, -) age; (last period of life) old age; **im ~ von** at the age of; **er ist in meinem ~** he's my age

alternativ adj alternative; (concerned for the environment) ecologically minded; (farming) organic; **Alternative** f alternative

Altersheim nt old people's home

Altglas nt used glass; **Altglascontainer** m bottle bank; **altmodisch** adj old-fashioned; **Altöl** nt used (or waste) oil; **Altpapier** nt waste paper; **Altstadt** f old town

Alt-Taste *f* Alt key

Alufolie *f* tin (*or* kitchen) foil

Aluminium *nt* (-s) aluminium (*Brit*), aluminum (*US*)

Alzheimerkrankheit *f* Alzheimer's (disease)

am *contr of* **an dem**; ~ **2. Januar** on January 2(nd); ~ **Morgen** in the morning; ~ **Strand** on the beach; ~ **Bahnhof** at the station; **was gefällt Ihnen ~ besten?** what do you like best?; ~ **besten bleiben wir hier** it would be best if we stayed here

Amateur(in) *m(f)* amateur

ambulant *adj* outpatient; **kann ich ~ behandelt werden?** can I have it done as an outpatient?; **Ambulanz** *f* ambulance; (*in hospital*) outpatients' department

Ameise *f* (-, -n) ant

amen *interj* amen

Amerika *nt* (-s) America; **Amerikaner(in)** *m(f)* (-s, -) American; **amerikanisch** *adj* American

Ampel *f* (-, -n) traffic lights *pl*

Amphitheater *nt* amphitheatre

Amsel *f* (-, -n) blackbird

Amt *nt* (-(e)s, Ämter) office, department; (*governmental agency*) office, department; (*position*) post; **amtlich** *adj* official; **Amtszeichen** *nt* TEL dialling tone (*Brit*), dial tone (*US*)

amüsant *adj* amusing; **amü-**

sieren **1.** *vt* amuse **2.** *vr* enjoy oneself, have a good time

an 1. *prep* + *dat* ~ **der Wand** on the wall; ~ **der Themse** on the Thames; **alles ist ~ seinem kalten Platz** everything is in its place; ~ **einem kalten Tag** on a cold day; ~ **Ostern** at Easter **2.** *prep* + *acc* ~ **die Tür klopfen** knock at the door; **ans Meer fahren** go to the seaside; ~ **die 40 Grad** nearly 40 degrees **3.** *adv* **von ... ~** from ... on; **das Licht/ Radio ist ~** the light/radio is on

anal *adj* anal

analog *adj* analogous; IT analog

Analyse *f* (-, -n) analysis; analysieren *vt* analyse

Ananas *f* (-, - *or* -se) pineapple

anbaggern *vt fam* chat up (*Brit*), come on to (*US*)

Anbau *m* AGR cultivation; (*building*) extension; **anbauen** *vt* AGR cultivate; (*garage etc*) build on

anbehalten *irr vt* keep on

anbei *adv* enclosed; ~ **sende ich ...** please find enclosed ...

anbeten *vt* worship

anbieten *irr* **1.** *vr* offer **2.** *vr* volunteer

anbinden *irr vt* tie up

Anblick *m* sight

anbraten *irr vt* brown

anbrechen *irr* **1.** *vt* start; (*reserves, savings*) break into;

(*bottle*, *packet*) open **2.** *vi*
start; (*day*) break; (*night*) fall
anbrennen *irr vt*, *vi* burn; **das
Fleisch schmeckt ange-
brannt** the meat tastes burnt
anbringen *irr vt* (*along with
one*) bring; (*fasten*) fix, attach

Andacht *f* (-, *-en*) devotion;
(*church service*) prayers *pl*
andauern *vi* continue, go on;
andauernd *adj* continual
Andenken *nt* (*-s*, -) memory;
(*object*) souvenir
andere(r, s) *adj* other; (*not
the same*) different; (*following*) next; **am ~n Tag** the
next day; **von etw/jmd ~m
sprechen** talk about sth/sb
else; **unter ~m** among other
things; **andererseits** *adv* on
the other hand
ändern 1. *vt* alter, change **2.** *vr*
change
andernfalls *adv* otherwise
anders *adv* differently (*als
from*); **jemand/irgendwo ~**
someone/somewhere else;
sie ist ~ als ihre Schwester
she's not like her sister; **es
geht nicht ~** there's no other
way; **anders(he)rum** adv the
other way round; **anderswo**
adv somewhere else
anderthalb *num* one and a
half
Änderung *f* change, alteration
andeuten *vt* indicate; (*indirectly*) hint at

Andorra *nt* (-s) Andorra
Andrang *m* **es herrschte großer ~** there was a huge crowd
androhen *vt* **jdm etw ~** threat-
en sb with sth
aneinander *adv* at/on/to
one another (*or* each other);
~ denken think of each other; **~ geraten** clash; **sich ~
gewöhnen** get used to each
other; **~ legen** put together
Anemone *f* (-, -n) anemone
anerkennen *irr vt* (*country,
certificate etc*) recognize; (*efforts etc*) appreciate; **Anerkennung** *f* recognition; (*of
efforts etc*) appreciation
anfahren *irr* **1.** *vt* (*pedestrian*)
run into; (*place*, *port*) stop
(*or* call) at; (*goods*) deliver;
jdn ~ fig (*verbally*) jump on
sb **2.** *vi* start; (*in car*) drive
off
Anfall *m* MED attack; **anfällig**
adj delicate; (*machine*) temperamental; **~ für** prone to
Anfang *m* (-(*e*)*s*, *Anfänge*) beginning, start; **zu/am ~** to
start with; **~ Mai** at the beginning of May; **sie ist ~ 20**
she's in her early twenties;
anfangen *irr vt*, *vi* begin,
start; **damit kann ich nichts
~** that's no use to me; **Anfän-
ger(in)** *m(f)* (-s, -) beginner;
anfangs *adv* at first; **An-
fangsbuchstabe** *m* first (*or*
initial) letter
anfassen 1. *vt* touch **2.** *vi*
kannst du mal mit ~? can

you give me a hand? **3.** *vr* **sich weich ~** feel soft

Anflug *m* AVIAT approach; (*small amount*) trace

anfordern *vt* demand; **Anforderung** *f* request (*von* for); (*on sb or sth*) demand

Anfrage *f* inquiry

anfreunden *vr* **sich mit jdm ~** make (*or* become) friends with sb

anfühlen *vr* feel; **es fühlt sich gut an** it feels good

Anführungszeichen *pl* quotation marks *pl*

Angabe *f* TECH specification; *fam* (*swanking*) showing off; (*in tennis*) serve; **~n** *pl* (*information*) particulars *pl*; **die ~n waren falsch** the information was wrong; **angeben** *irr* **1.** *vt* (*name, reason*) give; (*temperature, time etc*) indicate; (*course, pace*) set **2.** *vi fam* boast; SPORT serve; **Angeber(in)** *m(f)* (*-s, -*) *fam* show-off; **angeblich** *adj* alleged

angeboren *adj* inborn

Angebot *nt* offer; COMM supply (*an* + *dat* of); **~ und Nachfrage** supply and demand

angebracht *adj* appropriate

angebunden *adj* **kurz ~** curt

angeheitert *adj* tipsy

angehen *irr vt* concern; **das geht dich nichts an** that's none of your business; **ein Problem ~** tackle a problem;

was ihn angeht as far as he's concerned, for him **2.** *vi* (*fire*) catch; *fam* (*start*) begin; **angehend** *adj* prospective

Angehörige(r) *mf* relative

Angeklagte(r) *mf* accused, defendant

Angel *f* (*-, -n*) fishing rod; (*of door*) hinge

Angelegenheit *f* affair, matter

Angelhaken *m* fish hook; **angeln 1.** *vt* catch **2.** *vi* fish; **Angeln** *nt* (*-s*) angling, fishing; **Angelrute** *f* (*-, -n*) fishing rod

angemessen *adj* appropriate, suitable

angenehm *adj* pleasant; **~!** pleased to meet you; **das ist mir gar nicht ~** I don't like the idea of that

angenommen 1. *adj* assumed **2.** *conj* **~, es regnet, was machen wir dann?** suppose it rains, what do we do then?

angesehen *adj* respected

angesichts *prep* + *gen* in view of, considering

Angestellte(r) *mf* employee

angetan *adj* **von jdm/ etw ~ sein** be impressed by (*or* taken with) sb/ sth

angewiesen *adj* **auf jdn/ etw ~ sein** be dependent on sb/ sth

angewöhnen *vt* **sich etw ~** get used to doing sth; **Angewohnheit** *f* habit

Angina f (-, Anginen) tonsillitis; **Angina Pectoris** f (-) angina

Angler(in) m(f) (-s, -) angler

Angora nt (-s) angora

angreifen irr vt attack; (with hand) touch; (harm) damage; **Angriff** m attack; **etw in ~ nehmen** get started on sth

Angst f (-, Ängste) fear; **~ haben** be afraid (or scared) (vor + dat of); **jdm ~ machen** scare sb; **ängstigen 1.** vt frighten **2.** vr worry (um, wegen + dat about); **ängstlich** adj nervous; (anxious) worried

anhaben irr vt (clothes) have on, wear; (light) have on

anhalten irr vi stop; (carry on) continue; **anhaltend** adj continuous; **Anhalter(in)** m(f) (-s, -) hitch-hiker; **per ~ fahren** hitch-hike

anhand prep + gen with; **~ von** by means of

anhängen vt hang up; RAIL (carriages) couple; (something extra) add (on); **jdm etw ~** (blame) pin sth on sb; **Anhänger** m (-s, -) AUTO trailer; (on suitcase) tag; (jewellery) pendant; **Anhänger(in)** m(f) (-s, -) supporter; **Anhängerkupplung** f towbar; **anhänglich** adj affectionate; pej clinging

Anhieb m **auf ~** straight away; **das kann ich nicht auf ~ sa-**

gen I can't say offhand

anhimmeln vt worship, idolize

anhören 1. vt listen to **2.** vr sound; **das hört sich gut an** that sounds good

Animateur(in) m(f) host/hostess

Anis m (-es, -e) aniseed

Anker m (-s, -) anchor; **ankern** vt, vi anchor; **Ankerplatz** m anchorage

Ankleidekabine f changing cubicle

anklicken vt IT click on

anklopfen vi knock (an + acc on)

ankommen irr vi arrive; **bei jdm gut ~** go down well with sb; **es kommt darauf an** it depends (ob on whether); **darauf kommt es nicht an** that doesn't matter

ankotzen vt vulg **es kotzt mich an** it makes me sick

ankreuzen vt mark with a cross

ankündigen vt announce

Ankunft f (-, Ankünfte) arrival; **Ankunftszeit** f arrival time

Anlage f (tendency) disposition; (aptitude) talent; (park) gardens pl, grounds pl; (in letter etc) enclosure; (for CDs etc) stereo (system); TECH plant; FIN investment

Anlass m (-es, Anlässe) cause (zu for); (event) occasion; **aus diesem ~** for this reason; **anlassen** irr vt (engine) start; (light, garment) leave on; **Anlasser** m (-s, -) AUTO starter; **anlässlich** prep + gen on the occasion of

Anlauf m run-up; **anlaufen** irr vi begin; (film) open; (window) mist up; (metal) tarnish

anlegen 1. vt put (an + acc against / on); (jewellery) put on; (garden) lay out; (money) invest; (gun) aim (auf + acc at); **es auf etw acc ~** be out for sth **2.** vi (ship) berth, dock **3.** vr **sich mit jdm ~** fam pick a quarrel with sb; **Anlegestelle** f moorings pl

anlehnen 1. vt lean (an + acc against); (door) leave ajar **2.** vr lean (an + acc against)

anleiern vt **etw ~** fam get sth going

Anleitung f instructions pl

Anliegen nt (-s, -) matter; (question) request

Anlieger(in) m(f) (-s, -) resident; **~ frei** residents only

anlügen vt irr lie to

anmachen vt (fasten) attach; (light, TV etc) switch on; (salad) dress; fam (excite) turn on; fam (talk to) chat up (Brit), come on to (US); fam (attack verbally) have a go at

Anmeldeformular nt application form; (for registering with the authorities) registration form; **anmelden 1.** vt

(visit etc) announce **2.** vr (with doctor etc) make an appointment; (with the authorities, for course etc) register; **Anmeldeschluss** m deadline for applications, registration deadline; **Anmeldung** f registration; (request) application

annähen vt **einen Knopf (an den Mantel) ~** sew a button on (one's coat)

annähernd adv roughly; **nicht ~** nowhere near

Annahme f (-, -n) acceptance; (supposition) assumption; **annehmbar** adj acceptable; **annehmen** irr vt accept; (name) take; (child) adopt; (take as true) suppose, assume

Annonce f (-, -n) advertisement

anöden vt fam bore stiff (or silly)

annullieren vt cancel

anonym adj anonymous

Anorak m (-s, -s) anorak

anpacken vt (problem, task) tackle; **mit ~** lend a hand

anpassen 1. vt fig adapt (dat to) **2.** vr adapt (an + acc to)

anpfeifen irr vt **das Spiel ~** start the game; **Anpfiff** m SPORT (starting) whistle; (start) kick-off; fam (reprimand) roasting

anprobieren vt try on

Anrede f form of address

anreden vt address

anregen vt stimulate; **Anregung** f stimulation; (idea) suggestion

Anreise f journey; **der Tag der ~** the day of arrival; **anreisen** vi arrive

Anreiz m incentive

anrichten vt (food) prepare; (damage) cause

Anruf m call; **Anrufbeantworter** m (-s, -) answering machine, answerphone; **anrufen** irr vt TEL call, phone, ring (Brit)

ans contr of **an das**

Ansage f announcement; (on answerphone) recorded message; **ansagen 1.** vt announce; **angesagt sein** be recommended; (fashionable) be the in thing; **Spannung ist angesagt** we are in for some excitement **2.** vr **er sagte sich an** he said he would come

anschaffen vt buy

anschauen vt look at

Anschein m appearance; **dem** (or **allem**) **~ nach ...** it looks as if ...; **den ~ erwecken, hart zu arbeiten** give the impression of working hard; **anscheinend 1.** adj apparent **2.** adv apparently

anschieben irr vt **könnten Sie mich mal ~?** AUTO could you give me a push?

Anschlag m notice; (on sb or sth) attack; **anschlagen** irr **1.** vt (poster) put up; (damage)

chip **2.** vi (medicine etc) take effect; **mit etw an etw** acc **~** bang sth against sth

anschließen irr **1.** vt ELEC, TECH connect (an + acc to); (into socket) plug in **2.** vi, vr (**sich**) **an etw** acc **~** (building etc) adjoin sth; (happen after) follow sth **3.** vr join (jdm / einer Gruppe sb / a group); **anschließend 1.** adj adjacent; (happening afterwards) subsequent **2.** adv afterwards; **~ an** + acc following; **Anschluss** m ELEC, RAIL connection; (of water, gas etc) supply; **im ~ an** + acc following; **kein ~ unter dieser Nummer** TEL the number you have dialled has not been recognized; **Anschlussflug** m connecting flight

anschnallen 1. vt (skis) put on **2.** vr fasten one's seat belt

Anschrift f address

anschwellen irr vi swell (up)

ansehen irr vt look at; (while sth happens) watch; **jdn / etw als etw ~** look on sb / sth as sth; **das sieht man ihm an** he looks it

an sein irr vi → **an**

ansetzen 1. vt (date) fix; (food) prepare **2.** vi start, begin; **zu etw ~** prepare to do sth

Ansicht f view, opinion; (act of seeing) sight; **meiner ~ nach** in my opinion; **zur ~**

on approval; **Ansichtskarte** *f* postcard

ansonsten *adv* otherwise

Anspiel *nt* SPORT start of play; **anspielen** *vi* **auf** + *acc* ~ allude to sth; **Anspielung** *f* allusion (*auf* + *acc* to)

ansprechen *irr* **1.** *vt* speak to; (*interest*) appeal to **2.** *vi* **auf etw** *acc* ~ (*patient*) respond to sth; **ansprechend** *adj* attractive; **Ansprechpartner(in)** *m(f)* contact

anspringen *irr vi* AUTO start

Anspruch *m* claim; (*entitlement*) right (*auf* + *acc* to); **etw in** ~ **nehmen** take advantage of sth; ~ **auf etw haben** be entitled to sth; **anspruchslos** *adj* undemanding; (*life, accommodation etc*) modest; **anspruchsvoll** *adj* demanding

Anstalt *f* (-, -en) institution

Anstand *m* decency; **anständig** *adj* decent; *fig fam* proper; (*large*) considerable

anstarren *vt* stare at

anstatt *prep* + *gen* instead of

anstecken 1. *vt* fasten on; MED infect; **jdn mit einer Erkältung** ~ pass one's cold on to sb **2.** *vr* **ich habe mich bei ihm angesteckt** I caught it from him **3.** *vi fig* be infectious; **ansteckend** *adj* infectious; **Ansteckungsgefahr** *f* danger of infection

anstehen *irr vi* queue (*Brit*), stand in line (*US*); (*task*

etc) be on the agenda

anstelle *prep* + *gen* instead of

anstellen 1. *vt* (*radio, heating etc*) turn on; (*worker*) employ; (*undertake*) do; **was hast du wieder angestellt?** what have you been up to now? **2.** *vr* queue (*Brit*), stand in line (*US*); *fam* **stell dich nicht so an!** stop making such a fuss

Anstoß *m* impetus; SPORT kick-off; **anstoßen** *irr* **1.** *vt* push; (*with foot*) kick **2.** *vi* knock, bump; (*chink glasses*) drink (a toast) (*auf* + *acc* to); **anstößig** *adj* offensive; (*clothes etc*) indecent

anstrengen 1. *vt* strain **2.** *vr* make an effort; **anstrengend** *adj* tiring

Antarktis *f* Antarctic

Anteil *m* share (*an* + *dat* in); ~ **nehmen** *an* + *dat* sympathize with; take an interest in

Antenne *f* (-, -n) aerial

Antibabypille *f* **die** ~ the pill; **Antibiotikum** *nt* (-*s*, *Antibiotika*) MED antibiotic

antik *adj* antique

Antilope *f* (-, -n) antelope

Antiquariat *nt* second-hand bookshop

Antiquitäten *pl* antiques *pl*; **Antiquitätenhändler(in)** *m(f)* antique dealer

antönen *vt fam* turn on

Antrag *m* (-(*e*)*s*, *Anträge*) proposal; POL motion; (*document*) application form; **ei-**

nen ~ stellen auf + *acc* make an application for

antreffen *irr vt* find

antreiben *irr vt* TECH drive; (*onto shore*) wash up; *jdn zur Arbeit ~* make sb work

antreten *irr vt eine Reise ~* set off on a journey

Antrieb *m* TECH drive; (*motivation*) impetus

antun *irr vt jdm etwas ~* do sth to sb; *sich dat etwas ~* (*commit suicide*) kill oneself

Antwort *f* (-, -en) answer, reply; *um ~ wird gebeten* RSVP (*répondez s'il vous plaît*); **antworten** *vi* answer, reply; *jdm ~* answer sb; *auf etw acc ~* answer sth

anvertrauen *vt jdm etw ~* entrust sb with sth

Anwalt *m* (-s, *Anwälte*), **Anwältin** *f* lawyer

anweisen *irr vt* instruct; (*flat, job etc*) allocate (*jdm etw* sth to sb); **Anweisung** *f* instruction; (*for making payment*) money order

anwenden *irr vt* use; (*law, rule*) apply; **Anwender(in)** *m(f)* (-s, -) user; **Anwendung** *f* use; IT application

anwesend *adj* present; **Anwesenheit** *f* presence

anwidern *vt* disgust

Anwohner(in) *m(f)* (-s, -) resident

Anzahl *f* number (*an* + *dat* of); **anzahlen** *vt* pay a deposit on; *100 Euro ~* pay 100 euros as a deposit; **Anzahlung** *f* deposit

Anzeichen *nt* sign; MED symptom

Anzeige *f* (-, -n) (*in newspaper*) advertisement; (*electronic*) display; (*made to the police*) report; **anzeigen** *vt* (*temperature, time*) indicate, show; (*electronically*) display; (*make known*) announce; *jdn/einen Autodiebstahl bei der Polizei ~* report sb/a stolen car to the police

anziehen *irr* **1.** *vt* attract; (*clothes*) put on; (*screw, rope*) tighten **2.** *vr* get dressed; **anziehend** *adj* attractive

Anzug *m* suit

anzüglich *adj* suggestive

anzünden *vt* light; (*house etc*) set fire to

anzweifeln *vt* doubt

Aperitif *m* (-s, -s (or -e)) aperitif

Apfel *m* (-s, *Äpfel*) apple; **Apfelbaum** *m* apple tree; **Apfelkuchen** *m* apple cake; **Apfelmus** *nt* apple purée; **Apfelsaft** *m* apple juice; **Apfelsine** *f* orange; **Apfelwein** *m* cider

Apostroph *m* (-s, -e) apostrophe

Apotheke *f* (-, -n) chemist's (shop) (*Brit*), pharmacy (*US*); **apothekenpflichtig** *adj* only available at the chemist's (*or* pharmacy); **Apotheker(in)** *m(f)* (-s, -)

Arm

Apparat m (-(e)s, -e) (piece of) apparatus; TEL telephone; RADIO, TV set; **am ~!** TEL speaking; **am ~ bleiben** TEL hold the line

Appartement nt (-s, -s) studio flat (Brit) (or apartment (US))

Appetit m (-(e)s, -e) appetite; **guten ~!** bon appétit

appetitlich adj appetizing

Applaus m (-es, -e) applause

Aprikose f (-, -n) apricot

April m (-(s), -e) April; → **Juni ~, ~!** April fool!; **Aprilscherz** m (-es, -e) April fool's joke

apropos adv by the way; **~ Urlaub ...** while we're on the subject of holidays ...

Aquaplaning nt (-(s)) aquaplaning

Aquarell nt (-s, -e) watercolour

Aquarium nt aquarium

Äquator m equator

Araber(in) m(f) (-s, -) Arab; **arabisch** adj Arab; (numeral, language) Arabic; (Sea, Desert) Arabian

Arbeit f (-, -en) work; (post) job; (product) piece of work; **arbeiten** vi work; **Arbeiter(in)** m(f) (-s, -) worker; (unskilled) labourer; **Arbeitgeber(in)** m(f) (-s, -) employer; **Arbeitnehmer(in)** m(f) (-s, -) employee; **Arbeitsamt** nt job centre (Brit),

employment office (US); **Arbeitserlaubnis** f work permit; **arbeitslos** adj unemployed; **Arbeitslose(r)** mf unemployed person; **die ~n** pl the unemployed pl; **Arbeitslosengeld** nt (income-related) unemployment benefit, job-seeker's allowance (Brit); **Arbeitslosenhilfe** f (non-income related) unemployment benefit; **Arbeitslosigkeit** f unemployment; **Arbeitsplatz** m job; (place) workplace; **Arbeitsspeicher** m IT main memory; **Arbeitszeit** f working hours pl; **gleitende ~** flexible working hours pl, flexitime; **Arbeitszimmer** nt study

Archäologe m (-n, -n), **Archäologin** f archaeologist

Architekt(in) m(f) (-en, -en) architect; **Architektur** f architecture

Archiv nt (-s, -e) archives pl

arg 1. adj bad; (unpleasant, intense) awful **2.** adv (very) terribly

Argentinien nt (-s) Argentina

Ärger m (-s) annoyance; (stronger) anger; (difficulties) trouble; **ärgerlich** adj angry; (irritating) annoying; **ärgern 1.** vt annoy **2.** vr get annoyed

Argument nt (-s, -e) argument

Arktis f (-) Arctic

arm adj poor

Arm m (-(e)s, -e) arm; (of river) branch

Armaturenbrett nt instrument panel; AUTO dashboard

Armband nt bracelet; **Armbanduhr** f (wrist)watch

Armee f (-, -n) army

Ärmel m (-s, -) sleeve; **Ärmelkanal** m (English) Channel

Armut f (-) poverty

Aroma m (-s, Aromen) aroma; **Aromatherapie** f aromatherapy

arrogant adj arrogant

Arsch m (-es, Ärsche) vulg arse (Brit), ass (US); **Arschloch** nt vulg (person) arsehole (Brit), asshole (US)

Art f (-, -en) (manner) way; (type) kind, sort; (of animal) species; **nach ~ des Hauses** à la maison; **auf diese ~ (und Weise)** in this way; **das ist nicht seine ~** that's not like him

Arterie f (-, -n) artery

artig adj good, well-behaved

Artikel m (-s, -) (product) article, item; (in newspaper) article

Artischocke f (-, -n) artichoke

Artist(in) m(f) (-en, -en) (circus) performer

Arznei f medicine; **Arzt** m (-es, Ärzte) doctor; **Arzthelfer(in)** m(f) doctor's assistant; **Ärztin** f (female) doctor; **ärztlich** adj medical; **sich ~ behandeln lassen** undergo medical treatment

Asche f (-, -n) ashes pl; (from cigarette) ash; **Aschenbecher** m ashtray; **Aschermittwoch** m Ash Wednesday

Asiat(in) m(f) (-en, -en) Asian; **asiatisch** adj Asian; **Asien** nt (-s) Asia

Aspekt m (-(e)s, -e) aspect

Asphalt m (-(e)s, -e) asphalt

Aspirin® nt (-s, -e) aspirin

aß imperf of **essen**

Ass nt (-es, -e) (in card game, tennis) ace

Assistent(in) m(f) assistant

Ast m (-(e)s, Äste) branch

Asthma nt (-s) asthma

Astrologie f astrology; **Astronaut(in)** m(f) (-en, -en) astronaut; **Astronomie** f astronomy

ASU f (-, -s) abbr = **Abgassonderuntersuchung**; exhaust emission test

Asyl nt (-s, -e) asylum; (place) home; (for the homeless) shelter; (for animals) m(f), **Asylbewerber(in)** m(f) asylum seeker

Atelier nt (-s, -s) studio

Atem m (-s) breath; **atemberaubend** adj breathtaking; **Atembeschwerden** pl breathing difficulties pl; **atemlos** adj breathless; **Atempause** f breather

Athen nt Athens

Äthiopien nt (-s) Ethiopia

Athlet(in) m(f) (-en, -en) athlete

Atlantik m (-s) Atlantic

(Ocean)

Atlas m (- or Atlasses, Atlanten) atlas

atmen vt, vi breathe; **Atmung** f breathing

Atom nt (-s, -e) atom; **Atombombe** f atom bomb; **Atomkraftwerk** nt nuclear power station; **Atommüll** m nuclear waste; **Atomwaffen** pl nuclear weapons pl

Attentat nt (-(e)s, -e) assassination (auf + acc of); (unsuccessful) assassination attempt

Attest nt (-(e)s, -e) certificate

attraktiv adj attractive

Attrappe f (-, -n) dummy

ätzend adj fam revolting; (bad) lousy

au interj ouch!; ~ **ja!** yeah

Aubergine f (-, -n) aubergine, eggplant (US)

auch conj also, too; even; (actually) really; **oder** ~ or; **ich** ~ **nicht** me neither; **wer/was** ~ **immer** whoever/whatever; **ich gehe jetzt - ich** ~ I'm going now - so am I; **das weiß ich** ~ **nicht** I don't know either

audiovisuell adj audiovisual

auf 1. prep + acc or dat on; ~ **der Reise/dem Tisch** on the way/the table; ~ **der Post®/der Party** at the post office/the party; **etw** ~ **den Tisch stellen** put sth on the table; ~ **Deutsch** in German **2.** prep + acc (mountain, tree etc) up; (direction) to; (following) after; ~ **eine Party gehen** go to a party; **bis** ~ **ihn** except for him; ~ **einmal** suddenly; (simultaneously, in one go) at once **3.** adv open; ~ **sein** be open; (person) be up; ~ **und ab** up and down; ~**!** come on!; ~ **dass** so that

aufatmen vi breathe a sigh of relief

aufbauen vt (erect) put up; (develop) build up; (form) construct; (establish) found, base (auf + acc on); **sich eine Existenz** ~ make a life for oneself

aufbewahren vt keep, store

aufbleiben irr vi (door, shop etc) stay open; (person) stay up

aufblenden vi, vt (die Scheinwerfer) ~ put one's headlights on full beam

aufbrechen irr **1.** vt break open **2.** vi burst open; (person) leave; (on journey) set off; **Aufbruch** m departure

aufdrängen 1. vt jdm etw ~ force sth on sb **2.** vr intrude (jdm on sb); **aufdringlich** adj pushy

aufeinander adv on top of each other; ~ **achten** look after each other; ~ **schießen** shoot at each other; ~ **vertrauen** trust each other; ~ **folgen** follow one another;

~ prallen crash into one another

Aufenthalt m stay; (of train) stop; **Aufenthaltsgenehmigung** f residence permit; **Aufenthaltsraum** m lounge

aufessen irr vt eat up

auffahren irr vi (car) run (or crash) (auf + acc into); (get closer) drive up; **Auffahrt** f (of building) drive; (onto motorway) slip road (Brit), ramp (US); **Auffahrunfall** m rear-end collision; (several vehicles) pile-up

auffallen irr vi stand out; **jdm ~ strike sb; das fällt gar nicht auf** nobody will notice; **auffallend** adj striking; **auffällig** adj conspicuous; (clothes, colour) striking

auffangen irr vt (ball) catch; (blow) cushion

auffassen vt understand; **Auffassung** f view; opinion; (interpretation) concept; (comprehension) grasp

auffordern vt (order) call upon; (request) ask

auffrischen vt (knowledge) brush up

aufführen 1. vt THEATER perform; (in table, index) list; (example) give 2. vr behave; **Aufführung** f THEATER performance

Aufgabe f job, task; (schoolwork) exercise; homework

Aufgang m (steps) staircase

aufgeben irr 1. vt (job, smo-

king, plan etc) give up; (parcel) post; (luggage) check in; (order) place; (advertisement) insert; (puzzle, problem) set 2. vi give up

aufgehen irr vi (sun, dough) rise; (door, flower) open; (become clear) dawn (jdm on sb)

aufgelegt adj **gut/schlecht ~** in a good/bad mood

aufgeregt adj excited

aufgeschlossen adj open (-minded)

aufgeschmissen adj fam in a fix

aufgrund, auf Grund prep + gen on the basis of; (reason) because of

aufhaben irr 1. vt (hat etc) have on; **viel ~** have a lot of homework to do 2. vi (shop) be open

aufhalten irr 1. vt (person) detain; (development) stop; (door, hand) hold open; (eyes) keep open 2. vr (reside) live; (temporarily) stay

aufhängen irr vt hang up

aufheben irr vt (from ground etc) pick up; (not throw away) keep

aufholen 1. vt (time) make up 2. vi catch up

aufhören vi stop; **~, etw zu tun** stop doing sth

aufklären vt (mystery etc) clear up; **jdn ~** enlighten sb; (about sex) tell sb the facts of life

Aufkleber *m* (*-s*, *-*) sticker

aufkommen *irr vi* (*wind*) come up; (*doubt*, *feeling*) arise; (*fashion etc*) appear on the scene; **für den Schaden ~** pay for the damage

aufladen *irr vt* load; (*mobile phone etc*) charge; **Aufladegerät** *nt* charger

Auflage *f* edition; (*of newspaper*) circulation; (*imposed on sb*) condition

auflassen *vt* (*hat*, *glasses*) keep on; (*door*) leave open

Auflauf *m* crowd; (*dish*) bake

auflegen 1. *vt* (*CD*, *make-up etc*) put on; (*receiver*) put down **2.** *vi* TEL hang up

aufleuchten *vi* light up

auflösen 1. *vt* (*in liquid*) dissolve **2.** *vr* (*in liquid*) dissolve; **der Stau hat sich aufgelöst** traffic is back to normal; **Auflösung** *f* (*of puzzle*) solution; (*of screen*) resolution

aufmachen 1. *vt* open; (*garment*) undo **2.** *vr* set out (*nach*) for

aufmerksam *adj* attentive; **jdn auf etw** *acc* **~ machen** draw sb's attention to sth; **Aufmerksamkeit** *f* attention; (*concentration*) attentiveness; (*present*) small token

aufmuntern *vt* encourage; (*make happier*) cheer up

Aufnahme *f* (*-*, *-n*) PHOT photo(graph); (*in film*) shot; (*to*

club, hospital etc) admission; (*start*) beginning; (*on tape etc*) recording; **Aufnahmeprüfung** *f* entrance exam; **aufnehmen** *irr vt* (*to hospital*, *club etc*) admit; (*music*) record; (*begin*) take up; (*in list*) include; (*understand*) take in; **mit jdm Kontakt ~** get in touch with sb

aufpassen *vi* pay attention; (*be careful*) take care; **auf jdn/etw ~** keep an eye on sb/sth

Aufprall *m* (*-s*, *-e*) impact; **aufprallen** *vi* **auf etw** *acc* **~** hit sth, crash into sth

Aufpreis *m* extra charge

aufpumpen *vt* pump up

Aufputschmittel *nt* stimulant

aufräumen *vt*, *vi* clear away; (*room*) tidy up

aufrecht *adj* upright

aufregen 1. *vt* excite; (*irritate*) annoy **2.** *vr* get worked up; **aufregend** *adj* exciting; **Aufregung** *f* excitement

aufreißen *irr vt* (*paper bag etc*) tear open; (*door*) fling open; (*person*) fam pick up

Aufruf *m* AVIAT, IT call; (*public request*) appeal; **aufrufen** *irr vt* (*request*) call upon (*zu* for); (*names*) call out; AVIAT call; IT call up

aufrunden *vt* (*amount*) round up

aufs *contr of* **auf das**

Aufsatz *m* essay

aufschieben *irr vt* postpone;

(delay doing) put off; *(door)* slide open

Aufschlag m *(on price)* extra charge; *(in tennis)* service; **aufschlagen** irr **1.** vt *(book, eyes)* open; *(knee etc)* cut open; *(tent)* pitch, put up; *(camp)* set up **2.** vi *(in tennis)* serve; **auf etw** acc ~ hit sth

aufschließen irr **1.** vt unlock, open up **2.** vi *(people in a row)* close up

aufschneiden irr **1.** vt cut open; *(bread, meat etc)* slice **2.** vi boast, show off

Aufschnitt m *(slices* pl *of)* cold meat; *(cheese)* *(assorted)* sliced cheeses pl

aufschreiben irr vt write down

Aufschrift f inscription; *(piece of paper)* label

Aufschub m delay; *(until a later date)* postponement

Aufsehen nt *(-s)* stir; **großes ~ erregen** cause a sensation; **Aufseher(in)** m(f) *(-s, -)* guard; *(in firm)* supervisor; *(in museum)* attendant; *(in park)* keeper

auf sein irr vi → **auf**

aufsetzen 1. vt put on; *(document)* draw up **2.** vi *(plane)* touch down

Aufsicht f supervision; *(in exam)* invigilation; **die ~ haben** be in charge

aufspannen vt *(umbrella)* put up

aufsperren vt *(mouth)* open wide; *(door, flat)* unlock

aufspringen irr vi jump *(auf + acc* onto)*; *(stand up quickly)* jump up; *(door, suitcase)* spring open

aufstehen irr vi get up; *(door)* be open

aufstellen vt put up; *(in a row)* line up; *(candidate)* put up; *(list, schedule)* draw up; *(record)* set up

Aufstieg m *(-(e)s, -e)* *(up mountain)* ascent; *(progress)* rise; *(in career, sport)* promotion

Aufstrich m spread

auftanken vt, vi *(car)* tank up; *(plane)* refuel

auftauchen vi turn up; *(from water etc)* surface; *(question, problem)* come up

auftauen 1. vt *(food)* defrost **2.** vi thaw; fig *(person)* unbend

Auftrag m *(-(e)s, Aufträge)* COMM order; *(allocated work)* job; *(orders)* instructions pl; *(mission)* task; **im ~ von** on behalf of; **auftragen** irr vt *(ointment etc)* apply; *(meal)* serve

auftreten irr vi appear; *(problem)* come up; *(act)* behave; **Auftritt** m *(of actor)* entrance; fig *(argument)* scene

aufwachen vi wake up

aufwachsen irr vi grow up

Aufwand m *(-(e)s)* expenditure; *(costs also)* expense;

(exertion) effort; **aufwändig** *adj* costly; **das ist zu ~** that's too much trouble

aufwärmen *vt, vr* warm up

aufwärts *adv* upwards; **mit etw geht es ~** things are looking up for sth

aufwecken *vt* wake up

aufwendig *adj* → **aufwändig**

aufwischen *vt* wipe up; *(floor)* wipe

aufzählen *vt* list; **Aufzählungszeichen** *nt* bullet

aufzeichnen *vt* sketch; *(write)* jot down; *(on tape etc)* record; **Aufzeichnung** *f* *(written)* note; *(on tape etc)* recording; *(on film)* record

aufziehen *irr* **1.** *vt* *(drawer, curtains etc)* pull open; *(watch)* wind (up); *fam (make fun of)* tease; *(children)* bring up; *(animals)* rear **2.** *vi* *(storm)* come up

Aufzug *m* lift *(Brit)*, elevator *(US)*; *(floor etc)* get-up; THEAT act

Auge *nt* (-s, -n) eye; **jdm aufs ~ drücken** *fam* force sth on sb; **ins ~ gehen** *fam* go wrong; **unter vier ~n** in private; **etw im ~ behalten** keep sth in mind; **Augenarzt** *m*, **Augenärztin** *f* eye specialist, eye doctor *(US)*; **Augenblick** *m* moment; **im ~** at the moment; **Augenbraue** *f* (-, -n) eyebrow; **Augenbrauenstift** *m* eyebrow pencil; **Augenfarbe** *f* eye colour;

seine ~ the colour of his eyes; **Augenlid** *nt* eyelid; **Augenoptiker(in)** *m(f)* (-s, -) optician; **Augentropfen** *pl* eyedrops *pl*; **Augenzeuge** *m*, **Augenzeugin** *f* eyewitness

August *m* (-(e)s *or* -, -e) August; → **Juni**

Auktion *f* auction

aus 1. *prep* + *dat* *(from inside)* out of; *(source)* from; *(material)* (made) of; **~ Berlin kommen** come from Berlin; **~ Versehen** by mistake; **~ Angst** out of fear **2.** *adv* out; *(ended)* finished, over; **ein/~** TECH on/off; **~ sein** *fam* *(school etc)* be over; *(finished)* be over; **auf etw** *acc* **~ sein** be after sth; **von mir ~** as far as I'm concerned; **von mir ~!** I don't care; **zwischen uns ist es ~** we're finished; **Aus** *nt* (-) SPORT touch; *fig* end

ausatmen *vi* breathe out

ausbauen *vt* *(house, road)* extend; *(engine etc)* remove

ausbessern *vt* repair; *(clothes)* mend

ausbilden *vt* educate; *(apprentice etc)* train; *(skills)* develop; **Ausbildung** *f* education; *(of apprentice etc)* training; *(of skills)* development

Ausblick *m* view; *fig* outlook

ausbrechen *irr vi* break out; **in Tränen ~** burst into tears; **in Gelächter ~** burst into laughing

ausbreiten 1. *vt* spread (out); *(arms)* stretch out **2.** *vr* spread

Ausbruch *m (of war, epidemic etc)* outbreak; *(of volcano)* eruption; *(of feelings)* outburst; *(from prison)* escape

ausbuhen *vt* boo

Ausdauer *f* perseverance; SPORT stamina

ausdehnen *vt* stretch; *fig (power)* extend

ausdenken *irr vt* **sich** *dat* **etw** ~ come up with sth

Ausdruck 1. *m (Ausdrücke pl)* expression **2.** *m (Ausdrucke pl) (from computer)* print-out; **ausdrucken** *vt* IT print (out)

ausdrücken 1. *vt (facts, feelings etc)* express; *(cigarette)* put out; *(lemon etc)* squeeze **2.** *vr* express oneself; **ausdrücklich 1.** *adj* express **2.** *adv* expressly

auseinander *adv* apart; ~ **gehen** *(people)* separate; *(opinions)* differ; *(object)* fall apart; ~ **halten** tell apart; ~ **schreiben** write as separate words; ~ **setzen** explain; **sich** ~ **setzen** look *(mit* at); *(disagree)* argue *(mit* with); **Auseinandersetzung** *f (row)* argument; *(discussion)* debate

Ausfahrt *f (of train etc)* departure; *(from motorway, garage etc)* exit

ausfallen *irr vi (hair)* fall out; *(concert, class etc)* be cancelled; *(machine)* break down; *(electricity)* turn off; *(well, badly etc)* turn out; **groß/klein** ~ *(clothes, shoes)* be too big/ too small

ausfindig machen *vt* discover

ausflippen *vi fam* freak out

Ausflug *m* excursion, outing; **Ausflugsziel** *nt* destination

Ausfluss *m* MED discharge

ausfragen *vt* question

Ausfuhr *f* (-, -en) export

ausführen *vt (order, task, plan)* carry out; *(person)* take out; COMM export; *(theory etc)* explain

ausführlich 1. *adj* detailed **2.** *adv* in detail

ausfüllen *vt* fill up; *(questionnaire etc)* fill in *(or* out)

Ausgabe *f (money)* expenditure; IT output; *(of book)* edition; *(of magazine)* issue

Ausgang *m* way out, exit; *(at airport)* gate; *(conclusion)* end; *(outcome)* result; **„kein** ~" 'no exit'

ausgeben *irr* **1.** *vt (money)* spend; *(share out)* distribute; **jdm etw** ~ *(treat sb)* buy sb sth **2.** *vr* **sich für etw/jdn** ~ pass oneself off as sth/sb

ausgebucht *adj* fully booked

ausgefallen *adj* unusual

ausgehen *irr vi (in the evening etc)* go out; *(petrol, cof-*

fee etc) run out; (*hair*) fall out; (*fire, light etc*) go out; (*well, badly etc*) turn out; **davon ~, dass** assume that; **ihm ging das Geld aus** he ran out of money

ausgelassen *adj* exuberant

ausgeleiert *adj* worn out

ausgenommen *conj, prep* + *gen or dat* except

ausgerechnet *adv* **~ du** of all people; **~ heute** today of all days

ausgeschildert *adj* signposted

ausgeschlafen *adj* **bist du ~?** have you had enough sleep?

ausgeschlossen *adj* impossible, out of the question

ausgesprochen 1. *adj* out-and-out; (*strong*) marked **2.** *adv* extremely; **~ gut** really good

ausgezeichnet *adj* excellent

ausgiebig *adj* (*use*) thorough; (*meal*) substantial

ausgießen *irr vt* (*drink*) pour out; (*jug, glass etc*) empty

ausgleichen *irr* **1.** *vt* even out **2.** *vi* SPORT equalize

Ausguss *m* sink; (*waste pipe*) outlet

aushalten *irr* **1.** *vt* bear, stand; **nicht auszuhalten sein** be unbearable **2.** *vi* hold out

aushändigen *vt* **jdm etw ~** hand sth over to sb

Aushang *m* notice

Aushilfe *f* temporary help; (*in office*) temp

auskennen *irr vr* know a lot (*bei, in* about); (*in a place*) know one's way around

auskommen *irr vi* **gut/ schlecht mit jdm ~** get on well/badly with sb; **mit etw ~** get by with sth

Auskunft *f* (-, *Auskünfte*) information; (*particulars*) details *pl*; (*counter*) information desk; TEL (*directory*) enquiries *sg* (*Brit*), information (*US*)

auslachen *vt* laugh at

ausladen *irr vt* (*luggage etc*) unload; **jdn ~** (*guest*) tell sb not to come

Auslage *f* window display; **~n** *pl* (*costs*) expenses

Ausland *nt* foreign countries *pl*; **im/ins ~** abroad; **Ausländer(in)** *m(f)* (-s, -) foreigner; **ausländerfeindlich** *adj* hostile to foreigners, xenophobic; **ausländisch** *adj* foreign; **Auslandsgespräch** *nt* international call; **Auslandskrankenschein** *m* health insurance certificate for foreign countries, ≈ E111 (*Brit*); **Auslandsschutzbrief** *m* international (*motor*) insurance cover (*documents pl*)

auslassen *irr* **1.** *vt* leave out; (*word etc also*) omit; (*do without*) skip; (*anger*) vent (*an* + *dat* on) **2.** *vr* **sich über etw** *acc* **~** speak one's mind about sth

auslaufen *irr vi* (*liquid*) run out; (*tank etc*) leak; (*ship*) leave port; (*contract*) expire

auslegen *vt* (*goods*) display; (*money*) lend; (*text etc*) interpret; (*machine, building*) design (*für, auf* + *acc* for)

ausleihen *irr vt* (*to sb*) lend; **sich** *dat* **etw** ~ borrow sth

ausloggen *vi* IT log out (*or* off)

auslösen *vt* (*explosion, alarm*) set off; (*bring about*) cause; **Auslöser** *m* (*-s, -*) PHOT shutter release

ausmachen *vt* (*light, radio*) turn off; (*fire*) put out; (*date, price*) fix; (*arrange*) agree; (*proportion, amount etc*) represent; (*be significant*) matter; **macht es Ihnen etwas aus, wenn ...?** would you mind if ...?; **das macht mir nichts aus** I don't mind

Ausmaß *nt* extent

Ausnahme *f* (*-, -n*) exception; **ausnahmsweise** *adv* as an exception, just this once

ausnutzen *vt* (*time, opportunity, influence*) use; (*person, sb's good nature*) take advantage of

auspacken *vt* unpack

ausprobieren *vt* try (out)

Auspuff *m* (*-(e)s, -e*) TECH exhaust; **Auspuffrohr** *nt* exhaust (*pipe*); **Auspufftopf** *m* AUTO silencer (*Brit*), muffler (*US*)

ausrauben *vt* rob

ausräumen *vt* clear away; (*cupboard, room*) empty; (*misgivings*) put aside

ausrechnen *vt* calculate, work out

Ausrede *f* excuse

ausreden 1. *vi* finish speaking **2.** *vt* **jdm etw** ~ talk sb out of sth

ausreichend *adj* sufficient, satisfactory; (*mark in school*) ≈ D

Ausreise *f* departure; **bei der** ~ on leaving the country; **Ausreiseerlaubnis** *f* exit visa; **ausreisen** *vi* leave the country

ausreißen *irr vi* **1.** *vt* tear out **2.** *vi* come off; *fam* (*abscond*) run away

ausrenken *vt* **sich** *dat* **den Arm** ~ dislocate one's arm

ausrichten *vt* (*message*) deliver; (*regards*) pass on; **ich konnte bei ihr nichts** ~ I couldn't get anywhere with her; **jdm etw** ~ tell sb sth

ausrufen *irr vt* (*over loudspeaker*) announce; **jdn** ~ **lassen** page sb; **Ausrufezeichen** *nt* exclamation mark

ausruhen *vi, vr* rest

Ausrüstung *f* equipment

ausrutschen *vi* slip

ausschalten *vt* switch off; *fig* eliminate

Ausschau *f* ~ **halten** look out (*nach* for)

ausscheiden *irr* **1.** *vt* MED

give off, secrete **2.** *vi* leave (*aus etw* sth); SPORT be eliminated

ausschlafen *irr* **1.** *vi, vr* have a lie-in **2.** *vt* sleep off

Ausschlag *m* MED rash; **den geben** *fig* tip the balance; **ausschlagen** *irr* **1.** *vt* (*tooth*) knock out; (*invitation*) turn down **2.** *vi* (*horse*) kick out; **ausschlaggebend** *adj* decisive

ausschließen *irr vt* lock out; *fig* exclude; **ausschließlich 1.** *adv* exclusively **2.** *prep* + *gen* excluding

Ausschnitt *m* (*part*) section; (*of dress*) neckline; (*from newspaper*) cutting

Ausschreitungen *pl* riots *pl*

ausschütten *vt* (*liquid*) pour out; (*container*) empty

aussehen *irr vi* look; **krank ~** look ill; **gut ~** (*person*) be good-looking; (*thing*) be looking good; **es sieht nach Regen aus** it looks like rain; **es sieht schlecht aus** things look bad

aus sein *irr vi* → **aus**

außen *adv* outside; **nach ~** outwards; **von ~** from (the) outside; **Außenbordmotor** *m* outboard motor; **Außenminister(in)** *m(f)* foreign minister, Foreign Secretary (*Brit*); **Außenseite** *f* outside; **Außenseiter(in)** *m(f)* outsider; **Außenspiegel** *m* wing mirror (*Brit*), side mirror

(*US*)

außer 1. *prep* + *dat* except (for); **nichts ~** nothing but; **~ Betrieb** out of order; **~ sich sein** be beside oneself (*vor* with); **~ Atem** out of breath **2.** *conj* except; **~ wenn** unless; **~ dass** except; **außerdem** *conj* besides

äußere(r, s) *adj* outer, external

außergewöhnlich 1. *adj* unusual **2.** *adv* exceptionally; **~ kalt** exceptionally cold; **außerhalb** *prep* + *gen* outside

äußerlich *adj* external

äußern 1. *vt* express; (*display*) show **2.** *vr* give one's opinion; (*be visible*) show itself

außerordentlich *adj* extraordinary; **außerplanmäßig** *adj* unscheduled

äußerst *adv* extremely; **äußerste(r, s)** *adj* utmost; (*in distance*) farthest; (*date*) last possible

Äußerung *f* remark

aussetzen 1. *vt* (*child, animal*) abandon; (*reward*) offer; **ich habe nichts daran auszusetzen** I have no objection to it **2.** *vi* stop; (*take a break*) drop out; (*in game*) miss a turn

Aussicht *f* view; (*chance*) prospect; **aussichtslos** *adj* hopeless; **Aussichtsplattform** *f* observation platform; **Aussichtsturm** *m* observation tower

Aussiedler(in) *m(f)* (*-s, -*) émigré (*person of German descent from Eastern Europe*)

ausspannen 1. *vi* relax **2.** *vt* **er hat ihm die Freundin ausgespannt** *fam* he's nicked his girlfriend

aussperren 1. *vt* lock out **2.** *vr* lock oneself out

Aussprache *f* (*of words*) pronunciation; (*talk*) (frank) discussion; **aussprechen** *irr* **1.** *vt* pronounce; (*thoughts etc*) express **2.** *vr* talk (*über + acc* about) **3.** *vi* finish speaking

ausspülen *vt* rinse (out)

Ausstattung *f* (*in hospital, office etc*) equipment; (*in flat etc*) furnishings *pl*; (*in car*) fittings *pl*

ausstehen *irr* **1.** *vt* endure; **ich kann ihn nicht ~** I can't stand him **2.** *vi* (*debt etc*) be outstanding

aussteigen *irr vi* get out (*aus* of); **aus dem Bus/Zug ~** get off the bus/train; **Aussteiger(in)** *m(f)* dropout

ausstellen *vt* display; (*at trade fair, in museum etc*) exhibit; *fam* (*radio, heating etc*) switch off; (*cheque etc*) make out; (*passport etc*) issue; **Ausstellung** *f* exhibition

aussterben *irr vi* die out

ausstrahlen *vt* radiate; (*programme*) broadcast; **Ausstrahlung** *f* RADIO, TV broadcast; *fig* (*of person*) charisma

ausstrecken 1. *vr* stretch out **2.** *vt* (*hand*) reach out (*nach* for)

aussuchen *vt* choose

Austausch *m* exchange; **austauschen** *vt* exchange (*gegen* for)

austeilen *vt* distribute; hand out

Auster *f* (*-, -n*) oyster; **Austernpilz** *m* oyster mushroom

austragen *irr vt* (*mail*) deliver; (*competition*) hold

Australien *nt* (*-s*) Australia; **Australier(in)** *m(f)* (*-s, -*) Australian; **australisch** *adj* Australian

austrinken *irr* **1.** *vt* (*glass*) drain; (*wine, coffee etc*) drink up **2.** *vi* finish one's drink

austrocknen *vi* dry out; (*river*) dry up

ausüben *vt* (*profession, sport*) practise; (*influence*) exert

Ausverkauf *m* sale; **ausverkauft** *adj* (*tickets, item*) sold out

Auswahl *f* selection, choice (*an + dat* of); **auswählen** *vt* select, choose

auswandern *vi* emigrate

auswärtig *adj* not local; (*relating to other countries*) foreign; **auswärts** *adv* out of town; SPORT **~ spielen** play away; **Auswärtsspiel** *nt* away match

auswechseln vt replace; SPORT substitute

Ausweg m way out

ausweichen irr vi get out of the way; *jdm/einer Sache* ~ move aside for sb/sth; fig avoid sb/sth

Ausweis m (-es, -e) (for individual) identity card, ID; (for library etc) card; **ausweisen** irr 1. vt expel 2. vr prove one's identity; **Ausweiskontrolle** f ID check; **Ausweispapiere** pl identification documents pl

auswendig adv by heart

auswuchten vt AUTO (wheels) balance

auszahlen 1. vt (money) pay (out); (person) pay off 2. vr be worth it

auszeichnen 1. vt (special person) honour; COMM price 2. vr distinguish oneself

ausziehen irr 1. vt (clothes) take off 2. vr undress 3. vi (from flat) move out

Auszubildende(r) mf trainee

Auto nt (-s, -s) car; ~ **fahren** drive; **Autoatlas** m road atlas; **Autobahn** f motorway (Brit), freeway (US); **Autobahnauffahrt** f motorway access road (Brit), on-ramp (US); **Autobahnausfahrt** f motorway exit (Brit), off-ramp (US); **Autobahngebühr** f toll; **Autobahnkreuz** nt motorway interchange; **Autobahnring** m motorway

ring (Brit), beltway (US); **Autobombe** f car bomb; **Autofähre** f car ferry; **Autofahrer(in)** m(f) driver, motorist; **Autofahrt** f drive

Autogramm nt (-s, -e) autograph

Automarke f make of car

Automat m (-en, -en) vending machine

Automatik f (-, -en) AUTO automatic transmission; **Automatikschaltung** f automatic gear change (Brit) (or shift (US)); **Automatikwagen** m automatic

automatisch 1. adj automatic 2. adv automatically

Automechaniker(in) m(f) car mechanic; **Autonummer** f registration (Brit) (or license (US)) number; **Autoradio** nt car radio; **Autoreifen** m car tyre; **Autoreisezug** m Motorail train® (Brit), auto train (US); **Autorennen** nt motor racing; (single event) motor race; **Autoschlüssel** m car key; **Autotelefon** nt car phone; **Autounfall** m car accident; **Autoverleih** m, **Autovermietung** f car hire (Brit) (or rental (US)); (firm) car hire (Brit) (or rental (US)) company; **Autowaschanlage** f car wash; **Autowerkstatt** f car repair shop, garage; **Autozubehör** nt car accessories pl

Avocado f (-, -s) avocado

Axt f (-, Äxte) axe

Azubi m (-s, -s) f (-, -s) acr = *Auszubildende*; trainee

B

B abbr = *Bundesstraße*

Baby nt (-s, -s) baby; **Babybett** nt cot (Brit), crib (US); **Babyfläschchen** nt baby's bottle; **Babynahrung** f baby food; **Babysitter(in)** m(f) babysitter; **Babysitz** m child seat; **Babywickelraum** m baby-changing room

Bach m (-(e)s, Bäche) stream

Backblech nt baking tray (Brit), cookie sheet (US)

Backbord nt port (side)

Backe f (-, -n) cheek

backen (backte, gebacken) vt, vi bake

Backenzahn m molar

Bäcker(in) m(f) (-s, -) baker; **Bäckerei** f bakery; (selling bread) baker's (shop)

Backofen m oven; **Backpulver** nt baking powder

Backspace-Taste f IT backspace key

Backstein m brick

Backwaren pl bread, cakes and pastries pl

Bad nt (-(e)s, Bäder) bath; (in sea etc) swim; (resort) spa; *ein ~ nehmen* have (or take) a bath; **Badeanzug** m swimsuit, swimming costume (Brit); **Badehose** f swimming trunks pl; **Badekappe** f swimming cap; **Bademantel** m bathrobe; **Bademeister(in)** m(f) pool attendant; **Bademütze** f swimming cap

baden 1. vi have a bath; (in sea etc) swim, bathe (Brit) **2.** vt bath (Brit), bathe (US)

Baden-Württemberg nt (-s) Baden-Württemberg

Badeort m spa; **Badesachen** pl swimming things pl; **Badetuch** nt bath towel; **Badewanne** f bath (tub); **Badezimmer** nt bathroom

Badminton nt badminton

baff adj ~ *sein* fam be flabbergasted (or gobsmacked)

Bagger m (-s, -) excavator; **Baggersee** m artificial lake in quarry etc, used for bathing

Bahamas pl **die ~** the Bahamas pl

Bahn f (-, -en) railway (Brit), railroad (US); (racetrack) track; (for single runner) lane; ASTR orbit; **bahnbrechend** adj groundbreaking; **BahnCard®** f (-, -s) rail card (allowing 50% or 25% reduction on tickets); **Bahnfahrt** f railway (Brit) (or railroad (US)) journey; **Bahn-**

hof m station; **am** (or **auf dem**) ~ at the station; **Bahnlinie** f railway (Brit) (or railroad (US)) line; **Bahnpolizei** f railway (Brit) (or railroad (US)) police; **Bahnsteig** m (-(e)s, -e) platform; **Bahnstrecke** f railway (Brit) (or railroad (US)) line; **Bahnübergang** m level crossing (Brit), grade crossing (US)

Bakterien pl bacteria pl, germs pl

bald adv soon; almost; **bis ~!** see you soon (or later); **baldig** adj quick, speedy

Balkan m (-s) **der ~** the Balkans pl

Balken m (-s, -) beam

Balkon m (-s, -s or -e) balcony

Ball m (-(e)s, **Bälle**) ball; (event) dance, ball

Ballett nt (-s,) ballet

Ballon m (-s, -s) balloon

Ballspiel nt ball game

Ballungsgebiet nt conurbation

Baltikum nt (-s) **das ~** the Baltic States pl

Bambus m (-ses, -se) bamboo; **Bambussprossen** pl bamboo shoots pl

banal adj banal; (question, remark) trite

Banane f (-, -n) banana

band imperf of **binden**

Band **1.** m (-(e)s, **Bände**) (book) volume **2.** nt (-(e)s, **Bänder**) (of fabric) ribbon,

tape; (in factory) production line; (for recording) tape; ANAT ligament; **etw auf ~ aufnehmen** tape sth **3.** f (-, -s) (musicians) band

Bandage f (-, -n) bandage; **bandagieren** vt bandage

Bande f (-, -n) gang

Bänderriss m MED torn ligament

Bandscheibe f ANAT disc; **Bandwurm** m tapeworm

Bank **1.** f (-, **Bänke**) bench **2.** f (-, -en) FIN bank

Bankautomat m cash dispenser; **Bankkarte** f bank card; **Bankkonto** nt bank account; **Bankleitzahl** f bank sort code; **Banknote** f banknote; **Bankverbindung** f banking (or account) details pl

bar adj **~es Geld** cash; **etw (in) ~ bezahlen** pay sth (in) cash

Bar f (-, -s) bar

Bär m (-en, -en) bear

barfuß adj barefoot

barg imperf of **bergen**

Bargeld nt cash; **bargeldlos** adj non-cash

Barkeeper m (-s, -), **Barmann** m barman, bartender (US)

barock adj baroque

Barometer nt (-s, -) barometer

barsch adj brusque

Barsch m (-(e)s, -e) perch

Barscheck m open (or uncrossed) cheque

Bart m (-(e)s, **Bärte**) beard

bärtig

bärtig *adj* bearded

Barzahlung *f* cash payment

Basar *m* (-s, -e) bazaar

Baseballmütze *f* baseball cap

Basel *nt* (-s) Basle

Basilikum *nt* (-s) basil

Basis *f* (-, **Basen**) basis

Baskenland *nt* (-s) Basque region

Basketball *m* basketball

Bass *m* (-es, **Bässe**) bass

basta *interj* **und damit ~!** and that's that

basteln 1. *vt* make **2.** *vi* make things, do handicrafts

bat *imperf of* **bitten**

Batterie *f* battery; **batteriebetrieben** *adj* battery-powered

Bau 1. *m* (-(e)s) (*constructing*) building, construction; (*organization*) structure; (*place*) building site **2.** *m* (*Baue pl*) (*of animal*) burrow **3.** *m* (*Bauten pl*) (*edifice*) building; **Bauarbeiten** *pl* construction work *sg*; (*on road*) roadworks *pl* (*Brit*), roadwork (*US*); **Bauarbeiter(in)** *m(f)* construction worker

Bauch *m* (-(e)s, **Bäuche**) stomach; **Bauchnabel** *m* navel; **Bauchredner(in)** *m(f)* ventriloquist; **Bauchschmerzen** *pl* stomach-ache *sg*; **Bauchspeicheldrüse** *f* pancreas; **Bauchtanz** *m* belly dancing; **Bauchweh** *nt* (-s) stomach-ache

Baudenkmal *nt* monument

bauen *vt, vi* build; TECH construct

Bauer *m* (-n *or* -s, -n) farmer; (*in chess*) pawn; **Bäuerin** *f* farmer; farmer's wife; **Bauernhof** *m* farm

baufällig *adj* dilapidated; **Baujahr** *adj* year of construction; **der Wagen ist ~ 2002** the car is a 2002 model, the car was made in 2002

Baum *m* (-(e)s, **Bäume**) tree

Baumarkt *m* DIY centre

Baumwolle *f* cotton

Bauplatz *m* building site; **Baustein** *m* (*for building*) stone; (*toy*) brick; *fig* element; **elektronischer ~** chip; **Baustelle** *f* building site; (*on road*) roadworks *pl* (*Brit*), roadwork (*US*); **Bauteil** *nt* prefabricated part; **Bauunternehmer(in)** *m(f)* building contractor; **Bauwerk** *nt* building

Bayern *nt* (-s) Bavaria

beabsichtigen *vt* intend

beachten *vt* pay attention to; (*rule etc*) observe; **nicht ~** ignore; **beachtlich** *adj* considerable

Beachvolleyball *nt* beach volleyball

Beamte(r) *m* (-n, -n), **Beamtin** *f* official; (*employed by the state*) civil servant

beanspruchen *vt* claim; (*time, space*) take up; **jdn ~** keep sb busy

beanstanden *vt* complain

about

beantragen vt apply for

beantworten vt answer

bearbeiten vt work; (*material, data*) process; CHEM treat; (*case etc*) deal with; (*book etc*) revise; *fam* (*try to influence*) work on; **Bearbeitungsgebühr** f handling (*or* service) charge

beatmen vt **jdn ~** give sb artificial respiration

beaufsichtigen vt supervise; (*in exam*) invigilate

beauftragen vt instruct; **jdn mit etw ~** give sb the job of doing sth

Becher m (-s, -) mug; (*without handle*) tumbler; (*for yoghurt*) pot; (*made of cardboard*) tub

Becken nt (-s, -) basin; (*for washing*) sink; (*for swimming*) pool; MUS cymbal; ANAT pelvis

bedanken vr say thank you; **sich bei jdm für etw ~** thank sb for sth

Bedarf m (-(e)s) need (*an* + *dat* for); COMM demand (*an* + *dat* for); **je nach ~** according to demand; **bei ~** if necessary; **Bedarfshaltestelle** f request stop, flag stop (*US*)

bedauerlich adj regrettable; **bedauern** vt regret; (*person*) feel sorry for; **bedauernswert** adj regrettable; (*person*) unfortunate

bedeckt adj covered; (*sky*) overcast

bedenken irr vt consider; **Bedenken** n (-s, -) (*thought*) consideration; (*reservation*) doubt; (*moral doubt*) scruples pl; **bedenklich** adj dubious; (*condition, situation*) serious

bedeuten vt mean; **jdm nichts/viel ~** mean nothing/a lot to sb; **bedeutend** adj important; (*large*) considerable; **Bedeutung** f meaning; importance

bedienen 1. vt serve; (*machine*) operate **2.** vr (*when eating*) help oneself; **Bedienung** f service; (*person*) waiter/waitress; shop assistant; (*supplement*) service (charge); **Bedienungsanleitung** f operating instructions pl; **Bedienungshandbuch** nt instruction manual; **Bedingung** f condition; **unter der ~, dass** on condition that; **unter diesen ~en** under these circumstances

bedrohen vt threaten

Bedürfnis nt need

beeilen vr hurry

beeindrucken vt impress

beeinflussen vt influence

beeinträchtigen vt affect

beenden vt end; (*complete*) finish

beerdigen vt bury; **Beerdigung** f burial; (*ceremony*) funeral

Beere f (-, -n) berry; (for wine) grape

Beet nt (-(e)s, -e) bed

befahl imperf of **befehlen**

befahrbar adj passable; NAUT navigable; **befahren 1.** irr vt (road) use; (mountain pass) navigate; (river etc) navigate **2.** adj **stark/ wenig ~** busy/ quiet

Befehl m (-(e)s, -e) order; IT command; (army) command; (befahl, befohlen) **1.** vt order; **jdm ~, etw zu tun** order sb to do sth **2.** vi give orders

befestigen vt fix; (with string, rope) attach; (with glue) stick

befeuchten vt moisten

befinden irr vr be

befohlen pp of **befehlen**

befolgen vt (advice etc) follow

befördern vt transport; (at work) promote; **Beförderung** f transport; (at work) promotion; **Beförderungsbedingungen** pl conditions pl of carriage

Befragung f questioning; (survey) opinion poll

befreundet adj friendly; **~ sein** be friends (mit jdm with sb)

befriedigen vt satisfy; **befriedigend** adj satisfactory; (mark for schoolwork) ≈ C; **Befriedigung** f satisfaction

befristet adj limited (auf + acc to)

befruchten vt fertilize; fig stimulate

Befund m (-(e)s, -e) findings pl; MED diagnosis

befürchten vt fear

befürworten vt support

begabt adj gifted, talented; **Begabung** f talent, gift

begann imperf of **beginnen**

begegnen vt meet (jdm sb), meet with (einer Sache dat sth)

begehen irr vt (offence) commit; (anniversary etc) celebrate

begehrt adj sought-after; (bachelor) eligible

begeistern 1. vt fill with enthusiasm; (stimulate) inspire **2.** vr **sich für etw ~** be / get enthusiastic about sth; **begeistert** adj enthusiastic

Beginn m (-(e)s) beginning; **zu ~** at the beginning; **beginnen** (begann, begonnen) vt, vi start, begin

beglaubigen vt certify; **Beglaubigung** f certification

begleiten vt accompany; **Begleiter(in)** m(f) companion; **Begleitung** f company; MUS accompaniment

beglückwünschen vt congratulate (zu on)

begonnen pp of **beginnen**

begraben irr vt bury; **Begräbnis** nt burial; (ceremony) funeral

begreifen irr vt understand

Begrenzung f boundary; fig restriction

Begriff m (-(e)s, -e) concept;

(*mental impression*) idea; *im ~ sein, etw zu tun* be on the point of doing sth; *schwer von ~ sein* be slow on the uptake

begründen *vt* justify; **Begründung** *f* explanation; (*vindication*) justification

begrüßen *vt* greet; (*guest*) welcome; **Begrüßung** *f* greeting; (*reception*) welcome

behaart *adj* hairy

behalten *irr vt* keep; (*keep in head*) remember; *etw für sich ~* keep sth to oneself

Behälter *m* (*-s, -*) container

behandeln *vt* treat; **Behandlung** *f* treatment

behaupten 1. *vt* claim, maintain **2.** *vr* assert oneself; **Behauptung** *f* claim

beheizen *vt* heat

behelfen *irr vr* **sich mit/ohne etw ~** make do with/without sth

beherbergen *vt* accommodate

beherrschen 1. *vt* (*situation, feelings*) control; (*instrument*) master **2.** *vr* control oneself; **Beherrschung** *f* control (*über + acc* of); *die ~ verlieren* lose one's self-control

behilflich *adj* helpful; *jdm ~ sein* help sb (*bei* with)

behindern *vt* hinder; (*traffic, view*) obstruct; **Behinderte(r)** *mf* disabled person; **be-**

hindertengerecht *adj* suitable for disabled people

Behörde *f* (*-, -n*) authority; *die ~n pl* the authorities *pl*

bei *prep + dat* (*place*) near, by; (*stay*) at; (*time*) at, on; (*in the course of*) during; (*circumstance*) in; (*question*) at; *~m Friseur* at the hairdresser's; *~ uns zuhause* at our place; in our country; *~ Nacht* at night; *~ Tag* by day; *~ Nebel* in fog; *~ Regen findet die Veranstaltung im Saal statt* if it rains the event will take place in the hall; *etw ~ sich haben* have sth on one; *~m Fahren* while driving

beibehalten *irr vt* keep

Beiboot *nt* dinghy

beibringen *vt* (*tell*) break sth to sb; (*instruct*) teach sb sth

beide(s) *pron* both; *meine ~n Brüder* my two brothers, both my brothers; *wir ~* both (or the two) of us; *keiner von ~n* neither of them; *alle ~* both (of them); *~s ist sehr schön* both are very nice; *30 ~* (*in tennis*) 30 all

beieinander *adv* together

Beifahrer(in) *m(f)* passenger; **Beifahrerairbag** *m* passenger airbag; **Beifahrersitz** *m* passenger seat

Beifall *m* (*-(e)s*) applause

beige *adj inv* beige

Beigeschmack *m* aftertaste

Beil *nt* (*-(e)s, -e*) axe

Beilage f GASTR side dish; vegetables pl; (of newspaper) supplement

beiläufig 1. adj casual **2.** adv casually

Beileid nt condolences pl; (**mein**) **herzliches ~** please accept my sincere condolences

beiliegend adj enclosed

beim contr of **bei dem**

Bein nt (-(e)s, -e) leg

beinah(e) adv almost, nearly

beinhalten vt contain

Beipackzettel m instruction leaflet

beisammen adv together; **Beisammensein** nt (-s) get-together

Beischlaf m sexual intercourse

beiseite adv aside; **etw ~ legen** (save) put sth by

Beispiel nt (-(e)s, -e) example; **sich** dat **an jdm/etw ein ~ nehmen** take sb/sth as an example; **zum ~** for example

beißen (biss, gebissen) **1.** vt bite **2.** vi bite; (smoke, acid) sting **3.** vr (colours) clash

Beitrag m (-(e)s, Beiträge) contribution; (for membership) subscription; (for insurance) premium; **beitragen** irr vt, vi contribute (zu to)

bekannt adj well-known; (recognizable) familiar; **mit jdm ~ sein** know sb; **~ geben** announce; **jdn mit jdm ~ ma-** chen introduce sb to sb; **Bekannte(r)** mf friend; (less close) acquaintance; **bekanntlich** adv as everyone knows; **Bekanntschaft** f acquaintance

bekiffen vr fam get stoned

beklagen vr complain

Bekleidung f clothing

bekommen irr **1.** vt get; (letter, present etc) receive; (child) have; (train, cold) catch, get; **wie viel ~ Sie dafür?** how much is that? **2.** vi **jdm ~** (food) agree with sb; **wir ~ schon** we're being served

beladen irr vt load

Belag m (-(e)s, Beläge) coating; (on teeth) plaque; (on tongue) fur

belasten vt load; (body) strain; (environment) pollute; fig (with worries etc) burden; COMM (account) debit; LAW incriminate

belästigen vt bother; (stronger) pester; (sexually) harass; **Belästigung** f annoyance; **sexuelle ~** sexual harassment

belebt adj (street etc) busy

Beleg m (-(e)s, -e) COMM receipt; (written evidence) proof; **belegen** vt (bread) spread; (seat) reserve; (course) register for; (claim, expenditure etc) prove

belegt adj TEL engaged (Brit), busy (US); (hotel) full;

(*tongue*) coated; **~es Brötchen** sandwich; **der Platz ist ~** this seat is taken; **Belegtzeichen** *nt* TEL engaged tone (*Brit*), busy tone (*US*)

beleidigen *vt* insult; (*hurt feelings of*) offend; **Beleidigung** *f* insult; LAW slander; (*written*) libel

beleuchten *vt* light; (*light up*) illuminate; *fig* examine; **Beleuchtung** *f* lighting; (*lighting up*) illumination

Belgien *nt* (*-s*) Belgium; **Belgier(in)** *m(f)* (*-s, -*) Belgian; **belgisch** *adj* Belgian

belichten *vt* expose; **Belichtung** *f* exposure; **Belichtungsmesser** *m* (*-s, -*) light meter

Belieben *nt* (**ganz**) **nach ~** (just) as you wish

beliebig 1. *adj* **jedes ~e Muster** any pattern; **jeder ~e** anyone **2.** *adv* **~ lange** as long as you like; **~ viel** as many (*or* much) as you like

beliebt *adj* popular

beliefern *vt* supply

bellen *vi* bark

Belohnung *f* reward

Belüftung *f* ventilation

belügen *irr vt* lie to

bemerkbar *adj* noticeable; **sich ~ machen** (*person*) attract attention; (*thing*) become noticeable; **bemerken** *vt* notice; (*say*) remark; **bemerkenswert** *adj* remarkable; **Bemerkung** *f* remark

bemitleiden *vt* pity

bemühen *vr* try (hard), make an effort; **Bemühung** *f* effort

bemuttern *vt* mother

benachbart *adj* neighbouring

benachrichtigen *vt* inform; **Benachrichtigung** *f* notification

benachteiligen *vt* (put at a) disadvantage; (*racially etc*) discriminate against

benehmen *irr vr* behave; **Benehmen** *nt* (*-s*) behaviour

beneiden *vt* envy; **jdm um etw ~** envy sb sth

Beneluxländer *pl* Benelux countries *pl*

benommen *adj* dazed

benötigen *vt* need

benutzen *vt* use; **Benutzer(in)** *m(f)* (*-s, -*) user; **benutzerfreundlich** *adj* user-friendly; **Benutzerhandbuch** *nt* user's guide; **Benutzerkennung** *f* user ID; **Benutzeroberfläche** *f* IT user / system interface

Benzin *nt* (*-s, -e*) AUTO petrol (*Brit*), gas (*US*); **Benzinkanister** *m* petrol (*Brit*) (*or* gas (*US*)) can; **Benzinpumpe** *f* petrol (*Brit*) (*or* gas (*US*)) pump; **Benzintank** *m* petrol (*Brit*) (*or* gas (*US*)) tank; **Benzinuhr** *f* fuel gauge

beobachten *vt* observe; **Beobachtung** *f* observation

bequem *adj* comfortable; (*excuse*) convenient; (*idle*) lazy;

Bequemlichkeit

machen Sie es sich ~ make yourself at home; **Bequemlichkeit** f comfort; laziness

beraten irr **1.** vt advise; (plan etc) discuss **2.** vr consult; **Beratung** f advice; (at doctor's etc) consultation

berauben vt rob

berechnen vt calculate; COMM charge; **berechnend** adj (person) calculating

berechtigen vt entitle (zu to); fig justify; **berechtigt** adj justified; **zu etw ~ sein** be entitled to sth

bereden vt discuss

Bereich m (-(e)s, -e) area; (sphere) field

bereisen vt travel through

bereit adj ready; **zu etw ~ sein** be ready for sth; **sich ~ erklären, etw zu tun** agree to do sth

bereiten vt prepare; (grief) cause; (pleasure) give

bereitlegen vt lay out

bereitmachen vr get ready

bereits adv already

Bereitschaft f readiness; **~ haben** (doctor) be on call

bereitstehen vi be ready

bereuen vt regret

Berg m (-(e)s, -e) mountain; (smaller) hill; **in die ~e fahren** go to the mountains; **bergab** adv downhill; **bergauf** adv uphill; **Bergbahn** f mountain railway (Brit) (or railroad (US))

bergen (barg, geborgen) vt (person) rescue

Bergführer(in) m(f) mountain guide; **Berghütte** f mountain hut; **bergig** adj mountainous; **Bergkette** f mountain range; **Bergschuh** m climbing boot; **Bergsteigen** nt (-s) mountaineering; **Bergsteiger(in)** m(f) (-s, -) mountaineer; **Bergtour** f mountain hike

Bergung f rescue; (of body, vehicle) recovery

Bergwacht f (-, -en) mountain rescue service; **Bergwerk** nt mine

Bericht m (-(e)s, -e) report; **berichten** vt, vi report

berichtigen vt correct

Bermudadreieck nt Bermuda triangle; **Bermudainseln** pl Bermuda Isles; **Bermudashorts** pl Bermuda shorts pl

Bernstein m amber

berüchtigt adj notorious, infamous

berücksichtigen vt take into account; (application, applicant) consider

Beruf m (-(e)s, -e) occupation; (requiring academic training) profession; (skilled, self-employed) trade; **was sind Sie von ~?** what do you do (for a living)?; **beruflich** adj professional

Berufsausbildung f vocational training; **Berufsschule** f vocational college; **berufstätig** adj employed; **Be-**

56

rufsverkehr m commuter traffic

beruhigen 1. vt calm **2.** vr (*person, situation*) calm down; **beruhigend** adj reassuring; **Beruhigungsmittel** nt sedative

berühmt adj famous

berühren 1. vt touch; (*emotionally*) move; (*be important for*) affect; (*subject*) mention, touch on **2.** vr touch

besaufen irr vr fam get plastered

beschädigen vt damage

beschäftigen 1. vt occupy; (*worker*) employ **2.** vr **sich mit etw ~** occupy oneself with sth; (*problem etc*) deal with sth; **beschäftigt** adj busy, occupied; **Beschäftigung** f (*work*) employment; (*activity*) occupation; (*with problem etc*) preoccupation (*mit* with)

Bescheid m (-(e)s, -e) information; **~ wissen** be informed (*or* know) (*über* + acc about); **ich weiß ~** I know; (*jdm* **~ geben** (*or* **sagen**) let sb know

bescheiden adj modest

bescheinigen vt certify; (*confirm*) acknowledge; **Bescheinigung** f certificate; (*for money*) receipt

bescheißen irr vt vulg cheat (*um* out of)

beschimpfen vt swear at

Beschiss m (-es) **das ist ~**

vulg that's a rip-off; **beschissen** adj vulg shitty

beschlagnahmen vt confiscate

Beschleunigung f acceleration; **Beschleunigungsspur** f acceleration lane

beschließen irr vt decide on; (*conclude*) end; **Beschluss** m decision

beschränken 1. vt limit, restrict (*auf* + acc to) **2.** vr restrict oneself (*auf* + acc to); **Beschränkung** f limitation, restriction

beschreiben irr vt describe; (*paper*) write on; **Beschreibung** f description

beschuldigen vt accuse (*gen* of); **Beschuldigung** f accusation

beschummeln vt, vi fam cheat (*um* out of)

beschützen vt protect (*vor* + dat from)

Beschwerde f (-, -n) complaint; **~n** pl (*illness*) trouble sg; **beschweren 1.** vt weigh down; fig burden **2.** vr complain

beschwipst adj tipsy

beseitigen vt remove; (*problem*) get rid of; (*rubbish*) dispose of; **Beseitigung** f removal; (*of rubbish*) disposal

Besen m (-s, -) broom

besetzen vt (*house, country*) occupy; (*seat*) take; (*post*) fill; (*role*) cast; **besetzt** adj full; TEL engaged (*Brit*), busy

(*US*); (*seat*) taken; (*toilet*) engaged; **Besetztzeichen** *nt* engaged tone (*Brit*), busy tone (*US*)

besichtigen *vt* (*museum*) visit; (*sights*) have a look at; (*town*) tour

besiegen *vt* defeat

Besitz *m* (*-es*) possession; (*objects*) property; **besitzen** *irr vt* own; (*quality*) have; **Besitzer(in)** *m(f)* (*-s, -*) owner

besoffen *adj fam* plastered

besondere(r, s) *adj* special; (*specific, more than usual*) particular; (*strange*) peculiar; **nichts ~s** nothing special; **Besonderheit** *f* special feature; (*unusual characteristic*) peculiarity; **besonders** *adv* especially, particularly; (*individually*) separately

besorgen *vt* (*obtain*) get (*jdm* for sb); (*buy also*) purchase; (*task etc*) deal with

besprechen *irr vt* discuss; **Besprechung** *f* discussion; (*conference*) meeting

besser *adj* better; **es geht ihm ~** he feels better; **~ gesagt** or rather; **~ werden** improve; **bessern 1.** *vt* improve **2.** *vr* improve; (*person*) mend one's ways; **Besserung** *f* improvement; **gute ~!** get well soon

beständig *adj* constant; (*weather*) settled

Bestandteil *m* component

bestätigen *vt* confirm; (*receipt, letter*) acknowledge; **Bestätigung** *f* confirmation; (*of letter*) acknowledgement

beste(r, s) *adj* best; **das ~ wäre, wir ...** it would be best if we ... **2.** *adv* **sie singt am ~n** she sings best; **so ist es am ~n** it's best that way; **am ~n gehst du gleich** you'd better go at once

bestechen *irr vt* bribe; **Bestechung** *f* bribery

Besteck *nt* (*-(e)s, -e*) cutlery

bestehen *irr* **1.** *vi* be, exist; (*continue*) last; **~ auf +** *dat* insist on; **~ aus** consist of **2.** *vt* (*test, exam*) pass; (*fight*) win

bestehlen *irr vt* rob

bestellen *vt* order; (*reserve*) book; (*regards, message*) pass on (*jdm* to sb); (*person*) send for (*jdm* sb); **Bestellnummer** *f* order number; **Bestellung** *f* COMM order; (*action*) ordering

bestens *adv* very well

bestimmen *vt* determine; (*rules*) lay down; (*day, place*) fix; (*person to a post*) appoint; (*intend*) mean (*für* for); **bestimmt 1.** *adj* definite; (*left unspecified*) certain; (*resolute*) firm **2.** *adv* definitely; (*know*) for sure; **Bestimmung** *f* (*rule*) regulation; (*intended use*) purpose

Best.-Nr. *abbr* = **Bestellnummer**; order number

bestrafen *vt* punish

bestrahlen vt illuminate; MED treat with radiotherapy

bestreiten irr vt (assertion etc) deny

Bestseller m (-s, -) bestseller

bestürzt adj dismayed

Besuch m (-(e)s, -e) visit; (person) visitor; ~ **haben** have visitors / a visitor; **besuchen** vt visit; (school, cinema etc) go to; **Besucher(in)** m(f) (-s, -) visitor; **Besuchszeit** f visiting hours pl

betäuben vt MED anaesthetize; **Betäubungsmittel** nt anaesthetic

Bete f (-, -n) **Rote** ~ beetroot

beteiligen 1. vr **sich an etw** dat ~ take part in sth, participate in sth 2. vr **jdn an etw** dat ~ involve sb in sth; **Beteiligung** f participation; (portion) share; (number of people present) attendance

beten vi pray

Beton m (-s, -s) concrete

betonen vt stress; (give prominence to) emphasize; **Betonung** f stress; fig emphasis

Betr. abbr = **Betreff**: re

Betracht m **in** ~ **ziehen** take into consideration; **in** ~ **kommen** be a possibility; **nicht in** ~ **kommen** be out of the question; **betrachten** vt look at; ~ **als** regard as; **beträchtlich** adj considerable

Betrag m (-(e)s, Beträge) amount, sum; **betragen** irr 1. vt (or come) to

2. vr behave

betreffen irr vt concern; (regulation etc) affect; **was mich betrifft** as for me; betreffend adj relevant, in question

betreten irr vt enter; (stage etc) step onto; „**Betreten verboten**" 'keep off / out'

betreuen vt look after; (party of tourists, department) be in charge of; **Betreuer(in)** m(f) (-s, -) (of invalid, old person) carer; (of child) child minder; (of party of tourists) groupleader

Betrieb m (-(e)s, -e) (company) firm; (buildings etc) plant; (of machine, factory) operation; (in shops etc) bustle; **außer** ~ **sein** be out of order; **in** ~ **sein** be in operation; **betriebsbereit** adj operational; **Betriebsrat** m works council; **Betriebssystem** nt IT operating system

betrinken irr vr get drunk

betroffen adj (upset) shaken; **von etw** ~ **werden / sein** be affected by sth

betrog imperf of **betrügen**; **betrogen** pp of **betrügen**

Betrug m (-(e)s) deception; LAW fraud; **betrügen** (betrog, betrogen) vt deceive; LAW defraud; (partner) cheat on; **Betrüger(in)** m(f) (-s, -) cheat

betrunken adj drunk

Bett nt (-(e)s, -en) bed; **ins** (or

zu) ~ gehen go to bed; **das ~ machen** make the bed; Bettbezug *m* duvet cover; Bettdecke *f* blanket

betteln *vi* beg

Bettlaken *nt* sheet

Bettler(in) *m(f)* (*-s, -*) beggar

Bettsofa *nt* sofa bed; Betttuch *nt* sheet; Bettwäsche *f* bed linen; Bettzeug *m* bedding

beugen 1. *vt* bend **2.** *vr* bend; (*yield*) submit (*dat* to)

Beule *f* (*-, -n*) bump; (*in car etc*) dent

beunruhigen *vt, vr* worry

beurteilen *vt* judge

Beute *f* (*-*) (*of thief*) booty, loot; (*of animal*) prey

Beutel *m* (*-s, -*) bag

Bevölkerung *f* population

bevollmächtigt *adj* authorized (*zu etw* to do sth)

bevor *conj* before; bevorstehen *irr vi* (*difficulties*) lie ahead; (*danger*) be imminent; **jdm ~** (*surprise etc*) be in store for sb; bevorstehend *adj* forthcoming; bevorzugen *vt* prefer

bewachen *vt* guard; bewacht *adj* **~er Parkplatz** supervised car park (*Brit*), guarded parking lot (*US*)

bewegen *vt, vr* move; **jdn dazu ~, etw zu tun** get sb to do sth; **es bewegt sich etwas** *fig* things are beginning to happen; **Bewegung** *f* movement; PHYS motion; (*inner*) emotion; (*bodily*) exercise; Bewegungsmelder *m* (*-s, -*) sensor (*which reacts to movement*)

Beweis *m* (*-es, -e*) proof; (*material, facts*) evidence; beweisen *irr vt* prove; (*demonstrate*) show

bewerben *irr vr* apply (*um* for); Bewerbung *f* application; Bewerbungsunterlagen *pl* application documents *pl*

bewilligen *vt* allow; (*money*) grant

bewirken *vt* cause, bring about

bewohnen *vt* live in; Bewohner(in) *m(f)* (*-s, -*) inhabitant; (*of house*) resident

bewölkt *adj* cloudy, overcast; Bewölkung *f* clouds *pl*

bewundern *vt* admire; bewundernswert *adj* admirable

bewusst 1. *adj* conscious; (*intentional*) deliberate; **sich** *dat* **einer Sache gen ~ sein** be aware of sth **2.** *adv* consciously; (*intentionally*) deliberately; bewusstlos *adj* unconscious; Bewusstlosigkeit *f* unconsciousness; Bewusstsein *nt* (*-s*) consciousness; **bei ~** conscious

bezahlen *vt* pay; (*goods, service*) pay for; **sich bezahlt machen** be worth it

Bezahlung *f* payment

bezeichnen *vt* (*with sign etc*)

mark; (*give name to*) call; (*categorize*) describe; **Bezeichnung** f name; (*expression*) term

beziehen *irr* **1.** *vt* (*bed*) change; (*house, position*) move into; (*get*) receive; (*newspaper*) take; **einen Standpunkt ~** *fig* take up a position **2.** *vr* refer (*auf + acc* to); **Beziehung** f (*between two things*) connection; (*between lovers*) relationship; **~en haben** (*influential*) have connections (*or* contacts); **in dieser ~** in this respect; **beziehungsweise** *adv* or; (*more precisely*) or rather

Bezirk m (*-(e)s, -e*) district

Bezug m (*-(e)s, Bezüge*) (*for cushion etc*) cover; (*for pillow*) pillowcase; **in ~ auf + acc** with regard to; **bezüglich** *prep + gen* concerning

bezweifeln *vt* doubt

BH m (*-s, -s*) bra

Bhf. *abbr* = **Bahnhof**; station

Biathlon nt (*-s, -s*) biathlon

Bibel f (*-, -n*) Bible

Biber m (*-s, -*) beaver

Bibliothek f (*-, -en*) library

biegen (*bog, gebogen*) **1.** *vt, vr* bend **2.** *vi* turn (*in + acc* into); **Biegung** f bend

Biene f (*-, -n*) bee

Bier nt (*-(e)s, -e*) beer; **helles ~** ≈ lager (*Brit*), beer (*US*); **dunkles ~** ≈ brown ale (*Brit*), dark beer (*US*); **zwei**

~, bitte! two beers, please; **Biergarten** m beer garden; **Bierzelt** nt beer tent

bieten (*bot, geboten*) **1.** *vt* offer; (*at auction*) bid; **sich dat etw ~ lassen** put up with sth **2.** *vr* (*opportunity*) present itself (*dat* to)

Bikini m (*-s, -s*) bikini

Bild nt (*-(e)s, -er*) picture; (*in one's mind*) image; PHOT photo

bilden 1. *vt* form; (*intellectually*) educate; (*rule, basis etc*) constitute **2.** *vr* form; (*learn*) educate oneself

Bilderbuch nt picture book **Bildhauer(in)** m(f) (*-s, -*) sculptor

Bildschirm m screen; **Bildschirmschoner** m (*-s, -*) screen saver; **Bildschirmtext** m viewdata, videotext

Bildung f formation; (*knowledge, manners*) education; **Bildungsurlaub** m educational holiday; (*of employee*) study leave

Billard nt billiards *sg*

billig *adj* cheap; (*just*) fair

Binde f (*-, -n*) bandage; (*worn on arm*) band; (*for woman's period*) sanitary towel (*Brit*), sanitary napkin (*US*)

Bindehautentzündung f conjunctivitis

binden (*band, gebunden*) *vt* tie; (*book*) bind; (*sauce*) thicken

Bindestrich m hyphen

Bindfaden m string

Bindung f bond, tie; (on ski) binding

Bio- in cpds bio-; **Biokost** f health food; **Biologie** f biology; **biologisch** adj biological; (cultivation) organic

Birke f (-, -n) birch

Birne f (-, -n) pear; ELEC (light) bulb

bis 1. prep + acc (space) to, as far as; (time) till, until; (at the latest) by; **Sie haben ~ Dienstag Zeit** you have until (or till) Tuesday; **~ Dienstag muss es fertig sein** it must be ready by Tuesday; **~ hierher** this far; **~ in die Nacht** into the night; **~ auf weiteres** until further notice; **~ bald/gleich!** see you later/soon; **~ auf etw** acc including sth; (excluding) except sth; **~ zu** up to; **von ... ~ ...** from ... to ... **2.** conj (numbers) to; (time) until, till

Bischof m (-s, Bischöfe) bishop

bisher adv up to now, so far

Biskuit nt (-(e)s, -s or -e) sponge

biss imperf of **beißen**

Biss m (-es, -e) bite

bisschen 1. adj **ein ~** a bit of; **ein ~ Salz/Liebe** a bit of salt/love; **ich habe kein ~ Hunger** I'm not a bit hungry **2.** adv **ein ~** a bit; **kein ~** not at all

bissig adj (dog) vicious; (re-

mark) cutting

Bit nt (-s, -s) IT bit

bitte interj please; **(wie) ~?** (I beg your) pardon?; **~ (schön)!** (replying to thanks) you're welcome, that's alright; **hier, ~** here you are; **Bitte** f (-, -n) request; **bitten** (bat, gebeten) vt, vi ask (um for)

bitter adj bitter

Blähungen pl MED wind sg

blamieren 1. vr make a fool of oneself 2. vt **jdn ~** make sb look a fool

Blankoscheck m blank cheque

Blase f (-, -n) bubble; MED blister; ANAT bladder

blasen (blies, geblasen) vi blow; **jdm einen ~** vulg give sb a blow job

Blasenentzündung f cystitis

blass adj pale

Blatt nt (-(e)s, Blätter) leaf; (of paper) sheet; **blättern** vi IT scroll; **in etw** dat **~** leaf through sth; **Blätterteig** m puff pastry; **Blattsalat** m green salad; **Blattspinat** m spinach

blau adj blue; fam (drunk) plastered; GASTR boiled; **~es Auge** black eye; **~er Fleck** bruise; **Blaubeere** f bilberry, blueberry; **Blaulicht** nt flashing blue light; **blaumachen** vi skip work; (pupil) skip school; **Blauschimmelkäse** m blue cheese

Blazer m (-s, -) blazer

Blech nt (-(e)s, -e) sheet metal; (*for oven*) baking tray (*Brit*), cookie sheet (*US*); **Blechschaden** m AUTO damage to the bodywork

Blei nt (-(e)s, -e) lead

bleiben (blieb, geblieben) vi stay; **lass das ~!** stop it; **das bleibt unter uns** that's (just) between ourselves; **mir bleibt keine andere Wahl** I have no other choice

bleich adj pale; **bleichen** vi bleach

bleifrei adj (*petrol*) unleaded; **bleihaltig** adj (*petrol*) leaded

Bleistift m pencil

Blende f (-, -n) PHOT aperture

Blick m (-(e)s, -e) look; (*brief*) glance; (*from a place*) view; **auf den ersten ~** at first sight; **einen ~ auf etw acc werfen** have a look at sth; **blicken** vi look; **sich ~ lassen** show up

blieb imperf of **bleiben**

blies imperf of **blasen**

blind adj blind; (*glass etc*) dull; **Blinddarm** m appendix; **Blinddarmentzündung** f appendicitis; **Blinde(r)** mf blind person/man/woman; **die ~n** pl the blind pl; **Blindenhund** m guide dog; **Blindenschrift** f braille

blinken vi (*star, lights*) twinkle; (*brightly, briefly*) flash;

AUTO indicate; **Blinker** m (-s, -) AUTO indicator (*Brit*), turn signal (*US*)

blinzeln vi blink

Blitz m (-es, -e) (flash of) lightning; PHOT flash; **blitzen** vi PHOT use a/the flash; **es blitzte und donnerte** there was thunder and lightning; **Blitzlicht** nt flash

Block m (-(e)s, Blöcke) block; (*of paper*) pad; **Blockflöte** f recorder; **Blockhaus** nt log cabin; **blockieren** 1. vt block 2. vi jam; (*wheels*) lock; **Blockschrift** f block letters pl

blöd adj stupid; **blödeln** vi fam fool around

blond adj blond; (*woman*) blonde

bloß 1. adj (*without covering*) bare; (*nothing more than*) mere 2. adv only; **geh mir ~ aus dem Weg** just get out of my way

blühen vi bloom; fig flourish

Blume f (-, -n) flower; (*of wine*) bouquet; **Blumenkohl** m cauliflower; **Blumenladen** m flower shop; **Blumenstrauß** m bunch of flowers; **Blumentopf** m flowerpot; **Blumenvase** f vase

Bluse f (-, -n) blouse

Blut nt (-(e)s) blood; **Blutbild** nt blood count; **Blutdruck** m blood pressure

Blüte f (-, -n) (*part of plant*) flower, bloom; (*on tree*) blossom; *fig* prime

bluten *vi* bleed

Blütenstaub *m* pollen

Bluter *m* (*-s*, *-*) MED haemophiliac; **Blutguss** *m* haematoma; (*on skin*) bruise; **Blutgruppe** *f* blood group; **blutig** *adj* bloody; **Blutkonserve** *f* unit of stored blood; **Blutprobe** *f* blood sample; **Blutspende** *f* blood donation; **Bluttransfusion** *f* blood transfusion; **Blutung** *f* bleeding; **Blutvergiftung** *f* blood poisoning; **Blutwurst** *f* black pudding (*Brit*), blood sausage (*US*)

BLZ *abbr* = **Bankleitzahl**

Bob *m* (*-s*, *-s*) bob (sleigh)

Bock *m* (*-(e)s*, *Böcke*) (*deer*) buck; (*sheep*) ram; (*goat*) trestle; SPORT vaulting horse; **ich hab keinen ~ (drauf** *fam* I don't feel like it

Boden *m* (*-s*, *Böden*) ground; (*of room*) floor; (*of sea, barrel*) bottom; (*loft*) attic; **Bodennebel** *m* ground mist; **Bodenpersonal** *nt* ground staff; **Bodenschätze** *pl* mineral resources *pl*

Bodensee *m* **der ~** Lake Constance

Body *m* (*-s*, *-s*) body; **Bodybuilding** *nt* (*-s*) bodybuilding

bog *imperf of* **biegen**

Bogen *m* (*-s*, *-*) curve; (*in architecture*) arch; (*weapon, for violin etc*) bow; (*of paper*)

sheet

Bohne *f* (*-*, *-n*) bean; **grüne ~n** *pl* green (*or* French (*Brit*)) beans *pl*; **weiße ~n** *pl* haricot beans *pl*; **Bohnenkaffee** *m* real coffee; **Bohnensprosse** *f* bean sprout

bohren *vt* drill; **Bohrer** *m* (*-s*, *-*) drill

Boiler *m* (*-s*, *-*) water heater

Boje *f* (*-*, *-n*) buoy

Bolivien *nt* (*-s*) Bolivia

Bombe *f* (*-*, *-n*) bomb

Bon *m* (*-s*, *-s*) receipt; (*exchangeable for goods etc*) voucher, coupon

Bonbon *nt* (*-s*, *-s*) sweet (*Brit*), candy (*US*)

Bonus *m* (*-* *or* *-ses*, *-se* or *Boni*) bonus; (*in sport, school*) bonus points *pl*; (*in insurance*) no-claims bonus

Boot *nt* (*-(e)s*, *-e*) boat; **Bootsverleih** *m* boat hire (*Brit*) (*or* rental (*US*))

Bord *m* (*-(e)s*, *-e*) **an ~ (eines Schiffes)** on board (a ship); **an ~ gehen** (*ship*) go on board; (*plane*) board; **von ~ gehen** disembark; **Bordcomputer** *m* dashboard computer

Bordell *nt* (*-s*, *-e*) brothel

Bordkarte *f* boarding card

Bordstein *m* kerb (*Brit*), curb (*US*)

borgen *vt* borrow; **jdm etw ~** lend sb sth; **sich** *dat* **etw ~** borrow sth

Börse *f* (*-*, *-n*) stock exchange;

(for coins) purse

bös *adj* → **böse**; **bösartig** *adj* malicious; MED malignant

Böschung *f* slope; *(along river)* embankment

böse *adj* bad; *(stronger)* evil; *(wound)* nasty; *(annoyed)* angry; *bist du mir ~?* are you angry with me?

boshaft *adj* malicious

Bosnien *f* (*-s*) Bosnia; **Bosnien-Herzegowina** *nt* (*-s*) Bosnia-Herzegowina

böswillig *adj* malicious

bot *imperf of* **bieten**

botanisch *adj* **~er Garten** botanical gardens *pl*

Botschaft *f* message; POL embassy; **Botschafter(in)** *m(f)* ambassador

Botsuana *nt* (*-s*) Botswana

Bouillon *f* (*-*, *-s*) stock

Boutique *f* (*-*, *-n*) boutique

Bowle *f* (*-*, *-n*) punch

Box *f* (*-*, *-en*) *(container, for horse)* box; *(of stereo system)* speaker; *(in motor racing)* pit

boxen *vi* box; **Boxer** *m* (*-s*, *-*) *(dog, sportsman)* boxer; **Boxershorts** *pl* boxer shorts *pl*; **Boxkampf** *m* boxing match

Boykott *m* (*-s*, *-e*) boycott

brach *imperf of* **brechen**

brachte *imperf of* **bringen**

Brainstorming *nt* (*-s*) brainstorming

Branchenverzeichnis *nt* yellow pages® *pl*

Brand *m* (*-(e)s*, *Brände*) fire

Brandenburg *nt* (*-s*) Brandenburg

Brandsalbe *f* ointment for burns

Brandung *f* surf

Brandwunde *f* burn

brannte *imperf of* **brennen**

Brasilien *nt* (*-s*) Brazil

braten *(briet, gebraten)* *vt* roast; grill; fry; **Braten** *m* (*-s*, *-*) roast; *(uncooked)* joint; **Bratensoße** *f* gravy; **Brathähnchen** *nt* roast chicken; **Bratkartoffeln** *pl* fried potatoes *pl*; **Bratpfanne** *f* frying pan; **Bratspieß** *m* spit; **Bratwurst** *f* fried sausage; grilled sausage

Brauch *m* (*-s*, *Bräuche*) custom

brauchen *vt* need *(für, zu* for); *(patience, care etc)* require; *(time)* take; *(make use of)* use; *wie lange wird er ~?* how long will it take him?; *du brauchst es nur zu sagen* you only need to say; *das braucht (seine) Zeit* it takes time; *ihr braucht es nicht zu tun* you don't have (*or* need) to do it; *sie hätte nicht zu kommen ~* she needn't have come

brauen *vt* brew; **Brauerei** *f* brewery

braun *adj* brown; *(from sun)* tanned; **Bräune** *f* (*-*, *-n*) brownness; *(from sun)* tan; **Bräunungsstudio** *nt* tanning studio

Brause f (-, -n) (*apparatus*) shower; (*drink*) fizzy drink (*Brit*), soda (*US*)

Braut f (-, *Bräute*) bride; **Bräutigam** m (-s, -e) bridegroom

brav adj (*child*) good, well-behaved

bravo interj well done

brechen (*brach, gebrochen*) **1.** vt break; (*vomit*) bring up; **sich** dat **den Arm ~** break one's arm **2.** vi break; (*when unwell*) vomit, be sick; **Brechreiz** m nausea

Brei m (-(e)s, -e) mush, pulp; (*oats*) porridge; (*for children*) pap

breit adj wide; (*shoulders*) broad; **zwei Meter ~** two metres wide; **Breite** f (-, -n) breadth; (*in measurements*) width; GEO latitude; **der ~ nach** widthways; **Breitengrad** m (degree of) latitude

Bremen nt (-s) Bremen

Bremsbelag m brake lining; **Bremse** f (-, -n) brake; ZOOL horsefly; **bremsen 1.** vi brake **2.** vt (*car*) brake; fig slow down; **Bremsflüssigkeit** f brake fluid; **Bremslicht** nt brake light; **Bremspedal** nt brake pedal; **Bremsspur** f tyre marks pl; **Bremsweg** m braking distance

brennen (*brannte, gebrannt*) vi burn; (*house, forest*) be

on fire; **es brennt!** fire!; **mir ~ die Augen** my eyes are smarting; **das Licht ~ lassen** leave the light on; **Brennholz** nt firewood; **Brennnessel** f stinging nettle; **Brennspiritus** m methylated spirits pl; **Brennstab** m fuel rod; **Brennstoff** m fuel

Brett nt (-(e)s, -er) board; (*longer*) plank; (*for books etc*) shelf; (*for game*) board; **schwarzes ~** notice board, bulletin board (*US*); **~er** pl skis pl; **Brettspiel** nt board game

Brezel f (-, -n) pretzel

Brief m (-(e)s, -e) letter; **Briefbombe** f letter bomb; **Brieffreund(in)** m(f) penfriend, pen pal; **Briefkasten** m letterbox (*Brit*), mailbox (*US*); **Briefmarke** f stamp; **Briefpapier** nt writing paper; **Brieftasche** f wallet; **Briefträger(in)** m(f) postman/-woman; **Briefumschlag** m envelope; **Briefwaage** f letter scales pl

brief imperf of **braten**

Brille f (-, -n) glasses pl; (*protective*) goggles pl; **Brillenetui** nt glasses case

bringen (*brachte, gebracht*) vt bring; (*somewhere else*) take; (*go and come back with*) get, fetch; THEAT, FILM show; RADIO, TV broadcast; **~ Sie mir bitte noch ein Bier** could you bring me another beer, please?; **jdn nach Hause ~** take sb home; **jdn dazu ~, etw zu tun** make sb do sth; **jdn auf eine Idee ~** give sb an idea

Brise f (-, -n) breeze
Brite m (-n, -n), Britin f British person, Briton; **er ist ~** he is British; **die ~n** the British; **britisch** adj British
Brocken m (-s, -) bit; (larger) lump, chunk
Brokkoli m broccoli
Brombeere f blackberry
Bronchitis f (-) bronchitis
Bronze f (-, -n) bronze
Brosche f (-, -n) brooch
Brot nt (-(e)s, -e) bread; loaf; Brotaufstrich m spread; Brötchen nt roll; Brotzeit f break; (food) snack; **~ machen** have a snack
Browser m (-s, -) IT browser
Bruch m (-(e)s, Brüche) (action) breaking; (crack etc; with party, tradition etc) break; MED rupture, hernia; (of bone) fracture; MATH fraction; **brüchig** adj brittle
Brücke f (-, -n) bridge
Bruder m (-s, Brüder) brother
Brühe f (-, -n) (clear) soup; (basis for soup) stock; pej (drink) muck; Brühwürfel m stock cube
brüllen vi roar; (bull) bellow; (in agony) scream (with pain)
brummen 1. vi (bear, person) growl; (mumble) mutter; (insect) buzz; (engine, radio) drone 2. vt growl

brünett adj brunette
Brunnen m (-s, -) fountain; (deep) well; (natural) spring
Brust f (-, Brüste) breast; (of man) chest; Brustschwimmen nt (-s) breaststroke; Brustwarze f nipple
brutal adj brutal
brutto adv gross
BSE nt (-) abbr = **bovine spongiforme Enzephalopathie**; BSE
Bube m (-n, -n) boy, lad; (playing card) jack
Buch nt (-(e)s, Bücher) book
Buche f (-, -n) beech (tree)
buchen vt book; (amount) enter
Bücherei f library
Buchfink m chaffinch
Buchhalter(in) m(f) accountant
Buchhandlung f bookshop
Büchse f (-, -n) tin (Brit), can; Büchsenfleisch nt tinned meat (Brit), canned meat; Büchsenmilch f tinned milk (Brit), canned milk; Büchsenöffner m tin opener (Brit), can opener
Buchstabe m (-ns, -n) letter; buchstabieren vt spell
Bucht f (-, -en) bay
Buchung f booking; COMM entry
Buckel m (-s, -) hump
bücken vr bend down
Buddhismus m (-) Bud-

Bude

dhism

Bude f (-, -en) (at market) stall; fam (flat) pad, place

Büfett nt (-s, -s) sideboard; **kaltes ~** cold buffet

Büffel m (-s, -) buffalo

Bügel m (-s, -) (for clothes) hanger; (on saddle) stirrup; (of glasses) sidepiece; (of ski-lift) T-bar; **Bügelbrett** nt ironing board; **Bügeleisen** nt iron; **Bügelfalte** f crease; **bügelfrei** adj non--iron; **bügeln** vt, vi iron

buh interj boo

Bühne f (-, -n) stage; **Bühnenbild** nt set

Bulgare m (-n, -n) Bulgarian; **Bulgarien** nt (-s) Bulgaria; **bulgarisch** adj Bulgarian; **Bulgarisch** nt Bulgarian

Bulimie f (-) bulimia

Bulle m (-n, -n) bull; fam (policeman) cop

Bummel m (-s, -) stroll; **bummeln** vi stroll; fam (do things slowly) dawdle; (be idle) loaf around; **Bummelzug** m slow train

bums interj bang

bumsen vi vulg screw

Bund 1. m (-(e)s, Bünde) (of trousers, skirt) waistband; (between friends) bond; (organization) association; POL confederation; **der ~** fam (German military) the army 2. nt (-(e)s, -e) bunch; (of straw etc) bundle

Bundes- in cpds Federal; (referring to Germany also) German; **Bundesbahn** f German railway company; **Bundeskanzler(in)** m(f) Chancellor; **Bundesland** nt state, Land; **Bundesliga** f **erste/zweite ~** First/Second Division; **Bundespräsident(in)** m(f) President; **Bundesrat** m Upper House (of the German Parliament); (in Switzerland) Council of Ministers; **Bundesregierung** f Federal Government; **Bundesrepublik** f Federal Republic; **~ Deutschland** Federal Republic of Germany; **Bundesstraße** f ≈ A road (Brit), ≈ state highway (US); **Bundestag** m Lower House (of the German Parliament); **Bundeswehr** f (German) armed forces pl

Bündnis f alliance

Bungalow m (-s, -s) bungalow

Bungeejumping nt (-s) bungee jumping

bunt 1. adj colourful; (programme etc) varied; **~e Farben** bright colours 2. adv (paint) in bright colours; **Buntstift** m crayon, coloured pencil

Burg f (-, -en) castle

Bürger(in) m(f) (-s, -) citizen; **bürgerlich** adj (rights, marriage etc) civil; (in social hierarchy) middle-class; pej bourgeois; **Bürgermeis-**

ter(in) *m(f)* mayor; **Bürgersteig** *m* (-(e)s, -e) pavement (*Brit*), sidewalk (*US*)
Büro *nt* (-s, -s) office; **Büroklammer** *f* paper clip
Bürokratie *f* bureaucracy
Bursche *m* (-n, -n) lad; (*man*) guy
Bürste *f* (-, -n) brush; **bürsten** *vt* brush
Bus *m* (-ses, -se) bus; (*long-distance*) coach (*Brit*), bus; **Busbahnhof** *m* bus station
Busch *m* (-(e)s, *Büsche*) bush; shrub
Busen *m* (-s, -) breasts *pl*, bosom
Busfahrer(in) *m(f)* bus driv-

er; **Bushaltestelle** *f* bus stop
Businessclass *f* (-) business class
Busreise *f* coach tour (*Brit*), bus tour
Büßgeld *nt* fine
Büstenhalter *m* (-s, -) bra
Busverbindung *f* bus connection
Butter *f* (-) butter; **Butterbrot** *nt* slice of bread and butter; **Buttermilch** *f* buttermilk
Button *m* (-s, -s) badge (*Brit*), button (*US*)
b. w. *abbr* = *bitte wenden*; pto
Byte *nt* (-s, -s) byte
bzw. *adv abbr* = *beziehungsweise*

C

ca. *adv abbr* = *circa*; approx
Cabrio *nt* (-s, -s) convertible
Café *nt* (-s, -s) café
Cafeteria *f* (-, -s) cafeteria
Call-Center *nt* (-s, -) call centre
campen *vi* camp; **Camping** *nt* (-s) camping; **Campingbus** *m* camper; **Campingplatz** *m* campsite, camping ground (*US*)
Cappuccino *m* (-s, -s) cappuccino
Carving *nt* (-s) (*in skiing*) carving; **Carvingski** *m* carving ski
CD *f* (-, -s) *abbr* = *Compact Disc*; CD; **CD-Brenner** *m*

(-s, -) CD burner, CD writer; **CD-Player** *m* (-s, -) CD player; **CD-ROM** *f* (-, -s) *abbr* = *Compact Disc Read Only Memory*; CD-ROM; **CD-ROM-Laufwerk** *nt* CD-ROM drive, **CD-Spieler** *m* CD player
Cello *nt* (-s, -s *or Celli*) cello
Celsius *nt* celsius; *20 Grad ~* 20 degrees Celsius, 68 degrees Fahrenheit
Cent *m* (-, -s) (*of dollar and euro*) cent
Chamäleon *nt* (-s, -s) chameleon
Champagner *m* (-s, -) champagne

Champignon m (-s, -s) mushroom

Champions League f (-, -s) Champions League

Chance f (-, -n) chance; **die~n stehen gut** the prospects are good

Chaos nt (-) chaos; **Chaot(in)** m(f) (-en, -en) disorganized person, scatterbrain; **chaotisch** adj chaotic

Charakter m (-s, -e) character; **charakteristisch** adj characteristic (für + dat)

Charisma nt (-s, Charismen or Charismata) charisma

charmant adj charming

Charterflug m charter flight; **chartern** vt charter

checken vt check; fam (understand) get

Check-in m (-s, -s) check-in; **Check-in-Schalter** m check-in desk

Chef(in) m(f) (-s, -s) boss; **Chefarzt** m, **Chefärztin** f senior consultant (Brit), medical director (US)

Chemie f (-) chemistry; **chemisch** adj chemical; **~e Reinigung** dry cleaning

Chemotherapie f chemotherapy

Chicorée m (-s, -s) chicory

Chiffre f (-, -n) cipher; (in newspaper) box number

Chile nt (-s) Chile

Chili m (-s, -s) chilli

China nt (-s) China; **Chinakohl** m Chinese leaves pl (Brit), bok choy (US); **Chinarestaurant** nt Chinese restaurant; **Chinese** m (-n, -n) Chinese; **Chinesin** f (-, -nen) Chinese (woman); **sie ist ~** she's Chinese; **chinesisch** adj Chinese; **Chinesisch** nt Chinese

Chip m (-s, -s) IT chip; **Chipkarte** f smart card

Chips pl (snack) crisps pl (Brit), chips pl (US)

Chirurg(in) m(f) (-en, -en) surgeon

Chlor nt (-s) chlorine

Choke m (-s, -s) choke

Cholera f (-) cholera

Cholesterin nt (-s) cholesterol

Chor m (-(e), Chöre) choir; THEAT chorus

Choreografie f choreography

Christ(in) m(f) (-en, -en) Christian; **Christbaum** m Christmas tree; **Christi Himmelfahrt** f the Ascension (of Christ); **Christkind** nt baby Jesus; (bringing presents) ≈ Father Christmas, Santa Claus; **christlich** adj Christian

Chrom nt (-s) chrome; CHEM chromium

chronisch adj chronic

chronologisch 1. adj chronological **2.** adv in chronological order

Chrysantheme f (-, -n) chrysanthemum

circa adv about, approximately

City f (-) city centre, downtown (US)

Clementine f (-, -n) clementine

clever adj clever, smart

Clique f (-, -n) group; pej clique; *David und seine ~* David and his friends or crowd

Clown m (-s, -s) clown

Club m (-s, -s) club; **Cluburlaub** m club holiday (Brit), club vacation (US)

Cocktail m (-s, -s) cocktail; **Cocktailtomate** f cherry tomato

Cognac m (-s) cognac

Cola f (-, -s) Coke®, cola

Comic m (-s, -s) comic strip; (magazine) comic

Compact Disc f (-, -s) compact disc

Computer m (-s, -) computer; **Computerfreak** m computer nerd; **computergesteuert** adj computer-controlled; **Computergrafik** f computer graphics pl; **computerlesbar** adj machine-readable; **Computerspiel** nt computer game; **Computertomogra-**

fie f computer tomography, scan; **Computervirus** m computer virus

Container m (-s, -) (for transporting goods) container; (for refuse) skip

Control-Taste f control key

Cookie nt (-s, -s) IT cookie

cool adj fam cool

Cornflakes pl cornflakes pl

Couch f (-, -en) couch; **Couchtisch** m coffee table

Coupé nt (-s, -s) coupé

Coupon m (-s, -s) coupon

Cousin m (-s, -s) cousin; **Cousine** f cousin

Crack nt (-s) (drug) crack

Creme f (-, -s) cream; GASTR mousse

Creutzfeld-Jakob-Krankheit f Creutzfeld-Jakob disease, CJD

Croissant nt (-s, -s) croissant

Curry 1. m (-s) curry powder **2.** nt (-s) (dish) curry; **Currywurst** f fried sausage with ketchup and curry powder

Cursor m (-s, -) IT cursor

Cybercafé nt cybercafé; **Cyberspace** m (-) cyberspace

D

da 1. adv there; here; (time) then; **~ oben/drüben** up/over there; **~, wo** where; **~ sein** be there; **ist jemand ~?** is there anybody there?;

ich bin gleich wieder ~ I'll be right back; *ist noch Brot ~?* is there any bread left?; *es ist keine Milch mehr ~* we've run out of milk; **~, bit-**

te! there you are; **~ kann man nichts machen** there's nothing you can do to 2. *conj* as

dabei *adv* (*position*) close to it; (*simultaneously*) at the same time; (*but*) though; **sie hörte Radio und rauchte ~** she was listening to the radio and smoking (at the same time); **~ fällt mir ein ...** that reminds me ...; **~ kam es zu einem Unfall** this led to an accident; **... und ~ hat er gar keine Ahnung ...** even though he has no idea; **ich finde nichts ~** I find nothing wrong with it; **es bleibt ~** that's settled; **~ sein** be present; (*taking part*) be involved; **ich bin ~!** count me in; **er war gerade ~ zu gehen** he was just (*or* on the point of) leaving

dabeibleiben *irr vi* stick with it; **ich bleibe dabei** I'm not changing my mind

dabeihaben *irr vt* **er hat seine Schwester dabei** he's brought his sister; **ich habe kein Geld dabei** I haven't got any money on me

Dach *nt* (-(e)s, Dächer) roof; **Dachboden** *m* attic; loft; **Dachgepäckträger** *m* roofrack; **Dachrinne** *f* gutter

Dachs *m* (-es, -e) badger

dachte *imperf of* **denken**

Dackel *m* (-s, -) dachshund

dadurch **1.** *adv* (*space*) through it; (*means*) in that

way; (*cause*) because of that, for that reason **2.** *conj* **~, dass** because; **~, dass er hart arbeitete** (*means*) by working hard

dafür *adv* for it; (*in place of it*) instead; **~ habe ich 50 Euro bezahlt** I paid 50 euros for it; **ich bin ~ zu bleiben** I'm for (*or* in favour of) staying; **~ ist er ja da** that's what he's there for; **er kann nichts ~** he can't help it

dagegen *adv* against it; (*dissimilarity*) in comparison; (*exchange*) for it; **ich habe nichts ~** I don't mind

daheim *adv* at home

daher **1.** *adv* from there; (*reason*) that's why **2.** *conj* that's why

dahin *adv* there; (*time*) then; (*past, used up*) gone; **bis ~** till then; (*place*) up to there; **bis ~ muss die Arbeit fertig sein** the work must be finished by then

dahinter *adv* behind it

dahinterkommen *vi* find out

Dahlie *f* dahlia

Dalmatiner *m* (-s, -) dalmatian

damals *adv* at that time, then

Dame *f* (-, -n) lady; (*card*) queen; (*game*) draughts *sg* (*Brit*), checkers *sg* (*US*); **Damenbinde** *f* sanitary towel (*Brit*), sanitary napkin (*US*); **Damenfriseur** *m* ladies' hairdresser; **Damen-**

darstellen

kleidung f ladies' wear; **Damentoilette** f ladies' toilet (*or* restroom (*US*))

damit 1. *adv* with it; (*as a result*) by that; **was meint er ~?** what does he mean by that?; **genug ~!** that's enough **2.** *conj* so that

Damm m (-(e)s, **Dämme**) dyke; (*creating reservoir*) dam; (*in harbour*) mole; (*for railway, road*) embankment

Dämmerung f twilight; (*in morning*) dawn; (*in evening*) dusk

Dampf m (-(e)s, **Dämpfe**) steam; (*haze*) vapour; **Dampfbad** nt Turkish bath; **Dampfbügeleisen** nt steam iron; **dampfen** vi steam

dämpfen vt GASTR steam; (*sound*) deaden; (*enthusiasm*) dampen

Dampfer m (-s, -) steamer

Dampfkochtopf m pressure cooker

danach adv after that; (*time also*) afterwards; (*rules etc*) accordingly; **mir ist nicht ~** I don't feel like it; **~ sieht es aus** that's what it looks like

Däne m (-n, -n) Dane

daneben adv beside it; (*dissimilarity*) in comparison

Dänemark nt (-s) Denmark; **Dänin** f Dane, Danish woman / girl; **dänisch** adj Danish; **Dänisch** nt Danish

dank prep + dat or gen thanks to; **Dank** m (-(e)s) thanks pl; **vielen ~!** thank you very much; **jdm ~ sagen** thank sb; **dankbar** adj grateful; (*task*) rewarding; **danke** interj thank you, thanks; **nein ~!** no, thank you; **~, gerne!** yes, please; **~, gleichfalls!** thanks, and the same to you; **danken** vi **jdm für etw ~** thank sb for sth; **nichts zu ~!** you're welcome

dann adv then; **bis ~!** see you (later); **~ eben nicht** okay, forget it, suit yourself

daran adv on it; (*fix*) to it; (*bang*) against it; **es liegt ~, dass ...** it's because ...

darauf adv on it; (*direction*) towards it; (*time*) afterwards; **es kommt ganz ~ an, ob ...** it all depends whether ...; **ich freue mich ~** I'm looking forward to it; **am Tag ~** the next day

darauffolgend adj (*day, year*) next, following

daraus adv from it; **was ist ~ geworden?** what became of it?

darin adv in it; **das Problem liegt ~, dass ...** the basic problem is that ...

Darlehen nt (-s, -) loan

Darm m (-(e)s, **Därme**) intestine; (*of sausage*) skin; **Darmgrippe** f gastroenteritis

darstellen vt represent; THEAT play; (*of account of*) de-

scribe; **Darsteller(in)** *m(f)*
actor/actress; **Darstellung**
f representation; (*account*)
description

darüber *adv* above it, over it;
(*drive*) over it; (*amount*)
more; (*time*) meanwhile;
(*talk, argue, be pleased*)
about it

darum *adv* (*reason*) that's
why; **es geht ~, dass ...**
the point (*or* thing) is that ...

darunter *adv* under it;
(*group*) among them;
(*amount*) less; **was verstehen Sie ~?** what do you understand by that?

darunterfallen *vi* be included

das 1. *art* the; **er hat sich ~
Bein gebrochen** he's bro-
ken his leg; **vier Euro ~ Kilo**
four euros a kilo **2.** *pron* that
(one), this (one); **~ Auto da**
that car; **ich nehme ~ da**
I'll take that one; **~ heißt**
that is; **~ sind Amerikaner**
they're American **3.** *pron*
(*thing*) that, which; (*person*)
who, that; **~ Auto, ~ er kauf-
te** the car (that *or* which)
he bought; **~ Mädchen, ~
nebenan wohnt** the girl
who (*or* that) lives next door

da sein *irr vi* → **da**

dass *conj* that; **so ~** so that;
es sei denn, ~ unless; **ohne
~ grüßte** without saying
hello

dasselbe *pron* the same

Datei *f* IT file; **Dateimanager**

m file manager

Daten *pl* data *pl*; **Datenbank** *f*
database; **Datenmiss-
brauch** *m* misuse of data;
Datenschutz *m* data protection; **Datenträger** *m* data
carrier; **Datenverarbeitung**
f data processing

datieren *vt* date

Dativ *m* dative (case)

Dattel *f* (-, -n) date

Datum *nt* (-s, **Daten**) date

Dauer *f* (-, -n) duration; (*of
film, visit etc*) length; **auf
die ~** in the long run; **für
die ~ von zwei Jahren** for
(a period of) two years; **Dauerauftrag** *m* IT standing order; **dauerhaft** *adj* lasting;
(*material*) durable; **Dauerkarte** *f* season ticket; **dauern**
vi last; (*require time*) take;
**es hat sehr lange gedauert,
bis er ...** it took him a long
time to ...; **wie lange dauert
es denn noch?** how much
longer will it be?; **das dauert mir zu lange** I can't wait
that long; **dauernd 1.** *adj*
lasting; (*continual*) constant
2. *adv* always, constantly;
er lachte ~ he kept laughing;
unterbrich mich nicht ~
stop interrupting me; **Dauerwelle** *f* perm (*Brit*), permanent (*US*)

Daumen *m* (-s, -) thumb

Daunendecke *f* eiderdown

davon *adv* (*distance*)
away; (*separation*) from it;

(*reason*) because of it; **ich hätte gerne ein Kilo ~** I'd like one kilo of that; **~ habe ich gehört** I've heard of it; (*event*) I've heard about it; **das kommt ~, wenn ...** that's what happens when ...; **was habe ich ~?** what's the point?; **auf und ~ und away; davonlaufen** *irr vi* run away

davor *adv* in front of it; (*time*) before; **ich habe Angst ~** I'm afraid of it

dazu *adv* (*in addition*) on top of that, as well; (*suitability*) for it, for that purpose; **ich möchte Reis ~** I'd like rice with it; **und ~ noch** in addition; **~ fähig sein, etw zu tun** be capable of doing sth; **wie kam es ~?** how did it happen?; **dazugehören** *vi* belong to it; **dazukommen** *irr vi* join sth; **kommt noch etwas dazu?** anything else?

dazwischen *adv* in between; (*difference etc*) between them; (*in group*) among them

dazwischenkommen *irr vi* **wenn nichts dazwischenkommt** if all goes well; **mir ist etwas dazwischengekommen** something has cropped up

dealen *vi* fam deal in drugs; **Dealer(in)** *m(f)* (*-s, -*) *fam* dealer, pusher

Deck *nt* (*-(e)s, -s or -e*) deck; **an ~** on deck

Decke *f* (*-, -n*) cover; (*for bed*) blanket; (*for table*) tablecloth; (*of room*) ceiling

Deckel *m* (*-s, -*) lid

decken 1. *vt* cover; (*table*) lay, set **2.** *vr* (*interests*) coincide; (*statements*) correspond **3.** *vi* lay (*or* set) the table

Decoder *m* (*-s, -*) decoder

defekt *adj* faulty; **Defekt** *m* (*-(e)s, -e*) fault, defect

definieren *vt* define; **Definition** *f* (*-, -en*) definition

deftig *adj* (*prices*) steep; **ein ~es Essen** a good solid meal

dehnbar *adj* flexible, elastic; **dehnen** *vt, vr* stretch

Deich *m* (*-(e)s, -e*) dyke

dein *pron* (*as adj*) your; **deine(r, s)** *pron* (*as noun*) yours, of you; **deinetwegen** *adv* because of you; (*to please you*) for your sake

deinstallieren *vt* (*program*) uninstall

Dekolleté *nt* (*-s, -s*) low neckline

Dekoration *f* decoration; (*in shop*) window dressing; **dekorativ** *adj* decorative; **dekorieren** *vt* decorate; (*shop window*) dress

Delfin *m* (*-s, -e*) dolphin

delikat *adj* (*food*) delicious; (*problem*) delicate

Delikatesse *f* (*-, -n*) delicacy

Delle *f* (*-, -en*) *fam* dent

Delphin *m* (*-s, -e*) dolphin

dem dat sg of **der/das; wie ~ auch sein mag** be that as it may

demnächst adv shortly, soon

Demo f (-, -s) fam demo

Demokratie f (-, -n) democracy; **demokratisch** adj democratic

demolieren vt demolish

Demonstration f Demonstration; **demonstrieren** vt, vi demonstrate

den 1. art acc sg, dat pl of **der; sie hat sich ~ Arm gebrochen** she's broken her arm **2.** pron (person) that one; **~ hab ich schon ewig nicht mehr gesehen** I haven't seen him in ages **3.** pron (person) who, that, whom; (thing) which, that; **der Typ, auf ~ sie steht** the guy (who) she fancies; **der Berg, auf ~ wir geklettert sind** the mountain (that) we climbed

denkbar 1. adj **das ist ~** that's possible **2.** adv **~ einfach** extremely simple; **denken** (dachte, gedacht) **1.** vt, vi think (über + acc about); **an jdn/etw ~** think of sb/sth; (recall, take into consideration) remember sb/sth; **woran denkst Du?** what are you thinking about?; **denk an den Kaffee!** don't forget the coffee **2.** vr imagine; **das kann ich mir ~** I can (well) imag-

ine

Denkmal nt (-s, Denkmäler) monument; **Denkmalschutz** m monument preservation; **unter ~ stehen** be listed

denn 1. conj for, because **2.** adv then; (after comparative) than; **was ist ~?** what's wrong?; **ist das ~ so schwierig?** is it really that difficult?

dennoch conj still, nevertheless

Deo nt (-s, -s), **Deodorant** nt (-s, -s) deodorant; **Deoroller** m roll-on deodorant; **Deospray** m or nt deodorant spray

Deponie f (-, -n) waste disposal site, tip

Depressionen pl **an ~ leiden** suffer from depressions sg; **deprimieren** vt depress

der 1. art the; (dative) to the; (genitive) of the; **~ arme Marc** poor Marc; **ich habe es ~ Kundin geschickt** I sent it to the client; **~ Vater ~ Besitzerin** the owner's father **2.** pron that (one), this (one); **~ mit ~ Brille** the one (or him) with the glasses; **~ schreibt nicht mehr** (pen etc) that one doesn't write any more **3.** pron (person) who, that; (thing) which, that; **jeder, ~ ...** anyone who ...; **er war ~ erste, ~ es erfuhr** he was the first

dicht

to know

derart *adv* so; *(before adj)* such; **derartig** *adj* **ein ~er Fehler** such a mistake, a mistake like that

deren *gen of* **die 1.** *pron (person)* her; *(thing)* its; *(pl)* their **2.** *pron (person)* whose; *(thing)* of which

dergleichen *pron* **und ~ mehr** and the like, and so on; **nichts ~** no such thing

derjenige *pron* the one; **~, der** the one who (or that)

dermaßen *adv* so much; *(with adj)* so

derselbe *pron* the same (person / thing)

deshalb *adv* therefore; **~ frage ich ja** that's why I'm asking

Design *nt* (-s, -s) design; **Designer(in)** *m(f)* (-s, -) designer

Desinfektionsmittel *nt* disinfectant; **desinfizieren** *vt* disinfect

dessen *gen of* **der, das 1.** *pron (person)* his; *(thing)* its; **ich bin mir ~ bewusst** I'm aware of that **2.** *pron (person)* whose; *(thing)* of which

Dessert *nt* (-s, -s) dessert; **zum** (or **als**) **~** for dessert

destillieren *vt* distilled

desto *adv* **je eher, ~ besser** the sooner, the better

deswegen *conj* therefore

Detail *nt* (-s, -s) detail; **ins ~ gehen** go into detail

Detektiv(in) *m(f)* (-s, -e) detective

deutlich *adj* clear; *(difference)* distinct

deutsch *adj* German; **Deutsch** *nt* German; **auf ~** in German; **ins ~e übersetzen** translate into German; **Deutsche(r)** *mf* German; **Deutschland** *nt* Germany

Devise *f* (-, -n) motto; **~n** *pl* FIN foreign currency *sg*; **Devisenkurs** *m* exchange rate

Dezember *m* (-(s), -) December; → **Juni**

dezent *adj* discreet

d.h. *abbr of* **das heißt**; i.e.

Dia *nt* (-s, -s) slide

Diabetes *m* (-, -) MED diabetes; **Diabetiker(in)** *m(f)* (-s, -) diabetic

Diagnose *f* (-, -n) diagnosis

diagonal *adj* diagonal

Dialekt *m* (-(e)s, -e) dialect

Dialog *m* (-(e)s, -e) dialogue; IT dialog

Dialyse *f* (-, -n) MED dialysis

Diamant *m* (-en, -en) diamond

Diaprojektor *m* slide projector

Diät *f* (-, -en) diet; **eine ~ machen** be on a diet; *(start)* go on a diet

dich *pron acc of* **du**; you; **~ (selbst)** yourself; **pass auf ~ auf** look after yourself; **reg ~ nicht auf** don't get upset

dicht 1. *adj* dense; *(fog)* thick;

(*weave*) close; (*shoes, boat etc*) watertight; (*traffic*) heavy **2.** *adv* ~ **an/bei** close to; ~ **bevölkert** densely populated

Dichter(in) *m(f)* (*-s, -*) poet; (*author*) writer

Dichtung *f* AUTO gasket; (*for tap etc*) washer; (*verse*) poetry

Dichtungsring *m* TECH washer

dick *adj* thick; (*person*) fat; **jdn** ~ **haben** be sick of sb; **Dickdarm** *m* colon; **Dickkopf** *m* stubborn (*or* pig-headed) person; **Dickmilch** *f* sour milk

die 1. *art* the; ~ **arme Sarah** poor Sarah **2.** *pron* (*sg*) that (one), this (one); (*pl*) these (ones); ~ **mit den langen Haaren** the one (*or* that) with the long hair; **ich nehme** ~ **da** I'll take that one / those **3.** *pron* (*person*) who, that; (*thing*) which, that; **sie war** ~ **erste,** ~ **es erfuhr** she was the first to know **4.** *pl of* **der, die, das**

Dieb(in) *m(f)* (*-(e)s, -e*) thief; **Diebstahl** *m* (*-(e)s, Diebstähle*) theft; **Diebstahlsicherung** *f* burglar alarm

diejenige *pron* the one; ~, **die** the one who (*or* that); ~**n** (*pl*) those *pl,* the ones

Diele *f* (*-, -n*) hall

Dienst *m* (*-(e)s, -e*) service; **außer** ~ retired; ~ **haben**

be on duty; **der** ~ **habende Arzt** the doctor on duty

Dienstag *m* Tuesday; → **Mittwoch**; **dienstags** *adv* on Tuesdays; → **mittwochs**

Dienstbereitschaft *f* ~ **haben** (*doctor*) be on call; **Dienstleistung** *f* service; **dienstlich** *adj* official; **er ist** ~ **unterwegs** he's away on business; **Dienstreise** *f* business trip; **Dienststelle** *f* department; **Dienstwagen** *m* company car; **Dienstzeit** *f* office hours *pl;* MIL period of service

diesbezüglich *adj* (*formal*) on this matter

diese(r, s) *pron* this (one); (*pl*) these; ~ **Frau** this woman; ~**r Mann** this man; ~**s Mädchen** this girl; ~ **Leute** these people; **ich nehme** ~/~**n/**~**s** I'll take this one; (*there*) I'll take this one; **ich nehme** ~ *pl* I'll take these (ones); (*there*) I'll take those (ones)

Diesel *m* (*-s, -*) AUTO diesel

dieselbe *pron* the same; **es sind immer** ~**n** it's always the same people

Dieselmotor *m* diesel engine; **Dieselöl** *nt* diesel (oil)

diesig *adj* hazy, misty

diesmal *adv* this time

Dietrich *m* (*-s, -e*) skeleton key

Differenz *f* (*-, -en*) difference

digital *adj* digital; **Digital-** *in*

cpds (*camera, display etc*) digital

Diktat *nt* (-(*e*)*s*, -*e*) dictation

Diktatur *f* dictatorship

Dill *m* (-*s*) dill

DIN *abbr* = *Deutsche Industrienorm*; DIN; → *A4* A4

Ding *nt* (-(*e*)*s*, -*e*) thing; *vor allen ~en* above all; *der Stand der ~e* the state of affairs; *das ist nicht mein ~* it's not my sort of thing (*or* cup of tea); **Dingsbums** *nt* (-) *fam* thingy, thingummybob

Dinosaurier *m* dinosaur

Diphtherie *f* diphtheria

Diplom *nt* (-(*e*)*s*, -*e*) diploma

Diplomat(in) *m*(*f*) (-*en*, -*en*) diplomat

dir *pron dat of du*; (to) you; *hat er ~ geholfen?* did he help you?; *ich werde es ~ erklären* I'll explain it to you; *wasch ~ die Hände* go and wash your hands; *ein Freund von ~* a friend of yours

direkt 1. *adj* direct; (*question*) straight; *~e Verbindung* through service **2.** *adv* directly; (*straightaway*) immediately; *~ am Bahnhof* right next to the station; **Direktflug** *m* direct flight

Direktor(in) *m*(*f*) director; (*of school*) headmaster / -mistress (*Brit*), principal (*US*)

Direktübertragung *f* live broadcast

Dirigent(in) *m*(*f*) conductor; **dirigieren** *vt* direct; *MUS* conduct

Discman® *m* (-*s*, -*s*) Discman®

Diskette *f* disk, diskette; **Diskettenlaufwerk** *nt* disk drive

Diskjockey *m* (-*s*, -*s*) disc jockey; **Disko** *f* (-, -*s*) *fam* disco, club; **Diskothek** *f* (-, -*en*) discotheque, club

diskret *adj* discreet

diskriminieren *vt* discriminate against

Diskussion *f* discussion; **diskutieren** *vt*, *vi* discuss

Display *nt* (-*s*, -*s*) display

disqualifizieren *vt* disqualify

Distanz *f* distance

Distel *f* (-, -*n*) thistle

Disziplin *f* (-, -*en*) discipline

divers *adj* various

dividieren *vt* divide (*durch* by); *8 dividiert durch 2 ist 4* 8 divided by 2 is 4

DJ *m* (-*s*, -*s*) *abbr* = *Diskjockey*; DJ

doch 1. *adv* *das ist nicht wahr! — ~!* that's not true — yes it is; *nicht ~!* oh no; *er kommt ~?* he will come, won't he?; *er hat es ~ gemacht* he did it after all; *setzen Sie sich ~* do sit down, please **2.** *conj* but

Doktor(in) *m*(*f*) doctor

Dokument *nt* document; **Dokumentarfilm** *m* documentary (film); **dokumentieren** *vt* document; **Dokumentvorlage** *f* IT document template

Dolch *m* (-(e)s, -e) dagger

Dollar *m* (-(s), -s) dollar

dolmetschen *vt, vi* interpret; **Dolmetscher(in)** *m(f)* (-s, -/-) interpreter

Dolomiten *pl* Dolomites *pl*

Dom *m* (-(e)s, -e) cathedral

Domäne *f* (-, -n) domain, province; IT domain

Dominikanische Republik *f* Dominican Republic

Domino *nt* (-s, -s) dominoes *sg*

Donau *f* (-) Danube

Döner *m* (-s, -), **Döner Kebab** *m* (-(s), -s) doner kebab

Donner *m* (-s, -) thunder; **donnern** *vi* **es donnert** it's thundering

Donnerstag *m* Thursday; → **Mittwoch**; **donnerstags** *adv* on Thursdays; → **mittwochs**

doof *adj fam* stupid

dopen *vt* dope; **Doping** *nt* (-s) doping; **Dopingkontrolle** *f* drugs test

Doppel *nt* (-s, -) duplicate; SPORT doubles *sg*; **Doppelbett** *nt* double bed; **Doppeldecker** *m* double-decker; **Doppelhaushälfte** *f* semi--detached house (*Brit*), duplex (*US*); **doppelklicken** *vi* double-click; **Doppelname** *m* double-barrelled name; **Doppelpunkt** *m* colon; **Doppelstecker** *m* two--way adaptor; **doppelt** *adj*

double; **in ~er Ausführung** in duplicate; **Doppelzimmer** *nt* double room

Dorf *nt* (-(e)s, **Dörfer**) village

Dorn *m* (-(e)s, -en) BOT thorn

Dörrobst *nt* dried fruit

Dorsch *m* (-(e)s, -e) cod

dort *adv* there; ~ **drüben** over there; **dorther** *adv* from there

Dose *f* (-, -n) box; (*for food*) tin (*Brit*), can; (*for beer*) can

dösen *vi* doze

Dosenbier *nt* canned beer; **Dosenmilch** *f* canned milk, tinned milk (*Brit*); **Dosenöffner** *m* tin opener (*Brit*), can opener

Dotter *m* (-s, -) (egg) yolk

downloaden *vt* download

Downsyndrom *nt* (-(e)s, -e) MED Down's syndrome

Dozent(in) *m(f)* lecturer

Dr. *abbr* = **Doktor**

Drache *m* (-n, -n) dragon; **Drachen** *m* (-s, -) (*toy*) kite; SPORT hang-glider; **Drachenfliegen** *nt* (-s) hang-gliding; **Drachenflieger(in)** *m(f)* (-s, -/-) hang-glider

Draht *m* (-(e)s, **Drähte**) wire; **Drahtseilbahn** *f* cable railway

Drama *nt* (-s, **Dramen**) drama; **dramatisch** *adj* dramatic

dran *adv fam contr of* **daran**; **gut ~ sein** (*rich*) be well-off; (*lucky*) be fortunate; (*healthy*) be well; **schlecht ~ sein** be in a bad way; **wer ist ~?**

whose turn is it?; **ich bin ~** it's my turn; **bleib ~!** TEL hang on

drang imperf of **dringen**

Drang m (-(e)s, **Dränge**) urge (nach for); (of circumstances etc) pressure

drängeln vt, vi push

drängen 1. vt push; (try to persuade) urge **2.** vi be urgent; (time) press; **auf etw** acc ~ press for sth

drankommen irr vi **wer kommt dran?** who's turn is it?, who's next?

drauf fam contr of **darauf**; **gut/ schlecht ~ sein** be in a good/ bad mood

Draufgänger(in) m(f) (-s, -) daredevil

draufkommen irr vi remember; **ich komme nicht drauf** I can't think of it

draufmachen vi fam **einen ~** go on a binge

draußen adv outside

Dreck m (-(e)s) dirt, filth; **dreckig** adj dirty, filthy

drehen vt, vi turn; (cigarette) roll; (film) shoot **2.** vr turn; (revolve) rotate; **sich ~ um** (concern) be about

Drehstrom m three-phase current; **Drehtür** f revolving door; **Drehzahlmesser** m rev counter

drei num three; **~ viertel voll** three-quarters full; **es ist ~ viertel neun** it's a quarter to nine; **Drei** f (-, -en) three;

(mark in school) ≈ C; **Dreieck** nt triangle; **dreieckig** adj triangular; **dreifach 1.** adj triple **2.** adv three times; **dreihundert** num three hundred; **Dreikönigstag** m Epiphany; **dreimal** adv three times; **Dreirad** nt tricycle; **dreispurig** adj three-lane

dreißig num thirty; **dreißigste(r, s)** adj thirtieth; → **dritte**

Dreiviertelstunde f **eine ~** three quarters of an hour

dreizehn num thirteen; **dreizehnte(r, s)** adj thirteenth; → **dritte**

dressieren vt train

Dressing nt (-s, -s) (salad) dressing

Dressman m (-s, **Dressmen**) (male) model

Dressur f (-, -en) training

drin fam contr of **darin**; in it; **mehr war nicht ~** that was the best I could do

dringen (drang, gedrungen) vi (water, filter, cold) penetrate (durch through, in + acc into); **auf etw** acc ~ insist on sth; **dringend, dringlich** adj urgent

drinnen adv inside

dritt adv **wir sind zu ~** there are three of us; **dritte(r, s)** adj third; **die Dritte Welt** the Third World; **3. September** 3(rd) September; **am 3. September** on 3(rd) September, on September 3(rd); **München, den 3. September** Munich, September 3(rd); **Drittel** nt (-s, -) (fraction) third; **drittens** adv thirdly

Droge f (-, -n) drug; **drogenabhängig, drogensüchtig** adj addicted to drugs

Drogerie f chemist's (Brit), drugstore (US); **Drogeriemarkt** m discount chemist's (Brit) (or drugstore (US))

drohen vi threaten (jdm sb); **mit etw ~** threaten to do sth

dröhnen vi (engine) roar; (voice, music) boom; (room) resound

Drohung f threat

Drossel f (-, -n) thrush

drüben adv over there; on the other side

drüber fam contr of **darüber**

Druck 1. m (-(e)s, Drücke) PHYS pressure; fig (strain) stress; **jdn unter ~ setzen** put sb under pressure **2.** m (-(e)s, -e) TYPO printing; (product, typeface) print; **Druckbuchstabe** m block letter; **in ~n schreiben** print; **drucken** vt, vi print

drücken 1. vt, vi (button, hand) press; (garment) pinch; fig (prices) keep down; **jdm etw in die Hand ~** press sth into sb's hand **2.** vr **sich vor etw** dat **~** get out of sth; **drückend** adj op-

pressive

Drucker m (-s, -) IT printer; **Druckertreiber** m printer driver

Druckknopf m press stud (Brit), snap fastener (US); **Drucksache** f printed matter; **Druckschrift** f block letters pl

drunten adv down there

drunter fam contr of **darunter**

Drüse f (-, -n) gland

Dschungel m (-s, -) jungle

du pron you; **bist ~ es?** is it you?; **wir sind per ~** we're on first-name terms

Dübel m (-s, -) Rawlplug®

ducken vt, vr duck

Dudelsack m bagpipes pl

Duett nt (-s, -e) duet

Duft m (-(e)s, Düfte) scent; **duften** vi smell nice; **es duftet nach ...** it smells of ...

dulden vt tolerate

dumm adj stupid; **Dummheit** f stupidity; (act) stupid thing; **Dummkopf** m idiot

dumpf adj (sound) muffled; (memory) vague; (pain) dull

Düne f (-, -n) dune

Dünger m (-s, -) fertilizer

dunkel adj dark; (voice) deep; (suspicion) vague; (mysterious) obscure; (suspicious) dubious; **im Dunkeln tappen** fig be in the dark; **dunkelblau** adj dark blue; **dunkelblond** adj light brown;

dunkelhaarig adj dark-haired; **Dunkelheit** f darkness

dünn adj thin; (coffee) weak

Dunst m (-es, Dünste) haze; (light fog) mist; CHEM vapour

dünsten vt GASTR steam

Duo nt (-s, -s) duo

Dur nt (-) MUS major (key); *in G~* in G major

durch 1. prep + acc through; (means) by; (time) during; *~ Amerika reisen* travel across the USA; *er verdient seinen Lebensunterhalt ~ den Verkauf von Autos* he makes his living by selling cars **2.** adv (meat) cooked through, well done; *das ganze Jahr ~* all through the year, the whole year long; *darf ich bitte ~?* can I get through, please?

durchaus adv absolutely; *~ nicht* not at all

Durchblick m view; *den ~ haben* fig know what's going on; **durchblicken** vi look through; fam understand (bei etw sth); *etw ~ lassen* fig hint at sth

Durchblutung f circulation

durchbrennen irr vi (fuse) blow; (wire) burn through; fam (abscond) run away

durchdacht adv gut ~ well thought-out

durchdrehen 1. vt (meat) mince **2.** vi (wheels) spin; fam (under stress) crack up

durcheinander adv in a mess; fam (person) confused; *~ bringen* mess up; (person) confuse; *~ reden* talk all at the same time; *~ trinken* mix one's drinks; **Durcheinander** nt (-s) (of people) confusion; (of things) mess

Durchfahrt f way through; *„~ verboten!"* 'no thoroughfare'

Durchfall m MED diarrhoea

durchfallen irr vi fall through; (in exam) fail

durchfragen vr ask one's way

durchführen vt carry out

Durchgang m passage; SPORT round; (in election) ballot; **Durchgangsverkehr** m through traffic

durchgebraten adj well done

durchgefroren adj frozen to the bone

durchgehen irr vi go through (durch etw sth); (horse) break loose; (make off) run away; **durchgehend** adj (train) through; *~ geöffnet* open all day

durchhalten irr **1.** vi hold out **2.** vt (pace) keep up; *etw ~* (not give up) see sth through

durchkommen irr vi get through; (patient) pull through

durchlassen irr vt (person) let through; (water) let in

Durchlauf(wasser)erhitzer m (-s, -) instantaneous water heater

durchlesen *irr vt* read through

durchleuchten *vt* X-ray

durchmachen *vt* go through; (*development*) undergo; **die Nacht ~** make a night of it, have an all-nighter

Durchmesser *m (-s, -)* diameter

Durchreise *f* journey through; **auf der ~** passing through; (*goods*) in transit; **Durchreisevisum** *nt* transit visa

durchreißen *irr vt, vi* tear (in two)

durchs *contr of* **durch das**

Durchsage *f (-, -n)* announcement

durchschauen *vt* (*person, lie*) see through

durchschlagen *irr vr* struggle through

durchschneiden *irr vt* cut (in two)

Durchschnitt *m* average; **im ~** on average; **durchschnittlich 1.** *adj* average **2.** *adv* on average

durchsetzen 1. *vt* get through **2.** *vr* (*be successful*) succeed; (*assert oneself*) get one's way

durchsichtig *adj* transparent, see-through

durchstellen *vt* TEL put through

durchstreichen *irr vt* cross out

durchsuchen *vt* search (*nach* for); **Durchsuchung** *f* search

Durchwahl *f* direct dialling; (*number*) extension

durchziehen *irr vt* (*plan*) carry through

Durchzug *m* draught

dürfen (*durfte, gedurft*) *vi* **etw tun ~** (*permission*) be allowed to do sth; **darf ich?** may I?; **das darfst du nicht (tun)!** you mustn't do that; **was darf es sein?** what can I do for you?; **er dürfte schon dort sein** he should be there by now

dürr *adj* (*thin*) skinny

Durst *m (-(e)s)* thirst; **~ haben** be thirsty; **durstig** *adj* thirsty

Dusche *f (-, -n)* shower; **duschen** *vi, vr* have a shower; **Duschgel** *nt* shower gel

Düse *f (-, -n)* nozzle; TECH jet; **Düsenflugzeug** *nt* jet (aircraft)

düster *adj* dark; (*thoughts, future*) gloomy

Dutyfreeshop *m (-s, -s)* duty-free shop

duzen 1. *vt* address as 'du' **2.** *vr* **sich ~ (mit jdm)** address each other as 'du', be on first-name terms

DVD *f (-, -s)* *abbr* = **Digital Versatile Disk**; DVD

dynamisch *adj* dynamic

Dynamo *m (-s, -s)* dynamo

E

Ebbe f (-, -n) low tide
eben 1. adj level; (even) smooth **2.** adv just; (confirming sth) exactly
ebenfalls adv also, as well; (reply) you too; **ebenso** adv just as well; **~ gut** just as well; **~ viel** just as much
EC m (-, -s) abbr = **Eurocityzug**
Echo nt (-s, -s) echo
echt adj (leather, gold) real, genuine; **ein ~er Verlust** a real loss
EC-Karte f ≈ debit card
Ecke f (-, -n) corner; MATH angle; **an der ~** at the corner; **gleich um die ~** just round the corner; **eckig** adj rectangular
Economyclass f (-) coach (class), economy class
Ecstasy f (-) (drug) ecstasy
Efeu m (-s) ivy
Effekt m (-s, -e) effect
egal adj **das ist ~** it doesn't matter; **das ist mir ~** I don't care, it's all the same to me; **~ wie teuer** no matter how expensive
egoistisch adj selfish
ehe conj before
Ehe f (-, -n) marriage; **Ehefrau** f wife
ehemalig adj former; **ehemals** adv formerly

Ehemann m husband; **Ehepaar** nt married couple
eher adv (time) sooner; (preference) rather; (passing judgment) more; **je ~, desto besser** the sooner the better
Ehering m wedding ring
eheste(r, s) 1. adj (earliest) first **2.** adv **am ~n** (probably) most likely
Ehre f (-, -n) honour; **ehren** vt honour; **Ehrenwort** nt word of honour; **~!** I promise
ehrgeizig adj ambitious
ehrlich adj honest
Ei nt (-(e)s, -er) egg
Eiche f (-, -n) oak (tree); **Eichel** f (-, -n) acorn
Eichhörnchen nt squirrel
Eid m (-(e)s, -e) oath
Eidechse f (-, -n) lizard
Eierbecher m eggcup; **Eierstock** m ovary; **Eieruhr** f egg timer
Eifersucht f jealousy; **eifersüchtig** adj jealous (auf + acc of)
Eigelb nt (-(e)s, -) egg yolk
eigen adj own; (typical) characteristic (jdm of sb); (strange) peculiar; **eigenartig** adj peculiar; **Eigenschaft** f quality; CHEM, PHYS property
eigentlich 1. adj actual, real **2.** adv actually, really; **was denken Sie sich ~ dabei?**

what on earth do you think you're doing?

Eigentum nt property; **Eigentümer(in)** m(f) owner; **Eigentumswohnung** f owner-occupied flat (*Brit*), condominium (*US*)

eignen vr **sich ~ für** be suited for; **er würde sich als Lehrer ~** he'd make a good teacher

Eilbrief m express letter, special-delivery letter; **Eile** f (-) hurry; **eilen** vi (*letter, matter*) be urgent; **es eilt nicht** there's no hurry; **eilig** adj hurried; (*pressing*) urgent; **es ~ haben** be in a hurry

Eimer m (-s, -) bucket

ein adv **nicht ~ noch aus wissen** not know what to do; **~ - aus** (*switch*) on - off

ein(e) art a; an; **~ Mann** a man; **~ Apfel** an apple; **~e Stunde** an hour; **~ Haus** a house; **~ (gewisser) Herr Miller** a (certain) Mr Miller; **~es Tages** one day

einander pron one another, each other

einarbeiten 1. vt train 2. vr get used to the work

einatmen vt, vi breathe in

Einbahnstraße f one-way street

einbauen vt build in; (*engine etc*) install, fit; **Einbauküche** f fitted kitchen

einbiegen irr vi turn (*in* + *acc* into)

einbilden vt **sich** dat **etw ~** imagine sth

einbrechen irr vi (*into house*) break in; (*roof etc*) fall in, collapse; **Einbrecher(in)** m(f) (-s, -) burglar

einbringen irr 1. vt (*harvest*) bring in; (*profit*) yield; **jdm etw ~** bring (or earn) sb sth 2. vr **sich in** acc **etw ~** make a contribution to sth

Einbruch m break-in, burglary; **bei ~ der Nacht** at nightfall

Einbürgerung f naturalization

einchecken vt check in

eincremen vt, vr put some cream on

eindeutig 1. adj clear, obvious 2. adv clearly; **~ falsch** clearly wrong

eindringen irr vi force one's way in (*in* + *acc* -to); (*into house*) break in (*in* + *acc* -to); (*gas, water*) get in (*in* + *acc* -to)

Eindruck m impression; **großen ~ auf jdn machen** make a big impression on sb

eine(r, s) pron one; someone; **~r meiner Freunde** one of my friends; **~r nach dem andern** one after the other

eineiig adj (*twins*) identical

eineinhalb num one and a half

einerseits adv on the one hand

einfach 1. adj (*not complica-*

ted) simple; (*person*) ordinary; (*food*) plain; (*not multiple*) single; **~e Fahrkarte** single ticket (*Brit*), one-way ticket (*US*) **2.** *adv* simply; (*single time*) once

Einfahrt *f* (*in car*) driving in; (*of train*) arrival; (*place*) entrance

Einfall *m* idea; **einfallen** *irr vi* (*light etc*) fall in; (*roof, house*) collapse; **ihm fiel ein, dass ...** it occurred to him that ...; **ich werde mir etwas ~ lassen** I'll think of something; **was fällt Ihnen ein!** what do you think you're doing?

Einfamilienhaus *nt* detached house

einfarbig *adj* all one colour; (*fabric etc*) self-coloured

Einfluss *m* influence

einfrieren *irr vt, vi* freeze

einfügen *vt* fit in; add; IT insert; **Einfügetaste** *f* IT insert key

Einfuhr *f* (-, -en) import; **Einfuhrbestimmungen** *pl* import regulations *pl*

einführen *vt* introduce; (*goods*) import; **Einführung** *f* introduction

Eingabe *f* (*of data*) input; **Eingabetaste** *f* IT return (*or* enter) key

Eingang *m* entrance; **Eingangshalle** *f* entrance hall, lobby (*US*)

eingeben *irr vt* (*data etc*) en-

ter, key in

eingebildet *adj* imaginary; (*conceited*) arrogant

Eingeborene(r) *mf* native

eingehen *irr* **1.** *vi* (*letter, money*) come in, arrive; (*animal, plant*) die; (*fabric*) shrink; **auf etw** *acc* **~** agree to sth; **auf jdn ~** respond to sb **2.** *vt* (*contract*) enter into; (*bet*) make; (*risk*) take

eingelegt *adj* (*in vinegar*) pickled

eingeschaltet *adj* (switched) on

eingeschlossen *adj* locked in; (*in price*) included

eingewöhnen *vr* settle in

eingießen *irr vt* pour

eingreifen *irr vi* intervene; **Eingriff** *m* intervention; (*surgical*) operation

einhalten *irr vt* (*promise etc*) keep

einhängen *vt* (**den Hörer**) **~** hang up

einheimisch *adj* (*product, team*) local; **Einheimische(r)** *mf* local person

Einheit *f* unity; (*measurement*) unit; **einheitlich** *adj* uniform

einholen *vt* (*car, person*) catch up with; (*lateness*) make up for; (*advice, permission*) ask for

Einhorn *nt* unicorn

einhundert *num* one (*or* a) hundred

einig *adj* united; **sich** *dat* **~**

sein agree

einige 1. *pron pl* some; *(quite a few)* several **2.** *adj* some; *nach ~er Zeit* after some time; *~e hundert Euro* some hundred euros

einigen *vr* agree *(auf + acc* on)

einigermaßen *adv* fairly, quite; *(passably)* reasonably

einiges *pron* something; *(amount)* quite a bit; *(number)* a few things; *es gibt noch ~ zu tun* there's still a fair bit to do

Einkauf *m* purchase; *Einkäufe (machen)* (to do one's) shopping; **einkaufen 1.** *vt* buy **2.** *vi* go shopping; **Einkaufsbummel** *m* shopping trip; **Einkaufstasche** *f*, **Einkaufstüte** *f* shopping bag; **Einkaufswagen** *m* shopping trolley *(Brit)* (or cart *(US)*); **Einkaufszentrum** *nt* shopping centre *(Brit)* (or mall *(US)*)

einklemmen *vt* jam; *er hat sich dat den Finger eingeklemmt* he got his finger caught

Einkommen *nt* (-s, -) income

einladen *irr vt (person)* invite; *(things)* load; *jdn zum Essen ~* take sb out for a meal; *ich lade dich ein* (I'm paying) it's my treat; **Einladung** *f* invitation

Einlass *m* (-es, *Einlässe*) admittance; *~ ab 18 Uhr* doors

open at 6 pm; **einlassen** *irr vr sich mit jdm/auf etw acc ~* get involved with sb/sth

einleben *vr* settle down

einlegen *vt (film etc)* put in; *(food before cooking)* marinate; *eine Pause ~* take a break

einleiten *vt* start; *(measures)* introduce; *(birth)* induce; **Einleitung** *f* introduction; *(of birth)* induction

einleuchten *vi jdm ~* be (or become) clear to sb; **einleuchtend** *adj* clear to sb

einloggen *vi* IT log on (or in)

einlösen *vt (cheque)* cash; *(voucher)* redeem; *(promise)* keep

einmal *adv* once; *(at earlier time)* before; *(in the future)* some day; *(to begin with)* first; *~ im Jahr* once a year; *noch ~* once more, again; *ich war schon ~ hier* I've been here before; *warst du schon ~ in London?* have you ever been to London?; *nicht ~* not even; *auf ~* suddenly; *(simultaneously, in one go)* at once; **einmalig** *adj* unique; *(occurring only once)* single; *(excellent)* fantastic

einmischen *vr* interfere *(in + acc* with)

Einnahme *f* (-, *-n*) *(money)* takings *pl*; *(of medicine)* taking; **einnehmen** *irr vt (medi-*

cine) take; (money) take in; (attitude, space) take up; **jdn für sich** ~ win sb over

einordnen 1. vt put in order; (categorize) classify; (documents) file **2.** vr AUTO get in lane; **sich rechts/links** ~ get into the right/left lane

einpacken vt pack (up)

einparken vt, vi park

einplanen vt allow for

einprägen vr **sich dat etw** ~ remember (or memorize) sth

einräumen vt (books, crockery) put away; (cupboard) put things in

einreden vt jdm/sich etw ~ talk sb/oneself into (believing) sth

einreiben irr vt **sich mit etw** ~ rub sth into one's skin

einreichen vt hand in; (application) submit

Einreise f entry; **Einreisebestimmungen** pl entry regulations pl; **Einreiseerlaubnis** f, **Einreisegenehmigung** f entry permit; **einreisen** vi enter (in ein Land a country); **Einreisevisum** nt entry visa

einrenken vt (arm, leg) set

einrichten 1. vt (house) furnish; (business etc) establish, set up; (fix) arrange **2.** vr furnish one's home; (get ready) prepare oneself (auf + acc for); (adjust) adapt (auf + acc to); **Einrichtung** f (in house) furnishings pl; (orga-

nization) institution; (swimming pool etc) facility

eins num one; **Eins** f (-, -en) one; (mark in school) ≈ A

einsam adj lonely

einsammeln vt collect

Einsatz m (component) insert; (of machine, troops etc) use; (in gambling) stake; (of one's life) risk; MUS entry

einschalten vt ELEC switch on

einschätzen vt estimate, assess

einschenken vt pour

einschiffen vr embark (nach for)

einschlafen irr vi fall asleep, drop off; **mir ist der Arm eingeschlafen** my arm's gone to sleep

einschlagen irr **1.** vt (window) smash; (teeth, skull) smash in; (path, direction) take **2.** vi hit (in etw acc sth, auf jdn sb); (lightning) strike; (film, song etc) be a success

einschließen irr vt (person) lock in; (object) lock away; (encircle) surround; fig include; **einschließlich 1.** adv inclusive **2.** prep + gen including; **von Montag bis ~ Freitag** from Monday up to and including Friday, Monday through Friday (US)

einschränken vt limit, restrict; (reduce) cut down on **2.** vr cut down (on expenditure)

einschreiben irr vr register; (for school) enrol; **Einschreiben** nt (-s, -) registered letter; **etw per ~ schicken** send sth by special delivery

einschüchtern vt intimidate

einsehen irr vt (understand) see; (error) recognize; (files) have a look at

einseitig adj one-sided

einsenden irr vt send in

einsetzen 1. vt put in; (to a post) appoint; (money) stake; (machine, troops etc) use **2.** vi (rain etc) set in; MUS enter, come in **3.** vr work hard; **sich für jdn/etw ~** support sb/sth

Einsicht f insight; **zu der ~ kommen, dass ...** come to realize that ...

einsperren vt lock up

einspielen vt (money) bring in

einspringen irr vi (help out) step in (für for)

Einspruch m objection (gegen to)

einspurig adj single-lane

Einstand m (in tennis) deuce

einstecken vt pocket; ELEC plug in; (letter) post, mail (US); (keys, passport etc) take; (accept) swallow

einsteigen irr vi (into car) get in; (onto bus, train, plane) get on; (in business, project etc) get involved

einstellen 1. vt (end) stop; (de-

vice etc) adjust; (camera) focus; (station, radio) tune in; (car, bicycle etc) put; (worker) employ, take on **2.** vr **sich auf jdn/etw ~** adapt to sb/prepare oneself for sth; **Einstellung** f (of device etc) adjustment; (of camera) focusing; (of worker) taking on; (opinion) attitude

einstürzen vi collapse

eintägig adj one-day

eintauschen vt exchange (gegen for)

eintausend num one (or a) thousand

einteilen vt divide (up) (in + acc into); (time) organize

eintönig adj monotonous

Eintopf m stew

eintragen irr **1.** vt (in list) put down, enter **2.** vr put one's name down, register

eintreffen irr vi happen; (person, train, letter etc) arrive

eintreten irr vi enter (in etw acc sth); (club, party) join (in etw acc sth); (event) occur; **~ für** support; **Eintritt** m admission; **„~ frei"** 'admission free'; **Eintrittskarte** f (entrance) ticket; **Eintrittspreis** m admission charge

einverstanden **1.** interj okay, all right **2.** adj **mit etwas sein** agree to sth, accept sth

Einwanderer m, **Einwanderin** f immigrant; **einwandern** vi immigrate

einwandfrei adj perfect,

flawless

Einwegflasche f non-return-able bottle; **Einwegwaschlappen** m disposable flannel (*Brit*) (or washcloth (*US*))

einweichen vt soak

einweihen vt (*building*) inaugurate, open; **jdn in etw** acc ~ let sb in on sth; **Einweihungsparty** f housewarming party

einwerfen irr vt (*ball, remark etc*) throw in; (*letter*) post, mail (*US*); (*money*) put in, insert; (*window*) smash

einwickeln vt wrap up; fig **jdn** ~ take sb in

Einwohner(in) m(f) (-s, -) inhabitant; **Einwohnermeldeamt** nt registration office for residents

Einwurf m (*opening*) slot; SPORT throw-in

Einzahl f singular

einzahlen vt pay in (*auf ein Konto* -to an account)

Einzel nt (-s, -) (*in tennis*) singles sg; **Einzelbett** nt single bed; **Einzelfahrschein** m single ticket (*Brit*), one-way ticket (*US*); **Einzelgänger(in)** m(f) loner; **Einzelhandel** m retail trade; **Einzelkind** nt only child

einzeln 1. adj individual; (*not together*) separate; (*solitary*) single; **~e** several ..., some ...; **der/die Einzelne** the individual; **im Einzelnen** in detail 2. adv separately;

(*pack, list*) individually; ~ **angeben** specify; ~ **eintreten** enter one by one

Einzelzimmer nt single room; **Einzelzimmerzuschlag** m single-room supplement

einzeihen irr 1. vt **den Kopf** ~ duck 2. vi (*into house*) move in

einzig 1. adj only; (*solitary*) single; (*special*) unique; **kein ~er Fehler** not a single mistake; **das Einzige** the only thing; **der/die Einzige** the only person 2. adv only; **die ~ richtige Lösung** the only correct solution; **einzigartig** adj unique

Eis nt (-es, -) ice; (*food*) ice-cream; ~ **laufen** skate; **Eisbahn** f ice(-skating) rink; **Eisbär** m polar bear; **Eisbecher** m (ice-cream) sundae; **Eisberg** m iceberg; **Eiscafé** nt, **Eisdiele** f ice-cream parlour

Eisen nt (-s, -) iron; **Eisenbahn** f railway (*Brit*), railroad (*US*); **eisern** adj iron

eisgekühlt adj chilled; **Eishockey** nt ice hockey; **Eiskaffee** m iced coffee; **eiskalt** adj ice-cold; (*temperature*) freezing; **Eiskunstlauf** m figure skating; **Eissalat** m iceberg lettuce; **Eisschokolade** f iced chocolate; **Eisschrank** m fridge, ice-box (*US*); **Eistee** m iced tea; **Eiswürfel** m ice cube; **Eiszap-**

fen *m* icicle

eitel *adj* vain

Eiter *m* (-s) pus

Eiweiß *nt* (-es, -e) egg white;
CHEM, BIO protein

ekelhaft, ek(e)lig *adj* disgusting, revolting; **ekeln** *vr* be
disgusted (*vor* + *dat* at)

EKG *nt* (-s, -s) *abbr* = **Elektrokardiogramm**; ECG

Ekzem *nt* (-s, -e) MED eczema

Elastikbinde *f* elastic bandage; **elastisch** *adj* elastic

Elch *m* (-(e)s, -e) elk; (*North American*) moose

Elefant *m* elephant

elegant *adj* elegant

Elektriker(in) *m(f)* (-s, -)
electrician; **elektrisch** *adj*
electric; **Elektrizität** *f* electricity; **Elektroauto** *nt* electric car; **Elektrogerät** *nt*
electrical appliance; **Elektrogeschäft** *nt* electrical
shop; **Elektroherd** *m* electric
cooker; **Elektromotor** *m*
electric motor; **Elektronik** *f*
electronics *sg*; **elektronisch**
adj electronic; **Elektrorasierer** *m* (-s, -) electric razor

Element *nt* (-s, -e) element

elend *adj* miserable; **Elend** *nt*
(-(e)s) misery

elf *num* eleven; **Elf** *f* (-, -en)
SPORT eleven

Elfenbein *nt* ivory

Elfmeter *m* SPORT penalty
(kick)

elfte(r, s) *adj* eleventh; → **dritte**

Ell(en)bogen *m* elbow

Elster *f* (-, -n) magpie

Eltern *pl* parents *pl*

EM *f* *abbr* = **Europameisterschaft**; European Championship(s)

Email *nt* (-s, -s) enamel

E-Mail *f* (-, -s) IT e-mail; *jdm*
eine ~ schicken e-mail sb,
send sb an e-mail; *jdm et-*
was per ~ schicken e-mail
sth to sb; **E-Mail-Adresse** *f*
e-mail address; **e-mailen** *vt*
e-mail

Emoticon *nt* (-s, -s) emoticon

emotional *adj* emotional

empfahl *imperf of* **empfehlen**

empfand *imperf of* **empfinden**

Empfang *m* (-(e)s, *Empfänge*)
(*party; in hotel, office*) reception; (*of letter, goods*) receipt; *in ~ nehmen* receive;
empfangen (*empfing, empfangen*) *vt* receive; **Empfänger(in)** **1.** *m(f)* (-s, -) recipient; addressee **2.** *m* TECH receiver; **Empfängnisverhütung** *f* contraception; **Empfangshalle** *f* reception area

empfehlen (*empfahl, empfohlen*) *vt* recommend; **Empfehlung** *f* recommendation

empfinden (*empfand, empfunden*) *vt* feel; **empfindlich**
adj (*person*) sensitive; (*spot*)
sore; (*easily offended*)
touchy; (*material*) delicate

empfing *imperf of* **empfangen**

empfohlen pp of **empfehlen**

empfunden pp of **empfinden**

empört adj indignant (über + acc at)

Ende nt (-s, -n) end; (of film, novel) ending; **am ~** at the end; (when all is said and done) in the end; **~ Mai** at the end of May; **~ der Achtzigerjahre** in the late eighties; **sie ist ~ zwanzig** she's in her late twenties; **zu ~** over, finished; **enden** vi end; **der Zug endet hier** this service (or train) terminates here; **endgültig** adj final; (proof) conclusive

Endivie f endive

endlich adv at last, finally; (in the end) eventually; **Endspiel** nt final; (last round) finals pl; **Endstation** f terminus; **Endung** f ending

Energie f energy; **~ sparend** energy-saving; **Energiebedarf** m energy requirement; **Energieverbrauch** m energy consumption

energisch adj (firm) forceful

eng 1. adj narrow; (clothes) tight; fig (friendship, relationship) close; **das wird ~** fam (deadline) we're running out of time, it's getting tight 2. adv **~ befreundet sein** to be close friends

engagieren 1. vt engage 2. vr commit oneself, be committed (für to)

Engel m (-s, -) angel

England nt England; **Engländer(in)** m(f) (-s, -) Englishman / -woman; **die ~** pl the English pl; **englisch** adj English; GASTR rare; **Englisch** nt English; **ins ~e übersetzen** translate into English

Enkel m (-s, -) grandson; **Enkelin** f granddaughter

enorm adj enormous; fig tremendous

Entbindung f MED delivery

entdecken vt discover; **Entdeckung** f discovery

Ente f (-, -n) duck

entfernen 1. vt remove; IT delete 2. vr go away; **entfernt** adj distant; **15 km von X ~** 15 km away from X; **20 km voneinander ~** 20 km apart; **Entfernung** f distance; **aus der ~** from a distance

entführen vt kidnap; **Entführer(in)** m(f) kidnapper; **Entführung** f kidnapping

entgegen 1. prep + dat contrary to 2. adv towards; **dem Wind ~** against the wind; **entgegengesetzt** adj (direction) opposite; (view) opposing; **entgegenkommen** irr vi jdm ~ come to meet sb; fig accommodate sb; **entgegenkommend** adj (traffic) oncoming; fig obliging

entgegnen vt reply (auf + acc to)

entgehen irr vi jdm ~ escape

sb's notice; **sich** dat **etw ~ lassen** miss sth

entgleisen vi RAIL be derailed; fig (person) misbehave

Enthaarungscreme f hair remover

enthalten irr **1.** vt contain; (price) include **2.** vr abstain (gen from)

entkoffeiniert adj decaffeinated

entkommen irr vi escape

entkorken vt uncork

entlang prep + acc or dat **~ dem Fluss, den Fluss ~** along the river; **entlanggehen** irr vi walk along

entlassen irr vt (patient) discharge; (worker) dismiss

entlasten vt jdn~ relieve sb of some of his/her work

entmutigen vt discourage

entnehmen vt take (dat from)

entrahmt adj (milk) skimmed

entschädigen vt compensate; **Entschädigung** f compensation

entscheiden irr vt, vi, vr decide; **sich für/gegen etw ~** decide on/against sth; **wir haben uns entschieden, nicht zu gehen** we decided not to go; **das entscheidet sich morgen** that'll be decided tomorrow; **entscheidend** adj decisive; (question, problem) crucial; **Entscheidung** f decision

entschließen irr vr decide

(zu, für on), make up one's mind; **Entschluss** m decision

entschuldigen 1. vt excuse **2.** vr apologize; **sich bei jdm für etw ~** apologize to sb for sth **3.** vi **entschuldige!, ~ Sie!** (introducing question) excuse me; (apology) (I'm) sorry, excuse me (US); **Entschuldigung** f apology; (justification) excuse; **jdn um ~ bitten** apologize to sb; **~!** (colliding with sb) (I'm) sorry, excuse me (US); (introducing question) excuse me; (could you repeat that?) (I beg your) pardon?

entsetzlich adj dreadful, appalling

entsorgen vt dispose of

entspannen 1. vt (body) relax; POL (situation) ease **2.** vr relax; fam chill out; **Entspannung** f relaxation

entsprechen irr vi + dat correspond to; (requirements, wishes etc) comply with; **entsprechend 1.** adj appropriate **2.** adv accordingly **3.** prep + dat according to, in accordance with

entstehen vi (difficulties) arise; (town, building etc) be built; (work of art) be created

enttäuschen vt disappoint; **Enttäuschung** f disappointment

entweder conj **~ ... oder ...** either ... or ...; **~ oder!** take it or leave it

entwerfen *irr vt* (*furniture, clothes*) design; (*plan, contract*) draft

entwerten *vt* devalue; (*ticket*) cancel; **Entwerter** *m* (*-s, -*) ticket-cancelling machine

entwickeln *vt* a. PHOT develop; (*courage, energy*) show, display; **Entwicklung** *f* development; PHOT developing; **Entwicklungshelfer(in)** *m(f)* (*-s, -*) development worker; **Entwicklungsland** *nt* developing country

Entwurf *m* outline; (*of product*) design; (*of contract, novel etc*) draft

entzückend *adj* delightful, charming

Entzug *m* withdrawal; (*treatment*) detox; **Entzugserscheinung** *f* withdrawal symptom

entzünden *vt* catch fire; MED become inflamed; **Entzündung** *f* MED inflammation

Epidemie *f* epidemic

Epilepsie *f* epilepsy

er *pron* he; (*thing*) it; **er ist** it's him; **wo ist mein Mantel? – ~ ist ...** where's my coat? – it's ...

Erbe1. *m* (*-n, -n*) heir **2.** *nt* (*-s*) inheritance; *fig* heritage; **erben** *vt* inherit; **Erbin** *f* heiress; **erblich** *adj* hereditary

erbrechen *irr vt, vr* vomit; **Er-**

brechen *nt* vomiting

Erbschaft *f* inheritance

Erbse *f* (*-, -n*) pea

Erdapfel *m* potato; **Erdbeben** *nt* earthquake; **Erdbeere** *f* strawberry; **Erde** *f* (*-, -n*) (*planet*) earth; (*earth's surface*) ground; **Erdgas** *nt* natural gas; **Erdgeschoss** *nt* ground floor (*Brit*), first floor (*US*); **Erdkunde** *f* geography; **Erdnuss** *f* peanut; **Erdöl** *nt* (*mineral*) oil; **Erdrutsch** *m* landslide; **Erdteil** *m* continent

ereignen *vr* happen, take place; **Ereignis** *nt* event

erfahren 1. *irr vt* learn, find out; (*feeling*) experience **2.** *adj* experienced; **Erfahrung** *f* experience

erfinden *irr vt* invent; **erfinderisch** *adj* inventive, creative; **Erfindung** *f* invention

Erfolg *m* (*-(e)s, -e*) success; (*consequence*) result; **~ versprechend** promising; **viel ~!** good luck; **erfolglos** *adj* unsuccessful; **erfolgreich** *adj* successful

erforderlich *adj* necessary

erforschen *vt* explore; (*problem etc*) investigate

erfreulich *adj* pleasing, pleasant; (*news*) good; **erfreulicherweise** *adv* fortunately

erfrieren *irr vi* freeze to death; (*plants*) be killed by frost

Erfrischung *f* refreshment

erfüllen 1. vt (room) fill; (request, wish etc) fulfil **2.** vr come true

ergänzen 1. vt (remark) add; (collection etc) complete **2.** vr complement one another; **Ergänzung** f completion; (thing added) supplement

ergeben irr vt (amount) come to; (lead to) result in **2.** irr vr surrender; (arise) result (aus from) **3.** adj devoted; (unassuming) humble

Ergebnis nt result

ergreifen irr vt seize; (career) take up; (measure, opportunity) take; (fill with pity etc) move

erhalten irr vt receive; (building, custom etc) preserve; **gut ~ sein** in good condition; **erhältlich** adj available

erheblich adj considerable

erhitzen vt heat (up)

erhöhen 1. vt raise; (in amount, degree) increase **2.** vr increase

erholen vr recover; (relax) have a rest; **erholsam** adj restful; **Erholung** f recovery; (on holiday etc) relaxation, rest

erinnern 1. vt remind (an + acc of) **2.** vr remember (an etw acc sth); **Erinnerung** f memory; (object) souvenir; (letter etc) reminder

erkälten vr catch a cold; **erkältet** adj (stark) **~ sein** have a (bad) cold; **Erkältung** f cold

erkennen irr vt recognize; (discern, understand) see; **~, dass ...** realize that ...; **erkenntlich** adj **sich ~ zeigen** show one's appreciation

Erker m (-s, -) bay

erklären vt explain; (announce) declare; **Erklärung** f explanation; (announcement) declaration

erkundigen vr enquire (nach about)

erlauben vt allow, permit; **jdm ~, etw zu tun** allow (or permit) sb to do sth; **sich dat etw ~** permit oneself sth; ~ **Sie, dass ich rauche)?** do you mind (if I smoke)?; **was ~ Sie sich?** what do you think you're doing?; **Erlaubnis** f permission

Erläuterung f explanation; (on text) comment

erleben vt experience; (pleasant time etc) have; (bad experience etc) go through; (scene etc) witness; (be still alive for) live to see; **Erlebnis** nt experience

erledigen vt (matter, task) deal with; (tire) (exhaust) wear out; fam (ruin) finish; **erledigt** adj finished; (sorted out) dealt with; fam (exhausted) whacked, knackered (Brit)

erleichtert adj relieved

Erlös m (-es, -e) proceeds pl

ermahnen vt (against sth)

warn

ermäßigt *adj* reduced; Ermäßigung *f* reduction

ermitteln 1. *vt* find out; (*culprit*) trace **2.** *vi* LAW investigate

ermöglichen *vt* make possible (*dat* for)

ermorden *vt* murder

ermüdend *adj* tiring

ermutigen *vt* encourage

ernähren 1. *vt* feed; (*family*) support **2.** *vr* support oneself; **sich ~ von** live on; Ernährung *f* food; Ernährungsberater(in) *m(f)* nutritional (*or* dietary) adviser

erneuern *vt* renew; (*to original condition*) restore; (*to good condition*) renovate; (*with new one*) replace

ernst 1. *adj* serious **2.** *adv* **jdn/etw ~ nehmen** take sb/sth seriously; Ernst *m* (*-es*) seriousness; **das ist mein ~** I'm quite serious; **im ~?** really?; ernsthaft **1.** *adj* serious **2.** *adv* seriously

Ernte *f* (*-, -n*) harvest; Erntedankfest *nt* harvest festival (*Brit*), Thanksgiving (Day) (*US*); ernten *vt* harvest; (*praise etc*) earn

erobern *vt* conquer

eröffnen *vt* open; Eröffnung *f* opening

erogen *adj* erogenous

erotisch *adj* erotic

erpressen *vt* (*person*) black-

mail; (*money etc*) extort; Erpressung *f* blackmail; (*of money*) extortion

erraten *irr vt* guess

erregen 1. *vt* excite; (*sexually*) arouse; (*make angry*) annoy; (*cause*) arouse **2.** *vr* get worked up; Erreger *m* (*-s, -*) MED germ; virus

erreichbar *adj* **~ sein** be within reach; (*person*) be available; **das Stadtzentrum ist zu Fuß/mit dem Wagen leicht ~** the city centre is within easy walking/driving distance; erreichen *vt* reach; (*train etc*) catch

Ersatz *m* (*-es*) replacement; (*temporary*) substitute; (*for loss etc*) compensation; Ersatzreifen *m* AUTO spare tyre; Ersatzteil *nt* spare (part)

erscheinen *irr vi* appear; (*give impression*) seem

erschöpft *adj* exhausted; Erschöpfung *f* exhaustion

erschrecken 1. *vt* frighten **2.** (*erschrak, erschrocken*) *vi* get a fright; erschreckend *adj* alarming; erschrocken *adj* frightened

erschwinglich *adj* affordable

ersetzen *vt* replace; (*expenses*) reimburse

erst *adv* first; (*initially*) at first; (*as recently as, merely*) only; (*no earlier than*) not until; **~ jetzt/gestern** only now/yesterday; **~ morgen**

not until tomorrow; **es ist ~ 10 Uhr** it's only ten o'clock; **~ recht** all the more; **~ recht nicht** even less

erstatten vt (costs) refund; **Bericht ~** report (über + acc on) **Anzeige gegen jdn ~** report sb to the police

erstaunlich adj astonishing; **erstaunt** adj surprised

erstbeste(r, s) adj **das ~ Hotel** any old hotel; **der Erstbeste** just anyone

erste(r, s) adj first; → **dritte zum ~n Mal** for the first time; **er wurde Erster** he came first; **auf den ~n Blick** at first sight

erstens adv first(ly), in the first place

ersticken vi (person) suffocate; **in Arbeit ~** be snowed under with work

erstklassig adj first-class

erstmals adv for the first time

erstrecken vr extend, stretch (auf + acc to; über + acc over)

ertappen vt catch

erteilen vt (advice, permission) give

Ertrag m (-(e)s, Erträge) yield; (profit) proceeds pl; **ertragen** irr vt (pain) bear, stand; (tolerate) put up with; (erträglich) adj bearable; (fairly good) tolerable

ertrinken irr vi drown

erwachsen adj grown-up; **~ werden** grow up; **Erwach-**

sene(r) mf adult, grown-up

erwähnen vt mention

erwarten vt expect; wait for; **ich kann den Sommer kaum ~** I can hardly wait for the summer

erwerbstätig adj employed

erwidern vt reply; (greeting, visit) return

erwischen vt fam catch (bei etw doing sth)

erwünscht adj desired; (person) welcome

Erz nt (-es, -e) ore

erzählen vt tell (jdm etw sb sth); **Erzählung** f story, tale

erzeugen vt produce; (electricity) generate; **Erzeugnis** nt product

erziehen irr vt bring up; (intellectually) educate; (animal) train; **Erzieher(in)** m(f) (-s, -) educator; (in kindergarten) nursery school) teacher; **Erziehung** f upbringing; (intellectual) education

es pron it; (baby, animal) he / she; **ich bin ~** it's me; **~ ist kalt** it's cold; **~ gibt ...** there is ... / there are ...; **ich hoffe ~** I hope so; **ich kann ~** I can do it

Escape-Taste f IT escape key

Esel m (-s, -) donkey

Espresso m (-s, -) espresso

essbar adj edible; **essen** (aß, gegessen) vi, vt eat; **zu Mittag / Abend ~** have lunch / dinner; **was gibt's zu ~?** what's for lunch / dinner?; ~

gehen eat out; **Essen** nt (-s, -) meal; food

Essig m (-s, -e) vinegar; **Essiggurke** f gherkin

Esslöffel m dessert spoon; **Esszimmer** nt dining room

Estland nt Estonia

Etage f (-, -n) floor, storey; **in** (or **auf**) **der ersten** ~ on the first (Brit) (or second (US)) floor; **Etagenbett** nt bunk bed

Etappe f (-, -n) stage

ethnisch adj ethnic

Etikett nt (-(e)s, -e) label

etliche pron several, quite a few; **etliches** pron quite a lot

etwa adv (approximation) about; (possibility) perhaps; (example) for instance

etwas 1. pron something; (with negative, question) anything; (small amount) a little; ~ **Neues** something/anything new; ~ **zu essen** something to eat; ~ **Salz** some salt; **wenn ich noch** ~ **tun kann** ... if I can do anything else ... **2.** adv a bit, a little; ~ **mehr** a little more

EU f (-) abbr = **Europäische Union**; EU

euch pron acc, dat of **ihr**; you; (to) you; ~ (**selbst**) yourselves; **wo kann ich** ~ **treffen?** where can I meet you?; **sie schickt es** ~ she'll send it to you; **ein Freund von** ~ a friend of yours; **setzt** ~ **bitte** please sit down; **habt**

ihr ~ **amüsiert?** did you enjoy yourselves?

euer pron (as adj) your; ~ **David** (at end of letter) Yours, David; **euere(r, s)** pron → **eure**

Eule f (-, -n) owl

eure(r, s) pron (as noun) yours; **das ist** ~ that's yours; **euretwegen** adv because of you; (to please you) for your sake

Euro m (-, -) (currency) euro; **Eurocent** m eurocent; **Eurocity** m (-(s), -s), **Eurocityzug** m European Intercity train; **Europa** f (-s) Europe; **Europäer(in)** m(f) (-s, -) European; **europäisch** adj European; **Europäische Union** European Union; **Europameister(in)** m(f) European champion; (team) European champions pl; **Europaparlament** nt European Parliament

Euter nt (-s, -) udder

evangelisch adj Protestant

eventuell 1. adj possible **2.** adv possibly, perhaps

ewig adj eternal; **er hat** ~ **gebraucht** it took him ages; **Ewigkeit** f eternity

Ex- in cpds ex-, former; ~**frau** ex-wife; ~**minister** former minister

exakt adj precise

Examen nt (-s, -) exam

Exemplar nt (-s, -e) specimen; (book) copy

Exil *nt* (-s, -e) exile
Existenz *f* existence; *(financial means)* livelihood, living; existieren *vi* exist
exklusiv *adj* exclusive; exklusive *adv*, *prep* + *gen* excluding
exotisch *adj* exotic
Experte *m* (-n, -n), Expertin *f* expert
explodieren *vi* explode; Explosion *f* explosion
Export *m* (-(e)s, -e) export; exportieren *vt* export

Express *m* (-es), Expresszug *m* express (train)
extra **1.** *adj inv fam* separate; *(additional)* extra **2.** *adv* separately; *(for particular person or purpose)* specially; *(intentionally)* on purpose; Extra *nt* (-s, -s) extra
extrem **1.** *adj* extreme **2.** *adv* extremely; **~ kalt** extremely cold
exzellent *adj* excellent
Eyeliner *m* (-s, -) eyeliner

F

fabelhaft *adj* fabulous, marvellous
Fabrik *f* factory
Fach *nt* (-(e)s, Fächer) compartment; *(area of knowledge)* subject; Facharzt *m*, Fachärztin *f* specialist; Fachausdruck *m* (-s, Fachausdrücke) technical term
Fächer *m* (-s, -) fan
Fachfrau *f* specialist, expert; Fachmann *m* *(-leute pl)* specialist, expert; Fachwerkhaus *nt* half-timbered house
Fackel *f* (-, -n) torch
fad(e) *adj* *(food)* bland; *(boring)* dull
Faden *m* (-s, Fäden) thread
fähig *adj* capable *(zu, gen* of); Fähigkeit *f* ability
Fahndung *f* search
Fahne *f* (-, -n) flag

Fahrausweis *m* ticket; Fahrausweisautomat *m* ticket machine; Fahrausweiskontrolle *f* ticket inspection
Fahrbahn *f* road; *(between lines)* lane
Fähre *f* (-, -n) ferry
fahren *(fuhr, gefahren)* **1.** *vt* drive; *(bicycle)* ride; *(convey)* drive, take; **50 km/h ~** drive at (*or* do) 50 kph **2.** *vi* go; *(in car)* drive; *(ship)* sail; *(depart)* leave; **mit dem Auto/Zug ~** go by car/train; **rechts ~!** keep to the right; Fahrer(in) *m(f)* (-s, -) driver; Fahrerflucht *f ~* **begehen** fail to stop after an accident; Fahrersitz *m* driver's seat
Fahrgast *m* passenger; Fahrgeld *nt* fare; Fahrgemein-

schaft f car pool; **Fahrkarte**
f ticket

Fahrkartenautomat m ticket
machine; **Fahrkartenschal-**
ter m ticket office

fahrlässig adj negligent

Fahrlehrer(in) m(f) driving
instructor; **Fahrplan** m
timetable; **Fahrpreis** m fare;
Fahrpreisermäßigung f
fare reduction

Fahrrad nt bicycle; **Fahrrad-**
schloss nt bicycle lock;
Fahrradverleih m cycle hire
(*Brit*) (or rental (*US*)); **Fahr-**
radweg m cycle path

Fahrschein m ticket; **Fahr-**
scheinautomat m ticket machine; **Fahrscheinentwerter**
m ticket-cancelling machine

Fahrschule f driving school;
Fahrschüler(in) m(f) learner (driver) (*Brit*), student
driver (*US*)

Fahrstuhl m lift (*Brit*), elevator (*US*)

Fahrt f (-, -en) journey; (*short*)
trip; AUTO drive; **auf der ~**
nach London on the way
to London; **nach drei Stun-**
den ~ after travelling for
three hours; **gute ~!** have a
good trip; **Fahrtkosten** pl
travelling expenses pl

fahrtüchtig f (*person*) fit to
drive; (*vehicle*) roadworthy

Fahrtunterbrechung f break
in the journey, stop

Fahrverbot nt **~ erhalten/ ha-**
ben be banned from driving;

Fahrzeug nt vehicle; **Fahr-**
zeugbrief m (vehicle) registration document; **Fahr-**
zeughalter(in) m(f) registered owner; **Fahrzeugpa-**
piere pl vehicle documents
pl

fair adj fair

Fakultät f faculty

Falke m (-n, -n) falcon

Fall m (-(e)s, Fälle) (*accident*)
fall; (*instance, in law*) case;
auf jeden ~, auf alle Fälle
in any case; (*without fail*)
definitely; **auf keinen ~** on
no account; **für den ~, dass**
... in case ...

Falle f (-, -n) trap

fallen (*fiel, gefallen*) vi fall;
etw ~ lassen drop sth

fällig adj due

falls adv if; (*allowing for even-*
tuality) in case

Fallschirm m parachute;
Fallschirmspringen nt
parachuting, parachute
jumping; **Fallschirmsprin-**
ger(in) m(f) parachutist

falsch adj wrong; (*dishonest,*
not genuine) false; **~ verbun-**
den sorry, wrong number;
fälschen vt forge; **Falsch-**
geld nt counterfeit money;
Fälschung f forgery, fake

Faltblatt nt leaflet

Falte f (-, -n) fold; (*in skin*)
wrinkle; (*in skirt*) pleat; **fal-**
ten vt fold; **faltig** adj
creased; (*skin, face*)
wrinkled

Familie f family; **Familienangehörige(r)** f m family member; **Familienname** m surname; **Familienstand** m marital status

Fan m (-s, -s) fan

fand imperf of **finden**

fangen (fing, gefangen) **1.** vt catch **2.** vr (not fall) steady oneself; fig compose oneself

Fantasie f imagination

fantastisch adj fantastic

Farbbild nt colour photograph; **Farbe** f (-, -n) colour; (substance) paint; (for fabric) dye; **farbecht** adj colourfast; **färben** vt colour; (fabric, hair) dye; **Farbfilm** m colour film; **Farbfoto** nt colour photo; **farbig** adj coloured; **Farbkopierer** m colour copier; **Farbstoff** m dye; (for food) colouring

Farn m (-(e)s, -e) fern

Fasan m (-(e)s, -e(n)) pheasant

Fasching m (-s, -e) carnival, Mardi Gras (US); **Faschingsdienstag** m (-s, -e) Shrove Tuesday, Mardi Gras (US)

Faschismus m fascism

Faser f (-, -n) fibre

Fass nt (-es, Fässer) barrel; (for oil) drum

fassen 1. vt (take hold of) grasp; (be able to contain) hold; (decision) take; (comprehend) understand; **nicht zu ~!** unbelievable **2.** vr compose oneself; **Fassung** f (of jewel) mount; (of glasses) frame; (of lamp) socket; (of text) version; (self-control) composure; **jdn aus der ~ bringen** throw sb; **die ~ verlieren** lose one's cool

fast adv almost, nearly

fasten vi fast; **Fastenzeit** f **die ~** (Christian) Lent; (Muslim) Ramadan

Fast Food nt (-s) fast food

Fastnacht f carnival

faul adj (fruit, vegetables) rotten; (person) lazy; (excuse) lame; **faulen** vi rot

faulenzen vi do nothing, hang around; **Faulheit** f laziness

faulig adj rotten; (smell, taste) foul

Faust f (-, Fäuste) fist; **Fausthandschuh** m mitten

Fax nt (-, -(e)) fax; **faxen** vi, vt fax; **Faxgerät** nt fax machine; **Faxnummer** f fax number

FCKW m (-s, -s) abbr = **Fluorchlorkohlenwasserstoff**; CFC

Februar m (-(s), -e) February; → **Juni**

Fechten nt fencing

Feder f (-, -n) feather; (for writing) (pen-)nib; TECH spring; **Federball** m shuttlecock; (game) badminton; **Federung** f suspension

Fee f (-, -n) fairy

fegen vi, vt sweep

fehlen vi (from school etc) be

absent; *etw fehlt jdm* sb lacks sth; *was fehlt ihm?* what's wrong with him?; *du fehlst mir* I miss you; *es fehlt an ...* there's no...

Fehler *m* (-s, -) mistake, error; *(defect, failing)* fault; **Fehlermeldung** *f* IT error message

Fehlzündung *f* AUTO misfire

Feier *f* (-, -n) celebration; *(get--together)* party; **feierlich** *adj* solemn; **feiern** *vt, vi* celebrate, have a party; **Feiertag** *m* holiday; *gesetzlicher ~* public *(or* bank *(Brit) or* legal *(US))* holiday

feig(e) *adj* cowardly

Feige *f* (-, -n) fig

Feigling *m* coward

Feile *f* (-, -n) file

fein *adj* fine; *(gentleman, manners)* refined

Feind(in) *m(f)* (-(e)s, -e) enemy; **feindlich** *adj* hostile

Feinkost *f* (-) delicacies *pl*; **Feinkostladen** *m* delicatessen

Feinwaschmittel *nt* washing powder for delicate fabrics

Feld *nt* (-(e)s, -er) field; *(in chess)* square; SPORT pitch; **Feldweg** *m* path across the fields

Felge *f* (-, -n) (wheel) rim

Fell *nt* (-(e)s, -e) fur; *(of sheep)* fleece

Fels *m* (-en, -en), **Felsen** *m* (-s, -) rock; *(rock face)* cliff; **felsig** *adj* rocky

feministisch *adj* feminist

Fenchel *m* (-s, -) fennel

Fenster *nt* (-s, -) window; **Fensterbrett** *nt* windowsill; **Fensterladen** *m* shutter; **Fensterplatz** *m* windowseat; **Fensterscheibe** *f* windowpane

Ferien *pl* holidays *pl* *(Brit)*, vacation *sg* *(US)*; *~ haben/ machen* be/go on holiday *(Brit)* *(or* vacation *(US))*; **Ferienhaus** *nt* holiday *(Brit)* *(or* vacation *(US))* home; **Ferienkurs** *m* holiday *(Brit)* *(or* vacation *(US))* course; **Ferienlager** *nt* holiday camp *(Brit)*, vacation camp *(US)*; *(for children in summer)* summer camp; **Ferienort** *m* holiday *(Brit)* *(or* vacation *(US))* resort; **Ferienwohnung** *f* holiday flat *(Brit)*, vacation apartment *(US)*

fern *adj* distant, far-off; *von ~* from a distance; **Fernabfrage** *f* remote-control access; **Fernbedienung** *f* remote control; **Ferne** *f* distance; *aus der ~* from a distance

ferner *adj, adv* further; *(in addition)* besides

Fernflug *m* long-distance flight; **Ferngespräch** *nt* long-distance call; **ferngesteuert** *adj* remote-controlled; **Fernglas** *nt* binoculars *pl*; **Fernlicht** *nt* full beam *(Brit)*, high beam *(US)* fernsehen *irr vi* watch television; Fernsehen *nt* television; **im ~** on television; Fernseher *m* TV (set); Fernsehkanal *m* TV channel; Fernsehprogramm *nt* TV programme; *(magazine)* TV guide; Fernsehserie *f* TV series *sg*; Fernsehturm *m* TV tower

Fernstraße *f* major road; Fernverkehr *m* long-distance traffic

Ferse *f (-, -n)* heel

fertig *adj* ready; *(completed)* finished; **~ machen** *(task etc)* finish; **jdn ~ machen** *(criticize)* give sb hell; *(annoy)* drive sb mad; **sich ~ machen** get ready; **mit etw ~ werden** be able to cope with sth; **auf die Plätze, ~, los!** on your marks, get set, go!; Fertiggericht *nt* ready meal

fest *adj* firm; *(food)* solid; *(salary)* regular; *(shoes)* sturdy; *(sleep)* sound

Fest *nt (-(e)s, -e)* party; REL festival

Festbetrag *m* fixed amount

festbinden *irr vt* tie *(an + dat* to); festhalten *irr* **1.** *vt* hold onto **2.** *vr* hold on *(an + dat* to)

Festival *nt (-s, -s)* festival

festlegen **1.** *vt* fix **2.** *vr* commit oneself

festlich *adj* festive

festmachen *vt* fasten; *(date etc)* fix; festnehmen *irr vt* arrest

Festnetz *nt* TEL fixed-line network; Festplatte *f* IT hard disk

festsetzen *vt* fix

Festspiele *pl* festival *sg*

feststehen *irr vi* be fixed

feststellen *vt* establish; *(say)* remark

Festung *f* fortress

Festzelt *nt* marquee

Fete *f (-, -n)* party

fett *adj (person)* fat; *(food etc)* greasy; *(type)* bold; Fett *nt (-(e)s, -e)* fat; TECH grease; fettarm *adj* low-fat; fettig *adj* fatty; *(dirty)* greasy

fetzig *adj fam (music)* funky

feucht *adj* damp; *(air)* humid; Feuchtigkeit *f* dampness; *(of air)* humidity; Feuchtigkeitscreme *f* moisturizing cream

Feuer *nt (-s, -)* fire; **haben Sie ~?** have you got a light?; Feueralarm *m* fire alarm; feuerfest *adj* fireproof; feuergefährlich *adj* inflammable; Feuerlöscher *m (-s, -)* fire extinguisher; Feuermelder *m (-s, -)* fire alarm; Feuertreppe *f* fire escape; Feuerwehr *f (-, -en)* fire brigade; Feuerwerk *nt* fireworks *pl*; Feuerzeug *nt* (cigarette) lighter

Fichte *f (-, -n)* spruce

ficken *vt, vi vulg* fuck

Fieber *nt (-s, -)* temperature,

fever; **~ haben** have a high temperature; **Fieberthermometer** *nt* thermometer

fiel *imperf of* **fallen**

fies *adj fam* nasty

Figur *f* (-, -en) figure; (*in chess*) piece

Filet *nt* (-s, -s) COMM branch

Filiale *f* (-, -n) COMM branch

Film *m* (-(e)s, -e) film, movie; **filmen** *vt, vi* film

Filter *m* (-s, -) filter; **Filterkaffee** *m* filter coffee; **filtern** *vt* filter; **Filterpapier** *nt* filter paper

Filz *m* (-es, -e) felt; **Filzschreiber** *m*, **Filzstift** *m* felt(-tip) pen, felt-tip

Finale *nt* (-s, -) SPORT final

Finanzamt *nt* tax office; **finanziell** *adj* financial; **finanzieren** *vt* finance

finden (*fand, gefunden*) *vt* find; (*have opinion*) think; **ich finde nichts dabei, wenn ...** I don't see what's wrong if ...; **ich finde es gut/schlecht** I like/don't like it

fing *imperf of* **fangen**

Finger *m* (-s, -) finger; **Fingerabdruck** *m* fingerprint; **Fingernagel** *m* fingernail

Fink *m* (-en, -en) finch

Finne *f* (-n, -n), **Finnin** *f* Finn, Finnish man/woman; **finnisch** *adj* Finnish; **Finnisch** *nt* Finnish; **Finnland** *nt* Finland

finster *adj* dark; (*suspicious*) dubious; (*morose*) grim; (*thought*) dark; **Finsternis** *f* darkness

Firewall *f* (-, -s) IT firewall

Firma *f* (-, **Firmen**) firm

Fisch *m* (-(e)s, -e) fish; **~e** *pl* ASTR Pisces *sg*; **fischen** *vt, vi* fish; **Fischer(in)** *m(f)* (-s, -) fisherman/-woman; **Fischerboot** *nt* fishing boat; **Fischgericht** *nt* fish dish; **Fischhändler(in)** *m(f)* fishmonger; **Fischstäbchen** *nt* fish finger (*Brit*) (*or* stick (*US*))

Fisole *f* (-, -n) French bean

fit *adj* fit; **Fitness** *f* (-) fitness; **Fitnesscenter** *nt* (-s, -) fitness centre

fix *adj* quick; **~ und fertig** exhausted

fixen *vi fam* shoot up; **Fixer(in)** *m(f)* (-s, -) *fam* junkie

FKK *f abbr* = **Freikörperkultur**; nudism; **FKK-Strand** *m* nudist beach

flach *adj* flat; (*water, plate*) shallow; **~er Absatz** low heel; **Flachbildschirm** *m* flat screen

Fläche *f* (-, -n) area; (*of object*) surface

Flagge *f* (-, -n) flag

flambiert *adj* flambé(ed)

Flamme *f* (-, -n) flame

Flasche *f* (-, -n) bottle; **eine ~ sein** *fam* be useless; **Flaschenöffner** *m* bottle opener; **Flaschenpfand** *nt* deposit

flatterhaft *adj* fickle; **flattern** *vi* flutter

flauschig *adj* fluffy

Flaute *f* (-, *-n*) calm; COMM recession

Flechte *f* (-, *-n*) plait; MED scab; BOT lichen; **flechten** (*flocht, geflochten*) *vt* plait; (*wreath*) bind

Fleck *m* (-(*e*)*s*, *-e*), **Flecken** *m* (-*s*, *-*) spot; (*dirt*) stain; **Fleckentferner** *m* (-*s*, *-*) stain remover; **fleckig** *adj* spotted; (*with dirt*) stained

Fledermaus *f* bat

Fleisch *nt* (-(*e*)*s*) flesh; (*food*) meat

Fleischbrühe *f* meat stock

Fleischer(in) *m(f)* (-*s*, *-*) butcher; **Fleischerei** *f* butcher's (shop)

fleißig *adj* diligent, hard-working

flexibel *adj* flexible

flicken *vt* mend; **Flickzeug** *nt* repair kit

Flieder *m* (-*s*, *-*) lilac

Fliege *f* (-, *-n*) fly; (*clothing*) bow tie

fliegen (*flog, geflogen*) *vt, vi* fly

Fliese *f* (-, *-n*) tile

Fließband *nt* conveyor belt; (*system*) production (*or* assembly) line; **fließen** (*floss, geflossen*) *vi* flow; **fließend** *adj* (*speech, German*) fluent; (*transition*) smooth; *~(es)* **Wasser** running water

flippig *adj fam* eccentric

flirten *vi* flirt

Flitterwochen *pl* honeymoon *sg*

flocht *imperf of* **flechten**

Flocke *f* (-, *-n*) flake

flog *imperf of* **fliegen**

Floh *m* (-(*e*)*s*, *Flöhe*) flea; **Flohmarkt** *m* flea market

Flop *m* (-*s*, *-s*) flop

Floskel *f* (-, *-n*) empty phrase

floss *imperf of* **fließen**

Floß *nt* (-*es*, *Flöße*) raft

Flosse *f* (-, *-n*) fin; (*of swimmer*) flipper

Flöte *f* (-, *-n*) flute; (*held vertically*) recorder

Fluch *m* (-(*e*)*s*, *Flüche*) curse; **fluchen** *vi* swear, curse

Flucht *f* (-, *-en*) flight; **flüchten** *vi* flee (*vor + dat* from); **flüchtig** *adj* **ich kenne ihn nur ~** I don't know him very well at all; **Flüchtling** *m* refugee

Flug *m* (-(*e*)*s*, *Flüge*) flight; **Flugbegleiter(in)** *m(f)* (-*s*, *-*) flight attendant; **Flugblatt** *nt* leaflet

Flügel *m* (-*s*, *-*) wing; MUS grand piano

Fluggast *m* passenger (*on a plane*); **Fluggesellschaft** *f* airline; **Flughafen** *m* airport; **Fluglotse** *m* air-traffic controller; **Flugnummer** *f* flight number; **Flugplan** *m* flight schedule; **Flugplatz** *m* airport; (*small*) airfield; **Flugschein** *m* plane ticket; **Flugschreiber** *m* flight recorder, black box; **Flugsteig** *m* (*-s*, *-e*) gate; **Flugticket** *nt* plane ticket; **Flugverbindung** *f* flight connection; **Flugverkehr** *m* air traffic; **Flugzeit** *f* flying time; **Flugzeug** *nt* plane; **Flugzeugentführung** *f* hijacking

Flunder *f* (*-*, *-n*) flounder

Fluor *nt* (*-s*) fluorine

Flur *m* (*-(e)s*, *-e*) hall

Fluss *m* (*-es*, *Flüsse*) river; (*movement*) flow

flüssig *adj* liquid; **Flüssigkeit** *f* liquid

flüstern *vt*, *vi* whisper

Flut *f* (*-*, *-en*) flood; (*in sea*) high tide; **Flutlicht** *nt* floodlight

Fohlen *nt* (*-s*, *-*) foal

Föhn *m* (*-(e)s*, *-e*) hairdryer; (*wind*) foehn; **föhnen** *vt* dry; (*at hairdresser's*) blow-dry

Folge *f* (*-*, *-n*) (*one after another*) series *sg*; (*belonging together*) sequence; (*of novel*) instalment; (*of TV series*) episode; (*consequence*) result; **~n haben** have consequences; **folgen** *vi* follow (*jdm* sb); (*do as told*) obey (*jdm* sb); **jdm ~ können** *fig* be able to follow sb; **folgend** *adj* following; **folgendermaßen** *adv* as follows; **folglich** *adv* consequently

Folie *f* foil; (*for projector*) transparency

Fön® *m* → **Föhn**

Fondue *nt* (*-s*, *-s*) fondue

fönen *vt* → **föhnen**

fordern *vt* demand

fördern *vt* promote; (*support*) help

Forderung *f* demand

Forelle *f* trout

Form *f* (*-*, *-en*) form; (*outer form*) shape; (*for casting*) mould; (*for baking*) baking tin (*Brit*) (*or* pan (*US*)); **in ~ sein** be in good form; **Formalität** *f* formality; **Format** *nt* format; **formatieren** *vt* (*disk*) format; (*text*) edit; **formen** *vt* form, shape; **förmlich** *adj* formal; (*proper*) real; **formlos** *adj* informal; **Formular** *nt* (*-s*, *-e*) form; **formulieren** *vt* formulate

forschen *vi* search (*nach* for); (*academic*) research; **Forscher(in)** *m(f)* researcher; **Forschung** *f* research

Förster(in) *m(f)* (*-s*, *-*) forester; (*for animals*) gamekeeper

fort *adv* away; (*missing*) gone; **fortbewegen 1.** *vt* move away **2.** *vr* move; **Fortbildung** *f* further education; (*vocational*) further training; **fortfahren** *irr vi* go away; (*carry on*) continue; **fortgehen** *irr vi* go away; **fortgeschritten** *adj* advanced; **Fortpflanzung** *f* reproduction

Fortschritt *m* progress; **~e**

machen make progress; fortschrittlich *adj* progressive

fortsetzen *vt* continue; Fortsetzung *f* continuation; (*episode*) instalment; **~ folgt** to be continued

Foto **1.** *nt* (-s, -s) photo **2.** *m* (-s, -s) camera; Fotograf(in) *m(f)* (-en, -en) photographer; Fotografie *f* photography; (*picture*) photograph; fotografieren **1.** *vt* photograph **2.** *vi* take photographs; Fotokopie *f* photocopy; fotokopieren *vt* photocopy

Foul *nt* (-s, -s) foul

Foyer *nt* (-s, -s) foyer

Fr. *f abbr* = ***Frau***; Mrs; (*unmarried, neutral*) Ms

Fracht *f* (-, -en) freight; NAUT cargo; Frachter *m* (-s, -) freighter

Frack *m* (-(e)s, Fräcke) tails *pl*

Frage *f* (-, -n) question; **das ist eine ~ der Zeit** that's a matter (*or* question) of time; **das kommt nicht in ~** that's out of the question; Fragebogen *m* questionnaire; fragen *vt, vi* ask; Fragezeichen *nt* question mark; fragwürdig *adj* dubious

Franken **1.** *m* (-s, -) Swiss franc **2.** *nt* (-s) (*region*) Franconia

frankieren *vt* stamp; (*with machine*) frank

Frankreich *nt* (-s) France;

Franzose *m* (-n, -n), Französin *f* Frenchman /-woman; ***die ~n*** *pl* the French *pl*; französisch *adj* French; Französisch *nt* French

fraß *imperf of* ***fressen***

Frau *f* (-, -en) woman; (*spouse*) wife; (*form of address*) Mrs; (*unmarried, neutral*) Ms; Frauenarzt *m*, Frauenärztin *f* gynaecologist

Fräulein *nt* young lady; (*old-fashioned form of address*) Miss

Freak *m* (-s, -s) *fam* freak

frech *adj* cheeky; Frechheit *f* cheek; **so eine ~!** what a cheek

Freeclimbing *nt* (-s) free climbing

frei *adj* free; (*road*) clear; (*worker*) freelance; **~ er Tag** a day off; **~e Arbeitsstelle** vacancy; **Zimmer ~** room(s) to let (*Brit*), room(s) for rent (*US*); **im Freien** in the open air

Freibad *nt* open-air (swimming) pool; freiberuflich *adj* freelance; freig(i)ebig *adj* generous; Freiheit *f* freedom; Freikarte *f* free ticket; freilassen *irr vt* (set) free

freilich *adv* of course

Freilichtbühne *f* open-air theatre; freimachen *vr* undress; freinehmen *irr vt* **sich *dat* einen Tag ~** take a day off; Freisprechanlage *f* hands-free phone; Freistoß *m* free kick

Freitag *m* Friday; → *Mittwoch*; freitags *adv* on Fridays; → *mittwochs*

freiwillig *adj* voluntary

Freizeit *f* spare (or free) time; Freizeithemd *nt* sports shirt; Freizeitkleidung *f* leisure wear; Freizeitpark *m* leisure park

fremd *adj* (unfamiliar) strange; (of another country) foreign; (not one's own) someone else's; Fremde/r *mf* stranger; (from another country) foreigner; Fremdenführer(in) *m(f)* (tourist) guide; Fremdenverkehr *m* tourism; Fremdenverkehrsamt *nt* tourist information office; Fremdsprache *f* foreign language; Fremdsprachenkenntnisse *pl* knowledge *sg* of foreign languages; Fremdwort *nt* foreign word

Frequenz *f* RADIO frequency

fressen (fraß, gefressen) *vt, vi* (animal) eat; (person) guzzle

Freude *f* (-, -n) joy, delight; freuen 1. *vt* please; *es freut mich, dass ...* I'm pleased that ... 2. *vr* be pleased (*über + acc* about); *sich auf etw acc ~* look forward to sth

Freund *m* (-(e)s, -e) friend; (in relationship) boyfriend; Freundin *f* friend; (in relationship) girlfriend; freundlich *adj* friendly; (helpful etc) kind; freundlicherwei-

se *adv* kindly; Freundschaft *f* friendship

Frieden *m* (-s, -) peace; Friedhof *m* cemetery; friedlich *adj* peaceful

frieren (fror, gefroren) *vt, vi* freeze; *ich friere, es friert mich* I'm freezing

Frikadelle *f* rissole

Frisbeescheibe® *f* frisbee®

frisch *adj* fresh; (full of life) lively; *„~ gestrichen"* "wet paint"; *sich ~ machen* freshen up; Frischhaltefolie *f* clingfilm® (Brit), plastic wrap (US); Frischkäse *m* cream cheese

Friseur *m*, Friseuse *f* hairdresser; frisieren 1. *vt jdn ~* do sb's hair 2. *vr* do one's hair; Frisör *m* (-s, -e), Frisöse *f* (-, -n) hairdresser

Frist *f* (-, -en) period; (last date) deadline; *innerhalb einer ~ von zehn Tagen* within a ten-day period; *eine ~ einhalten* meet a deadline; *die ~ ist abgelaufen* the deadline has expired; fristlos *adj* *~e Entlassung* dismissal without notice

Frisur *f* hairstyle

frittieren *vt* deep-fry

Frl. *f abbr* = *Fräulein*; Miss

froh *adj* happy; *~e Weihnachten!* Merry Christmas

fröhlich *adj* happy, cheerful

Frontalzusammenstoß *m* head-on collision

fror *imperf of frieren*

Frosch m (-(e)s, Frösche) frog

Frost m (-(e)s, Fröste) frost; **bei ~** in frosty weather; **Frostschutzmittel** nt anti-freeze

Frottee nt terry(cloth); **frottieren** vt rub down; **Frottier(hand)tuch** nt towel

Frucht f (-, Früchte) fruit; (grain) corn; **Fruchteis** nt fruit-flavoured ice-cream; **fruchtig** adj fruity; **Fruchtsaft** m fruit juice; **Fruchtsalat** m fruit salad

früh adj, adv early; **heute ~** this morning; **um fünf Uhr ~** at five (o'clock) in the morning; **~ genug** soon enough; **früher 1.** adj earlier; (ex-) former **2.** adv formerly, in the past; **frühestens** adv at the earliest

Frühjahr nt, **Frühling** m spring; **Frühlingsrolle** f spring roll; **Frühlingszwiebel** f spring onion (Brit), scallion (US)

Frühschicht f ~ **haben** be on the early shift

Frühstück nt breakfast; **frühstücken** vi have breakfast; **Frühstücksbüffett** nt breakfast buffet

frühzeitig adj early

Frust m (-s) fam frustration; **frustrieren** vt frustrate

Fuchs m (-es, Füchse) fox

fühlen vt, vi, vr feel

fuhr imperf of **fahren**

führen 1. vt lead; (business) run; (accounts) keep **2.** vi lead, be in the lead **3.** vr behave; **Führerschein** m driving licence (Brit), driver's license (US); **Führung** f leadership; (of company) management; MIL command; (in museum, town) guided tour; **in ~ liegen** be in the lead

füllen vt, vr fill; GASTR stuff; **Füllung** f filling

Füller m (-s, -), **Füllfederhalter** m (-s, -) fountain pen

Fund m (-(e)s, -e) find; **Fundbüro** nt lost property office (Brit), lost and found (US); **Fundsachen** pl lost property sg

fünf num five; **Fünf** f (-, -en) five; (mark in school) ≈ E; **fünfhundert** num five hundred; **fünfmal** adv five times; **fünfte(r, s)** adj fifth; → **dritte**; **fünftel** nt (-s, -) fifth; **fünfzehn** num fifteen; **fünfzehnte(r, s)** adj fifteenth; → **dritte**; **fünfzig** num fifty; **fünfzigste(r, s)** adj fiftieth

Funk m (-s) radio; **über ~** by radio

Funke m (-ns, -n) spark; **funkeln** vi sparkle

Funkgerät nt radio set; **Funktaxi** nt radio taxi, radio cab

Funktion f function; **funktionieren** vi work, function

für prep + acc for; **was ~ (ein) ...?** what kind (or sort) of ...?; **Tag ~ Tag** day after day

Furcht f (-) fear; **furchtbar** adj terrible; **fürchten 1.** vt be afraid of, fear **2.** vr be afraid (vor + dat of); **fürchterlich** adj awful

füreinander adv for each other

fürs contr of **für das**

Fürst(in) m(f) (-en, -en) prince/princess; **Fürstentum** nt principality

Furunkel nt (-s, -) boil

Furz m (-es, -e) vulg fart; **furzen** vi vulg fart

Fuß m (-es, Füße) foot; (of glass, column etc) base; (of furniture) leg; **zu ~** on foot; **zu ~ gehen** walk; **Fußball** m football (Brit), soccer

Fußballmannschaft f football (Brit) (or soccer) team; **Fußballplatz** m football pitch (Brit), soccer field (US); **Fußballspiel** nt foot-ball (Brit) (or soccer) match; **Fußballspieler(in)** m(f) footballer (Brit), soccer player; **Fußboden** m floor; **Fußgänger(in)** m(f) (-s, -), pedestrian; **Fußgängerüberweg** m pedestrian crossing (Brit), crosswalk (US); **Fußgängerzone** f pedestrian precinct (Brit) (or zone (US)); **Fußgelenk** nt ankle; **Fußpilz** m athlete's foot; **Fußtritt** m kick; **jdm einen ~ geben** give sb a kick, kick sb; **Fußweg** m footpath

futsch adj fam broken; (in pieces) smashed; (lost, vanished) gone

Futter nt (-s, -) feed; (hay etc) fodder; (material) lining; **füttern** vt feed; (garment) line

Fuzzi m (-s, -s) fam guy

G

gab imperf of **geben**

Gabe f (-, -n) gift

Gabel f (-, -n) fork; **Gabelung** f fork

gaffen vi gape

Gage f (-, -n) fee

gähnen vi yawn

Galerie f gallery

Galle f (-, -n) gall; (organ) gall bladder; **Gallenstein** m gall-stone

Galopp m (-s) gallop; galop-pieren vi gallop

galt imperf of **gelten**

gammeln vi loaf (or hang) around

Gang m (-(e)s, Gänge) walk; (in plane) aisle; (of meal, events etc) course; (in building) corridor; (connecting way) passage; AUTO gear; **den zweiten ~ einlegen** change into second (gear); **etw in ~ bringen** get sth go-

ing; **Gangschaltung** f gears
pl; **Gangway** f (-, -s) AVIAT
steps pl; NAUT gangway
Gans f (-, *Gänse*) goose; **Gänseblümchen** nt daisy; **Gänsehaut** f goose pimples pl
(*Brit*), goose bumps pl (*US*)
ganz 1. adj whole; (*set etc*)
complete; **~ Europa** all of
Europe; **sein ~es Geld** all
his money; **den ~en Tag** all
day; **die ~e Zeit** all the time
2. adv quite; (*totally*) completely; **es hat mir ~ gut gefallen** I quite liked it; **~
schön viel** quite a lot; ganz-
tägig adj all-day; (*work, job*)
full-time
gar 1. adj done, cooked **2.** adv
at all; **nicht/nichts/kei-
ner** not/nothing/nobody at
all; **~ nicht schlecht** not
bad at all
Garage f (-, -n) garage
Garantie f guarantee; garantieren vt guarantee
Garderobe f (-, -n) (*clothes*)
wardrobe; (*in theatre, museum etc*) cloakroom
Gardine f curtain
Garn nt (-(e)s, -e) thread
Garnele f (-, -n) shrimp
garnieren vt decorate; (*food*)
garnish
Garten m (-s, *Gärten*) garden;
Gärtner(in) m(f) (-s, -) gardener; **Gärtnerei** f market
garden (*Brit*), truck farm
(*US*)
Garzeit f cooking time

Gas nt (-es, -e) gas; **~ geben**
AUTO accelerate; fig get a
move on; **Gasanzünder** m
gas lighter; **Gasheizung** f
gas heating; **Gasherd** m
gas stove, gas cooker (*Brit*);
Gaskocher m camping
stove; **Gaspedal** nt accelera-
tor, gas pedal (*US*)
Gasse f (-, -n) alley
Gast m (-es, *Gäste*) guest;
Gäste haben have guests;
Gästebett nt spare bed;
Gästebuch nt visitors' book;
Gästehaus nt guest house;
Gästezimmer nt guest room;
gastfreundlich adj hospitable; **Gastgeber(in)** m(f)
(-s, -) host/hostess; **Gasthaus** nt, **Gasthof** m inn;
Gastland nt host country
Gastritis f (-) gastritis
Gastronomie f catering trade
Gastspiel nt SPORT away
game; **Gaststätte** f restaurant; pub (*Brit*), bar; **Gast-
wirt(in)** m(f) landlord /-lady
Gaumen m (-s, -) palate
geb. **1.** adj abbr = **geboren:**
2. adj abbr = **geborene:** née
→ **geboren**
Gebäck nt (-(e)s, -e) pastries
pl, biscuits pl (*Brit*), cookies
pl (*US*)
gebacken pp of **backen**
Gebärmutter f womb
Gebäude nt (-s, -) building
geben (*gab, gegeben*) **1.** vt, vi
give (*jdm etw* sb sth, sth to
sb); (*cards*) deal; **lass dir ei-**

ne Quittung ~ ask for a receipt **2.** vt impers **es gibt** there is/are; (in the future) there will be; **das gibt's nicht** I don't believe it **3.** vr (person) behave, act; **das gibt sich wieder** it'll sort itself out

Gebet nt (-(e)s, -e) prayer

gebeten pp of **bitten**

Gebiet nt (-(e)s, -e) area; (British etc) territory; fig field

gebildet adj educated; (with book learning) well-read

Gebirge nt (-s, -) mountains pl

Gebiss nt (-es, -e) teeth pl; (false) dentures pl; **gebissen** pp of **beißen**; **Gebissreiniger** m denture tablets pl

Gebläse nt (-s, -) fan, blower

geblasen pp of **blasen**

geblieben pp of **bleiben**

gebogen pp of **biegen**

geboren 1. pp of **gebären 2.** adj born; **Andrea Jordan, ~e Christian** Andrea Jordan, née Christian

geborgen 1. pp of **bergen 2.** adj secure, safe

geboten pp of **bieten**

gebracht pp of **bringen**

gebrannt pp of **brennen**

gebraten pp of **braten**

gebrauchen vt use; **Gebrauchsanweisung** f directions pl for use; **gebraucht** adj used; **etw ~ kaufen** buy sth secondhand; **Gebrauchtwagen** m secondhand (or

used) car

gebrochen pp of **brechen**

Gebühr f (-, -en) charge; (for using road) toll; (for doctor, lawyer etc) fee; **gebührenfrei** adj free of charge; (number) freefone® (Brit), toll-free (US); **gebührenpflichtig** adj subject to charges; **~e Straße** toll road

gebunden pp of **binden**

Geburt f (-, -en) birth; **gebürtig** adj **er ist ~er Schweizer** he is Swiss by birth; **Geburtsdatum** nt date of birth; **Geburtsjahr** nt year of birth; **Geburtsname** m birth name; (of woman) maiden name; **Geburtsort** m birthplace; **Geburtstag** m birthday; **herzlichen Glückwunsch zum ~!** Happy Birthday; **Geburtsurkunde** f birth certificate

Gebüsch nt (-(e)s, -e) bushes pl

gedacht pp of **denken**

Gedächtnis nt memory; **im ~ behalten** remember

Gedanke m (-ns, -n) thought; **sich dat über etw** acc **~n machen** think about sth; (anxiously) be worried about sth; **Gedankenstrich** m dash

Gedeck nt (-(e)s, -e) place setting; (on menu) set meal

Gedenkstätte f memorial

Gedicht nt (-(e)s, -e) poem

Gedränge nt (-s) crush, crowd

gedrungen pp of **dringen**

Geduld f (-) patience; **geduldig** adj patient

gedurft pp of **dürfen**

geehrt adj **Sehr ~er Herr Young** Dear Mr Young

geeignet adj suitable

Gefahr f (-, -en) danger; **auf eigene ~** at one's own risk; **gefährden** vt endanger

gefahren vi of **fahren**

gefährlich adj dangerous

Gefälle nt (-s, -) gradient, slope

gefallen 1. pp of **fallen 2.** irr vi **jdm ~** please sb; **er/es gefällt mir** I like him/it; **sich dat etw~ lassen** put up with sth

Gefallen m (-s, -) favour; **jdm einen ~ tun** do sb a favour

gefangen pp of **fangen**

Gefängnis nt prison

Gefäß nt (-es, -e) container, receptacle; ANAT, BOT vessel

gefasst adj composed, calm; **auf etw** acc **~ sein** be prepared (or ready) for sth

geflochten pp of **flechten**

geflogen pp of **fliegen**

geflossen pp of **fließen**

Geflügel nt (-s) poultry

gefragt adj in demand

gefressen pp of **fressen**

Gefrierbeutel m freezer bag; **Gefrierfach** nt freezer compartment; **Gefrierschrank** m (upright) freezer; **Gefriertruhe** f (chest) freezer

gefroren pp of **frieren**

Gefühl nt (-(e)s, -e) feeling

gefunden pp of **finden**

gegangen pp of **gehen**

gegeben pp of **geben**

gegebenenfalls adv if need be

gegen prep + acc against; (exchange) (in return) for; **~ 8 Uhr** about 8 o'clock; **Deutschland ~ England** Germany versus England; **etwas ~ Husten** something for coughs

Gegend f (-, -en) area; **hier in der ~** around here

gegeneinander adv against one another

Gegenfahrbahn f opposite lane; **Gegenmittel** nt remedy (**gegen** for); **Gegenrichtung** f opposite direction; **Gegensatz** m contrast; **im ~ zu** in contrast to; **gegensätzlich** adj conflicting; **gegenseitig** adj mutual; **sich ~ helfen** help each other

Gegenstand m object; (topic) subject

Gegenteil nt opposite; **im ~** on the contrary; **gegenteilig** adj opposite, contrary

gegenüber 1. prep + dat opposite; (with regard to person) to(wards) **2.** adv opposite; **gegenüberstehen** vt face; (problems) be faced with; **gegenüberstellen** vt confront (dat with); fig compare (dat with)

Gegenverkehr m oncoming traffic; **Gegenwart** f (-) pre-

sent (tense)
gegessen pp of **essen**
geglichen pp of **gleichen**
geglitten pp of **gleiten**
Gegner(in) m(f) (-s, -) opponent
gegolten pp of **gelten**
gegossen pp of **gießen**
gegraben pp of **graben**
gegriffen pp of **greifen**
gehabt pp of **haben**
Gehalt 1. m (-(e)s, -e) content **2.** nt (-(e)s, Gehälter) salary
gehalten pp of **halten**
gehangen pp of **hängen**
gehässig adj spiteful, nasty
gehauen pp of **hauen**
gehbehindert adj **sie ist ~** she can't walk properly
geheim adj secret; **etw ~ halten** keep sth secret; **Geheimnis** nt secret; (puzzling) mystery; **geheimnisvoll** adj mysterious; **Geheimnummer** f, **Geheimzahl** f (of credit card) PIN number
geheißen pp of **heißen**
gehen (ging, gegangen) **1.** vt, vi go; (on foot) walk; (function) work; **über die Straße ~** cross the street **2.** vi impers **wie geht es dir?** how are you (or things)?; **mir/ihm geht es gut** I'm/he's (doing) fine; **geht das?** is that possible?; **geht's noch?** can you still manage?; **es geht** not too bad, OK; **es geht um ...** it's about ...
Gehirn nt (-(e)s, -e) brain; Ge-

hirnerschütterung f concussion
gehoben pp of **heben**
geholfen pp of **helfen**
Gehör nt (-(e)s) hearing
gehorchen vi obey (jdm sb)
gehören 1. vi belong (jdm to sb); **wem gehört das Buch?** whose book is it?; **gehört es dir?** is it yours? **2.** vr impers **das gehört sich nicht** it's not done
Gehweg m (-s, -e) pavement (Brit), sidewalk (US)
Geier m (-s, -) vulture
Geige f (-, -n) violin
geil adj randy (Brit), horny (US); fam (wonderful) fantastic
Geisel f (-, -n) hostage
Geist m (-(e)s, -er) spirit; (phantom) ghost; (intellect) mind; **Geisterbahn** f ghost train, tunnel of horror (US); **Geisterfahrer(in)** m(f) person driving the wrong way on the motorway
geizig adj stingy
gekannt pp of **kennen**
geklungen pp of **klingen**
gekniffen pp of **kneifen**
gekommen pp of **kommen**
gekonnt 1. pp of **können 2.** adj skilful
gekrochen pp of **kriechen**
Gel nt (-s, -s) gel
Gelächter nt (-s, -) laughter
geladen 1. pp of **laden 2.** adj loaded; ELEC live; fig furious
gelähmt adj paralysed

Gelände nt (-s, -) land, terrain; (of factory, for sport) grounds pl; (being built on) site

Geländer nt (-s, -) railing; (on stairs) banister

Geländewagen m off-road vehicle

gelang imperf of **gelingen**

gelassen 1. pp of **lassen** 2. adj calm, composed

Gelatine f gelatine

gelaufen pp of **laufen**

gelaunt adj **gut**/ **schlecht** ~ in a good/bad mood

gelb adj yellow; (traffic light) amber, yellow (US); **gelblich** adj yellowish; **Gelbsucht** f jaundice

Geld nt (-(e)s, -er) money; **Geldautomat** m cash machine (or dispenser (Brit)), ATM (US); **Geldbeutel** m, **Geldbörse** f purse; **Geldschein** m (bank)note (Brit), bill (US); **Geldstrafe** f fine; **Geldstück** nt coin; **Geldwechsel** m exchange of money; **Geldwechselautomat** m, **Geldwechsler** m (-s, -) change machine

Gelee nt (-s, -s) jelly

gelegen pp of **liegen**

Gelegenheit f opportunity; (event) occasion

gelegentlich 1. adj occasional 2. adv occasionally

Gelenk nt (-(e)s, -e) joint

gelernt adj skilled

gelesen pp of **lesen**

geliehen pp of **leihen**

gelingen (gelang, gelungen) vi succeed; **es ist mir gelungen, ihn zu erreichen** I managed to get hold of him

gelitten pp of **leiden**

gelogen pp of **lügen**

gelten (galt, gegolten) 1. vt be worth; **jdm viel**/ **wenig** ~ mean a lot/not mean much to sb 2. vi be valid; (in game etc) be allowed; **etw** ~ **lassen** accept sth

gelungen pp of **gelingen**

gemahlen pp of **mahlen**

Gemälde nt (-s, -) painting, picture

gemäß 1. prep + dat in accordance with 2. adj appropriate (dat to)

gemein adj mean, nasty

Gemeinde f (-, -n) district, community; (church district) parish; (people in church) congregation

gemeinsam 1. adj joint, common 2. adv together, jointly; **das Haus gehört uns beiden** ~ the house belongs to both of us

Gemeinschaft f community

gemeint pp of **meinen**; **das war nicht so** ~ I didn't mean it like that

gemessen pp of **messen**

gemieden pp of **meiden**

gemischt adj mixed

gemocht pp of **mögen**

Gemüse nt (-s, -) vegetables pl; **Gemüsehändler(in)**

m(f) greengrocer

gemusst *pp of* **müssen**

gemustert *adj* patterned

gemütlich *adj* comfortable, cosy; (*person*) good-natured, easy-going; **mach es dir~** make yourself at home

genannt *pp of* **nennen**

genau 1. *adj* exact, precise **2.** *adv* exactly, precisely; **~ in der Mitte** right in the middle; **es mit etw~ nehmen** be particular about sth; **~ genommen** strictly speaking; **ich weiß es~** I know for certain (*or* for sure); **genauso** *adv* exactly the same (way); **~ gut/viel/viele Leute** just as well/much/many people (*wie as*)

genehmigen *vt* approve; **sich** *dat* **etw ~** indulge in sth; **Genehmigung** *f* approval

Generalkonsulat *nt* consulate general

Generation *f* generation

Genf *nt* (*-s*) Geneva; **~er See** Lake Geneva

genial *adj* brilliant

Genick *nt* (*-(e)s, -e*) (back of the) neck

Genie *nt* (*-s, -s*) genius

genieren *vt* feel awkward; **ich geniere mich vor ihm** he makes me feel embarrassed

genießen (*genoss, genossen*) *vt* enjoy

Genitiv *m* genitive (case)

genommen *pp of* **nehmen**

genoss *imperf of* **genießen**

genossen *pp of* **genießen**

genug *adv* enough

genügen *vi* be enough (*jdm* for sb); **danke, das genügt** thanks, that's enough (*or* that will do)

Genuss *m* (*-es, Genüsse*) pleasure; (*eating, drinking*) consumption

geöffnet *adj* (*shop etc*) open

Geografie *f* geography

Geologie *f* geology

Georgien *nt* (*-s*) Georgia

Gepäck *nt* (*-(e)s*) luggage (*Brit*), baggage; **Gepäckabfertigung** *f* luggage (*Brit*) (*or* baggage) check-in; **Gepäckannahme** *f* (*for forwarding*) luggage (*Brit*) (*or* baggage) office; (*for safekeeping*) left-luggage office (*Brit*), baggage checkroom (*US*); **Gepäckaufbewahrung** *f* left-luggage office (*Brit*), baggage checkroom (*US*); **Gepäckausgabe** *f* luggage (*Brit*) (*or* baggage) office; (*at airport*) baggage reclaim; **Gepäckband** *nt* luggage (*Brit*) (*or* baggage) conveyor; **Gepäckkontrolle** *f* luggage (*Brit*) (*or* baggage) check; **Gepäckstück** *nt* item of luggage (*Brit*) (*or* baggage); **Gepäckträger** *m* porter; (*fixed to bicycle*) carrier; **Gepäckwagen** *m* luggage van (*Brit*), baggage car (*US*)

gepfiffen *pp of* **pfeifen**

gepflegt *adj* well-groomed; (*park*) well looked after

gequollen *pp of* **quellen**

gerade **1.** *adj* straight; (*number*) even **2.** *adv* exactly; (*a short while ago*) just; **warum ~ ich?** why me (of all people)?; **~ weil** precisely because; **~ noch** only just; **~ neben** right next to; gerade- aus *adv* straight ahead

gerannt *pp of* **rennen**

Gerät *nt* (-(e)s, -e) device, gadget; (*implement*) tool; (*radio, television*) set; (*gear*) equipment

geraten **1.** *pp of* **raten 2.** *irr vi* turn out; **gut/schlecht ~** turn out well/badly; **an jdn ~** come across sb; **in etw** *acc* **~** get into sth

geräuchert *adj* smoked

geräumig *adj* roomy

Geräusch *nt* (-(e)s, -e) sound; (*unpleasant*) noise

gerecht *adj* fair; (*punishment, reward*) just

gereizt *adj* irritable

Gericht *nt* (-(e)s, -e) LAW court; (*food*) dish

gerieben *pp of* **reiben**

gering *adj* small; (*minor*) slight; (*temperature, price etc*) low; (*time*) short; ge- ringfügig **1.** *adj* slight, minor **2.** *adv* slightly

gerissen *pp of* **reißen**

geritten *pp of* **reiten**

gern(e) *adv* willingly, gladly; **~**

haben, ~ mögen like; **etw ~ tun** like doing sth; **~ gesche- hen** you're welcome

gerochen *pp of* **riechen**

Gerste *f* (-, -n) barley; Gers- tenkorn *nt* (*on eyelid*) stye

Geruch *m* (-(e)s, Gerüche) smell

Gerücht *nt* (-(e)s, -e) rumour

gerufen *pp of* **rufen**

Gerümpel *nt* (-s) junk

gerungen *pp of* **ringen**

Gerüst *nt* (-(e)s, -e) (*around building*) scaffolding; *fig* framework (*zu* of)

gesalzen *pp of* **salzen**

gesamt *adj* whole, entire; (*costs*) total; (*works*) com- plete; **Gesamtschule** *f* ≈ comprehensive school

gesandt *pp of* **senden**

Gesäß *nt* (-es, -e) bottom

geschaffen *pp of* **schaffen**

Geschäft *nt* (-(e)s, -e) busi- ness; shop; (*transaction*) deal; **geschäftlich 1.** *adj* commercial **2.** *adv* on busi- ness; **Geschäftsführer(in)** *m(f)* managing director; (*of shop*) manager; Ge- schäftsmann *m* business- man; Geschäftsreise *f* busi- ness trip; Geschäftszeiten *pl* business (*or* opening) hours *pl*

geschehen (*geschah, gesche- hen*) *vi* happen

Geschenk *nt* (-(e)s, -e) pre- sent, gift; Geschenkgut- schein *m* gift voucher; Ge-

schenkpapier *nt* giftwrap
Geschichte *f* (-, *-n*) story; (*matter*) affair; HIST history
geschickt *adj* skilful
geschieden 1. *pp of scheiden* 2. *adj* divorced
geschienen *pp of scheinen*
Geschirr *nt* (-(e)s, -e) crockery; (*for cooking*) pots and pans *pl*; (*of horse*) harness; ~ **spülen** do (*or* wash) the dishes, do the washing-up (*Brit*); Geschirrspülmaschine *f* dishwasher; Geschirrspülmittel *nt* washing-up liquid (*Brit*), dishwashing liquid (*US*); Geschirrtuch *nt* tea towel (*Brit*), dish towel (*US*)
geschissen *pp of scheißen*
geschlafen *pp of schlafen*
geschlagen *pp of schlagen*
Geschlecht *nt* (-(e)s, *-er*) sex; LING gender; Geschlechtskrankheit *f* sexually transmitted disease, STD; Geschlechtsverkehr *m* sexual intercourse
geschlichen *pp of schleichen*
geschliffen *pp of schleifen*
geschlossen *adj* closed
Geschmack *m* (-(e)s, Geschmäcke) taste; geschmacklos *adj* tasteless; Geschmack(s)sache *f das ist ~* that's a matter of taste; geschmackvoll *adj* tasteful
geschmissen *pp of schmeißen*

geschmolzen *pp of schmelzen*
geschnitten *pp of schneiden*
geschoben *pp of schieben*
Geschoss *nt* (-es, -e) (*storey*) floor
geschossen *pp of schießen*
Geschrei *nt* (-s) cries *pl*; *fig* fuss
geschrieben *pp of schreiben*
geschrie(e)n *pp of schreien*
geschützt *adj* protected
Geschwätz *nt* (-es) chatter; (*about other people*) gossip; geschwätzig *adj* talkative, gossipy
geschweige *adv* ~ (**denn**) let alone
geschwiegen *pp of schweigen*
Geschwindigkeit *f* speed; PHYS velocity; Geschwindigkeitsbegrenzung *f* speed limit
Geschwister *pl* brothers and sisters *pl*
geschwollen *adj* swollen; (*speech*) pompous
geschwommen *pp of schwimmen*
geschworen *pp of schwören*
Geschwulst *f* (-, Geschwülste) growth
Geschwür *nt* (-(e)s, -e) ulcer
gesehen *pp of sehen*
gesellig *adj* sociable; Gesellschaft *f* society; (*people with sb*) company
gesessen *pp of sitzen*

Gesetz nt (-es, -e) law; **gesetzlich** adj legal; **gesetzwidrig** adj illegal

Gesicht nt (-(e)s, -er) face; (look) expression; **mach doch nicht so ein ~!** stop pulling such a face; **Gesichtscreme** f face cream; **Gesichtswasser** nt toner

gesoffen pp of **saufen**

gesogen pp of **saugen**

gespannt adj tense; (keen) eager; **ich bin ~, ob ...** I wonder if ...; **auf etw/jdn ~ sein** look forward to sth/to seeing sb

Gespenst nt (-(e)s, -er) ghost

gesperrt adj closed

gesponnen pp of **spinnen**

Gespräch nt (-(e)s, -e) talk, conversation; discussion; (by phone) call

gesprochen pp of **sprechen**

gesprungen pp of **springen**

Gestalt f (-, -en) form, shape; (person) figure

gestanden pp of **stehen, gestehen**

Gestank m (-(e)s) stench

gestatten vt permit, allow; **~ Sie?** may I?

Geste f (-, -n) gesture

gestehen irr vt confess

gestern adv yesterday; **~ Abend/Morgen** yesterday evening/morning

gestiegen pp of **steigen**

gestochen pp of **stechen**

gestohlen pp of **stehlen**

gestorben pp of **sterben**

gestört adj disturbed; (radio reception) poor

gestoßen pp of **stoßen**

gestreift adj striped

gestrichen pp of **streichen**

gestritten pp of **streiten**

gestunken pp of **stinken**

gesund adj healthy; **wieder ~ werden** get better; **Gesundheit** f health; **~!** bless you!

gesundheitsschädlich adj unhealthy

gesungen pp of **singen**

gesunken pp of **sinken**

getan pp of **tun**

getragen pp of **tragen**

Getränk nt (-(e)s, -e) drink; **Getränkeautomat** m drinks machine; **Getränkekarte** f list of drinks

Getreide nt (-s, -) cereals pl, grain

getrennt adj separate; **~ leben** live apart; **~ zahlen** pay separately

getreten pp of **treten**

Getriebe nt (-s, -) AUTO gearbox

getrieben pp of **treiben**

getroffen pp of **treffen**

getrunken pp of **trinken**

Getue nt fuss

geübt adj experienced

Gewähr f (-) guarantee

Gewalt f (-, -en) power; (influence) control; (brute strength) force; (brutality) violence; **mit aller ~** with all one's might; **gewaltig** adj tremendous; (mistake) huge gewandt **1.** *pp of* **wenden 2.** *adj* (*physically*) nimble; (*talented*) skilful; (*practised*) experienced

gewann *imperf of* **gewinnen**

gewaschen *pp of* **waschen**

Gewebe *nt* (-s, -) fabric; BIO tissue

Gewehr *nt* (-(e)s, -e) rifle, gun

Geweih *nt* (-(e)s, -e) antlers *pl*

gewellt *adj* (*hair*) wavy

gewendet *pp of* **wenden**

Gewerbe *nt* (-s, -) trade; Gewerbegebiet *nt* industrial estate (*Brit*) (*or* park (*US*)); gewerblich *adj* commercial

Gewerkschaft *f* trade union

gewesen *pp of* **sein**

Gewicht *nt* (-(e)s, -e) weight; *fig* importance

gewiesen *pp of* **weisen**

Gewinn *m* (-(e)s, -e) profit; (*from gambling*) winnings *pl*; gewinnen (**gewann**, **gewonnen**) *vt* **1.** *vt* win; (*acquire*) gain; (*coal, oil*) extract **2.** *vt* win; (*profit*) gain; Gewinner(in) *m(f)* (-s, -) winner

gewiss **1.** *adj* certain **2.** *adv* certainly

Gewissen *nt* (-s, -) conscience; **ein gutes/ schlechtes ~ haben** have a clear/ bad conscience

Gewitter *nt* (-s, -) thunderstorm

gewogen *pp of* **wiegen**

gewöhnen *vt* **jdn an etw** *acc* **~** accustom sb to sth **2.** *vr* **sich an jdn/etw ~** get

used (*or* accustomed) to sb / sth; Gewohnheit *f* habit; (*tradition*) custom; gewöhnlich *adj* usual; (*average*) ordinary; (*pej*) common; **wie ~ as** usual; gewohnt *adj* usual; **etw ~ sein** be used to sth

Gewölbe *nt* (-s, -) vault

gewonnen *pp of* **gewinnen**

geworben *pp of* **werben**

geworden *pp of* **werden**

geworfen *pp of* **werfen**

Gewürz *nt* (-es, -e) spice; Gewürznelke *f* clove; gewürzt *adj* seasoned

gewusst *pp of* **wissen**

Gezeiten *pl* tides *pl*

gezogen *pp of* **ziehen**

gezwungen *pp of* **zwingen**

Gibraltar *nt* (-s) Gibraltar

Gicht *f* (-) gout

Giebel *m* (-s, -) gable

gierig *adj* greedy

gießen (**goss**, **gegossen**) *vt* pour; (*flowers*) water; (*metal*) cast; Gießkanne *f* watering can

Gift *nt* (-(e)s, -e) poison; giftig *adj* poisonous

Gigabyte *nt* gigabyte

Gin *m* (-s, -s) gin

ging *imperf of* **gehen**; Gin Tonic *m* (-(s), -s) gin and tonic

Gipfel *m* (-s, -) summit, peak; POL summit; *fig* (*culmination*) height

Gips *m* (-es, -e) *a.* MED plaster; Gipsverband *m* plaster cast

Giraffe *f* (-, -n) giraffe

Girokonto *nt* current account

(*Brit*), checking account (*US*)

Gitarre *f* (-, -*n*) guitar

Gitter *nt* (-*s*, -) bars *pl*

glänzen *vi a. fig* shine; **glänzend** *adj* shining; *fig* brilliant

Glas *nt* (-*es*, *Gläser*) glass; (*for jam*) jar; **Glascontainer** *m* bottle bank; **Glaser(in)** *m(f)* glazier; **Glasscheibe** *f* pane (*of glass*); **Glassplitter** *m* splinter of glass

Glasur *f* glaze; GASTR icing

glatt *adj* smooth; (*floor, road etc*) slippery; (*lie*) downright; **Glatteis** *nt* (black) ice

Glatze *f* (-, -*n*) bald head

glauben *vt, vi* believe (*an + acc* in); (*have opinion*) think; *jdm* ~ believe sb

gleich **1.** *adj* equal; (*similar*) same, identical; **es ist mir ~** it's all the same to me **2.** *adv* equally; (*immediately*) straight away; (*soon*) in a minute; ~ **groß/alt** the same size/age; ~ **nach/an** right after/at; **Gleichberechtigung** *f* equal rights *pl*; **gleichen** (*glich, geglichen*) **1.** *vi* *jdm/einer Sache* ~ be like sb/sth **2.** *vr* be alike; **gleichfalls** *adv* likewise; **danke ~!** thanks, and the same to you; **gleichgültig** *adj* indifferent; (*immaterial*) unimportant; **gleichmäßig** *adj* regular; (*distribution*) even, equal; **gleichzeitig** **1.** *adj* simultaneous **2.** *adv* at the same time

Gleis *nt* (-*es*, -*e*) track, rails *pl*; (*area in station*) platform

gleiten (*glitt, geglitten*) *vi* glide; (*slip down*) slide; **Gleitschirmfliegen** *nt* (-*s*) paragliding

Gletscher *m* (-*s*, -) glacier

glich *imperf of* **gleichen**

Glied *nt* (-(*e*)*s*, -*er*) (*arm, leg*) limb; (*of chain*) link; (*male organ*) penis; **Gliedmaßen** *pl* limbs *pl*

glitschig *adj* slippery

glitt *imperf of* **gleiten**

glitzern *vi* glitter; (*stars*) twinkle

Glocke *f* (-, -*n*) bell; **Glockenspiel** *nt* chimes *pl*

Glotze *f* (-, -*n*) *fam* (*TV*) box; **glotzen** *vi fam* stare

Glück *nt* (-(*e*)*s*) luck; (*pleasure*) happiness; ~ **haben** be lucky; **viel ~!** good luck; **zum ~** fortunately; **glücklich** *adj* lucky; (*pleased*) happy; **glücklicherweise** *adv* fortunately; **Glückwunsch** *m* congratulations *pl*; **herzlichen ~ zur bestandenen Prüfung** congratulations on passing your exam; **herzlichen ~ zum Geburtstag!** Happy Birthday

Glühbirne *f* light bulb; **glühen** *vi* glow; **Glühwein** *m* mulled wine

GmbH *f* (-, -*s*) *abbr* = **Gesellschaft mit beschränkter Haftung;** ≈ Ltd (*Brit*), ≈

Inc (US)

Gokart m (-(s), -s) go-kart

Gold nt (-(e)s) gold; **golden** adj gold; fig golden; **Goldfisch** m goldfish; **Goldmedaille** f gold medal; **Goldschmied**(in) m(f) goldsmith

Golf 1. m (-(e)s, -e) gulf; **der ~ von Biskaya** the Bay of Biscay **2.** nt (-s) golf; **Golfplatz** m golf course; **Golfschläger** m golf club

Gondel f (-, -n) gondola; (of cable railway) cable-car

gönnen vt **ich gönne es ihm** I'm really pleased for him; **sich** dat **etw ~** allow oneself sth

goss imperf of **gießen**

gotisch adj Gothic

Gott m (-es, Götter) God; (deity) god; **Gottesdienst** m service; **Göttin** f goddess

Grab nt (-(e)s, Gräber) grave

graben (grub, gegraben) vt dig; **Graben** m (-s, Gräben) ditch

Grabstein m gravestone

Grad m (-(e)s, -e) degree; **wir haben 30 ~ Celsius** it's 30 degrees Celsius; **es ist 86 degrees Fahrenheit; bis zu einem gewissen ~** up to a certain extent

Graf m (-en, -en) count; (in Britain) earl

Graffiti pl graffiti sg

Grafik f (-, -en) graph; (work of art) graphic; (illustration) diagram; **Grafikkarte** f IT

graphics card

Gräfin f (-, -nen) countess

Gramm nt (-s) gram(me)

Grammatik f grammar

Grapefruit f (-, -s) grapefruit

Graphik f → **Grafik**

Gras nt (-es, Gräser) grass

grässlich adj horrible

Gräte f (-, -n) (fish)bone

gratis adj, adv free (of charge)

gratulieren vi **jdm** (**zu etw**) ~ congratulate sb (on sth); (**ich**) **gratuliere!** congratulations!

grau adj grey, gray (US); **grauhaarig** adj grey-haired

grausam adj cruel

gravierend adj (error) serious

greifen (griff, gegriffen) **1.** vt seize; **nach etw ~** reach for sth **2.** vi (rule etc) have an effect (bei on)

grell adj harsh

Grenze f (-, -n) boundary; (of country) border; (on sth) limit; **grenzen** vi border (an + acc on); **Grenzkontrolle** f border control

Grieche m (-n, -n) Greek; **Griechenland** nt Greece; **Griechin** f Greek; **griechisch** adj Greek; **Griechisch** nt Greek

Grieß m (-es, -e) GASTR semolina

griff imperf of **greifen**

Griff m (-(e)s, -e) grip; (of door etc) handle; **griffbereit** adj handy

Grill m (-s, -s) grill; (outdoors)

barbecue

Grille f (-, -n) cricket

grillen 1. vt grill 2. vi have a barbecue; Grillfest nt, Grillfete f barbecue; Grillkohle f charcoal

grinsen vi grin; (mockingly) sneer

Grippe f (-, -n) flu; Grippeschutzimpfung f flu vaccination

grob adj coarse; (error, breach) gross; (estimate) rough

Grönland nt (-s) Greenland

groß 1. adj big, large; (person) tall; fig great; (letter) capital; (adult) grown-up; im Großen und Ganzen on the whole 2. adv greatly; großartig adj wonderful

Großbritannien nt (-s) (Great) Britain

Großbuchstabe m capital letter

Größe f (-, -n) size; (of person) height; fig greatness; welche ~ haben Sie? what size do you take?

Großeltern pl grandparents pl; Großhandel m wholesale trade; Großmarkt m hypermarket; Großmutter f grandmother; großschreiben irr vt write with a capital letter; Großstadt f city; Großvater m grandfather; großzügig adj generous

Grotte f (-, -n) grotto

grub imperf of graben

Grübchen nt dimple

Grube f (-, -n) pit

grüezi interj (Swiss) hello

grün adj green; ~er Salat lettuce; ~e Bohnen French beans; die Bananen sind noch zu ~ the bananas aren't ripe yet

Grund m (-(e)s, Gründe) reason; (earth's surface) ground; (of sea, container) bottom; (belonging to sb) land, property; aus gesundheitlichen Gründen for health reasons; aus diesem ~ for this reason

gründen vt found; Gründer(in) m(f) founder

Grundgebühr f basic charge

gründlich adj thorough

grundsätzlich adj fundamental, basic; sie kommt ~ zu spät she's always late; Grundschule f primary school; Grundstück nt plot; (land) estate; (for building on) site

Grüne(r) mf POL Green; die ~n the Green Party

Gruppe f (-, -n) group; Gruppenermäßigung f group discount; Gruppenreise f group tour

Gruß m (-es, Grüße) greeting; viele Grüße best wishes; Grüße an + acc regards to; mit freundlichen Grüßen Yours sincerely (Brit), Sincerely yours (US); grüßen vt greet; grüß deine Mutter von mir give your mother my regards; *Julia lässt (euch)* ~ Julia sends (you) her regards

gucken *vi* look

Gulasch *nt* (-(e)s, -e) goulash

gültig *adj* valid

Gummi *nt or m* (-s, -s) rubber; Gummistiefel *m* wellington (boot) (*Brit*), rubber boot (*US*)

günstig *adj* favourable; (*price*) good

gurgeln *vi* gurgle; (*with mouthwash*) gargle

Gurke *f* (-, -*n*) cucumber; *saure* ~ gherkin

Gurt *m* (-(e)s, -e) belt

Gürtel *m* (-s, -) belt; GEO zone; Gürtelrose *f* shingles *sg*

gut 1. *adj* good; (*mark in school*) ≈ B; *sehr* ~ very good, excellent; (*mark in school*) ≈ A; *alles Gute!* all the best 2. *adv* well; ~ *gehen* (*business etc*) go well; *es geht ihm* ~ he's doing fine;

jdm ~ *tun* do sb good; ~ *aussehend* good-looking; ~ *gelaunt* in a good mood; ~ *gemeint* well meant; *schon ~!* it's all right; *machs ~!* take care, bye

Gutachten *nt* (-s, -) report; Gutachter(in) *m(f)* (-s, -) expert

gutartig *adj* MED benign

Güter *pl* goods *pl*; Güterzug *m* goods train

gutgläubig *adj* trusting

Guthaben *nt* (-s) (credit) balance

gutmütig *adj* good-natured

Gutschein *m* voucher

Gutschrift *f* credit

Gymnasium *nt* ≈ grammar school (*Brit*), ≈ high school (*US*)

Gymnastik *f* exercises *pl*, gymnastics *sg*

Gynäkologe *m*, Gynäkologin *f* gynaecologist

Gyros *nt* (-, -) doner kebab

H

Haar *nt* (-(e)s, -e) hair; *um ein* ~ nearly; *sich auf die ~e schneiden lassen* have one's hair cut; Haarbürste *f* hairbrush; Haarfestiger *m* setting lotion; Haargel *nt* hair gel; haarig *adj* hairy; *fig* nasty; Haarschnitt *m* haircut; Haarspange *f* hair slide (*Brit*), barrette (*US*);

Haarspliss *m* split ends *pl*; Haarspray *nt* hair spray; Haartrockner *m* (-s, -) hairdryer; Haarwaschmittel *nt* shampoo

haben (*hatte, gehabt*) *vt*, *vaux* have; *Hunger/Angst* ~ be hungry/afraid; *Ferien* ~ be on holiday (*Brit*) (or vacation (*US*)); *welches Datum*

~ wir heute? what's the date today?; **ich hätte gerne ...** I'd like ...; **hätten Sie etwas dagegen, wenn ...?** would you mind if ...?; **was hast du denn?** what's the matter (with you?)

Haben nt COMM credit

Habicht m (-(e)s, -e) hawk

Hacke f (-, -n) hoe; (of foot, shoe) heel; **hacken** vt chop; (hole) hack; (soil) hoe; **Hacker(in)** m(f) (-s, -) IT hacker; **Hackfleisch** nt mince(d meat) (Brit), ground meat (US)

Hafen m (-s, Häfen) harbour; (larger) port; **Hafenstadt** f port

Hafer m (-s, -) oats pl; **Haferflocken** pl rolled oats pl

Haft f (-) custody; **haftbar** adj liable, responsible; **haften** vi stick; **~ für** to be liable (or responsible) for; **Haftnotiz** f Post-it®; **Haftpflichtversicherung** f third party insurance; **Haftung** f liability

Hagebutte f (-, -n) rose hip

Hagel m (-(e)s, -) hail; **hageln** vi impers hail

Hahn m (-(e)s, Hähne) cock; (for water) tap (Brit), faucet (US); **Hähnchen** nt cockerel; GASTR chicken

Hai(fisch) m (-(e)s, -e) shark

Haken m (-s, -) hook; (mark) tick

halb adj half; **~ eins** half past twelve; fam half twelve; **eine**

~e Stunde half an hour; **~ offen** half-open; **Halbfinale** nt semifinal; **halbieren** vt halve; **Halbinsel** f peninsula; **Halbjahr** nt half-year; **Halbmond** m ASTR half-moon; (symbol) crescent; **Halbpension** f half board; **halbtags** adv (work) part-time; **halbwegs** adv (fairly) reasonably; **Halbzeit** f half; (interval) half-time

half imperf of **helfen**; **Hälfte** f (-, -n) half

Halle f (-, -n) hall; **Hallenbad** nt indoor (swimming) pool

hallo interj hello, hi

Halogenlampe f halogen lamp

Hals m (-es, Hälse) neck; (inside) throat; **Halsband** nt (for animal) collar; **Halsentzündung** f sore throat; **Halskette** f necklace; **Hals-Nasen-Ohren-Arzt** m, **Hals-Nasen-Ohren-Ärztin** f ear, nose and throat specialist; **Halsschmerzen** pl sore throat sg; **Halstuch** nt scarf

halt 1. interj stop **2.** adv das ist **~ so** that's just the way it is; **Halt** m (-(e)s, -e) stop; (grip) hold; (inner strength) stability

haltbar adj durable; (food) non-perishable; **Haltbarkeitsdatum** nt best-before date

halten (hielt, gehalten) **1.** vt keep; (grip) hold; **~ für** regard as; **~ von** think of; **den Elfmeter ~** save the penalty; **eine Rede ~** give (or make) a speech **2.** vi hold; *(stay fresh)* keep; *(come to standstill)* stop; **zu jdm ~** stand by sb **3.** vr *(stay fresh)* keep

Haltestelle f stop; **Halteverbot ist hier nicht ~** you can't stop here

Haltung f *(of body)* posture; *fig* attitude; *(self-control)* composure

Hamburg nt; **Hamburger m** *(-s, -)* GASTR hamburger

Hammelfleisch nt mutton

Hammer m *(-s, Hämmer)* hammer; *fig fam (mistake)* howler

Hämorrho(o)iden pl haemorrhoids pl, piles pl

Hamster m *(-s, -)* hamster

Hand f *(-, Hände)* hand; **jdm die ~ geben** shake hands with sb; **zu Händen von** attention; **Handarbeit** f *(school subject)* handicraft; **~ sein** be handmade; **Handball** m handball; **Handbremse** f handbrake; **Handbuch** nt handbook, manual; **Handcreme** f hand cream

Handel m *(-s)* trade; *(deal)* transaction; **handeln 1.** vi act; COMM trade; **~ von** be about **2.** vr impers **es handelt sich um ...** it's about ...

Handfeger m *(-s, -)* brush; **Handfläche** f palm; **Hand-**

gelenk nt wrist; **handgemacht** adj handmade; **Handgepäck** nt hand luggage *(Brit)* (or baggage)

Händler(in) m(f) *(-s, -)* dealer

handlich adj handy

Handlung f act, action; *(of novel, film)* plot

Handschellen pl handcuffs pl; **Handschrift** f handwriting; **Handschuh** m glove; **Handschuhfach** nt glove compartment; **Handtasche** f handbag, purse *(US)*; **Handtuch** nt towel; **Handwerk** nt trade; **Handwerker** m *(-s, -)* workman

Handy nt *(-s, -s)* mobile (phone), cell phone *(US)*

Hang m *(-(e)s, Hänge)* slope; *fig* tendency

Hängematte f hammock

hängen 1. *(hing, gehangen)* vi hang; **an der Wand / an der Decke ~** hang on the wall / from the ceiling; **an jdm ~** fig be attached to sb; **~ bleiben** get caught (an + dat on); *fig* get stuck **2.** vt hang (an + acc on)

Hantel f *(-, -n)* dumbbell

Hardware f *(-, -s)* IT hardware

Harfe f *(-, -n)* harp

harmlos adj harmless

harmonisch adj harmonious

Harn m *(-(e)s, -e)* urine; **Harnblase** f bladder

hart adj hard; *fig* harsh; **~ gekocht** *(egg)* hard-boiled; **hartnäckig** adj stubborn

Haschisch nt (-) hashish

Hase m (-n, -n) hare

Haselnuss f hazelnut

Hass m (-es) hatred (auf + acc, gegen of), hate; hassen vt hate

hässlich adj ugly; (mean) nasty

Hast f (-) haste, hurry; hastig adj hasty

hatte imperf of haben

Haube f (-, -n) hood; (hat) cap; AUTO bonnet (Brit), hood (US)

hauchdünn adj (layer, slice) wafer-thin

hauen (haute, gehauen) vt hit

Haufen m (-s, -) pile; ein ~ Geld a lot of money

häufig 1. adj frequent 2. adv frequently, often

Haupt- in cpds main; Hauptbahnhof m central (or main) station; Haupteingang m main entrance; Hauptgericht nt main course

Häuptling m chief

Hauptquartier nt headquarters pl; Hauptrolle f leading role; Hauptsache f main thing; hauptsächlich adv mainly, chiefly; Hauptsaison f high (or peak) season; Hauptsatz m main clause; Hauptschule f ≈ secondary school (Brit), ≈ junior high school (US); Hauptstadt f capital; Hauptstraße f main road; (in town centre) main street; Hauptverkehrszeit f

rush hour

Haus nt (-es, Häuser) house; nach ~e home; zu ~e at home; jdn nach ~e bringen take sb home; Hausarbeit f housework; Hausaufgabe f homework; ~n pl homework sg; Hausbesitzer(in) m(f) (-s, -) house owner; (renting out) landlord / -lady; Hausbesuch m home visit; Hausflur m hall; Hausfrau f housewife; hausgemacht adj homemade; Haushalt m household; POL budget

häuslich adj domestic

Hausmann m house-husband; Hausmannskost f good plain cooking; Hausmeister(in) m(f) caretaker (Brit), janitor (US); Hausnummer f house number; Hausschlüssel m frontdoor key; Hausschuh m slipper; Haustier nt pet; Haustür f front door

Haut f (-, Häute) skin; Hautarzt m, Hautärztin f dermatologist; Hautausschlag m skin rash; Hautcreme f skin cream; Hautfarbe f skin colour

Hawaii nt (-s) Hawaii

Hebamme f (-, -n) midwife

Hebel m (-s, -) lever

heben (hob, gehoben) vt raise, lift

Hebräisch nt (-) Hebrew

Hecht m (-(e)s, -e) pike

Heck nt (-(e)s, -e) (of boat)

stern; (of car) rear; **Heckantrieb** m rear-wheel drive

Hecke f (-, -n) hedge

Heckklappe f tailgate; **Heckscheibe** f rear window; **Heckscheibenheizung** f rear-window defroster

Hefe f (-, -n) yeast

Heft nt (-(e)s, -e) notebook, exercise book; (of magazine) issue

heftig adj violent; (criticism, argument) fierce

Heftklammer f paper clip; **Heftpflaster** nt plaster (Brit), Band-Aid® (US)

Heide f (-, -n) heath, moor; **Heidekraut** nt heather

Heidelbeere f bilberry, blueberry

heidnisch adj (custom) pagan

heikel adj (matter) awkward; (person) fussy

heil adj (thing) in one piece, intact; **heilbar** adj curable

Heilbutt m (-(e)s, -e) halibut

heilen 1. vt cure 2. vi heal

heilig adj holy; **Heiligabend** m Christmas Eve; **Heilige(r)** mf saint

Heilpraktiker(in) m(f) (-s, -) non-medical practitioner

heim adv home; **Heim** nt (-(e), -e) home

Heimat f (-, -en) home (town / country)

heimfahren irr vi drive home / **Heimfahrt** f journey home; **heimisch** adj (population, customs) local; (animal,

plant) native; **heimkommen** irr vi come (or return) home

heimlich adj secret

Heimreise f journey home; **Heimspiel** nt SPORT home game; **Heimweg** m way home; **Heimweh** nt (-s) homesickness; **~ haben** be homesick

Heirat f (-, -en) marriage; **heiraten** 1. vi get married 2. vt marry; **Heiratsantrag** m proposal; **er hat ihr einen ~ gemacht** he proposed to her

heiser adj hoarse

heiß adj hot; (discussion) heated; **mir ist ~** I'm hot

heißen (hieß, geheißen) 1. vi be called; (have sense, consequence) mean; **ich heiße Tom** my name is Tom; **wie ~ Sie?** what's your name?; **wie heißt sie mit Nachnamen?** what's her surname?; **wie heißt das auf Englisch?** what's that in English? 3. vi impers **es heißt** (people say) it is said; **es heißt in dem Brief ...** it says in the letter ...; **das heißt** that is

Heißluftherd m fan-assisted oven

heiter adj cheerful; (weather) bright

heizen vt heat; **Heizkissen** m MED heated pad; **Heizkörper** m radiator; **Heizöl** nt fuel oil; **Heizung** f heating

Hektar nt (-s, -) hectare

Hektik f (-, -en) **nur keine ~!**

take it easy; **hektisch** *adj* hectic

Held *m* (-en, -en) hero; **Heldin** *f* heroine

helfen (*half, geholfen*) **1.** *vi* help (*jdm bei etw* sb with sth); (*be*) of use 2. *vi impers* **es hilft nichts, du musst** ... it's no use, you have to ...; **Helfer(in)** *m(f)* helper; (*at work*) assistant

hell *adj* bright; (*colour*) light; (*complexion*) fair; **hellblau** *adj* light blue; **hellblond** *adj* ash-blond; **hellgelb** *adj* pale yellow; **hellgrün** *adj* light green; **Hellseher(in)** *m(f)* clairvoyant

Helm *m* (-(e)s, -e) helmet; **Helmpflicht** *f* compulsory wearing of helmets

Hemd *nt* (-(e)s, -en) shirt

hemmen *vt* check; (*hinder*) hamper; **gehemmt sein** be inhibited; **Hemmung** *f* inhibition; (*moral*) scruple

Henkel *m* (-s, -) handle

Henna *nt* (-s) henna

Henne *f* (-, -n) hen

Hepatitis *f* (-, *Hepatitiden*) hepatitis

her *adv* here; **wo ist sie ~?** where is she from?; **das ist zehn Jahre ~** that was ten years ago

herab *adv* down; **herablassend** *adj* (*remark*) condescending; **herabsehen** *irr vt auf jdn ~* look down on sb; **herabsetzen** *vt* reduce;

fig disparage

heran *adv* **näher ~!** come closer; **herankommen** *irr vi* approach; **~ an** + *acc* be able to get at; *fig* be able to get hold of; **heranwachsen** *irr vi* grow up

herauf *adv* up; **heraufbeschwören** *irr vt* evoke; (*crisis, dispute etc*) cause; **heraufziehen** *irr* **1.** *vt* pull up **2.** *vi* approach; (*storm*) gather

heraus *adv* out; **herausbekommen** *irr vt* (*secret*) find out; (*puzzle*) solve; **herausbringen** *irr vt* bring out; **herausfinden** *irr vt* find out; **herausfordern** *vt* challenge; **Herausforderung** *f* challenge; **herausgeben** *irr vt* (*book*) edit; (*issue*) publish; **jdm zwei Euro ~** give sb two euros change; **herausholen** *vt* get out (*aus* of); **herauskommen** *irr vi* come out; **dabei kommt nichts heraus** nothing will come of it; **herausstellen** *vr* turn out (*als* to be); **herausziehen** *irr vt* pull out

Herbst *m* (-(e)s, -e) autumn, fall (*US*)

Herd *m* (-(e)s, -e) cooker, stove

Herde *f* (-, -n) herd; (*of sheep*) flock

herein *adv* in; **~!** come in; **hereinfallen** *irr vi* **wir sind auf einen Betrüger hereingefallen** we were taken in by a swindler; **hereinlegen** vt **jdn ~ fig** take sb for a ride

Herfahrt f journey here; **auf der ~** on the way here

Hergang m course (of events); **schildern Sie mir den ~** tell me what happened

Hering m (-s, -e) herring

herkommen vi come; **wo kommt sie her?** where does she come from?

Heroin nt (-s) heroin

Herpes m (-) MED herpes

Herr m (-(e)n, -en) (before name) Mr; (person) gentleman; (nobleman, God) Lord; **mein ~!** sir; **meine ~en!** gentlemen; **Sehr geehrte Damen und ~en** Dear Sir or Madam; **Herrentoilette** f men's toilet, gents

herrichten vt prepare

herrlich adj marvellous, splendid

Herrschaft f rule; power

herrschen vi rule; (exist) be

herstellen vt make; (industrially) manufacture; **Hersteller(in)** m(f) manufacturer; **Herstellung** f production

herüber adv over

herum adv around; (in a circle) round; **um etw ~** around sth; **du hast den Pulli falsch ~ an** you're wearing your sweater inside out; **anders ~** the other way round; **herumfahren** irr vi drive around; **herumkommen** irr vi **sie ist viel in der Welt he-**

rumgekommen she's been around the world; **um etw ~** (avoid) get out of sth; **herumkriegen** vt talk round; **herumtreiben** irr vr hang around

herunter adv down; **heruntergekommen** adj (building, area) run-down; (person) down-at-heel; **herunterhandeln** vt get down; **herunterholen** vt bring down; **herunterkommen** irr vi come down; **herunterladen** irr vt IT download

hervor adv out; **hervorbringen** irr vt produce; (word) utter; **hervorheben** irr vt emphasize, stress; **hervorragend** adj excellent; **hervorrufen** irr vt cause, give rise to

Herz nt (-ens, -en) heart; (card suit) hearts; **von ganzem ~en** wholeheartedly; **sich** dat **etw zu ~en nehmen** take sth to heart; **Herzanfall** m heart attack; **Herzbeschwerden** pl heart trouble sg; **herzhaft** adj (meal) substantial; **~ lachen** have a good laugh; **Herzinfarkt** m heart attack; **Herzklopfen** nt (-s) MED palpitations pl; **ich hatte ~ (vor Aufregung)** my heart was pounding (with excitement); **herzkrank** adj **sie ist ~** she's got a heart condition; **herzlich** adj (reception, person) warm; **~en Glückwunsch**

congratulations

Herzog(in) m(f) (-s, Herzöge) duke / duchess

Herzschlag m heartbeat; (stopping) heart failure; **Herzschrittmacher** m pacemaker

Hessen nt (-s) Hessen

heterosexuell adj heterosexual

Hetze f (-, -n) rush; **hetzen** vt, vr rush

Heu nt (-(e)s) hay

heuer adv this year

heulen vi howl; (weep) cry

Heuschnupfen m hay fever

Heuschrecke f (-, -n) grasshopper; (larger) locust

heute adv today; **~ Abend / früh** this evening / morning; **~ Nacht** tonight; (just gone) last night; **~ in acht Tagen** a week (from) today; **sie hat bis ~ nicht bezahlt** she hasn't paid to this day; **heutig** adj **die ~e Zeitung / Generation** today's paper / generation; **heutzutage** adv nowadays

Hexe f (-, -n) witch; **Hexenschuss** m lumbago

hielt imperf of **halten**

hier adv here; **~ entlang** this way; **~ bleiben** stay here; **~ lassen** leave here; **ich bin auch nicht von ~** I'm a stranger here myself; **hierher** adv here; **das gehört nicht ~** that doesn't belong here; **hiermit** adv with this

hiesig adj local

hieß imperf of **heißen**

Hi-Fi-Anlage f hi-fi (system)

high adj fam high; **Highlife** nt (-s) high life; **~ machen** live it up; **Hightech** nt (-s) high tech

Hilfe f (-, -n) help; (financial, for those in need) aid; **~!** help!; **erste ~ leisten** give first aid; **um ~ bitten** ask for help; **hilflos** adj helpless; **hilfsbereit** adj helpful; **Hilfsmittel** nt aid

Himbeere f raspberry

Himmel m (-s, -) sky; REL heaven; **Himmelfahrt** f Ascension; **Himmelsrichtung** f direction; **himmlisch** adj heavenly

hin adv there; **~ und her** to and fro; **~ und zurück** there and back; **bis zur Mauer** up to the wall; **das ist noch lange ~** (in the future) that's a long way off

hinab adv down; **hinabgehen** irr vi go down

hinauf adv up; **hinaufgehen** irr vi, vt go up; **hinaufsteigen** irr vi climb (up)

hinaus adv out; **hinausgehen** irr vi go out; **~ über** + acc exceed; **hinauslaufen** irr vi run out; **~ auf** + acc come to, amount to; **hinausschieben** irr vi put off, postpone; **hinauswerfen** irr vt throw out; (employee) fire, sack (Brit); **hinauszögern**

vr take longer than expected

hinbringen *irr vt* **ich bringe Sie hin** I'll take you there

hindern *vt* prevent; **jdn daran ~, etw zu tun** stop (or prevent) sb from doing sth; **Hindernis** *nt* obstacle

Hinduismus *m* Hinduism

hindurch *adv* through; **das ganze Jahr ~** throughout the year, all year round; **die ganze Nacht ~** all night (long)

hinein *adv* in; hineingehen *irr vi* go in; **~ in +** *acc* go into, enter; **hineinpassen** *vi* fit in; **~ in +** *acc* fit into

hinfahren *irr* **1.** *vi* go there **2.** *vt* take there; **Hinfahrt** *f* outward journey

hinfallen *irr vi* fall (down)

Hinflug *m* outward flight

hing *imperf of* **hängen**

hingehen *irr vi* go there; (*time*) pass; **hinhalten** *irr vt* hold out; (*keep waiting*) put off

hinken *vi* limp; **der Vergleich hinkt** the comparison doesn't work

hinlegen **1.** *vt* put down **2.** *vr* lie down; **hinnehmen** *irr vt fig* put up with, take; **Hinreise** *f* outward journey; **hinsetzen** *vr* sit down; **hinsichtlich** *prep* + *gen* with regard to; **hinstellen** **1.** *vt* put (down) **2.** *vr* stand

hinten *adv* at the back; (*in car*) in the back; (*sth / sb else*) behind

hinter *prep* + *dat or acc* behind; (*beyond, of importance*) after; **~ jdm her sein** be after sb; **etw ~ sich** *acc* **bringen** get sth over (and done) with; **Hinterachse** *f* rear axle; **Hinterbein** *nt* hind leg; **Hinterbliebene(r)** *mf* surviving relative; **hintere(r, s)** *adj* rear, back; **hintereinander** *adv* (*in a row*) one behind the other; (*in continuous sequence*) one after the other; **drei Tage ~** three days running (or in a row); **Hintergedanke** *m* ulterior motive; **hintergehen** *irr vt* deceive; **Hintergrund** *m* background; **hinterher** *adv* afterwards; **los, ~!** come on, after him / her / them; **Hinterkopf** *m* back of the head; **hinterlassen** *vt* leave; **jdm eine Nachricht ~** leave a message for sb; **hinterlegen** *vt* leave (*bei* with)

Hintern *m* (-, -) *fam* backside, bum

Hinterradantrieb *m* AUTO rear-wheel drive; **Hinterteil** *nt* back (part); (*of person*) behind; **Hintertür** *f* back door

hinüber *adv* over; **~ sein** *fam* (*broken*) be ruined; (*food*) have gone bad; **hinübergehen** *irr vi* go over

hinunter *adv* down; **hinuntergehen** *irr vi, vt* go down; hinunterschlucken vt a. fig swallow

Hinweg m outward journey

hinwegsetzen vr sich über etw acc ~ ignore sth

Hinweis m (-es, -e) (suggestion) hint; (for user etc) instruction; hinweisen irr vi jdn auf etw acc ~ point sth out to sb

hinzu adv in addition; hinzufügen vt add

Hirn nt (-(e)s, -e) brain; (intellect) brains pl; Hirnhautentzündung f meningitis

Hirsch m (-(e)s, -e) deer; (meat) venison

Hirse f (-, -n) millet

Hirte m (-n, -n) shepherd

historisch adj historical

Hit m (-s, -s) MUS, IT hit; Hitliste f, Hitparade f charts pl

Hitze f (-) heat; hitzebeständig adj heat-resistant; Hitzewelle f heatwave; hitzig adj hot-tempered; (debate) heated; Hitzschlag m heatstroke

HIV nt (-(s), -(s)) abbr = Human Immunodeficiency Virus; HIV; HIV-negativ adj HIV-negative; HIV-positiv adj HIV-positive

H-Milch f long-life milk

hob imperf of heben

Hobby nt (-s, -s) hobby

Hobel m (-s, -) plane

hoch adj high; (tree, house) tall; (snow) deep; der Zaun ist drei Meter ~ the fence is three metres high; ~ be-

gabt extremely gifted; das ist mir zu ~ that's above my head; ~ soll sie leben!, sie lebe ~! three cheers for her; 4 ~ 2 ist 16 4 squared is 16; 4 ~ 5 4 to the power of 5

Hoch nt (-s, -s) METEO high; hochachtungsvoll adv Yours faithfully; Hochbetrieb m es herrscht ~ they / we are extremely busy; Hochdeutsch nt High German; Hochgebirge nt high mountains pl; Hochhaus nt high rise; hochheben irr vt lift (up); Hochschule f college; university; Hochsommer m midsummer; Hochsprung m high jump

höchst adv highly, extremely; höchste(r, s) adj highest; (very great) extreme; höchstens adv at the most; Höchstgeschwindigkeit f maximum speed

höchstwahrscheinlich adv very probably

Hochwasser nt high water; floods pl

Hochzeit f (-, -en) wedding; Hochzeitsnacht f wedding night; Hochzeitsreise f honeymoon; Hochzeitstag m wedding day; (yearly) wedding anniversary

hocken vi, vr squat, crouch

Hocker m (-s, -) stool

Hockey nt (-s) hockey

Hoden m (-s, -) testicle

Hof m (-(e)s, Höfe) yard; (*surrounded by building*) courtyard; (*agricultural*) farm; (*royal*) court

hoffen vi hope (auf + acc for); **ich hoffe es** I hope so; hoffentlich adv hopefully; ~ **nicht** I hope not; **Hoffnung** f hope; **hoffnungslos** adj hopeless

höflich adj polite; **Höflichkeit** f politeness

hohe(r, s) adj → **hoch**

Höhe f (-, -n) height; (*high land*) hill; (*of sum of money*) amount; (*flying height*) altitude; **Höhenangst** f vertigo; **Höhensonne** f sun lamp

Höhepunkt m (*of trip*) high point; (*of show etc*) highlight; (*sexual, of film*) climax

höher adj, adv higher

hohl adj hollow

Höhle f (-, -n) cave

holen vt get, fetch; (*collect*) pick up; (*breath*) catch; **die Polizei** ~ call the police; **jdn/etw** ~ **lassen** send for sb/sth

Holland nt Holland; **Holländer(in)** m(f) (-s, -) Dutchman/-woman; **holländisch** adj Dutch

Hölle f (-, -n) hell

Hologramm nt hologram

holperig adj bumpy

Holunder m (-s, -) elder

Holz nt (-es, Hölzer) wood; **Holzboden** m wooden floor; **hölzern** adj wooden; **holzig**

adj (*stem*) woody; **Holzkohle** f charcoal

Homebanking nt (-s) home banking, online banking; **Homepage** f (-, -s) home page; **Hometrainer** m exercise machine

homöopathisch adj homeopathic

homosexuell adj homosexual

Honig m (-s, -e) honey; **Honigmelone** f honeydew melon

Honorar nt (-s, -e) fee

Hopfen m (-s, -) BOT hop; (*in brewing*) hops pl

hoppla interj whoops, oops

horchen vi listen (auf + acc to); (*at door*) eavesdrop

hören vt, vi hear; (*by chance*) overhear; (*attentively; radio, music*) listen to; **ich habe schon viel von Ihnen gehört** I've heard a lot about you; **Hörer** m TEL receiver; **Hörer(in)** m(f) listener; **Hörgerät** nt hearing aid

Horizont m (-(e)s, -e) horizon; **das geht über meinen ~** that's beyond me

Hormon nt (-s, -e) hormone

Hornhaut f hard skin; (*of eye*) cornea

Horoskop nt (-s, -e) horoscope

Hörsaal m lecture hall; **Hörsturz** m acute hearing loss

Hose f (-, -n) trousers pl (Brit), pants pl (US); (*undergar-*

ment) (under)pants pl; **eine ~** a pair of trousers/pants; **kurze ~** (pair of) shorts pl; Hosenanzug m trouser suit (Brit), pantsuit (US); Hosenschlitz m fly, flies (Brit); Hosentasche f trouser pocket (Brit), pant pocket (US); Hosenträger m braces pl (Brit), suspenders pl (US)

Hospital nt (-s, -e, Hospitäler) hospital

Hotdog nt or m (-s, -s) hot dog

Hotel nt (-s, -s) hotel; **in welchem ~ seid ihr?** which hotel are you staying at?; Hoteldirektor(in) m(f) hotel manager; Hotelkette f hotel chain; Hotelzimmer nt hotel room

Hotline f (-, -s) hot line

Hubraum m cubic capacity

hübsch adj (girl, child, dress) pretty; (man, woman) good-looking, cute

Hubschrauber m (-s, -) helicopter

Huf m (-(e)s, -e) hoof; Hufeisen nt horseshoe

Hüfte f (-, -n) hip

Hügel m (-s, -) hill; hügelig adj hilly

Huhn nt (-(e)s, Hühner) hen; GASTR chicken; Hühnchen nt chicken; Hühnerauge nt corn; Hühnerbrühe f chicken broth

Hülle f (-, -n) cover; (for ID) case; (cellophane) wrapping

Hummel f (-, -n) bumblebee

Hummer m (-s, -) lobster; Hummerkrabbe f king prawn

Humor m (-s) humour; **~ haben** have a sense of humour; humorvoll adj humorous

humpeln vi hobble

Hund m (-(e)s, -e) dog; Hundeleine f dog lead (Brit), dog leash (US)

hundert num hundred; hundertprozentig adj, adv one hundred per cent; hundertste(r, s) adj hundredth

Hündin f bitch

Hunger m (-s) hunger; **~ haben/bekommen** be/get hungry; hungern vi go hungry; (seriously, constantly) starve

Hupe f (-, -n) horn; hupen vi sound one's horn

Hüpfburg f bouncy castle®; hüpfen vi hop; jump

Hürde f (-, -n) hurdle

Hure f (-, -n) whore

hurra interj hooray

husten vi cough; Husten m (-s) cough; Hustenbonbon nt cough sweet; Hustensaft m cough mixture

Hut m (-(e)s, Hüte) hat

hüten 1. vt look after 2. vr watch out; **sich ~, etw zu tun** take care not to do sth; **sich ~ vor** + dat beware of

Hütte f (-, -n) hut, cottage

Hyäne f (-, -n) hyena

Hydrant m hydrant

hygienisch adj hygienic

Hyperlink *m* (-*s*, -*s*) hyperlink

Hypnose *f* (-, -*n*) hypnosis; **Hypnotiseur(in)** *m(f)* hypnotist; **hypnotisieren** *vt*

hypnotize

Hypothek *f* (-, -*en*) mortgage

hysterisch *adj* hysterical

I

IC *m* (-, -*s*) *abbr* = **Intercityzug**; Intercity (train)

ICE *m* (-, -*s*) *abbr* = **Intercityexpresszug**; German high-speed train

ich *pron* I; ~ **bin's** it's me; ~ **nicht** not me; **du und** ~ you and me; **hier bin** ~! here I am; ~ **Idiot!** stupid me

Icon *nt* (-*s*, -*s*) IT icon

ideal *adj* ideal; **Ideal** *nt* (-*s*, -*e*) ideal

Idee *f* (-, -*n*) idea

identifizieren *vt*, *vr* identify

identisch *adj* identical

Idiot(in) *m(f)* (-*en*, -*en*) idiot; **idiotisch** *adj* idiotic

Idol *nt* (-*s*, -*e*) idol

Idylle *f* idyll; **idyllisch** *adj* idyllic

Igel *m* (-*s*, -) hedgehog

ignorieren *vt* ignore

ihm *pron dat sg of* **er**/**es**; (to) him; (*thing*) (to) it; **wie geht es** ~? how is he?; **ein Freund von** ~ a friend of his

ihn *pron acc sg of* **er**; him; (*thing*) it

ihnen *pron dat pl of* **sie**; (to) them; **wie geht es** ~? how are they?; **ein Freund von** ~ a friend of theirs

Ihnen *pron dat sg and pl of* **Sie**; (to) you; **wie geht es** ~? how are you?; **ein Freund von** ~ a friend of yours

ihr 1. *pron* (2nd person pl) you; ~ **seid's** it's you **2.** *pron* (*dat sg*) *of* **sie**; (to) her; (*thing*) (to) it; **er schickte es** ~ he sent it to her; **er hat** ~ **die Haare geschnitten** he cut her hair; **wie geht es** ~? how is she?; **ein Freund von** ~ a friend of hers **3.** *pron* (*as adj*) her; (*thing*) its; (*pl*) their; ~ **Vater** her father; ~ **Auto** (several owners) their car

Ihr *pron of* **Sie**; (*as adj*) your; ~**(e) XY** (at end of letter) Yours, XY

ihre(r, s) *pron* (*as noun, sg*) hers; (*pl*) theirs; **das ist** ~/~**r/ihr(e)s** that's hers; (*pl*) that's theirs

Ihre(r, s) *pron* (*as noun*) yours; **das ist** ~/~**r/Ihr(e)s** that's yours

ihretwegen 1. *adv* (*sg*) because of her; (*to please her*) for her sake **2.** *adv* (*pl*) because of them; (*to please them*) for their sake;

Ihretwegen adv because of you; (to please you) for your sake

Ikone f (-, -n) icon

illegal adj illegal

Illusion f illusion; **sich** dat **~en machen** delude oneself; **illusorisch** adj illusory

Illustration f illustration

Illustrierte f (-n, -n) (glossy) magazine

im contr f in dem; **~ Bett** in bed; **~ Fernsehen** on TV; **~ Radio** on the radio; **~ Bus/Zug** on the bus/train; **~ Januar** in January; **~ Stehen** (while) standing up

Imbiss m (-es, -e) snack; **Imbissbude** f snack bar

Imbussschlüssel m hex key

immer adv always; **~ mehr** more and more; **~ wieder** again and again; **~ noch** still; **~ noch nicht** still not; **für ~** forever; **~ wenn ich ...** every time I ...; **~ schöner/trauriger** more and more beautiful/sadder and sadder; **was/wer/wo/wann (auch) ~** whatever/whoever/wherever/whenever; **immerhin** adv after all; **immerzu** adv all the time

Immigrant(in) m(f) immigrant

Immobilien pl property sg, real estate sg; **Immobilienmakler(in)** m(f) estate agent (Brit), realtor (US)

immun adj immune (gegen

to); **Immunschwäche** f immunodeficiency; **Immunschwächekrankheit** f immune deficiency syndrome; **Immunsystem** nt immune system

impfen vt vaccinate; **Impfpass** m vaccination card; **Impfstoff** m vaccine; **Impfung** f vaccination

imponieren vi impress (jdm sb)

Import m (-(e)s, -e) import; **importieren** vt import

impotent adj impotent

imstande adj **~ sein** be in a position; (capable) be able

in 1. prep + acc in(to); to; **~ die Stadt** into town; **~ die Schule gehen** go to school **2.** prep + dat in; (with time) in; (in the course of) during; (before the end of) within; **~ der Stadt** in town; **~ der Schule** at school; **noch ~ dieser Woche** by the end of this week; **heute ~ acht Tagen** a week (from) today; **Dienstag ~ einer Woche** a week on Tuesday **3.** adv **~ sein** (fashionable) be in

inbegriffen adj included

indem conj **sie gewann, ~ sie mogelte** she won by cheating

Inder(in) m(f) (-s, -) Indian

Indianer(in) m(f) (-s, -) American Indian, Native American; **indianisch** adj American Indian, Native

American

Indien nt (-s) India
indirekt adj indirect
indisch adj Indian
individuell adj individual
Indonesien nt (-s) Indonesia
Industrie f industry; **Industrie-** in cpds industrial
ineinander adv in(to) one another (or each other)
Infarkt m (-(e)s, -e) heart attack
Infektion f infection; **Infektionskrankheit** f infectious disease; **infizieren 1.** vt infect **2.** vr be infected
Info f (-, -s) fam info
infolge prep + gen as a result of, owing to; **infolgedessen** adv consequently
Informatik f computer science; **Informatiker(in)** m(f) (-s, -) computer scientist
Information f information; **Informationsschalter** m information desk; **informieren 1.** vt inform; **falsch ~** misinform **2.** vr find out (über + acc about)
infrage adv **das kommt nicht ~** that's out of the question; **etw ~ stellen** question sth
Infrastruktur f infrastructure
Infusion f infusion
Ingenieur(in) m(f) engineer
Ingwer m (-s) ginger
Inhaber(in) m(f) (-s, -) owner; (of licence) holder
Inhalt m (-(e)s, -e) contents pl; (of book etc) content; MATH

volume; (two-dimensional) area; **Inhaltsangabe** f summary; **Inhaltsverzeichnis** nt table of contents
Initiative f initiative; **die ~ ergreifen** take the initiative
Injektion f injection
inklusive adv, prep inclusive (gen of)
inkonsequent adj inconsistent
Inland nt POL, COMM home; **im ~** at home; GEO inland; **Inlandsflug** m domestic flight; **Inlandsgespräch** nt national call
Inlineskates pl inline skates pl
innen adv inside; **Innenarchitekt(in)** m(f) interior designer; **Innenhof** m (inner) courtyard; **Innenminister(in)** m(f) minister of the interior, Home Secretary (Brit); **Innenseite** f inside; **Innenspiegel** m rearview mirror; **Innenstadt** f town centre; city centre
innere(r, s) adj inner; (in body, own country) internal; **Innere(s)** nt inside; (middle) centre; fig heart
innerhalb adv, prep + gen within; (with space) inside
innerlich adj internal; (calm etc) inner
innerste(r, s) adj innermost
Innovation f innovation
inoffiziell adj unofficial; (party etc) informal

ins contr of **in das**

Insasse m (-n, -n), **Insassin** f AUTO passenger; (of mental hospital, prison) inmate

insbesondere adv particularly, in particular

Inschrift f inscription

Insekt nt (-(e)s, -en) insect, bug (US); **Insektenschutzmittel** nt insect repellent; **Insektenstich** m insect bite

Insel f (-, -) island

Inserat nt advertisement

insgesamt adv altogether, all in all

Insider(in) m(f) (-s, -) insider

insofern 1. adv in that respect; (therefore) (and) so 2. conj if; ~ **als** in so far as

Installateur(in) m(f) plumber; electrician; **installieren** vt IT install

Instinkt m (-(e)s, -e) instinct

Institut nt (-(e)s, -e) institute

Institution f institution

Instrument nt instrument

Insulin nt (-s) insulin

Inszenierung f production

intakt adj intact

intellektuell adj intellectual

intelligent adj intelligent; **Intelligenz** f intelligence

intensiv adj intensive; (feeling, pain) intense; **Intensivkurs** m crash course; **Intensivstation** f intensive care unit

interaktiv adj interactive

interessant adj interesting; **Interesse** nt (-s, -n) interest;

~ **haben an** + dat be interested in; **interessieren 1.** vt interest **2.** vr be interested (für in)

Interface nt (-, -s) IT interface

Internat nt boarding school

international adj international

Internet nt (-s) Internet, Net; **im ~** on the Internet; **im ~ surfen** surf the Net; **Internetcafé** nt Internetcafé, cybercafé; **Internetfirma** f dotcom company; **Internethandel** m e-commerce; **Internetseite** f web page

interpretieren vt interpret (als as)

Interpunktion f punctuation

Interregio m (-s, -s) regional train

Interview nt (-s, -s) interview; **interviewen** vt interview

intim adj intimate

intolerant adj intolerant

investieren vt invest

inwiefern adv in what way; (how far) to what extent; **inwieweit** adv to what extent

inzwischen adv meanwhile

Irak m (-(s)) **(der) ~** Iraq

Iran m (-(s)) **(der) ~** Iran

Ire m (-n, -n) Irishman

irgend adv **so ein Idiot** some idiot; **wenn ~ möglich** if at all possible; **irgendein** pron, **irgendeine(r, s)** adj some; (with question, conditional clause; whichever) any; **irgendetwas** pron something; (with question, conditional clause) anything; **irgendjemand** pron somebody; (with question, conditional clause) anybody; **irgendwann** adv sometime; (whenever you like) any time; **irgendwie** adv somehow; **irgendwo** adv somewhere; (with question, conditional clause) anywhere

Irin f Irishwoman; **irisch** adj Irish; **Irland** nt Ireland

ironisch adj ironic

irre adj crazy, mad; (wonderful) terrific; **Irre(r)** mf lunatic; **irreführen** irr vt mislead; **irren** vi, v refl be mistaken; **wenn ich mich nicht irre** if I'm not mistaken; **irrsinnig** adj mad, crazy; **Irrtum** m (-s, -tümer) mistake, error; **irrtümlich 1.** adj mistaken

2. adv by mistake

Ischias m (-) sciatica

Islam m (-s) Islam; **islamisch** adj Islamic

Island nt Iceland; **Isländer(in)** m(f) (-s, -) Icelander; **isländisch** adj Icelandic; **Isländisch** nt Icelandic

Isolierband nt insulating tape; **isolieren** vt isolate; ELEC insulate

Isomatte f thermomat, karrymat®

Israel nt (-s) Israel; **Israeli** m (-(s), -(s)) f (-, -(s)) Israeli; **israelisch** adj Israeli

IT f (-) abbr = Informationstechnologie; IT

Italien nt (-s) Italy; **Italiener(in)** m(f) (-s, -) Italian; **italienisch** adj Italian; **Italienisch** nt Italian

J

ja adv yes; **aber ∼!** yes, of course; **∼, wissen Sie ...** well, you know ...; **ich glaube ∼** I think so; **∼?** (on phone) hello?; **sag's ihr ∼ nicht!** don't you dare tell her; **das sag ich ∼** that's what I'm trying to say

Jacht f (-, -en) yacht; **Jachthafen** m marina

Jacke f (-, -n) jacket; (knitted) cardigan

Jackett nt (-s, -s or -e) jacket

Jagd f (-, -en) hunt; (activity) hunting; **jagen 1.** vi hunt **2.** vt hunt; (pursue) chase; **Jäger(in)** m(f) hunter

Jaguar m (-s, -e) jaguar

Jahr nt (-(e)s, -e) year; **ein halbes ∼** six months pl; **Anfang der neunziger ∼e** in the early nineties; **mit sechzehn ∼en** (at the age of) sixteen; **Jahrestag** m anniversary; **Jahreszahl** f date, year; **Jahreszeit** f season; Jahrgang m (of wine) year, vintage; **der ~ 1989** (people) those born in 1989; Jahrhundert nt (-s, -e) century; jährlich adj yearly, annual; Jahrmarkt m fair; Jahrtausend nt millennium; Jahrzehnt nt decade

jähzornig adj hot-tempered
Jakobsmuschel f scallop
Jalousie f (venetian) blind
Jamaika nt (-s) Jamaica
jämmerlich adj pathetic
jammern vi moan
Januar m (-(s), -e) January; → **Juni**
Japan nt (-s) Japan; Japaner(in) m(f) (-s, -) Japanese; japanisch adj Japanese; Japanisch nt Japanese
jaulen vi howl
jawohl adv yes (of course)
Jazz m (-) jazz
je adv ever; (for every one) each; **~ nach** depending on; **~ nachdem** it depends; **~ schneller desto besser** the faster the better
Jeans f (-, -) jeans pl
jede(r, s) **1.** indef num every; (considered singly) each; (whichever you like) any; **~s Mal** every time, each time; **~n zweiten Tag** every other day; **bei ~m Wetter** in any weather **2.** pron everybody; (every single one) each; **~r von euch/uns** each of you/us; jedenfalls adv in any case; jederzeit adv at

any time; jedesmal adv every time
jedoch adv however
jemals adv ever
jemand pron somebody; (with question or negative) anybody
Jemen m (-(s)) Yemen
jene(r, s) pron that (one), those pl
jenseits **1.** adv on the other side **2.** prep + gen on the other side of; fig beyond
Jetlag m (-s) jet lag
jetzig adj present
jetzt adv now; **erst~** only now; **~ gleich** right now; **bis ~** so far, up to now; **von~ an** from now on
jeweils adv **~ zwei zusammen** two at a time; **zu ~ 5 Euro** at 5 euros each
Job m (-s, -s) job; jobben vi fam work, have a job
Jod nt (-(e)s) iodine
Joga m (-s) yoga
joggen vi jog; Jogging nt (-s) jogging; Jogginghose f jogging pants pl
Jog(h)urt m or nt (-s, -s) yoghurt
Johannisbeere f **Schwarze ~** blackcurrant; **Rote ~** redcurrant
Joint m (-s, -s) fam joint
jonglieren vi juggle
Jordanien nt (-s) Jordan
Joule nt (-(s), -) joule
Journalist(in) m(f) journalist
Joystick m (-s, -s) IT joystick

jubeln *vi* cheer

Jubiläum *nt* (-s, Jubiläen) jubilee; *(date)* anniversary

jucken 1. *vi* itch **2.** *vt* **es juckt mich am Arm** my arm is itching; *das juckt mich nicht jam* I couldn't care less; **Juckreiz** *m* itch

Jude *m* (-n, -n), **Jüdin** *f* Jew; **sie ist Jüdin** she's Jewish; **jüdisch** *adj* Jewish

Judo *nt* (-(s)) judo

Jugend *f* (-) youth; **Jugendherberge** *f* (-, -n) youth hostel; **jugendlich** *adj* youthful; **Jugendliche(r)** *mf* young person; **Jugendstil** *m* art nouveau; **Jugendzentrum** *nt* youth centre

Jugoslawien *nt* (-s) HIST Yugoslavia

Juli *m* (-(s), -s) July; → **Juni**

jung *adj* young

Junge *m* (-n, -n) boy

Junge(s) *nt* (-n, -n) young animal; *die ~n pl* the young *pl*

Jungfrau *f* virgin; ASTR Virgo

Junggeselle *m* (-n, -n) bachelor

Juni *m* (-(s), -s) June; *im ~* in June; *am 4. ~* on 4(th) June, on June 4(th) ; *Anfang/Mitte/Ende ~* at the beginning/in the middle/ at the end of June; *letzten/nächsten ~* last/next June

Jupiter *m* (-s) Jupiter

Jura *no article (subject)* law; *~ studieren* study law; **Jurist(in)** *m(f)* lawyer; **juristisch** *adj* legal

Justiz *f* (-) justice; **Justizminister(in)** *m(f)* minister of justice

Juwel *nt* (-s, -en) jewel; **Juwelier(in)** *m(f)* (-s, -e) jeweller

Jux *m* (-es, -e) joke, lark

K

Kabel *nt* (-s, -) ELEC wire; *(thick)* cable; **Kabelfernsehen** *nt* cable television

Kabeljau *m* (-s, -e or -s) cod

Kabine *f* cabin; *(at swimming pool)* cubicle

Kabrio *nt* (-s, -s) convertible

Kachel *f* (-, -n) tile; **Kachelofen** *m* tiled stove

Käfer *m* (-s, -) beetle, bug (US)

Kaff *nt* (-s, -s) dump, hole

Kaffee *m* (-s, -s) coffee; *~ kochen* make some coffee; **Kaffeekanne** *f* coffeepot; **Kaffeelöffel** *m* coffee spoon; **Kaffeemaschine** *f* coffee maker (or machine); **Kaffeetasse** *f* coffee cup

Käfig *m* (-s, -e) cage

kahl *adj (person, head)* bald; *(tree, wall)* bare

Kahn *m* (-(e)s, Kähne) boat; *(for goods)* barge

Kai m (-s, -e or -s) quay

Kaiser m (-s, -) emperor; Kaiserin f empress; Kaiserschnitt m MED caesarean (section)

Kajak nt (-s, -s) kayak

Kajüte f (-, -n) cabin

Kakao m (-s, -s) cocoa; (drink) (hot) chocolate

Kakerlake f (-, -n) cockroach

Kaki f (-, -s) kaki

Kaktee f (-, -n), Kaktus m (-, -se) cactus

Kalb nt (-(e)s, Kälber) calf; Kalbfleisch nt veal; Kalbsbraten m roast veal; Kalbsschnitzel nt veal cutlet; (in breadcrumbs) escalope of veal

Kalender m (-s, -) calendar; (book) diary

Kalk m (-(e)s, -e) lime; (in bones) calcium

Kalorie f calorie; kalorienarm adj low-calorie

kalt adj cold; mir ist(es) ~ I'm cold; kaltblütig adj cold-blooded; Kälte f (-) cold; fig coldness

kam imperf of kommen

Kambodscha nt (-s) Cambodia

Kamel nt (-(e)s, -e) camel

Kamera f (-, -s) camera

Kamerad(in) m(f) (-en, -en) friend; (accompanying sb) companion

Kamerafrau f, Kameramann m camerawoman / -man

Kamille f (-, -n) camomile;

Kamillentee m camomile tea

Kamin m (-s, -e) (outside) chimney; (inside) fireplace

Kamm m (-(e)s, Kämme) comb; (of mountain) ridge; (of cock) crest; kämmen vr sich ~, sich dat die Haare ~ comb one's hair

Kampf m (-(e)s, Kämpfe) fight; (in war) battle; (in sport etc) contest; fig struggle; kämpfen vi fight (für, um for); Kampfsport m martial art

Kanada nt (-s) Canada; Kanadier(in) m(f) (-s, -) Canadian; kanadisch adj Canadian

Kanal m (-s, Kanäle) canal; (ditch, on TV) channel; der ~ the (English) Channel; Kanalinseln pl Channel Islands pl; Kanaltunnel m Channel Tunnel

Kanarienvogel m canary

Kandidat(in) m(f) (-en, -en) candidate

Kandis(zucker) m (-) rock candy

Känguru nt (-s, -s) kangaroo

Kaninchen nt rabbit

Kanister m (-s, -) can

Kännchen nt pot; ein ~ Kaffee/Tee a pot of coffee/tea; Kanne f (-, -n) jug; (for coffee) pot; (for milk) churn; (for watering plants) can

kannte imperf of kennen

Kante f (-, -n) edge

Kantine f canteen

Kanton m (-s, -e) canton

Kanu nt (-s, -s) canoe

Kanzler(in) m(f) (-s, -) chancellor

Kap nt (-s, -s) cape

Kapelle f chapel; MUS band

Kaper f (-, -n) caper

kapieren vt, vi fam understand; **kapiert?** got it?

Kapital nt (-s, -e or -ien) capital

Kapitän m (-s, -e) captain

Kapitel nt (-s, -) chapter

Kappe f (-, -n) cap

Kapsel f (-, -n) capsule

kaputt adj fam broken; (person) exhausted; kaputtgehen irr vi break; (shoes) fall apart; kaputtmachen vt break; (person) wear out

Kapuze f (-, -n) hood

Karaffe f (-, -n) carafe; (with stopper) decanter

Karambole f (-, -n) star fruit, carambola

Karamell m (-s) caramel, toffee

Karaoke nt (-(s)) karaoke

Karat nt (-s, -e) carat

Karate nt (-s) karate

Kardinal m (-s, Kardinäle) cardinal

Karfreitag m Good Friday

kariert adj checked; (paper) squared

Karies f (-) (tooth) decay

Karikatur f caricature

Karneval m (-s, -e or -s) carnival

Kärnten nt (-s) Carinthia

Karo nt (-s, -s) square; (card suit) diamonds pl

Karosserie f AUTO body (-work)

Karotte f (-, -n) carrot

Karpfen m (-s, -) carp

Karriere f (-, -n) career

Karte f (-, -n) card; (of country etc) map; (in restaurant) menu; (for theatre, train etc) ticket; **mit ~ bezahlen** pay by credit card; **~n spielen** play cards; **die ~n mischen/ geben** shuffle / deal the cards

Kartei f card index; Karteikarte f index card

Kartenspiel nt card game; Kartentelefon nt cardphone; Kartenvorverkauf m advance booking

Kartoffel f (-, -n) potato; Kartoffelbrei m mashed potatoes pl; Kartoffelchips pl crisps pl (Brit), chips pl (US); Kartoffelsalat m potato salad

Karton m (-s, -s) cardboard; (container) (cardboard) box

Karussell nt (-s, -s) roundabout (Brit), merry-go-round

Kaschmir m (-s, -e) cashmere

Käse m (-s, -) cheese; Käsekuchen m cheesecake; Käseplatte f cheeseboard

Kasino nt (-s, -s) casino

Kasper(l) m (-s, -) Punch; fig clown; Kasperl(e)theater nt Punch and Judy show

Kasse f (-, -n) (in shop) till, cash register; (in supermarket) checkout; (container) cashbox; (at theatre) box office; (at cinema) ticket office; (insurance scheme) health insurance; **Kassenbon** m (-s, -s), **Kassenzettel** m receipt

Kassette f (small) box; (tape) cassette; **Kassettenrekorder** m cassette recorder

kassieren 1. vt take 2. vi **darf ich ~?** would you like to pay now?; **Kassierer(in)** m(f) cashier

Kastanie f chestnut

Kasten m (-s, **Kästen**) box; (for bottles) crate

Kat m abbr = **Katalysator**

Katalog m (-(e)s, -e) catalogue

Katalysator m AUTO catalytic converter

Katar nt (-s) Qatar

Katarr(h) m (-s, -e) catarrh

Katastrophe f (-, -n) catastrophe, disaster

Kategorie f (-, -n) category

Kater m (-s, -) tomcat; fam hangover

Kathedrale f (-, -n) cathedral

Katholik(in) m(f) Catholic; **katholisch** adj Catholic

Katze f (-, -n) cat

Kauderwelsch nt (-(s)) gibberish

kauen vt, vi chew

Kauf m (-(e)s, **Käufe**) purchase; (action) buying; **ein guter ~** a bargain; **etw in ~**

nehmen put up with sth; **kaufen** vt buy; **Käufer(in)** m(f) buyer; **Kauffrau** f businesswoman; **Kaufhaus** nt department store; **Kaufmann** m businessman; (retailer) shopkeeper (Brit), storekeeper (US)

Kaugummi m chewing gum

Kaulquappe f (-, -n) tadpole

kaum adv hardly, scarcely

Kaution f deposit; LAW bail

Kaviar m caviar

KB nt (-, -), **Kbyte** nt (-, -) abbr = **Kilobyte**; KB

Kebab m (-(s), -s) kebab

Kegel m (-s, -) skittle; (in tenpin bowling) pin; MATH cone; **Kegelbahn** f bowling alley; **kegeln** vi play skittles; (in tenpin bowling) bowl

Kehle f (-, -n) throat; **Kehlkopf** m larynx

kehren vt (with brush) sweep

Keilriemen m AUTO fan belt

kein pron no, not ... any; **ich habe ~ Geld** I have no money, I don't have money; **keine(r, s)** pron no one, nobody; (thing) not ... any, none; **~r von ihnen** none of them; (two people / things) neither of them; **ich will keins von beiden** I don't want either (of them); **keinesfalls** adv on no account, under no circumstances

Keks m (-es, -e) biscuit (Brit), cookie (US); **jdm auf den ~ gehen** fam get on sb's nerves

Keller m (-s, -) cellar; (storey) basement

Kellner m (-s, -) waiter; **Kellnerin** f waitress

Kenia nt (-s) Kenya

kennen (kannte, gekannt) vt know; **wir ~ uns seit 1990** we've known each other since 1990; **~ lernen** get to know; **sich ~ lernen** get to know each other; (for the first time) meet

Kenntnis f knowledge; **seine ~se** his knowledge

Kennwort nt a. IT password; **Kennzeichen** nt mark, sign; AUTO number plate (Brit), license plate (US)

Kerl m (-s, -e) guy, bloke (Brit)

Kern m (-(e)s, -e) (of fruit) pip; (of peach, cherry etc) stone; (of nut) kernel; (of atom) nucleus; fig heart, core

Kernenergie f nuclear energy; **Kernkraft** f nuclear power; **Kernkraftwerk** nt nuclear power station

Kerze f (-, -n) candle; (in engine) plug

Ket(s)chup m or nt (-(s), -s) ketchup

Kette f (-, -n) chain; (jewellery) necklace

keuchen vi pant; **Keuchhusten** m whooping cough

Keule f (-, -n) club; GASTR leg; (of chicken also) drumstick

Keyboard nt (-s, -s) MUS keyboard

Kfz nt abbr = **Kraftfahrzeug**

Kfz-Brief m ≈ logbook

Kfz-Steuer f ≈ road tax (Brit), vehicle tax (US)

Kichererbse f chick pea

kichern vi giggle

Kickboard® nt (-s, -s) micro scooter

Kicker m (-s, -) table football (Brit), foosball (US)

kidnappen vt kidnap

Kidney-Bohne f kidney bean

Kiefer 1. m (-s, -) jaw **2.** f (-, -n) pine

Kieme f (-, -n) gill

Kies m (-es, -e) gravel; **Kiesel** m (-s, -), **Kieselstein** m pebble

kiffen vi fam smoke pot

Kilo nt (-s, -(s)) kilo; **Kilobyte** nt kilobyte; **Kilogramm** nt kilogram; **Kilojoule** nt kilojoule; **Kilometer** m kilometre; **Kilometerstand** m ≈ mileage; **Kilowatt** nt kilowatt

Kind nt (-(e)s, -er) child; **sie bekommt ein ~** she's having a baby; **Kinderarzt** m, **Kinderärztin** f paediatrician; **Kinderbetreuung** f childcare; **Kinderbett** nt cot (Brit), crib (US); **Kinderfahrkarte** f child's ticket; **Kindergarten** m nursery school, kindergarten; **Kindergärtnerin** f nursery-school teacher; **Kindergeld** nt child benefit; **Kinderkrankheit** f children's illness;

Kinderkrippe f crèche (Brit), daycare center (US); **Kinderlähmung** f polio; **Kindermädchen** nt nanny (Brit), nurse(maid); **kindersicher** adj childproof; **Kindersicherung** f childproof safety catch; (on bottle) childproof cap; **Kindersitz** m child seat; **Kinderteller** m (in restaurant) children's portion; **Kinderwagen** m pram (Brit), baby carriage (US); **Kinderzimmer** nt children's (bed)room; **Kindheit** f childhood; **kindisch** adj childish; **kindlich** adj childlike

Kinn nt (-(e)s, -e) chin

Kino nt (-s, -s) cinema (Brit), movie theater (US); **ins ~ gehen** go to the cinema (Brit) (or to the movies (US))

Kiosk m (-s, -e) kiosk

Kippe f fam cigarette end, fag end (Brit)

Kirche f (-, -n) church; **Kirchturm** m church tower; (pointed) steeple

Kirmes f (-, -sen) fair

Kirsche f (-, -n) cherry; **Kirschtomate** f cherry tomato

Kissen nt (-s, -) cushion; (on bed) pillow

Kiste f (-, -n) box; (trunk) chest

kitschig adj kitschy, cheesy

kitzelig adj a. fig ticklish; **kit-**

zeln vt, vi tickle

Kiwi f (-, -s) kiwi (fruit)

Klage f (-, -n) complaint; LAW lawsuit; **klagen** vi complain (über + acc about, bei to); **kläglich** adj wretched

Klammer f (-, -n) (in text) bracket; (on documents) clip; (for washing) peg (Brit), clothespin (US); (on teeth) brace; **Klammeraffe** m fam at-sign, @; **klammern** vr cling (an + acc to)

klang imperf of **klingen**

Klang m (-(e)s, Klänge) sound

Klappbett nt folding bed

klappen vi impers (succeed) work; **es hat gut geklappt** it went well

klappern vi rattle; (pots and pans) clatter; **Klapperschlange** f rattlesnake

Klappstuhl m folding chair

klar adj clear; **sich** dat **im Klaren sein** (über + acc about); **alles ~?** everything okay?

klären 1. vt (liquid) purify; (problem, issue) clarify **2.** vr clear itself up

Klarinette f (-, -n) clarinet

klarkommen irr vi **mit etw ~** cope with something; **kommst du klar?** are you managing all right?; **mit jdm ~** get along with sb; **klarmachen** vt **jdm etw ~** make sth clear to sb; **Klarsichtfolie** f clingfilm® (Brit), plastic wrap (US); **klarstellen** vt clarify

Klärung f (of problem, issue) clarification

klasse adj inv fam great, brilliant

Klasse f (-, -n) class; (year in school) form (Brit), grade (US); **erster ~ reisen** travel first class; **in welche ~ gehst du?** which form (Brit) (or grade (US)) are you in?; **Klassenarbeit** f test; **Klassenlehrer(in)** m(f) class teacher; **Klassenzimmer** nt classroom

Klassik f classical period; classical music

Klatsch m (-(e)s, -e) (talk) gossip; **klatschen** vi (hit) smack; (after concert etc) applaud, clap; (talk) gossip; **klatschnass** adj soaking (wet)

Klaue f (-, -n) claw; fam (handwriting) scrawl

klauen vt fam pinch

Klavier nt (-s, -e) piano

Klebeband nt adhesive tape; **kleben 1.** vt stick (an + acc to) **2.** vi (unpleasantly) be sticky; **klebrig** adj sticky; **Klebstoff** m glue; **Klebstreifen** m adhesive tape

Klecks m (-es, -e) blob; (of ink) blot

Klee m (-s) clover

Kleid nt (-(e)s, -er) dress; **~er** pl clothes pl; **Kleiderbügel** m coat hanger; **Kleiderschrank** m wardrobe (Brit),

closet (US); **Kleidung** f clothing

klein adj small, little; (finger) little; **mein ~er Bruder** my little (or younger) brother; **als ich noch ~ war** when I was a little boy/girl; **etw ~ schneiden** chop sth up; **Kleinanzeige** f classified ad; **Kleinbuchstabe** m small letter; **Kleinbus** m minibus; **Kleingeld** nt change; **Kleinigkeit** f trifle; (meal) snack; **Kleinkind** nt toddler; **kleinschreiben** vt write with a small letter; **Kleinstadt** f small town

Klempner(in) m(f) plumber

klettern vi climb

Klettverschluss m Velcro® fastening

klicken vi a. IT click

Klient(in) m(f) (-en, -en) client

Klima nt (-s, -s) climate; **Klimaanlage** f air conditioning; **klimatisiert** adj air-conditioned

Klinge f (-, -n) blade

Klingel f (-, -n) bell; **klingeln** vi ring

klingen (klang, geklungen) vi sound

Klinik f clinic; (non-specialist) hospital

Klinke f (-, -n) handle

Klippe f (-, -n) cliff; (in sea) reef; fig hurdle

Klischee nt (-s, -s) fig cliché

Klo nt (-s, -s) fam loo (Brit),

john (US); **Klobrille** f toilet seat; **Klopapier** nt toilet paper

klopfen vt, vi knock; (heart) thump

Kloß m (-es, Klöße) (in throat) lump; GASTR dumpling

Kloster nt (-s, Klöster) monastery; (for women) convent

Klub m (-s, -s) club

klug adj clever

knabbern vt, vi nibble

Knäckebrot nt crispbread

knacken vt, vi crack

Knall m (-(e)s, -e) bang; **Knallbonbon** m cracker; **knallen** vi bang

knapp adj (in short supply) scarce; (victory) narrow; ~ **bei Kasse sein** be short of money; ~ **zwei Stunden** just under two hours

Knautschzone f AUTO crumple zone

kneifen (kniff, gekniffen) vt, vi pinch; (shirk) back out (vor + dat of)

Kneipe f (-, -n) fam pub (Brit), bar

Knete f (-) fam (money) dough; **kneten** vt knead; (shape) mould

knicken vt, vi break; (paper) fold

Knie nt (-s, -) knee; **in die gehen** bend one's knees; **Kniebeuge** f knee bend; **Kniegelenk** nt knee joint; **Kniekehle** f back of the knee; **knien** vi kneel; **Knie-**

scheibe f kneecap; **Knieschoner** m (-s, -), **Knieschützer** m (-s, -) knee pad

kniff imperf of **kneifen**

knipsen 1. vt punch; PHOT snap 2. vi PHOT take snaps

knirschen vi crunch; **mit den Zähnen ~** grind one's teeth

knitterfrei adj non-crease; **knittern** vi crease

Knoblauch m garlic; **Knoblauchbrot** nt garlic bread; **Knoblauchzehe** f clove of garlic

Knöchel m (-s, -) knuckle; (of foot) ankle

Knochen m (-s, -) bone; **Knochenbruch** m fracture; **Knochenmark** nt marrow

Knödel m (-s, -) dumpling

Knopf m (-(e)s, Knöpfe) button; **Knopfdruck** m **auf ~** at the touch of a bottin; **Knopfloch** nt buttonhole

Knospe f (-, -n) bud

knoten vt knot; **Knoten** m (-s, -) knot; MED lump

Know-how nt (-(s)) know-how, expertise

knurren vi (dog) growl; (stomach) rumble; (person) grumble

knusprig adj crisp; (biscuit) crunchy

knutschen vi fam smooch

k. o. adj inv SPORT knocked out; fig knackered

Koalition f coalition

Koch m (-(e)s, Köche) cook; **Kochbuch** nt cookery book, cookbook; **kochen** vt, vi cook; (water) boil; (coffee, tea) make; **Köchin** f cook; **Kochlöffel** m wooden spoon; **Kochnische** f kitchenette; **Kochplatte** f hotplate; **Kochrezept** nt recipe; **Kochtopf** m saucepan

Kode m (-s, -s) code

Köder m (-s, -) bait

Koffein nt (-s) caffeine; **koffeinfrei** adj decaffeinated

Koffer m (-s, -) (suit)case; **Kofferraum** m AUTO boot (Brit), trunk (US)

Kognak m (-s, -s) brandy

Kohl m (-(e)s, -e) cabbage

Kohle f (-, -n) coal; (made from wood) charcoal; (Fam (money) cash, dough; **Kohlehydrat** nt carbohydrate; **Kohlendioxid** nt carbon dioxide; **Kohlensäure** f (in drinks) fizz; **ohne ~** still, non-carbonated (US); **mit ~** sparkling, carbonated (US)

Kohlrabi m (-(s), -(s)) kohlrabi

Kohlrübe f swede (Brit), rutabaga (US)

Koje f (-, -n) cabin; (bed) bunk

Kokain nt (-s) cocaine

Kokosnuss f coconut

Kolben m (-s, -) TECH piston

Kolik f (-, -en) colic

Kollaps m (-es, -e) collapse

Kollege m (-n, -n), **Kollegin** f colleague

Köln nt (-s) Cologne

Kolonne f (-, -n) convoy

Kolumbien nt (-s) Columbia

Koma nt (-s, -s) coma

Kombi m (-(s), -s) estate (car) (Brit), station wagon (US); **Kombination** f combination; (reasoning) deduction; **kombinieren 1.** vt combine **2.** vi reason; (suspect) guess

Komfort m (-s) conveniences pl; (of guest, room etc) comfort

Komiker(in) m(f) comedian, comic; **komisch** adj funny

Komma nt (-s, -s) comma

kommen (kam, gekommen) vi come; (come closer) approach; (occur) happen; (reach, begin) get; (become visible) appear; (to school, prison etc) go; **zu ~** come round (or to); **zu etw ~** (get) acquire sth; (find time for) get round to sth; **wer kommt zuerst?** who's first?; **kommend** adj coming; **~e Woche** next week; **in den ~en Jahren** in the years to come

Kommentar m commentary; **kein ~** no comment

Kommilitone m (-n, -n), **Kommilitonin** f fellow student

Kommissar(in) m(f) inspector

Kommode f (-, -n) chest of drawers

Kommunikation f communication

Kommunion f REL communion

Kommunismus *m* communism

Komödie *f* comedy

kompakt *adj* compact

Kompass *m* (-es, -e) compass

kompatibel *adj* compatible

kompetent *adj* competent

komplett *adj* complete

Kompliment *nt* compliment; **jdm ein ~ machen** pay sb a compliment; **~!** congratulations

kompliziert *adj* complicated

Komponist(in) *m(f)* composer

Kompost *m* (-(e)s, -e) compost; **Komposthaufen** *m* compost heap

Kompott *nt* (-(e)s, -e) stewed fruit

Kompresse *f* (-, -n) compress

Kompromiss *m* (-es, -e) compromise

Kondition *f* condition; **sie hat eine gute ~** she's in good shape

Konditorei *f* cake shop; (*serving coffee etc*) café

Kondom *nt* (-s, -e) condom

Konfektionsgröße *f* size

Konferenz *f* conference

Konfession *f* religion; (*within Christianity*) denomination

Konfetti *nt* (-(s)) confetti

Konfirmation *f* REL confirmation

Konflikt *m* (-(e)s, -e) conflict

konfrontieren *vt* confront

Kongo *m* (-s) Congo

Kongress *m* (-es, -e) confer-ence; **der ~** (*US parliament*) Congress

König *m* (-(e)s, -e) king; **Königin** *f* queen; **Königinpastete** *f* vol-au-vent; **königlich** *adj* royal; **Königreich** *nt* kingdom

Konkurrenz *f* competition

können (*konnte, gekonnt*) *vt, vi* be able to, can; (*poem, song*) know; **~ Sie Deutsch?** can (*or* do) you speak German?; **ich kann nicht kommen** I can't come; **das kann sein** that's possible; **ich kann nichts dafür** it's not my fault

konsequent *adj* consistent

konservativ *adj* conservative

Konserven *pl* tinned food *sg* (*Brit*), canned food *sg*; **Konservendose** *f* tin (*Brit*), can

konservieren *vt* preserve; **Konservierungsmittel** *nt* preservative

Konsonant *m* consonant

Konsul(in) *m(f)* (-s, -n) consul; **Konsulat** *nt* consulate

Kontakt *m* (-(e)s, -e) contact; **kontaktarm** *adj* **er ist ~** he lacks contact with other people; **kontaktfreudig** *adj* sociable; **Kontaktlinsen** *pl* contact lenses *pl*

Kontinent *m* continent

Konto *nt* (-s, Konten) account; **Kontoauszug** *m* (bank) statement; **Kontoinhaber(in)** *m(f)* account holder; **Kontonummer** *f* account number; **Kontostand** m balance

Kontrabass m double bass

Kontrast m (-(e)s, -e) contrast

Kontrolle f (-, -n) control; (*checking*) supervision; (*at airport etc*) passport control; **kontrollieren** vt control; (*verify*) check

Konzentration f concentration; **Konzentrationslager** nt HIST concentration camp; **konzentrieren** vt, vr concentrate

Konzept nt (-(e)s, -e) rough draft

Konzert nt (-(e)s, -e) concert; (*piece of music*) concerto; **Konzertsaal** m concert hall

koordinieren vt coordinate

Kopf m (-(e)s, Köpfe) head; **Kopfhörer** m headphones pl; **Kopfkissen** nt pillow; **Kopfsalat** m lettuce; **Kopfschmerzen** pl headache sg; **Kopfstütze** f headrest; **Kopftuch** nt headscarf

Kopie f copy; **kopieren** vt a. IT copy; **Kopierer** m (-s, -), **Kopiergerät** nt copier

Kopilot(in) m(f) co-pilot

Koralle f (-, -n) coral

Koran m (-s) REL Koran

Korb m (-(e)s, Körbe) basket; **jdm einen ~ geben** fig turn sb down

Kord m (-(e)s, -e) corduroy

Kordel f (-, -n) cord

Korinthe f (-e, -n) currant

Kork m (-(e)s, -e) cork; **Korken** m (-s, -) cork; **Korkenzieher** m (-s, -) corkscrew

Korn nt (-(e)s, Körner) grain; **Kornblume** f cornflower

Körper m (-s, -) body; **Körperbau** m build; **körperbehindert** adj disabled; **Körpergeruch** m body odour; **körperlich** adj physical; **Körperverletzung** f physical injury

korrekt adj correct

Korrespondent(in) m(f) correspondent; **Korrespondenz** f correspondence

korrigieren vt correct

Kosmetik f cosmetics pl; **Kosmetikkoffer** m vanity case; **Kosmetiksalon** m beauty parlour

Kost f (-) food; (*meals*) board

kostbar adj precious; (*dear*) costly, expensive

kosten 1. vt cost **2.** vt, vi (*sample*) taste; **Kosten** pl costs pl, cost; (*money spent*) expenses pl; **auf ~ von** at the expense of; **kostenlos** adj free (of charge); **Kostenvoranschlag** m estimate

köstlich adj (*food*) delicious; **sich ~ amüsieren** have a marvellous time

Kostprobe f taster; fig sample; **kostspielig** adj expensive

Kostüm nt (-s, -e) costume; (*jacket and skirt*) suit

Kot m (-(e)s) excrement

Kotelett nt (-(e)s, -e or -s)

chop, cutlet
Koteletten pl sideboards pl (Brit), sideburns pl (US)
Kotflügel m AUTO wing
kotzen vi vulg puke, throw up
Krabbe f (-, -n) shrimp; (larger) prawn; (with pincers) crab
krabbeln vi crawl
Krach m (-(e)s, -s or -e) crash; (continuous) noise; fam (argument) row
Kraft f (-, Kräfte) strength; POL, PHYS force; (ability) power; **in ~ treten** come into effect; **Kraftausdruck** m swearword; **Kraftfahrzeug** nt motor vehicle; **Kraftfahrzeugbrief** m ≈ logbook; **Kraftfahrzeugschein** m vehicle registration document; **Kraftfahrzeugsteuer** f ≈ road tax (Brit), vehicle tax (US); **Kraftfahrzeugversicherung** f car insurance; **kräftig** adj strong; healthy; (colour) intense; strong; **Kraftstoff** m fuel; **Kraftwerk** nt power station
Kragen m (-s, ~) collar
Krähe f (-, -n) crow
Kralle f (-, -n) claw; (on car) wheel clamp
Kram m (-(e)s) stuff
Krampf m (-(e)s, Krämpfe) cramp; (twitching) spasm; **Krampfader** f varicose vein
Kran m (-(e)s, Kräne) crane
Kranich m (-s, -e) ZOOL crane
krank adj ill, sick

kränken vt hurt
Krankengymnastik f physiotherapy; **Krankenhaus** nt hospital; **Krankenkasse** f health insurance; **Krankenpfleger** m (-s, -) (male) nurse; **Krankenschein** m health insurance certificate; **Krankenschwester** f nurse; **Krankenversicherung** f health insurance; **Krankenwagen** m ambulance; **Krankheit** f illness; (infectious) disease
Kränkung f insult
Kranz m (-es, Kränze) wreath
krass adj crass; fam (wonderful) wicked
kratzen vt/i scratch; **Kratzer** m (-s, -) scratch
kraulen 1. vi (swim) do the crawl **2.** vt (stroke) pet
Kraut nt (-(e)s, Kräuter) cabbage; **Kräuter** pl herbs pl; **Kräuterbutter** f herb butter; **Kräutertee** m herbal tea; **Krautsalat** m coleslaw
Krawatte f tie
kreativ adj creative
Krebs m (-es, -e) ZOOL crab; MED cancer; ASTR Cancer
Kredit m (-(e)s, -e) credit; **auf ~** on credit; **einen ~ aufnehmen** take out a loan; **Kreditkarte** f credit card
Kreide f (-, -n) chalk
Kreis m (-es, -e) circle; (administrative area) district
Kreisel m (-s, -) (toy) top; (on road) roundabout (Brit),

traffic circle (US)

Kreislauf m MED circulation; fig (of nature etc) cycle; **Kreislaufstörungen** pl MED **ich habe ~** I've got problems with my circulation; **Kreisverkehr** m roundabout (Brit), traffic circle (US)

Kren m (-s) horseradish

Kresse f (-, -n) cress

Kreuz nt (-es, -e) cross; ANAT small of the back; (card suit) clubs pl; **mir tut das ~ weh** I've got backache; **Kreuzband** nt cruciate ligament; **Kreuzfahrt** f cruise; **Kreuzgang** m cloisters pl; **Kreuzotter** f (-, -n) adder; **Kreuzschlüssel** m AUTO wheel brace; **Kreuzschmerzen** pl backache sg; **Kreuzung** f crossroads sg, intersection; (animal, plant) cross; **Kreuzworträtsel** nt crossword (puzzle)

kriechen (kroch, gekrochen) vi crawl; (unobtrusively) creep; fig pej (vor jdm) crawl to sb)

Krieg m (-(e)s, -e) war

kriegen vt fam get; (rascal, bus etc) catch; **sie kriegt ein Kind** she's having a baby; **ich kriege noch Geld von dir** you still owe me some money

Krimi m (-s, -s) fam thriller; **Kriminalität** f criminality; **Kriminalpolizei** f detective force, ≈ CID (Brit), ≈ FBI (US); **Kriminalroman** m detective novel; **kriminell** adj criminal

Krippe f (-, -n) manger; (Nativity scene) crib (Brit), crèche (US); (nursery) crèche (Brit), daycare center (US)

Krise f (-, -n) crisis

Kristall 1. m (-s, -e) crystal **2.** nt (-s) (glass) crystal

Kritik f criticism; (of film, book etc) review; **Kritiker(in)** m(f) critic; **kritisch** adj critical

kritzeln vt, vi scribble, scrawl

Kroate m (-n, -n) Croat; **Kroatien** nt (-s) Croatia; **Kroatin** f Croat; **kroatisch** adj Croatian; **Kroatisch** nt Croatian

kroch imperf of **kriechen**

Krokodil nt (-s, -e) crocodile

Krokus m (-, - or -se) crocus

Krone f (-, -n) crown

Kröte f (-, -n) toad

Krücke f (-, -n) crutch

Krug m (-(e)s, Krüge) jug; (for beer) mug

Krümel m (-s, -) crumb

krumm adj crooked

Kruste f (-, -n) crust

Kruzifix nt (-es, -e) crucifix

Kuba nt (-s) Cuba

Kübel m (-s, -) tub; (with handle) bucket

Kubikmeter m cubic metre

Küche f (-, -n) kitchen; (activity) cooking

Kuchen m (-s, -) cake; **Kuchengabel** f cake fork

Küchenmaschine f food processor; **Küchenpapier** nt kitchen roll; **Küchenschrank** m (kitchen) cupboard

Kuckuck m (-s, -e) cuckoo

Kugel f (-, -n) ball; MATH sphere; MIL bullet; (on Christmas tree) bauble; **Kugellager** nt ball bearing; **Kugelschreiber** m (ball-point) pen, biro® (Brit); **Kugelstoßen** nt (-s) shot put

Kuh f (-, Kühe) cow

kühl adj cool; **Kühlbox** f cool box; **kühlen** vt cool; **Kühler** m (-s, -) AUTO radiator; **Kühlerhaube** f AUTO bonnet (Brit), hood (US); **Kühlschrank** m fridge, refrigerator; **Kühltasche** f cool bag; **Kühltruhe** f freezer

Kuhstall m cowshed

Küken nt (-s, -) chick

Kuli m (-s, -s) fam pen, biro® (Brit)

Kulisse f (-, -n) scenery

Kult m (-(e)s, -e) cult; **Kultfigur** f cult figure

Kultur f culture; (way of life) civilization; **Kulturbeutel** m toilet bag (Brit), washbag; **kulturell** adj cultural

Kümmel m (-s, -) caraway seeds pl

Kummer m (-s) grief, sorrow

kümmern 1. vr **sich um jdn ~** look after sb; **sich um etw ~** see to sth 2. vt concern; **das kümmert mich nicht** that

doesn't worry me

Kumpel m (-s, -) fam mate, pal

Kunde m (-n, -n) customer; **Kundendienst** m after-sales (or customer) service; **Kunden(kredit)karte** f storecard, chargecard; **Kundennummer** f customer number

kündigen 1. vi hand in one's notice; (tenant) give notice that one is moving out; **jdm ~** give sb his/ her notice; (landlord) give sb notice to quit **2.** vt cancel; (contract) terminate; **jdm die Stellung ~** give sb his/ her notice; **Kündigung** f (from job) dismissal; (of contract) termination; (of subscription) cancellation; (period of notification) notice

Kundin f customer; **Kundschaft** f customers pl

künftig adj future

Kunst f (-, Künste) art; (ability) skill; **Kunstausstellung** f art exhibition; **Kunstgewerbe** nt arts and crafts pl; **Künstler(in)** m(f) (-s, -) artist; **künstlerisch** adj artistic

künstlich adj artificial

Kunststoff m synthetic material; **Kunststück** nt trick; **Kunstwerk** nt work of art

Kupfer nt (-s, -) copper

Kuppel f (-, -n) dome

kuppeln vi AUTO operate the clutch; **Kupplung** f coupling; AUTO clutch

Kur f (-, -en) course of treatment; (*at health resort*) cure

Kür f (-, -en) SPORT free programme

Kurbel f (-, -n) winder

Kürbis m (-ses, -se) pumpkin

Kurierdienst m courier service

Kurort m health resort

Kurs m (-es, -e) course; FIN rate; (*for foreign currency*) exchange rate

kursiv 1. adj italic **2.** adv in italics

Kursleiter(in) m(f) course tutor; **Kursteilnehmer(in)** m(f) (course) participant

Kurve f (-, -n) curve; (*in road*) bend; **kurvenreich** adj (*road*) winding

kurz adj short; (*with time also*) brief; **~ vorher / darauf** shortly before / after; **kannst du ~ kommen?** could you come here for a minute?; **~ gesagt** in short; **kurzärmelig** adj short-sleeved; **kürzen** vt cut short; (*in length*) shorten; (*salary*) reduce; **kurzer-**

hand adv on the spot; **kurzfristig** adj short-term; **das Konzert wurde ~ abgesagt** the concert was called off at short notice; **Kurzgeschichte** f short story; **kürzlich** adv recently; **Kurznachrichten** pl news summary sg; **Kurzparkzone** f short-stay (*Brit*) (*or* short-term (*US*)) parking zone; **Kurzschluss** m ELEC short circuit; **kurzsichtig** adj short-sighted; **Kurzurlaub** m short holiday (*Brit*), short vacation (*US*)

Kusine f cousin

Kuss m (-es, Küsse) kiss; **küssen** vt, vr kiss

Küste f (-, -n) coast; (*strip of land*) shore; **Küstenwache** f coastguard

Kutsche f (-, -n) carriage; (*enclosed*) coach

Kuvert nt (-s, -s) envelope

Kuvertüre f (-, -n) coating

Kuwait nt (-s) Kuwait

KZ nt (-s, -s) abbr = **Konzentrationslager**; HIST concentration camp

L

Labor nt (-s, -e *or* -s) lab

Labyrinth nt (-s, -e) maze

lächeln vi smile; **Lächeln** nt (-s) smile; **lachen** vi laugh; **lächerlich** adj ridiculous

Lachs m (-es, -e) salmon

Lack m (-(e)s, -e) varnish; (*co-*

loured) lacquer; (*for car*) paint; **lackieren** vt varnish; (*car*) spray; **Lackschaden** m scratch (on the paintwork)

Ladegerät nt (battery) charger; **laden** (lud, geladen) vt a. IT load; (*guest*) invite; (*mo-*

bile phone etc) charge

Laden *m* (-s, *Läden*) shop; *(on window)* shutter; **Ladendieb(in)** *m(f)* shoplifter; **Ladendiebstahl** *m* shoplifting

Ladung *f* load; NAUT, AVIAT cargo

lag *imperf of* **liegen**

Lage *f* (-, -n) position, situation

Lager *nt* (-s, -) camp; COMM warehouse; TECH bearing; **Lagerfeuer** *nt* campfire; **lagern** *vt* store

Lagune *f* lagoon

lahm *adj* lame; *(dreary)* dull; **lähmen** *vt* paralyse; **Lähmung** *f* paralysis

Laib *m* (-s, -e) loaf

Laie *m* (-n, -n) layman

Laken *nt* (-s, -) sheet

Lakritze *f* (-, -n) liquorice

Lamm *nt* (-(e)s, *Lämmer*) *(also meat)* lamb

Lampe *f* (-, -n) lamp; *(in lamp)* bulb; **Lampenfieber** *nt* stage fright; **Lampenschirm** *m* lampshade

Lampion *m* (-s, -s) Chinese lantern

Land *nt* (-(e)s, *Länder*) land; *(nation)* country; *(German federal division)* state, Land; **auf dem ~(e)** in the country **Landebahn** *f* runway; **landen** *vt, vi* land

Länderspiel *nt* international *(match)*

Landesgrenze *f* national border, frontier; **Landeswäh-**

rung *f* national currency; **landesweit** *adj* nationwide

Landhaus *nt* country house; **Landkarte** *f* map; **Landkreis** *m* administrative region, ≈ district

ländlich *adj* rural

Landschaft *f* countryside; *(beautiful)* scenery; ART landscape; **Landstraße** *f* country road, B road *(Brit)*

Landung *f* landing; **Landungsbrücke** *f*, **Landungssteg** *m* gangway

Landwirt(in) *m(f)* farmer; **Landwirtschaft** *f* agriculture, farming; **landwirtschaftlich** *adj* agricultural

lang *adj* long; *(person)* tall; **ein zwei Meter ~er Tisch** a table two metres long; **den ganzen Tag ~** all day long; **langärmelig** *adj* long-sleeved; **lange** *adv* (for) a long time; **ich musste ~ warten** I had to wait (for) a long time; **ich bleibe nicht ~** I won't stay long; **es ist ~ her, dass wir uns gesehen haben** it's a long time since we saw each other; **Länge** *f* (-, -n) length; GEO longitude **langen** *vi fam* be enough; *fam (with hand)* reach *(nach* for); **mir langt's** I've had enough

Langeweile *f* boredom

langfristig 1. *adj* long-term **2.** *adv* in the long term

Langlauf *m* cross-country skiing

langsam 1. *adj* slow **2.** *adv* slowly

Langschläfer(in) *m(f)* (*-s, -*) late riser

längst *adv* **das ist ~ fertig** that was finished a long time ago; **sie sollte ~ da sein** she should have been here long ago; **als sie kam, waren wir ~ weg** when she arrived we had long since left

Langstreckenflug *m* long-haul flight

Languste *f* (*-, -n*) crayfish, crawfish (*US*)

langweilen *vt* bore; **ich langweile mich** I'm bored; **langweilig** *adj* boring

Laos *nt* (*-*) Laos

Lappen *m* (*-s, -*) cloth, rag; (*for dusting*) duster

läppisch *adj* silly; (*amount of money*) ridiculous

Laptop *m* (*-s, -s*) laptop

Lärche *f* (*-, -n*) larch

Lärm *m* (*-(e)s*) noise

las *imperf of* **lesen**

Lasche *f* (*-, -n*) flap

Laser *m* (*-s, -*) laser; **Laserdrucker** *m* laser printer

lassen (*ließ, gelassen*) *vi, vt* (*allow*) let; (*in a place, a condition*) leave; (*cease*) stop; **etw machen ~** have sth done; **sich** *dat* **die Haare schneiden ~** have one's hair cut; **jdn etw machen ~** make sb do sth; **lass das!** stop it!

lässig *adj* casual

Last *f* (*-, -en*) load; (*duty, obligation etc*) burden

Laster *nt* (*-s, -*) vice; *fam* truck, lorry (*Brit*)

lästern *vi* **über jdn/etw ~** make nasty remarks about sb/sth

lästig *adj* annoying; (*person*) tiresome

Last-Minute-Flug *m* last-minute flight; **Last-Minute-Ticket** *nt* last-minute ticket

Lastwagen *m* truck, lorry (*Brit*)

Latein *nt* (*-s*) Latin

Laterne *f* (*-, -n*) lantern; (*in street*) streetlight

Latte *f* (*-, -n*) slat; SPORT bar

Latz *m* (*-es, Lätze*) bib; **Lätzchen** *nt* bib; **Latzhose** *f* dungarees *pl*

lau *adj* (*wind, air*) mild

Laub *nt* (*-(e)s*) foliage; **Laubfrosch** *m* tree frog

Lauch *m* (*-(e)s, -e*) leeks *pl*; **eine Stange ~** a leek; **Lauchzwiebel** *f* spring onions *pl* (*Brit*), scallions *pl* (*US*)

Lauf *m* (*-(e)s, Läufe*) run; (*contest*) race; (*development*) course; **laufen** (*lief, gelaufen*) *vi, vt* run; walk; (*function*) work; **mir läuft die Nase** my nose is running; **was läuft im Kino?** what's on at the cinema?; **wie läuft's so?** how are things?; **laufend** *adj* running; (*month, expenses*) current; **auf dem Laufenden sein/halten** be/keep up-to-date; **Läufer** m (-s, -) (*carpet*) rug; (*in chess*) bishop; **Läufer(in)** m(f) SPORT runner; **Laufmasche** f ladder (*Brit*), run (*US*); **Laufwerk** nt IT drive

Laune f (-, -n) mood; **gute/schlechte ~ haben** be in a good / bad mood; **launisch** adj moody

Laus f (-, **Läuse**) louse

lauschen vi listen; (*secretly*) eavesdrop

laut 1. adj loudly; (*read*) aloud **3.** prep + gen or dat according to

läuten vt, vi ring

lauter adv fam nothing but

Lautsprecher m loudspeaker; **Lautstärke** f loudness; RADIO, TV volume

lauwarm adj lukewarm

Lava f (-, **Laven**) lava

Lavendel m (-s, -) lavender

Lawine f avalanche

leasen vt lease; **Leasing** nt (-s) leasing

leben vt, vi live; (*not be dead*) be alive; **wie lange ~ Sie schon hier?** how long have you been living here?; **von ... ~** (*food etc*) live on ...; (*~ occupation, activity*) make one's living from ...; **Leben** nt (-s, -) life; **lebend** adj living; **lebendig** adj alive; (*full of live*) lively; **lebensgefährlich** adj very dangerous; (*injury*) critical; **Lebensgefährte** m, **Lebensgefährtin** f

partner; **Lebenshaltungskosten** pl cost sg of living; **lebenslänglich** adj for life; **~ bekommen** get life; **Lebenslauf** m curriculum vitae (*Brit*), CV (*Brit*), resumé (*US*); **Lebensmittel** pl food sg; **Lebensmittelgeschäft** nt grocer's (shop); **Lebensmittelvergiftung** f food poisoning; **lebensnotwendig** adj vital; **Lebensretter(in)** m(f) rescuer; **Lebensstandard** m standard of living; **Lebenszeichen** nt sign of life

Leber f (-, -n) liver; **Leberfleck** m mole; **Leberpastete** f liver pâté

Lebewesen nt living being

lebhaft adj lively; (*memory, impression*) vivid

Lebkuchen m gingerbread

leblos adj lifeless

Leck nt leak

lecken 1. vi (*container, ship*) leak **2.** vt, vi lick

lecker adj delicious, tasty

Leder nt (-s, -) leather

ledig adj single

legal adj legal, lawful

leer adj empty; (*page*) blank; (*battery*) dead; **leeren** vt, vr empty; **Leerlauf** m (*gear*) neutral; **Leerung** f emptying; (*from postbox*) collection

legen 1. vt put, place; (*eggs*) lay **2.** vr lie down; (*storm, excitement*) die down; (*pain,* *feeling*) wear off

leger *adj* casual

Lehm *m* (-(e)s, -e) loam; (*for bricks etc*) clay

Lehne *f* (-, -n) arm(rest); back(rest); **lehnen** *vt, vr* lean

Lehrbuch *nt* textbook; **Lehre** *f* (-, -n) teaching; (*vocational*) apprenticeship; (*moral*) lesson; **lehren** *vt* teach; **Lehrer(in)** *m(f)* (-s, -) teacher; **Lehrgang** *m* course; **Lehrling** *m* apprentice; **lehrreich** *adj* instructive

Leibwächter(in) *m(f)* bodyguard

Leiche *f* (-, -n) corpse; **Leichenwagen** *m* hearse

leicht 1. *adj* light; (*task etc*) easy, simple; (*illness*) slight; **jdm ~ fallen** be easy for sb; **es sich** *dat* **~ machen** take the easy way out **2.** *adv* easily; (*a bit*) slightly; **Leichtathletik** *f* athletics *sg*; **Leichtsinnig** *adj* careless; (*stronger*) reckless

leid *adj* **jdn/etw ~ sein** be tired of sth/sb; **Leid** *nt* (-(e)s) grief, sorrow; **~ tun** → **leidtun**; **leiden** (*litt, gelitten*) *vi, vt* suffer (*an, unter* + *dat* from); **ich kann ihn/es nicht ~** I can't stand him/it; **Leiden** *nt* (-s, -) suffering; (*medical*) illness

Leidenschaft *f* passion; **leidenschaftlich** *adj* passionate

leider *adv* unfortunately; **wir**

müssen jetzt ~ gehen I'm afraid we have to go now; **~ ja/nein** I'm afraid so/not

leidtun *vi* **es tut mir/ihm ~** I'm/he's sorry; **er tut mir ~** I'm sorry for him

leihen (*lieh, geliehen*) *vt* **jdm etw ~** lend sb sth; **sich** *dat* **etw von jdm ~** borrow sth from sb; **Leihwagen** *m* hire car (*Brit*), rental car (*US*)

Leim *m* (-(e)s, -e) glue

Leine *f* (-, -n) cord; (*for washing*) line; (*for dog*) lead (*Brit*), leash (*US*)

Leinen *nt* (-s, -) linen; **Leinwand** *f* ART canvas; FILM screen

leise 1. *adj* quiet; (*music, steps etc*) soft **2.** *adv* quietly

Leiste *f* (-, -n) ledge; (*decorative*) strip; ANAT groin

leisten *vt* (*work*) do; (*accomplish*) achieve; **jdm Gesellschaft ~** keep sb company; **sich** *dat* **etw ~** (*as reward etc*) treat oneself to sth; **ich kann es mir nicht ~** I can't afford it

Leistenbruch *m* hernia

Leistung *f* performance; (*remarkable*) achievement

leiten *vt* lead; (*firm*) run; (*guide*) direct; ELEC conduct

Leiter *f* (-, -n) ladder

Leiter(in) *m(f)* (-s, -) (*of business*) manager

Leitplanke *f* (-, -n) crash barrier

Leitung *f* (*guidance*) direction; TEL line; (of firm) management; (for water) pipe; (for electricity) cable; **eine lange ~ haben** be slow on the uptake; Leitungswasser nt tap water

Lektion f lesson

Lektüre f (-, -n) reading; (books etc) reading matter

Lende f (-, -n) (meat) loin; (of beef) sirloin

lenken vt steer; (gaze) direct (auf + acc towards); **jds Aufmerksamkeit auf etw** acc ~ draw sb's attention to sth; Lenker m handlebars pl; Lenkrad nt steering wheel; Lenkradschloss nt steering lock; Lenkstange f handlebars pl

Leopard m (-en, -en) leopard

Lepra f (-) leprosy

Lerche f (-, -n) lark

lernen vt, vi learn; (for exam) study, revise

lesbisch adj lesbian

Lesebuch nt reader; lesen (las, gelesen) vi, vt read; (fruit) pick; Leser(in) m(f) reader; leserlich adj legible; Lesezeichen nt bookmark

Lettland nt Latvia

letzte(r, s) adj last; (most recent) latest; (definitive) final; **zum ~n Mal** for the last time; **am ~n Montag** last Monday; **in ~r Zeit** lately, recently; letztens adv recently

Leuchte f (-, -n) lamp, light; leuchten vi shine; (fire, dial) glow; Leuchter m (-s, -) candlestick; Leuchtreklame f neon sign; Leuchtstift m highlighter; Leuchtturm m lighthouse

leugnen 1. vt deny 2. vi deny everything

Leukämie f leukaemia (Brit), leukemia (US)

Leukoplast® nt (-(e)s, -e) Elastoplast® (Brit), Band--Aid® (US)

Leute pl people pl

Lexikon nt (-s, Lexika) encyclopaedia (Brit), encyclopedia (US)

Libanon m (-s) **der** ~ Lebanon

Libelle f dragonfly

liberal adj liberal

Libyen nt (-s) Libya

Licht nt (-(e)s, -er) light; Lichtblick m ray of hope; lichtempfindlich adj sensitive to light; Lichtempfindlichkeit f PHOT speed; Lichthupe f **die ~ betätigen** flash one's lights; Lichtjahr nt light year; Lichtmaschine f dynamo; Lichtschalter m light switch; Lichtschranke f light barrier; Lichtschutzfaktor m sun protection factor, SPF

Lichtung f clearing

Lid nt (-(e)s, -er) eyelid; Lidschatten m eyeshadow

lieb adj (kind) nice; (loved) dear; (lovely) sweet; **das ist ~ von dir** that's nice of you; **Lieber Herr X** Dear

Mr X; **Liebe** f (-, -n) love; **lieben** vt love; (sexually) make love to; **liebenswürdig** adj kind; **lieber** adv rather; **ich möchte ~ nicht** I'd rather not; **welches ist dir ~?** which one do you prefer?; → **gern, lieb**; **Liebesbrief** m love letter; **Liebeskummer m ~ haben** be lovesick; **Liebespaar** nt lovers pl; **liebevoll** adj loving; **Liebhaber(in)** m(f) (-s, -) lover; **lieblich** adj lovely; (wine) sweet; **Liebling** m darling; **Lieblings-** in cpds favourite; **liebste(r, s)** adj favourite; **liebsten** adv **am ~ esse ich ...** my favourite food is ...; **am ~ würde ich bleiben** I'd really like to stay

Liechtenstein nt (-s) Liechtenstein

Lied nt (-(e)s, -er) song; REL hymn

lief imperf of **laufen**

liefern vt deliver; (provide) supply; **Lieferung** f delivery

Liege f (-, -n) (at doctor's) couch; (for overnight stay) campbed; (in garden) lounger; **liegen** (lag, gelegen) vi lie; (be situated) be; **mir liegt nichts/ viel daran** it doesn't matter to me/ it matters a lot to me; **woran liegt es nur, dass ...?** why is it that ...?; **~ bleiben** (person) stay lying down; stay in bed; (thing) be left (behind); **~ lassen** (for-

get) leave behind; **Liegestuhl** m deck chair; **Liegestütz** m press-up (Brit), push-up (US); **Liegewagen** n RAIL couchette car

lieh imperf of **leihen**

ließ imperf of **lassen**

Lift m (-(e)s, -e or -s) lift, elevator (US)

Liga f (-, Ligen) league, division

light adj (cola) diet; (food) low-fat; low-calorie; (cigarettes) mild

Likör m (-s, -e) liqueur

lila adj inv purple

Lilie f lily

Limette f (-, -n) lime

Limo f (-, -s) fam fizzy drink (Brit), soda (US); **Limonade** f fizzy drink (Brit), soda (US); (lemon-flavoured) lemonade

Limone f (-, -n) lime

Limousine f (-, -n) saloon (car) (Brit), sedan (US); fam limo

Linde f (-, -n) lime tree

lindern vt relieve, soothe

Lineal nt (-s, -e) ruler

Linie f line; **Linienflug** m scheduled flight; **Linienrichter** m linesman; **liniert** adj ruled, lined

Linke f (-n, -n) left-hand side; (hand) left hand; POL left (wing); **linke(r, s)** adj left; **auf der ~n Seite** on the left, on the left-hand side; **links** adv on the left; **~ abbiegen**

turn left; **~ von** to the left of; **~ oben** at the top left; **Linksaußen** *m* left winger; **Linkshänder(in)** *m(f)* (-s, -) left-hander; **linksherum** *adv* to the left, anticlockwise; **Linksverkehr** *m* driving on the left

Linse *f* (-, -n) lentil; *(optical)* lens; **Linsensuppe** *f* lentil soup

Lippe *f* (-, -n) lip; **Lipgloss** *m* lip gloss; **Lippenstift** *m* lipstick

lispeln *vi* lisp

List *f* (-, -en) cunning; *(ruse)* trick

Liste *f* (-, -n) list

Litauen *nt* (-s) Lithuania

Liter *m* or *nt* (-s, -) litre

literarisch *adj* literary; **Literatur** *f* literature

Litschi *f* (-, -s) lychee, litchi

litt *imperf of* **leiden**

live *adv* RADIO, TV live

Lizenz *f* licence

Lkw *m* (-(s), -(s)) *abbr* = **Lastkraftwagen**; truck, lorry *(Brit)*

Lob *nt* (-(e)s) praise; **loben** *vt* praise

Loch *nt* (-(e)s, Löcher) hole; **lochen** *vt* punch; **Locher** *m* (-s, -) (hole) punch

Locke *f* (-, -n) curl; **locken** *vt* lure; *(hair)* curl; **Lockenstab** *m* curling tongs *pl* (*Brit*), curling irons *pl* (*US*); **Lockenwickler** *m* (-s, -) curler

locker *adj* *(screw, tooth)* loose; *(posture)* relaxed; *(person)* easy-going; **lockern** *vt, vr* loosen

lockig *adj* curly

Löffel *m* (-s, -) spoon; *einen ~ Mehl zugeben* add a spoonful of flour

log *imperf of* **lügen**

Loge *f* (-, -n) THEAT box

logisch *adj* logical

Lohn *m* (-(e)s, Löhne) reward; *(for work)* pay, wages *pl*

lohnen *vr* be worth it; *es lohnt sich nicht zu warten* it's no use waiting

Lohnerhöhung *f* pay rise (*Brit*), pay raise (*US*); **Lohnsteuer** *f* income tax

Lokal *nt* (-(e)s, -e) restaurant; pub (*Brit*), bar

Lokomotive *f* locomotive

London *nt* (-s) London

Lorbeer *m* (-s, -en) laurel; **Lorbeerblatt** *nt* GASTR bay leaf

los *adj* loose; *~!* go on!; *jdn/ etw ~ sein* be rid of sb/sth; *was ist ~?* what's the matter?, what's up?; *dort ist nichts/viel ~* there's nothing/a lot going on there

Los *nt* (-es, -e) lot, fate; *(in lottery etc)* ticket

löschen *vt* *(fire, light)* put out, extinguish; *(thirst)* quench; *(tape)* erase; *(data, line)* delete

lose *adj* loose

Lösegeld *nt* ransom

losen vi draw lots

lösen 1. vt (*knot, screw etc*) loosen; (*puzzle*) solve; CHEM dissolve; (*ticket for train etc*) buy **2.** vr (*wallpaper, paint etc*) come off; (*sugar etc*) dissolve; (*problem, difficulty*) (re)solve itself

losfahren irr vi leave; **losgehen** irr vi set out; (*begin*) start; **loslassen** irr vt let go

löslich adj soluble

Lösung f (*liquid, of puzzle, problem*) solution

loswerden irr vt get rid of

Lotterie f lottery; **Lotto** nt (*-s*) National Lottery; ~ **spielen** play the lottery

Löwe m (*-n, -n*) ZOOL lion; ASTR Leo; **Löwenzahn** m dandelion

Luchs m (*-es, -e*) lynx

Lücke f (*-, -n*) gap

lud imperf of **laden**

Luft f (*-, Lüfte*) air; (*of person*) breath; **Luftballon** m balloon; **luftdicht** adj airtight; **Luftdruck** m METEO atmospheric pressure; (*in tyre*) air pressure

lüften vt air; (*secret*) reveal

Luftfahrt f aviation; **Luftfeuchtigkeit** f humidity; **Luftfilter** m air filter; **Luftfracht** f air freight; **Luftmatratze** f airbed; **Luftpirat(in)** m(f) hijacker; **Luftpost** f air-mail; **Luftpumpe** f (*bicycle*) pump; **Luftröhre** f windpipe

Lüftung f ventilation

Luftverschmutzung f air pollution; **Luftwaffe** f air force; **Luftzug** m draught (*Brit*), draft (*US*)

Lüge f (*-, -n*) lie; **lügen** (*log, gelogen*) vi lie; **Lügner(in)** m(f) (*-s, -*) liar

Luke f (*-, -n*) hatch

Lumpen m (*-s, -*) rag

Lunchpaket nt packed lunch

Lunge f (*-, -n*) lungs pl; **Lungenentzündung** f pneumonia

Lupe f (*-, -n*) magnifying glass; **etw unter die ~ nehmen** fig have a close look at sth

Lust f (*-, Lüste*) joy, delight; (*inclination*) desire; ~ **auf etw** acc **haben** feel like sth; ~ **haben, etw zu tun** feel like doing sth

lustig adj amusing, funny; (*jovial*) cheerful

lutschen 1. vt suck **2.** vi ~ **an** + dat suck; **Lutscher** m (*-s, -*) lollipop

Luxemburg nt (*-s*) Luxembourg

luxuriös adj luxurious

Luxus m (*-*) luxury

Lymphdrüse f lymph gland; **Lymphknoten** m lymph node

Lyrik f (*-*) poetry

M

machbar *adj* feasible

machen 1. *vt* (*produce, cause*) make; (*carry out, accomplish*) do; (*cost*) be; *das Essen/einen Fehler ~* make dinner/a mistake; *ein Foto ~* take a photo; *was machst du?* what are you doing? (*as job*) what do you do (for a living)?; *das kann man doch nicht ~!* you can't do that; *das Bett ~* make the bed; *das Zimmer ~* do (or tidy (up)) the room; *was macht das?* how much is that?; *das macht zwanzig Euro* that's twenty euros; *einen Spaziergang ~* go for a walk; *Urlaub ~* go on holiday; *eine Pause ~* take a break; *einen Kurs ~* take a course; *das macht nichts* it doesn't matter 2. *vr sich an die Arbeit ~* get down to work

Macht *f* (*-s, Mächte*) power; mächtig *adj* powerful; *fam* enormous; machtlos *adj* powerless; *da ist man ~* there's nothing you can do (about it)

Mädchen *nt* girl; Mädchenname *m* maiden name

Made *f* (*-, -n*) maggot

Magazin *nt* (*-s, -e*) magazine

Magen *m* (*-s, - or Mägen*) stomach; Magenbeschwerden *pl* stomach trouble *sg*; Magen-Darm-Infektion *f* gastroenteritis; Magengeschwür *nt* stomach ulcer; Magenschmerzen *pl* stomachache *sg*

mager *adj* (*meat*) lean; (*person*) thin; (*cheese, yoghurt*) low-fat; Magermilch *f* skimmed milk; Magersucht *f* anorexia; magersüchtig *adj* anorexic

magisch *adj* magical

Magnet *m* (*-s or -en, -en*) magnet

mähen *vt, vi* mow

mahlen (*mahlte, gemahlen*) *vt* grind

Mahlzeit 1. *f* meal; (*for baby*) feed 2. *interj* enjoy your meal

mahnen *vt* urge; *jdn schriftlich ~* send sb a reminder; Mahngebühr *f* fine; Mahnung *f* warning; (*written*) reminder

Mai *m* (*-(s), -e*) May; → *Juni*; Maifeiertag *m* May Day; Maiglöckchen *nt* lily of the valley; Maikäfer *m* cockchafer

Mail *f* (*-, -s*) e-mail; Mailbox *f* IT mailbox; mailen *vi, vt* e-mail

Mais *m* (*-es, -e*) maize, corn (*US*); Maiskolben *m* corn cob; GASTR corn on the cob

Majestät f (-, -en) Majesty

Majonäse f (-, -n) mayonnaise

Majoran m (-s, -e) marjoram

Make-up nt (-s, -s) make-up

Makler(in) m(f) (-s, -) broker; (for houses etc) estate agent (Brit), realtor (US)

Makrele f (-, -n) mackerel

Makrone f (-, -n) macaroon

mal adv (in calculation) times, multiplied by; (in measurement) by; fam (in past) once; (in future) some day; **4~3 ist 12** 4 times 3 is (or equals) twelve; **da habe ich ~ gewohnt** I used to live there one day

Mal nt (-(e)s, -e) time; (on skin) mark; **jedes ~** every time; **ein paar ~** a few times

Malaria f (-, -) malaria

Malaysia nt (-s) Malaysia

Malbuch nt colouring book

Malediven pl Maldives pl

malen vt, vi paint; **Maler(in)** m(f) (-s, -) painter; **Malerei** f painting; **malerisch** adj picturesque

Mallorca nt (-s) Majorca, Mallorca

malnehmen irr vt multiply (mit by)

Malta nt (-s) Malta

Malz nt (-es) malt; **Malzbier** nt malt beer

Mama f (-, -s) mum(my) (Brit), mom(my) (US)

man pron you; (formal) one; (unspecified person) someone, somebody; (unspecified persons) they, people pl; **wie schreibt ~ das?** how do you spell that?; **~ sagt, dass ...** they (or people) say that ...

managen vt fam manage; **Manager(in)** m(f) (-s, -) manager

manche(r, s) pron some; (large number) many; **~ Politiker** many politicians pl, many a politician; **manchmal** adv sometimes

Mandant(in) m(f) client

Mandarine f mandarin, tangerine

Mandel f (-, -n) almond; **~n** ANAT tonsils pl; **Mandelentzündung** f tonsillitis

Manege f (-, -n) ring

Mangel m (-s, Mängel) lack; (scarcity) shortage (an + dat of); (imperfection) defect, fault; **mangelhaft** adj (goods) faulty; (mark in school) ≈ E

Mango f (-, -s) mango

Manieren pl manners pl

Maniküre f (-, -n) manicure

manipulieren vt manipulate

Manko nt (-s, -s) deficiency

Mann m (-(e)s, Männer) man; (spouse) husband; **Männchen** nt **es ist ein ~** (animal) it's a he; **männlich** adj masculine; BIO male

Mannschaft f SPORT, fig team; NAUT, AVIAT crew

Mansarde f (-, -n) attic
Manschettenknopf m cufflink
Mantel m (-s, Mäntel) coat
Mappe f (-, -n) briefcase; (cardboard, plastic) folder
Maracuja f (-, -s) passion fruit
Marathon m (-s, -s) marathon
Märchen nt fairy tale
Marder m (-s, -) marten
Margarine f margarine
Marienkäfer m ladybird (Brit), ladybug (US)
Marihuana nt (-s) marijuana
Marille f (-, -n) apricot
Marine f navy
marinieren vt marinate
Marionette f puppet
Mark nt (-(e)s) (in bone) marrow; (from fruit) pulp
Marke f (-, -n) (of food, cigarettes etc) brand; (of car, cooker etc) make; (for letter) stamp; (for meal) voucher, ticket; (made of metal etc) disc; (of water level etc) mark
markieren vt mark; **Markierung** f marking; (sign) mark
Markise f (-, -n) awning
Markt m (-(e)s, Märkte) market; **auf den ~ bringen** launch; **Markthalle** f covered market; **Marktlücke** f gap in the market; **Marktplatz** m market place; **Marktwirtschaft** f market economy
Marmelade f jam; (orange) marmalade
Marmor m (-s, -e) marble; **Marmorkuchen** m marble cake

Marokko nt (-s) Morocco
Marone f (-, -n) chestnut
Mars m (-) Mars
Marsch m (-(e)s, Märsche) march
Märtyrer(in) m(f) (-s, -) martyr
März m (-(es), -e) March; → **Juni**
Marzipan nt (-s, -e) marzipan
Maschine f machine; (of car) engine; **Maschinenbau** m mechanical engineering
Masern pl MED measles sg
Maske f (-, -n) mask; **Maskenball** m fancy-dress ball
Maskottchen nt mascot
maß imperf of **messen**
Maß nt (-es, -e) measure; (restraint) moderation; (scale) degree, extent; **~e** (of person) measurements; (of room) dimensions; **in gewissem/ hohem ~e** to a certain / high degree
Mass f (-, -(en)) litre of beer
Massage f (-, -n) massage
Masse f (-, -n) mass; (of people) crowd; (most) majority; **massenhaft** adv masses (or loads) of; **Massenkarambolage** f pile-up; **Massenmedien** pl mass media pl
Masseur(in) m(f) masseur / masseuse
maßgeschneidert adj (clothes) made-to-measure
massieren vt massage
mäßig adj moderate

medium

massiv *adj* solid; *fig* massive
maßlos *adj* extreme
Maßnahme *f* (-, *-n*) measure, step
Maßstab *m* rule, measure; *fig* standard; **im ~ von 1:5** on a scale of 1:5
Mast *m* (-(*e*)*s, -e(n)*) mast; ELEC pylon
Material *nt* (-*s, -ien*) material; (*for one's work*) materials *pl*; **materialistisch** *adj* materialistic
Materie *f* matter
Mathematik *f* mathematics *sg*; **Mathematiker(in)** *m(f)* mathematician
Matinee *f* (-, *-n*) ≈ matinee
Matratze *f* (-, *-n*) mattress
Matrose *m* (-*n, -n*) sailor
Matsch *m* (-(*e*)*s*) mud; (*snow*) slush; **matschig** *adj* (*ground*) muddy; (*snow*) slushy; (*fruit*) mushy
matt *adj* weak; (*not shiny*) dull; PHOT matt; (*in chess*) mate
Matte *f* (-, *-n*) mat
Matura *f* (-) *Austrian school-leaving examination*, ≈ A-levels (*Brit*), ≈ High School Diploma (*US*)
Mauer *f* (-, *-n*) wall
Maul *nt* (-(*e*)*s, Mäuler*) mouth; *fam* gob; **halt's ~!** shut your face (*or* gob); **Maulesel** *m* mule; **Maulkorb** *m* muzzle; **Maulwurf** *m* mole
Maurer(in) *m(f)* (-*s, -*) bricklayer

Mauritius *nt* (-) Mauritius
Maus *f* (-, *Mäuse*) mouse; **Mausefalle** *f* mousetrap; **Mausklick** *m* (-*s, -s*) mouse click; **Mauspad** *nt* (-*s, -s*) mouse mat (*or* pad); **Maustaste** *f* mouse key (*or* button)
Maut *f* (-, *-en*) toll; **Mautgebühr** *f* toll; **mautpflichtig** *adj* **~e Straße** toll road, turnpike (*US*); **Mautstelle** *f* tollbooth, tollgate; **Mautstraße** *f* toll road, turnpike (*US*)
maximal *adv* **ihr habt ~ zwei Stunden Zeit** you've got two hours at (the) most; **~ vier Leute** a maximum of four people
Mayonnaise *f* → **Majonäse**
Mazedonien *nt* (-*s*) Macedonia
MB *nt* (-, *-*), **Mbyte** *nt* (-, *-*) *abbr* = **Megabyte**; MB
Mechanik *f* mechanics *sg*; (*mechanism*) mechanics *pl*; **Mechaniker(in)** *m(f)* (-*s, -*) mechanic; **mechanisch** *adj* mechanical; **Mechanismus** *m* mechanism
meckern *vi* (*goat*) bleat; *fam* (*person*) moan
Mecklenburg-Vorpommern *nt* (-*s*) Mecklenburg-Western Pomerania
Medaille *f* (-, *-n*) medal
Medien *pl* media *pl*
Medikament *nt* medicine
Meditation *f* meditation; **meditieren** *vi* meditate
medium *adj* (*steak*) medium

Medizin f (-, -en) medicine (*gegen* for); **medizinisch** adj medical

Meer nt (-(e)s, -e) sea; **am ~** by the sea; **Meerenge** f straits pl; **Meeresfrüchte** pl seafood sg; **Meeresspiegel** m sea level; **Meerrettich** m horseradish; **Meerschweinchen** nt guinea pig

Megabyte nt megabyte

Mehl nt (-(e)s, -e) flour; **Mehlspeise** f sweet dish made from flour, eggs and milk

mehr 1. pron more; **~ will ich nicht ausgeben** I don't want to spend any more, that's as much as I want to spend; **was willst du ~** what do you want? 2. adv **immer ~** (**Leute**) more and more (people); **~ als fünf Minuten** more than five minutes; **es ist kein Brot ~ da** there's no bread left; **nie ~** never again; **mehrdeutig** adj ambiguous; **mehrere** pron several; **mehreres** pron several things; **mehrfach** adj multiple; (*done again*) repeated; **Mehrfachstecker** m multiple plug; **Mehrheit** f majority; **mehrmals** adv repeatedly; **mehrsprachig** adj multilingual; **Mehrwertsteuer** f value added tax, VAT; **Mehrzahl** f majority; (*in grammar*) plural

meiden (**mied**, **gemieden**) vt avoid

Meile f (-, -n) mile

mein pron my; **meine(r, s)** pron mine

meinen vt, vi think; say; (*want to say, intend*) mean; **das war nicht so gemeint** I didn't mean it like that

meinetwegen adv because of me; (*to please me*) for my sake; (*for my part*) as far as I'm concerned

Meinung f opinion; **meiner nach** in my opinion; **Meinungsumfrage** f opinion poll; **Meinungsverschiedenheit** f disagreement (*über* + acc about)

Meise f (-, -n) tit; **eine ~ haben** fam be crazy

Meißel m (-s, -) chisel

meist adv mostly; **meiste(r, s)** pron most; **die ~n** (**Leute**) most people; **die ~ Zeit** most of the time; **das ~** (**davon**) most of it; **die ~n von ihnen** most of them; **meistens** adv mostly; (*largely*) for the most part

Meister(in) m(f) (-s, -) master; SPORT champion; **Meisterschaft** f championship; **Meisterwerk** nt masterpiece

melden 1. vt report 2. vr report (*bei* to); (*in class*) put one's hand up; (*offer one's services*) volunteer; (*on phone, in response to advert*) answer; **Meldung** f announcement; (*account*) report; IT message

Melodie f tune, melody

Melone f (-, -n) melon

Memoiren pl memoirs pl

Menge f (-, -n) quantity; (of people) crowd; **eine ~** a lot (gen of)

Meniskus m (-, Menisken) meniscus

Mensa f (-, Mensen) canteen, cafeteria (US)

Mensch m (-en, -en) human being, man; (individual) person; **kein ~** nobody; **~!** wow!; (annoyed) bloody hell!; **Menschenmenge** f crowd; **Menschenrechte** pl human rights pl; **Menschenverstand** m **gesunder ~** common sense; **Menschheit** f humanity, mankind; **menschlich** adj human; (kind) humane

Menstruation f menstruation

Mentalität f mentality, mindset

Menthol nt (-s) menthol

Menü nt (-s, -s) set meal; IT menu; **Menüleiste** f IT menu bar

Merkblatt nt leaflet; **merken** vt notice; **sich** dat **etw ~** remember sth; **Merkmal** nt feature

Merkur m (-s) Mercury

merkwürdig adj odd

Messbecher m measuring jug

Messe f (-, -n) fair; REL mass

messen (maß, gemessen) **1.** vt measure; (temperature, pul-

se) take **2.** vr compete

Messer nt (-s, -) knife

Messing nt (-s) brass

Metall nt (-s, -e) metal

Meteorologe m, **Meteorologin** f meteorologist

Meter m or nt (-s, -) metre; **Metermaß** nt tape measure

Methode f (-, -n) method

Metzger(in) m(f) (-s, -) butcher; **Metzgerei** f butcher's (shop)

Mexiko nt (-s) Mexico

MEZ f abbr = **mitteleuropäische Zeit** = CET

miau interj miaow

mich pron acc of **ich**; me; **~ (selbst)** myself; **stell dich hinter ~** stand behind me; **ich fühle ~ wohl** I feel fine

mied imperf of **meiden**

Miene f (-, -n) look, expression

mies adj fam lousy

Miesmuschel f mussel

Mietauto nt → **Mietwagen**; **Miete** f (-, -n) rent; **mieten** vt rent; (car) hire (Brit), rent (US); **Mieter(in)** m(f) (-s, -) tenant; **Mietshaus** nt block of flats (Brit), apartment house (US); **Mietvertrag** m rental agreement; **Mietwagen** m hire car (Brit), rental car (US); **sich** dat **einen ~ nehmen** hire (Brit) (or rent (US)) a car

Migräne f (-, -n) migraine

Mikrofon nt (-s, -e) microphone

Mikrowelle f (-, -n), **Mikro-**

wellenherd *m* microwave (oven)

Milch *f* (-) milk; **Milcheis** *nt* ice-cream (*made with milk*); **Milchkaffee** *m* milky coffee; **Milchpulver** *nt* powdered milk; **Milchreis** *m* rice pudding; **Milchshake** *m* milk shake; **Milchstraße** *f* Milky Way

mild *adj* mild; (*judge*) lenient; (*friendly*) kind

Militär *nt* (-s) military, army

Milliarde *f* (-, -n) billion; **Milligramm** *nt* milligram; **Milliliter** *m* millilitre; **Millimeter** *m* millimetre; **Million** *f* million; **Millionär(in)** *m(f)* millionaire

Milz *f* (-, -en) spleen

Minderheit *f* minority

minderjährig *adj* underage

minderwertig *adj* inferior

Mindest- *in cpds* minimum; **mindeste(r, s)** *adj* least; **mindestens** *adv* at least

Mine *f* (-, -n) mine; (*in pencil*) lead; (*in ballpoint pen*) refill

Mineralwasser *nt* mineral water

Minibar *f* minibar; **Minigolf** *nt* miniature golf, crazy golf (*Brit*)

minimal *adj* minimal

Minimum *nt* (-s, *Minima*) minimum

Minirock *m* miniskirt

Minister(in) *m(f)* (-s, -) minister; **Ministerium** *nt* ministry; **Ministerpräsident(in)** *m(f)* Minister President (*Prime Minister of a Bundesland*)

minus *adv* minus; **Minus** *nt* (-, -) deficit; **im ~ sein** be in the red; (*account*) be overdrawn

Minute *f* (-, -n) minute

Minze *f* (-, -n) mint

mir *pron dat of ich*; (to) me; **kannst du ~ helfen?** can you help me?; **kannst du es ~ erklären?** can you explain it to me?; **ich habe ~ einen neuen Rechner gekauft** I bought (myself) a new computer; **ein Freund von ~** a friend of mine

mischen *vt* mix; (*cards*) shuffle; **Mischung** *f* mixture (*aus of*)

missachten *vt* ignore; **Missbrauch** *m* abuse; (*wrong use*) misuse; **missbrauchen** *vt* misuse (*zu for*); (*sexually*) abuse; **Misserfolg** *m* failure; **Missgeschick** *nt* mishap; **misshandeln** *vt* ill-treat

Mission *f* mission

misslingen (*misslang, misslungen*) *vi* fail; **misstrauen** *vt + dat* distrust; **Misstrauen** *nt* (-s) mistrust, suspicion (*gegenüber of*); **misstrauisch** *adj* distrustful; (*suspecting sth*) suspicious; **Missverständnis** *nt* misunderstanding; **missverstehen** *irr vt* misunderstand

Mist *m* (-(e)s) *fam* rubbish; (*from cows*) dung; (*as fertilizer*) manure

Mistel f (-, -n) mistletoe
mit 1. prep + dat with; (by means of) by; ~ **der Bahn** by train; ~ **der Kreditkarte bezahlen** pay by credit card; ~ **10 Jahren** at the age of 10; **wie wärs ~ ...?** how about ...? **2.** adv along, too; **wollen Sie ~?** do you want to come along?
Mitarbeiter(in) m(f) employee
mitbekommen irr vt fam catch; (learn about) hear; (understand) get
mitbenutzen vt share
Mitbewohner(in) m(f) flatmate (Brit), roommate (US)
mitbringen irr vt bring along; **Mitbringsel** nt (-s, -) small present
miteinander adv with one another; (jointly) together
miterleben vt see (with one's own eyes)
Mitesser m (-s, -) blackhead
Mitfahrgelegenheit f ≈ lift, ride (US); **Mitfahrzentrale** f agency for arranging lifts
mitgeben irr vt jdm etw ~ give sb sth (to take along)
Mitgefühl nt sympathy
mitgehen irr vi go/come along
mitgenommen adj worn out, exhausted
Mitglied nt member
mithilfe prep + gen or ~ **von** with the help of
mitkommen irr vi come

along; (understand) follow
Mitleid nt pity; ~ **haben mit** feel sorry for
mitmachen 1. vt take part in **2.** vi take part
mitnehmen irr vt take along; (tire) wear out, exhaust
mitschreiben irr **1.** vi take notes **2.** vt take down
Mitschüler(in) m(f) schoolmate
mitspielen vi (in team) play; (in game) join in; **in einem Film/Stück ~** act in a film/play
Mittag m midday; **gestern ~** at midday yesterday, yesterday lunchtime; **zu ~ essen** have lunch; **Mittagessen** nt lunch; **mittags** adv at lunchtime, at midday; **Mittagspause** f lunch break
Mitte f (-, -n) middle; ~ **Juni** in the middle of June; **sie ist ~ zwanzig** she's in her mid-twenties
mitteilen vt jdm etw ~ inform sb of sth; **Mitteilung** f notification
Mittel nt (-s -) means sg; (practical measure, way) method; MED remedy (gegen for)
Mittelalter nt Middle Ages pl; **mittelalterlich** adj medieval; **Mittelamerika** nt Central America; **Mitteleuropa** nt Central Europe; **Mittelfeld** nt midfield; **Mittelfinger** m middle finger; **mittelmäßig** adj mediocre; **Mittelmeer**

nt Mediterranean (Sea); Mittelohrentzündung *f* inflammation of the middle ear; Mittelpunkt *m* centre; **im ~ stehen** be the centre of attention

mittels *prep* + *gen* by means of

Mittelstürmer(in) *m(f)* striker, centre-forward

mitten *adv* in the middle; **auf der Straße/ in der Nacht** in the middle of the street/ night

Mitternacht *f* midnight

mittlere(r, s) *adj* middle; (*ordinary*) average

mittlerweile *adv* meanwhile

Mittwoch *m* (-s, -e) Wednesday; (**am**) **~** on Wednesday; (**am**) **~ Morgen/ Nachmittag/ Abend** (on) Wednesday morning/ afternoon/ evening; **diesen/ letzten/ nächsten ~** this/ last/ next Wednesday; **jeden ~** every Wednesday; **~ in einer Woche** a week on Wednesday, Wednesday week; mittwochs *adv* on Wednesdays; **~ abends** on Wednesday evenings

mixen *vt* mix; Mixer *m* (-s, -) (*kitchen appliance*) blender

mobben *vt* harass (or bully) (at work)

Möbel *nt* (-s, -) piece of furniture; **die ~** *pl* the furniture *sg*; Möbelwagen *m* removal van

mobil *adj* mobile; Mobiltelefon *nt* mobile phone

möblieren *vt* furnish

mochte *imperf of* **mögen**

Mode *f* (-, -*n*) fashion

Model *nt* (-s, -s) model

Modell *nt* (-s, -e) model

Modem *nt* (-s, -s) IT modem

Mode(n)schau *f* fashion show

Moderator(in) *m(f)* presenter

modern *adj* modern; (*stylish*) fashionable; modisch *adj* fashionable

Modus *m* (-, *Modi*) IT mode; *fig* way

Mofa *nt* (-s, -s) moped

mogeln *vi* cheat

mögen (*mochte, gemocht*) *vt*, *vi* like; **ich möchte ...** I would like ...; **ich möchte lieber bleiben** I'd rather stay; **möchtest du lieber Tee oder Kaffee?** would you prefer tea or coffee?

möglich *adj* possible; **so bald wie ~** as soon as possible; möglicherweise *adv* possibly; Möglichkeit *f* possibility; möglichst *adv* as ... as possible

Mohn *m* (-(e)s, -e) poppy; (*for cake etc*) poppy seed

Möhre *f* (-, -*n*), Mohrrübe *f* carrot

Mokka *m* (-s, -s) mocha

Moldawien *nt* (-s) Moldova

Molkerei *f* (-, -en) dairy

Moll *nt* (-) minor (key); **a~** A

minor

mollig *adj* cosy; (*person*) plump

Moment *m* (*-(e)s, -e*) moment; *im ~* at the moment; *einen ~ bitte!* just a minute; **momentan 1.** *adj* momentary **2.** *adv* at the moment

Monaco *nt* (*-s*) Monaco

Monarchie *f* monarchy

Monat *m* (*-(e)s, -e*) month; *sie ist im dritten ~* she's three months pregnant; **monatlich** *adj, adv* monthly; *~ 100 Euro zahlen* pay 100 euros a month (*or* every month); **Monatskarte** *f* monthly season ticket

Mönch *m* (*-s, -e*) monk

Mond *m* (*-(e)s, -e*) moon; **Mondfinsternis** *f* lunar eclipse

Mongolei *f* (*-*) **die ~** Mongolia

Monitor *m* IT monitor

monoton *adj* monotonous

Monsun *m* (*-s, -e*) monsoon

Montag *m* Monday; → **Mittwoch**; **montags** *adv* on Mondays; → **mittwochs**

Montenegro *nt* (*-s*) Montenegro

Monteur(in) *m(f)* (*-s, -e*) fitter; **montieren** *vt* assemble, set up

Monument *nt* monument

Moor *nt* (*-(e)s, -e*) moor

Moos *nt* (*-es, -e*) moss

Moped *nt* (*-s, -s*) moped

Moral *f* (*-*) morals *pl*; **moralisch** *adj* moral

Mord *m* (*-(e)s, -e*) murder; **Mörder(in)** *m(f)* (*-s, -*) murderer / murderess

morgen *adv* tomorrow; *~ früh* tomorrow morning

Morgen *m* (*-s, -*) morning; *am ~* in the morning; **Morgenmantel** *m* dressing gown; **Morgenmuffel** *m* **er ist ein ~** he's not a morning person; **morgens** *adv* in the morning; *um 3 Uhr ~* at 3 (o'clock) in the morning, at 3 am

Morphium *nt* (*-s*) morphine

morsch *adj* rotten

Mosaik *nt* (*-s, -e(n)*) mosaic

Mosambik *nt* (*-s*) Mozambique

Moschee *f* (*-, -n*) mosque

Moskau *nt* (*-s*) Moscow

Moskito *m* (*-s, -s*) mosquito; **Moskitonetz** *nt* mosquito net

Moslem *m* (*-s, -s*), **Moslime** *f* (*-, -n*) Muslim

Most *m* (*-(e)s, -e*) (unfermented) fruit juice; (*fermented, from apples*) cider

Motel *nt* (*-s, -s*) motel

motivieren *vt* motivate

Motor *m* engine; ELEC motor; **Motorboot** *nt* motorboat; **Motorenöl** *nt* engine oil; **Motorhaube** *f* bonnet (*Brit*), hood (*US*); **Motorrad** *nt* motorbike, motorcycle; **Motorradfahrer(in)** *m(f)* motorcyclist; **Motorroller** *m* (motor) scooter; **Motorschaden** *m* engine trouble

Motte f (-, -n) moth

Motto nt (-s, -s) motto

Mountainbike nt (-s, -s) mountain bike

Möwe f (-, -n) (sea)gull

Mücke f (-, -n) midge; (in the tropics) mosquito; **Mückenstich** m mosquito bite

müde adj tired

muffig adj (smell) musty; (face, person) grumpy

Mühe f (-, -n) trouble, pains pl; **sich** dat **große ~ geben** go to a lot of trouble

Mühle f (-, -n) mill; (for coffee) grinder

Mull m (-(e)s, -e) muslin; MED gauze

Müll m (-(e)s) rubbish (Brit), garbage (US)

Mullbinde f gauze bandage

Müllcontainer m waste container; **Mülleimer** m rubbish bin (Brit), garbage can (US); **Mülltonne** f dustbin (Brit), garbage can (US); **Müllwagen** m dustcart (Brit), garbage truck (US)

multikulturell adj multicultural

Multimedia- in cpds multimedia

Multiple-Choice-Verfahren nt multiple choice

multiple Sklerose f (-n, -n) multiple sclerosis

Multiplexkino nt multiplex (cinema)

multiplizieren vt multiply (mit by)

Mumie f mummy

Mumps m (-) mumps sg

München nt (-s) Munich

Mund m (-(e)s, Münder) mouth; **halt den ~!** shut up; **Mundart** f dialect; **Munddusche** f dental water jet

münden vi flow (in + acc into)

Mundgeruch m bad breath; **Mundharmonika** f (-, -s) mouth organ

mündlich adj oral

Mundschutz m mask; **Mundwasser** nt mouthwash

Munition f ammunition

Münster nt (-s, -) minster, cathedral

munter adj lively

Münzautomat m vending machine; **Münze** f (-, -n) coin; **Münzeinwurf** m slot; **Münzrückgabe** f coin return; **Münztelefon** nt pay phone; **Münzwechsler** m change machine

murmeln vt, vi murmur, mutter

Murmeltier nt marmot

mürrisch adj sullen, grumpy

Muschel f (-, -n) mussel; (empty) shell

Museum nt (-s, Museen) museum

Musical nt (-s, -s) musical

Musik f music; **musikalisch** adj musical; **Musiker(in)** m(f) (-s, -) musician; **Musikinstrument** nt musical in-

nachgeben

strument; **musizieren** *vi* play music

Muskat *m* (-(e)s) nutmeg

Muskel *m* (-s, -n) muscle; **Muskelkater** *m* ~ **haben** be stiff; **Muskelriss** *m* torn muscle; **Muskelzerrung** *f* pulled muscle; **muskulös** *adj* muscular

Müsli *nt* (-s, -) muesli

Muslim(in) *m(f)* (-s, -s) Muslim

Muss *nt* (-) must

müssen (musste, gemusst) *vi* must, have to; **er hat gehen ~** he (has) had to go; **sie müsste schon längst hier sein** she should have arrived a long time ago; **du musst**

es nicht tun you don't have to do it, you needn't do it; **ich muss mal** I need to got to the loo (*Brit*), I have to go to the bathroom (*US*)

Muster *nt* (-s, -) pattern, design; (*small quantity*) sample

Mut *m* (-(e)s) courage; **jdm ~ machen** encourage sb; **mutig** *adj* brave, courageous

Mutter 1. *f* (-, *Mütter*) mother **2.** *f* (-, -n) (*for bolt*) nut; **Muttersprache** *f* mother tongue; **Muttertag** *m* Mother's Day; **Mutti** *f* mum(my) (*Brit*), mom(my) (*US*)

mutwillig *adj* deliberate

Mütze *f* (-, -n) cap

Myanmar *nt* (-s) Myanmar

N

na *interj* ~ **also!**, ~ **bitte!** see?, what did I tell you?; ~ **ja** well; ~ **und?** so what?

Nabel *m* (-s, -) navel

nach *prep* + *dat* after; (*direction*) to; (*consistent with*) according to; ~ **zwei Stunden** after two hours, two hours later; **es ist fünf ~ sechs** it's five past (*Brit*) or after (*US*)) six; **der Zug ~ London** the train for (*or* to) London; ~ **rechts/links** to the right/left; ~ **Hause** home; ~ **oben/hinten/unten** up/back/down; ~ **und ~** gradually

nachahmen *vt* imitate

Nachbar(in) *m(f)* (-n, -n) neighbour; **Nachbarschaft** *f* neighbourhood

nachdem *conj* after; (*because*) since; **je ~ (ob/wie)** depending on (whether/how)

nachdenken *irr vi* think (*über* + *acc* about); **nachdenklich** *adj* thoughtful

nacheinander *adv* one after another (*or* the other)

Nachfolger(in) *m(f)* (-s, -) successor

nachforschen *vt* investigate

Nachfüllpack *m* refill pack

nachgeben *irr vi* give in (*jdm* to sb)

nachgehen *irr vi* follow (*jdm* sb); (*investigate*) inquire (*einer Sache dat* into sth); **die Uhr geht** (*zehn Minuten*) **nach** this watch is (ten minutes) slow

nachher *adv* afterwards; **bis ~!** see you later

Nachhilfe *f* extra tuition

nachholen *vt* catch up with; (*what one has missed*) make up for

nachkommen *irr vi* follow; **einer Verpflichtung ~** fulfil an obligation

nachlassen *irr* **1.** *vt* (*sum of money*) take off **2.** *vi* decrease, ease off; (*get worse*) deteriorate; **nachlässig** *adj* negligent, careless

nachlaufen *irr vi* run after, chase (*jdm* sb)

nachmachen *vt* imitate, copy (*jdm etw* sth from sb); (*fake*) counterfeit

Nachmittag *m* afternoon; **heute ~** this afternoon; **am ~** in the afternoon; **nachmittags** *adv* in the afternoon; **um 3 Uhr ~** at 3 (o'clock) in the afternoon, at 3 pm

Nachnahme *f* (-, -*n*) cash on delivery; **per ~** COD

Nachname *m* surname

Nachporto *nt* excess postage

nachprüfen *vt* check

nachrechnen *vt* check

Nachricht *f* (-, -*en*) (*piece of*) news *sg*; (*notification*) message; **Nachrichten** *pl* news *sg*

Nachsaison *f* off-season

nachschauen 1. *vi* **jdm ~** gaze after sb **2.** *vt* check

nachschicken *vt* forward

nachschlagen *irr vt* look up

nachsehen *irr vt* check

nachsenden *irr vt* forward

Nachspeise *f* dessert

nächste(r, s) *adj* next; (*in space*) nearest

Nacht *f* (-, *Nächte*) night; **in der ~** during the night; (*when dark*) at night; **Nachtclub** *m* nightclub; **Nachtdienst** *m* night duty; **~ haben** (*chemist's*) be open all night

Nachteil *m* disadvantage

Nachtflug *m* night flight; **Nachthemd** *nt* nightdress; (*for men*) nightshirt

Nachtigall *f* (-, -*en*) nightingale

Nachtisch *m* dessert, sweet (*Brit*); pudding (*Brit*)

Nachtleben *nt* nightlife

nachträglich *adv* **~ alles Gute zum Geburtstag!** Happy belated birthday

nachts *adv* at night; **um 11 Uhr ~** at 11 (o'clock) at night, at 11 pm; **um 2 Uhr ~** at 2 (o'clock) in the morning, at 2 am; **Nachtschicht** *f* night shift; **Nachttisch** *m* bedside table; **Nachtzug** *m* night train

Nachweis *m* (-*es*, -*e*) proof

Nachwirkung *f* after-effect

nachzahlen 1. *vi* pay extra **2.** *vt* **20 Euro ~** pay 20 euros extra

nachzählen *vt* check

Nacken *m* (-s, -) (nape of the) neck

nackt *adj* naked; (*facts*) plain, bare; **Nacktbadestrand** *m* nudist beach

Nadel *f* (-, -n) needle; (*with head*) pin

Nagel *m* (-s, *Nägel*) nail; **Nagelfeile** *f* nail-file; **Nagellack** *m* nail varnish (*or* polish); **Nagellackentferner** *m* (-s, -) nail-varnish (*or* nail-polish) remover; **Nagelschere** *f* nail scissors *pl*

nah(e) 1. *adj, adv* near(by); (*in time*) near; (*relative, friend*) close; **jdm ~e gehen** upset sb; **~e liegen** be obvious **2.** *prep + dat* near (to); close to; **Nähe** *f* (-) vicinity; **in der ~** nearby; **in der ~ von** near to

nähen *vt, vi* sew

nähere(r, s) *adj* (*explanation, investigation*) more detailed; **die ~ Umgebung** the immediate area; **Nähere(s)** *nt* details *pl*; **nähern** *vr* approach

nahezu *adv* virtually, almost

nahm *imperf of* **nehmen**

Nähmaschine *f* sewing machine; **Nähnadel** *f* (sewing) needle

nahrhaft *adj* nourishing, nutritious; **Nahrung** *f* food; **Nahrungsmittel** *nt* food

Naht *f* (-, *Nähte*) seam; MED stitches *pl*, suture; TECH join

Nahverkehr *m* local traffic

Nähzeug *nt* sewing kit

naiv *adj* naive

Name *m* (-ns, -n) name

nämlich *adv* that is to say, namely; (*because*) since

nannte *imperf of* **nennen**

Napf *m* (-(e)s, *Näpfe*) bowl, dish

Narbe *f* (-, -n) scar

Narkose *f* (-, -n) anaesthetic

Narzisse *f* (-, -n) narcissus

naschen *vt, vi* nibble

Nase *f* (-, -n) nose; **Nasenbluten** *nt* (-s) nosebleed; **~ haben** have a nosebleed; **Nasenloch** *nt* nostril; **Nasentropfen** *pl* nose drops *pl*

Nashorn *nt* rhinoceros

nass *adj* wet; **Nässe** *f* (-) wetness; **nässen** *vi* (*wound*) weep

Nation *f* (-, -en) nation; **national** *adj* national; **Nationalfeiertag** *m* national holiday; **Nationalhymne** *f* (-, -n) national anthem; **Nationalität** *f* nationality; **Nationalmannschaft** *f* national team; **Nationalspieler(in)** *m(f)* international (player)

NATO *f* (-) *abbr* = **North Atlantic Treaty Organization**; NATO, Nato

Natur *f* nature; **Naturkost** *f* health food; **natürlich 1.** *adj* natural **2.** *adv* naturally; (*certainly, obviously*) of course; **Naturpark** m nature reserve; **Naturschutz** m conservation; **Naturschutzgebiet** nt nature reserve; **Naturwissenschaft** f (natural) science; **Naturwissenschaftler(in)** m(f) scientist

Navigationssystem nt AUTO navigation system

n. Chr. abbr = **nach Christus**; AD

Nebel m (-s, -) fog, mist; **nebelig** adj foggy, misty; **Nebelscheinwerfer** m foglamp; **Nebelschlussleuchte** f AUTO rear fog-lamp

neben prep + acc or dat next to; (in addition to) apart from, besides; **nebenan** adv next door; **nebenbei** adv at the same time; (as an extra) additionally; (by the way) incidentally; **nebeneinander** adv side by side; **Nebenfach** nt subsidiary subject

nebenher adv (in addition) besides; (simultaneously) at the same time; (at the side) alongside

Nebenkosten pl extra charges pl, extras pl; **nebensächlich** adj minor; **Nebensaison** f low season; **Nebenstelle** f (of phone) extension; **Nebenstraße** f side street; **Nebenwirkung** f side effect

neblig adj foggy, misty

necken vt tease

Neffe m (-n, -n) nephew

negativ adj negative; **Negativ**

nt PHOT negative

nehmen (nahm, genommen) vt take; **jdm etw ~** take sth (away) from sb; **den Bus/ Zug ~** take the bus/train; **jdn/etw ernst ~** take sb/sth seriously

neidisch adj envious

neigen vi **zu etw ~** tend towards sth; **Neigung** f slope; (tendency) inclination; (interest) liking

nein adv no

Nektarine f nectarine

Nelke f (-, -n) carnation; (spice) clove

nennen (nannte, genannt) vt name; (by a name) call

Neonlicht nt neon light; **Neonröhre** f neon tube

Nepal nt (-s) Nepal

Neptun m (-s) Neptune

Nerv m (-s, -en) nerve; **jdm auf die ~en gehen** get on sb's nerves; **jdn ~** fam get on sb's nerves; **Nervenzusammenbruch** m nervous breakdown; **nervös** adj nervous

Nest nt (-(e)s, -er) nest; pej (place) dump

nett adj nice; (friendly) kind; **sei so ~ und ...** do me a favour and ...

netto adv net

Netz nt (-es, -e) net; (system) network; (electricity supply) mains, power (US); **Netzanschluss** m mains connection; **Netzwerk** nt IT network

neu adj new; (languages, history) modern; **die ~esten Nachrichten** the latest news; **Neubau** m new building; **neuerdings** adv recently; **Neuerung** f innovation; (change) reform

Neugier f curiosity; **neugierig** adj curious (auf + acc about); **ich bin ~, ob ...** I wonder whether (or if) ...

Neuheit f novelty; **Neuigkeit** f news sg; **Neujahr** nt New Year; **prosit ~!** Happy New Year; **neulich** adv recently, the other day

neun num nine; **neunhundert** num nine hundred; **neunmal** adv nine times; **neunte(r, s)** adj ninth; → **dritte; Neuntel** nt (-s, -) (fraction) ninth; **neunzehn** num nineteen; **neunzehnte(r, s)** adj nineteenth; → **dritte; neunzig** num ninety; **in den ~er Jahren** in the nineties; **Neunzigerjahre** pl nineties pl; **neunzigste(r, s)** adj ninetieth

neureich adj nouveau riche

Neurologe m, **Neurologin** f neurologist; **Neurose** f (-, -n) neurosis; **neurotisch** adj neurotic

Neuseeland nt New Zealand

Neustart m IT restart, reboot

neutral adj neutral

neuwertig adj nearly new

Nicaragua nt (-s) Nicaragua

nicht 1. adv not; **er kommt ~** he doesn't come; (on this occasion) he isn't coming; **sie wohnt ~ mehr hier** she doesn't live here any more; **gar ~** not at all; **ich kenne ihn auch ~** I don't know him either; **noch ~** not yet; **~ berühren!** do not touch **2.** pref non-

Nichte f (-, -n) niece

Nichtraucher(in) m(f) non-smoker; **Nichtraucherzone** f non-smoking area

nichts pron nothing; **ich habe ~ gesagt** I didn't say anything; **~ sagend** meaningless; **macht ~** never mind

Nichtschwimmer(in) m(f) non-swimmer

nicken vi nod

Nickerchen nt nap

nie adv never; **~ wieder** (or **mehr**) never again; **fast ~** hardly ever

nieder 1. adj low; (in status) inferior **2.** adv down; **niedergeschlagen** adj depressed; **Niederlage** f defeat

Niederlande pl Netherlands pl; **Niederländer(in)** m(f) Dutchman / Dutchwoman; **niederländisch** adj Dutch; **Niederländisch** nt Dutch

Niederlassung f branch

Niederösterreich nt Lower Austria; **Niedersachsen** nt Lower Saxony

Niederschlag m METEO precipitation; rainfall

niedlich adj sweet, cute

niedrig adj low

niemals adv never

niemand pron nobody, no one; **ich habe ~en gesehen** I haven't seen anyone; **~ von ihnen** none of them

Niere f (-, -n) kidney; **Nierensteine** pl kidney stones pl

nieseln vi impers drizzle; **Nieselregen** m drizzle

niesen vi sneeze

Niete f (-, -n) (losing ticket) blank; pej (person) failure; TECH rivet

Nigeria nt (-s) Nigeria

Nikotin nt (-s) nicotine; **nikotinarm** adj low in nicotine

Nilpferd nt hippopotamus

nippen vi sip; **an etw** dat **~** sip sth

nirgends adv nowhere

Nische f (-, -n) niche

Nitrat nt nitrate

Niveau nt (-s, -s) level; **sie hat ~** she's got class

nobel adj generous; fam classy, posh

Nobelpreis m Nobel Prize

noch 1. adv still; (in addition) else; **wer kommt ~?** who else is coming?; **~ nie** never; **~ nicht** not yet; **immer ~** still; **~ einmal** (once) again; **~ am selben Tag** that (very) same day; **~ besser/mehr/ jetzt** even better/more/ now; **wie heißt sie ~?** what's her name again?; **~ ein Bier, bitte** another beer, please **2.** conj nor; **nochmal(s)** adv

again, once more

Nominativ m nominative (case)

Nonne f (-, -n) nun

Non-Stop-Flug m nonstop flight

Nord north; **Nordamerika** nt North America; **Norddeutschland** nt Northern Germany; **Norden** m (-s) north; **Nordeuropa** nt Northern Europe; **Nordirland** nt Northern Ireland; **nordisch** adj Nordic; **Nordkorea** nt (-s) North Korea; **nördlich** adj northern; (course, direction) northerly; **Nordost(en)** m northeast; **Nordpol** m North Pole; **Nordrhein-Westfalen** nt (-s) North Rhine-Westphalia; **Nordsee** f North Sea; **nordwärts** adv north, northwards; **Nordwest(en)** m northwest; **Nordwind** m north wind

nörgeln vi grumble

Norm f (-, -en) norm; (technical, industrial) standard

normal adj normal; **normalerweise** adv normally

Norwegen nt (-s) Norway; **Norweger(in)** m(f) Norwegian; **norwegisch** adj Norwegian; **Norwegisch** nt Norwegian

Not f (-, Nöte) need; poverty; (distress) hardship; (emergency situation) trouble; **zur ~** if necessary; (with little *to spare*) just about

Notar(in) *m(f)* public notary

Notarzt *m*, **Notärztin** *f* emergency doctor; **Notarztwagen** *m* emergency ambulance; **Notausgang** *m* emergency exit; **Notbremse** *f* emergency brake; **Notdienst** *m* emergency service, after-hours service; **notdürftig** *adj* scanty; (*rough and ready*) makeshift

Note *f* (-, -*n*) (*in school*) mark, grade (*US*); MUS note

Notebook *nt* (-(*s*), -*s*) IT notebook

Notfall *m* emergency; **notfalls** *adv* if necessary

notieren *vt* note down

nötig *adj* necessary; **etw ~ haben** need sth

Notiz *f* (-, -*en*) note; **Notizblock** *m* notepad; **Notizbuch** *nt* notebook

notlanden *vi* make a forced (*or* emergency) landing; **Notruf** *m* emergency call; **Notrufnummer** *f* emergency number; **Notrufsäule** *f* emergency telephone

notwendig *adj* necessary

Nougat *m or nt* (-*s*, -*s*) nougat

November *m* (-(*s*), -) November; → **Juni**

Nr. *abbr* = **Nummer**; No., no.

Nu *m* **im ~** in no time

nüchtern *adj* sober; (*sto-*

mach) empty

Nudel *f* (-, -*n*) noodle; **~n** *pl* (*Italian*) pasta *sg*; **Nudelsuppe** *f* noodle soup

null *num* zero; TEL O (*Brit*), zero (*US*); **~ Fehler** no mistakes; **~ Uhr** midnight; **Null** *f* (-, -*en*) nought, zero; *pej* (*person*) dead loss; **Nulltarif** *m* **zum ~** free of charge

Nummer *f* (-, -*n*) number; **nummerieren** *vt* number; **Nummernschild** *nt* AUTO number plate (*Brit*), license plate (*US*)

nun 1. *adv* now; **von ~ an** from now on **2.** *interj* well; **~ gut!** all right, then; **es ist ~ mal so** that's the way it is

nur *adv* only; **nicht ~ ..., sondern auch ...** not only ..., but also ...

Nürnberg *nt* (-*s*) Nuremberg

Nuss *f* (-, *Nüsse*) nut; **Nussknacker** *m* (-*s*, -) nutcracker

Nutte *f* (-, -*n*) *fam* tart

nutz, nütze *adj* **zu nichts ~ sein** be useless; **nutzen, nützen 1.** *vt* use (*zu etw* for sth); **was nützt es?** what use is it? **2.** *vi* be of use; **das nützt nicht viel** that doesn't help much; **Nutzen** *m* (-*s*, -) usefulness; (*financial*) profit; **nützlich** *adj* useful

Nylon *nt* (-*s*) nylon

O

o *interj* oh

Oase *f* (-, -n) oasis

ob *conj* if, whether; **so als ~** as if; **und ~!** you bet

obdachlos *adj* homeless

oben *adv* at the top; (*in pile, on cupboard etc*) on (the) top; (*in house*) upstairs; (*in text*) above; **da ~** up there; **von ~ bis unten** from top to bottom; **siehe ~** see above

Ober *m* (-s, -) waiter

obere(r, s) *adj* upper, top

Oberfläche *f* surface; **oberflächlich** *adj* superficial; **Obergeschoss** *nt* upper floor

oberhalb *adv, prep + gen* above

Oberkörper *m* upper body; **Oberlippe** *f* upper lip; **Oberösterreich** *nt* Upper Austria; **Oberschenkel** *m* thigh

oberste(r, s) *adj* very top, topmost

Oberteil *nt* top; **Oberweite** *f* bust / chest measurement

Objekt *nt* (-(e)s, -e) object

objektiv *adj* objective

Objektiv *nt* lens

obligatorisch *adj* compulsory, obligatory

Oboe *f* (-, -n) oboe

Observatorium *nt* observatory

Obst *nt* (-(e)s) fruit; **Obstku-**chen *m* fruit tart; **Obstsalat** *m* fruit salad

obwohl *conj* although

Ochse *m* (-n, -n) ox

ocker *adj* ochre

öd(e) *adj* waste; (*fig*) dull

oder *conj* or; **~ aber** or else; **er kommt doch, ~?** he's coming, isn't he?

Ofen *m* (-s, Öfen) oven; (*for heating*) heater; (*using coal etc*) stove; (*kitchen appliance*) cooker, stove; **Ofenkartoffel** *f* baked (*or* jacket) potato

offen 1. *adj* open; (*honest*) frank; (*job*) vacant **2.** *adv* frankly; **~ gesagt** to be honest

offenbar *adj* obvious; **offensichtlich** *adj* evident, obvious

öffentlich *adj* public; **Öffentlichkeit** *f* public

offiziell *adj* official

offline *adj* IT offline

öffnen *vt, vr* open; **Öffner** *m* (-s, -) opener; **Öffnung** *f* opening; **Öffnungszeiten** *pl* opening times *pl*

oft *adv* often; **schon ~** many times; **öfter** *adv* more often (*or* frequently); **öfters** *adv* often, frequently

ohne *conj, prep + acc* without; **~ weiteres** without a second thought; (*without delay*) immediately; **~ mich** count me out

Ohnmacht f (*-machten pl*) unconsciousness; **in ~ fallen** faint; **ohnmächtig** *adj* unconscious; **sie ist ~** she has fainted

Ohr *nt* (*-(e)s, -en*) ear; (*faculty*) hearing

Öhr *nt* (*-(e)s, -e*) eye

Ohrenarzt *m*, **Ohrenärztin** f ear specialist; **Ohrenschmerzen** *pl* earache; **Ohrentropfen** *pl* ear drops *pl*; **Ohrfeige** f slap (in the face); **Ohrläppchen** *nt* earlobe; **Ohrringe** *pl* earrings *pl*

oje *interj* oh dear

okay *interj* OK, okay

Ökoladen *m* health food store; **ökologisch** *adj* ecological; **~e Landwirtschaft** organic farming

ökonomisch *adj* economic; (*money-saving*) economical

Ökosystem *nt* ecosystem

Oktober *m* (*-(s), -*) October; → **Juni**

Öl *nt* (*-(e)s, -e*) oil; **Ölbaum** *m* olive tree; **ölen** *vt* oil; TECH lubricate; **Ölfarbe** f oil paint; **Ölfilter** *m* oil filter; **Ölgemälde** *nt* oil painting; **Ölheizung** f oil-fired central heating; **ölig** *adj* oily

oliv *adj inv* olive-green; **Olive** f (*-, -n*) olive; **Olivenöl** *nt* olive oil

Ölsardine f sardine in oil; **Öl-**

teppich *m* oil slick; **Ölwechsel** *m* oil change

Olympiade f Olympic Games *pl*; **olympisch** *adj* Olympic

Oma f, **Omi** f (*-s, -s*) grandma, gran(ny)

Omelett *nt* (*-(e)s, -s*), **Omelette** f omelette

Omnibus *m* bus

onanieren *vi* masturbate

Onkel *m* (*-s, -*) uncle

online *adv* IT online

OP *m* (*-s, -s*) *abbr* = **Operationssaal**; operating theatre (*Brit*) (*or* room (*US*))

Opa *m*, **Opi** *m* (*-s, -s*) grandpa, grandad

Openairkonzert *nt* open-air concert

Oper f (*-, -n*) opera; (*building*) opera house

Operation f operation

Operette f operetta

operieren 1. *vi* operate **2.** *vt* operate on

Opernsänger(in) *m(f)* opera singer

Opfer *nt* (*-s, -*) sacrifice; (*person*) victim; **ein ~ bringen** make a sacrifice

Opium *nt* (*-s*) opium

Opposition f opposition

Optiker(in) *m(f)* (*-s, -*) optician

optimal *adj* optimal, optimum

optimistisch *adj* optimistic

oral *adj* oral; **Oralverkehr** *m* oral sex

orange *adj inv* orange; **Orange** f (*-, -n*) orange; **Oran-**

genmarmelade f marmalade; Orangensaft m orange juice

Orchester nt (-s, -) orchestra

Orchidee f (-, -n) orchid

Orden m (-s, -) REL order; MIL decoration

ordentlich 1. adj respectable; (orderly) tidy, neat 2. adv properly

ordinär adj common, vulgar; (joke) dirty

ordnen vt sort out; Ordner m (-s, -) (at events) steward; (for documents) file; Ordnung f order; (orderliness) tidiness; (geht) in ~! (that's) all right

Oregano m (-s) oregano

Organ nt (-s, -e) organ; voice

Organisation f organization; organisieren 1. vt organize; fam (obtain) get hold of 2. vr organize

Organismus m organism

Orgasmus m orgasm

Orgel f (-, -n) organ

Orgie f orgy

orientalisch adj oriental

orientieren vr get one's bearings; Orientierung f orientation; Orientierungssinn m sense of direction

original adj original; (real) genuine; Original nt (-s, -e) original; Originalfassung f original version

originell adj original; (humorous) witty

Orkan m (-(e)s, -e) hurricane

Ort m (-(e)s, -e) place; (small town) village

Orthopäde m (-n, -n), Orthopädin f orthopaedist

örtlich adj local; Ortschaft f village, small town; Ortsgespräch nt local call; Ortstarif m local rate; Ortszeit f local time

Ost east; Ostdeutschland nt Eastern Germany; HIST East Germany; Osten m (-s) east

Osterei nt Easter egg; Osterglocke f daffodil; Osterhase m Easter bunny; Ostermontag m Easter Monday; Ostern nt (-, -) Easter; an (or zu) ~ at Easter; frohe ~ Happy Easter

Österreich nt (-s) Austria; Österreicher(in) m(f) (-s, -) Austrian; österreichisch adj Austrian

Ostersonntag m Easter Sunday

Osteuropa nt Eastern Europe; Ostküste f east coast; östlich adj eastern; (course, direction) easterly; Ostsee f die ~ the Baltic (Sea); Ostwind m east(erly) wind

Otter m (-s, -) otter

out adj fam out; outen vt out

oval adj oval

Overheadprojektor m overhead projector

Ozean m (-s, -e) ocean; der Stille ~ the Pacific (Ocean)

Ozon nt (-s) ozone; Ozonloch

nt hole in the ozone layer; **Ozonschicht** *f* ozone layer;

Ozonwerte *pl* ozone levels *pl*

P

paar *adj inv* **ein ~** a few; **ein ~ Mal** a few times; **ein ~ Äpfel** some apples

Paar *nt* (-(e)s, -e) pair; (*married*) couple

pachten *vt* lease

Päckchen *nt* package; (*of cigarettes*) packet; (*sent by post*) small parcel; **packen** *vt* pack; (*get hold of*) grasp, seize; *fam* (*succeed with*) manage; *fig* (*film, story etc*) grip; **Packpapier** *nt* brown paper; **Packung** *f* packet, pack (*US*); **Packungsbeilage** *f* package insert

Pädagoge *m* (-n, -n), **Pädagogin** *f* teacher; **pädagogisch** *adj* educational

Paddel *nt* (-s, -) paddle; **Paddelboot** *nt* canoe; **paddeln** *vi* paddle

Paket *nt* (-(e)s, -e) packet; (*sent by post*) IT package; **Paketbombe** *f* parcel bomb

Pakistan *nt* (-s) Pakistan

Palast *m* (-es, **Paläste**) palace

Palästina *nt* (-s) Palestine; **Palästinenser(in)** *m(f)* (-s, -) Palestinian

Palatschinken *pl* filled pancakes *pl*

Palette *f* (*of painter*) palette;

(*for moving goods*) pallet; (*variety*) range

Palme *f* (-, -n) palm (tree); **Palmsonntag** *m* Palm Sunday

Pampelmuse *f* (-, -n) grapefruit

pampig *adj fam* cheeky; (*food etc*) gooey

Panda(bär) *m* (-s, -s) panda

panieren *vt* GASTR coat with breadcrumbs; **paniert** *adj* breaded

Panik *f* panic

Panne *f* (-, -n) AUTO breakdown; (*mishap*) slip; **Pannendienst** *m*, **Pannenhilfe** *f* breakdown (*or* rescue) service

Pant(h)er *m* (-s, -) panther

Pantoffel *m* (-s, -n) slipper

Pantomime *f* (-, -n) mime

Panzer *m* (-s, -) MIL (*vehicle*) tank

Papa *m* (-s, -s) dad(dy), pa (*US*)

Papagei *m* (-s, -en) parrot

Papaya *f* (-, -s) papaya

Papier *nt* (-s, -e) paper; **~e** *pl* (*ID*) papers *pl*; (*official texts*) papers, documents *pl*; **Papierkorb** *m* wastepaper basket; IT recycle bin; **Papiertaschentuch** *nt* (paper) tissue; **Papiertonne** *f* paper bank

Pappbecher *m* paper cup; **Pappe** *f* (-, -n) cardboard; **Pappkarton** *m* cardboard box; **Pappteller** *m* paper plate

Paprika *m* (-s, -s) *(spice)* paprika; *(vegetable)* pepper

Papst *m* (-(e)s, *Päpste)* pope

Paradeiser *m* (-s, -s) tomato

Paradies *nt* (-es, -e) paradise

Paragliding *nt* (-s) paragliding

Paragraph *m* (-en, -en) paragraph; LAW section

parallel *adj* parallel

Paranuss *f* Brazil nut

Parasit *m* (-en, -en) parasite

parat *adj* ready; *etw ~ haben* have sth ready

Pärchen *nt* couple

Parfüm *nt* (-s, -s *or -e)* perfume

Park *m* (-s, -s) park; **Parkanlage** *f* park; *(around building)* grounds *pl*; **Parkbank** *f* park bench

Parkdeck *nt* parking level; **parken** *vt, vi* park

Parkett *nt* (-s, -e) parquet flooring; THEAT stalls *pl* *(Brit)*, parquet *(US)*

Parkhaus *nt* multi-storey car park *(Brit)*, parking garage *(US)*

parkinsonsche Krankheit *f* Parkinson's disease

Parkkralle *f* AUTO wheel clamp; **Parklicht** *nt* parking

light; **Parklücke** *f* parking space; **Parkplatz** *m* parking space; *(for many cars)* car park *(Brit)*, parking lot *(US)*; **Parkscheibe** *f* parking disc; **Parkscheinautomat** *m* pay point; *(issuing ticket)* ticket machine; **Parkuhr** *f* parking meter; **Parkverbot** *nt* no-parking zone; *hier ist ~* you can't park here

Parlament *nt* parliament

Parmesan *m* (-s) Parmesan *(cheese)*

Partei *f* party

Parterre *nt* (-s, -s) ground floor *(Brit)*, first floor *(US)*

Partitur *f* MUS score

Partizip *nt* (-s, *-ien)* participle

Partner(in) *m(f)* (-s, -) partner; **Partnerschaft** *f* partnership; *eingetragene ~* civil partnership; **Partnerstadt** *f* twin town

Party *f* (-, -s) party; **Partymuffel** *m* (-s, -) party pooper; **Partyservice** *m* catering service

Pass *m* (-es, *Pässe)* pass; *(ID)* passport

passabel *adj* reasonable

Passagier *m* (-s, -e) passenger

Passamt *nt* passport office;

Passbild *nt* passport photo

passen *vi (size)* fit; *(colour, style)* go *(zu* with); *(not answer)* pass; *passt (es) dir morgen?* does tomorrow suit you?; *das passt mir gut* that suits me fine; passend *adj* suitable; (*in colour, style*) matching; (*appropriate*) fitting; (*time*) convenient

passieren *vi* happen

passiv *adj* passive

Passkontrolle *f* passport control

Passwort *nt* password

Paste *f* (-, -n) paste

Pastete *f* (-, -n) pie; (*small*) vol-au-vent; (*for spreading*) pâté

Pastor, in *m(f)* (-s, -en) minister, vicar

Pate *m* (-n, -n) godfather; **Patenkind** *nt* godchild

Patient(in) *m(f)* patient

Patin *f* godmother

Patrone *f* (-, -n) cartridge

Patsche *f* (-, -n) (*difficult situation*) mess; **patschnass** *adj* soaking wet

pauschal *adj* (*cost*) inclusive; (*judgment*) sweeping; **Pauschale** *f* (-, -n) flat rate; **Pauschalgebühr** *f* flat rate (charge); **Pauschalpreis** *m* flat rate; (*for hotel, trip*) all-inclusive price; **Pauschalreise** *f* package tour

Pause *f* (-, -n) break; THEAT interval; (*in cinema*) intermission; (*when speaking*) pause

Pavian *m* (-s, -e) baboon

Pavillon *m* (-s, -s) pavilion

Pay-TV *nt* (-s) pay-per-view television, pay TV

Pazifik *m* (-s) Pacific (Ocean)

PC *m* (-s, -s) *abbr* = **Personalcomputer**; PC

Pech *nt* (-s, -e) *fig* bad luck; **~ haben** be unlucky; **~ gehabt!** tough (luck)

Pedal *nt* (-s, -e) pedal

Pediküre *f* (-, -en) pedicure

Peeling *nt* (-s, -s) (facial / body) scrub

peinlich *adj* embarrassing, awkward; (*conscientious*) painstaking; **es war mir sehr ~** I was totally embarrassed

Peitsche *f* (-, -n) whip

Pelikan *m* (-s, -e) pelican

Pellkartoffeln *pl* potatoes *pl* boiled in their skins

Pelz *m* (-es, -e) fur; **pelzig** *adj* (*tongue*) furred

pendeln *vi* (*train, bus*) shuttle; (*person*) commute; **Pendelverkehr** *m* shuttle traffic; (*for commuters*) commuter traffic; **Pendler(in)** *m(f)* (-s, -) commuter

Penis *m* (-, -se) penis

Pension *f* (*money*) pension; (*period*) retirement; (*building*) guesthouse, B&B; **pensioniert** *adj* retired

Peperoni *f* (-, -) chilli

per *prep* + *acc* by, per; (*each*) per; (*not later than*) by

perfekt *adj* perfect

Periode *f* (-, -n) period

Perle *f* (-, -n) a. *fig* pearl

perplex *adj* dumbfounded

Person *f* (-, -en) person; **ein Tisch für drei ~en** a table for three; **Personal** *nt* (-s) staff, personnel; **Personalausweis** *m* identity card;

Personalien pl particulars pl; **Personenschaden** m injury to persons; **persönlich 1.** adj personal; (on letter) private **2.** adv personally; (oneself) in person; **Persönlichkeit** f personality

Peru nt (-s) Peru

Perücke f (-, -n) wig

pervers adj perverted

pessimistisch adj pessimistic

Pest f (-) plague

Petersilie f parsley

Petroleum nt (-s) paraffin (Brit), kerosene (US)

Pfad m (-(e)s, -e) path; **Pfadfinder** m (-s, -) boy scout; **Pfadfinderin** f girl guide

Pfahl m (-(e)s, **Pfähle**) post, stake

Pfand nt (-(e)s, **Pfänder**) security; (on bottle) deposit; (in game) forfeit; **Pfandflasche** f returnable bottle

Pfanne f (-, -n) (frying) pan

Pfannkuchen m pancake

Pfarrei f parish; **Pfarrer(in)** m(f) (-s, -) priest

Pfau m (-(e)s, -en) peacock

Pfeffer m (-s, -) pepper; **Pfefferkuchen** m gingerbread; **Pfefferminze** f (-e) peppermint; **Pfefferminztee** m peppermint tea; **Pfeffermühle** f pepper mill; **Pfefferstreuer** m (-s, -) pepper pot

Pfeife f (-, -n) (for tobacco, of organ) whistle; pfeifen (pfiff, gepfiffen) vt, vi whistle

Pfeil m (-(e)s, -e) arrow

Pferd nt (-(e)s, -e) horse; **Pferdeschwanz** m ponytail; **Pferdestall** m stable

pfiff imperf of **pfeifen**

Pfifferling m chanterelle

Pfingsten nt (-, -) Whitsun, Pentecost (US); **Pfingstmontag** m Whit Monday; **Pfingstsonntag** m Whit Sunday, Pentecost (US); **Pfingstrose** f peony

Pfirsich m (-s, -e) peach

Pflanze f (-, -n) plant; pflanzen vt plant; **Pflanzenfett** nt vegetable fat

Pflaster nt (-s, -) (for wound) plaster, Band Aid® (US); (on road) road surface, pavement (US)

Pflaume f (-, -n) plum

Pflege f (-, -n) care; (of patient) nursing; (of car, machine) maintenance; **pflegebedürftig** adj in need of care; **pflegeleicht** adj easy-care; pflegen vt look after; (patient) nurse; (relations) foster; (fingernails, face) take care of; (data) maintain; **Pflegepersonal** nt nursing staff; **Pflegeversicherung** f long-term care insurance

Pflicht f (-, -en) duty; SPORT compulsory section; **pflichtbewusst** adj conscientious; **Pflichtfach** nt compulsory subject

pflücken vt pick

Pforte f (-, -n) gate; **Pförtner(in)** m(f) (-s, -) porter

Pfosten m (-s, -) post

Pfote f (-, -n) paw

pfui interj ugh

Pfund nt (-(e)s, -e) pound

pfuschen vi fam be sloppy

Pfütze f (-, -n) puddle

Phantasie f → **Fantasie**; **phantastisch** adj → **fantastisch**

Phase f (-, -n) phase

Philippinen pl Philippines pl

Philosophie f philosophy

Photo nt → **Foto**

pH-neutral adj pH-balanced; **pH-Wert** m pH-value

Physalis f (-, Physalen) physalis

Physik f physics sg

physisch adj physical

Pianist(in) m(f) (-en, -en) pianist

Pickel m (-s, -) pimple; (tool) pickaxe

Picknick nt (-s, -e or -s) picnic; **ein ~ machen** have a picnic

piepsen vi chirp

piercen vt **sich die Nase ~ lassen** have one's nose pierced; **Piercing** nt (-s) (body) piercing

pieseln vi fam pee

Pik nt (-, -) (card suit) spades pl

pikant adj spicy

Pilger(in) m(f) pilgrim; **Pilgerfahrt** f pilgrimage

Pille f (-, -n) pill; **sie nimmt die ~** she's on the pill

Pilot(in) m(f) (-en, -en) pilot

Pilz m (-es, -e) mushroom; (poisonous) toadstool; MED fungus

PIN f (-, -s) PIN (number)

pingelig adj fam fussy

Pinguin m (-s, -e) penguin

Pinie f pine; **Pinienkern** m pine nut

pink adj shocking pink

pinkeln vi fam pee

Pinsel m (-s, -) (paint)brush

Pinzette f tweezers pl

Pistazie f pistachio

Piste f (-, -n) piste; AVIAT runway

Pistole f (-, -n) pistol

Pixel nt (-s) IT pixel

Pizza f (-, -s) pizza; **Pizzaservice** m pizza delivery service; **Pizzeria** f (-, Pizzerien) pizzeria

Pkw m (-(s), -(s)) abbr = **Personenkraftwagen**; car

Plakat nt poster

Plan m (-(e)s, Pläne) plan; (of town) map; **planen** vt plan

Planet m (-en, -en) planet; **Planetarium** nt planetarium

planmäßig adj scheduled

Plan(t)schbecken nt paddling pool; **plan(t)schen** vi splash around

Planung f planning

Plastik 1. f sculpture **2.** nt (-s) plastic; **Plastikfolie** f plastic film; **Plastiktüte** f plastic bag

Platin nt (-s) platinum

platsch interj splash

platt adj flat; fam (surprised)

flabbergasted; *fig (remarks etc)* flat, boring

Platte f (-, -n) PHOT, TECH, GASTR plate; *(stone slab)* flag; *(LP)* record; **Plattenspieler** m record player

Plattform f platform; **Plattfuß** m flat foot; *(on vehicle)* flat (tyre)

Platz m *(-es, Plätze)* place; *(in train, theatre etc)* seat; *(vacant area)* space, room; *(in town)* square; *(for sports)* playing field; **nehmen Sie ~** please sit down, take a seat; **ist dieser ~ frei?** is this seat taken?

Plätzchen nt spot; *(sweet food)* biscuit

platzen vi burst; *(bomb)* explode

Platzkarte f seat reservation; **Platzreservierung** f seat reservation; **Platzverweis** m **er erhielt einen ~** he was sent off; **Platzwunde** f laceration, cut

plaudern vi chat, talk

pleite adj fam broke; **Pleite** f (-, -n) bankruptcy; fam *(party, play etc)* flop

Plombe f (-, -n) lead seal; *(in tooth)* filling; **plombieren** vt *(tooth)* fill

plötzlich **1.** adj sudden **2.** adv suddenly, all at once

plumps interj thud; *(in liquid)* plop

Plural m *(-s, -e)* plural

plus adv plus; **fünf ~ sieben**

ist zwölf five plus seven is *(or are)* twelve; **zehn Grad ~** ten degrees above zero; **Plus** nt (-, -) plus; FIN profit; *(benefit)* advantage

Plüsch m *(-(e)s, -e)* plush

Pluto m Pluto

Po m *(-s, -s)* fam bottom, bum

Pocken pl smallpox sg

poetisch adj poetic

Pointe f (-, -n) punch line

Pokal m *(-s, -e)* goblet; SPORT cup

pökeln vt pickle

Pol m *(-s, -e)* pole

Pole m *(-n, -n)* Pole; **Polen** nt *(-s)* Poland

Police f (-, -n) *(insurance)* policy

polieren vt polish

Polin f Pole, Polish woman

Politik f politics sg; *(course of action)* policy; **Politiker(in)** m(f) politician; **politisch** adj political

Politur f polish

Polizei f police pl; **Polizeibeamte(r)** m, **Polizeibeamtin** f police officer; **Polizeirevier** nt, **Polizeiwache** f police station; **Polizist(in)** m(f) policeman/ -woman

Pollen m *(-s, -)* pollen; **Pollenflug** m *(-s)* pollen count

polnisch adj Polish; **Polnisch** nt Polish

Polo nt *(-s)* polo; **Polohemd** nt polo shirt

Polterabend m party prior to a wedding, at which old

crockery is smashed to bring good luck

Polyester *m* (-s, -) polyester

Polypen *pl* MED adenoids *pl*

Pommes frites *pl* chips *pl* (*Brit*), French fries *pl* (*US*)

Pony 1. *m* (-s, -s) (*hairstyle*) fringe (*Brit*), bangs *pl* (*US*) **2.** *nt* (-s, -s) (*horse*) pony

Popcorn *nt* (-s) popcorn

Popmusik *f* pop (music)

populär *adj* popular

Pore *f* (-, -n) pore

Pornografie *f* pornography

Porree *m* (-s, -s) leeks *pl*; *eine Stange ~* a leek

Portemonnaie, Portmonee *nt* (-s, -s) purse

Portion *f* portion, helping

Porto *nt* (-s, -s) postage

Portrait, Porträt *nt* (-s, -s) portrait

Portugal *nt* (-s) Portugal; **Portugiese** *m* (-n, -n) Portuguese; **Portugiesin** *f* (-, -nen) Portuguese; **portugiesisch** *adj* Portuguese; **Portugiesisch** *nt* Portuguese

Portwein *m* (-s, -e) port

Porzellan *nt* (-s, -e) china

Posaune *f* (-, -n) trombone

Position *f* position

positiv *adj* positive

Post® *f* (-, -en) post office; (*letters*) post (*Brit*), mail; **Postamt** *nt* post office; **Postanweisung** *f* postal order (*Brit*), money order (*US*); **Postbank** *f* German post office bank; **Postbote** *m*, **-bo-**

tin *f* postman / -woman

Posten *m* (-s, -) post, position

Poster *nt* (-s, -) poster

Postfach *nt* post-office box, PO box; **Postkarte** *f* postcard; **Postleitzahl** *f* postcode (*Brit*), zip code (*US*)

Poststempel *m* postmark

Potenz *f* MATH power; (*of man*) potency

PR *f* (-, -s) *abbr* = *Public Relations*; PR

prächtig *adj* splendid

prahlen *vi* boast, brag

Praktikant(in) *m(f)* trainee; **Praktikum** *nt* (-s, Praktika) practical training; **praktisch** *adj* practical; *~er Arzt* general practitioner

Praline *f* chocolate

Prämie *f* (*for insurance*) premium; (*as recompense*) reward; (*from employer*) bonus

Präservativ *nt* condom

Präsident(in) *m(f)* president

Praxis *f* (-, Praxen) practice; (*treatment room*) surgery; (*of lawyer*) office

präzise *adj* precise, exact

predigen *vt, vi* preach; **Predigt** *f* (-, -en) sermon

Preis *m* (-es, -e) price; (*for winner*) prize; **Preisausschreiben** *nt* competition

Preiselbeere *f* cranberry

preisgünstig *adj* inexpensive; **Preisschild** *nt* price tag; **Preisträger(in)** *m(f)* prizewinner; **preiswert** *adj* inexpensive

Prellung f bruise

Premiere f (-, -n) premiere, first night

Premierminister(in) m(f) prime minister, premier

Presse f (-, -n) press

pressen vt press

prickeln vi tingle

Priester(in) m(f) (-s, -) priest / (woman) priest

Primel f (-, -n) primrose

primitiv adj primitive

Prinz m (-en, -en) prince; **Prinzessin** f princess

Prinzip nt (-s, -ien) principle; **im ~** basically; **aus ~** on principle

privat adj private; **Privatfernsehen** nt commercial television; **Privatgrundstück** nt private property; **privatisieren** vt privatize; **Privatquartier** nt private accommodation

pro prep + acc per; **5 Euro ~ Stück/ Person** 5 euros each/ per person; **Pro** nt (-s) pro

Probe f (-, -n) test; (small quantity) sample; THEAT rehearsal; **Probefahrt** f test drive; **eine ~ machen** go for a test drive; **Probezeit** f trial period; **probieren** vt, vi try; (wine, food) taste, sample

Problem nt (-s, -e) problem

Produkt nt (-(e)s, -e) product; **Produktion** f production;

(amount produced) output; **produzieren** vt produce

Professor(in) m(f) (-s, -en) professor

Profi m (-s, -s) pro

Profil nt (-s, -e) profile; (of tyre, sole of shoe) tread

Profit m (-(e)s, -e) profit; **profitieren** vi profit (von from)

Prognose f (-, -n) prediction; (of weather) forecast

Programm nt (-s, -e) programme; IT program; TV channel; **Programmheft** nt programme; **programmieren** vt program; **Programmierer(in)** m(f) (-s, -) programmer

Projekt nt (-(e)s, -e) project

Projektor m projector

Promenade f (-, -n) promenade

Promille nt (-(s), -) (blood) alcohol level; **0,8 ~** 0.08 per cent; **Promillegrenze** f legal alcohol limit

prominent adj prominent; **Prominenz** f VIPs pl, prominent figures pl; fam (celebrities) the glitterati pl

Propeller m (-s, -) propeller

prosit interj cheers

Prospekt m (-(e)s, -e) leaflet, brochure

prost interj cheers

Prostituierte(r) mf prostitute

Protest m (-(e)s, -e) protest

Protestant(in) m(f) Protestant; **protestantisch** adj Protestant

protestieren vi protest (*gegen* against)
Prothese f (-, -n) artificial arm/leg; (*false teeth*) dentures pl
Protokoll nt (-s, -e) (*of meeting*) minutes pl; IT protocol; (*given to police*) statement
protzen vi show off; **protzig** adj flashy
Proviant m (-s, -e) provisions pl
Provider m (-s, -) IT (service) provider
Provinz f (-, -en) province
Provision f COMM commission
provisorisch adj provisional
provozieren vt provoke
Prozent nt (-(e)s, -e) per cent
Prozess m (-es, -e) process; LAW trial; (*lawsuit*) (court) case; **prozessieren** vi go to law (*mit* against)
Prozession f procession
Prozessor m (-s, -en) IT processor
prüde adj prudish
prüfen vt test; (*verify*) check; **Prüfung** f exam; (*verification*) check; **eine ~ machen** take an exam
Prügelei f fight; **prügeln 1.** vt beat **2.** vr fight
PS 1. abbr = **Pferdestärke**; hp **2.** abbr = **Postskript(um)**; PS
pseudo- pref pseudo; **Pseudonym** nt (-s, -e) pseudonym
pst interj ssh
Psychiater(in) m(f) (-s, -) psychiatrist; **psychisch** adj

psychological; (*illness*) mental; **Psychoanalyse** f psychoanalysis; **Psychologe** m (-n, -n), **Psychologin** f psychologist; **Psychologie** f psychology; **psychosomatisch** adj psychosomatic; **Psychoterror** m psychological intimidation; **Psychotherapie** f psychotherapy
Pubertät f puberty
Publikum nt (-s) audience; SPORT crowd
Pudding m (-s, -e *or* -s) blancmange
Pudel m (-s, -) poodle
Puder m (-s, -) powder; **Puderzucker** m icing sugar
Puerto Rico nt (-s) Puerto Rico
Pulli m (-s, -s), **Pullover** m (-s, -) sweater, pullover, jumper (*Brit*)
Puls m (-es, -e) pulse
Pulver nt (-s, -) powder; **Pulverkaffee** m instant coffee; **Pulverschnee** m powder snow
Pumpe f (-, -n) pump; **pumpen** vt pump; fam (*to sb*) lend; fam (*from sb*) borrow
Pumps pl court shoes pl (*Brit*), pumps pl (*US*)
Punk m (-s, -s) (*music, person*) punk
Punkt m (-(e)s, -e) point; (*in pattern*) dot; (*punctuation mark*) full stop (*Brit*), period (*US*); **~ zwei Uhr** at two o'clock sharp

pünktlich *adj* punctual, on time; Pünktlichkeit *f* punctuality

Punsch *m* (-(e)s, -e) punch

Pupille *f* (-, -n) pupil

Puppe *f* (-, -n) doll

pur *adj* pure; (*absolute*) sheer; (*whisky*) neat

Püree *nt* (-s, -s) puree; mashed potatoes *pl*

Puste *f* (-) *fam* puff; **außer ~ sein** be puffed; pusten *vi* blow; (*pant*) puff

Pute *f* (-, -n) turkey

Putz *m* (-es) (*on wall*) plaster

putzen *vt* clean; **sich** *dat* **die Nase ~** blow one's nose; **sich** *dat* **die Zähne ~** brush one's teeth; Putzfrau *f* cleaner; Putzlappen *m* cloth; Putzmittel *nt* cleaning agent, cleaner

Puzzle *nt* (-s, -s) jigsaw (puzzle)

Pyjama *m* (-s, -s) pyjamas *pl*

Pyramide *f* (-, -n) pyramid

Python *m* (-s, -s) python

Q

Quadrat *nt* square; quadratisch *adj* square; Quadratmeter *m* square metre

quaken *vi* (*frog*) croak; (*duck*) quack

Qual *f* (-, -en) pain, agony; (*mental*) anguish; quälen **1.** *vt* torment **2.** *vr* struggle; (*mentally*) torment oneself; Quälerei *f* torture, torment

qualifizieren *vt*, *vr* qualify; (*classify*) label

Qualität *f* quality

Qualle *f* (-, -n) jellyfish

Qualm *m* (-(e)s) thick smoke; qualmen *vi*, *vi* smoke

Quantität *f* quantity

Quarantäne *f* (-, -n) quarantine

Quark *m* (-s) quark; *fam* (*nonsense*) rubbish

Quartett *nt* (-s, -e) quartet;

(*card game*) happy families *sg*

Quartier *nt* (-s, -e) accommodation

quasi *adv* more or less

Quatsch *m* (-es) *fam* rubbish; quatschen *vi fam* chat

Quecksilber *nt* mercury

Quelle *f* (-, -n) spring; (*of river*) source

quer *adv* crossways, diagonally; at right angles; Querflöte *f* flute; Querschnitt *m* cross section; querschnittsgelähmt *adj* paraplegic; Querstraße *f* side street

quetschen *vt* squash, crush; MED bruise; Quetschung *f* bruise

Queue *m* (-s, -s) (*billiard*) cue

quietschen *vi* squeal; (*door, bed*) squeak; (*brakes*)

screech
Quirl m (-s, -e) whisk
quitt adj quits, even
Quitte f (-, -n) quince

Quittung f receipt
Quiz nt (-, -) quiz
Quote f (-, -n) rate; COMM quota

R

Rabatt m (-(e)s, -e) discount
Rabbi m (-(s), -s) rabbi; Rabbiner m (-s, -) rabbi
Rabe m (-n, -n) raven
Rache f (-) revenge, vengeance
Rachen m (-s, -) throat
rächen 1. vt avenge 2. vr take (one's) revenge (an + dat on)
Rad nt (-(e)s, Räder) wheel; (vehicle) bike; ~ fahren cycle; mit dem ~ fahren go by bike
Radar m or nt (-s) radar; Radarfalle f speed trap; Radarkontrolle f radar speed check
radeln vi fam cycle; Radfahrer(in) m(f) (-s, -) cyclist; Radfahrweg m cycle track (or path)
Radicchio m (-s) radicchio
radieren vt rub out, erase; Radiergummi m rubber (Brit), eraser; Radierung f ART etching
Radieschen nt radish
radikal adj radical
Radio nt (-s, -s) radio; im ~ on the radio
radioaktiv adj radioactive
Radiologe m (-n, -n), Radio-

login f radiologist
Radiowecker m radio alarm (clock)
Radkappe f AUTO hub cap
Radler(in) m(f) (-s, -) cyclist
Radlerhose f cycling shorts pl; Radrennen nt cycle racing; (single event) cycle race; Radtour f cycling tour; Radweg m cycle track (or path)
raffiniert adj crafty, cunning; (sugar) refined
Rafting nt (-s) white water rafting
Ragout nt (-s, -s) ragout
Rahm m (-s, -) cream
rahmen vt frame; Rahmen m (-s, -) frame
Rakete f (-, -n) rocket
rammen vt ram
Rampe f (-, -n) ramp
ramponieren vt fam damage, batter
Ramsch m (-(e)s, -e) junk
ran adv contr of heran
Rand m (-(e)s, Ränder) edge; (of spectacles, cup etc) rim; (on paper) margin; (of dirt, under eyes) ring; fig verge, brink
randalieren vi (go on the)

rampage

rang imperf of **ringen**

Rang m (-(e)s, Ränge) rank; (in competition) place; THEAT circle

rannte imperf of **rennen**

ranzig adj rancid

Rap m (-(s), -s) MUS rap; **rappen** vi MUS rap; **Rapper(in)** m(f) (-s, -) MUS rapper

rar adj rare, scarce

rasant adj quick, rapid

rasch adj quick

rascheln vi rustle

rasen vi (rush) race; (behave wildly) rave; **gegen einen Baum ~** crash into a tree

Rasen m (-s, -) lawn

rasend adj furious

Rasenmäher m (-s, -) lawnmower

Rasierapparat m razor; (electric) shaver; **Rasiercreme** f shaving cream; **rasieren** vt, vr shave; **Rasierer** m shaver; **Rasiergel** nt shaving gel; **Rasierklinge** f razor blade; **Rasiermesser** nt (cutthroat) razor; **Rasierpinsel** m shaving brush; **Rasierschaum** m shaving foam

Rasse f (-, -n) race; (animals) breed

Rassismus m racism; **Rassist(in)** m(f) racist; **rassistisch** adj racist

Rast f (-, -en) rest, break; **~ machen** have a rest (or break); **Raststätte** f AUTO service area; (café) motor-

way (Brit) (or highway (US)) restaurant

Rasur f shave

Rat m (-(e)s, Ratschläge) (piece of) advice; **um ~ fragen** ask for advice

Rate f (-, -n) instalment; **etw auf ~n kaufen** buy sth in instalments (Brit), buy sth on the instalment plan (US)

raten (riet, geraten) vt, vi guess; (recommend) advise (jdm sb)

Rathaus nt town hall

Ration f ration

ratlos adj at a loss, helpless; **ratsam** adj advisable

Rätsel nt (-s, -) puzzle; (word puzzle) riddle; **das ist mir ein ~** it's a mystery to me; **rätselhaft** adj mysterious

Ratte f (-, -n) rat

rau adj rough, coarse; (weather) harsh

Raub m (-(e)s) robbery; (stolen things) loot, booty; **rauben** vt steal; **jdm etw ~** rob sb of sth; **Räuber(in)** m(f) (-s, -) robber; **Raubkopie** f pirate copy; **Raubmord** m robbery with murder; **Raubtier** nt predator; **Raubüberfall** m mugging; **Raubvogel** m bird of prey

Rauch m (-(e)s) smoke; (from exhaust) fumes pl; **rauchen** vt, vi smoke; **Raucher(in)** m(f) (-s, -) smoker

Räucherlachs m smoked salmon; **räuchern** vt smoke

rauchig *adj* smoky; **Rauch-melder** *m* smoke detector; **Rauchverbot** *nt* smoking ban; **hier ist ~** there's no smoking here

rauf *fam contr of* **herauf**

rauh *adj* → **rau;** Rauhreif *m* → **Raureif**

Raum *m* (-(e)s, Räume) space; (*part of building, space for a purpose*) room; (*district*) area

räumen *vt* clear; (*house, seat*) vacate; (*take away*) shift, move; (*into cupboard etc*) put away

Raumfähre *f* space shuttle; **Raumfahrt** *f* space travel; **Raumschiff** *nt* spacecraft, spaceship; **Raumsonde** *f* space probe; **Raumstation** *f* space station

Raupe *f* (-, -n) caterpillar

Raureif *m* hoarfrost

raus *contr of* **heraus, hinaus; ~!** (get) out!

Rausch *m* (-(e)s, Räusche) intoxication; **einen ~ haben/kriegen** be/get drunk; **Rauschgift** *nt* drug; **Rauschgiftsüchtige(r)** *mf* drug addict

rausfliegen *irr vi fam* be kicked out

raushalten *irr vr fam* **halt du dich da raus!** you (just) keep out of it

räuspern *vr* clear one's throat

rausschmeißen *irr vt fam* throw out

Razzia *f* (-, *Razzien*) raid

reagieren *vi* react (*auf* + *acc* to); **Reaktion** *f* reaction

real *adj* real; **realisieren** *vt* (*danger, problem*) realize; (*plan, idea*) implement; **realistisch** *adj* realistic; **Realität** *f* (-, -en) reality; **Reality-TV** *nt* (-s) reality TV

Realschule *f* ≈ secondary school, junior high (school) (*US*)

rebellieren *vi* rebel

Rebhuhn *nt* partridge

rechnen 1. *vt, vi* calculate; **~ mit** expect; (*rely on*) count on **2.** *vr* pay off, turn out to be profitable; **Rechner** *m* (-s, -) calculator; (*larger*) computer; **Rechnung** *f* calculation(s); comm bill (*Brit*), check (*US*); **die ~, bitte!** can I have the bill, please?; **das geht auf meine ~** this is on me

recht 1. *adj* right; **mir soll's ~ sein** it's alright by me; **mir ist es ~** I don't mind **2.** *adv* really, quite; (*correctly*) right(ly); **ich weiß nicht ~** I don't really know; **es geschieht ihm ~** it serves him right

Recht *nt* (-(e)s, -e) right; law law; **~ haben** be right; **jdm ~ geben** agree with sb

Rechte *f* (-n, -n) right-hand side; (*hand*) right hand; pol right (wing); **rechte(r, s)** *adj* right; **auf der ~n Seite**

on the right, on the right-hand side

Rechteck *nt* (*-s, -e*) rectangle; **rechteckig** *adj* rectangular

rechtfertigen 1. *vt* justify **2.** *vr* justify oneself

rechtlich *adj* legal; **rechtmäßig** *adj* legal, lawful

rechts *adv* on the right; **~ abbiegen** turn right; **~ von** to the right of; **~ oben** at the top right

Rechtsanwalt *m*, **-anwältin** *f* lawyer

Rechtschreibung *f* spelling

Rechtshänder(in) *m(f)* (*-s, -*) right-hander; **rechtsherum** *adv* to the right, clockwise; **rechtsradikal** *adj* POL extreme right-wing

Rechtsschutzversicherung *f* legal costs insurance

Rechtsverkehr *m* driving on the right

rechtswidrig *adj* illegal

rechtwinklig *adj* right-angled; **rechtzeitig 1.** *adj* timely **2.** *adv* in time

recyceln *vt* recycle; **Recycling** *nt* (*-s*) recycling

Redakteur(in) *m(f)* editor; **Redaktion** *f* editing; (*people*) editorial staff; (*place*) editorial office(s)

Rede *f* (*-, -n*) speech; (*conversation*) talk; **eine ~ halten** make a speech; **reden 1.** *vi* talk, speak **2.** *vt* say; (*nonsense etc*) talk; **Redewendung** *f* idiom; **Redner(in)**

m(f) speaker

reduzieren *vt* reduce

Referat *nt* (*-s, -e*) paper; **ein ~ halten** give a paper (*über + acc* on)

reflektieren *vt* reflect

Reform *f* (*-, -en*) reform; **Reformhaus** *nt* health food shop; **reformieren** *vt* reform

Regal *nt* (*-s, -e*) shelf; (*piece of furniture*) shelves *pl*

Regel *f* (*-, -n*) rule; MED period; **regelmäßig** *adj* regular; **regeln** *vt* regulate, control; (*matter*) settle; **Regelung** *f* regulation

Regen *m* (*-s, -*) rain; **Regenbogen** *m* rainbow; **Regenmantel** *m* raincoat; **Regenschauer** *m* shower; **Regenschirm** *m* umbrella; **Regenwald** *m* rainforest; **Regenwurm** *m* earthworm

Regie *f* direction

regieren *vt, vi* govern, rule; **Regierung** *f* government; (*of monarch*) reign

Region *f* region; **regional** *adj* regional

Regisseur(in) *m(f)* director

regnen *vi impers* rain; **regnerisch** *adj* rainy

regulär *adj* regular; **regulieren** *vt* regulate, adjust

Reh *nt* (*-(e)s, -e*) deer; (*meat*) venison

Reibe *f* (*-, -n*), **Reibeisen** *nt* grater; **reiben** (*rieb, gerieben*) *vt* rub; GASTR grate; **reibungslos** *adj* smooth

reich adj rich
Reich nt (-(e)s, -e) empire; (of king) kingdom
reichen 1. vi reach; (money, food etc) be sufficient (jdm for sb) **2.** vt hold out; (give) pass, hand; (serve) offer
reichhaltig adj ample, rich; **reichlich** adj (tip) generous; (meal) ample; **~ Zeit** plenty of time; **Reichtum** m (-s, -tümer) wealth
reif adj ripe; (person, judgment) mature
Reif 1. m (-(e)s) hoarfrost **2.** m (-(e)s), -e) ring, hoop
reifen vi mature; (fruit) ripen
Reifen m (-s, -) ring, hoop; (of car) tyre; **Reifendruck** m tyre pressure; **Reifenpanne** f puncture; **Reifenwechsel** m tyre change
Reihe f (-, -n) row; (of days etc) series m (number) series sg; **der ~ nach** one after the other; **er ist an der ~** it's his turn; **Reihenfolge** f order, sequence; **Reihenhaus** nt terraced house (Brit), row house (US)
Reiher m (-s, -) heron
rein 1. fam contr of **herein, hinein 2.** adj pure; (shirt, air) clean
Reinfall m fam letdown; **reinfallen** irr vi fam **auf etw acc ~** fall for sth
reinigen vt clean; **Reinigung** f cleaning; (shop) (dry)

cleaner's; **Reinigungsmittel** nt cleaning agent, cleaner
reinlegen vt **jdn ~** take sb for a ride
Reis m (-es, -e) rice
Reise f (-, -n) journey; (on ship) voyage; **Reiseapotheke** f first-aid kit; **Reisebüro** nt travel agent's; **Reisebus** m coach; **Reiseführer(in)** m(f) courier; (book) guide(book); **Reisegepäck** nt luggage (Brit), baggage; **Reisegesellschaft** f tour company; **Reiseleiter(in)** m(f) courier; **reisen** vi travel; **~ nach** go to; **Reisende(r)** mf traveller; **Reisepass** m passport; **Reisescheck** m traveller's cheque; **Reisetasche** f holdall (Brit), carryall (US); **Reiseveranstalter** m tour operator; **Reiseverkehr** m holiday traffic; **Reiseversicherung** f travel insurance; **Reiseziel** nt destination
reißen (riss, gerissen) vt, vi tear; (move) pull, drag
Reißnagel m drawing pin (Brit), thumbtack (US); **Reißverschluss** m zip (Brit), zipper (US); **Reißzwecke** f drawing pin (Brit), thumbtack (US)
reiten (ritt, geritten) vt, vi ride; **Reiter(in)** m(f) rider
Reiz m (-es, -e) stimulus; (delightfulness) charm; (appeal) attraction; **reizen** vt stimu-

late; (*make angry*) annoy; (*interest*) appeal to, attract; **reizend** *adj* charming; **Reizung** *f* irritation

Reklamation *f* complaint

Reklame *f* (-, -n) advertising; (*on TV*) commercial

reklamieren *vi* complain (*wegen*, *about* for)

Rekord *m* (-(e)s, -e) record

relativ 1. *adj* relative **2.** *adv* relatively

relaxen *vi* relax, chill out

Religion *f* religion; **religiös** *adj* religious

Remoulade *f* (-, -n) tartar sauce

Renaissance *f* renaissance, revival; HIST Renaissance

rennen (*rannte, gerannt*) *vt, vi* run; **Rennen** *nt* (-s, -) running; (*competition*) race; **Rennrad** *nt* racing bike

renommiert *adj* famous, noted (*wegen*, HIST for)

renovieren *vt* renovate; **Renovierung** *f* renovation

rentabel *adj* profitable

Rente *f* (-, -n) pension; **Rentenversicherung** *f* pension scheme

Rentier *nt* reindeer

rentieren *vr* pay, be profitable

Rentner(in) *m(f)* (-s, -) pensioner, senior citizen

Reparatur *f* repair; **Reparaturwerkstatt** *f* repair shop; AUTO garage; **reparieren** *vt* repair

Reportage *f* report; **Repor-**ter(in) *m(f)* (-s, -) reporter

Republik *f* republic

Reservat *nt* (-s, -e) nature reserve; **Reserve** *f* (-, -n) reserve; **Reservekanister** *m* spare can; **Reserverad** *nt* AUTO spare wheel; **Reservespieler(in)** *m(f)* reserve; **reservieren** *vt* reserve; **Reservierung** *f* reservation

resignieren *vi* give up; **resigniert** *adj* resigned

Respekt *m* (-(e)s) respect; **respektieren** *vt* respect

Rest *m* (-(e)s, -e) rest, remainder; (*left over*) remains *pl*

Restaurant *nt* (-s, -s) restaurant

restaurieren *vt* restore

restlich *adj* remaining

Resultat *nt* result

retten *vt* save, rescue

Rettich *m* (-s, -e) radish (*large white or red variety*)

Rettung *f* rescue; (*assistance*) help; (*medical team*) ambulance service; **Rettungsboot** *nt* lifeboat; **Rettungshubschrauber** *m* rescue helicopter; **Rettungsring** *m* lifebelt, life preserver (*US*); **Rettungswagen** *m* ambulance

Reue *f* (-) remorse; regret

revanchieren *vr* (*for help etc*) return the favour

Revolution *f* revolution

Rezept *nt* (-(e)s, -e) GASTR recipe; MED prescription; **rezeptfrei** *adj* over-the-counter, non-prescription

Rezeption f (at hotel) reception

rezeptpflichtig adj available only on prescription

Rhabarber m (-s) rhubarb

Rhein m (-s) Rhine; **Rheinland-Pfalz** nt (-) Rhineland-Palatinate

Rheuma nt (-s) rheumatism

Rhythmus m rhythm

richten 1. vt direct (auf + acc to); (weapon, camera) point (auf + acc at); (letter, inquiry) address (an + acc to) **2.** vr **sich ~ nach** (rule etc) depend on; (fashion, example) follow; (vary according to) depend on

Richter(in) m(f) (-s, -) judge

Richtgeschwindigkeit f recommended speed

richtig adj right, correct; (genuine) proper; **etw ~ stellen** set sth right **2.** adv fam (very) really

Richtlinie f guideline

Richtung f direction; (trend) tendency

rieb imperf of **reiben**

riechen (roch, gerochen) vt, vi smell; **nach etw ~** smell of sth

rief imperf of **rufen**

Riegel m (-s, -) bolt; GASTR (of chocolate) bar

Riese m (-n, -n) giant; **Riesengarnele** f king prawn; **riesengroß** adj gigantic, huge; **Riesenrad** nt big

wheel; **riesig** adj enormous, huge

riet imperf of **raten**

Riff nt (-(e)s, -e) reef

Rind nt (-(e)s, -er) cow; (male) bull; GASTR beef; **~er** pl cattle pl

Rinde f (-, -n) (of tree) bark; (of cheese) rind; (of bread) crust

Rinderbraten m roast beef; **Rindfleisch** nt beef

Ring m (-(e)s, -e) ring; (round town) ring road; **Ringfinger** m ring finger; **ringsherum** adv round about

Rippe f (-, -n) rib

Risiko nt (-s, -s or Risiken) risk; **auf eigenes ~** at one's own risk; **riskant** adj risky; **riskieren** vt risk

riss imperf of **reißen**

Riss m (-es, -e) tear; (in wall, cup etc) crack; **rissig** adj cracked; (skin) chapped

ritt imperf of **reiten**

Ritter m (-s, -) knight

Rivale m (-n, -n), **Rivalin** f rival

Robbe f (-, -n) seal

Roboter m (-s, -) robot

robust adj robust

roch imperf of **riechen**

Rock m (-(e)s, Röcke) skirt

Rockmusik f rock (music)

Rodelbahn f toboggan run; **rodeln** vi toboggan

Roggen m (-s, -) rye; **Roggenbrot** nt rye bread

roh adj raw; (person) coarse,

crude; **Rohkost** f raw vegetables and fruit pl

Rohr nt (-(e)s, -e) pipe; **Röhre** f (-, -n) tube; (in cooker) oven; **Rohrzucker** m cane sugar

Rohstoff m raw material

Rokoko nt (-s) rococo

Rolle f (-, -n) roll; THEAT role

rollen vt, vi roll

Roller m (-s, -) scooter

Rollerskates pl roller skates pl

Rollkragenpullover m polo-neck (Brit) (or turtleneck (US)) sweater; **Rollladen** m, **Rollo** m (-s, -s) (roller) shutters pl; **Rollschuh** m roller skate; **Rollstuhl** m wheelchair; **rollstuhlgerecht** adj suitable for wheelchairs; **Rolltreppe** f escalator

Roman m (-s, -e) novel

Romantik f romance; **romantisch** adj romantic

römisch-katholisch adj Roman Catholic

röntgen vt X-ray; **Röntgenaufnahme** f, **Röntgenbild** nt X-ray; **Röntgenstrahlen** pl X-rays pl

rosa adj inv pink

Rose f (-, -n) rose

Rosenkohl m (Brussels) sprouts pl

Rosé(wein) m rosé (wine)

rosig adj rosy

Rosine f raisin

Rosmarin m (-s) rosemary

Rost m (-(e)s, -e) rust; (for roasting) grill, gridiron; **Rostbratwurst** f grilled sausage; **rosten** vi rust; **rösten** vt roast, grill; (bread) toast; **rostfrei** adj rustproof; (steel) stainless; **rostig** adj rusty

rot adj red; **~ werden** blush; **~e Karte** red card; **~e Be(e)te** beetroot; **bei Rot über die Ampel fahren** jump the lights; **das Rote Kreuz** the Red Cross

Röteln pl German measles sg

rothaarig adj red-haired

rotieren vi rotate

Rotkehlchen nt robin; **Rotkohl** m, **Rotkraut** nt red cabbage; **Rotlichtviertel** nt red-light district; **Rotwein** m red wine

Rouge nt (-s, -s) rouge

Route f (-, -n) route

Routine f experience; (drudgery) routine

Rubbellos nt scratchcard; **rubbeln** vt rub

Rübe f (-, -n) turnip; **Gelbe ~** carrot; **Rote ~** beetroot

rüber fam contr of **herüber, hinüber**

Rubin m (-s, -e) ruby

rücken vt, vi move; **könntest du ein bisschen ~?** could you move over a bit?

Rücken m (-s, -) back; **Rückenlehne** f back(rest); **Rückenmark** nt spinal cord; **Rückenschmerzen** pl backache sg; **Rückenschwim-**

men *nt* (*-s*) backstroke; **Rückenwind** *m* tailwind

Rückerstattung *f* refund; **Rückfahrkarte** *f* return ticket (*Brit*), round-trip ticket (*US*); **Rückfahrt** *f* return journey; **Rückfall** *m* relapse; **Rückflug** *m* return flight; **Rückgabe** *f* return; **rückgängig** *adj* **etw ~ machen** cancel sth; **Rückgrat** *nt* (*-(e)s, -e*) spine, backbone; **Rückkehr** *f* (*-, -en*) return; **Rücklicht** *nt* rear light; **Rückreise** *f* return journey; **auf der ~** on the way back

Rucksack *m* rucksack, backpack; **Rucksacktourist(in)** *m(f)* backpacker

Rückschritt *m* step back; **Rückseite** *f* back; **siehe ~** see overleaf

Rücksicht *f* consideration; **~ nehmen auf** + *acc* show consideration for; **rücksichtslos** *adj* inconsiderate; (*driving*) reckless; **rücksichtsvoll** *adj* considerate

Rücksitz *m* back seat; **Rückspiegel** *m* AUTO rear-view mirror; **Rückvergütung** *f* refund; **rückwärts** *adv* backwards, back; **Rückwärtsgang** *m* AUTO reverse (gear); **Rückweg** *m* return journey, way back; **Rückzahlung** *f* repayment; **Rückzieher** *m* **einen ~ machen** back out

Ruder *nt* (*-s, -*) oar; (*at back of boat*) rudder; **Ruderboot** *nt* rowing boat (*Brit*), rowboat (*US*); **rudern** *vt, vi* row

Ruf *m* (*-(e)s, -e*) call, cry; (*of artist, company etc*) reputation; (*cry*) (*rief, gerufen*) *vt, vi* call; (*shout*) cry; **Rufnummer** *f* telephone number

Ruhe *f* (*-*) rest; (*untroubled state*) peace, quiet; (*stillness*) calm; (*no talking*) silence; **lass mich in ~!** leave me alone; **ruhen** *vi* rest; **Ruhestand** *m* retirement; **im ~ sein** be retired; **Ruhetag** *m* closing day; **montags ~ haben** be closed on Mondays

ruhig *adj* quiet; (*motionless*) still; (*hand*) steady; (*composed, peaceful*) calm

Ruhm *m* (*-(e)s*) fame, glory

Rührei *nt* scrambled egg(s); **rühren 1.** *vt* move; (*with spoon etc*) stir **2.** *vr* move; (*speak*) say something; **rührend** *adj* touching, moving

Ruine *f* (*-, -n*) ruin; **ruinieren** *vt* ruin

rülpsen *vi* burp, belch

rum *fam contr of* **herum**

Rum *m* (*-s, -s*) rum

Rumänien *nt* (*-s*) Romania

Rummel *m* (*-s*) hustle and bustle; (*event*) fair; (*in the media*) hype; **Rummelplatz** *m* fairground

rumoren *vi* **es rumort in meinem Bauch/Kopf** my stomach is rumbling/my head is spinning

Rumpf m (-(e)s, Rümpfe) ANAT trunk; AVIAT fuselage; NAUT hull

Rumpsteak nt rump steak

rund 1. adj round **2.** adv (approximately) around; **~ um etw** (a)round sth; **~** on sth; **Runde** f (-, -n) round; (in race) lap; **Rundfahrt** f tour (durch of); **Rundfunk** m (organization) broadcasting service; **im ~** on the radio; **Rundgang** m tour (durch of); (of guard etc) round; **Rundreise** f tour (durch of)

runter fam contr of **herunter, hinunter**; **runterscrollen** vt IT scroll down

runzeln vt **die Stirn ~** frown;

runzelig adj wrinkled
ruppig adj gruff
Ruß m (-es) soot
Russe m (-n, -n) Russian
Rüssel m (-s, -) (of elephant) trunk; (of pig) snout
Russin f Russian; **russisch** adj Russian; **Russisch** nt Russian; **Russland** nt Russia
Rüstung f (of knight) armour; (weapons etc) armaments pl
Rutsch m (-(e)s, -e) **guten ~ (ins neue Jahr)!** Happy New Year; **Rutschbahn** f, **Rutsche** f (-, -n) slide; **rutschen** vi slide; (accidentally) slip; **rutschig** adj slippery
rütteln vt, vi shake

S

s. abbr = **siehe**; see; **S.** abbr = **Seite**; p.
Saal m (-(e)s, Säle) hall; (for meetings) room
Saarland nt Saarland
sabotieren vt sabotage
Sache f (-, -n) thing; (situation, event) affair, business; (issue) matter; **bei der ~ bleiben** keep to the point; **sachkundig** adj competent; **Sachlage** f situation; **sachlich** adj objective; (unemotional) matter-of-fact; (error, account) factual; **sächlich** adj LING neuter; **Sachschaden** m material damage

Sachsen nt (-s) Saxony; **Sachsen-Anhalt** nt (-s) Saxony-Anhalt
sacht(e) adv softly, gently
Sachverständige(r) mf expert
Sack m (-(e)s, Säcke) sack; pej bastard, bugger; **Sackgasse** f dead end, cul-de-sac
Safe m (-s, -s) safe
Safer Sex m safe sex
Safran m (-s, -e) saffron
Saft m (-(e)s, Säfte) juice; **saftig** adj juicy
Sage f (-, -n) legend
Säge f (-, -n) saw
sagen vt, vi say (jdm to sb),

tell (*jdm sb*); *wie sagt man ... auf Englisch?* what's ~ in English?; *ich will dir mal was ~* let me tell you something

sägen *vt, vi* saw

sah *imperf of* **sehen**

Sahne *f* (-) cream; **Sahnetorte** *f* gateau

Saison *f* (-, -s) season; *außerhalb der ~* out of season

Saite *f* (-, -n) string

Sakko *nt* (-s, -s) jacket

Salami *f* (-, -s) salami

Salat *m* (-(e)s, -e) salad; (*vegetable*) lettuce; **Salatbar** *f* salad bar; **Salatschüssel** *f* salad bowl; **Salatsoße** *f* salad dressing

Salbe *f* (-, -n) ointment

Salbei *m* (-s) sage

Salmonellenvergiftung *f* salmonella (poisoning)

Salsamusik *f* salsa (music)

Salto *m* (-s, -s) somersault

Salz *nt* (-es, -e) salt; **salzarm** *adj* low-salt; **salzen** (*salzte, gesalzen*) *vt* salt; **salzig** *adj* salty; **Salzkartoffeln** *pl* boiled potatoes *pl*; **Salzstange** *f* pretzel stick; **Salzstreuer** *m* salt cellar (*Brit*) *or* shaker (*US*)); **Salzwasser** *nt* salt water

Samba *f* (-, -s) samba

Samen *m* (-s, -) seed; (*of male*) sperm

sammeln *vt* collect; **Sammlung** *f* collection

Samstag *m* Saturday; → **Mitt-**

woch; **samstags** *adv* on Saturdays; → **mittwochs**

samt *prep* + *dat* (along) with, together with

Samt *m* (-(e)s, -e) velvet

sämtliche(r, s) *adj* all (the)

Sanatorium *nt* (-s, *Sanatorien*) sanatorium (*Brit*), sanitarium (*US*)

Sand *m* (-(e)s, -e) sand

Sandale *f* (-, -n) sandal

sandig *adj* sandy; **Sandkasten** *m* sandpit (*Brit*), sandbox (*US*); **Sandstrand** *m* sandy beach

sandte *imperf of* **senden**

sanft *adj* soft, gentle

sang *imperf of* **singen**

Sänger(in) *m(f)* (-s, -) singer

Sangria *f* (-, -s) sangria

sanieren *vt* redevelop; (*building*) renovate; (*business*) restore to profitability

sanitär *adj* sanitary; *~e Anlagen* *pl* sanitation

Sanitäter(in) *m(f)* (-s, -) ambulance man / woman, paramedic

sank *imperf of* **sinken**

Sardelle *f* anchovy

Sarg *m* (-(e)s, *Särge*) coffin

saß *imperf of* **sitzen**

Satellit *m* (-en, -en) satellite; **Satellitenfernsehen** *nt* satellite TV; **Satellitenschüssel** *f fam* satellite dish

satt *adj* full; (*colour*) rich, deep; *~ sein* (*after meal*) be full; *~ machen* be filling; *jdn / etw ~ sein* (*or* **haben**) be fed up with sb/sth

Sattel m (-s, Sättel) saddle

Saturn m (-s) Saturn

Satz m (-es, Sätze) LING sentence; MUS movement; (in tennis) set; (of coffee) grounds pl; (leap) jump; COMM rate

Sau f (-, Säue) sow; pej dirty bugger

sauber adj clean; (ironic) fine; ~ **machen** clean; **Sauberkeit** f cleanness; (hygiene) cleanliness; **säubern** vt clean

saublöd adj fam really stupid, dumb

Sauce f (-, -n) sauce; (with meat) gravy

Saudi-Arabien nt (-s) Saudi Arabia

sauer adj sour; CHEM acid; fam (annoyed) cross; **saurer Regen** acid rain; **Sauerkirsche** f sour cherry; **Sauerkraut** nt sauerkraut; **säuerlich** adj slighthly sour; **Sauerrahm** m sour cream; **Sauerstoff** m oxygen

saufen (soff, gesoffen) **1.** vt drink; (fam (person) knock back **2.** vi drink; fam (person) booze

saugen (sog or saugte, gesogen or gesaugt) vt, vi suck; (with cleaner) vacuum, hoover (Brit); **Säugetier** nt mammal; **Säugling** m infant, baby

Säule f (-, -n) column, pillar

Saum m (-s, Säume) hem;

(join) seam

Sauna f (-, -s) sauna

Säure f (-, -n) acid

Saustall m pigsty; **Sauwetter** nt **was für ein ~** fam what lousy weather

Saxophon nt (-s, -e) saxophone

S-Bahn f suburban railway; **S-Bahn-Haltestelle** f, **S-Bahnhof** m suburban (train) station

scannen vt scan; **Scanner** m (-s, -) scanner

schäbig adj shabby

Schach nt (-s, -s) chess; (position) check; **Schachbrett** nt chessboard; **Schachfigur** f chess piece; **schachmatt** adj checkmate

Schacht m (-(e)s, Schächte) shaft

Schachtel f (-, -n) box

schade interj what a pity

Schädel m (-s, -) skull; **Schädelbruch** m fractured skull

schaden vi damage, harm (jdm sb); **das schadet nichts** it won't do any harm; **Schaden** m (-s, Schäden) damage; (to body) injury; (bad thing) disadvantage; **einen ~ verursachen** cause damage; **Schadenersatz** m compensation, damages pl; **schadhaft** adj faulty; damaged; **schädigen** vt damage; (person) do harm to, harm; **schädlich** adj harmful (für to); **Schadstoff** m harmful substance; **schadstoffarm** adj low-emission

Schaf nt (-(e)s, -e) sheep; **Schäfer** m (-s, -) shepherd; **Schäferhund** m Alsatian (Brit), German shepherd; **Schäferin** f shepherdess

schaffen 1. (schuf, geschaffen) vt create; (room) make **2.** vt manage, do; (complete) finish; (exam) pass; **jdm zu ~ machen** cause sb trouble

Schaffner(in) m(f) (-s, -) (in bus) conductor/conductress; RAIL guard

Schafskäse m sheep's (milk) cheese

schal adj (drink) flat

Schal m (-s, -e or -s) scarf

Schale f (-, -n) skin; (removed) peel; (of nut, mussel, egg) shell; (container) bowl, dish

schälen 1. vt peel; (tomato, almonds) skin; (peas, eggs, nuts) shell; (grain) husk **2.** vr peel

Schall m (-(e)s, -e) sound; **Schalldämpfer** m (-s, -) AUTO silencer (Brit), muffler (US); **Schallplatte** f record

Schalotte f (-, -n) shallot

schalten 1. vt switch **2.** vi AUTO change gear; **Schalter** m (-s, -) (at post office, bank) counter; (electrical) switch; **Schalterhalle** f main hall; **Schalthebel** m gear lever (Brit) (or shift US)); **Schaltjahr** nt leap year; **Schalt-**

knüppel m gear lever (Brit) (or shift (US)); **Schaltung** f gear change (Brit), gearshift (US)

Scham f (-) shame; modesty; **schämen** vr be ashamed

Schande f (-) disgrace

Schanze f (-, -n) ski jump

Schar f (-, -en) (of birds) flock; (of people) crowd; **in ~en** in droves

scharf adj (knife; criticism) sharp; (spicy) hot; **auf etw acc ~ sein** fam be keen on sth

Schärfe f (-, -n) sharpness; (severity) rigour; PHOT focus

Scharlach m (-s) MED scarlet fever

Scharnier nt (-s, -e) hinge

Schaschlik m or nt (-s, -s) (shish) kebab

Schatten m (-s, -) shadow; **30 Grad im ~** 30 degrees in the shade; **schattig** adj shady

Schatz m (-es, Schätze) treasure; (person) love

schätzen vt estimate; (object) value; (appreciate) value, esteem; (think) reckon; **Schätzung** f estimate; (action) estimation; (of price) valuation; **schätzungsweise** adv roughly, approximately

schauen vi look; **ich schau mal, ob ...** I'll go and have a look whether ...; **schau, dass ...** see (to it) that ...

Schauer m (-s, -) (rain) shower; (shiver) shudder

Schaufel f (-, -n) shovel; **~ und Besen** dustpan and brush; **schaufeln** vt shovel

Schaufenster nt shop window

Schaukel f (-, -n) swing; **schaukeln** vi rock; (on a swing) swing; **Schaukelstuhl** m rocking chair

Schaum m (-(e)s, Schäume) foam; (from soap) lather; (on beer) froth; **Schaumbad** nt bubble bath; **schäumen** vi foam; **Schaumfestiger** m (-s, -) styling mousse; **Schaumgummi** m foam (rubber); **Schaumwein** m sparkling wine

Schauplatz m scene

Schauspiel nt spectacle; THEAT play; **Schauspieler(in)** m(f) actor/actress

Scheck m (-s, -s) cheque; **Scheckheft** nt chequebook; **Scheckkarte** f cheque card

Scheibe f (-, -n) disc; (of bread, cheese etc) slice; (of glass) pane; **Scheibenwischer** m (-s, -) AUTO windscreen (Brit) (or windshield (US)) wiper

Scheich m (-s, -e) sheik(h)

Scheide f (-, -n) ANAT vagina

scheiden (schied, geschieden) vt separate; **sich ~ lassen** get a divorce; **sie hat sich von ihm ~ lassen** she divorced him; **Scheidung** f divorce

Schein m (-(e)s, -e) light; (ex-

ternal impression) appearance; (money) (bank)note; **scheinbar** adj apparent; **scheinen** (schien, geschienen) vi (sun) shine; (appear) seem; **Scheinwerfer** m (-s, -) floodlight; THEAT spotlight; AUTO headlight

Scheiß- in cpds vulg damned, bloody (Brit); **Scheiße** f (-) vulg shit, crap; **scheißegal** adj vulg **das ist mir ~** I don't give a damn (or toss); **scheißen** (schiss, geschissen) vi vulg shit

Scheitel m (-s, -) parting (Brit), part (US)

scheitern vi fail (an + dat because of)

Schellfisch m haddock

Schema nt (-s, -s or Schemata) scheme, plan; (drawing) diagram

Schenkel m (-s, -) thigh

schenken vt give; **er hat es mir geschenkt** he gave it to me (as a present); **sich** dat etw ~ fam skip sth

Scherbe f (-, -n) broken piece, fragment

Schere f (-, -n) scissors pl; (large) shears pl; **eine ~** a pair of scissors/shears

Scherz m (-es, -e) joke

scheu adj shy

scheuen 1. vr **sich ~ vor** + dat be afraid of, shrink from **2.** vt shun **3.** vi (horse) shy

scheuern vt scrub; **jdm eine ~** fam slap sb in the face

Scheune *f* (-, -*n*) barn
scheußlich *adj* dreadful
Schi *m* (-*s*, -*er*) → **Ski**
Schicht *f* (-, -*en*) layer; (*in society*) class; (*in factory etc*) shift
schick *adj* stylish, chic
schicken 1. *vt* send **2.** *vr* hurry up
Schickimicki *m* (-(*s*), -*s*) *fam* trendy
Schicksal *nt* (-*s*, -*e*) fate
Schiebedach *nt* AUTO sunroof; **schieben** (*schob, geschoben*) *vt, vi* push; **die Schuld auf jdn ~** put the blame on sb; **Schiebetür** *f* sliding door
schied *imperf of* **scheiden**
Schiedsrichter(in) *m(f)* referee, umpire
schief 1. *adj* crooked **2.** *adv* crooked(ly); **~ gehen** go wrong
schielen *vi* squint
schien *imperf of* **scheinen**
Schienbein *nt* shin
Schiene *f* (-, -*n*) rail; MED splint
schießen (*schoss, geschossen*) **1.** *vt* shoot; (*ball*) kick; (*goal*) score; (*photo*) take **2.** *vi* shoot (*auf + acc* at)
Schiff *nt* (-(*e*)*s*, -*e*) ship; (*in church*) nave; **Schifffahrt** *f* shipping; **Schiffsreise** *f* voyage
schikanieren *vt* harass; (*at school*) bully
Schild 1. *m* (-(*e*)*s*, -*e*) (*of war-*

rior) shield **2.** *nt* (-(*e*)*s*, -*er*) sign; **was steht auf dem ~?** what does the sign say?
Schilddrüse *f* thyroid gland
schildern *vt* describe
Schildkröte *f* tortoise; (*living in water*) turtle
Schimmel *m* (-*s*, -) mould; (*animal*) white horse; **schimmeln** *vi* go mouldy
schimpfen 1. *vt* tell off **2.** *vi* complain; **mit jdm ~** tell sb off; **Schimpfwort** *nt* swearword
Schinken *m* (-*s*, -) ham
Schirm *m* (-(*e*)*s*, -*e*) umbrella; (*for sun*) parasol, sunshade
schiss *imperf of* **scheißen**
Schlacht *f* (-, -*en*) battle; **schlachten** *vt* slaughter; **Schlachter(in)** *m(f)* (-*s*, -) butcher; **Schlachtfeld** *nt* battlefield
Schlaf *m* (-(*e*)*s*) sleep; **Schlafanzug** *m* pyjamas *pl*; **Schlafcouch** *f* bed settee
Schläfe *f* (-, -*n*) temple
schlafen (*schlief, geschlafen*) *vi* sleep; **schlaf gut!** sleep well; **hast du gut geschlafen?** did you sleep all right?; **er schläft noch** he's still asleep; **~ gehen** go to bed
schlaff *adj* slack; (*weak*) limp; (*tired*) exhausted
Schlafgelegenheit *f* place to sleep; **Schlaflosigkeit** *f* sleeplessness; **schläfrig** *adj* sleepy; **Schlafsack** *m* sleeping bag; **Schlaftablette** *f*

sleeping pill; **Schlafwagen** *m* sleeping car, sleeper; **Schlafzimmer** *nt* bedroom

Schlag *m* (-(e)s, Schläge) blow; ELEC shock; **Schlagader** *f* artery; **Schlaganfall** *m* MED stroke; **schlagartig** *adj* sudden; **Schlagbohrmaschine** *f* hammer drill

schlagen (schlug, geschlagen) **1.** *vt* hit; (*hit repeatedly, defeat*) beat; (*cream*) whip **2.** *vi* (*heart*) beat; (*clock*) strike; **mit dem Kopf gegen etw ~** bang one's head against sth **3.** *vr* fight

Schläger *m* (-s, -) SPORT bat; racket; (*golf*) club; hockey stick; (*person*) brawler; **Schlägerei** *f* fight, brawl

schlagfertig *adj* quick-witted; **Schlagloch** *nt* pothole; **Schlagsahne** *f* whipping cream; (*beaten*) whipped cream; **Schlagzeile** *f* headline; **Schlagzeug** *nt* drums *pl*; (*in orchestra*) percussion

Schlamm *m* (-(e)s, -e) mud

schlampig *adj fam* sloppy

schlang *imperf of* **schlingen**

Schlange *f* (-, -n) snake; (*of people*) queue (*Brit*), line (*US*); **~ stehen** queue (*Brit*), stand in line (*US*)

schlank *adj* slim

schlapp *adj* limp

Schlappe *f* (-, -n) *fam* setback

schlau *adj* clever, smart; (*wily*) crafty, cunning

Schlauch *m* (-(e)s, Schläuche)

hose; (*in tyre*) inner tube; **Schlauchboot** *nt* rubber dinghy

schlecht 1. *adj* bad; **mir ist ~** I feel sick; **jdn ~ machen** run sb down; **die Milch ist ~** the milk has gone off **2.** *adv* badly; **es geht ihm ~** he's having a hard time; (*health-wise*) he's not feeling well; (*financially*) he's pretty hard up

schleichen (schlich, geschlichen) *vi* creep

Schleier *m* (-s, -) veil

Schleife *f* (-, -n) IT, AVIAT, ELEC loop; (*ribbon*) bow

Schleim *m* (-(e)s, -e) slime; MED mucus; **Schleimer** *m* (-s, -) *fam* creep; **Schleimhaut** *f* mucous membrane

schlendern *vi* stroll

schleppen *vt* drag; (*car, ship*) tow; (*carry*) lug; **Schlepplift** *m* ski tow

Schleswig-Holstein *nt* (-s) Schleswig-Holstein

Schleuder *f* (-, -n) catapult; (*for washing*) spin-dryer; **schleudern 1.** *vt* hurl; (*washing*) spin-dry **2.** *vi* AUTO skid; **Schleudersitz** *m* ejector seat

schleunigst *adv* straight away

schlich *imperf of* **schleichen**

schlicht *adj* simple, plain

schlichten *vt* (*dispute*) settle

schlief *imperf of* **schlafen**

schließen (schloss, geschlos-

sen) vt, vi, vr close, shut; *(bring to an end)* close; *(friendship, alliance, marriage)* enter into; *(deduce)* infer *(aus* from); **Schließfach** *nt* locker

schließlich *adv* finally; *(when all is said and done)* after all

schliff *imperf of* **schleifen**

schlimm *adj* bad; **schlimmer** *adj* worse; **schlimmste(r, s)** *adj* worst; **schlimmstenfalls** *adv* at (the) worst

Schlips *m (-es, -e)* tie

Schlitten *m (-s, -)* sledge, toboggan; *(with horses)* sleigh; **Schlittenfahren** *nt (-s)* tobogganing

Schlittschuh *m* ice skate; ~ **laufen** ice-skate

Schlitz *m (-es, -e)* slit; *(for coin)* slot; *(on trousers)* flies *pl*

schloss *imperf of* **schließen**

Schloss *nt (-es, Schlösser)* lock; *(building)* castle

Schlosser(in) *m(f)* mechanic

Schlucht *f (-, -en)* gorge, ravine

schluchzen *vi* sob

Schluckauf *m (-s)* hiccups *pl*;

schlucken *vt, vi* swallow

schlug *imperf of* **schlagen**

schlüpfrig *adj* slippery; *fig* risqué

schlürfen *vt, vi* slurp

Schluss *m (-es, Schlüsse)* end; *(deduction)* conclusion; **am** ~ at the end; **mit jdm** ~

machen finish *(or* split up) with sb

Schlüssel *m (-s, -) a. fig* key; **Schlüsselbein** *nt* collarbone; **Schlüsselblume** *f* cowslip; **Schlüsselbund** *m* bunch of keys; **Schlüsselloch** *nt* keyhole

Schlussfolgerung *f* conclusion; **Schlusslicht** *nt* tail-light; *fig* tail-ender; **Schlusspfiff** *m* final whistle; **Schlussverkauf** *m* clearance sale

schmal *adj* narrow; *(person, book etc)* slim

Schmalz *nt (-es, -e)* dripping, lard

schmatzen *vi* eat noisily

schmecken *vt, vi* taste *(nach* of); **es schmeckt ihm** he likes it; **lass es dir** ~**!** bon appétit

Schmeichelei *f* flattery; **schmeichelhaft** *adj* flattering; **schmeicheln** *vi* **jdm** ~ flatter sb

schmeißen *(schmiss, geschmissen) vt fam* chuck, throw

schmelzen *(schmolz, geschmolzen) vt, vi* melt

Schmerz *m (-es, -en)* pain; *(sorrow)* grief; ~**en haben** be in pain; ~**en im Rücken haben** have a pain in one's back; **schmerzen** *vt, vi* hurt; **Schmerzensgeld** *nt* compensation; **schmerzhaft**, **schmerzlich** *adj* painful;

Schmerzmittel nt painkiller; **schmerzstillend** adj painkilling; **Schmerztablette** f painkiller

Schmetterling m butterfly

schmieden vt forge; (plans) make

schmieren 1. vt smear; (machine, bicycle etc) lubricate, grease; (person) bribe **2.** vt, vi (write) scrawl; **Schmiergeld** nt fam bribe; **schmierig** adj greasy; **Schmiermittel** nt lubricant; **Schmierpapier** nt scrap paper

Schminke f (-, -n) make-up; **schminken** vr put one's make-up on

schmiss imperf of **schmeißen**

schmollen vi sulk

schmolz imperf of **schmelzen**

Schmuck m (-(e)s, -e) jewellery (Brit), jewelry (US); (ornament) decoration; **schmücken** vt decorate

schmuggeln vt, vi smuggle

schmunzeln vi smile

schmusen vi (kiss and) cuddle

Schmutz m (-es) dirt, filth; **schmutzig** adj dirty

Schnabel m (-s, Schnäbel) beak, bill; (for pouring) spout

Schnake f (-, -n) mosquito

Schnäppchen nt fam bargain; **schnappen 1.** vt catch **2.** vi **nach Luft ~** gasp for

breath; **Schnappschuss** m PHOT snap(shot)

Schnaps m (-es, Schnäpse) schnapps

schnarchen vi snore

schnaufen vi puff, pant

Schnauzbart m moustache; **Schnauze** f (-, -n) snout, muzzle; (for pouring) spout; fam (mouth) trap; **die ~ voll haben** have had enough

schnäuzen vr blow one's nose

Schnecke f (-, -n) snail; **Schneckenhaus** nt snail's shell

Schnee m (-s) snow; **Schneeball** m snowball; **Schneebrille** f snow goggles pl; **Schneeflocke** f snowflake; **Schneeglöckchen** nt snowdrop; **Schneegrenze** f snowline; **Schneekanone** f snow thrower; **Schneekette** f AUTO snow chain; **Schneemann** m snowman; **Schneematsch** m slush; **Schneepflug** m snowplough; **Schneeregen** m sleet; **Schneesturm** m snowstorm, blizzard; **Schneetreiben** nt light blizzards pl; **Schneewehe** f snowdrift

Schneide f (-, -n) edge; (part of knife) blade; **schneiden** (schnitt, geschnitten) **1.** vt cut; **sich dat die Haare ~ lassen** have one's hair cut **2.** vr cut oneself; **Schneider(in)** m(f) (-s, -) tailor; dressmaker; **Schneidezahn** *m* incisor

schneien *vi impers* snow

schnell 1. *adj* quick, fast **2.** *adv* quickly, fast; **mach ~!** hurry up; **Schnelldienst** *m* express service; **Schnellhefter** *m* loose-leaf binder; **Schnellimbiss** *m* snack bar; **Schnellstraße** *f* expressway

schneuzen *vr* → **schnäuzen**

schnitt *imperf of* **schneiden**

Schnitt *m* (-(e)s, -e) cut; (*where lines cross*) intersection; (*diagram*) (cross) section; (*of quantities*) average; **Schnittblume** *f* cut flower; **Schnitte** *f* (-, -n) slice; (*with filling*) sandwich; **Schnittkäse** *m* cheese slices *pl*; **Schnittlauch** *m* chives *pl*; **Schnittstelle** *f* IT, *fig* interface; **Schnittwunde** *f* cut, gash

Schnitzel *nt* (-s, -) (*of paper*) scrap; GASTR escalope

schnitzen *vt* carve

Schnorchel *m* (-s, -) snorkel; **schnorcheln** *vi* go snorkeling, snorkel; **Schnorcheln** *nt* (-s) snorkelling

schnüffeln *vi* sniff

Schnuller *m* (-s, -) dummy (*Brit*), pacifier (*US*)

Schnulze *f* (-, -n) (*film, novel*) weepie

Schnupfen *m* (-s, -) cold

schnuppern *vi* sniff

Schnur *f* (-, Schnüre) string, cord; ELEC lead; **schnurlos**

adj cordless

Schnurrbart *m* moustache

schnurren *vi* purr

Schnürschuh *m* lace-up (shoe); **Schnürsenkel** *m* (-s, -) shoelace

schob *imperf of* **schieben**

Schock *m* (-(e)s, -e) shock; **unter ~ stehen** be in a state of shock; **schockieren** *vt* shock

Schokolade *f* chocolate; **Schokoriegel** *m* chocolate bar

Scholle *f* (-, -n) plaice; (*on sea*) ice floe

schon *adv* already; **ist er ~ da?** is he here yet?; **warst du ~ einmal da?** have you ever been there?; **ich war ~ einmal da** I've been there before; **~ damals** even then; **~ 1999** as early (*or* as long ago) as 1999

schön *adj* beautiful; (*kind*) nice; (*woman*) beautiful, pretty; (*man*) beautiful, handsome; (*weather*) fine; **~e Grüße** best wishes; **~es Wochenende** have a nice weekend

schonen 1. *vt* look after **2.** *vr* take it easy

Schönheit *f* beauty

Schonkost *f* light diet

Schöpfung *f* creation

Schoppen *m* (-s, -) glass (of wine)

Schorf *m* (-(e)s, -e) scab

Schorle *f* (-, -n) spritzer

Schornstein *m* chimney; **Schornsteinfeger(in)** *m(f)* (*-s, -*) chimney sweep

schoss *imperf of* **schießen**

Schoß *m* (*-es, Schöße*) lap

Schotte *m* (*-n, -n*) Scot, Scotsman; **Schottin** *f* Scot, Scotswoman; **schottisch** *adj* Scottish, Scots; **Schottland** *nt* Scotland

schräg *adj* slanting; (*roof*) sloping; (*line*) diagonal; *fam* (*unconventional*) wacky

Schrank *m* (*-(e)s, Schränke*) cupboard; (*for clothes*) wardrobe (*Brit*), closet (*US*)

Schranke *f* (*-, -n*) barrier

Schrankwand *f* wall unit

Schraube *f* (*-, -n*) screw; **schrauben** *vt* screw; **Schraubenschlüssel** *m* spanner; **Schraubenzieher** *m* (*-s, -*) screwdriver; **Schraubverschluss** *m* screw top, screw cap

Schreck *m* (*-(e)s, -e*), **Schrecken** *m* (*-s, -*) terror; (*momentary*) fright; *jdm einen ~ einjagen* give sb a fright; **schreckhaft** *adj* jumpy; **schrecklich** *adj* terrible, dreadful

Schrei *m* (*-(e)s, -e*) scream; (*call*) shout

Schreibblock *m* writing pad; **schreiben** (*schrieb, geschrieben*) *vt, vi* spell; *wie schreibt man ...?* how do you spell ...?; **Schreiben** *nt* (*-s, -*) writing; (*sent to*

sb) letter; **Schreibfehler** *m* spelling mistake; **schreibgeschützt** *adj* write-protected; **Schreibtisch** *m* desk; **Schreibwaren** *pl* stationery *sg*; **Schreibwarenladen** *m* stationer's

schreien (*schrie, geschrie(e)n*) *vt, vi* scream; (*call*) shout

Schreiner(in) *m(f)* joiner; **Schreinerei** *f* joiner's workshop

schrie *imperf of* **schreien**

schrieb *imperf of* **schreiben**

Schrift *f* (*-, -en*) (*by hand*) handwriting; (*printing style*) typeface; (*type*) font; **schriftlich 1.** *adj* written **2.** *adv* in writing; *würden Sie uns das bitte ~ geben?* could we have that in writing, please?; **Schriftsteller(in)** *m(f)* (*-s, -*) writer

Schritt *m* (*-(e)s, -e*) step; *für ~* step by step; **Schrittgeschwindigkeit** *f* walking speed; **Schrittmacher** *m* MED pacemaker

Schrott *m* (*-(e)s, -e*) scrap metal; *fig* rubbish

schrubben *vi, vt* scrub; **Schrubber** *m* (*-s, -*) scrubbing brush

schrumpfen *vi* shrink

Schubkarren *m* (*-s, -*) wheelbarrow; **Schublade** *f* drawer

schubsen *vt* shove, push

schüchtern *adj* shy

schuf *imperf of* **schaffen**

Schuh *m* (*-(e)s, -e*) shoe;

Schuhcreme f shoe polish; **Schuhgeschäft** nt shoe shop; **Schuhgröße** f shoe size; **Schuhlöffel** m shoehorn; **Schuhsohle** f sole

Schulabschluss m school-leaving qualification

schuld adj **wer ist ~ daran?** whose fault is it?; **er ist ~** it's his fault, he's to blame; **Schuld** f (-) guilt; (blame) fault; **~ haben** to be blame (an + dat for); **er hat ~** it's his fault; **Schulden** pl (jdm etw sb sth); **Schulden** pl debts pl; **~ haben** be in debt; **~ machen** run up debts; **seine ~ bezahlen** pay off one's debts; **schuldig** adj guilty (an + dat of); (proper) due; **jdm etw ~ sein** owe sb sth

Schule f (-, -n) school; **in der ~** at school; **in die ~ gehen** to go to school; **Schüler(in)** m(f) (-s, -) pupil; (older) student; **Schüleraustausch** m school exchange; **Schulfach** nt subject; **Schulferien** pl school holidays pl (Brit) or vacation (US)); **schulfrei** adj **morgen ist ~** there's no school tomorrow; **Schulfreund(in)** m(f) schoolmate; **Schuljahr** nt school year; **Schulkenntnisse** pl **~ in Französisch** school(-level) French; **Schulklasse** f class; **Schulleiter(in)** m(f) headmaster / headmistress (Brit),

principal (US)

Schulter f (-, -n) shoulder

Schulung f training; (event) training course

Schund m (-(e)s) trash

Schuppe f (-, -n) (of fish) scale; **Schuppen** pl dandruff sg

Schürfwunde f graze

Schürze f (-, -n) apron

Schuss m (-es, Schüsse) shot; **mit einem ~ Wodka** with a dash of vodka

Schüssel f (-, -n) bowl

Schuster(in) m(f) (-s, -) shoemaker

Schutt m (-(e)s) rubble

Schüttelfrost m shivering fit; **schütteln** vt, vr shake

schütten 1. vt pour; (sugar, gravel etc) tip **2.** vi impers pour (down)

Schutz m (-es) protection (gegen, vor against, from); (place) shelter; **jdn in ~ nehmen** stand up for sb; **Schutzblech** nt mudguard

Schütze m (-n, -n) (in football) scorer; ASTR Sagittarius

schützen vt **jdn gegen/ vor etw ~** protect sb against / from sth; **Schutzimpfung** f inoculation, vaccination

schwach adj weak; **~e Augen** poor eyesight sg; **Schwäche** f (-, -n) weakness; **Schwachstelle** f weak point

Schwager m (-s, Schwäger) brother-in-law; **Schwägerin** f sister-in-law

Schwalbe   218

Schwalbe f (-, -n) swallow; (in football) dive
schwamm imperf of **schwimmen**
Schwamm m (-(e)s, Schwämme) sponge
Schwan m (-(e)s, Schwäne) swan
schwanger adj pregnant; **im vierten Monat ~ sein** be four months pregnant; Schwangerschaft f pregnancy; Schwangerschaftsabbruch m abortion; Schwangerschaftstest m pregnancy test
schwanken vi sway; (prices, figures) fluctuate; (be uncertain) hesitate; (drunkard etc) stagger
Schwanz m (-es, Schwänze) tail; vulg (penis) cock
Schwarm m (-(e)s, Schwärme) swarm; fam (pop star etc) heartthrob; schwärmen vi swarm; ~ **für** be mad about
schwarz adj black; ~ **sehen** fam be pessimistic (für about); **mir wurde ~ vor Augen** everything went black; Schwarzarbeit f illicit work; Schwarzbrot nt black bread; schwarzfahren irr vi travel without a ticket; Schwarzfahrer(in) m(f) fare-dodger; Schwarzmarkt m black market; Schwarzwald m Black Forest; schwarzweiß adj black and white

schwatzen vi chatter; Schwätzer(in) m(f) (-s, -) chatterbox; (long-winded) gasbag; (about other people) gossip
schweben vi float; (upwards) soar
Schwede m (-n, -n) Swede; Schweden nt (-s) Sweden; Schwedin f Swede; schwedisch adj Swedish; Schwedisch nt Swedish
Schwefel m (-s) sulphur
schweigen (schwieg, geschwiegen) vi be silent; stop talking; Schweigen nt (-s) silence
Schwein nt (-(e)s, -e) pig; fam luck; fam (vile person) swine; Schweinebraten m roast pork; Schweinefleisch nt pork; Schweinerei f mess; (act) dirty trick
Schweiß m (-es) sweat
schweißen vt, vi weld
Schweißfüße pl sweaty feet pl
Schweiz f (-) **die ~** Switzerland; Schweizer(in) m(f) (-s, -) Swiss; Schweizerdeutsch nt Swiss German; schweizerisch adj Swiss
Schwelle f (-, -n) doorstep; a. fig threshold
schwellen vi swell (up); Schwellung f swelling
schwer 1. adj heavy; (task, life, question) difficult, hard; (illness, mistake) serious, bad 2. adv (very) really; (injured

etc) seriously, badly; **jdm ~ fallen** be difficult for sb; **Schwerbehinderte(r)** *mf* severely disabled person; **schwerhörig** *adj* hard of hearing

Schwert *nt* (-(e)s, -er) sword

Schwester *f* (-, -n) sister; MED nurse

schwieg *imperf of* **schweigen**

Schwiegereltern *pl* parents--in-law *pl*; **Schwiegermutter** *f* mother-in-law; **Schwiegersohn** *m* son-in-law; **Schwiegertochter** *f* daughter-in--law; **Schwiegervater** *m* father-in-law

schwierig *adj* difficult, hard; **Schwierigkeit** *f* difficulty; **in ~en kommen** get into trouble; **jdm ~en machen** make things difficult for sb

Schwimmbad *nt* swimming pool; **Schwimmbecken** *nt* swimming pool; **schwimmen** (*schwamm, geschwommen*) *vi* swim; (*drift, not sink*) float; *fig* be all at sea; **Schwimmer(in)** *m(f)* swimmer; **Schwimmflosse** *f* flipper; **Schwimmflügel** *m* water wing; **Schwimmreifen** *m* rubber ring; **Schwimmweste** *f* life jacket

Schwindel *m* (-s) dizziness; (*fit*) dizzy spell; (*deception*) swindle; **schwindelfrei** *adj* **nicht ~ sein** suffer from vertigo; **~ sein** have a head for

heights; **schwindlig** *adj* dizzy; **mir ist ~** I feel dizzy

Schwips *m* **einen ~ haben** be tipsy

schwitzen *vi* sweat

schwoll *imperf of* **schwellen**

schwor *imperf of* **schwören**

schwören (*schwor, geschworen*) *vt, vi* swear; **einen Eid ~** take an oath

schwul *adj* gay

schwül *adj* close

Schwung *m* (-(e)s, *Schwünge*) swing; (*force when moving*) momentum; *fig* energy; *fam* (*quantity*) batch; **in ~ kommen** get going

Schwur *m* (-s, *Schwüre*) oath

scrollen *vi* IT scroll

sechs *num* six; **Sechs** *f* (-, -en) six; (*mark in school*) ≈ F; **sechshundert** *num* six hundred; **sechsmal** *adv* six times; **sechste(r, s)** *adj* sixth; → **dritte**; **Sechstel** *nt* (-s, -) (*fraction*) sixth; **sechzehn** *num* sixteen; **sechzehnte(r, s)** *adj* sixteenth; → **dritte**; **sechzig** *num* sixty; **in den ~er Jahren** in the sixties; **sechzigste(r, s)** *adj* sixtieth

Secondhandladen *m* secondhand shop

See **1.** *f* (-, -n) sea; **an der ~** by the sea **2.** *m* (-s, -n) lake; **am ~** by the lake; **Seehund** *m* seal; **Seeigel** *m* sea urchin; **seekrank** *adj* seasick

Seele *f* (-, -n) soul

Seeleute *pl* seamen *pl*, sailors *pl*

seelisch *adj* mental, psychological

Seelöwe *m* sea lion; **Seemann** *m* sailor, seaman; **Seemeile** *f* nautical mile; **Seemöwe** *f* seagull; **Seepferdchen** *nt* seahorse; **Seerose** *f* water lily; **Seestern** *m* starfish; **Seezunge** *f* sole

Segel *nt* (-s, -) sail; **Segelboot** *nt* yacht; **Segelfliegen** *nt* (-s) gliding; **Segelflugzeug** *nt* glider; **segeln** *vt, vi* sail; **Segelschiff** *nt* sailing ship

sehbehindert *adj* partially sighted

sehen (*sah, gesehen*) *vt, vi* see; *(in specific direction)* look; **gut/schlecht ~** have good/bad eyesight; **kann ich das mal ~?** can I have a look at it?; **wir ~ uns morgen!** see you tomorrow; **Sehenswürdigkeiten** *pl* sights *pl*

Sehne *f* (-, -n) tendon; *(on bow)* string

sehnen *vr* long *(nach* for)

Sehnenzerrung *f* MED pulled tendon

Sehnsucht *f* longing; **sehnsüchtig** *adj* longing

sehr *adv* very; *(with verbs)* a lot, very much; **zu ~** too much

seicht *adj* shallow

Seide *f* (-, -n) silk

Seife *f* (-, -n) soap; **Seifenoper** *f* soap (opera); **Seifenschale** *f* soap dish

Seil *nt* (-(e)s, -e) rope; *(metal)* cable; **Seilbahn** *f* cable railway

sein (*war, gewesen*) *vi, vaux* be; **lass das ~!** leave that!; *(sth annoying)* stop that!; **das kann ~** that's possible

sein *pron* his; her; its; **das ist ~e Tasche** that's his bag; **jeder hat ~e Sorgen** everyone has their problems; **seine(r, s)** *pron* his; hers; **das ist ~r/~/~s** that's his/hers; **seinetwegen** *adv* because of him; *(to please him)* for his sake

seit *conj* since; *(period)* for; **er ist ~ Montag hier** he's been here since Monday; **er ist ~ einer Woche hier** he's been here for a week; **~ langem** for a long time; **seitdem** *adv, conj* since

Seite *f* (-, -n) side; *(in book)* page; **zur ~ gehen** step aside; **Seitensprung** *m* affair; **Seitenstechen** *nt* (-s) **~ haben/bekommen** have/get a stitch; **Seitenstraße** *f* side street; **Seitenstreifen** *m* hard shoulder *(Brit)*, shoulder *(US)*; **seitenverkehrt** *adj* the wrong way round; **Seitenwind** *m* crosswind

seither *adv* since (then)

seitlich *adj* side

Sekretär(in) *m(f)* secretary

Sekt *m* (-(e)s, -e) sparkling wine

Sekte *f* (-, -n) sect

Sekunde *f* (-, -n) second; **Sekundenkleber** *m* (-s, -) superglue

selbst 1. *pron* **ich** ... I ... myself; **du/Sie** ~ you ... yourself; **er** ~ he ... himself; **sie** ~ she ... herself; **they** ... themselves; **wir haben es** ~ **gemacht** we did it ourselves; **mach es** ~ do it yourself; **das versteht sich ja von** ~ that goes without saying **2.** *adv* even; **mir gefiel's** even I liked it

selbständig *adj* → **selbstständig**

Selbstauslöser *m* (-s, -) PHOT self-timer; **Selbstbedienung** *f* self-service; **Selbstbefriedigung** *f* masturbation; **Selbstbeherrschung** *f* self-control; **Selbstbeteiligung** *f* (on insurance) excess; **selbstbewusst** *adj* (self-)confident; **selbstgemacht** *adj* self-made; **Selbstgespräch** *nt* ~**e führen** talk to oneself; **selbstklebend** *adj* self-adhesive; **Selbstkostenpreis** *m* cost price; **Selbstlaut** *m* vowel; **Selbstmord** *m* suicide; **selbstsicher** *adj* self-assured; **selbstständig** *adj* independent; (working) self-em-ployed; **selbstverständlich 1.** *adj* obvious; **ich halte das für** ~ I take that for granted **2.** *adv* naturally; **Selbstvertrauen** *nt* self-confidence

Sellerie *m* (-s, -(s)) *f* (-, -n) celeriac; (in sticks) celery

selten 1. *adj* rare **2.** *adv* seldom, rarely

seltsam *adj* strange; ~ **schmecken/riechen** taste/smell strange

Semester *nt* (-s, -) semester; **Semesterferien** *pl* vacation *sg*

Seminar *nt* (-s, -e) seminar

Semmel *f* (-, -n) roll; **Semmelbrösel** *pl* breadcrumbs *pl*

Senat *m* (-(e)s, -e) senate

senden 1. (sandte, gesandt) *vt* send **2.** *vt, vi* RADIO, TV broadcast; **Sender** *m* (-s, -) (TV) channel; (radio) station; (apparatus) transmitter; **Sendung** *f* RADIO, TV broadcasting; (single broadcast) programme

Senf *m* (-(e)s, -e) mustard

Senior(in) *m(f)* senior citizen; **Seniorenpass** *m* senior citizen's travel pass

senken 1. *vt* lower **2.** *vr* sink

senkrecht *adj* vertical

Sensation *f* (-, -en) sensation

sensibel *adj* sensitive

sentimental *adj* sentimental

separat *adj* separate

September *m* (-(s), -) September; → **Juni**

Serbien nt (-s) Serbia

Serie f series sg

seriös adj serious; (firm, people) respectable

Serpentine f hairpin (bend)

Serum nt (-s, Seren) serum

Server m (-s, -) IT server

Service 1. nt (-(s), -) (crockery) service **2.** m (-, -s) service

servieren vt, vi serve

Serviette f napkin, serviette

Servolenkung f AUTO power steering

Sesam m (-s, -s) sesame seeds pl

Sessel m (-s, -) armchair; **Sessellift** m chairlift

Set m or nt (-s, -s) set; (under plate etc) tablemat

setzen 1. vt put; (sail) **2.** vr settle; (person) sit down; ~ **Sie sich doch** please sit down

Seuche f (-, -n) epidemic

seufzen vt, vi sigh

Sex m (-(es)) sex; **sexistisch** adj sexist; **Sexualität** f sexuality; **sexuell** adj sexual

Seychellen pl Seychelles pl

sfr abbr = **Schweizer Franken**; Swiss franc(s)

Shampoo nt (-s, -s) shampoo

Shorts pl shorts pl

Shuttlebus m shuttle bus

sich pron himself; herself; itself; (plural) themselves; (after 'Sie') yourself; yourselves; (indefinite, after 'man') oneself; **er hat ~ ver-**letzt he hurt himself; **sie kennen ~** they know each other; **sie hat ~ sehr gefreut** she was very pleased; **er hat ~ das Bein gebrochen** he's broken his leg

sicher adj safe (vor + dat from); (sure) certain (gen of); (method, source) reliable; (self-assured) confident; **aber ~!** of course, sure; **Sicherheit** f safety; (protective measures) FIN security; (sureness) certainty; (self-assurance) confidence; **mit ~** definitely; **Sicherheitsabstand** m safe distance; **Sicherheitsgurt** m seat belt; **sicherheitshalber** adv just to be on the safe side; **Sicherheitsnadel** f safety pin; **Sicherheitsvorkehrung** f safety precaution; **sicherlich** adv certainly; (in all likelihood) probably

sichern vt secure (gegen against); (guard) IT protect; (data) back up; **Sicherung** f securing; (on machine etc) safety device; (on gun) safety catch; ELEC fuse; IT backup; **die ~ ist durchgebrannt** the fuse has blown

Sicht f (-) sight; (scene) view; **sichtbar** adj visible; **sichtlich** adj evident, obvious; **Sichtverhältnisse** pl visibility sg; **Sichtweite** f **in/außer ~** within/out of sight

sie pron she; (plural) they;

(*accusative*) her; them; (*thing*) it; **da ist ~ ja** there she is; **da sind ~ ja** there they are; **ich kenne ~** I know her; I know them

Sie *pron* you

Sieb *nt* (-(e)s, -e) sieve; (*for tea*) strainer

sieben *num* seven; **siebenhundert** *num* seven hundred; **siebenmal** *adv* seven times; **siebte(r, s)** *adj* seventh; → **dritte**; **Siebtel** *nt* (-s, -) (*fraction*) seventh; **siebzehn** *num* seventeen; **siebzehnte(r, s)** *adj* seventeenth; → **dritte**; **siebzig** *num* seventy; **in den ~er Jahren** in the seventies; **siebzigste(r, s)** *adj* seventieth

Siedlung *f* (-, -en) housing estate (*Brit*) (*or* development (*US*))

Sieg *m* (-(e)s, -e) victory; **siegen** *vi* win; **Sieger(in)** *m(f)* (-s, -) winner; **Siegerehrung** *f* presentation ceremony

siezen *vt* address as 'Sie'

Signal *nt* (-s, -e) signal

Silbe *f* (-, -n) syllable

Silber *nt* (-s) silver; **Silberhochzeit** *f* silver wedding; **Silbermedaille** *f* silver medal

Silikon *nt* (-s, -e) silicone

Silvester *nt* (-s, -), **Silvesterabend** *m* New Year's Eve, Hogmanay (*Scot*)

Simbabwe *nt* (-s) Zimbabwe

simpel *adj* simple

simultan *adj* simultaneous

simsen *vt*, *vi fam* text

Sinfonie *f* (-, -n) symphony; **Sinfonieorchester** *nt* symphony orchestra

Singapur *nt* (-s) Singapore

singen (*sang, gesungen*) *vt*, *vi* sing; **richtig/falsch ~** sing in tune/out of tune

Single 1. *f* (-, -s) (*CD*) single **2.** *m* (-s, -s) (*person*) single

Singular *m* singular

sinken (*sank, gesunken*) *vi* sink; (*prices etc*) fall, go down

Sinn *m* (-(e)s, -e) (*of word, speech etc*) sense, meaning; **~ machen** make sense; **das hat keinen ~** it's no use; **sinnlich** *adj* sensuous; (*erotic*) sensual; (*perception*) sensory; **sinnlos** *adj* stupid; (*behaviour*) senseless; (*futile*) pointless; (*talk etc*) meaningless; **sinnvoll** *adj* meaningful; (*reasonable*) sensible

Sirup *m* (-s, -e) syrup

Sitte *f* (-, -n) custom

Situation *f* situation

Sitz *m* (-es, -e) seat; **sitzen** (*saß, gesessen*) *vi* sit; (*remark, blow*) strike home; (*what one has learnt*) have sunk in; **der Rock sitzt gut** the skirt is a good fit; **Sitzgelegenheit** *f* place to sit down; **Sitzplatz** *m* seat; **Sitzung** *f* meeting

Sizilien *nt* (-s) Sicily

Skandal *m* (-s, -e) scandal

Skandinavien *nt* (-s) Scandinavia

Skateboard *nt* (-s, -s) skateboard; Skateboardfahrer(in) *m(f)* skateboarder

Skelett *nt* (-(e)s, -e) skeleton

skeptisch *adj* sceptical

Ski *m* (-s, -er) ski; ~ laufen (or fahren) ski; Skianzug *m* ski suit; Skibrille *f* ski goggles *pl*; Skifahren *nt* (-s, -) skiing; Skigebiet *nt* (-(e)s, -e) skiing area; Skihose *f* skiing trousers *pl*; Skikurs *m* skiing course; Skiläufer(in) *m(f)* skier; Skilehrer(in) *m(f)* ski instructor; Skilift *m* ski-lift

Skinhead *m* (-s, -s) skinhead

Skischuh *m* ski boot; Skispringen *nt* (-s, -n) ski jumping; Skistiefel *m* (-s, -) ski boot; Skistock *m* ski pole; Skiurlaub *m* skiing holiday (*Brit*) or vacation (*US*))

Skizze *f* (-, -n) sketch

Skonto *m* or *nt* (-s, -s) discount

Skorpion *m* (-s, -e) ZOOL scorpion; ASTR Scorpio

Skulptur *f* (-, -en) sculpture

S-Kurve *f* double bend

Slalom *m* (-s, -s) slalom

Slip *m* (-s, -s) (pair of) briefs *pl*; Slipeinlage *f* panty liner

Slowakei *f* (-) Slovakia; slowakisch *adj* Slovakian; Slowakisch *nt* Slovakian

Slowenien *nt* (-s) Slovenia; slowenisch *adj* Slovenian;

Slowenisch *nt* Slovenian

Smiley *m* (-s, -s) smiley

Smog *m* (-s) smog; Smogalarm *m* smog alert

Smoking *m* (-s, -s) dinner jacket (*Brit*), tuxedo (*US*)

SMS 1. *nt abbr* = **Short Message Service** 2. *f* text message; **ich schicke dir eine** ~ I'll text you, I'll send you a text (message)

Snowboard *nt* (-s, -s) snowboard; Snowboardfahren *nt* (-s) snowboarding; Snowboardfahrer(in) *m(f)* snowboarder

so 1. *adv* so; (*in this way*) like this; (*approximately*) about; **fünf Euro oder** ~ five euros or so; ~ **ein** such a; ~ ... **wie** ... as ... as ...; und ~ **weiter** and so on; ~ **genannt** so-called; ~ **viel** as much (*wie* as); ~ **weit sein** be ready; ~ **weit wie** (or **als**) **möglich** as far as possible 2. *conj* so; (*before adjective*) as

sobald *conj* as soon as

Socke *f* (-, -n) sock

Sodbrennen *nt* (-s) heartburn

Sofa *nt* (-s, -s) sofa

sofern *conj* if, provided (that)

soff *imperf of* **saufen**

sofort *adv* immediately, at once

Softeis *nt* soft ice-cream

Software *f* (-, -s) software

sog *imperf of* **saugen**

sogar *adv* even; **kalt, ~ sehr**

kalt cold, in fact very cold
Sohle f (-, -n) sole
Sohn m (-(e)s, Söhne) son
Soja f (-, Sojen) soya; **Sojasprossen** pl bean sprouts pl
solang(e) conj as long as
Solarium nt solarium
Solarzelle f solar cell
solche(r, s) pron such; **eine ~ Frau, solch eine Frau** such a woman, a woman like that; **~ Sachen** things like that, such things; **ich habe ~ Kopfschmerzen** I've got such a headache; **ich habe ~n Hunger** I'm so hungry
Soldat(in) m(f) (-en, -en) soldier
solidarisch adj showing solidarity
solid(e) adj solid; (life, person) respectable
Soll nt (-(s), -(s)) FIN debit; (amount of work) quota, target
sollen vi be supposed to; (obligation) shall, ought to; **soll ich?** shall I?; **du solltest besser nach Hause gehen** you'd better go home; **sie soll sehr reich sein** she's said to be very rich; **was soll das?** what's all that about?
Solo nt (-s, -s) solo
Sommer m (-s, -) summer; **Sommerfahrplan** m summer timetable; **Sommerferien** pl summer holidays pl (Brit) (or vacation sg (US)); **sommerlich** adj sum-

mery; (clothes) summer; **Sommerreifen** m normal tyre; **Sommersprossen** pl freckles pl; **Sommerzeit** f summertime; (by the clock) daylight saving time
Sonderangebot nt special offer; **sonderbar** adj strange, odd; **Sondermüll** m hazardous waste
sondern conj but; **nicht nur ..., ~ auch** not only ..., but also
Sonderpreis m special price; **Sonderschule** f special school; **Sonderzeichen** nt IT special character
Song m (-s, -s) song
Sonnabend m Saturday; → **Mittwoch**; **sonnabends** adv on Saturdays; → **mittwochs**
Sonne f (-, -n) sun; **sonnen** vr sunbathe; **Sonnenaufgang** m sunrise; **Sonnenblume** f sunflower; **Sonnenbrand** m sunburn; **Sonnenbrille** f sunglasses pl, shades pl; **Sonnencreme** f sun cream; **Sonnendach** nt (of car) sunroof; **Sonnendeck** nt sun deck; **Sonnenmilch** f suntan lotion; **Sonnenöl** nt suntan oil; **Sonnenschein** m sunshine; **Sonnenschirm** m parasol, sunshade; **Sonnenstich** m sunstroke; **Sonnenstudio** nt solarium; **Sonnenuhr** f sundial; **Sonnenuntergang** m sunset; **sonnig** adj

sunny

Sonntag *m* Sunday; → **Mittwoch**; sonntags *adv* on Sundays; → **mittwochs**

sonst *adv* else; (*if not*) otherwise, (or) else; (*at other times*) normally, usually; ~ **noch etwas?** anything else?; ~ **nichts** nothing else

sooft *conj* whenever

Sopran *m* (*-s, -e*) soprano

Sorge *f* (*-, -n*) worry; (*looking after*) care; **sich** *dat* **um jdn ~n machen** be worried about sb; sorgen 1. *vi* **für jdn** ~ look after sb; **für etw** ~ take care of sth, see to sth 2. *vr* worry (*um* about); sorgfältig *adj* careful

sortieren *vt* sort (out)

sosehr *conj* however much

Soße *f* (*-, -n*) sauce; (*with meat*) gravy

Soundkarte *f* IT sound card

Souvenir *nt* (*-s, -s*) souvenir

soviel *conj* as far as

soweit *conj* as far as

sowie *conj* as well as; (*with time*) as soon as

sowohl *conj* ~ ... **als** (*or* **wie**) **auch** both ... and

sozial *adj* social; Sozialhilfe *f* income support (*Brit*), welfare (aid) (*US*); Sozialismus *m* socialism; Sozialversicherung *f* social security; Sozialwohnung *f* council flat (*Brit*), state-subsidized apartment (*US*)

Soziologie *f* sociology

sozusagen *adv* so to speak

Spachtel *m* (*-s, -*) spatula

Spag(h)etti *pl* spaghetti *sg*

Spalte *f* (*-, -n*) crack; (*in glacier*) crevasse; (*in text*) column

spalten *vt, vr* split

Spange *f* (*-, -n*) clasp; (*for hair*) hair slide (*Brit*), barrette (*US*)

Spanien *nt* (*-s*) Spain; Spanier(in) *m(f)* (*-s, -*) Spaniard; spanisch *adj* Spanish; Spanisch *nt* Spanish

spann *imperf von* **spinnen**

spannen 1. *vt* (*make taut*) tighten 2. *vi* be tight

spannend *adj* exciting, gripping; Spannung *f* tension; ELEC voltage; *fig* suspense

Sparbuch *nt* savings book; (*account*) savings account; sparen *vt, vi* save

Spargel *m* (*-s, -*) asparagus; Spargelsuppe *f* asparagus soup

Sparkasse *f* savings bank; Sparkonto *f* savings account

spärlich *adj* meagre; (*clothing*) scanty

sparsam *adj* economical; Sparschwein *nt* piggy bank

Spaß *m* (*-es, Späße*) joke; (*pleasure*) fun; **es macht mir** ~ I enjoy it, it's (great) fun; **viel** ~! have fun

spät *adj, adv* late; **zu** ~ **kommen** be late

Spaten *m* (*-s, -*) spade

später *adj, adv* later; spätes-

tens *adv* at the latest; **Spät-
vorstellung** *f* late-night performance

Spatz *m* (-en, -en) sparrow

spazieren *vi* stroll, walk; ~
gehen go for a walk; **Spaziergang** *m* walk

Specht *m* (-(e)s, -e) woodpecker

Speck *m* (-(e)s, -e) bacon fat;
(streaky) bacon

Spedition *f* removal firm

Speiche *f* (-, -n) spoke

Speichel *m* (-s) saliva

Speicher *m* (-s, -) *(in building)* attic; IT memory; **speichern** *vt* IT store; *(send to
disk etc)* save

Speise *f* (-, -n) food; *(prepared)* dish; **Speisekarte** *f*
menu; **Speiseröhre** *f* gullet,
oesophagus; **Speisesaal** *m*
dining hall; **Speisewagen**
m dining car

Spende *f* (-, -n) donation;
spenden *vt* donate, give

spendieren *vt* *jdm etw ~* treat
sb to sth

Sperre *f* (-, -n) barrier; *(on ski
or sth)* ban; **sperren** *vt* block;
SPORT suspend; *(exports etc)*
ban; **Sperrstunde** *f* closing
time; **Sperrung** *f* closing

Spesen *pl* expenses *pl*

spezialisieren *vr* specialize
(auf + acc in); **Spezialist(in)**
m(f) specialist; **Spezialität** *f*
speciality *(Brit)*, specialty
(US); **speziell 1.** *adj* special
2. *adv* especially

Spiegel *m* (-s, -) mirror; **Spiegelei** *nt* fried egg (sunny-side
up *(US)*); **spiegelglatt** *adj*
very slippery; **Spiegelre-
flexkamera** *f* reflex camera

Spiel *nt* (-(e)s, -e) game; *(activity)* play(ing); *(of playing
cards)* pack, deck; **Spielautomat** *m* gaming machine;
(with cash payout) slot machine; **spielen** *vt*, *vi* play;
(for money) gamble; THEAT
perform, act; **Klavier ~** play
the piano; **spielend** *adv* easily; **Spieler(in)** *m(f)* (-s, -)
player; *(for money)* gam-
bler; **Spielfeld** *nt* *(for football, hockey)* field; *(for basketball)* court; **Spielfilm** *m*
feature film; **Spielkasino** *nt*
casino; **Spielplatz** *m* playground; **Spielraum** *m* room
to manoeuvre; **Spielregel** *f*
rule; **sich an die ~n halten**
stick to the rules; **Spielsa-
chen** *f* toys *pl*; **Spielverder-
ber(in)** *m(f)* (-s, -) spoil-
sport; **Spielzeug** *nt* toys *pl*;
(single item) toy

Spieß *m* (-es, -e) spear; *(for
roasting)* spit; **Spießer(in)**
m(f) (-s, -) square, stuffy
type; **spießig** *adj* square, un-
cool

Spikes *pl* SPORT spikes *pl*;
AUTO studs *pl*

Spinat *m* (-(e)s, -e) spinach

Spinne *f* (-, -n) spider; **spinnen** *(spann, gesponnen)* *vt*,
vi spin; *fam* talk rubbish;

be crazy; **du spinnst!** you must be mad; **Spinnwebe** f (-, -n) cobweb

Spion(in) m(f) (-s, -e) spy; **spionieren** vi spy; fig snoop around

Spirale f (-, -n) spiral; MED coil

Spirituosen pl spirits pl, liquor sg (US)

Spiritus m (-, -se) spirit

spitz adj (nose, chin) pointed; (pencil, knife) sharp; (angle) acute; **Spitze** f (-, -n) point; (of finger, nose) tip; (remark) taunt, dig; (in race etc) lead; (fabric) lace; **Spitzengeschwindigkeit** f top speed; **Spitzer** m (-s, -) pencil sharpener; **Spitzname** m nickname

Spliss m (-es, -se) split ends pl

sponsern vt sponsor; **Sponsor(in)** m(f) (-s, -en) sponsor

spontan adj spontaneous

Sport m (-(e)s, -e) sport; **~ treiben** do sport; **Sportanlage** f sports grounds pl; **Sportart** f sport; **Sportbekleidung** f sportswear; **Sportgeschäft** nt sports shop; **Sporthalle** f gymnasium, gym; **Sportlehrer(in)** m(f) (-s, -) sports instructor, PE teacher; **Sportler(in)** m(f) (-s, -) sportsman/-woman; **sportlich** adj sporting; (person) sporty; **Sportplatz** m playing field; **Sportverein** m sports club; **Sportwagen** m sports car

sprach imperf of **sprechen**

Sprache f (-, -n) language; (faculty) speech; **Sprachenschule** f language school; **Sprachkurs** m language course; **Sprachunterricht** m language teaching

sprang imperf of **springen**

Spray m or nt (-s, -s) spray

Sprechanlage f intercom; **sprechen** (sprach, gesprochen) vt, vi speak (jdn, mit jdm to sb); (converse) talk (mit to, über, von about); **~ Sie Deutsch?** do you speak German?; **kann ich bitte mit David ~?** (on phone) can I speak to David, please?; **Sprecher(in)** m(f) (-s, -) speaker; (on TV, radio) announcer; **Sprechstunde** f consultation; (of doctor) surgery hours pl; (of solicitor etc) office hours pl; **Sprechzimmer** nt consulting room

Sprichwort nt proverb

Springbrunnen m fountain

springen (sprang, gesprungen) vi jump; (glass) crack; (headfirst) dive

Sprit m (-(e)s, -e) fam petrol (Brit), gas (US)

Spritze f (-, -n) syringe; (jab) injection; (on hose) nozzle; **spritzen 1.** vt spray; MED inject **2.** vi splash; MED give injections

Spruch m (-(e)s, Sprüche) saying

Sprudel m (-s, -) sparkling

mineral water; (sweet) fizzy drink (Brit), soda (US); **sprudeln** vi bubble

Sprühdose f aerosol (can); **sprühen** vt, vi spray; fig sparkle; **Sprühregen** m drizzle

Sprung m (-(e)s, Sprünge) jump; (in glass etc) crack; **Sprungbrett** nt springboard; **Sprungschanze** f ski jump; **Sprungturm** m diving platforms pl

Spucke f (-) spit; **spucken** vt, vi spit

spuken vi (ghost) walk; **hier spukt es** this place is haunted

Spülbecken nt sink

Spule f (-, -n) spool; ELEC coil

Spüle f (-, -n) sink; **spülen** vt, vi rinse; (after meal) wash up; (toilet) flush; **Spülmaschine** f dishwasher; **Spülmittel** nt washing-up liquid (Brit), dishwashing liquid (US); **Spültuch** nt dishcloth; **Spülung** f (of toilet) flush

Spur f (-, -en) trace; (of feet, wheels) track; (followed by police etc) trail; (on road) lane; **die ~ wechseln** change lanes pl

spüren vt feel; (observe) notice; **Spürhund** m sniffer dog

Squash nt (-) squash; **Squashschläger** m squash racket

Sri Lanka nt (-s) Sri Lanka

Staat m (-(e)s, -en) state; **staatlich** adj state(-); (industry, museum etc) state--run; **Staatsangehörigkeit** f nationality; **Staatsanwalt** m, **-anwältin** f prosecuting counsel (Brit), district attorney (US); **Staatsbürger(in)** m(f) citizen; **Staatsbürgerschaft** f nationality

Stab m (-(e)s, Stäbe) rod; (of cage, window) bar; **Stäbchen** nt chopstick; **Stabhochsprung** m pole vault

stabil adj stable; (furniture) sturdy

stach imperf of **stechen**

Stachel m (-s, -n) spike; (of animal) spine; (of insect) sting; **Stachelbeere** f gooseberry; **Stacheldraht** m barbed wire; **stachelig** adj prickly

Stadion nt (-s, Stadien) stadium

Stadt f (-, Städte) town; (large) city; **in der ~** in town; **Stadtautobahn** f urban motorway (Brit) (or expressway (US)); **Städtepartnerschaft** f twinning; **Stadtführer** m (booklet) city guide; **Stadtführung** f city sightseeing tour; **Stadthalle** f municipal hall; **städtisch** adj municipal; **Stadtmauer** f city wall(s); **Stadtmitte** f town / city centre, downtown (US); **Stadtplan** m (street) map; **Stadtrand** m outskirts pl; **Stadt-**

rundfahrt f city tour

stahl imperf of **stehlen**

Stahl m (-(e)s, Stähle) steel

Stall m (-(e)s, Ställe) stable; (for rabbit) hutch; (for pigs) pigsty; (for poultry) henhouse

Stamm m (-(e)s, Stämme) (of tree) trunk; (people) tribe; stammen vi **~ aus** come from; Stammgast m regular (guest); Stammkunde m, Stammkundin f regular (customer); Stammtisch m table reserved for regulars

stand imperf of **stehen**

Stand m (-(e)s, Stände) (of water, petrol) level; (posture) standing position; (situation) state; (in game) score; (at fair etc) stand

Standby-Betrieb m stand-by; Standby-Ticket nt stand-by ticket

Ständer m (-s, -) stand; fam (erection) hard-on

Standesamt nt registry office

ständig adj permanent; (uninterrupted) constant, continual

Standlicht nt sidelights pl (Brit), parking lights pl (US); Standort m position; Standpunkt m standpoint; Standspur f AUTO hard shoulder (Brit), shoulder (US)

Stange f (-, -n) stick; (long, round) pole; (metal) bar; (of cigarettes) carton

stank imperf of **stinken**

Stapel m (-s, -) pile

Star 1. m (-(e)s, -e) (bird) starling; MED cataract 2. m (-s, -s) (in film etc) star

starb imperf of **sterben**

stark adj strong; (intense, big) heavy; (in measurements) thick; Stärke f (-, -n) strength; (dimension) thickness; (in washing, food) starch; stärken vt strengthen; (washing) starch; Stärkung f strengthening; (food) refreshment

starr adj stiff; (unyielding) rigid; (look) staring

starren vi stare

Start m (-(e)s, -e) start; AVIAT takeoff; Startbahn f runway; starten vi, vt start; AVIAT take off; Startmenü nt IT start menu

Station f stop; (on railway) station; (in hospital) ward; stationär adj stationary; **~e Behandlung** in-patient treatment; **jdn ~ behandeln** treat sb as an in-patient

Statistik f statistics pl

Stativ nt tripod

statt conj, prep + gen or dat instead of; **~ zu arbeiten** instead of working

stattfinden irr vi take place

Statue f (-, -n) statue

Statusleiste f, Statuszeile f IT status bar

Stau m (-(e)s, -e) (traffic) jam; **im ~ stehen** be stuck in a traffic jam

Staub m (-(e)s) dust; **~ wischen** dust; **staubig** adj dusty; **staubsaugen** vt, vi vacuum, hoover (BRIT); **Staubsauger** m vacuum cleaner, hoover® (BRIT); **Staubtuch** nt duster

Staudamm m dam

staunen vi be astonished (über + acc an)

Stausee m reservoir; **Stauung** f (of water) damming-up; (of blood, traffic) congestion

Stauwarnung f traffic report

Steak nt (-s, -s) steak

stechen (stach, gestochen) vt, vi (with needle etc) prick; (with knife) stab; (with finger) poke; (bee) sting; (mosquito) bite; (sun) burn; (in card game) trump; **Stechen** nt (-s, -) sharp pain, stabbing pain; **Stechmücke** f mosquito

Steckdose f socket; **stecken 1.** vt put; (pin) stick; (in sewing) pin **2.** vi (not move) be stuck; (pin) be sticking; **der Schlüssel steckt** the key is in the door; **Stecker** m (-s, -) plug; **Stecknadel** f pin

Steg m (-s, -e) bridge

stehen (stand, gestanden) **1.** vi stand (zu by); (with location, circumstance) be; (watch, machine, traffic) have stopped; **was steht im**

Brief? what does it say in the letter?; **jdm (gut) ~ suit** sb; **~ bleiben** (clock) stop; **~ lassen** leave **2.** vi impers **wie steht's?** what's the score?; **Stehlampe** f standard lamp (BRIT), floor lamp (US)

stehlen (stahl, gestohlen) vt steal

Stehplatz m (in concert etc) standing ticket

Steiermark f (-) Styria

steif adj stiff

steigen (stieg, gestiegen) vi (prices, temperature) rise; (person) climb

steigern vt, vi increase

Steigung f incline, gradient

steil adj steep; **Steilhang** m steep slope; **Steilküste** f steep coast

Stein m (-(e)s, -e) stone; **Steinbock** m ZOOL ibex; ASTR Capricorn; **Steinbutt** m (-s, -e) turbot; **steinig** adj stony; **Steinschlag** m falling rocks pl

Stelle f (-, -n) place, spot; (work) post, job; (department) office; **ich an deiner ~** if I were you; **stellen 1.** vt put; (clock etc) set (auf + acc to); (make available) provide **2.** vr (to the police) give oneself up; **sich schlafend ~** pretend to be asleep; **Stellenangebot** nt job offer, vacancy; **stellenweise** adv in places; **Stellplatz** m parking space; **Stellung** f position; **zu etw ~ nehmen** comment on sth; **Stellvertreter(in)** m(f) representative; (as official post) deputy

Stempel m (-s, -) stamp; **stempeln** vt stamp; (postage stamp) cancel

sterben (starb, gestorben) vi die

Stereoanlage f stereo (system)

steril adj sterile; **sterilisieren** vt sterilize

Stern m (-(e)s, -e) star; **Sternbild** nt constellation; (in astrology) star sign, sign of the zodiac; **Sternfrucht** f star fruit; **Sternschnuppe** f (-, -n) shooting star; **Sternwarte** f (-e, -n) observatory; **Sternzeichen** nt star sign, sign of the zodiac; **welches ~ bist du?** what's your star sign?

stets adv always

Steuer 1. nt (-s, -) AUTO steering wheel **2.** f (-, -n) tax; **Steuerberater(in)** m(f) tax adviser; **Steuerbord** nt starboard; **Steuererklärung** f tax declaration; **steuerfrei** adj tax-free; (goods) duty-free; **Steuerknüppel** m control column; AVIAT, IT joystick; **steuern** vt, vi steer; (plane) pilot; (development, volume) IT control; **steuerpflichtig** adj taxable; **Steuerung** f AUTO steering; (instru-

ments) controls pl; AVIAT piloting; fig control

Stich m (-(e)s, -e) (of insect) sting; (of mosquito) bite; (with knife) stab; (in sewing) stitch; (of colour) tinge; (in card game) trick; ART engraving; **Stichprobe** f spot check

sticken vt, vi embroider

Sticker m (-s, -) sticker

Stickerei f embroidery

stickig adj stuffy, close

Stiefbruder m stepbrother

Stiefel m (-s, -) boot

Stiefmutter f stepmother

Stiefmütterchen nt pansy

Stiefschwester f stepsister; **Stiefsohn** m stepson; **Stieftochter** f stepdaughter; **Stiefvater** m stepfather

stieg imperf of **steigen**

Stiege f (-, -n) steps pl

Stiel m (-(e)s, -e) handle; BOT stalk; **ein Eis am ~** an ice lolly (Brit), a Popsicle® (US)

Stier m (-(e)s, -e) ZOOL bull; ASTR Taurus; **Stierkampf** m bullfight; **Stierkämpfer(in)** m(f) bullfighter

stieß imperf of **stoßen**

Stift m (-(e)s, -e) (wooden) peg; (nail) tack; (for writing, drawing) pen; crayon; pencil

Stil m (-s, -e) style

still adj quiet; (motionless) still

stillen vt breast-feed

stillhalten irr vi keep still; **Stillleben** nt still life; **stillstehen** irr vi stand still

Stimme f (-, -n) voice; (in election) vote

stimmen vi be right; **stimmt!** that's right; **hier stimmt was nicht** there's something wrong here; **stimmt so!** keep the change

Stimmung f mood; (in group etc) atmosphere

stinken (stank, gestunken) vi stink (nach of)

Stipendium nt scholarship; (as means of support) grant

Stirn f (-, -en) forehead; **Stirnhöhle** f sinus

Stock 1. m (-(e)s, Stöcke) stick; BOT stock 2. m (Stockwerke pl) floor, storey; **Stockbett** nt bunk bed; **Stöckelschuhe** pl high-heels; **Stockwerk** nt floor; **im ersten ~** on the first floor (Brit), on the second floor (US)

Stoff m (-(e)s, -e) (fabric) material; (substance) matter; (of book etc) subject (matter); fam (drugs) stuff

stöhnen vi groan (vor with)

stolpern vi stumble, trip

stolz adj proud

stopp interj hold it; (introducing new thought) hang on a minute; **stoppen** vt, vi stop; (with watch) time; **Stoppschild** nt stop sign; **Stoppuhr** f stopwatch

Stöpsel m (-s, -) plug; (for bottle) stopper

Storch m (-(e)s, Störche) stork

stören vt disturb; (hinder) in-

terfere with; **darf ich dich kurz ~?** can I trouble you for a minute?; **stört es dich, wenn ...?** do you mind if ...?

stornieren vt cancel

Störung f disturbance; (on phone line) fault

Stoß m (-es, Stöße) push; (with fist, elbow) blow; (with foot) kick; (of books, washing) pile; **Stoßdämpfer** m (-s, -) shock absorber

stoßen (stieß, gestoßen) 1. vt shove, push; (with a blow) knock; (with foot) kick; (head etc) bump 2. vr bang oneself

Stoßstange f AUTO bumper

stottern vt, vi stutter

Strafe f (-, -n) punishment; SPORT penalty; (in prison) sentence; (money) fine; **strafen** vt punish; **Strafraum** m penalty area; **Strafstoß** m penalty kick; **Straftat** f (criminal) offence; **Strafzettel** m ticket

Strahl m (-s, -en) ray, beam; (of water) jet; **strahlen** vi radiate; fig beam

Strähne f (-, -n) strand; (white, coloured) streak

Strand m (-(e)s, Strände) beach; **am ~** on the beach; **Strandcafé** nt beach café

strapazieren vt be hard on; (person, nerves) be a strain on

Straße f (-, -n) road; (in town) street; **Straßenarbeiten** pl roadworks *pl* (*Brit*), road repairs *pl* (*US*); Straßenbahn *f* tram (*Brit*), streetcar (*US*); Straßencafé *nt* pavement café (*Brit*), sidewalk café (*US*); Straßenfest *nt* street party; Straßenglätte *f* slippery roads *pl*; Straßenrand *m am ~* at the roadside; Straßenschild *nt* street sign; Straßensperre *f* roadblock; Straßenverhältnisse *pl* road conditions *pl*

Strategie *f* (-, -n) strategy
Strauch *m* (-(e)s, Sträucher) bush, shrub
Strauß 1. *m* (-es, Sträuße) bunch; (*as gift*) bouquet 2. *m* (Sträuße *pl*) ostrich
Strecke *f* (-, -n) route; distance; RAIL line
strecken *vt, vr* stretch
streckenweise *adv* in parts; (*occasionally*) at times
Streich *m* (-(e)s, -e) trick, prank
streicheln *vt* stroke
streichen (strich, gestrichen) *vt* paint; (*word etc*) delete; (*flight, race etc*) cancel
Streichholz *nt* match; Streichholzschachtel *f* matchbox; Streichkäse *m* cheese spread
Streifen *m* (-s, -) stripe; (*piece*) strip; (*movie*) film
Streifenwagen *m* patrol car
Streik *m* (-(e)s, -s) strike; streiken *vi* be on strike
Streit *m* (-(e)s, -e) argument

(*um, wegen* about, over); streiten (stritt, gestritten) *vi, vr* argue (*um, wegen* about, over)
streng *adj* (*look, appearance*) severe; (*teacher, measure*) strict; (*smell etc*) sharp
Stress *m* (-es) stress; stressen *vt* stress (out); stressig *adj fam* stressful
Stretching *nt* (-s) SPORT stretching exercises *pl*
streuen *vt* scatter
strich *imperf of* *streichen*
Strich *m* (-(e)s, -e) line; Stricher *m fam* rent boy (*Brit*), boy prostitute; Strichkode *m* (-s, -s) bar code; Stricherin *f fam* hooker; Strichpunkt *m* semicolon
Strick *m* (-(e)s, -e) rope
stricken *vt, vi* knit; Strickjacke *f* cardigan; Stricknadel *f* knitting needle
Stripper(in) *m(f)* stripper; Striptease *m* (-) striptease
stritt *imperf of* *streiten*
Stroh *nt* (-(e)s) straw; Strohdach *nt* thatched roof; Strohhalm *m* (drinking) straw; Strohhut *m* straw hat
Strom *m* (-(e)s, Ströme) river; *fig* stream; ELEC current; Stromanschluss *m* connection; Stromausfall *m* power failure
strömen *vi* stream; pour; Strömung *f* current
Stromzähler *m* electricity meter

Strophe f (-, -n) verse

Strudel m (-s, -) (in river) whirlpool; (dessert) strudel

Struktur f structure; (of material) texture

Strumpf m (-(e)s, Strümpfe) stocking; sock; **Strumpfhose** f (pair of) tights pl (Brit), pantyhose (US)

Stück nt (-(e)s, -e) piece; (some) bit; (of sugar) lump; THEAT play

Student (in) m(f) student; **Studentenausweis** m student card; **Studentenwohnheim** nt hall of residence (Brit), dormitory (US); **Studienabschluss** m qualification (at the end of a course of higher education); **Studienfahrt** f study trip; **Studienplatz** m university/college place; **studieren** vt, vi study; **Studium** nt studies pl; **während seines ~s** while he is/was studying

Stufe f (-, -n) step; (in development) stage

Stuhl m (-(e)s, Stühle) chair

stumm adj silent; MED dumb

stumpf adj blunt; (apathetic, not shiny) dull; **stumpfsinnig** adj dull

Stunde f (-, -n) hour; (in school etc) lesson; **eine halbe ~** half an hour; **Stundenkilometer** m **80 ~** 80 kilometres an hour; **stundenlang** adv for hours; **Stundenplan** m timetable;

stündlich adj hourly

Stuntman m (-s, Stuntmen) stuntman; **Stuntwoman** f (-, Stuntwomen) stuntwoman

stur adj stubborn; (stronger) pigheaded

Sturm m (-(e)s, Stürme) storm; **stürmen** vi (wind) blow hard; (rush) storm; **Stürmer**(in) m(f) striker, forward; **Sturmflut** f storm tide; **stürmisch** adj stormy; fig tempestuous; (time) turbulent; (lover) passionate; (applause, welcome) tumultuous; **Sturmwarnung** f gale warning

Sturz m (-es, Stürze) fall; POL overthrow; **stürzen 1.** vt hurl; POL overthrow; (container) overturn **2.** vi fall; (rush) dash; **Sturzhelm** m crash helmet

Stute f (-, -n) mare

Stütze f (-, -n) support; (person who helps) help; fam (for unemployed person) dole (Brit), welfare (US)

stutzig adj perplexed, puzzled; (distrustful) suspicious

Styropor® nt (-s) polystyrene (Brit), styrofoam (US)

subjektiv adj subjective

Substanz f (-, -en) substance

subtrahieren vt subtract

Subvention f subsidy; **subventionieren** vt subsidize

Suche f search (nach for); **auf**

der ~ nach etw sein be looking for sth; **suchen 1.** *vt* look for; IT search **2.** *vi* look, search (*nach* for); **Suchmaschine** *f* IT search engine

Sucht *f* (-, *Süchte*) mania; MED addiction; **süchtig** *adj* addicted; **Süchtige(r)** *mf* addict

Süd south; **Südafrika** *nt* South Africa; **Südamerika** *nt* South America; **Süddeutschland** *nt* Southern Germany; **Süden** *m* (-s) south; ***im ~ Deutschlands*** in the south of Germany; **Südeuropa** *nt* Southern Europe; **Südkorea** *nt* (-s) South Korea; **südlich** *adj* southern; (*course, direction*) southerly; **Südost(en)** *m* southeast; **Südpol** *m* South Pole; **Südstaaten** *pl* (*in USA*) the Southern States *pl*, the South *sg*; **südwärts** *adv* south, southwards; **Südwest(en)** *m* southwest; **Südwind** *m* south wind

Sultanine *f* sultana

Sülze *f* (-, -n) jellied meat

Summe *f* (-, -n) sum; (*altogether*) total

summen *vi, vt* hum; (*insect*) buzz

Sumpf *m* (-(e)s, *Sümpfe*) marsh; (*in the tropics*) swamp; **sumpfig** *adj* marshy

Sünde *f* (-, -n) sin

super *adj fam* super, great; **Super** *nt* (-s) four star (petrol) (*Brit*), premium (*US*); **Supermarkt** *m* supermarket

Suppe *f* (-, -n) soup; **Suppengrün** *nt* bunch of herbs and vegetables for flavouring soup; **Suppenwürfel** *m* stock cube

Surfbrett *nt* surfboard; **surfen** *vi* surf; ***im Internet ~*** surf the Internet; **Surfer(in)** *m(f)* (-s, -) surfer

Surrealismus *m* surrealism

süß *adj* sweet; **süßen** *vt* sweeten; **Süßigkeit** *f* sweet (*Brit*), candy (*US*); **süßsauer** *adj* sweet-and-sour; **Süßspeise** *f* dessert; **Süßstoff** *m* sweetener; **Süßwasser** *nt* fresh water

Sweatshirt *nt* (-s, -s) sweatshirt

Swimmingpool *m* (-s, -s) (swimming) pool

Sylvester *nt* → *Silvester*

Symbol *nt* (-s, -e) symbol; **Symbolleiste** *f* IT toolbar

Symmetrie *f* (-, -n) symmetry; **symmetrisch** *adj* symmetrical

sympathisch *adj* nice; ***jdn ~ finden*** like sb

Symphonie *f* (-, -n) symphony

Symptom *nt* (-s, -e) symptom (*für* of)

Synagoge *f* (-, -n) synagogue

synchronisiert *adj* (*film*) dubbed; **Synchronstimme** *f* dubbing voice

Synthesizer *m* (-s, -) MUS syn-

thesizer
Synthetik f (-, -en) synthetic (fibre); **synthetisch** adj synthetic

Syrien nt (-s) Syria

System nt (-s, -e) system; **systematisch** adj systematic; **Systemsteuerung** f IT control panel

Szene f (-, -n) scene

T

Tabak m (-s, -e) tobacco; **Tabakladen** m tobacconist's

Tabelle f table

Tablett nt (-s, -e) tray

Tablette f tablet, pill

Tabulator m tabulator, tab

Tacho(meter) m (-s, -) AUTO speedometer

Tafel f (-, -n) a. MATH table; (for notices) board; (in classroom) blackboard; (commemorative) plaque; **eine ~ Schokolade** a bar of chocolate

Tag m (-(e)s, -e) day; daylight; **guten ~!** good morning / afternoon; **am ~** during the day; **sie hat ihre ~e** she's got her period; **eines ~es** one day; **Tagebuch** nt diary; **tagelang** adv for days (on end); **Tagesanbruch** m daybreak; **Tagesausflug** m day trip; **Tagescreme** f day cream; **Tagesgericht** nt dish of the day; **Tageskarte** f day ticket; **die ~** (in restaurant) today's menu; **Tageslicht** nt daylight; **Tagesordnung** f agenda; **Tagestour** f day trip; **Tageszeitung** f daily newspaper; **täglich** adj, adv daily; **tags(über)** adv during the day; **Tagung** f conference

Tai Chi nt (-) tai chi

Taille f (-, -n) waist; **tailliert** adj fitted

Taiwan nt (-s) Taiwan

Takt m (-(e)s, -e) tact; MUS time

Taktik f (-, -en) tactics pl

Tal nt (-(e)s, Täler) valley

Talent nt (-(e)s, -e) talent; **talentiert** adj talented

Talkmaster(in) m(f) (-s, -) talk-show host; **Talkshow** f (-, -s) talkshow

Tampon m (-s, -s) tampon

Tandem nt (-s, -s) tandem

Tang m (-s, -e) seaweed

Tank m (-s, -s) tank; **Tankanzeige** f fuel gauge; **Tankdeckel** m fuel cap; **tanken** vi get some petrol (Brit) (or gas (US)); AVIAT refuel; **Tanker** m (-s, -) (oil) tanker; **Tankstelle** f petrol station (Brit), gas station (US)

Tanne f (-, -n) fir; **Tannenzapfen** m fir cone

Tansania nt (-s) Tanzania

Tante f (-, -n) aunt; **Tante-Emma-Laden** m corner shop

(Brit), grocery store *(US)*

Tanz m *(-es, Tänze)* dance; **tanzen** vi, vi dance; **Tänzer(in)** m(f) dancer; **Tanzfläche** f dance floor; **Tanzkurs** m dancing course; **Tanzlehrer(in)** m(f) dancing instructor; **Tanzstunde** f dancing lesson

Tapete f *(-, -n)* wallpaper; **tapezieren** vt, vi wallpaper

Tarif m *(-s, -e)* tariff, (scale of) fares / charges pl

Tasche f *(-, -n)* bag; (in trousers etc) pocket; (handbag) bag *(Brit)*, purse *(US)*; **Taschen-** in cpds pocket; **Taschenbuch** nt paperback; **Taschendieb(in)** m(f) pickpocket; **Taschengeld** nt pocket money; **Taschenlampe** f torch *(Brit)*, flashlight *(US)*; **Taschenmesser** nt penknife; **Taschenrechner** m pocket calculator; **Taschentuch** nt handkerchief

Tasse f *(-, -n)* cup; **eine ~ Kaffee** a cup of coffee

Tastatur f keyboard; **Taste** f *(-, -n)* button; (of piano, computer) key; **Tastenkombination** f IT shortcut; **Tastentelefon** nt push-button telephone

tat imperf of **tun**

Tat f *(-, -en)* action

Tatar nt *(-s, -s)* raw minced beef

Täter(in) m(f) *(-s, -)* culprit

Tätigkeit f activity; (job) oc-

cupation

tätowieren vt tattoo; **Tätowierung** f tattoo (an + dat on)

Tatsache f fact; **tatsächlich 1.** adj actual **2.** adv really

Tau 1. nt *(-(e)s, -e)* rope **2.** m *(-(e)s)* dew

taub adj deaf

Taube f *(-, -n)* pigeon, dove

taubstumm adj deaf-and-dumb; **Taubstumme(r)** mf deaf-mute

tauchen 1. vt dip **2.** vi dive; NAUT submerge; **Tauchen** nt *(-s)* diving; **Taucher(in)** m(f) *(-s, -)* diver; **Taucheranzug** m diving (or wet) suit; **Taucherbrille** f diving goggles pl; **Tauchermaske** f diving mask; **Tauchkurs** m diving course

tauen vi impers thaw

Taufe f *(-, -n)* baptism; **taufen** vt baptize; (name) christen

taugen vi be suitable (für for); **nichts ~** be no good

Tausch m *(-(e)s, -e)* exchange; **tauschen** vt exchange, swap

täuschen 1. vt deceive **2.** vi be deceptive **3.** vr be wrong; **täuschend** adj deceptive; **Täuschung** f deception; (optical) illusion

tausend num a thousand; **vier~** four thousand; **~ Dank!** thanks a lot; **tausendmal** adv a thousand times; **tausendste(r, s)** adj thousandth; **Tausendstel** nt *(-s,*

-) (*fraction*) thousandth

Tauwetter *nt* thaw

Taxi *nt* taxi; **Taxifahrer(in)** *m(f)* taxi driver; **Taxistand** *m* taxi rank (*Brit*), taxi stand (*US*)

Team *nt* (*-s, -s*) team; **Teamarbeit** *f* team work; **teamfähig** *adj* able to work in a team

Technik *f* technology; (*applied*) engineering; (*method, skill*) technique; **Techniker(in)** *m(f)* (*-s, -*) engineer; SPORT, MUS technician; **technisch** *adj* technical

Techno *m* (*-s*) MUS techno

Teddybär *m* teddy bear

Tee *m* (*-s, -s*) tea; **Teebeutel** *m* teabag; **Teekanne** *f* teapot; **Teelöffel** *m* teaspoon

Teer *m* (*-s, -e*) tar

Teesieb *nt* tea strainer; **Teetasse** *f* teacup

Teich *m* (*-(e)s, -e*) pond

Teig *m* (*-(e)s, -e*) dough; **Teigwaren** *pl* pasta *sg*

Teil 1. *m* (*-(e)s, -e*) part; (*due to sb*) share; **zum ~** partly **2.** *nt* (*-(e)s, -e*) part; (*part of whole*) component; **teilen** *vt, vr* divide; (*with sb*) share (*mit* with); **20 durch 4 ~** divide 20 by 4

Teilnahme *f* (*-, -n*) participation (*an + dat* in); **teilnehmen** *irr vi* take part (*an + dat* in); **Teilnehmer(in)** *m(f)* (*-s, -*) participant

teils *adv* partly; **teilweise** *adv* partially, in part; **Teilzeit** *f ~*

arbeiten work part-time

Teint *m* (*-s, -s*) complexion

Telefon *nt* (*-s, -e*) telephone; **Telefonanruf** *m*, **Telefonat** *nt* (*-(e)s*) (tele)phone call; **Telefonanschluss** *m* telephone connection; **Telefonauskunft** *f* directory enquiries *pl* (*Brit*), directory assistance (*US*); **Telefonbuch** *nt* telephone directory; **Telefongebühren** *pl* telephone charges *pl*; **Telefongespräch** *nt* telephone conversation; **telefonieren** *vi* **ich telefoniere gerade (mit ...)** I'm on the phone (to ...); **telefonisch** *adj* telephone; (*notification*) by telephone; **Telefonkarte** *f* phonecard; **Telefonnummer** *f* (tele)phone number; **Telefonrechnung** *f* phone bill; **Telefonverbindung** *f* telephone connection; **Telefonzelle** *f* phone box (*Brit*), phone booth

Telegramm *nt* telegram; **Teleobjektiv** *nt* telephoto lens; **Teleshopping** *nt* (*-s*) teleshopping; **Teleskop** *nt* (*-s, -e*) telescope

Teller *m* (*-s, -*) plate

Temperament *nt* temperament; liveliness; **temperamentvoll** *adj* lively

Temperatur *f* temperature; **bei ~en von 30 Grad** at temperatures of 30 degrees

Tempo *nt* (*-s, -s*) speed; **Tem-**

polimit *nt* (-s, -s) speed limit
Tempotaschentuch® *nt* (paper) tissue, ≈ Kleenex®
Tendenz *f* tendency; intention
Tennis *nt* (-) tennis; **Tennisball** *m* tennis ball; **Tennisplatz** *m* tennis court; **Tennisschläger** *m* tennis racket; **Tennisspieler(in)** *m(f)* tennis player; **Tennisturnier** *nt* tennis tournament
Tenor *m* (-s, *Tenöre*) tenor
Teppich *m* (-s, -e) carpet; **Teppichboden** *m* (wall-to-wall) carpet
Termin *m* (-s, -e) date; (*for finishing sth*) deadline; (*with doctor etc*) appointment
Terminal *nt* (-s, -s) IT, AVIAT terminal
Terminkalender *m* diary; **Terminplaner** *m* personal organizer, Filofax®; (*pocket computer*) personal digital assistant, PDA
Terrasse *f* (-, -n) terrace; (*adjoining house*) patio
Terror *m* (-s) terror; **Terroranschlag** *m* terrorist attack; **terrorisieren** *vt* terrorize; **Terrorismus** *m* terrorism; **Terrorist(in)** *m(f)* terrorist
Tesafilm® *m* ≈ sellotape® (*Brit*), ≈ Scotch tape® (*US*)
Test *m* (-s, -s) test
Testament *nt* will; *das Alte/ Neue* ~ the Old/New Testament
testen *vt* test; **Testergebnis** *nt* test results *pl*

Tetanus *m* (-) tetanus; **Tetanusimpfung** *f* (anti-)tetanus injection
teuer *adj* expensive, dear (*Brit*)
Teufel *m* (-s, -) devil; **Teufelskreis** *m* vicious circle
Text *m* (-(e)s, -e) text; (*of song*) words *pl*, lyrics *pl*; **Textmarker** *m* (-s, -) highlighter; **Textverarbeitung** *f* word processing
Thailand *nt* Thailand
Theater *nt* (-s, -) theatre; *fam* fuss; *ins ~ gehen* go to the theatre; **Theaterkasse** *f* box office; **Theaterstück** *nt* (stage) play
Theke *f* (-, -n) bar; (*in shop*) counter
Thema *nt* (-s, *Themen*) subject, topic; *kein ~!* no problem
Themse *f* (-) Thames
Theologie *f* theology
theoretisch *adj* theoretical; ~ *stimmt das* that's right in theory; **Theorie** *f* theory
Therapeut(in) *m(f)* therapist; **Therapie** *f* therapy; *eine ~ machen* undergo therapy
Thermalbad *nt* thermal bath; (*resort*) thermal spa; **Thermometer** *nt* (-s, -) thermometer; **Thermoskanne®** *f* Thermos® (flask); **Thermostat** *m* (-(e)s, -e) thermostat
These *f* (-, -n) theory
Thron *m* (-(e)s, -e) throne
Thunfisch *m* tuna

Thüringen *nt* (-s) Thuringia

Thymian *m* (-s, -e) thyme

Tick *m* (-(e)s, -s) tic; (*idiosyncrasy*) quirk; (*mania*) craze; **ticken** *vi* tick; **er tickt nicht ganz richtig** he's off his rocker

Ticket *nt* (-s, -s) (plane) ticket

Tiebreak *m* (-s, -s) tie break(-er)

tief *adj* deep; (*neckline, note, sun*) low; **2 Meter ~** 2 metres deep; **Tief** *nt* (-s, -s) METEO low; (*mood*) depression; **Tiefdruck** *m* METEO low pressure; **Tiefe** *f* (-, -n) depth; **Tiefgarage** *f* underground car park (*Brit*) (*or* garage (*US*)); **tiefgekühlt** *adj* frozen; **Tiefkühlfach** *nt* freezer compartment; **Tiefkühlkost** *f* frozen food; **Tiefkühltruhe** *f* freezer; **Tiefpunkt** *m* low

Tier *nt* (-(e)s, -e) animal; **Tierarzt** *m*, **Tierärztin** *f* vet; **Tiergarten** *m* zoo; **Tierhandlung** *f* pet shop; **Tierheim** *nt* animal shelter; **tierisch 1.** *adj* animal **2.** *adv fam* really; **~ ernst** deadly serious; **ich hatte ~ Angst** I was dead scared; **Tierkreiszeichen** *nt* sign of the zodiac; **Tierpark** *m* zoo; **Tierquälerei** *f* cruelty to animals; **Tierschützer(in)** *m(f)* (-s, -) animal rights campaigner; **Tierversuch** *m* animal experiment

Tiger *m* (-s, -) tiger

timen *vt* time; **Timing** *nt* (-s) timing

Tinte *f* (-, -n) ink; **Tintenfisch** *m* cuttlefish; (*small*) squid; (*with eight arms*) octopus; **Tintenfischringe** *pl* calamari *pl*

Tipp *m* (-s, -s) tip; **tippen** *vt, vi* tap; *fam* type; *fam* guess

Tirol *nt* (-s) Tyrol

Tisch *m* (-(e)s, -e) table; **Tischdecke** *f* tablecloth; **Tischtennis** *nt* table tennis; **Tischtennisschläger** *m* table-tennis bat

Titel *m* (-s, -) title; **Titelbild** *nt* cover picture; **Titelmusik** *f* theme music; **Titelverteidiger(in)** *m(f)* defending champion

Toast *m* (-(e)s, -s) toast; **toasten** *vt* toast; **Toaster** *m* (-s, -) toaster

Tochter *f* (-, *Töchter*) daughter

Tod *m* (-(e)s, -e) death; **Todesopfer** *nt* casualty; **Todesstrafe** *f* death penalty; **todkrank** *adj* terminally ill; (*not life-threatening*) seriously ill; **tödlich** *adj* deadly, fatal; **er ist ~ verunglückt** he was killed in an accident; **todmüde** *adj fam* dead tired; **todsicher** *adj fam* dead certain

Tofu *m* (-(s)) tofu, bean curd

Toilette *f* toilet, restroom (*US*); **Toilettenpapier** *nt* toilet paper

toi, toi, toi *interj* good luck

tolerant adj tolerant (gegen of)

toll adj mad; (activity) wild; fam (wonderful) great; Tollwut f rabies sg

Tomate f (-, -n) tomato; Tomatenmark nt tomato purée (Brit) (or paste (US)); Tomatensaft m tomato juice

Tombola f (-, -s) raffle, tombola (Brit)

Ton 1. m (-(e)s, -e) clay 2. m (Töne pl) sound; MUS note; (in voice) tone; (hue, nuance) shade

tönen 1. vi sound 2. vt shade; (hair) tint

Toner m (-s, -) toner; Tonerkassette f toner cartridge

Tonne f (-, -n) barrel; (weight) tonne, metric ton

Tontechniker(in) m(f) sound engineer

Tönung f hue; (for hair) rinse

Top nt (-s, -s) top

Topf m (-(e)s, Töpfe) pot

Töpfer(in) m(f) (-s, -) potter; Töpferei f pottery; (item) piece of pottery

Tor nt (-(e)s, -e) gate; SPORT goal; ein ~ schießen score a goal; Torhüter(in) m(f) goalkeeper

torkeln vi stagger

Torlinie f goal line

Tornado m (-s, -s) tornado

Torpfosten m goalpost; Torschütze m, Torschützin f (goal)scorer

Torte f (-, -n) cake; (fruit tart)

flan; (with layers of cream) gateau

Torwart(in) m(f) (-s, -e) goalkeeper

tot adj dead; ~er Winkel blind spot

total adj total, complete; Totalschaden m complete write-off

Tote(r) mf dead man/woman; (body) corpse; töten vt, vi kill; Totenkopf m skull

totlachen vr kill oneself laughing

Toto m or nt (-s, -s) pools pl

totschlagen irr vt beat to death; die Zeit ~ kill time

Touchscreen m (-s, -s) touch screen

Toupet nt (-s, -s) toupee

Tour f (-, -en) trip; (circular) tour

Tourismus m tourism; Tourist(in) m(f) tourist; touristisch adj tourist; pej touristy

traben vi trot

Tournee f (-, -n) tour

Tracht f (-, -en) traditional costume

Tradition f tradition; traditionell adj traditional

traf imperf of treffen

Trafik f (-, -en) tobacconist's

tragbar adj portable

träge adj sluggish, slow

tragen (trug, getragen) vt carry; (clothes, glasses, hair) wear; (name, fruit) bear; Träger m (-s, -) (on dress etc) strap; Tragflügelboot *nt* hydrofoil

tragisch *adj* tragic; **Tragödie** *f* tragedy

Trainer(in) *m(f)* (-s, -) trainer, coach; **trainieren** *vt, vi* train; (*person also*) coach; (*exercise*) practise; **Training** *nt* (-s, -s) training; **Trainingsanzug** *m* tracksuit

Traktor *m* tractor

Trambahn *f* tram (*Brit*), streetcar (*US*)

trampen *vi* hitchhike; **Tramper(in)** *m(f)* hitchhiker

Träne *f* (-, -n) tear; **tränen** *vi* water; **Tränengas** *nt* teargas

trank *imperf of* **trinken**

Transfusion *f* transfusion

Transitverkehr *m* transit traffic; **Transitvisum** *nt* transit visa

Transplantation *f* transplant; (*of skin*) graft

Transport *m* (-(e)s, -e) transport; **transportieren** *vt* transport

Transvestit *m* (-en, -en) transvestite

trat *imperf of* **treten**

Traube *f* (-, -n) grape; bunch of grapes; **Traubensaft** *m* grape juice; **Traubenzucker** *m* glucose

trauen (1.) *vi* **jdm/einer Sache ~** trust sb/sth 2. *vr* dare 3. *vt* marry; **sich ~ lassen** get married

Trauer *f* (-) sorrow; (*for deceased person*) mourning

Traum *m* (-(e)s, **Träume**) dream; **träumen** *vt, vi* dream (*von* of, about); **traumhaft** *adj* dreamlike; *fig* wonderful

traurig *adj* sad (*über* + *acc* about)

Trauschein *m* marriage certificate; **Trauung** *f* wedding ceremony; **Trauzeuge** *m*, **Trauzeugin** *f* witness (*at wedding ceremony*), ≈ best man/maid of honour

Travellerscheck *m* traveller's cheque

treffen (*traf, getroffen*) **1.** *vr* meet **2.** *vt, vi* hit; (*remark*) hurt; (*friend etc*) meet; (*decision*) make; (*measures*) take; **Treffen** *nt* (-s, -) meeting; **Treffer** *m* (-s, -) goal; **Treffpunkt** *m* meeting place

treiben (*trieb, getrieben*) **1.** *vt* drive; (*sport*) do **2.** *vi* (*on water*) drift; (*plant*) sprout; (*tea, coffee*) be diuretic; **Treiber** *m* (-s, -) IT driver; **Treibhaus** *nt* greenhouse; **Treibstoff** *m* fuel

trennen 1. *vt* separate; (*split into parts*) divide **2.** *vr* separate; **sich von jdm ~** leave sb; **sich von etw ~** part with sth; **Trennung** *f* separation

Treppe *f* (-, -n) stairs *pl*; (*outside*) steps *pl*

Tresen *m* (-s, -) bar; (*in shop*) counter

Tresor *m* (-s, -e) safe

Tretboot *nt* pedal boat; **treten** (*trat, getreten*) **1.** *vi* step; **~ nach** kick at **2.** *vt* kick

treu adj (to partner) faithful; (customer, fan) loyal; **Treue** f (-) (in marriage) faithfulness; (of customer, fan) loyalty

Triathlon m (-s, -s) triathlon

Tribüne f (-, -n) stand; (for speaker) platform

Trick m (-s, -e or -s) trick; **Trickfilm** m cartoon

trieb imperf of **treiben**

Trieb m (-(e)s, -e) urge; (instinct) drive; (on tree etc) shoot; **Triebwerk** nt engine

Trikot nt (-s, -s) shirt, jersey

trinkbar adj drinkable; **trinken** (trank, getrunken) vt, vi drink; **einen ~ gehen** go out for a drink; **Trinkgeld** nt tip

Trinkhalm m (drinking) straw; **Trinkschokolade** f drinking chocolate; **Trinkwasser** nt drinking water

Trio nt (-s, -s) trio

Tritt m (-(e)s, -e) step; kick

Triumph m (-(e)s, -e) triumph; **triumphieren** vi triumph (über + acc over)

trivial adj trivial

trocken adj dry; **Trockenheit** f dryness; **trockenlegen** vt (baby) change; **trocknen** vt, vi dry; **Trockner** m (-s, -) dryer

Trödel m (-s) fam junk; **Trödelmarkt** m flea market

trödeln vi fam dawdle

Trommel f (-, -n) drum; **Trommelfell** nt eardrum; **trommeln** vt, vi drum

Trompete f (-, -n) trumpet

Tropen pl tropics f

Tropf m (-(e)s, -e) MED drip; **am ~ hängen** be on a drip; **tröpfeln** vi drip; **es tröpfelt** it's drizzling; **tropfen** vt, vi drip; **Tropfen** m (-s, -) drop; **tropfenweise** adv drop by drop; **tropfnass** adj dripping wet; **Tropfsteinhöhle** f stalactite cave

tropisch adj tropical

Trost m (-es) consolation, comfort; **trösten** vt console, comfort; **trostlos** adj bleak; (conditions) wretched; **Trostpreis** m consolation prize

trotz prep + gen or dat in spite of; **Trotz** m (-es) defiance; **trotzdem 1.** adv nevertheless **2.** conj although; **trotzig** adj defiant

trüb adj dull; (liquid, glass) cloudy; fig gloomy

Trüffel f (-, -n) truffle

trug imperf of **tragen**

trügerisch adj deceptive

Truhe f (-, -n) chest

Trumpf m (-(e)s, **Trümpfe**) trump

Trunkenheit f intoxication; **~ am Steuer** drink driving (Brit), drunk driving (US)

Truthahn m turkey

Tscheche m (-n, -n), **Tschechin** f Czech; **Tschechien** nt (-s) Czech Republic; **tschechisch** adj Czech;

Tschechisch nt Czech
Tschetschenien nt (-s)
Chechnya
tschüs(s) interj bye
T-Shirt nt (-s, -s) T-shirt
Tube f (-, -n) tube
Tuberkulose f (-, -n) tuberculosis, TB
Tuch nt (-(e)s, Tücher) cloth; (for neck) scarf; (for head) headscarf
tüchtig adj competent; (hard-working) efficient
Tugend f (-, -en) virtue; tugendhaft adj virtuous
Tulpe f (-, -n) tulip
Tumor m (-s, -en) tumour
Tümpel m (-s, -) pond
tun (tat, getan) 1. vt do; (sth somewhere) put; **was tust du da?** what are you doing?; **das tut man nicht** you shouldn't do that; **jdm etw ~** (harm) do sth to sb 2. vi act; **so ~, als ob** act as if 3. vr impers **es tut sich etwas/ viel** something/ a lot is happening
Tuner m (-s, -) tuner
Tunesien nt (-s) Tunisia
Tunfisch m tuna
Tunnel m (-s, -(s)) tunnel
Tunte f (-, -n) pej fam fairy
tupfen vt, vi dab; (with colour) dot; Tupfen m (-s, -) dot
Tür f (-, -en) door; **vor/ an der ~** at the door; **an die ~ gehen**

answer the door
Türke m (-n, -n) Turk; Türkei f (-) **die ~** Turkey; Türkin f Turk
Türkis m (-es, -e) turquoise
türkisch adj Turkish; Türkisch nt Turkish
Turm m (-(e)s, Türme) tower; (pointed church tower) steeple; (in chess) rook, castle
turnen vi do gymnastics; Turnen nt (-s) gymnastics sg, physical education, PE; Turner(in) m(f) gymnast; Turnhalle f gym(nasium); Turnhose f gym shorts pl
Turnier nt (-s, -e) tournament
Turnschuh m (-s, -e) gym shoe, sneaker (US)
Türschild nt doorplate; Türschloss nt lock
tuscheln vt, vi whisper
Tussi f (-, -s) pej fam chick
Tüte f (-, -n) bag
TÜV m (-s, -s) acr = **Technischer Überwachungsverein;** ≈ MOT (Brit), vehicle inspection (US)
Tweed m (-s, -s) tweed
Typ m (-s, -en) type; (car) model; (man) guy, bloke
Typhus m (-) typhoid
typisch adj typical (für of); **ein ~er Fehler** a common mistake; **~ Marcus!** that's just like Marcus; **~ amerikanisch!** that's so American

U

u. a. *abbr* = **und andere(s)**; and others; = **unter anderem, unter anderen**; among other things

u. A. w. g. *abbr* = **um Antwort wird gebeten**; RSVP

U-Bahn *f* underground (*Brit*), subway (*US*)

übel *adj* bad; (*morally*) wicked; **mir ist ~** I feel sick; **diese Bemerkung hat er mir ~ genommen** he took offence at my remark; Übelkeit *f* nausea

üben *vt, vi* practise

über *prep + dat or acc* (*throw, jump*) over; (*with position also*) above; (*from one side to the other*) across; (*farther up from*) above; (*route*) via; (*concerning*) about; (*quantity*) over, more than; **~ das Wochenende** over the weekend

überall *adv* everywhere

überbacken *adj* (**mit Käse**) **~** au gratin; überbelichten *vt* PHOT overexpose; überbieten *irr vt* outbid; (*be better than*) surpass; (*record*) break

Überbleibsel *nt* (-s, -) remnant

Überblick *m* overview; *fig* survey; (*understanding*) grasp (*über* + *acc* of)

überbuchen *vt* overbook;

Überbuchung *f* overbooking

übereinander *adv* on top of each other; (*talk etc*) about each other

übereinstimmen *vi* agree (*mit* with)

überfahren *irr vt* AUTO run over; Überfahrt *f* crossing

Überfall *m* robbery; MIL raid; (*on sb*) assault; überfallen *irr vt* attack; (*bank*) raid

überfällig *adj* overdue

überfliegen *irr vt* fly over; (*book*) skim through

überflüssig *adj* superfluous

überfordern *vt* demand too much of; (*strength etc*) overtax; **da bin ich überfordert** you've got me there

Überführung *f* flyover (*Brit*), overpass (*US*)

überfüllt *adj* overcrowded

Übergabe *f* handover

Übergang *m* crossing; (*change, passing*) transition; Übergangslösung *f* temporary solution, stopgap

übergeben *irr* 1. *vt* hand over 2. *vr* be sick, vomit

Übergepäck *nt* excess baggage

Übergewicht *nt* excess weight; (**10 Kilo**) **~ haben** be (10 kilos) overweight

überglücklich *adj* overjoyed;

fam over the moon

überhaupt *adv* at all; in general

überheblich *adj* arrogant

überholen *vt* overtake; TECH overhaul; **Überholspur** *f* overtaking (*Brit*) (*or* passing (*US*)) lane; **überholt** *adj* outdated

überhören *vt* miss, not catch; (*deliberately*) ignore; **überladen 1.** *irr vt* overload **2.** *adj fig* cluttered; **überlassen** *irr vt* **jdm etw ~** leave sth to sb; **überlaufen** *irr vi* (*liquid*) overflow

überleben *vt, vi* survive; **Überlebende(r)** *mf* survivor

überlegen 1. *vt* consider; *sich dat etw ~* think about sth; *er hat es sich dat anders überlegt* he's changed his mind **2.** *adj* superior (*dat* to); **Überlegung** *f* consideration

übermäßig *adj* excessive

übermorgen *adv* the day after tomorrow

übernächste(r, s) *adj ~ Woche* the week after next

übernachten *vi* spend the night (*bei jdm* at sb's place); **Übernachtung** *f* overnight stay; **~ mit Frühstück** bed and breakfast

übernehmen *irr* **1.** *vt* take on; (*post, business*) take over **2.** *vr* take on too much

überprüfen *vt* check; **Überprüfung** *f* check; (*action*) checking

überqueren *vt* cross

überraschen *vt* surprise; **Überraschung** *f* surprise

überreden *vt* persuade; *er hat mich überredet* he talked me into it

überreichen *vt* hand over

überschätzen *vt* overestimate; **überschlagen** *irr* **1.** *vt* estimate **2.** *vr* somersault; (*car*) overturn; (*voice*) crack; **überschneiden** *irr vr* (*lines etc*) intersect; (*dates*) clash

Überschrift *f* heading

Überschwemmung *f* flood

übersehen *irr vt* look (out) over; (*ignore*) overlook

übersetzen *vt* translate (*aus* from, *in* + *acc* into); **Übersetzer(in)** *m(f)* (*-s, -*) translator; **Übersetzung** *f* translation

Übersicht *f* overall view; (*résumé*) survey; **übersichtlich** *adj* clear

überstehen *irr vt* get over

Überstunden *pl* overtime *sg*

überstürzt *adj* hasty

übertragbar *adj* transferable; MED infectious; **übertragen** *irr* **1.** *vt* transfer (*auf* + *acc* to); RADIO broadcast; (*disease*) transmit **2.** *vr* spread (*auf* + *acc* to) **3.** *adj* figurative; **Übertragung** *f* RADIO broadcast; (*of data*) transmission

übertreffen *irr vt* surpass

übertreiben *irr vt, vi* exaggerate, overdo; **Übertreibung** *f* exaggeration; **übertrieben**

adj exaggerated, overdone

überwachen *vt* supervise; (*suspect*) keep under surveillance

überwand *imperf of* **überwinden**

überweisen *irr vt* transfer; (*patient*) refer (*an + acc* to); **Überweisung** *f* transfer; (*of patient*) referral

überwiegend *adv* mainly

überwinden (*überwand*, *überwunden*) **1.** *vt* overcome **2.** *vr* make an effort, force oneself; **überwunden** *pp of* **überwinden**

überzeugen *vt* convince; **Überzeugung** *f* conviction

überziehen *irr vt* cover; (*jacket etc*) put on; (*account*) overdraw; **die Betten frisch ~** change the sheets; **Überziehungskredit** *m* overdraft facility

üblich *adj* usual

übrig *adj* remaining; **ist noch Saft ~?** is there any juice left?; **für jdn etwas ~ haben** *fam* have a soft spot for sb; **die Übrigen** *pl* the rest *pl*; **im Übrigen** besides; **~ bleiben** be left (over); **übrigens** *adv* besides; (*incidentally*) by the way

Übung *f* practice; (*set of movements, task etc*) exercise

Ufer *nt* (-s, -) (*of river*) bank; (*of sea, lake*) shore; **am ~** on the bank / shore

Uhr *f* (-, -en) clock; watch; **wie**

viel ~ ist es? what time is it?; **1 ~** 1 o'clock; **20 ~** 8 o'clock, 8 pm; **Uhrzeit** *f* time (of day)

Ukraine *f* (-) **die ~** the Ukraine

UKW *abbr = Ultrakurzwelle*; VHF

Ulme *f* (-, -n) elm

Ultrakurzwelle *f* very high frequency; **Ultraschalluntersuchung** *f* MED scan

um 1. *prep + acc* (*space*) (a)round; (*time*) at; **~ etw kämpfen** fight for sth **2.** *conj* (in order) to; **zu klug, ~ zu ...** too clever to ... **3.** *adv* (approximately) about; **die Ferien sind ~** the holidays are over; **die Zeit ist ~** time's up; → **umso**

umarmen *vt* embrace

Umbau *m* rebuilding; (*into sth*) conversion (*zu* into); **umbauen** *vt* rebuild; (*into sth*) convert (*zu* into)

umblättern *vt, vi* turn over

umbringen *irr vt* kill

umbuchen *vi* change one's reservation / flight

umdrehen *vt, vr* turn (round); (*retrace steps*) turn back; **Umdrehung** *f* turn; PHYS, AUTO revolution

umfahren *irr vt* knock down

umfallen *irr vi* fall over

Umfang *m* extent; (*of book*) size; (*of voice, instrument*) range; MATH circumference; **umfangreich** *adj* extensive

Umfrage *f* survey

Umgang *m* company; (*with sb*) dealings *pl*; **umgänglich** *adj* sociable; **Umgangssprache** *f* colloquial language, slang

Umgebung *f* surroundings *pl*; (*social*) environment; (*friends, colleagues etc*) people around one

umgehen 1. *irr vi* go round; ~ (**können**) **mit** (know how to) handle 2. *irr vt* avoid; (*problems*) get round; **Umgehungsstraße** *f* bypass

umgekehrt 1. *adj* reverse; (*contrary*) opposite **2.** *adv* the other way round; **und** ~ and vice versa

umhören *vr* ask around; **umkehren 1.** *vi* turn back **2.** *vt* reverse; **umkippen 1.** *vi* tip over **2.** *vt* overturn; *fig* change one's mind; *fam* (*faint*) pass out

Umkleidekabine *f* changing cubicle (*Brit*), dressing room (*US*); **Umkleideraum** *m* changing room

umleiten *vt* divert; **Umleitung** *f* diversion

umrechnen *vt* convert (*in* + *acc* into); **Umrechnung** *f* conversion; **Umrechnungskurs** *m* rate of exchange

Umriss *m* outline

umrühren *vi, vt* stir

ums *contr of* **um das**

Umsatz *m* turnover

umschalten *vi* turn over

Umschlag *m* cover; (*of book*)

jacket; MED compress; (*of letter*) envelope

Umschulung *f* retraining

umsehen *irr vr* look around; (*search*) look out (*nach* for)

umso *adv* all the; ~ **mehr** all the more; ~ **besser** so much the better

umsonst *adv* in vain; (*free*) for nothing

Umstand *m* circumstance; **Umstände** *pl fig* fuss; **in anderen Umständen sein** be pregnant; **jdm Umstände machen** cause sb a lot of trouble; **unter diesen/keinen Umständen** under these/no circumstances; **unter Umständen** possibly; **umständlich** *adj* (*method*) complicated; (*way of expressing oneself*) long-winded; (*person*) ponderous

umsteigen *irr vi* change (trains/buses)

umstellen 1. *vt* (*move*) change round **2.** *vr* adapt (*auf* + *acc* to); **Umstellung** *f* change; (*adapting*) adjustment

Umtausch *m* exchange; **umtauschen** *vt* exchange; (*currency*) change

Umweg *m* detour

Umwelt *f* environment; **Umweltbelastung** *f* ecological damage; **Umweltschutz** *m* environmental protection; **Umweltschützer(in)** *m(f)* (*-s, -*) environmentalist; **Umweltverschmutzung** *f* pollution; **umweltverträglich** *adj* environment-friendly

umwerfen *irr vt* knock over; *fig* (*change*) upset; *fig fam* flabbergast

umziehen *irr* **1.** *vt*, *vr* change **2.** *vi* move (house); **Umzug** *m* procession; (*to new house*) move

unabhängig *adj* independent; **Unabhängigkeitstag** *m* Independence Day, Fourth of July (*US*)

unabsichtlich *adv* unintentionally

unangenehm *adj* unpleasant; **Unannehmlichkeit** *f* inconvenience; **~en** *pl* trouble *sg*

unanständig *adj* indecent; **unappetitlich** *adj* (*food*) unappetizing; (*repulsive*) off-putting; **unbeabsichtigt** *adj* unintentional; **unbedeutend** *adj* insignificant, unimportant; (*error*) slight

unbedingt **1.** *adj* unconditional **2.** *adv* absolutely

unbefriedigend *adj* unsatisfactory; **unbegrenzt** *adj* unlimited; **unbekannt** *adj* unknown; **unbeliebt** *adj* unpopular; **unbemerkt** *adj* unnoticed; **unbequem** *adj* (*chair, person*) uncomfortable; **unbeständig** *adj* (*weather*) unsettled; (*situation*) unstable; (*person*) unreliable; **unbestimmt** *adj* indefinite; **unbewusst** *adj* uncon-

scious; **unbezahlt** *adj* unpaid; **unbrauchbar** *adj* useless

und *conj* and; **~ so weiter** and so on; **na ~?** so what?

undankbar *adj* (*person*) ungrateful; (*task*) thankless; **undenkbar** *adj* inconceivable; **undeutlich** *adj* indistinct; **undicht** *adj* leaky; **uneben** *adj* uneven; **unecht** *adj* (*jewellery etc*) fake; **unehelich** *adj* (*child*) illegitimate; **unendlich** *adj* endless; MATH infinite; **unentbehrlich** *adj* indispensable; **unentgeltlich** *adj* free (of charge)

unentschieden *adj* undecided; **~ enden** SPORT end in a draw

unerfreulich *adj* unpleasant; **unerlässlich** *adj* indispensable; **unerträglich** *adj* unbearable; **unerwartet** *adj* unexpected; **unfähig** *adj* incompetent; **~ sein, etw zu tun** be incapable of doing sth; **unfair** *adj* unfair

Unfall *m* accident; **Unfallstation** *f* casualty ward; **Unfallstelle** *f* scene of the accident; **Unfallversicherung** *f* accident insurance

unfreundlich *adj* unfriendly

Ungarn *nt* (*-s*) Hungary

Ungeduld *f* impatience; **ungeduldig** *adj* impatient

ungeeignet *adj* unsuitable

ungefähr **1.** *adj* approximate **2.** *adv* approximately; **~ 10**

Kilometer about 10 kilometres; ***wann ~?*** about what time?; ***wo ~?*** whereabouts?

ungefährlich *adj* harmless; *(involving no danger)* safe

ungeheuer 1. *adj* huge **2.** *adv fam* enormously; **Ungeheuer** *nt (-s, -)* monster

ungehorsam *adj* disobedient *(gegenüber* to); **ungemütlich** *adj* unpleasant; *(person)* disagreeable; **ungenießbar** *adj* inedible; *(drink)* undrinkable; **ungenügend** *adj* unsatisfactory; *(mark in school)* ≈ F; **ungepflegt** *adj (garden)* untended; *(appearance)* unkempt; *(hands)* neglected; **ungerade** *adj* odd

ungerecht *adj* unjust; **ungerechtfertigt** *adj* unjustified; **Ungerechtigkeit** *f* injustice, unfairness

ungern *adv* reluctantly; **ungeschickt** *adj* clumsy; **ungeschminkt** *adj* without make-up; **ungesund** *adj* unhealthy; **ungewiss** *adj* uncertain; **ungewöhnlich** *adj* unusual

Ungeziefer *nt (-s)* vermin *pl* **ungezwungen** *adj* relaxed

unglaublich *adj* incredible

Unglück *nt (-(e)s, -e)* misfortune; *(in game, career etc)* bad luck; *(train or plane crash)* disaster; ***das bringt ~*** that's unlucky; **unglücklich** *adj* unhappy; *(unsuccessful)* unlucky; *(unfavou-*

rable) unfortunate; **unglücklicherweise** *adv* unfortunately

ungültig *adj* invalid

ungünstig *adj* inconvenient

unheilbar *adj* incurable; **~ krank sein** be terminally ill

unheimlich 1. *adj* eerie **2.** *adv fam* incredibly

unhöflich *adj* impolite

uni *adj* plain

Uni *f (-, -s)* uni

Uniform *f (-, -en)* uniform

Universität *f* university

Unkenntnis *f* ignorance

unklar *adj* unclear

Unkosten *pl* expenses *pl*

Unkraut *nt* weeds *pl*

unlogisch *adj* illogical

unmissverständlich *adj* unambiguous

unmittelbar *adj* immediate; **~ darauf** immediately afterwards

unmöbliert *adj* unfurnished

unmöglich *adj* impossible

unnötig *adj* unnecessary

UNO *f (-)* acr = **United Nations Organization**; UN

unordentlich *adj* untidy; **Unordnung** *f* disorder

unpassend *adj* inappropriate; *(time)* inconvenient; **unpersönlich** *adj* impersonal; **unpraktisch** *adj* impractical

Unrecht *nt* wrong; **zu ~** wrongly; **~ haben, im ~ sein** be wrong

unregelmäßig *adj* irregular; **unreif** *adj* unripe; **unruhig**

adj restless; **~ schlafen** have a bad night

uns *pron acc, dat of* **wir**; us, (to) us; **~ (selbst)** *(reflexive)* ourselves; **sehen Sie ~?** can you see us?; **er schickte es ~** he sent it to us; **lasst ~ in Ruhe** leave us alone; **ein Freund von ~** a friend of ours; **wir haben ~ hingesetzt** we sat down; **wir haben ~ amüsiert** we enjoyed ourselves; **wir mögen ~** we like each other

unscharf *adj* PHOT blurred, out of focus

unschlüssig *adj* undecided

unschuldig *adj* innocent

unser *pron* our; **unsere(r, s)** *pron* ours; **unseretwegen** *adv* because of us; *(to please us)* for our sake

unseriös *adj* dubious; **unsicher** *adj* uncertain; *(lacking confidence)* insecure

Unsinn *m* nonsense

unsterblich *adj* immortal; **~ verliebt** madly in love

unsympathisch *adj* unpleasant; **er ist mir ~** I don't like him

unten *adv* below; *(in house)* downstairs; *(at lower end)* at the bottom; **nach ~** down; **unter** *prep* + *acc or dat* under, below; *(people)* among; *(time)* during

Unterarm *m* forearm

Unterbewusstsein *nt* subconscious

unterbrechen *irr vt* interrupt; **Unterbrechung** *f* interruption; **ohne ~** nonstop

unterdrücken *vt* suppress; *(people)* oppress

untere(r, s) *adj* lower

untereinander *adv* *(in space)* one below the other; *(reciprocally)* each other; among themselves / yourselves / ourselves

Unterführung *f* underpass

untergehen *irr vi* go down; *(sun also)* set; *(nation)* perish; *(world)* come to an end; *(by noise)* be drowned out

Untergeschoss *nt* basement; **Untergewicht** *nt* **(10 Kilo) ~ haben** be (10 kilos) underweight; **Untergrund** *m* foundation; POL underground; **Untergrundbahn** *f* underground *(Brit)*, subway *(US)*

unterhalb *adv, prep* + *gen* below; **~ von** below

Unterhalt *m* maintenance; **unterhalten** *irr* **1.** *vt* maintain; *(audience, guest)* entertain **2.** *vr* talk; *(have a good time)* enjoy oneself; **Unterhaltung** *f* entertainment; talk, conversation

Unterhemd *nt* vest *(Brit)*, undershirt *(US)*; **Unterhose** *f* underpants *pl*; *(for women)* briefs *pl*

unterirdisch *adj* underground

Unterkiefer *m* lower jaw

Unterkunft f (-, -künfte) accommodation

Unterlage f document; (for resting on when writing) pad

unterlassen irr vt **es ~, etw zu tun** fail to do sth; (hold back) refrain from doing sth

unterlegen adj inferior (dat to); (beaten) defeated

Unterleib m abdomen

Unterlippe f lower lip

Untermiete f **zur ~ wohnen** be a subtenant; **Untermieter(in)** m(f) subtenant

unternehmen irr vt (trip) go on; (attempt) make; **etwas ~** do something (gegen about); **Unternehmen** nt (-s, -) undertaking; (COMM company); **Unternehmensberater(in)** m(f) (-s, -) management consultant; **Unternehmer(in)** m(f) (-s, -) entrepreneur

Unterricht m (-(e)s, -e) lessons pl; **unterrichten** vt teach

unterschätzen vt underestimate

unterscheiden irr **1.** vt distinguish (von from, zwischen + dat between) **2.** vr differ (von from)

Unterschenkel m lower leg

Unterschied m (-(e)s, -e) difference; **im ~ zu dir** unlike you; **unterschiedlich** adj different

unterschreiben irr vt sign; **Unterschrift** f signature

Untersetzer m (-s, -) table-

mat; (for glass) coaster

unterste(r, s) adj lowest, bottom

unterstellen vr take shelter

unterstreichen irr vt a. fig underline

unterstützen vt support; **Unterstützung** f support

untersuchen vt MED examine; (police) investigate; **Untersuchung** f examination; (by police) investigation

Untertasse f saucer; **Unterteil** nt lower part, bottom; **Untertitel** m subtitle

untervermieten vt sublet

Unterwäsche f underwear

unterwegs adv on the way

unterzeichnen vt sign

untreu adj unfaithful; **unüberlegt 1.** adj ill-considered **2.** adv without thinking; **unüblich** adj unusual; **unverantwortlich** adj irresponsible

unverbindlich 1. adj not binding; (reply) noncommittal **2.** adv COMM without obligation

unverbleit adj unleaded; **unverheiratet** adj unmarried, single; **unvermeidlich** adj unavoidable; **unvernünftig** adj silly; **unverschämt** adj impudent; **unverständlich** adj incomprehensible; **unverträglich** adj (food) indigestible; **unverzüglich** adj immediate; **unvollständig** adj incomplete; **unvorsich-**

tig *adj* careless
unwahrscheinlich 1. *adj* improbable, unlikely 2. *adv*
fam incredibly
Unwetter *nt* thunderstorm
unwichtig *adj* unimportant
unwiderstehlich *adj* irresistible
unwillkürlich 1. *adj* involuntary 2. *adv* instinctively
unwohl *adj* unwell, ill
unzählig *adj* innumerable,
countless
unzerbrechlich *adj* unbreakable; unzertrennlich *adj* inseparable; unzufrieden *adj*
dissatisfied; unzugänglich
adj inaccessible; unzumutbar *adj* unacceptable; unzutreffend *adj* inapplicable;
(*wrong*) incorrect; unzuverlässig *adj* unreliable
Update *nt* (-s, -s) IT update
üppig *adj* (*meal*) lavish; (*vegetation*) lush
uralt *adj* ancient, very old
Uran *nt* (-s) uranium
Uranus *m* (-) Uranus
Uraufführung *f* premiere
Urenkel *m* great-grandson;
Urenkelin *f* great-granddaughter; Urgroßeltern *pl*
great-grandparents *pl*; Urgroßmutter *f* great-grandmother; Urgroßvater *m*
great-grandfather

Urheber(in) *m(f)* (-s, -) originator; (*writer*) author
Urin *m* (-s, -e) urine; Urinprobe *f* urine specimen
Urkunde *f* (-, -n) document
Urlaub *m* (-(e)s, -e) holiday
(*Brit*), vacation (*US*); im ~
on holiday (*Brit*), on vacation (*US*); in ~ fahren go
on holiday (*Brit*) (*or* vacation (*US*)); Urlauber(in)
m(f) (-s, -) holiday-maker
(*Brit*), vacationer (*US*); Urlaubsort *m* holiday resort;
urlaubsreif *adj* ready for a
holiday (*Brit*) (*or* vacation
(*US*)); Urlaubszeit *f* holiday
season (*Brit*), vacation period (*US*)
Urologe *m*, Urologin *f* urologist
Ursache *f* cause (*für* of); keine ~! not at all; (*in reply to
apology*) that's all right
Ursprung *m* origin; ursprünglich 1. *adj* original
2. *adv* originally
Urteil *nt* (-s, -e) opinion; LAW
verdict; (*penalty*) sentence;
urteilen *vi* judge
Uruguay *nt* (-s) Uruguay
Urwald *m* jungle
USA *pl* USA *sg*
User(in) *m(f)* (-s, -) IT user
usw. *abbr* = und so weiter;
etc

V

vage *adj* vague

Vagina *f* (-, *Vaginen*) vagina

vakuumverpackt *adj* vacuum-packed

Valentinstag *m* St Valentine's Day

Vandalismus *m* vandalism

Vanille *f* (-) vanilla

variieren *vt, vi* vary

Vase *f* (-, *-n*) vase

Vater *m* (*-s, Väter*) father; väterlich *adj* paternal; Vaterschaft *f* fatherhood; LAW paternity; Vatertag *m* Father's Day; Vaterunser *nt das ~* (**beten**) (to say) the Lord's Prayer

V-Ausschnitt *m* V-neck

v. Chr. *abbr = vor Christus*; BC

Veganer(in) *m(f)* (*-s, -*) vegan; Vegetarier(in) *m(f)* (*-s, -*) vegetarian; vegetarisch *adj* vegetarian

Veilchen *nt* violet

Velo *nt* (*-s, -s*) (*Swiss*) bicycle

Vene *f* (-, *-n*) vein

Venedig *nt* (*-s*) Venice

Venezuela *nt* (*-s*) Venezuela

Ventil *nt* (*-s, -e*) valve

Ventilator *m* ventilator

Venus *f* (-) Venus

Venusmuschel *f* clam

verabreden **1.** *vt* arrange **2.** *vr* arrange to meet (*mit jdm* sb); *ich bin schon verabredet*

I'm already meeting someone; Verabredung *f* arrangement; (*meeting*) appointment; (*with friend*) date

verabschieden **1.** *vt* say goodbye to; (*law*) pass **2.** *vr* say goodbye

verachten *vt* despise; verächtlich *adj* contemptuous; (*deserving contempt*) contemptible; Verachtung *f* contempt

verallgemeinern *vt* generalize

Veranda *f* (-, *Veranden*) veranda, porch (*US*)

veränderlich *adj* changeable; verändern *vt, vr* change; Veränderung *f* change

veranlassen *vt* cause

veranstalten *vt* organize; Veranstalter(in) *m(f)* (*-s, -*) organizer; Veranstaltung *f* event; Veranstaltungsort *m* venue

verantworten **1.** *vt* take responsibility for **2.** *vr sich für etw ~* answer for sth; verantwortlich *adj* responsible (*für* for); Verantwortung *f* responsibility (*für* for)

verärgern *vt* annoy

verarschen *vt fam* take the piss out of (*Brit*), make a sucker out of (*US*)

Verb *nt* (*-s, -en*) verb

Verband *m* MED bandage; *(organization)* association; **Verband(s)kasten** *m* first-aid box; **Verband(s)zeug** *nt* dressing material

verbergen *irr vt, vr* hide *(vor + dat* from)

verbessern 1. *vt* improve; *(error, person speaking)* correct 2. *vr* improve; *(when speaking)* correct oneself; **Verbesserung** *f* improvement; *(of error)* correction

verbiegen *irr vt, vr* bend

verbieten *irr vt* forbid; **jdm ~, etw zu tun** forbid sb to do sth

verbilligt *adj* reduced

verbinden *irr* 1. *vt* connect; *(do or have at the same time)* combine; MED bandage; **können Sie mich mit ... ?** TEL can you put me through to ...?; **ich verbinde** TEL I'm putting you through 2. *vr* CHEM combine; **Verbindung** *f* connection

verbleit *adj* leaded

Verbot *nt* (-(e)s, -e) ban *(für, von* on); **verboten** *adj* forbidden; **es ist ~** it's not allowed; **es ist ~, hier zu parken** you're not allowed to park here; **Rauchen ~** no smoking

verbrannt *adj* burnt

Verbrauch *m* (-(e)s) consumption; **verbrauchen** *vt* use up; **Verbraucher(in)** *m(f)* (-s, -) consumer

Verbrechen *nt* (-s, -) crime;

Verbrecher(in) *m(f)* (-s, -) criminal

verbreiten *vt, vr* spread

verbrennen *irr vt* burn; **Verbrennung** *f* burning; *(in engine)* combustion

verbringen *irr vt* spend

verbunden *adj* **falsch ~** sorry, wrong number

Verdacht *m* (-(e)s) suspicion; **verdächtig** *adj* suspicious; **verdächtigen** *vt* suspect

verdammt *interj fam* damn

verdanken *vt* **jdm etw ~** owe sth to sb

verdarb *imperf of* **verderben**

verdauen *vt a. fig* digest; **Verdauung** *f* digestion

Verdeck *nt* (-(e)s, -e) top

verderben *(verdarb, verdorben)* 1. *vt* spoil; *(damage)* ruin; *(morally)* corrupt; **ich habe mir den Magen verdorben** I've got an upset stomach 2. *vi (food)* go off

verdienen *vt* earn; *(morally)* deserve; **Verdienst** 1. *m* (-(e)s, -e) earnings *pl* 2. *nt* (-(e)s, -e) merit; *(contribution)* service *(um* to)

verdoppeln *vt* double

verdorben 1. *pp of* **verderben** 2. *adj* spoilt; *(damaged)* ruined; *(morally)* corrupt

verdrehen *vt* twist; *(eyes)* roll; **jdm den Kopf ~** *fig* turn sb's head

verdünnen *vt* dilute

verdunsten *vi* evaporate

verdursten *vi* die of thirst

verehren vt admire; REL worship; **Verehrer(in)** m(f) (-s, -) admirer

Verein m (-(e)s, -e) association; (for sport, hobby) club

vereinbaren vt arrange; **Vereinbarung** f agreement, arrangement

vereinigen vt, vr unite; **Vereinigtes Königreich** nt United Kingdom; **Vereinigte Staaten** (von Amerika) pl United States sg (of America); **Vereinigung** f union; (organization) association; **Vereinte Nationen** pl United Nations pl

vereisen 1. vi (road) freeze over; (window) ice up **2.** vt MED freeze

verfahren irr **1.** vi proceed **2.** vr get lost; **Verfahren** nt (-s, -) procedure; TECH method; LAW proceedings pl

verfallen irr vi decline; (ticket etc) expire; ~ **in** + acc lapse into; **Verfallsdatum** nt expiry (Brit) (or expiration (US)) date; (of food) best-before date

verfärben vr change colour; (washing) discolour

Verfasser(in) m(f) (-s, -) author, writer; **Verfassung** f condition; POL constitution

verfaulen vi rot

verfehlen vt miss

Verfilmung f film (or screen) version

verfluchen vt curse

verfolgen vt pursue; POL persecute

verfügbar adj available; **verfügen** vi **über etw** acc ~ have sth at one's disposal; **Verfügung** f order; **jdm zur ~ stehen** be at sb's disposal

verführen vt tempt; (sexually) seduce; **verführerisch** adj seductive

vergangen adj past; **~e Woche** last week; **Vergangenheit** f past

Vergaser m (-s, -) AUTO carburettor

vergaß imperf of **vergessen**

vergeben irr vt forgive (jdm etw sb for sth); **vergebens** adv in vain; **vergeblich 1.** adv in vain **2.** adj vain, futile

vergehen irr **1.** vi pass **2.** vr **sich an jdm** ~ indecently assault sb; **Vergehen** nt (-s, -) offence

vergessen (vergaß, vergessen) vt forget; **vergesslich** adj forgetful

vergeuden vt squander, waste

vergewaltigen vt rape; **Vergewaltigung** f rape

vergewissern vr make sure

vergiften vt poison; **Vergiftung** f poisoning

Vergissmeinnicht nt (-(e)s, -e) forget-me-not

Vergleich m (-(e)s, -e) comparison; LAW settlement; **im ~ zu** compared to (or with); **vergleichen** irr vt compare

(*mit* to, with)

Vergnügen *nt* (-s, -) pleasure; **viel ~!** enjoy yourself; vergnügt *adj* cheerful; Vergnügungspark *m* amusement park

vergriffen *adj* (*book*) out of print; (*product*) out of stock

vergrößern *vt* enlarge; (*in quantity*) increase; (*with lens*) magnify; Vergrößerung *f* enlargement; (*in quantity*) increase; (*with lens*) magnification; Vergrößerungsglas *nt* magnifying glass

verhaften *vt* arrest

verhalten *irr vr* behave; Verhalten *nt* (-s) behaviour

Verhältnis *nt* relationship (*zu* with); MATH ratio; **~se** *pl* circumstances *pl*, conditions *pl*; **im ~ von 1 zu 2** in a ratio of 1 to 2; verhältnismäßig **1.** *adj* relative **2.** *adv* relatively

verhandeln *vi* negotiate (*über etw acc* sth); Verhandlung *f* negotiation

verheimlichen *vt* keep secret (*jdm* from sb)

verheiratet *adj* married

verhindern *vt* prevent; **sie ist verhindert** she can't make it

Verhör *nt* (-(e)s, -e) interrogation; (*in court*) examination; verhören **1.** *vt* interrogate; (*in court*) examine **2.** *vr* mishear

verhungern *vi* starve to death

verhüten *vt* prevent; Verhütung *f* prevention; (*with pill, condom etc*) contraception; Verhütungsmittel *nt* contraceptive

verirren *vr* get lost

Verkauf *m* sale; verkaufen *vt* sell; **zu ~** for sale; Verkäufer(in) *m(f)* seller; (*professional*) salesperson; (*in shop*) shop assistant (*Brit*), salesperson (*US*); verkäuflich *adj* for sale

Verkehr *m* (-s, -e) traffic; (*sexual*) intercourse; (*general use*) circulation; verkehren *vi* (*bus etc*) run; **~ mit** associate (*or* mix) with; Verkehrsampel *f* traffic lights *pl*; Verkehrsamt *nt* tourist information office; Verkehrsfunk *m* travel news *sg*; Verkehrsinsel *f* traffic island; Verkehrsmeldung *f* traffic report; Verkehrsmittel *nt* means of transport; **öffentliche ~** *pl* public transport *sg*; Verkehrsschild *nt* traffic sign; Verkehrsunfall *m* road accident; Verkehrszeichen *nt* traffic sign

verkehrt *adj* wrong; the wrong way round, inside out; **du machst es ~** you're doing it wrong

verklagen *vt* take to court

verkleiden 1. *vt, vr* dress up (*als* as) **2.** *vr* dress up (*als* as); (*to avoid being recognized*) disguise oneself; Verkleidung *f* fancy dress

verkleinern *vt* reduce; (*room, area etc*) make smaller; **verkommen 1.** *irr vi* deteriorate; (*person*) go downhill **2.** *adj* (*house etc*) dilapidated; (*morally*) depraved; **verkraften** *vt* cope with

verkratzt *adj* scratched

verkühlen *vr* get a chill

verkürzen *vt* shorten

Verlag *m* (-(*e*)*s*, -*e*) publishing company

verlangen 1. *vt* demand; want; (*price*) ask; (*expect*) ask (*von* of); (*person*) ask for; (*passport etc*) ask to see; ~ **Sie Herrn X** ask for Mr X **2.** *vi* ~ **nach** ask for

verlängern *vt* extend; (*passport, permit*) renew; **Verlängerung** *f* extension; SPORT extra time; (*of passport, permit*) renewal; **Verlängerungsschnur** *f* extension cable; **Verlängerungswoche** *f* extra week

verlassen 1. *irr vt* leave **2.** *irr vr* rely (*auf* + *acc* on) **3.** *adj* desolate; (*person*) abandoned; **verlässlich** *adj* reliable

Verlauf *m* course; **verlaufen** *irr* **1.** *vi* (*path, border*) run (*entlang* along); (*in time*) pass; (*colours*) run **2.** *vr* get lost; (*crowd*) disperse

verlegen 1. *vt* move; (*lose*) mislay; (*book*) publish **2.** *adj* embarrassed; **Verlegenheit** *f* embarrassment; (*situa-*

tion) difficulty

Verleih *m* (-(*e*)*s*, -*e*) hire company (*Brit*), rental company (*US*); **verleihen** *irr vt* lend; (*commercially*) hire (out) (*Brit*), rent (out) (*US*); (*prize, medal*) award

verleiten *vt* **jdn dazu** ~, **etw zu tun** induce sb to do sth

verlernen *vt* forget

verletzen *vt* injure; *fig* hurt; **Verletzte(r)** *mf* injured person; **Verletzung** *f* injury; (*of law etc*) violation

verlieben *vr* fall in love (*in jdn* with sb); **verliebt** *adj* in love

verlieren (*verlor, verloren*) *vt*, *vi* lose

verloben *vr* get engaged (*mit* to); **Verlobte(r)** *mf* fiancé / fiancée; **Verlobung** *f* engagement

verlor *imperf of* **verlieren**

verloren *pp of* **verlieren**

verlosen *vt* raffle; **Verlosung** *f* raffle

Verlust *m* (-(*e*)*s*, -*e*) loss

vermehren *vt*, *vr* multiply; (*amount*) increase

vermeiden *irr vt* avoid

vermeintlich *adj* supposed

vermieten *vt* rent (out), let (out) (*Brit*), (*car*) hire (out) (*Brit*), rent (out) (*US*); **Vermieter(in)** *m*(*f*) landlord / landlady

vermischen *vt*, *vr* mix

vermissen *vt* miss; **vermisst** *adj* missing; **jdn als** ~ **melden** report sb missing

Vermögen *nt* (-s, -) fortune

vermuten *vt* suppose; (*sth bad*) suspect; **vermutlich 1.** *adj* probable **2.** *adv* probably; **Vermutung** *f* supposition; (*of sth bad*) suspicion

vernachlässigen *vt* neglect

vernichten *vt* destroy; **vernichtend** *adj fig* crushing; (*look*) withering; (*criticism*) scathing

Vernunft *f* (-) reason; **vernünftig** *adj* sensible; (*price*) reasonable

veröffentlichen *vt* publish

verordnen *vt* MED prescribe; **Verordnung** *f* order; MED prescription

verpachten *vt* lease (out) (*an + acc* to)

verpacken *vt* pack; (*in paper*) wrap up

Verpackung *f* packaging

verpassen *vt* miss

verpflegen *vt* feed; **Verpflegung** *f* feeding; food; (*in hotel*) board

verpflichten 1. *vt* oblige; (*employ*) engage **2.** *vr* commit oneself (*etw zu tun* to doing sth)

verpfuschen *vt fam* make a mess of; *vulg* fuck up

verprügeln *vt* beat up

verraten 1. *vt* betray; (*secret*) divulge; **aber nicht ~!** but don't tell anyone **2.** *vr* give oneself away

verrechnen 1. *vt* ~ **mit** set off against **2.** *vr* miscalculate;

Verrechnungsscheck *m* crossed cheque (*Brit*), check for deposit only (*US*)

verregnet *adj* rainy

verreisen *vi* go away (*nach* to); **sie ist** (**geschäftlich**) **verreist** she's away (on business); **verrenken** *vt* contort; MED dislocate; **sich** *dat* **den Knöchel ~** sprain (*or* twist) one's ankle; **verringern** *vt* reduce

verrostet *adj* rusty

verrückt *adj* mad, crazy; **es macht mich ~** it's driving me mad

versagen *vi* fail; **Versagen** *nt* (-s) failure; **Versager(in)** *m(f)* (-s, -) failure

versalzen *irr vt* put too much salt in/on

versammeln *vt*, *vr* assemble, gather; **Versammlung** *f* meeting

Versand *m* (-(e)s) dispatch; (*in company*) dispatch department; **Versandhaus** *nt* mail-order company

versäumen *vt* miss; (*not do*) neglect; **~, etw zu tun** fail to do sth

verschätzen *vr* miscalculate

verschenken *vt* give away; (*chance*) waste

verschicken *vt* send off

verschieben *vt irr* postpone, put off; (*push*) move

verschieden *adj* different; (*several*) various; **sie sind ~ groß** they are of different sizes; **Verschiedene** pl various people / things pl; **Verschiedenes** various things pl

verschimmelt adj mouldy

verschlafen irr 1. vt sleep through; fig miss 2. vi, vr oversleep

verschlechtern vr deteriorate, get worse; **Verschlechterung** f deterioration

verschließbar adj lockable; **verschließen** irr vt close; (with key) lock

verschlimmern 1. vt make worse 2. vr get worse

verschlossen adj locked; fig reserved

verschlucken 1. vt swallow 2. vr choke (an + dat on)

Verschluss m loss; (on dress) fastener; PHOT shutter; (bung) stopper

verschmutzen vt get dirty; (environment) pollute

verschnaufen vi **ich muss mal ~** I need to get my breath back

verschneit adj snow-covered

verschnupft adj ~ **sein** have a cold; fam be peeved

verschonen vt spare (jdn mit etw sth with)

verschreiben irr vt MED prescribe; **verschreibungspflichtig** adj available only on prescription

verschwand imperf of **verschwinden**

verschweigen irr vt keep secret; **jdm etw ~** keep sth from sb

verschwenden vt waste; **Verschwendung** f waste

verschwiegen adj discreet; (place) secluded

verschwinden (verschwand, verschwunden) vi disappear, vanish; **verschwinde!** get lost!; **verschwunden** pp of **verschwinden**

Versehen nt (-s, -) **aus ~** by mistake; **versehentlich** adv by mistake

versenden irr vt send off

versetzen 1. vt transfer; (jewellery etc) pawn; fam (on a date) stand up 2. vr **sich in jdn** (or **jds Lage**) ~ put oneself in sb's place

verseuchen vt contaminate

versichern vt insure; (confirm) assure; **versichert sein** be insured; **Versichertenkarte** f health-insurance card; **Versicherung** f insurance; **Versicherungskarte** f **grüne ~** green card (Brit), insurance document for driving abroad; **Versicherungspolice** f insurance policy

versilbert adj silver-plated

versinken irr vi sink

versöhnen 1. vt reconcile 2. vr become reconciled

versorgen 1. vt provide, supply (mit with); (family) look after 2. vr look after oneself; **Versorgung** f provision; (care) maintenance; (money) benefit

verspäten *vr* be late; Verspätung *f* delay; (*eine Stunde*) ~ *haben* be (an hour) late

versprechen *irr* 1. *vt* promise 2. *vr ich habe mich versprochen* I didn't mean to say that

Verstand *m* mind; (common) sense; *den* ~ *verlieren* lose one's mind; verständigen 1. *vt* inform 2. *vr* communicate; (*agree*) come to an understanding; Verständigung *f* communication; verständlich *adj* understandable; Verständnis *nt* understanding (*für* of); verständnisvoll *adj* understanding

Verstärker *m* (-s, -) amplifier

verstauchen *vt* sprain

Versteck *nt* (-(e)s, -e) hiding place; ~ *spielen* play hide-and-seek; verstecken *vt*, *vr* hide (*vor* + *dat* from)

verstehen *irr* 1. *vt* understand; *falsch* ~ misunderstand 2. *vr* get on (*mit* with)

verstellbar *adj* adjustable; verstellen 1. *vt* move; (*clock*) adjust; (*obstruct*) block; (*voice*, *handwriting*) disguise 2. *vr* pretend, put on an act

verstopfen *vt* block up; MED constipate; Verstopfung *f* obstruction; MED constipation

Verstoß *m* infringement, violation (*gegen* of)

Versuch *m* (-(e)s, -e) attempt; (*scientific*) experiment; versuchen *vt* try

vertauschen *vt* exchange; (*by mistake*) mix up

verteidigen *vt* defend

verteilen *vt* distribute

Vertrag *m* (-(e)s, Verträge) contract; POL treaty

vertragen *irr* 1. *vt* stand, bear 2. *vr* get along (with each other); (*be reconciled*) make it up

vertrauen *vi jdm*/*einer Sache* ~ trust sb/sth; Vertrauen *nt* (-s) trust (*in* + *acc* in, *zu* in); *ich habe kein* ~ *zu ihm* I don't trust him; *ich hab's ihm im* ~ *gesagt* I told him in confidence; vertraulich *adj* confidential; vertraut *adj sich mit etw* ~ *machen* familiarize oneself with sth

vertreten *irr* *vt* represent; (*opinion*) hold; Vertreter(in) *m(f)* (-s, -) representative

Vertrieb *m* (-(e)s, -e) sales department

verunglücken *vi* have an accident; *tödlich* ~ be killed in an accident

verursachen *vt* cause

verurteilen *vt* condemn

verwackeln *vt* (*photo*) blur

verwählen *vr* dial the wrong number

verwalten *vt* manage; (*offi-*

cials) administer; **Verwalter(in)** *m(f)* (*-s, -*) manager; **Verwaltung** *f* management; (*by officials*) administration

verwandt *adj* related (*mit* to); **Verwandte(r)** *mf* relative, relation; **Verwandtschaft** *f* relationship; (*people*) relations *pl*

verwarnen *vt* warn; SPORT caution

verwechseln *vt* confuse (*mit* with); (*for sb or sth else*) mistake (*mit* for)

verweigern *vt* refuse

verwenden *vt* use; **Verwendung** *f* use

verwirklichen *vt* realize; **sich selbst ~** fulfil oneself

verwirren *vt* confuse; **Verwirrung** *f* confusion

verwöhnen *vt* spoil

verwunderlich *adj* surprising; **Verwunderung** *f* astonishment

verwüsten *vt* devastate

verzählen *vr* miscount

verzehren *vt* consume

Verzeichnis *nt* list; (*of books, products*) catalogue; (*in book*) index; IT directory

verzeihen (*verzieh, verziehen*) *vt, vi* forgive (*jdm etw* sb for sth); **~ Sie bitte,** ... excuse me, ...; **~ Sie die Störung** sorry to disturb you; **Verzeihung** *f* **~!** sorry; **~,** ... excuse me, ...; (*jdn*) **um ~ bitten** apologize (to sb)

verzichten *vi* **auf etw** *acc* **~** do

without sth; (*abandon*) give sth up

verzieh *imperf of* **verzeihen**

verziehen *pp of* **verzeihen**

verziehen *irr* **1.** *vt* (*child*) spoil; **das Gesicht ~** pull a face **2.** *vr* go out of shape; (*go away*) disappear

verzieren *vt* decorate

verzögern 1. *vt* delay **2.** *vr* be delayed; **Verzögerung** *f* delay

verzweifeln *vi* despair (*an + dat* of); **verzweifelt** *adj* desperate; **Verzweiflung** *f* despair

vgl. *abbr* = **vergleiche**; cf

Viagra® *nt* (*-s*) Viagra®

Vibrator *m* (*-s, -en*) vibrator; **vibrieren** *vi* vibrate

Video *nt* (*-s, -s*) video; **auf ~ aufnehmen** record on video; **Videoclip** *m* (*-s, -s*) video clip; **Videofilm** *m* video; **Videogerät** *nt* video (recorder); **Videokamera** *f* video camera; **Videokassette** *f* video (cassette); **Videorekorder** *m* video recorder; **Videospiel** *nt* video game; **Videothek** *f* (*-, -en*) video library

Vieh *nt* (*-(e)s*) cattle

viel 1. *pron* a lot of, lots of; **~ Arbeit** a lot of work; lots of work; **~e Leute** a lot of people, lots of people, many people; **zu ~** too much; **zu ~e** too many; **sehr ~** a great deal of; **sehr ~e** a great many; **ziemlich ~/~e** quite a lot of; **nicht ~** not much, not a lot of; **nicht ~e** not many, not a lot of; **sie sagt nicht ~** she doesn't say a lot; **gibt es ~?** is there much?, is there a lot?; **gibt es ~e?** are there many?, are there a lot? **2.** adv a lot; **er geht ~ ins Kino** he goes a lot to the cinema; **sehr ~** a great deal; **ziemlich ~** quite a lot; **~ besser** much better; **~ teurer** much more expensive; **~ zu ~** far too much

vielleicht adv perhaps; **~ ist sie krank** perhaps she's ill, she might be ill; **weißt du ~, wo er ist?** do you know where he is (by any chance)?

vielmal(s) adv many times; **danke vielmals** many thanks; **vielmehr** adv rather; **vielseitig** adj very varied; (person, device) versatile

vier num four; **auf allen ~en** on all fours; **unter ~ Augen** in private, privately; **Vier** f (-, -en) four; (mark in school) ≈ D; **Vierbettzimmer** nt four-bed room; **Viereck** nt (-(e)s, -e) four-sided figure; square; **viereckig** adj four-sided; square; **vierfach** adj **die ~e Menge** four times the amount; **vierhundert** num four hundred; **viermal** adv four times; **vierspurig** adj four-lane

viert adv **wir sind zu ~** there are four of us; **vierte(r, s)** adj fourth; → **dritte**

Viertel nt (-s, -) (of town) quarter, district; (fraction) quarter; (of wine etc) quarter-litre; **~ vor/nach drei** a quarter to/past three; **viertel drei** a quarter past two; **drei viertel drei** a quarter to three; **Viertelfinale** nt quarter-final; **vierteljährlich** adj quarterly; **Viertelstunde** f quarter of an hour

vierzehn num fourteen; **in ~ Tagen** in two weeks, in a fortnight (Brit); **vierzehntägig** adj two-week, fortnightly (Brit); **vierzehnte(r, s)** adj fourteenth; → **dritte**; **vierzig** num forty; **vierzigste(r, s)** adj fortieth

Vietnam nt (-s) Vietnam

Vignette f motorway (Brit) (or freeway (US)) permit

Villa f (-, Villen) villa

violett adj purple

Violine f violin

Virus m or nt (-, Viren) virus

Visitenkarte f card

Visum nt (-s, Visa or Visen) visa

Vitamin nt (-s, -e) vitamin

Vitrine f (-, -n) (glass) cabinet; (in museum etc) display case

Vogel m (-s, Vögel) bird; **vögeln** vi, vt vulg screw

Voicemail f (-, -s) voice mail

Vokal m (-s, -e) vowel

Volk nt (-(e)s, Völker) people pl; (community) nation;

Volksfest nt festival; (with rides etc) funfair; Volkshochschule f adult education centre; Volkslied nt folksong; Volksmusik f folk music; volkstümlich adj popular; traditional; (art) folk

voll adj full (von of); ~ machen fill up; ~ tanken fill up; Vollbremsung f eine ~ machen slam on the brakes; vollends adv completely

Vollgas nt mit ~ at full throttle; ~ geben step on it

völlig 1. adj complete 2. adv completely

volljährig adj of age; Vollkaskoversicherung f fully comprehensive insurance; vollklimatisiert adj fully air-conditioned; vollkommen 1. adj perfect; ~er Unsinn complete rubbish 2. adv completely

Vollkornbrot nt wholemeal (Brit) (or whole wheat (US)) bread

Vollmacht f (-, -en) authority; (document) power of attorney

Vollmilch f full-fat milk (Brit), whole milk (US); Vollmilchschokolade f milk chocolate; Vollmond m full moon; Vollnarkose f general anaesthetic; Vollpension f full board

vollständig adj complete

Vollwaschmittel nt all-purpose washing powder; Voll

wertkost f wholefood; vollzählig adj complete

Volt nt (-, -) volt

Volumen nt (-s, -) volume

vom contr of von dem; (with space, time, cause) from; ich kenne sie nur ~ Sehen I only know her by sight

von prep + dat (with space, time) from; (replacing genitive, consisting of) of; (passive) by; ein Freund ~ mir a friend of mine; ~ mir aus fam I don't mind; ~ wegen! no way; voneinander adv from each other

vor prep + dat or acc before; (in space) in front of; fünf ~ drei five to three; ~ 2 Tagen 2 days ago; ~ Wut/ Liebe with rage / love; ~ allem above all

vorangehen irr vi go ahead; einer Sache dat ~ precede sth; vorankommen irr vi make progress

voraus adv jdm ~ sein be ahead of sb; im Voraus in advance; vorausfahren irr vi drive on ahead; vorausgesetzt conj provided (that); Voraussage f prediction; (for weather) forecast; voraussagen vt predict; voraussehen irr vt foresee; voraussetzen vt assume; Voraussetzung f requirement, prerequisite; voraussichtlich 1. adj expected 2. adv probably; vorauszahlen vt pay in advance

vorbei *adv* past, over, finished; **vorbeibringen** *irr vt* drop by (*or* in); **vorbeifahren** *irr vi* drive past; **vorbeigehen** *irr vi* pass by, go past; (*elapse, end*) pass; **vorbeikommen** *irr vi* drop by; **vorbeilassen** *irr vt* **kannst du die Leute ~?** would you let these people pass?; **lässt du mich bitte mal vorbei?** can I get past, please?

vorbereiten 1. *vt* prepare **2.** *vr* get ready (*auf* + *acc, für* for); **Vorbereitung** *f* preparation

vorbestellen *vt* book in advance; (*meal*) order in advance; **Vorbestellung** *f* booking, reservation

vorbeugen *vi* prevent (*dat* sth); **vorbeugend** *adj* preventive; **Vorbeugung** *f* prevention

Vorbild *nt* (role) model; **vorbildlich** *adj* exemplary, ideal

Vorderachse *f* front axle; **vordere(r, s)** *adj* front; **Vordergrund** *m* foreground; **Vorderradantrieb** *m* AUTO front-wheel drive; **Vorderseite** *f* front; **Vordersitz** *m* front seat; **Vorderteil** *m or nt* front (part)

vordrängen *vr* push forward

voreilig *adj* hasty, rash; **~e Schlüsse ziehen** jump to conclusions; **voreingenommen** *adj* biased

vorenthalten *irr vt* **jdm etw ~**

withhold sth from sb

vorerst *adv* for the moment

vorfahren *irr vi* drive on ahead; **vor das Haus ~** drive up to the house; **fahren Sie bis zur Ampel vor** drive as far as the traffic lights

Vorfahrt *f* AUTO right of way; **~ achten** give way (*Brit*), yield (*US*); **Vorfahrtsschild** *nt* give way (*Brit*) (*or* yield (*US*)) sign; **Vorfahrtsstraße** *f* major road

Vorfall *m* incident

vorführen *vt* demonstrate; (*film*) show; THEAT perform

Vorgänger(in) *m(f)* predecessor

vorgehen *irr vi* go on ahead; (*to the front*) go forward; (*take action*) act, proceed; (*clock, watch*) be fast; (*be more important*) take precedence; (*happen*) go on; **Vorgehen** *nt* (*-s*) procedure

Vorgesetzte(r) *mf* superior

vorgestern *adv* the day before yesterday

vorhaben *irr vt* plan; **hast du schon was vor?** have you got anything on?; **ich habe vor, nach Rom zu fahren** I'm planning to go to Rome

vorhalten *irr vt* **jdm etw ~** accuse sb of sth

Vorhand *f* forehand

vorhanden *adj* existing; available

Vorhang *m* curtain

Vorhängeschloss *nt* padlock

Vorhaut f foreskin

vorher adv before; **zwei Tage ~** two days before; **~ essen wir** we'll eat first; **Vorhersage** f forecast; **vorhersehen** irr vt foresee

vorhin adv just now, a moment ago

vorig adj previous; (week etc) last

vorkommen irr vi come forward; (take place) happen; (appear) seem (to be); **sich** dat **dumm ~** feel stupid

Vorlage f model

vorlassen irr vt **jdn ~** let sb go first

vorläufig adj temporary

vorlesen irr vt read out

vorletzte(r, s) adj last but one; **am ~n Samstag** (on) the Saturday before last

Vorliebe f preference

vormachen vt **kannst du es mir ~?** can you show me how to do it?; **jdm etwas ~** fig fool sb

Vormittag m morning; **am ~ in** the morning; **heute ~** this morning; **vormittags** adv in the morning; **um 9 Uhr ~** at 9 (o'clock) in the morning, at 9 am

vorn(e) adv in front; **von~ anfangen** start at the beginning; **nach ~** to the front; **weiter ~** further up; **von ~ bis hinten** from beginning to end

Vorname m first name; **wie**

heißt du mit ~ what's your first name?

vornehm adj distinguished; (behaviour) refined; (clothes, hotel etc) elegant

vornehmen irr vt **sich** dat **etw ~** start on sth; **sich** dat **etw zu tun** decide to do sth

vornherein adv **von ~** from the start

Vorort m suburb

vorrangig adj priority

Vorrat m stock, supply; **vorrätig** adj in stock; **Vorratskammer** f pantry

Vorrecht nt privilege; **Vorruhestand** m early retirement; **Vorsaison** f early season

Vorsatz m intention; LAW intent; **vorsätzlich** adj intentional; LAW premeditated

Vorschau f preview; (for film) trailer

Vorschlag m suggestion, proposal; **vorschlagen** irr vt suggest, propose; **ich schlage vor, dass wir gehen** I suggest we go

vorschreiben irr vt stipulate; **jdm etw ~** dictate sth to sb

Vorschrift f regulation, rule; instruction; **vorschriftsmäßig** adj correct

Vorsicht f care; **~!** look out; (on sign) caution; **~ Stufe!** mind the step; **vorsichtig** adj careful; **vorsichtshalber** adv just in case

Vorsorge f precaution; (stopping) prevention; **Vorsorge-**

untersuchung f checkup;
vorsorglich adv as a precaution

Vorspeise f starter

vorstellen vt (person) introduce, put forward; (in front of sth else) put in front; **sich dat etw ~** imagine sth; Vorstellung f (to sb) introduction; THEAT performance; (concept) idea; Vorstellungsgespräch nt interview

vortäuschen vt feign

Vorteil m advantage (gegenüber over); **die Vor- und Nachteile** the pros and cons; vorteilhaft adj advantageous

Vortrag m (-(e)s, Vorträge) talk (über + acc on); (academic) lecture; **einen ~ halten** give a talk

vorüber adv over; vorübergehen irr vi pass; vorübergehend **1.** adj temporary **2.** adv temporarily, for the time being

Vorurteil nt prejudice

Vorverkauf m advance booking

vorverlegen vt bring forward

Vorwahl f TEL dialling code (Brit), area code (US)

Vorwand m (-(e)s, Vorwände) pretext, excuse; **unter dem ~, dass** with the excuse that

vorwärts adv forward; **~ gehen** fig progress; Vorwärtsgang m AUTO forward gear

vorweg adv in advance; vorwegnehmen irr vt anticipate

vorwerfen irr vt **jdm etw ~** accuse sb of sth

vorwiegend adv mainly

Vorwort nt preface

Vorwurf m reproach; **sich dat Vorwürfe machen** reproach oneself; **jdm Vorwürfe machen** accuse sb; vorwurfsvoll adj reproachful

vorzeigen vt show

vorzeitig adj premature, early

vorziehen irr vt prefer

vorzüglich adj excellent

vulgär adj vulgar

Vulkan m (-s, -e) volcano; Vulkanausbruch m volcanic eruption

W

Waage f (-, -n) scales pl; ASTR Libra; waagerecht adj horizontal

wach adj awake; **~ werden** wake up; Wache f (-, -n) guard

Wachs nt (-es, -e) wax

wachsen (wuchs, gewachsen) vi grow

wachsen vt (skis) wax

Wachstum nt growth

Wächter(in) m(f) (-s, -) guard; (of car park) attendant

wandeln

wackelig *adj* wobbly; *fig* shaky; **Wackelkontakt** *m* loose connection; **wackeln** *vi* (*chair*) be wobbly; (*tooth, screw*) be loose; *mit dem Kopf ~* waggle one's head

Wade *f* (-, -*n*) calf

Waffe *f* (-, -*n*) weapon

Waffel *f* (-, -*n*) waffle; (*biscuit, for ice cream*) wafer

wagen *vt* risk; *es ~, etw zu tun* dare to do sth

Wagen *m* (-*s*, -) AUTO car; RAIL carriage; **Wagenheber** *m* (-*s*, -) jack; **Wagentyp** *m* model, make

Wahl *f* (-, -*en*) choice; POL election

wählen 1. *vt* choose; TEL dial; POL vote for; (*as president, to board etc*) elect **2.** *vi* choose; TEL dial; POL vote; **Wähler(in)** *m(f)* (-*s*, -) voter; **wählerisch** *adj* choosy

Wahlkampf *m* election campaign; **wahllos** *adv* at random; **Wahlwiederholung** *f* redial

Wahnsinn *m* madness; *~!* amazing!; **wahnsinnig 1.** *adj* insane, mad **2.** *adv fam* incredibly

wahr *adj* true; *das darf doch nicht ~ sein!* I don't believe it; *nicht ~?* that's right, isn't it?

während 1. *prep + gen* during **2.** *conj* while; **währenddessen** *adv* meanwhile, in the meantime

Wahrheit *f* truth

wahrnehmbar *adj* noticeable, perceptible; **wahrnehmen** *irr vt* perceive

Wahrsager(in) *m(f)* (-*s*, -) fortune-teller

wahrscheinlich 1. *adj* probable, likely **2.** *adv* probably; *ich komme ~ zu spät* I'll probably be late; **Wahrscheinlichkeit** *f* probability

Währung *f* currency

Wahrzeichen *nt* symbol

Waise *f* (-, -*n*) orphan

Wal *m* (-(*e*)*s*, -*e*) whale

Wald *m* (-(*e*)*s*, *Wälder*) wood; (*extensive*) forest; **Waldbrand** *m* forest fire; **Waldlauf** *m* cross-country run; **Waldsterben** *nt* (-*s*) forest dieback

Wales *nt* (-) Wales; **Waliser(in)** *m(f)* Welshman/ Welshwoman; **walisisch** *adj* Welsh; **Walisisch** *nt* Welsh

Walkman® *m* (-*s*, -*s*) walkman®, personal stereo

Wallfahrt *f* pilgrimage; **Wallfahrtsort** *m* place of pilgrimage

Walnuss *f* walnut

Walross *nt* (-*es*, -*e*) walrus

wälzen 1. *vt* roll; (*books*) pore over; (*problems*) deliberate on **2.** *vr* wallow; (*in pain*) roll about; (*in bed*) toss and turn

Walzer *m* (-*s*, -) waltz

Wand *f* (-, *Wände*) wall

Wandel *m* (-*s*) change; **wandeln** *vt*, *vr* change

Wanderer *m (-s, -)*, Wanderin *f* hiker; Wanderkarte *f* hiking map; wandern *vi* hike; *(gaze)* wander; *(thoughts)* stray; Wanderschuh *m* walking shoe; Wanderstiefel *m* hiking boot; Wanderung *f* hike; *eine ~ machen* go on a hike; Wanderweg *m* walking *(or* hiking) trail; Wandschrank *m* built-in cupboard *(Brit)*, closet *(US)*; wandte *imperf of* wenden

Wange *f (-, -n)* cheek

wann *adv* when; *seit ~ ist sie da?* how long has she been here?; *bis ~ bleibt ihr?* how long are you staying?

Wanne *f (-, -n)* (bath) tub

Wappen *nt (-s, -)* coat of arms

war *imperf of* sein

warb *imperf of* werben

Ware *f (-, -n)* product; *~n* goods *pl*; Warenhaus *nt* department store; Warenprobe *f* sample; Warensendung *f* consignment; Warenzeichen *nt* trademark

warf *imperf of* werfen

warm *adj* warm; *(meal)* hot; *~ laufen* warm up; *mir ist es zu ~* I'm too warm; Wärme *f (-, -n)* warmth; wärmen 1. *vt* warm; *(food)* warm *(or* heat) up 2. *vi* be warm 3. *vr* warm up; *(by holding each other)* keep each other warm; Wärmflasche *f* hot-water bottle

Warnblinkanlage *f* AUTO warning flasher; Warndreieck *nt* AUTO warning triangle; warnen *vt* warn *(vor + dat* about, of); Warnung *f* warning

Warteliste *f* waiting list; warten 1. *vi* wait *(auf + acc* for); *warte mal!* wait *(or* hang on) a minute 2. *vt* TECH service

Wärter(in) *m(f)* attendant

Wartesaal *m*, Wartezimmer *nt* waiting room

Wartung *f* service; *(action)* servicing

warum *adv* why

Warze *f (-, -n)* wart

was 1. *pron* what; *~ kostet das?* what does it cost?, how much is it?; *~ für ein Auto ist das?* what kind of car is that?; *~ für eine Farbe/Größe?* what colour/size?; *fam ~?*, what?; *~ ist/gibt's?* what is it?, what's up? 2. *pron du weißt, ~ ich meine* you know what I mean; *~ (auch) immer* whatever this; *~ soll ich dir ~ mitbringen?* do you want me to bring you anything?

Waschanlage *f* AUTO car wash; waschbar *adj* washable; Waschbecken *nt* washbasin

Wäsche *f (-, -n)* washing; *(dirty)* laundry; *in der ~* in the wash; Wäscheklammer *f* clothes peg *(Brit)* (or pin *(US)*); Wäscheleine *f* clothesline waschen (*wusch, gewaschen*) **1.** *vt*, *vi* wash; *Waschen und Legen* shampoo and set **2.** *vr* (have a) wash; *sich dat die Haare ~* wash one's hair

Wäscherei *f* laundry; Wäscheschleuder *f* spin-drier; Wäscheständer *m* clothes horse; Wäschetrockner *m* tumble-drier

Waschgelegenheit *f* washing facilities *pl*; Waschlappen *m* flannel (*Brit*), washcloth (*US*); *fam* (person) wet blanket; Waschmaschine *f* washing machine; Waschmittel *nt*, Waschpulver *nt* washing powder; Waschraum *m* washroom; Waschsalon *m* (*-s, -s*) launderette (*Brit*), laundromat (*US*); Waschstraße *f* car wash

Wasser *nt* (*-s, -*) water; *flie-Bendes ~* running water; Wasserball *m* SPORT water polo; wasserdicht *adj* watertight; (*fabric, watch*) waterproof; Wasserfall *m* waterfall; Wasserfarbe *f* watercolour; wasserfest *adj* watertight, waterproof; Wasserhahn *m* tap (*Brit*), faucet (*US*); wässerig *adj* watery; Wasserkessel *m* kettle; Wasserkocher *m* electric kettle; Wasserleitung *f* water pipe; wasserlöslich *adj* water-soluble; Wassermann *m* ASTR Aquarius; Wassermelone *f* water melon; Was-serrutschbahn *f* water chute; Wasserschaden *m* water damage; wasserscheu *adj* scared of water; Wasserski *m* water-skiing; Wassersport *m* water sports *pl*; Wasserspülung *f* flush; wasserundurchlässig *adj* watertight, waterproof; Wasserverbrauch *m* water consumption; Wasserversorgung *f* water supply; Wasserwerk *nt* waterworks *pl*

waten *vi* wade

Watt **1.** *nt* (*-(e)s, -en*) GEO mud flats *pl* **2.** *nt* (*-s, -*) ELEC watt

Watte *f* (*-, -n*) cotton wool; Wattestäbchen *nt* cotton bud, Q-tip® (*US*)

WC *nt* (*-s, -s*) toilet, restroom (*US*); WC-Reiniger *m* toilet cleaner

Web *nt* (*-s*) IT Web; Webseite *f* IT web page

Wechsel *m* (*-s, -*) change; SPORT substitution; Wechselgeld *nt* change; wechselhaft *adj* (*weather*) changeable; Wechseljahre *pl* menopause *sg*; Wechselkurs *m* exchange rate; wechseln **1.** *vt* change; (*looks*) exchange; *Geld ~* change some money; (*into smaller coins or notes*) get some change; *Euro in Pfund ~* change euros into pounds **2.** *vi* change; *kannst du ~?* can you change this?; Wechselstrom *m* alternat-

ing current, AC; **Wechselstube** f bureau de change
Weckdienst m wake-up call
service; **wecken** vt wake
(up); **Wecker** m (-s, -) alarm
clock; **Weckruf** m wake-up
call
wedeln vi SKI wedel; **der
Hund wedelte mit dem
Schwanz** the dog wagged
its tail
weder conj ~ ... **noch** ... neither ... nor ...
weg adv away; (leaving, removed) off; **er war schon ~**
he had already left (or gone);
Hände ~! hands off; **weit ~** a
long way away (or off)
Weg m (-(e)s, -e) way; (for
walking) path; (way travelled) route; **jdn nach dem ~
fragen** ask sb the way; **auf
dem ~ sein** be on the way
wegbleiben irr vi stay away;
wegbringen irr vt take away
wegen prep + gen or dat because of
wegfahren irr vi drive away;
(depart) leave; (on holiday)
go away; **Wegfahrsperre** f
AUTO (engine) immobilizer;
weggehen irr vi go away;
wegkommen irr vi come off,
fig **gut / schlecht ~** come off
well / badly; **weglassen** irr
vt leave out; **weglaufen** irr
vi run away; **weglegen** irr vt
put aside; **wegmüssen** irr
vi **ich muss weg** I've got
to go; **wegnehmen** irr vt

take away; **wegräumen** vt
clear away; **wegrennen** irr
vi run away; **wegschicken**
vt send away; **wegschmei-
ßen** irr vt throw away; **wegsehen** irr vi look away; **weg-
tun** irr vt put away
Wegweiser m (-s, -) signpost
wegwerfen irr vt throw away;
Wegwerfflasche f non-returnable bottle; **wegwi-
schen** vt wipe (off); **wegziehen** irr vi move (away)
weh adj sore; → **wehtun**
wehen vt, vi blow; (flag) flutter
Wehen pl labour pains pl
Wehrdienst m military service
wehren vr defend oneself
wehtun irr vi hurt; **jdm / sich
~** hurt sb / oneself
Weibchen nt **es ist ein ~** (animal) it's a she; **weiblich** adj
feminine; BIO female
weich adj soft; **~ gekocht**
(egg) soft-boiled
Weichspüler m (-s, -) (fabric)
softener
Weide f (-, -n) (tree) willow;
(field) meadow
weigern vr refuse; **Weigerung** f refusal
Weiher m (-s, -) pond
Weihnachten nt (-, -) Christmas; **Weihnachtsabend** m
Christmas Eve; **Weih-
nachtsbaum** m Christmas
tree; **Weihnachtsfeier** f
Christmas party; **Weih-**

nachtsferien pl Christmas holidays pl (Brit), Christmas vacation sg (US); **Weihnachtsgeschenk** nt Christmas present; **Weihnachtslied** nt Christmas carol; **Weihnachtsmann** m Father Christmas, Santa (Claus); **Weihnachtstag** m **erster ~** Christmas Day; **zweiter ~** Boxing Day; **Weihnachtszeit** f Christmas season

weil conj because

Weile f (-) while, short time; **es kann noch eine ~ dauern** it could take some time

Wein m (-(e)s, -e) wine; (plant) vine; **Weinbrand** m brandy

weinen vt, vi cry

Weinglas nt wine glass; **Weinkarte** f wine list; **Weinkeller** m wine cellar; **Weinprobe** f wine tasting; **Weintraube** f grape

weise adj wise

Weise f (-, -n) manner, way; **auf diese (Art und) ~** this way

weisen (wies, gewiesen) vt show

Weisheit f wisdom; **Weisheitszahn** m wisdom tooth

weiß adj white; **Weißbier** nt ≈ wheat beer; **Weißbrot** nt white bread; **Weißkohl** m, **Weißkraut** nt (white) cabbage; **Weißwein** m white wine

weit 1. adj wide; (concept) broad; (journey, throw) long; (dress) loose; **wie ~ ist es ...?** how far is it ...?; **so ~ sein** be ready 2. adv far; **~ verbreitet** widespread; **~ gereist** widely travelled; **~ offen** wide open; **das geht zu ~** that's going too far, that's pushing it

weiter 1. adj (more distant) farther (away); (additional) further; **~e Informationen** further information sg 2. adv further; **~f** go on; (to people walking) keep moving; **~ nichts/niemand** nothing/nobody else; **und so ~** and so on; **Weiterbildung** f further training (or education); **weiterempfehlen** irr vt recommend; **weitererzählen** vt **~f** I don't tell anyone; **weiterfahren** irr vi go on (nach to, bis as far as); **weitergeben** irr vt pass on; **weitergehen** irr vi go on; **weiterhelfen** irr vi **jdm ~** help sb

weiterhin adv **etw ~ tun** go on doing sth

weitermachen vt, vi continue; **weiterreisen** vi continue one's journey

weitgehend 1. adj considerable 2. adv largely; **weitsichtig** adj long-sighted; fig far-sighted; **Weitspringer(in)** m(f) long jumper; **Weitsprung** m long jump; **Weitwinkelobjektiv** nt PHOT wide-angle lens

Weizen *m* (-s, -) wheat; Weizenbier *nt* ≈ wheat beer

welche(r, s) 1. *pron* what; *(when choosing)* which (one); **~ Geschmacksrichtung willst du?** which flavour do you want?; **~r ist es?** which (one) is it? 2. *pron (relative, person)* who; *(relative, thing)* which, that; **zeig mir, ~r es war** show me which one of them it was 3. *pron fam* some; **hast du Kleingeld? - ja, ich hab' ~** have you got any change? - yes, I've got some

welk *adj* withered; welken *vi* wither

Welle *f* (-, -n) wave; Wellengang *m* waves *pl*; **stärker ~** heavy seas *pl*; Wellenlänge *f* wavelength; Wellenreiten *nt* surfing; Wellensittich *m* (-s, -e) budgerigar, budgie

Welpe *m* (-n, -n) puppy

Welt *f* (-, -en) world; **auf der ~** in the world; **auf die ~ kommen** be born; Weltall *nt* universe; weltbekannt *adj*, weltberühmt *adj* world-famous; Weltkrieg *m* world war; Weltmacht *f* world power; Weltmeister(in) *m(f)* world champion; Weltmeisterschaft *f* world championship; *(in football)* World Cup; Weltraum *m* space; Weltreise *f* trip round the world; Weltrekord *m* world record; Weltstadt *f* metrop-

olis; weltweit *adj* worldwide, global

wem *pron dat of* wer; who ... to, (to) whom; **~ hast du's gegeben?** who did you give it to?; **~ gehört es?** who does it belong to?, whose is it?; **~ auch immer es gehört** whoever it belongs to

wen *pron acc of* wer; who, whom; **~ hast du besucht?** who did you visit?; **~ möchten Sie sprechen?** who would you like to speak to?; **~ auch immer du gesprochen hast** whoever you talked to

Wende *f* (-, -n) turning point; *(transformation)* change; **die ~** HIST the fall of the Berlin Wall; Wendekreis *m* AUTO turning circle

wenden *(wendete or* wandte, *gewendet or* gewandt) *vt, vi, vr* turn (round); *(by 180°)* make a U-turn; **sich an jdn ~** turn to sb; **bitte ~!** please turn over, PTO

wenig 1. *pron* little; **~(e)** *pl* few; **(nur) ein (klein) ~** (just) a little (bit); **ein ~ Zucker** a little bit of sugar, a little sugar; **wir haben ~ Zeit** we haven't got much time; **zu ~** too little; *pl* too few; **nur ~ wissen** only a few know 2. *adv* **er spricht ~** he doesn't talk much; **~ bekannt** little known; wenigstens *adv* at least

wenn conj if; (with time) when; **wennschon** adv **na ~ so** what?

wer 1. pron who; **~ war das?** who was that?; **~ von euch?** which (one) of you? **2.** pron anybody who, anyone who; **~ das glaubt, ist dumm** anyone who believes that is stupid; **~ auch immer** whoever **3.** pron somebody, someone; anybody, anyone; **ist da~?** is (there) anybody there?

Werbefernsehen nt TV commercials pl; **werben** (warb, geworben) **1.** vt win; (member) recruit **2.** vi advertise; **Werbespot** m (-s, -s) commercial; **Werbung** f advertising

werden (wurde, geworden) **1.** vi get, become; **alt/müde/reich ~** get old / tired / rich; **was willst du ~?** what do you want to be?; vaux (future) will; (definitely) be going to; (passive) be; **er wird uns (schon) fahren** he'll drive us; **ich werde kommen** I'll come; **er wird uns abholen** he's going to pick us up; **wir ~ dafür bezahlt** we're paid for it; **er wird gerade diskutiert** he's being discussed

werfen (warf, geworfen) vt throw

Werft f (-, -en) shipyard, dockyard

Werk nt (-(e)s, -e) (of art, literature etc) work; (industrial) factory; (mechanism) works pl; **Werkstatt** f (-, -stätten) workshop; AUTO garage; **Werktag** m working day; **werktags** adv on weekdays, during the week; **Werkzeug** nt tool; **Werkzeugkasten** m toolbox

wert adj worth; **es ist etwa 50 Euro ~** it's worth about 50 euros; **das ist nichts ~** it's worthless; **Wert** m (-(e)s, -e) worth; FIN value; **~ legen auf** + acc attach importance to; **es hat doch keinen ~** (sense) it's pointless; **Wertangabe** f declaration of value; **Wertbrief** m insured letter; **Wertgegenstand** m valuable object; **wertlos** adj worthless; **Wertmarke** f token; **Wertpapiere** pl securities pl; **Wertsachen** pl valuables pl; **Wertstoff** m recyclable waste; **wertvoll** adj valuable

Wesen nt (-s, -) being; (character) nature

wesentlich 1. adj significant; (substantial) considerable **2.** adv considerably

weshalb adv why

Wespe f (-, -n) wasp

wessen pron gen of **wer**; whose

West west; **Westdeutschland** nt Western Germany; HIST West Germany

Weste f (-, -n) waistcoat (Brit),

vest (US); (woollen) cardigan

Westen m (-s) west; **im ~ England** in the west of England; **Westeuropa** nt Western Europe; **Westküste** f west coast; **westlich** adj western; (course, direction) westerly; **Westwind** m west(erly) wind

weswegen adv why

Wettbewerb m competition; **Wettbüro** nt betting office; **Wette** f (-, -n) bet; **eine ~ abschließen** make a bet; **die ~ gilt!** you're on; **wetten** vt, vi bet (auf + acc on); **ich habe mit ihm gewettet, dass ...** I bet him that ...; **ich wette mit dir um 50 Euro** I'll bet you 50 euros; **~, dass?** wanna bet?

Wetter nt (-s, -) weather; **Wetterbericht** m, **Wettervorhersage** f weather forecast

Wettkampf m contest; **Wettlauf** m, **Wettrennen** nt race

WG f (-, -s) abbr = **Wohngemeinschaft**

Whirlpool® m (-s) jacuzzi®

Whisky m (-s, -s) (Scottish) whisky; (Irish, American) whiskey

wichtig adj important

wickeln vt (string) wind (um round); (paper, scarf, blanket) wrap (um round); **ein Baby ~** change a baby's nappy (Brit) (or diaper (US)); **Wickelraum** m baby-changing room; **Wickeltisch** m baby-changing table

Widder m (-s, -) ZOOL ram; ASTR Aries sg

wider prep + acc against

widerlich adj disgusting

widerrufen irr vt withdraw; (contract, order) cancel

widersprechen irr vi contradict (jdm sb); **Widerspruch** m contradiction

Widerstand m resistance; **widerstandsfähig** adj resistant (gegen to)

widerwärtig adj disgusting

widerwillig adj unwilling, reluctant

widmen 1. vt dedicate **2.** vr **sich jdm/etw ~** devote oneself to sb/sth; **Widmung** f dedication

wie 1. adv how; **~ viel** how much; **~ viele Leute?** how many people?; **~ gehts?** how are you?; **~ das?** how come?; **~ bitte?** pardon?, sorry? (Brit) **2.** (so) **schön ~ ...** as beautiful as ...; **~ du weißt** as you know; **~ ich das hörte** when I heard that; **ich sah, ~ er rauskam** I saw him coming out

wieder adv again; **~ ein(e) ...** another ...; **~ erkennen** recognize; **etw ~ gutmachen** make up for sth; **~ verwerten** recycle

wiederbekommen irr vt get back

wiederholen vt repeat; **Wie-**

derholung f repetition

Wiederhören nt TEL **auf ~** goodbye

wiederkommen irr vi come back

wiedersehen irr vt see again; (person) meet again; **Wiedersehen** nt (-s) reunion; **auf ~!** goodbye

Wiedervereinigung f reunification

Wiege f (-, -n) cradle; **wiegen** (wog, gewogen) vt, vi weigh

Wien nt (-s) Vienna

wies imperf of **weisen**

Wiese f (-, -n) meadow

Wiesel nt (-s, -) weasel

wieso adv why

wievielmal adv how often; **wievielte(r, s)** adj **zum ~n Mal?** how many times?; **den Wievielten haben wir heute?** what's the date today?; **am Wievielten hast du Geburtstag?** which day is your birthday?

wieweit conj to what extent

wild adj wild

Wild nt (-(e)s) game

wildfremd adj fam **ein ~er Mensch** a complete (or total) stranger; **Wildleder** nt suede; **Wildpark** m game park; **Wildschwein** nt (wild) boar; **Wildwasserfahren** nt (-s) whitewater canoeing (or rafting)

Wille m (-ns, -n) will

willen prep + gen **um ... ~** for the sake of ...; **um Himmels**

~! for heaven's sake; (shocked) goodness me

willkommen adj welcome

Wimper f (-, -n) eyelash; **Wimperntusche** f mascara

Wind m (-(e)s, -e) wind

Windel f (-, -n) nappy (Brit), diaper (US)

windgeschützt adj sheltered from the wind; **windig** adj windy; fig dubious; **Windjacke** f windcheater; **Windmühle** f windmill; **Windpocken** pl chickenpox sg; **Windschutzscheibe** f AUTO windscreen (Brit), windshield (US); **Windstärke** f wind force; **Windsurfen** nt (-s) windsurfing; **Windsurfer(in)** m(f) windsurfer

Winkel m (-s, -) MATH angle; (in room) corner

winken vt, vi wave

Winter m (-s, -) winter; **Winterausrüstung** f AUTO winter equipment; **Winterfahrplan** m winter timetable; **winterlich** adj wintry; **Wintermantel** m winter coat; **Winterreifen** m winter tyre; **Winterschlussverkauf** m winter sales pl; **Wintersport** m winter sports pl

Winterzeit f (by the clock) winter time (Brit), standard time (US)

winzig adj tiny

wir pron we; **~ alle** all of us; **~ drei** the three of us; **~ sind's** it's us; **~ nicht** not us

Wirbel m (-s, -) whirl; (*activity*) hurly-burly; (*about sb or sth*) fuss; ANAT vertebra; **Wirbelsäule** f spine

wirken vi be effective; (*be successful*) work; (*appear to be*) seem

wirklich adj real; **Wirklichkeit** f reality

wirksam adj effective; **Wirkung** f effect

wirr adj confused; **Wirrwarr** m (-s) confusion

Wirsing m (-s) savoy cabbage

Wirt m (-(e)s, -e) landlord; **Wirtin** f landlady

Wirtschaft f economy; (*place*) pub; **wirtschaftlich** adj economic; (*not wasteful*) economical

Wirtshaus nt pub

wischen vt, vi wipe; **Wischer** m (-s, -) wiper; **Wischlappen** m cloth

wissen (*wusste, gewusst*) vt know; **weißt du schon, ...?** did you know ...?; **woher weißt du das?** how do you know?; **das musst du selbst ~** that's up to you; **Wissen** nt (-s) knowledge

Wissenschaft f science; **Wissenschaftler(in)** m(f) (-s, -) scientist; (*in the arts*) academic; **wissenschaftlich** adj scientific; (*in the arts*) academic

Witwe f (-, -n) widow; **Witwer** m (-s, -) widower

Witz m (-(e)s, -e) joke; **mach keine ~e!** you're kidding!; **das soll wohl ein ~ sein** you've got to be joking; **witzig** adj funny

wo 1. adv where; **überall, ~ ich hingehe** wherever I go 2. conj **jetzt, ~ du da bist** now that you're here; **~ ich dich gerade spreche** while I'm talking to you; **woanders** adv somewhere else

wobei adv **~ mir einfällt ...** which reminds me ...

Woche f (-, -n) week; **während** (or **unter**) **der ~** during the week; **einmal die ~** once a week; **Wochenende** nt weekend; **am ~** at (*Brit*) (or on (*US*)) the weekend; **wir fahren übers ~ weg** we're going away for the weekend; **Wochenendhaus** nt weekend cottage; **Wochenkarte** f weekly (season) ticket; **wochenlang** adv for weeks (on end); **Wochenmarkt** m weekly market; **Wochentag** m weekday; **wöchentlich** adj, adv weekly

Wodka m (-s, -s) vodka

wodurch adv **~ unterscheiden sie sich?** what's the difference between them?; **~ hast du es gemerkt?** how did you notice?; **wofür** adv (*relative*) for which; (*question*) what ... for; **~ brauchst du das?** what do you need that for?

wog imperf of **wiegen**

woher *adv* where ... from; **wohin** *adv* where ... to

wohl *adv* well; at ease, comfortable; probably; certainly; **Wohl** *nt* (-(e)s) **zum ~!** cheers; **wohlbehalten** *adj* safe and sound; **wohlgemerkt** *adv* mind you; **Wohlstand** *m* prosperity, affluence

Wohnblock *m* block of flats (*Brit*), apartment house (*US*); **wohnen** *vi* live; **Wohngemeinschaft** *f* shared flat (*Brit*) (*or* apartment (*US*)); **ich wohne in einer ~** I share a flat (*or* an apartment); **wohnhaft** *adj* resident; **Wohnküche** *f* kitchen-cum-living-room; **Wohnmobil** *nt* (-s, -e) camper, RV (*US*); **Wohnort** *m* place of residence; **Wohnsitz** *m* place of residence; **Wohnung** *f* flat (*Brit*), apartment (*US*); **Wohnungstür** *f* front door; **Wohnwagen** *m* caravan; **Wohnzimmer** *nt* living room

Wolf *m* (-(e)s, **Wölfe**) wolf

Wolke *f* (-, -n) cloud; **Wolkenkratzer** *m* skyscraper; **wolkenlos** *adj* cloudless; **wolkig** *adj* cloudy

Wolldecke *f* (woollen) blanket; **Wolle** *f* (-, -n) wool

wollen 1. *vaux* want; **sie wollte ihn nicht sehen** she didn't want to see him; **~ wir gehen?** shall we go?; **~ Sie bitte ...** will (*or* would) you please ...; **2.** *vt* want; **ich will lieber bleiben** I'd prefer to stay; **er will, dass ich aufhöre** he wants me to stop; **ich wollte, ich wäre/ hätte ...** I wish I were/had ... **3.** *vi* want to; **ich will nicht** I don't want to; **was du willst** whatever you like; **ich will nach Hause** I want to go home; **wo willst du hin?** where do you want to go?; (*to person heading somewhere*) where are you going?

Wolljacke *f* cardigan

womit *adv* what ... with; **~ habe ich das verdient?** what have I done to deserve that?

womöglich *adv* possibly

woran *adv* **~ denkst du?** what are you thinking of?; **~ ist er gestorben?** what did he die of?; **~ sieht man das?** how can you tell?

worauf *adv* **~ wartest du?** what are you waiting for?

woraus *adv* **~ ist das gemacht?** what is it made of?

Wort 1. *nt* (-(e)s, **-e**) word **2.** *nt* (-(e)s, **-e**) word; **mit anderen ~en** in other words; **jdn beim ~ nehmen** take sb at his/her word; **Wörterbuch** *nt* dictionary; **wörtlich** *adj* literal

worüber *adv* **~ redet sie?** what is she talking about?

worum *adv* **~ geht's?** what is it about?

worunter adv ~ **leidet er?** what is he suffering from?

wovon adv (relative) from which; ~ **redest du?** what are you talking about?; **wozu** adv (relative) to/for which; (question) what ... for/to; (for what reason) why; ~? what for?; ~ **brauchst du das?** what do you need it for?; ~ **soll das gut sein?** what's it for?

Wrack nt (-(e)s, -s) wreck

wuchs imperf of **wachsen**

wühlen vi rummage; (animal) root; (mole) burrow

wund adj sore; **Wunde** f (-, -n) wound

Wunder nt (-s, -) miracle; **es ist kein ~** it's no wonder; **wunderbar** adj wonderful, marvellous; **Wunderkerze** f sparkler; **wundern 1.** vr be surprised (über + acc at) **2.** vt surprise; **wunderschön** adj beautiful; **wundervoll** adj wonderful

Wundsalbe f antiseptic ointment; **Wundstarrkrampf** m tetanus

Wunsch m (-(e)s, Wünsche) wish (nach for); **wünschen** vt wish; **sich** dat **etw ~** want sth; **ich wünsche dir alles Gute** I wish you all the best;

wünschenswert adj desirable

wurde imperf of **werden**

Wurf m (-s, Würfe) throw; ZOOL litter

Würfel m (-s, -) dice; MATH cube; **würfeln 1.** vi throw (the dice); (as game) play dice **2.** vt (number) throw; GASTR dice; **Würfelzucker** m lump sugar

Wurm m (-(e)s, Würmer) worm

Wurst f (-, Würste) sausage; **das ist mir ~** fam I couldn't care less

Würstchen nt frankfurter

Würze f (-, -n) seasoning, spice

Wurzel f (-, -n) root

würzen vt season, spice; **würzig** adj spicy

wusch imperf of **waschen**

wusste imperf of **wissen**

wüst adj (untidy) chaotic; (party, life, person) wild; (place) desolate; fam (intense) terrible

Wüste f (-, -n) desert

Wut f (-) rage, fury; **ich habe eine~ auf ihn** I'm really mad at him; **wütend** adj furious

WWW nt (-) abbr = World Wide Web; WWW

X, Y

X-Beine pl knock-knees pl; **x-beinig** adj knock-kneed

x-beliebig adj **ein ~es Buch** any book (you like)

x-mal adv umpteen times

Xylophon nt (-s, -e) xylophone

Yacht f (-, -en) yacht

Yoga m or nt (-(s)) yoga

Yuppie m (-s, -s) f (-, -s) yuppie

Z

Zacke f (-, -n) point; (of saw, comb) tooth; (of fork) prong; **zackig** adj (line etc) jagged; fam (speed) brisk

zaghaft adj timid

zäh adj tough

Zahl f (-, -en) number; **zahlbar** adj payable; **zahlen** vt, vi pay; **~ bitte!** could I have the bill (Brit) (or check (US)) please?; **bar ~** pay cash; **zählen** vt, vi count (auf + acc on); **~ zu** be one of; **Zahlenschloss** nt combination lock; **Zähler** m (-s, -) counter; (for electricity, water) meter; **zahlreich** adj numerous; **Zahlung** f payment

zahm adj tame; **zähmen** vt tame

Zahn m (-(e)s, Zähne) tooth; **Zahnarzt** m, **Zahnärztin** f dentist; **Zahnbürste** f toothbrush; **Zahncreme** f toothpaste; **Zahnersatz** m dentures pl; **Zahnfleisch** nt gums pl; **Zahnfleischbluten** nt bleeding gums pl; **Zahnfüllung** f filling; **Zahnklammer** f brace; **Zahnpasta** f, **Zahnpaste** f toothpaste; **Zahnschmerzen** pl toothache sg; **Zahnseide** f dental floss; **Zahnspange** f brace; **Zahnstocher** m (-s, -) toothpick

Zange f (-, -n) pliers pl; (for sugar) tongs pl; ZOOL pincers pl

zanken vi, vr quarrel

Zäpfchen nt ANAT uvula; MED suppository

zapfen vt (beer) pull; **Zapfsäule** f petrol (Brit) (or gas (US)) pump

zappeln vi wriggle; (be restless) fidget

zappen vi zap, channel-hop

zart adj soft; (meat etc) tender; (fine, weakly) delicate; **zartbitter** adj (chocolate) plain, dark

zärtlich adj tender, affectionate; **Zärtlichkeit** f tenderness; **~en** pl hugs and kisses pl

Zauber m (-s, -) magic; (magic power) spell; **Zauberei** f magic; **Zauberer** m (-s, -) magician; (entertainer) conjuror; **Zauberformel** f (magic) spell; **zauberhaft** adj enchanting; **Zauberin** f sorceress; **Zauberkünstler(in)** m(f) magician, conjuror; **Zaubermittel** nt magic cure; **zaubern** vi do magic; (entertainer) do conjuring tricks; **Zauberspruch** m (magic) spell

Zaun m (-(e)s, Zäune) fence

z. B. abbr = **zum Beispiel;** e.g., eg

Zebra nt (-s, -s) zebra; **Zebrastreifen** m zebra crossing (Brit), crosswalk (US)

Zechtour f pub crawl

Zecke f (-, -n) tick

Zehe f (-, -n) toe; (of garlic) clove; **Zehennagel** m toenail; **Zehenspitze** f tip of the toes

zehn num ten; **Zehnerkarte** f ticket valid for ten trips; **Zehnkampf** m decathlon; **Zehnkämpfer(in)** m(f) decathlete; **zehnmal** adv ten times; **zehntausend** num ten thousand; **zehnte(r, s)** adj tenth; → **dritte; Zehntel** nt (-s, -) tenth

Zeichen nt (-s, -) sign; (letter, numeral) character; **Zeichenblock** m sketch pad; **Zeichensetzung** f punctuation; **Zeichensprache** f sign language; **Zeichentrickfilm** m cartoon

zeichnen vt, vi draw; **Zeichnung** f drawing

Zeigefinger m index finger; **zeigen 1.** vt show; **sie zeigte uns die Stadt** she showed us around the town; **zeig mal!** let me see **2.** vi point (auf + acc to, at) **3.** vr show oneself; **es wird sich ~** time will tell; **Zeiger** m (-s, -) pointer; (of clock, watch) hand

Zeile f (-, -n) line

Zeit f (-, -en) time; **ich habe keine ~** I haven't got time; **lass dir ~** take your time; **von ~ zu ~** from time to time; **Zeitansage** f TEL speaking clock (Brit), correct time (US); **Zeitarbeit** f temporary work; **zeitgenössisch** adj contemporary, modern; **zeitgleich 1.** adj simultaneous **2.** adv at exactly the same time; **zeitig** adj early; **Zeitkarte** f season ticket; **zeitlich** adj (order) chronological; **es passt ~ nicht** it isn't a convenient time; **Zeitlupe** f slow motion; **Zeitplan** m schedule; **Zeitpunkt** m point in time; **Zeitraum** m period (of time)

Zeitschrift f magazine; (aca-

demic, scientific) periodical

Zeitung f newspaper; **es steht in der ~** it's in the paper(s); Zeitungsartikel m newspaper article; Zeitungskiosk m, Zeitungsstand m newsstand

Zeitunterschied m time difference; Zeitverschiebung f time lag; Zeitvertreib m (-(e)s, -e) **zum ~** to pass the time; Zeitzone f time zone

Zelle f (-, -n) cell

Zellophan® nt (-s) cellophane®

Zelt nt (-(e)s, -e) tent; zelten vi camp, go camping; Zeltplatz m campsite, camping site

Zement m (-(e)s, -e) cement

Zentimeter m or nt centimetre

Zentner m (-s, -) (metric) hundredweight; (in Germany) fifty kilos; (in Austria and Switzerland) one hundred kilos

zentral adj central; Zentrale f (-, -n) central office; TEL exchange; Zentralheizung f central heating; Zentralverriegelung f AUTO central locking; Zentrum nt (-s, Zentren) centre

zerbrechen irr vt, vi break; zerbrechlich adj fragile

Zeremonie f (-, -n) ceremony

zerkleinern vt cut up; (roughly) chop (up); zerkratzen vt scratch; zerlegen vt take to pieces; (meat) carve; (machi-

ne, engine) dismantle; zerquetschen vt squash; zerreißen irr 1. vt tear to pieces 2. vi tear

zerren 1. vt drag; **sich dat einen Muskel ~** pull a muscle 2. vi tug (an + dat at); Zerrung f MED pulled muscle

zerschlagen irr 1. vt smash 2. vr come to nothing

zerschneiden irr vt cut up

Zerstäuber m (-s, -) atomizer

zerstören vt destroy; Zerstörung f destruction

zerstreuen 1. vt scatter; (crowd) disperse; (doubts, fears) dispel 2. vr (crowd) disperse; zerstreut adj scattered; (person) absent-minded; (temporarily) distracted

zerteilen vt split up

Zertifikat nt (-(e)s, -e) certificate

Zettel m (-s, -) piece of paper; (message, reminder) note

Zeug nt (-(e)s, -e) fam stuff; (equipment) gear; **dummes ~** nonsense

Zeuge m (-n, -n), Zeugin f witness

Zeugnis nt certificate; (from school) report; (from former employer) reference

zickig adj fam touchy, bitchy

Zickzack m (-(e)s, -e) **im ~ fahren** zigzag (across the road)

Ziege f (-, -n) goat

Ziegel m (-s, -) brick; (on roof) tile

Ziegenkäse m goat's cheese

ziehen (zog, gezogen) **1.** vt draw; (tug, drag) pull; (piece in game) move; (breed) rear **2.** vi pull; (go) move; (smoke, cloud etc) drift; **den Tee ~ lassen** let the tea stand **3.** vi impers **es zieht** there's a draught **4.** vr (meeting, speech) drag on

Ziel nt (-(e)s, -e) (of journey) destination; SPORT finish; (intention) goal, aim; **zielen** vi aim (**auf** + acc at); **Zielgruppe** f target group; **ziellos** adj aimless; **Zielscheibe** f target

ziemlich **1.** adj considerable; **ein ~es Durcheinander** quite a mess; **mit ~er Sicherheit** with some certainty **2.** adv rather, quite; **~ viel** quite a lot

zierlich adj dainty; (woman) petite

Ziffer f (-, -n) figure; **arabische/römische ~n** pl Arabic/Roman numerals pl; **Zifferblatt** nt dial, face

zig adj fam umpteen

Zigarette f cigarette; **Zigarettenautomat** m cigarette machine; **Zigarettenschachtel** f cigarette packet; **Zigarettenstummel** m cigarette end; **Zigarillo** m (-s, -s) cigarillo; **Zigarre** f (-, -n) cigar

Zimmer nt (-s, -) room; **haben Sie ein ~ für zwei Personen?** do you have a room for two?; **Zimmerlautstärke** f reasonable volume; Zim-

mermädchen nt chambermaid; **Zimmermann** m carpenter; **Zimmerpflanze** f house plant; **Zimmerschlüssel** m room key; **Zimmerservice** m room service; **Zimmervermittlung** f accommodation agency

Zimt m (-(e)s, -e) cinnamon

Zink nt (-(e)s) zinc

Zinn nt (-(e)s) tin; (alloy) pewter

Zinsen pl interest sg

Zipfel m (-s, -) corner; (pointed) tip; (of shirt) tail; (of sausage) end; fam (penis) willy

zirka adv about, approximately

Zirkel m (-s, -) MATH (pair of) compasses pl

Zirkus m (-, -se) circus

zischen vi hiss

Zitat nt (-(e)s, -e) quotation (aus from); **zitieren** vt quote

Zitronat nt candied lemon peel; **Zitrone** f (-, -n) lemon; **Zitronenlimonade** f lemonade; **Zitronensaft** m lemon juice

zittern vi tremble (vor + dat with)

zivil adj civilian; (price) reasonable; **Zivil** nt (-s) plain clothes pl; MIL civilian clothes pl; **Zivildienst** m community service (for conscientious objectors)

zocken vi fam gamble

Zoff m (-s) fam trouble

zog imperf of **ziehen**

zögerlich *adj* hesitant; zögern *vi* hesitate

Zoll *m* (-(e)s, Zölle) customs *pl*; *(tax)* duty; Zollabfertigung *f* customs clearance; Zollamt *nt* customs office; Zollbeamte(r) *m*, Zollbeamtin *f* customs official; Zollerklärung *f* customs declaration; zollfrei *adj* duty-free; Zollgebühren *pl* customs duties *pl*; Zollkontrolle *f* customs check; Zöllner(in) *m(f)* customs officer; zollpflichtig *adj* liable to duty

Zone *f* (-, -n) zone

Zoo *m* (-s, -s) zoo

Zoom *nt* (-s, -s) zoom (shot); zoom (lens)

Zopf *m* (-(e)s, Zöpfe) plait (*Brit*), braid (*US*)

Zorn *m* (-(e)s) anger; zornig *adj* angry *(über etw ~* about sth, *auf jdn* with sb)

zu 1. *conj* (*with infinitive*) to 2. *prep + dat* (*direction, action*) to; (*place, time, price*) at; (*purpose*) for; *~r Post® gehen* go to the post office; *~ Hause* at home; *~ Weihnachten* at Christmas; *fünf Bücher ~ 20 Euro* five books at 20 euros each; *~m Fenster herein* through the window; *~ meiner Zeit* in my time 3. *adv* too; *~ viel* too much; *~ wenig* too little; *~ adj fam* shut; *Tür ~!* shut the door

zuallererst *adv* first of all; zu-

allerletzt *adv* last of all

Zubehör *nt* (-(e)s, -e) accessories *pl*

zubereiten *vt* prepare; Zubereitung *f* preparation

zubinden *irr vt* do (*or* tie) up

Zucchini *pl* courgettes *pl* (*Brit*), zucchini *pl* (*US*)

züchten *vt* (*animals*) breed; (*plants*) grow

zucken *vi* jerk; (*convulsively*) twitch; *mit den Schultern ~* shrug (one's shoulders)

Zucker *m* (-s, -) sugar; MED diabetes *sg*; Zuckerdose *f* sugar bowl; zuckerkrank *adj* diabetic; Zuckerrohr *nt* sugar cane; Zuckerwatte *f* candy-floss (*Brit*), cotton candy (*US*)

zudecken *vt* cover up

zudrehen *vt* turn off

zueinander *adv* to one other; (*as part of verb*) together; *~ halten* stick together

zuerst *adv* first; (*at the start*) at first; *~ einmal* first of all

Zufahrt *f* access; (*of house*) drive(way); Zufahrtsstraße *f* access road; (*onto motorway*) slip road (*Brit*), ramp (*US*)

Zufall *m* chance; (*event*) coincidence; *durch ~* by accident; *so ein ~!* what a coincidence; zufällig 1. *adj* chance 2. *adv* by chance; *weißt du ~, ob ...?* do you happen to know whether ...?

zufrieden *adj* content(ed);

(*with sth*) satisfied; **sich mit etw ~ geben** settle for sth; **lass sie ~** leave her alone (*or* in peace); **sie ist schwer ~ zu stellen** she is hard to please; Zufriedenheit *f* contentment; (*with sth*) satisfaction

zufügen *vt* add (*dat* to); **jdm Schaden/ Schmerzen ~** cause sb harm/pain

Zug *m* (-(e)s, Züge) RAIL train; (*air*) draught; (*tug*) pull; (*in chess*) move; (*of character*) trait; (*on cigarette*) puff, drag; (*swallow*) gulp

Zugabe *f* extra; (*at concert etc*) encore

Zugabteil *nt* train compartment

Zugang *m* access; **„kein ~!"** 'no entry'

Zugauskunft *f* train information office/ desk; Zugbegleiter(in) *m(f)* guard (*Brit*), conductor (*US*)

zugeben *irr vt* admit; zugegeben *adv* admittedly

zugehen *irr* **1.** *vi* (*door, cupboard etc*) shut; **auf jdn/ etw ~** walk towards sb/sth; **dem Ende ~** be coming to a close **2.** *vi impers* happen; **es ging lustig zu** we/they had a lot of fun

Zügel *m* (-s, -) rein

Zugführer(in) *m(f)* guard (*Brit*), conductor (*US*)

zugig *adj* draughty

zügig *adj* speedy

Zugluft *f* draught

Zugpersonal *nt* train staff

zugreifen *irr vi fig* seize the opportunity; (*when eating*) help oneself; **~ auf +** *acc* IT access

Zugrestaurant *nt* dining car, diner (*US*)

Zugriffsberechtigung *f* IT access right

zugrunde *adv* **~ gehen** perish; **~ gehen an +** *dat* die of

Zugschaffner(in) *m(f)* ticket inspector; Zugunglück *nt* train crash

zugunsten *prep* + *gen or dat* in favour of

Zugverbindung *f* train connection

zuhaben *irr vi* be closed

zuhalten *irr vi* **sich dat die Nase ~** hold one's nose; **sich dat die Ohren ~** hold one's hands over one's ears; **die Tür ~** hold the door shut

Zuhause *nt* (-s) home

zuhören *vi* listen (*dat* to); Zuhörer(in) *m(f)* listener

zukleben *vt* seal

zukommen *irr vi* come up (*auf +* *acc* to); **jdm etw ~ lassen** give/ send sb sth; **etw auf sich** *acc* **~ lassen** take sth as it comes

Zukunft *f* (-, Zukünfte) future; zukünftig **1.** *adj* future **2.** *adv* in future

zulassen *irr vt* (*let in*) admit; (*allow*) permit; (*car*) license; *fam* (*not open*) keep shut;

zulässig adj permissible, permitted

zuletzt adv finally, at last

zuliebe adv **jdm ~** for sb's sake

zum contr of **zu dem; ~ dritten Mal** for the third time; **~ Trinken** for drinking

zumachen 1. vt shut; (clothes) do up **2.** vi shut

zumindest adv at least

zumuten 1. vt **jdm etw ~** expect sth of sb **2.** vr **sich dat zu viel ~** overdo things

zunächst adv first of all; **~ einmal** to start with

Zunahme f (-, -n) increase

Zuname m surname, last name

zünden vt, vi AUTO ignite; fire; **Zündholz** nt match; **Zündkabel** f AUTO ignition cable; **Zündkerze** f AUTO spark plug; **Zündschloss** nt ignition lock; **Zündschlüssel** m ignition key; **Zündung** f ignition

zunehmen irr **1.** vi increase; (person) put on weight **2.** vt **5 Kilo ~** put on 5 kilos

Zunge f (-, -n) tongue

Zungenkuss m French kiss

zunichte adv **~ machen** ruin

zunutze adv **sich** dat **etw ~ machen** make use of sth

zuparken vt block

zur contr of **zu der**

zurechtfinden irr vr find one's way around; **zurechtkommen** irr vi cope (mit

etw with sth); **zurechtmachen 1.** vt prepare **2.** vr get ready

Zürich nt (-s) Zurich

zurück adv back

zurückbekommen irr vt get back; **zurückblicken** vi look back (auf + acc at); **zurückbringen** irr vt bring back; (somewhere else) take back; **zurückerstatten** vt refund; **zurückfahren** irr vi go back; **zurückgeben** irr vt give back; **zurückgehen** irr vi go back; (in time) date back (auf + acc to)

zurückhalten irr **1.** vt hold back; (hinder) prevent **2.** vr hold back; **zurückhaltend** adj reserved

zurückholen vt fetch back; **zurückkommen** irr vi come back; **auf etw acc ~** return (or get back) to sth; **zurücklassen** irr vt leave behind; **zurücklegen** vt put back; (money) put by; (keep in reserve) keep back; (distance) cover; **zurücknehmen** irr vt take back; **zurückrufen** irr vt call back; **zurückschicken** vt send back; **zurückstellen** vt put back; **zurücktreten** irr vi step back; (from office) retire; **zurückverlangen** vt **etw ~** ask for sth back; **zurückzahlen** vt pay back

zurzeit adv at present

Zusage f promise; (of invitation) acceptance; **zusagen**

1. vt promise **2.** vi accept; **jdm ~** (please) appeal to sb zusammen adv together
Zusammenarbeit f collaboration; zusammenarbeiten vi work together
zusammenbrechen irr vi collapse; (mentally) break down; Zusammenbruch m collapse; (mental) breakdown
zusammenfassen vt summarize; (bring together) unite; Zusammenfassung f summary
zusammengehören vi belong together; zusammenhalten irr vi stick together
Zusammenhang m connection; im/ aus dem ~ in/ out of context; zusammenhängen irr vi be connected; zusammenhängend adj coherent; zusammenhang(s-)los adj incoherent
zusammenklappen vi, vt fold up; zusammenlegen **1.** vt fold up **2.** vt club together; zusammennehmen irr **1.** vt summon up; **alles zusammengenommen** all in all **2.** vr pull oneself together; fam get a grip, get one's act together; zusammenpassen vi go together; (people) be suited; zusammenrechnen vt add up incoherent
Zusammensein nt (-s) get-together
zusammensetzen **1.** vt put

together **2.** vr sich ~ aus be composed of; Zusammensetzung f composition
Zusammenstoß m crash, collision; zusammenstoßen irr vi crash (mit into)
zusammenzählen vt add up
zusammenziehen irr vi (into flat etc) move in together
Zusatz m addition; Zusatzgerät nt attachment; IT add-on; zusätzlich **1.** adj additional **2.** adv in addition
zuschauen irr vi watch; Zuschauer(in) m(f) (-s, -) spectator; die ~ pl THEAT the audience sg; Zuschauertribüne f stand
zuschicken irr vt send
Zuschlag m extra charge; (on ticket) supplement
zuschlagpflichtig adj subject to an extra charge; RAIL subject to a supplement
zuschließen irr vt lock up
zusehen irr vi watch (jdm sb); ~, dass make sure that
zusichern vt jdm etw~ assure sb of sth
Zustand m state, condition
zustande adv ~ bringen bring about; ~ kommen come about
zuständig adj (authority) relevant; ~ für responsible for
Zustellung f delivery
zustimmen vi agree (einer Sache dat to sth, jdm with sb); Zustimmung f approval
zustoßen irr vi fig happen

Zwiebelsuppe

(jdm to sb)

Zutaten pl ingredients pl

zutrauen vt **jdm etw ~** think sb is capable of sth; **das hätte ich ihm nie zugetraut** I'd never have thought he was capable of it; **ich würde es ihr ~** (sth negative) I wouldn't put it past her; **Zutrauen** nt (-s) confidence (zu in); **zutraulich** adj trusting; (animal) friendly

zutreffen irr vi be correct; **~ auf + acc** apply to; **Zutreffendes bitte streichen** please delete as applicable

Zutritt m entry; (permission to enter) access; **„~ verboten!"** 'no entry'

zuverlässig adj reliable; **Zuverlässigkeit** f reliability

Zuversicht f confidence; **zuversichtlich** adj confident

zuvor adv before; (before anything else) first; **zuvorkommen** irr vi **jdm ~** beat sb to it

Zuwachs m (-es, Zuwächse) increase, growth; **fam** (baby) addition to the family

zuwider adv **es ist mir ~** I hate (or detest) it

zuzüglich prep + gen plus

zwang imperf of **zwingen**

Zwang m (-(e)s, Zwänge) (inner urge) compulsion; (against will) force; **zwängen** vt, vr squeeze (in + acc into); **zwanglos** adj informal

zwanzig num twenty; **zwan-**

zigste(r, s) adj twentieth; **→ dritte**

zwar adv **und ~ ..., ...**, to be precise; **das ist ~ schön, aber ...** it is nice, but ...

Zweck m (-(e)s, -e) purpose; **zwecklos** adj pointless

zwei num two; **Zwei** f (-, -en) two; (mark in school) ≈ B; **Zweibettzimmer** m twin room; **zweideutig** adj ambiguous; (indecent) suggestive; **zweifach** adj, adv double

Zweifel m (-s, -) doubt; **zweifellos** adv undoubtedly; **zweifeln** vi doubt (an etw dat sth); **Zweifelsfall** m **im ~** in case of doubt

Zweig m (-(e)s, -e) branch; **Zweigstelle** f branch

zweihundert num two hundred; **zweimal** adv twice; **zweisprachig** adj bilingual; **zweispurig** adj AUTO two-lane; **zweit wir sind zu ~** there are two of us; **zweite(r, s)** adj second; **→ dritte**; **zweitens** adv secondly; (when listing) second; **zweitgrößte(r, s)** adj second largest; **Zweitschlüssel** m spare key

Zwerg(in) m(f) (-(e)s, -e) dwarf

Zwetschge f (-, -n) plum

zwicken vt pinch

Zwieback m (-(e)s, -e) rusk

Zwiebel f (-, -n) onion; (of flower) bulb; **Zwiebelsuppe**

f onion soup
Zwilling *m* (*-s, -e*) twin; **~e** *pl*
ASTR Gemini *sg*
zwingen (*zwang, gezwungen*)
vt force
zwinkern *vi* blink; (*deliberately*) wink
zwischen *prep + acc or dat*
between; **Zwischenablage**
f IT clipboard; **zwischendurch** *adv* in between; **Zwischenlandung** *f* stopover;
Zwischenraum *m* space;

Zwischenstopp *m* (*-s, -s*)
stopover; **Zwischenzeit** *f* **in**
der ~ in the meantime
zwitschern *vt, vi* twitter,
chirp
zwölf *num* twelve; **zwölfte(r,**
s) *adj* twelfth; → *dritte*
Zylinder *m* (*-s, -*) cylinder; top
hat; **Zylinderkopfdichtung** *f*
cylinder-head gasket
zynisch *adj* cynical
Zypern *nt* (*-s*) Cyprus

A

a, an *art* ein / eine / ein; **~ man** ein Mann; **~ woman** eine Frau; **~n apple** ein Apfel; **he's ~ student** er ist Student; **three times ~ week** dreimal pro Woche / in der Woche

AA *abbr* = **Automobile Association**; *britischer Automobilklub*; ≈ ADAC *m*

aback *adv* **taken ~** erstaunt

abandon *vt* (*desert*) verlassen; (*give up*) aufgeben

abbey *n* Abtei *f*

abbreviation *n* Abkürzung *f*

abdication *n* Abdankung *f*

abdomen *n* Unterleib *m*

ability *n* Fähigkeit *f*; **able** *adj* fähig; **be ~ to do sth** etw tun können

aboard *adv*, *prep* an Bord + *gen*

abolish *vt* abschaffen

aborigine *n* Ureinwohner(in) *m(f)* (Australiens)

abortion *n* Abtreibung *f*

about 1. *adv* (*around*) herum, umher; (*approximately*) ungefähr; (*with time*) ungefähr; **be ~ to** im Begriff sein zu; **there are a lot of people ~** es sind eine Menge Leute da 2. *prep* (*concerning*) über + *acc*; **there is nothing you can do ~ it** da kann man nichts machen

above 1. *adv* oben; **children aged 8 and ~** Kinder ab 8 Jahren; **on the floor ~** ein Stockwerk höher 2. *prep* über; **~ 40 degrees** über 40 Grad; **~ all** vor allem 3. *adj* obig

abroad *adv* im Ausland; **go ~** ins Ausland gehen

absent *adj* abwesend; **be ~** fehlen; **absent-minded** *adj* zerstreut

absolute *adj* absolut; (*rubbish*) vollkommen, total; **absolutely** *adv* absolut; (*true, stupid*) vollkommen; **~!** genau!; **you're ~ right** du hast / Sie haben völlig Recht

absorb *vt* absorbieren; *fig* (*information*) in sich aufnehmen; **absorbed** *adj* **~ in sth** in etw vertieft; **absorbent** *adj* absorbierend; **~ cotton** (*US*) Watte *f*; **absorbing** *adj* *fig* faszinierend, fesselnd

abstract *adj* abstrakt

abundance *n* Reichtum *m* (*of* an + *dat*)

abuse 1. n (*rude language*) Beschimpfungen pl; (*mistreatment*) Missbrauch m **2.** vt (*misuse*) missbrauchen; **abusive** adj beleidigend

AC 1. abbr = *alternating current*; Wechselstrom m **2.** abbr = *air conditioning*; Klimaanlage f

a/c abbr = *account*; Kto.

academic 1. n Wissenschaftler(in) m(f) **2.** adj wissenschaftlich

accelerate vi (*car etc*) beschleunigen; (*driver*) Gas geben; **acceleration** n Beschleunigung f; **accelerator** n Gas(pedal) nt

accent n Akzent m

accept vt annehmen; (*agree to*) akzeptieren; (*responsibility*) übernehmen; **acceptable** adj annehmbar

access n Zugang m; ɪT Zugriff m; **accessible** adj (leicht) zugänglich/erreichbar; **accessory** n Zubehörteil nt; **access road** n Zufahrtsstraße f

accident n Unfall m; **by ~** zufällig; **accidental** adj unbeabsichtigt; (*meeting*) zufällig; (*death*) durch Unfall; **accident-prone** adj vom Pech verfolgt

acclimatize vt **~ oneself** sich gewöhnen (*to* an + acc)

accommodate vt unterbringen; **accommodation**, s n Unterkunft f

accompany vt begleiten

accomplish vt erreichen

accord n **of one's own ~** freiwillig; **according to** prep nach, laut + dat

account n (*in bank etc*) Konto nt; (*narrative*) Bericht m; **on ~ of** wegen; **on no ~** auf keinen Fall; **take into ~** berücksichtigen, in Betracht ziehen; **accountant** n Buchhalter(in) m(f); **account for** vt (*explain*) erklären; (*expenditure*) Rechenschaft ablegen für; **account number** n Kontonummer f

accurate adj genau

accusation n Anklage f, Beschuldigung f; **accuse** vt beschuldigen; ʟᴀᴡ anklagen (*of* wegen gen); **accused** n ʟᴀᴡ Angeklagte(r) m(f)

accustom vt gewöhnen (*to* an + acc); **accustomed** adj gewohnt; **get ~ to sth** sich an etw acc gewöhnen

ace 1. n Ass nt **2.** adj Star-

ache 1. n Schmerz m **2.** vi wehtun

achieve vt erreichen; **achievement** n Leistung f

acid 1. n Säure f **2.** adj sauer

acknowledge vt (*recognize*) anerkennen; (*admit*) zugeben; (*receipt of letter etc*) bestätigen; **acknowledgement** n Anerkennung f; (*of letter*) Empfangsbestätigung f

acne n Akne f

acorn n Eichel f

acoustic adj akustisch; **acoustics** npl Akustik f

acquaintance n (person) Bekannte(r) mf

acquire vt erwerben, sich aneignen; **acquisition** n (of skills etc) Erwerb m; (object) Anschaffung f

across 1. prep über + acc; **he lives ~ the street** er wohnt auf der anderen Seite der Straße **2.** adv hinüber, herüber; **100m ~** 100m breit

act 1. n (deed) Tat f; LAW Gesetz nt; THEAT Akt m; **be in the ~ of doing sth** gerade dabei sein, etw zu tun **2.** vi (take action) handeln; (behave) sich verhalten; THEAT spielen; **~ as** (person) fungieren als; (thing) dienen als **3.** vt (a part) spielen

action n (of play, novel etc) Handlung f; (in film etc) Action f; MIL Kampf m; **take ~** etwas unternehmen; **put a plan into ~** einen Plan in die Tat umsetzen; action replay n SPORT, TV Wiederholung f

active adj aktiv; (child) lebhaft; **activity** n Aktivität f; (occupation) Beschäftigung f; (organized event) Veranstaltung f

actor n Schauspieler(in) m(f); **actress** n Schauspielerin f

actual adj wirklich; **actually**

adv eigentlich; (said in surprise) tatsächlich

acupuncture n Akupunktur f

acute adj (pain) akut; MATH (angle) spitz

ad abbr = **advertisement**

AD abbr = **Anno Domini**; nach Christi, n. Chr.

adapt 1. vi sich anpassen (to + dat) **2.** vi sich anpassen (to + dat); (rewrite) bearbeiten (for für); **adaptation** n (of book etc) Bearbeitung f; **adapter** n ELEC Zwischenstecker m, Adapter m

add vt (ingredient) hinzufügen; (numbers) addieren; **add up 1.** vi (make sense) stimmen **2.** vt (numbers) addieren

addicted adj **~ to alcohol/ drugs** alkohol-/drogensüchtig

addition n Zusatz m; (to bill) Aufschlag m; MATH Addition f; **in ~** außerdem, zusätzlich (to zu); **additional** adj zusätzlich, weiter; **additive** n Zusatz m; **add-on** n Zusatzgerät nt

address 1. n Adresse f **2.** vt (letter) adressieren; (person) anreden

adequate adj (appropriate) angemessen; (sufficient) ausreichend

adhesive n Klebstoff m; **adhesive tape** n Klebstreifen m

adjacent adj benachbart

adjoining *adj* benachbart, Neben-

adjust 1. *vt* einstellen; (*put right also*) richtig stellen; (*speed, flow*) regulieren; (*in position*) verstellen 2. *vi* sich anpassen (*to + dat*); adjustable *adj* verstellbar

admin *n fam* Verwaltung *f*; administration *n* Verwaltung *f*; POL Regierung *f*

admirable *adj* bewundernswert; admiration *n* Bewunderung *f*; admire *vt* bewundern

admission *n* (*entrance*) Zutritt *m*; (*to university etc*) Zulassung *f*; (*fee*) Eintritt *m*; admission charge, admission fee *n* Eintrittspreis *m*; admit *vt* (*let in*) hereinlassen (*to in + acc*); (*to university etc*) zulassen; (*confess*) zugeben, gestehen; **be ~ted to hospital** ins Krankenhaus eingeliefert werden

adolescent *n* Jugendliche(r) *mf*

adopt *vt* (*child*) adoptieren; (*idea*) übernehmen; adoption *n* (*of child*) Adoption *f*; (*of idea*) Übernahme *f*

adorable *adj* entzückend; adore *vt* anbeten; (*person*) über alles lieben, vergöttern

adult 1. *adj* (*person*) erwachsen; (*film etc for*) für Erwachsene 2. *n* Erwachsene(r) *mf*

adultery *n* Ehebruch *m*

advance 1. *n* (*money*) Vor-

schuss *m*; (*progress*) Fortschritt *m*; **in ~** im Voraus; **book in ~** vorbestellen 2. *vi* (*move forward*) vorrücken 3. *vt* (*money*) vorschießen; advance booking *n* Reservierung *f*; THEAT Vorverkauf *m*; advanced *adj* (*modern*) fortschrittlich; (*course, study*) für Fortgeschrittene; advance payment *n* Vorauszahlung *f*

advantage *n* Vorteil *m*; **take ~ of** (*exploit*) ausnutzen; (*profit from*) Nutzen ziehen aus; **it's to your ~** es ist in deinem / Ihrem Interesse

adventure *n* Abenteuer *nt*; adventure holiday *n* Abenteuerurlaub *m*; adventure playground *n* Abenteuerspielplatz *m*

adverse *adj* (*conditions etc*) ungünstig; (*effect, comment etc*) negativ

advert *n* Anzeige *f*; advertise 1. *vt* werben für; (*in newspaper*) inserieren; (*job*) ausschreiben 2. *vi* Reklame machen; advertisement *n* Werbung *f*; (*announcement*) Anzeige *f*; advertising *n* Werbung *f*

advice *n* Rat(schlag) *m*; **take my ~** hör auf mich; advisable *adj* ratsam; advise *vt* raten (*sb* jdm); **~ sb to do sth / not to do sth** jdm zuraten / abraten, etw zu tun

aerial 1. *n* Antenne *f* 2. *adj*

Luft-
aerobics nsing Aerobic nt
aeroplane n Flugzeug nt
afaik abbr = **as far as I know**;
(SMS) ≈ soweit ich weiß
affair n (matter, business) Sache f, Angelegenheit f; (scandal) Affäre f; (love affair) Verhältnis nt
affect vt (influence) (ein)wirken auf + acc; (health, organ) angreifen; (move deeply) berühren; (concern) betreffen;
affection n Zuneigung f; affectionate adj liebevoll
affluent adj wohlhabend
afford vt sich leisten; **I can't ~ it** ich kann es mir nicht leisten; **affordable** adj erschwinglich
Afghanistan n Afghanistan nt
aforementioned adj oben genannt
afraid adj **be ~** Angst haben (of + dat); **be ~ that ...** fürchten, dass ...; **I'm ~ I don't know** das weiß ich leider nicht
Africa n Afrika nt; African **1.** adj afrikanisch **2.** n Afrikaner(in) m(f); African American adj, n Afro-American n Afroamerikaner(in) m(f)
after 1. prep nach; **ten ~ five** (US) zehn nach fünf; **be ~ sb/ sth** (following, seeking) hinter jdm/etw her sein; **~ all** schließlich **2.** conj nachdem **3.** adv **soon ~** bald danach; **aftercare** n Nachbehandlung f
afternoon n Nachmittag m; **in the ~** nachmittags
afters npl Nachtisch m; after-**-sales service** n Kundendienst m; **after-shave (lotion)** n Rasierwasser nt; after-sun lotion n After-Sun--Lotion f; **afterwards** adv nachher; (after that) danach
again adv wieder; (one more time) noch einmal; **~ and ~** immer wieder; **the same ~ please** das Gleiche noch mal bitte
against prep gegen; **~ my will** wider Willen; **~ the law** unrechtmäßig, illegal
age 1. n Alter nt; (period of history) Zeitalter nt; **at the ~ of four** im Alter von vier (Jahren); **what ~ is she?, what is her ~?** wie alt ist sie?; **under ~** minderjährig **2.** vi altern, alt werden; aged **1.** adj **~ thirty** dreißig Jahre alt; **a son ~ twenty** ein zwanzigjähriger Sohn **2.** adj (elderly) betagt; age group n Altersgruppe f; age limit n Altersgrenze f
agency n Agentur f
agenda n Tagesordnung f
agent n COMM Vertreter(in) m(f); (for writer, actor etc) Agent(in) m(f)
aggression n Aggression f; **aggressive** adj aggressiv
AGM abbr = **Annual General**

Meeting; JHV f

ago adv **two days ~** heute vor zwei Tagen; **not long ~** (erst) vor kurzem

agonize vi sich den Kopf zerbrechen (over über + acc); **agonizing** adj qualvoll; **agony** n Qual f

agree 1. vt (date, price etc) vereinbaren; **~ to do sth** sich bereit erklären, etw zu tun; **~ that ...** sich dat einig sein, dass ...; (decide) beschließen, dass ...; (admit) zugeben, dass ... **2.** vi (have same opinion, correspond) übereinstimmen (with mit); (consent) zustimmen; (come to an agreement) sich einigen (about, on auf + acc); (food) **not ~ with sb** jdm nicht bekommen; **agreement** n (agreeing) Übereinstimmung f; (contract) Abkommen nt, Vereinbarung f

agricultural adj landwirtschaftlich, Landwirtschafts-; **agriculture** n Landwirtschaft f

ahead adv **be ~** führen, vorne liegen; **~ of** vor + dat; **be 3 metres ~** 3 Meter Vorsprung haben

aid 1. n Hilfe f; **in ~ of** zugunsten + gen; **with the ~ of** mit-hilfe + gen **2.** vt helfen + dat; (support) unterstützen

Aids n acr = **acquired immune deficiency syndrome**; Aids nt

aim 1. vt (gun, camera) richten (at auf + acc) **2.** vi **~ at** (with gun etc) zielen auf + acc; fig abzielen auf + acc; **~ to do sth** beabsichtigen, etw zu tun **3.** n Ziel nt

air 1. n Luft f; **in the open ~** im Freien **2.** vt lüften; **airbag** n AUTO Airbag m; **air-conditioned** adj mit Klimaanlage; **air-conditioning** n Klimaanlage f; **aircraft** n Flugzeug nt; **airfield** n Flugplatz m; **air force** n Luftwaffe f; **airline** n Fluggesellschaft f; **airmail** n Luftpost f; **by ~** mit Luftpost; **airplane** n (US) Flugzeug nt; **air pollution** n Luftverschmutzung f; **airport** n Flughafen m; **airsick** adj luftkrank; **airtight** adj luftdicht; **air-traffic controller** n Fluglotse m, Fluglotsin f

aisle n Gang m; (in church) Seitenschiff nt; **~ seat** Sitz m am Gang

ajar adj (door) angelehnt

alarm 1. n (warning) Alarm m; (bell etc) Alarmanlage f **2.** vt beunruhigen; **alarm clock** n Wecker m; **alarmed** adj (protected) alarmgesichert; **alarming** adj beunruhigend

Albania n Albanien nt; **Albanian 1.** adj albanisch **2.** n (person) Albaner(in) m(f); (language) Albanisch nt

album n Album nt

alcohol n Alkohol m; **alco-**

hol-free adj alkoholfrei; **alcoholic 1.** adj (drink) alkoholisch **2.** n Alkoholiker(in) m(f)

ale n Ale nt (helles englisches Bier)

alert 1. adj wachsam **2.** n Alarm m **3.** vt warnen (to vor + dat)

algebra n Algebra f

Algeria n Algerien nt

alibi n Alibi nt

alien n (foreigner) Ausländer(in) m(f); (from space) Außerirdische(r) mf

alike adj, adv gleich; (similar) ähnlich

alive adj lebendig; **keep sth ~** etw am Leben erhalten; **he's still ~** er lebt noch

all 1. adj (plural, every one of) alle; (singular, the whole of) ganz; **~ the children** alle Kinder; **~ the time** die ganze Zeit; **~ his life** sein ganzes Leben; **why me of ~ people?** warum ausgerechnet ich? **2.** pron (everything) alles; (everybody) alle; **~ of** ganz; **~ of them came** sie kamen alle **3.** n alles **4.** adv (completely) ganz; **it's ~ over** es ist ganz aus; **~ along** von Anfang an; **~ at once** auf einmal

allegation n Behauptung f; **alleged** adj angeblich

allergic adj allergisch (to gegen); **allergy** n Allergie f

alleviate vt (pain) lindern

alley n (enge) Gasse; (passage) Durchgang m; (bowling) Bahn f

alliance n Bündnis nt

alligator n Alligator m

all-night adj (café, cinema) die ganze Nacht geöffnet

allocate vt zuweisen, zuteilen (to dat)

allotment n (plot) Schrebergarten m

allow vt (permit) erlauben (sb jdm); (grant) bewilligen; (time) einplanen; **allow for** vt berücksichtigen; (cost etc) einkalkulieren; **allowance** n (from state) Beihilfe f; (from parent) Unterhaltsgeld nt

all right 1. adj okay, in Ordnung; **I'm ~** mir geht's gut **2.** adv (satisfactorily) ganz gut **3.** interj okay

allusion n Anspielung f (to auf + acc)

all-wheel drive n AUTO Allradantrieb m

ally n Verbündete(r) mf; HIST Alliierte(r) mf

almond n Mandel f

almost adv fast

alone adj, adv allein

along 1. prep entlang + acc; **~ the river** den Fluss entlang; (position) am Fluss entlang **2.** adv (onward) weiter; **~ with** zusammen mit; **all ~** die ganze Zeit; **alongside 1.** prep neben + dat **2.** adv (walk) nebenher

aloud adv laut

alphabet n Alphabet nt

Alps npl **the ~** die Alpen

already adv schon, bereits

Alsace n Elsass nt; **Alsatian 1.**
adj elsässisch **2.** n Elsäs-
ser(in) m(f); (Brit, dog)
Schäferhund m

also adv auch

altar n Altar m

alter vt ändern; **alteration** n
Änderung f; **~s** (to building)
Umbau m

alternate 1. adj abwechselnd
2. vi abwechseln (with mit);
alternating current n Wechselstrom m; **alternative 1.** adj
Alternativ- **2.** n Alternative f

although conj obwohl

altitude n Höhe f

altogether adv (in total) insgesamt; (entirely) ganz und
gar

aluminium, **aluminum** (US)
n Aluminium nt

always adv immer

am present of **be**; bin

am, **a.m.** abbr = **ante meridiem**; vormittags, morgens

amateur 1. n Amateur(in)
m(f) **2.** adj Amateur-; (theatre, choir) Laien-

amazed adj erstaunt (at über
+ acc); **amazing** adj erstaunlich

Amazon n ~ (**river**) Amazo-
nas m

ambassador n Botschafter m

ambiguity n Zweideutigkeit
f; **ambiguous** adj zweideutig

ambition n Ambition f; (ambitious nature) Ehrgeiz m;
ambitious adj ehrgeizig

ambulance n Krankenwagen
m

America n Amerika nt;
American 1. adj amerikanisch **2.** n Amerikaner(in)
m(f); **native ~** Indianer(in)
m(f)

amiable adj liebenswürdig

amicable adj freundlich; (relations) freundschaftlich

amnesia n Gedächtnisverlust
m

among(st) prep unter + dat

amount 1. n (quantity) Menge
f; (of money) Betrag m; **a
large/ small ~ of ...** ziemlich
viel / wenig ... **2.** vi **~ to** (total)
sich belaufen auf + acc

amp, **ampere** n Ampere nt

amplifier n Verstärker m

Amtrak® n amerikanische Ei-
senbahngesellschaft

amuse vt amüsieren; (entertain) unterhalten; **amused**
adj **I'm not ~** das finde ich
gar nicht lustig; **amusement**
n (enjoyment) Vergnügen nt;
(recreation) Unterhaltung f;
amusement park n Vergnügungspark m; **amusing** adj
amüsant

an art ein(e)

anaemic adj blutarm

anaesthetic n Narkose f;
(substance) Narkosemittel
nt

analyse, **analyze** vt analysieren; **analysis** *n* Analyse *f*

anatomy *n* Anatomie *f*; (*structure*) Körperbau *m*

ancestor *n* Vorfahr *m*

anchor 1. *n* Anker *m* **2.** *vt* verankern

anchovy *n* Sardelle *f*

ancient *adj* alt; *fam* (*person, clothes etc*) uralt

and *conj* und

Andorra *n* Andorra *nt*

anemic *adj* (*US*) → **anaemic**

anesthetic *n* (*US*) → **anaesthetic**

angel *n* Engel *m*

anger 1. *n* Zorn *m* **2.** *vt* ärgern

angina *n*, **angina pectoris** *n* Angina Pectoris *f*

angle *n* Winkel *m*; *fig* Standpunkt *m*

angling *n* Angeln *nt*

angry *adj* verärgert; (*stronger*) zornig; **be ~ with sb** auf jdn böse sein

angular *adj* eckig; (*face*) kantig

animal *n* Tier *nt*; **animal rights** *npl* Tierrechte *pl*

animated *adj* lebhaft; **~ film** Zeichentrickfilm *m*

aniseed *n* Anis *m*

ankle *n* (Fuß)knöchel *m*

annex *n* Anbau *m*

anniversary *n* Jahrestag *m*

announce *vt* bekannt geben; RADIO, TV ansagen; **announcement** *n* Bekanntgabe *f*; (*official*) Bekanntmachung *f*; RADIO, TV Ansage *f*; **announcer** *n* RADIO, TV Ansager(in) *m(f)*

annoy *vt* ärgern; **annoyance** *n* Ärger *m*; **annoyed** *adj* ärgerlich; **be ~ with sb** (*about sth*) sich über jdn (über etw) ärgern; **annoying** *adj* ärgerlich; (*person*) lästig, nervig

annual 1. *adj* jährlich **2.** *n* Jahrbuch *nt*

anonymous *adj* anonym

anorak *n* Anorak *m*; (*Brit*) *fam pej* Freak *m*

anorexia *n* Magersucht *f*; **anorexic** *adj* magersüchtig

another *adj, pron* (*different*) ein(e) andere(r, s); (*additional*) noch eine(r, s); **let me put it ~ way** lass es mich anders sagen

answer 1. *n* Antwort *f* (*to* auf + *acc*) **2.** *vi* antworten; (*on phone*) sich melden **3.** *vt* (*person*) antworten + *dat*; (*letter, question*) beantworten; (*telephone*) gehen an + *acc*, abnehmen; (*door*) öffnen; **answering machine**, **answerphone** *n* Anrufbeantworter *m*

ant *n* Ameise *f*

Antarctic *n* Antarktis *f*; **Antarctic Circle** *n* südlicher Polarkreis

antelope *n* Antilope *f*

antenna *n* ZOOL Fühler *m*; RADIO Antenne *f*

anti- *pref* Anti-, anti-; **antibiotic** *n* Antibiotikum *nt*

anticipate *vt* (*expect: trouble, question*) erwarten, rechnen mit; **anticipation** n Erwartung f

anticlimax n Enttäuschung f; **anticlockwise** adv entgegen dem Uhrzeigersinn; **antifreeze** n Frostschutzmittel nt

Antipodes npl Australien und Neuseeland

antiquarian adj ~ **bookshop** Antiquariat nt

antique 1. n Antiquität f **2.** adj antik; **antique shop** n Antiquitätengeschäft nt

antiseptic 1. n Antiseptikum nt **2.** adj antiseptisch

antlers npl Geweih nt

anxiety n Sorge f (about um);
anxious adj besorgt (about um); (apprehensive) ängstlich

any 1. adj (in question: untranslated) **do you have ~ money?** hast du Geld?; (with negative) **I don't have ~ money** ich habe kein Geld; (whichever one likes) **take ~ card** nimm irgendeine Karte **2.** pron (in question) **do you want ~?** (singular) willst du etwas (davon)?; (plural) willst du welche?; (with negative) **I don't have ~** ich habe keine / keinen / keins; (whichever one likes) **you can take ~ of them** du kannst viele(n) beliebige(n) nehmen **3.** adv (in question) **are there ~ more strawberries?** gibt es noch Erdbeeren?; **can't you work**

~ faster? kannst du nicht schneller arbeiten?; (with negative) **not ~ longer** nicht mehr; **this isn't ~ better** das ist auch nicht besser; **anybody** pron (whoever one likes) irgendjemand; (everyone) jeder; (in question) jemand; **anyhow** adv **I don't want to talk about it, not now ~** ich möchte nicht darüber sprechen, jedenfalls nicht jetzt; **if I can help you ~** wenn ich Ihnen irgendwie helfen kann; **they asked me not to go, but I went ~** sie baten mich, nicht hinzugehen, aber ich bin trotzdem hingegangen; **anyone** pron (whoever one likes) irgendjemand; (everyone) jeder; (in question) jemand; **isn't there ~ you can ask?** gibt es denn niemanden, den du fragen kannst?; **anyplace** adv (US) irgendwo; (direction) irgendwohin; (everywhere) überall; **anything** pron (whatever one likes, in question) (irgend)etwas; (everything) alles; **~ else?** sonst noch etwas?; **~ but that** alles, nur das nicht; **she didn't tell me ~** sie hat mir nichts gesagt; **anytime** adv jederzeit; **anyway** adv **I didn't want to go there ~** ich wollte da sowieso nicht hingehen; **thanks ~** trotzdem danke; **~, as I was saying, ...** jeden-

falls, wie ich schon sagte, ...;
anywhere *adv* irgendwo;
(*direction*) irgendwohin; (*everywhere*) überall

apart *adv* auseinander; **~ from** außer; **live ~** getrennt leben

apartment *n* Wohnung *f*;
apartment block *n* Wohnblock *m*

ape *n* (Menschen)affe *m*

aperitif *n* Aperitif *m*

aperture *n* Öffnung *f*; PHOT Blende *f*

apologize *vi* sich entschuldigen; **apology** *n* Entschuldigung *f*

apostrophe *n* Apostroph *m*

appalled *adj* entsetzt (*at* über + *acc*); **appalling** *adj* entsetzlich

apparatus *n* Apparat *m*;
(*piece of apparatus*) Gerät *nt*

apparent *adj* (*obvious*) offensichtlich (*to* für); (*seeming*)
scheinbar; **apparently** *adv* anscheinend

appeal 1. *vi* (dringend) bitten
(*for* um, *to* + *acc*); LAW Berufung einlegen; **~ to sb** (*be attractive*) jdm zusagen **2.** *n* Aufruf *m* (*to* an + *acc*); LAW Berufung *f*; (*attraction*) Reiz *m*; **appealing** *adj* ansprechend, attraktiv

appear *vi* erscheinen; THEAT auftreten; (*seem*) scheinen; **appearance** *n* Erscheinen *nt*; THEAT Auftritt *m*; (*look*)
Aussehen *nt*

appendicitis *n* Blinddarm-

entzündung *f*; **appendix** *n*
Blinddarm *m*; (*to book*) Anhang *m*

appetite *n* Appetit *m*; *fig* (*desire*) Verlangen *nt*; **appetizing** *adj* appetitlich

applause *n* Beifall *m*, Applaus *m*

apple *n* Apfel *m*; **apple juice** *n* Apfelsaft *m*; **apple pie** *n*
gedeckter Apfelkuchen *m*;
apple puree, **apple sauce** *n* Apfelmus *nt*; **apple tart** *n* Apfelkuchen *m*; **apple tree** *n* Apfelbaum *m*

appliance *n* Gerät *nt*; **applicable** *adj* anwendbar; (*on forms*) zutreffend; **applicant** *n* Bewerber(in) *m(f)*; **application** *n* (*request*) Antrag *m* (*for* auf + *acc*); (*for job*)
Bewerbung *f* (*for* um); **application form** *n* Anmeldeformular *nt*; **apply 1.** *vi* (*be relevant*) zutreffen (*to* auf + *acc*); (*for job etc*) sich bewerben (*for* um) **2.** *vt* (*cream, paint etc*) auftragen; (*put into practice*) anwenden; (*brakes*)
betätigen

appoint *vt* (*to post*) ernennen;
appointment *n* Verabredung *f*; (*at doctor, hairdresser etc, in business*) Termin *m*; **by ~** nach Vereinbarung

appreciate 1. *vt* (*value*) zu schätzen wissen; (*understand*) einsehen **2.** *vi* (*increase in value*) im Wert steigen; **appreciation** *n* (*esteem*)

Anerkennung f, Würdigung f

apprehensive adj ängstlich

approach 1. vi sich nähern **2.** vt (place) sich nähern + dat; (person) herantreten an + acc

appropriate adj passend; (to occasion) angemessen; (remark) treffend; **appropriately** adv passend; (expressed) treffend

approval n (show of satisfaction) Anerkennung f; (permission) Zustimmung f (of zu); **approve 1.** vt billigen **2.** vi **of sth/sb** etw billigen/von jdm etwas halten; **I don't** ~ ich missbillige das

approx = **approximately**; ca.; **approximate** adj ungefähr; **approximately** adv ungefähr, circa

apricot n Aprikose f

April n April m; → **September**

apron n Schürze f

aptitude n Begabung f

aquaplaning n AUTO Aquaplaning nt

aquarium n Aquarium nt

Aquarius n ASTR Wassermann m

Arab n Araber(in) m(f); **Arabian** adj arabisch; **Arabic 1.** n (language) Arabisch nt **2.** adj arabisch

arbitrary adj willkürlich

arcade n Arkade f; (shopping arcade) Einkaufspassage f

arch n Bogen m

archaeologist, archeologist (US) n Archäologe m, Archäologin f; **archaeology, archeology** (US) n Archäologie f

archaic adj veraltet

archbishop n Erzbischof m

architect n Architekt(in) m(f); **architecture** n Architektur f

archive(s) n(pl) Archiv nt

archway n Torbogen m

Arctic n Arktis f; **Arctic Circle** n nördlicher Polarkreis

are present of **be**

area n (region, district) Gebiet nt, Gegend f; (amount of space) Fläche f; (part of building etc) Bereich m, Zone f; (fig field) Bereich m; **the London** ~ der Londoner Raum; **area code** n (US) Vorwahl f

aren't contr of **are not**

Argentina n Argentinien nt

argue vi streiten (about, over über + acc); ~ **that ...** behaupten, dass ...; ~ **for/against ...** sprechen für/gegen ...; **argument** n (reasons) Argument nt; (quarrel) Streit m; **have an** ~ sich streiten

Aries nsing ASTR Widder m

arise vi sich ergeben, entstehen; (problem, question, wind) aufkommen

aristocracy n (class) Adel m; **aristocrat** n Adlige(r) mf; **aristocratic** adj aristokratisch, adlig

arm 1. n Arm m; (sleeve) Ärmel m; (of armchair) Armlehne f **2.** vt bewaffnen; **armchair** n Lehnstuhl m

armed adj bewaffnet

armpit n Achselhöhle f

arms npl Waffen pl

army n Armee f

A road n (Brit) ≈ Bundesstraße f

aroma n Duft m, Aroma nt; **aromatherapy** n Aromatherapie f

arose pt of **arise**

around 1. adv herum, umher; (present) hier (irgendwo); (approximately) ungefähr; (with time) gegen; **he's ~ somewhere** er ist hier irgendwo in der Nähe **2.** prep (surrounding) um ... (herum); (about in) in ... herum

arr. abbr = **arrival, arrives**; Ank.

arrange vt (put in order) (an-) ordnen; (artistically) arrangieren; (agree to: meeting etc) vereinbaren, festsetzen; (organize) planen; ~ **that ...** es so einrichten, dass ...; **we ~d to meet at eight o'clock** wir haben uns für acht Uhr verabredet; **arrangement** n (layout) Anordnung f; (agreement) Vereinbarung f, Plan m; **make ~s** Vorbereitungen treffen

arrest 1. vt (person) verhaften **2.** n Verhaftung f

arrival n Ankunft f; **new ~** (person) Neuankömmling m; **arrivals** n (airport) Ankunftshalle f; **arrive** vi ankommen (at bei, in + dat); **~ at a solution** eine Lösung finden

arrogant adj arrogant

arrow n Pfeil m

arse n vulg Arsch m

art n Kunst f, **~s** pl Geisteswissenschaften pl

artery n Schlagader f, Arterie f

art gallery n Kunstgalerie f, Kunstmuseum nt

arthritis n Arthritis f

artichoke n Artischocke f

article n Artikel m; (object) Gegenstand m

artificial adj künstlich, Kunst-

artist n Künstler(in) m(f); **artistic** adj künstlerisch

as 1. adv (like) wie; (in role of) als; **such ~ (for example)** ... wie etwa ...; ~ ... ~ so ... wie; ~ **soon** ~ **he comes** sobald er kommt; **twice ~ much** zweimal so viel; ~ **for** ... was ... betrifft; ~ **of** ... (time) ab ... + dat **2.** conj (since) da, weil; (while) als, während; ~ **if,** ~ **though** als ob; **leave it** ~ **it is** lass es so (wie es ist); ~ **it were** sozusagen

asap acr = **as soon as possible**; möglichst bald

ash n (dust) Asche f; (tree) Esche f

ashamed adj beschämt; **be ~ (of sb/sth)** sich (für jdn/etw) schämen

ashore adv an Land

ashtray n Aschenbecher m

Asia n Asien nt; **Asian 1.** adj asiatisch **2.** n Asiat(in) m(f)

aside adv beiseite, zur Seite; **~ from** (esp, US) außer

ask vt, vi fragen; (question) stellen; (request) bitten um; **~ sb the way** jdn nach dem Weg fragen; **~ for** jdn bitten um; **~ sb to do sth** jdn darum bitten, etw zu tun; **ask for** et bitten um; **~ sb to do sth** jdn darum bitten, etw zu tun; **ask for** jdn bitten um

asleep adj, adv **be ~** schlafen; **fall ~** einschlafen

asparagus n Spargel m

aspirin n Aspirin nt

ass n a. fig Esel m; (US) vulg Arsch m

assassinate vt ermorden; **assassination** n Ermordung f

assault 1. n Angriff m; LAW Körperverletzung f **2.** vt überfallen, herfallen über + acc

assemble 1. vt (parts) zusammensetzen **2.** vi sich versammeln; **assembly** n (of people) Versammlung f; **assembly hall** n Aula f; **assertion** n Behauptung f

assess vt einschätzen; **assessment** n Einschätzung f

asset n Vermögenswert m; fig Vorteil m; **~s** pl Vermögen nt

assign vt zuweisen; **assignment** n Aufgabe f; (mission) Auftrag m

assist vt helfen + dat; **assistance** n Hilfe f; **assistant** n Assistent(in) m(f), Mitarbeiter(in) m(f); (in shop) Verkäufer(in) m(f)

associate 1. n (partner) Partner(in) m(f), Teilhaber(in) m(f) **2.** vt verbinden (with mit); **association** n (organization) Verband m, Vereinigung f; **in ~ with ...** in Zusammenarbeit mit ...

assorted adj gemischt; **assortment** n Auswahl f (of an + dat); (of sweets) Mischung f

assume vt annehmen (that ... dass ...); (role, responsibility) übernehmen; **assumption** n Annahme f

assurance n Versicherung f; (confidence) Zuversicht f; **assure** vt (say confidently) versichern + dat; **be ~d of sth** einer Sache sicher sein

asterisk n Sternchen nt

asthma n Asthma nt

astonished adj erstaunt (at über); **astonishing** adj erstaunlich; **astonishment** n Erstaunen nt

astound vt sehr erstaunen; **astounding** adj erstaunlich

astray adv **go ~** (letter etc) verloren gehen; (person) vom Weg abkommen

astrology n Astrologie f

astronaut n Astronaut(in) m(f)

astronomy n Astronomie f

asylum n (*home*) Anstalt f; (*political asylum*) Asyl nt; **asylum seeker** n Asylbewerber(in) m(f)

at prep (*place*) **~ the door** an der Tür; **~ home** zu Hause; **~ John's** bei John; **~ school** in der Schule; **~ the theatre/ cinema** im Theater / Kino; **~ lunch/ work** beim Essen / bei der Arbeit; (*direction*) **point ~ sb** auf jdn zeigen; **he looked ~ me** er sah mich an; (*time*) **~ 2 o'clock** um 2 Uhr; **~ Easter/ Christmas** zu Ostern / Weihnachten; **~ the moment** im Moment; **(the age of) 16** im Alter von 16 Jahren, mit 16; (*price*) **~ £5 each** zu je 5 Pfund; (*speed*) **~ 20 mph** mit 20 Meilen pro Stunde

ate pret of **eat**

athlete n Athlet(in) m(f); (*track and field*) Leichtathlet(in) m(f); **~'s foot** Fußpilz m; **athletic** adj sportlich; (*build*) athletisch; **athletics** npl Leichtathletik f

Atlantic n **the ~ (Ocean)** der Atlantik

atlas n Atlas m

ATM abbr = **automated teller machine** ; Geldautomat m

atmosphere n Atmosphäre f, Stimmung f

atom n Atom nt; **atom(ic) bomb** n Atombombe f; **atomic** adj Atom-; **~ energy** Atomenergie f; **~ power**

Atomkraft f

A to Z® n Stadtplan m (in Buchform)

atrocious adj grauenhaft; **atrocity** n Grausamkeit f; (*deed*) Gräueltat f

attach vt befestigen, anheften (*to an ~ed to sb/ sth* an jdm/etw hängen; attachment n (*affection*) Zuneigung f; IT Attachment nt, Anhang m

attack 1. vt, vi angreifen 2. n Angriff + acc (*on* auf m); MED Anfall m

attempt 1. n Versuch m 2. vt versuchen

attend vt (*go to*) teilnehmen an + dat; (*lectures, school*) besuchen 2. vi (*be present*) anwesend sein; **attend to** vt sich kümmern um; (*customer*) bedienen; **attendance** n (*presence*) Anwesenheit f; **attendant** n (*in car park etc*) Wächter(in) m(f); (*in museum*) Aufseher(in) m(f)

attention n Aufmerksamkeit f; (*your*) **~ please** Achtung!; **pay ~ to sth** etw beachten; **pay ~ to sb** jdm aufmerksam zuhören

attic n Dachboden m; (*lived in*) Mansarde f

attitude n (*mental*) Einstellung f (*to, towards* zu); (*more general, physical*) Haltung f

attorney n (US, *lawyer*) Rechtsanwalt m, Rechtsanwältin f

attract

attract vt anziehen; (attention) erregen; **be ..ed to** or **by sb** sich zu jdm hingezogen fühlen; **attraction** n Anziehungskraft f; (thing) Attraktion f; **attractive** adj attraktiv; (thing, idea) reizvoll

aubergine n Aubergine f

auction 1. n Versteigerung f, Auktion f 2. vt versteigern

audience n Publikum nt; RADIO Zuhörer pl; TV Zuschauer pl

audio adj Ton-

audition 1. n Probe f 2. vi THEAT vorspielen, vorsingen

auditorium n Zuschauerraum m

August n August m; → **September**

aunt n Tante f

au pair n Aupairmädchen nt, Aupairjunge m

Australia n Australien nt; **Australian** 1. adj australisch 2. n Australier(in) m(f)

Austria n Österreich nt; **Austrian** 1. adj österreichisch 2. n Österreicher(in) m(f)

authentic adj echt; (signature) authentisch; **authenticity** n Echtheit f

author n Autor(in) m(f); (of report etc) Verfasser(in) m(f)

authority n (power, expert) Autorität f; **the authorities** pl die Behörden pl; **authorize** vt (permit) genehmigen

auto n (US) Auto nt

autograph n Autogramm nt

automatic 1. adj automatisch; **~ gear change** (Brit), **~ gear shift** (US) Automatikschaltung f 2. n (car) Automatikwagen m

automobile n (US) Auto(mobil) nt; **autotrain** n (US) Autoreisezug m

autumn n (Brit) Herbst m

auxiliary 1. adj Hilfs- 2. n Hilfskraft f

availability n (of product) Lieferbarkeit f; (of resources) Verfügbarkeit f; **available** adj erhältlich; (existing) vorhanden; (product) lieferbar; (person) erreichbar; **be/ make ~ to sb** jdm zur Verfügung stehen/stellen

avalanche n Lawine f

Ave abbr = **avenue**

avenue n Allee f

average 1. n Durchschnitt m; **on ~** im Durchschnitt 2. adj durchschnittlich

aviation n Luftfahrt f

avocado n Avocado f

avoid vt vermeiden; **~ sb** jdm aus dem Weg gehen; **avoidable** adj vermeidbar

awake 1. vi aufwachen 2. adj wach

award 1. n (prize) Preis m; (for bravery etc) Auszeichnung f 2. vt zuerkennen (to sb jdm); (present) verleihen (to sb jdm)

aware adj bewusst; **be ~ of sth** sich dat einer Sache gen bewusst sein; **I was not ~ that ...**

es war mir nicht klar, dass ...
away adv weg; **look ~** wegsehen; **he's ~** er ist nicht da; (*on a trip*) er ist verreist; (*from school, work*) er fehlt; SPORT **they are (playing)** ~ sie spielen auswärts; (*with distance*) **three miles ~** drei Meilen (von hier) entfernt

awful adj schrecklich, furchtbar; **awfully** adv furchtbar
awkward adj (*clumsy*) ungeschickt; (*embarrassing*) peinlich; (*difficult*) schwierig
awning n Markise f
awoke pt of **awake**
awoken pp of **awake**
ax (US), **axe** n Axt f
axle n TECH Achse f

B

BA abbr = **Bachelor of Arts**
babe n fam Baby nt; (*affectionate*) Schatz m, Kleine(r) mf
baby n Baby nt; (*of animal*) Junge(s) nt; fam (*affectionate*) Schatz m, Kleine(r) mf; **have a ~** ein Kind bekommen; **baby carriage** n (US) Kinderwagen m; **baby food** n Babynahrung f; **baby shower** n (US) Party für die werdende Mutter; **baby-sit** irr vi babysitten; **baby-sitter** n Babysitter m
bachelor n Junggeselle m; **Bachelor of Arts / Science** erster akademischer Grad, ≈ Magister / Diplom; **bachelorette** n Junggesellin f; **bachelorette party** n (US) Junggesellinnenabschied; **bachelor party** n (US) Junggesellenabschied
back 1. n (*of person, animal*)

Rücken m; (*of house, coin etc*) Rückseite f; (*of chair*) Rückenlehne f; (*of car*) Rücksitz m; (*of train*) Ende nt; SPORT (*defender*) Verteidiger(in) m(f); **at the ~ of ...,** **in ~ of** (*inside*) hinten in ...; (*outside*) hinter ...; **~ to front** verkehrt herum 2. vt (*support*) unterstützen; (*car*) rückwärts fahren 3. vi (*go backwards*) rückwärts gehen or fahren 4. adj Hinter-; **~ wheel** Hinterrad nt 5. adv zurück; **they're ~** sie sind wieder da; **back down** vi nachgeben; **back up** 1. vi (*car*) zurücksetzen 2. vt (*support*) unterstützen; IT sichern; (*car*) zurückfahren

backache n Rückenschmerzen pl; **backbone** n Rückgrat nt; **backdoor** n Hintertür f; **backfire** vi (*plan*) fehlschlagen; AUTO fehlzünden;

background n Hintergrund m; backhand n SPORT Rückhand f; backlog n (of work) Rückstand m; backpack n (US) Rucksack m; backpacker n Rucksacktourist(in) m(f); backpacking n Rucksacktourismus m; back seat n Rücksitz m; backside n fam Po m; back street n Seitensträßchen nt; backstroke n Rückenschwimmen nt; back-up n (support) Unterstützung f; ~ (copy) IT Sicherungskopie f; backward adj (region) rückständig; ~ movement Rückwärtsbewegung f; backwards adv rückwärts; backyard n Hinterhof m

bacon n Frühstücksspeck m

bacteria npl Bakterien pl

bad adj schlecht, schlimm; (smell) übel; I have a ~ back mir tut der Rücken weh; I'm ~ at maths / sport ich bin schlecht in Mathe / Sport; go ~ schlecht werden, verderben

badge n Abzeichen nt

badger n Dachs m

badly adv schlecht; ~ wounded schwer verwundet; need sth ~ etw dringend brauchen; bad-tempered adj schlecht gelaunt

bag n (small) Tüte f; (larger) Beutel m; (handbag) Tasche f; it's not my ~ fam das ist nicht mein Ding

baggage n Gepäck nt; baggage (re)claim n Gepäckrückgabe f

baggy adj (zu) weit; (trousers, suit) ausgebeult

bagpipes npl Dudelsack m

Bahamas npl the ~ die Bahamas pl

bail n (money) Kaution f

bait n Köder m

bake vt, vi backen; baked beans npl weiße Bohnen in Tomatensoße; baked potato n in der Schale gebackene Kartoffel, Ofenkartoffel f; baker n Bäcker(in) m(f); bakery n Bäckerei f; baking powder n Backpulver nt

balance 1. n (equilibrium) Gleichgewicht nt 2. vt (make up for) ausgleichen; balance sheet n Bilanz f

balcony n Balkon m

bald adj kahl; be ~ eine Glatze haben

Balkans npl the ~ der Balkan, die Balkanländer pl

ball n Ball m; have a ~ fam sich prima amüsieren

ballet n Ballett nt; ballet dancer n Balletttänzer(in) m(f)

balloon n (Luft)ballon m

ballot n (geheime) Abstimmung

ballpoint (pen) n Kugelschreiber m

ballroom n Tanzsaal m

Baltic adj ~ Sea Ostsee f; the ~ States die baltischen Staaten

bamboo n Bambus m; **bamboo shoots** npl Bambussprossen pl

ban 1. n Verbot nt **2.** vt verbieten

banana n Banane f; **he's ~s** er ist völlig durchgeknallt; **banana split** n Bananensplit nt

band n (group) Gruppe f; (of criminals) Bande f; (pop, rock etc) Band f; (strip) Band nt

bandage 1. n Verband m; (elastic) Bandage f **2.** vt verbinden

B & B abbr = **bed and breakfast**

bang 1. n (noise) Knall m; (blow) Schlag m **2.** vt, vi knallen; (door) zuschlagen, zuknallen; **banger** n (Brit fam (firework) Knallkörper m; (sausage) Würstchen nt; (old car) Klapperkiste f

bangs npl (US, von Frisur) Pony m

banish vt verbannen

banister(s) n (Treppen)geländer nt

bank n FIN Bank f; (of river etc) Ufer nt; **bank account** n Bankkonto nt; **bank balance** n Kontostand m; **bank card** n Bankkarte f; **bank code** n Bankleitzahl f; **bank holiday** n gesetzlicher Feiertag

bankrupt vt ruinieren; **go ~** Pleite gehen

bank statement n Kontoauszug m

baptism n Taufe f; **baptize** vt taufen

bar 1. n (for drinks) Bar f; (less smart) Lokal nt; (rod) Stange f; (of chocolate etc) Riegel m, Tafel f; (of soap) Stück nt; (counter) Theke f **2.** prep außer; **~ none** ohne Ausnahme

barbecue n (device) Grill m; (party) Barbecue nt, Grillfete f; **have a ~** grillen

bar code n Strichkode m

bare adj nackt; **~ patch** kahle Stelle; **barefoot** adj, adv barfuß; **bareheaded** adj, adv ohne Kopfbedeckung; **barely** adv kaum; (with age) knapp

bargain 1. n (cheap offer) günstiges Angebot, Schnäppchen nt; (transaction) Geschäft nt; **what a ~** das ist aber günstig! **2.** vi (ver)handeln

barge n (for freight) Lastkahn m; (unpowered) Schleppkahn m

bark 1. n (of tree) Rinde f; (of dog) Bellen nt **2.** vi (dog) bellen

barley n Gerste f

barmaid n Bardame f; **barman** n Barkeeper m

barn n Scheune f

barometer n Barometer nt

baroque adj barock, Barock-

barracks npl Kaserne f

barrel n Fass nt; **barrel organ**

n Drehorgel *f*

barrier *n* (*obstruction*) Absperrung *f*; (*across road etc*) Schranke *f*

bartender *n* (*US*) Barkeeper *m*

base 1. *n* Basis *f*; (*of lamp, pillar etc*) Fuß *m*; MIL Stützpunkt *m* **2.** *vt* gründen (*on* auf + *acc*); **be ~d on sth** auf etw *dat* basieren

baseball *n* Baseball *m*; baseball cap *n* Baseballmütze *f*

basement *n* Kellergeschoss *nt*

bash *fam* **1.** *n* Schlag *m*, Party *f* **2.** *vt* hauen

basic *adj* einfach; (*fundamental*) Grund-; (*importance, difference*) grundlegend; (*in principle*) grundsätzlich; **basically** *adv* im Grunde; **basics** *npl* **the ~** das Wesentliche

basil *n* Basilikum *nt*

basin *n* (*for washing, valley*) (Wasch)becken *nt*

basis *n* Basis *f*; **on the ~ of** aufgrund + *gen*; **on a monthly ~** monatlich

basket *n* Korb *m*; **basketball** *n* Basketball *m*

Basque 1. *n* (*person*) Baske *m*, Baskin *f*; (*language*) Baskisch *nt* **2.** *adj* baskisch

bass 1. *n* MUS Bass *m*; (*cool*) Barsch *m* **2.** *adj* MUS Bass-

bastard *n* vulg (*awful person*) Arschloch *nt*

bat *n* ZOOL Fledermaus *f*; SPORT (*cricket, baseball*)

Schlagholz *nt*; (*table tennis*) Schläger *m*

bath 1. *n* Bad *nt*; (*tub*) Badewanne *f*; **have a ~** baden **2.** *vt* (*child etc*) baden

bathe *vt*, *vi* (*wound etc*) baden; **bathing cap** *n* Badekappe *f*; **bathing costume**, **bathing suit** (*US*) *n* Badeanzug *m*

bathmat *n* Badevorleger *m*; **bathrobe** *n* Bademantel *m*; **bathroom** *n* Bad(ezimmer) *nt*; **bath towel** *n* Badetuch *nt*; **bathtub** *n* Badewanne *f*

baton *n* MUS Taktstock *m*; (*police*) Schlagstock *m*

batter 1. *n* Teig *m* **2.** *vt* heftig schlagen; **battered** *adj* übel zugerichtet; (*hat, car*) verbeult; (*wife, baby*) misshandelt

battery *n* ELEC Batterie *f*; **battery charger** *n* Ladegerät *nt*

battle *n* Schlacht *f*; *fig* Kampf *m* (*for* um); **battlefield** *n* Schlachtfeld *nt*

Bavaria *n* Bayern *nt*

bay *n* (*of sea*) Bucht *f*; (*on house*) Erker *m*; (*tree*) Lorbeerbaum *m*; **bay leaf** *n* Lorbeerblatt *nt*; **bay window** *n* Erkerfenster *nt*

BBC *abbr* = **British Broadcasting Corporation**; BBC *f*

BC *abbr* = **before Christ**; vor Christi Geburt, v. Chr.

be 1. *vi* sein; (*become*) werden; (*be situated*) liegen, sein; **she's French** sie ist Französin; *he wants to ~ a doctor* er will Arzt werden; *I'm too hot* mir ist zu warm; *she's not well (health)* ihr geht's nicht gut; *the book is 5 dollars (cost)* das Buch kostet 5 Dollar; *how much is that altogether?* was macht das zusammen?; *how long have you been here?* wie lange sind Sie schon da?; *have you ever been to Rome?* warst du / waren Sie schon einmal in Rom?; *there is / are* es gibt, es ist / sind; *there are two left* es sind noch zwei übrig **2.** *vaux (passive)* werden; *he was run over* er ist überfahren worden, er wurde überfahren; *(continous tenses) I was walking on the beach* ich ging am Strand spazieren; *they're coming tomorrow* sie kommen morgen; *(infinitive: intention, obligation) the car is to ~ sold* das Auto soll verkauft werden; *you are not to mention it* du darfst es nicht erwähnen

beach *n* Strand *m*; **beachwear** *n* Strandkleidung *f*

bead *n (of glass, wood etc)* Perle *f*; *(drop)* Tropfen *m*

beak *n* Schnabel *m*

beam 1. *(of wood etc)* Balken *m*; *(of light)* Strahl *m* **2.** *vi (smile etc)* strahlen

bean *n* Bohne *f*; **bean curd** *n*

Tofu *m*

bear 1. *vt (carry)* tragen; *(tolerate)* ertragen **2.** *n* Bär *m*; **bearable** *adj* erträglich

beard *n* Bart *m*

beat 1. *vt* schlagen; *(as punishment)* prügeln; *~ sb at tennis* jdn im Tennis schlagen **2.** *n (of heart, drum etc)* Schlag *m*; MUS Takt *m*; **beat up** *vt* zusammenschlagen; **beaten** *pp of* **beat**; *of the ~ track* abgelegen

beautiful *adj* schön; *(splendid)* herrlich; **beauty** *n* Schönheit *f*; **beauty spot** *n (place)* lohnendes Ausflugsziel

beaver *n* Biber *m*

became *pt of* **become**

because *1. adv, conj* weil **2.** *prep ~ of* wegen + *gen or dat*

become *vt* werden; *what's ~ of him?* was ist aus ihm geworden?

bed *n* Bett *nt*; *(in garden)* Beet *nt*; **bed and breakfast** *n* Übernachtung *f* mit Frühstück; **bedding** *n* Bettzeug *nt*; **bed linen** *n* Bettwäsche *f*; **bedroom** *n* Schlafzimmer *nt*; **bed-sit(ter)** *n fam* möblierte Einzimmerwohnung; **bedspread** *n* Tagesdecke *f*; **bedtime** *n* Schlafenszeit *f*

bee *n* Biene *f*

beech *n* Buche *f*

beef *n* Rindfleisch *nt*; **beefburger** *n* Hamburger *m*;

beef tomato n Fleischtomate f

beehive n Bienenstock m

been pp of **be**

beer n Bier nt

beetle n Käfer m

beetroot n Rote Bete

before 1. prep vor; **the year ~ last** vorletztes Jahr; **the day ~ yesterday** vorgestern **2.** conj bevor **3.** adv (of time) vorher; **have you been there ~?** waren Sie schon einmal dort?; **beforehand** adv vorher

beg 1. vt **~ sb to do sth** jdn inständig bitten, etw zu tun **2.** vi (beggar) betteln (for um)

began pt of **begin**

beggar n Bettler(in) m(f)

begin vt, vi anfangen, beginnen; **beginner** n Anfänger(in) m(f); **beginning** n Anfang m; **begun** pp of **begin**

behalf n **on ~ of, in ~ of** (US) im Namen / Auftrag von; **on my ~** für mich

behave vi sich benehmen; **behavior** (US), **behaviour** n Benehmen nt

behind 1. prep hinter **2.** adv hinten; **be ~ with one's work** mit seiner Arbeit im Rückstand sein **3.** n fam Hinterteil nt

beige adj beige

being n (existence) Dasein nt; (person) Wesen nt

Belarus n Weißrussland nt

belch 1. n Rülpser m **2.** vi rülpsen

Belgian 1. adj belgisch **2.** n Belgier(in) m(f); **Belgium** n Belgien nt

belief n Glaube m (in an + acc); (conviction) Überzeugung f; **it's my ~ that ...** ich bin der Überzeugung, dass ...; **believe** vt glauben; **believe in** vi glauben an + acc

bell n (church) Glocke f; (bicycle, door) Klingel f; **bellboy** n (esp, US) Page m

bellows npl (for fire) Blasebalg m

belly n Bauch m; **bellyache 1.** n Bauchweh nt; **belly button** n fam Bauchnabel m; **bellyflop** n fam Bauchklatscher m

belong vi gehören (to sb jdm); (to club) angehören + dat; **belongings** npl Habe f

below 1. prep unter **2.** adv unten

belt 1. n (round waist) Gürtel m; (safety belt) Gurt m **2.** vi fam (go fast) rasen, düsen; **beltway** n (US) Umgehungsstraße f

bench n Bank f

bend 1. n Biegung f; (in road) Kurve f **2.** vt (curve) biegen; (head, arm) beugen **3.** vi sich biegen; (person) sich beugen; **bend down** vi sich bücken

beneath 1. prep unter **2.** adv darunter

beneficial adj gut, nützlich (to

bike

für); **benefit 1.** n (advantage)
Vorteil m; (profit) Nutzen m;
for your/his ~ deinetwegen/seinetwegen; **unemployment ~** Arbeitslosengeld nt **2.** vt gut tun + dat
3. vi Nutzen ziehen (from
aus)

Benelux n Beneluxländer pl

bent 1. pt, pp of **bend 2.** adj
krumm; fam korrupt

Bermuda 1. n **the ~s** pl die
Bermudas pl **2.** adj **~ shorts**
pl Bermudashorts pl

berry n Beere f

beside prep neben; **~ the
sea/lake** am Meer/See;
besides 1. prep außer **2.**
adv außerdem

best 1. adj beste(r, s); **my ~
friend** mein bester or engster
Freund; **the ~ thing (to do)
would be to ...** das Beste wäre zu ...; (on food packaging)
~ before ... mindestens haltbar bis ... **2.** n das Beste;
all the ~ alles Gute; **make
the ~ of it** das Beste daraus machen **3.** adv am
besten; **I like this ~** das
mag ich am liebsten; **best-before date** n Mindesthaltbarkeitsdatum nt; **best man**
n Trauzeuge m

bet 1. vt, vi wetten (on auf
+ acc); **you ~** fam und ob!;
I ~ he'll be late wette ich
mit Sicherheit zu spät **2.** n
Wette f

betray vt verraten

better adj, adv besser; **get ~**
(healthwise) sich erholen,
wieder gesund werden; (improve) sich verbessern; **I'm
much ~ today** es geht mir
heute viel besser; **you'd ~
go** du solltest lieber gehen;
a change for the ~ eine
Wendung zum Guten

between 1. prep zwischen;
(among) unter; **~ you and
me, ...** unter uns gesagt, ...
2. adv (in) **~** dazwischen

beverage n (formal) Getränk
nt

beware vt **~ of sth** sich vor etw
+ dat hüten; **"~ of the dog"**
„Vorsicht, bissiger Hund!"

beyond 1. prep (place) jenseits + gen; (time) über ... hinaus; (out of reach) außerhalb + gen; **it's ~ me** da habe
ich keine Ahnung, da bin ich
überfragt **2.** adv darüber hinaus

bias n (prejudice) Vorurteil nt,
Voreingenommenheit f; **biased** adj voreingenommen

bib n Latz m

Bible n Bibel f

bicycle n Fahrrad nt

bid 1. vt (offer) bieten **2.** n (attempt) Versuch m; (offer)
Gebot nt

big adj groß; **it's no ~ deal**
fam es ist nichts Besonderes; **big dipper** n (Brit)
Achterbahn f; **bigheaded**
adj eingebildet

bike n fam Rad nt

bikini n Bikini m

bilberry n Heidelbeere f

bilingual adj zweisprachig

bill n (account) Rechnung f; (US, banknote) Banknote f; POL Gesetzentwurf m; ZOOL Schnabel m; billfold n (US) Brieftasche f

billiards nsing Billard nt

billion n Billion f

bin n Behälter m; (rubbish bin) Mülleimer m; (for paper) Papierkorb m

bind vt binden; (bind together) zusammenbinden; (wound) verbinden; binding n (ski) Bindung f; (book) Einband m

binge n fam (drinking) Sauferei f; go on a ~ auf Saaftour gehen

bingo n Bingo nt

binoculars npl Fernglas nt

biological adj biologisch; biology n Biologie f

birch n Birke f

bird n Vogel m; (Brit) fam (girl, girlfriend) Tussi f; bird watcher n Vogelbeobachter(in) m(f)

birth n Geburt f; birth certificate n Geburtsurkunde f; birthday n Geburtstag m; happy ~ herzlichen Glückwunsch zum Geburtstag; birthday card n Geburtstagskarte f; birthday party n Geburtstagsfeier f; birthplace n Geburtsort m

biscuit n (Brit) Keks m

bisexual adj bisexuell

bishop n Bischof m; (in chess) Läufer m

bit 1. pt of bite 2. n (piece) Stück(chen) nt; IT Bit nt; a ~ (of ...) (small amount) ein bisschen ...; a ~ tired etwas müde; ~ by ~ allmählich; (time) for a ~ ein Weilchen; quite a ~ (a lot) ganz schön viel

bitch n (dog) Hündin f; pej (woman) Miststück nt, Schlampe f; son of a ~ (US) vulg Hurensohn m, Scheißkerl m; bitchy adj gemein, zickig

bite 1. vt, vi beißen 2. n Biss m; (mouthful) Bissen m; (insect) Stich m; have a ~ eine Kleinigkeit essen; bitten pp of bite

bitter 1. adj bitter; (memory etc) schmerzlich 2. n (Brit, beer) halbdunkles Bier; bitter lemon n Bitter Lemon nt

black adj schwarz; blackberry n Brombeere f; blackbird n Amsel f; blackboard n (Wand)tafel f; black box n AVIAT Flugschreiber m; blackcurrant n Schwarze Johannisbeere; black eye n blaues Auge; Black Forest n Schwarzwald m; blackmail 1. n Erpressung f 2. vt erpressen; black market n Schwarzmarkt m; blackout n MED Ohnmacht f; have a ~ ohnmächtig werden; black

pudding n ≈ Blutwurst f;
Black Sea n **the ~** das
Schwarze Meer; **blacksmith**
n Schmied(in) m(f); **black
tie** n Abendanzug m, Smoking m; **is it ~?** ist/besteht
da Smokingzwang?

bladder n Blase f

blade n (of knife) Klinge f; (of
propeller) Blatt nt; (of grass)
Halm m

blame 1. n Schuld f **2.** vt **sth
on sb** jdm die Schuld an etw
dat geben; **he is to ~** er ist daran schuld

bland adj (taste) fade; (comment) nichts sagend

blank adj (page, space) leer,
unbeschrieben; (look) aus-
druckslos; **~ cheque** Blankoscheck m

blanket n (Woll)decke f

blast 1. n (of wind) Windstoß
m; (of explosion) Druckwel-
le f **2.** vt (blow up) sprengen

blatant adj (undisguised) offen; (obvious) offensichtlich

blaze 1. vi lodern; (sun) brennen **2.** n (building) Brand m;
(other fire) Feuer nt

bleach 1. n Bleichmittel nt **2.**
vt bleichen

bleary adj (eyes) trübe, verschlafen

bleed vi bluten

bleep 1. n Piepton m **2.** vi pie-
pen; **bleeper** n fam Piepser
m

blend 1. n Mischung f **2.** vt mischen **3.** vi sich mischen;

blender n Mixer m

bless vt segnen; **~ you!** Gesundheit!; **blessing** n Segen
m

blew pt of **blow**

blind 1. adj blind; (corner) un-
übersichtlich; **turn a ~ eye to
sth** bei etw ein Auge zudrü-
cken **2.** n (for window) Rollo
nt **3.** vt blenden; **blind alley** n
Sackgasse f; **blind spot** n
AUTO toter Winkel; fig schwa-
cher Punkt

blink vi blinzeln; (light) blinken

bliss n (Glück)seligkeit f

blister n Blase f

blizzard n Schneesturm m

block 1. n (of wood, stone, ice)
Block m, Klotz m; (of buildings) Häuserblock m; **~ of
flats** (Brit) Wohnblock m **2.**
vt (road etc) blockieren;
(pipe, nose) verstopfen;
blockage n Verstopfung f;
blockbuster n Knüller m;
block letters npl Blockschrift f

bloke n (Brit) fam Kerl m, Typ
m

blonde 1. adj blond **2.** n (person) Blondine f, blonder Typ

blood n Blut nt; **blood count**
n Blutbild nt; **blood donor** n
Blutspender(in) m(f); **blood
group** n Blutgruppe f; **blood
poisoning** n Blutvergiftung
f; **blood pressure** n Blutdruck m; **blood sample** n
Blutprobe f; **bloodsports**

npl Sportarten, bei denen Tiere getötet werden; **bloody** *adj* (Brit) fam verdammt, Scheiß-; (literal sense) blutig

bloom 1. *n* Blüte *f* **2.** *vi* blühen

blossom 1. *n* Blüte *f* **2.** *vi* blühen

blouse *n* Bluse *f*; **big girl's ~** fam Schwächling *m*, femininer Typ

blow 1. *n* Schlag *m* **2.** *vi, vt* (wind) wehen, blasen; (person: trumpet etc) blasen; **~ one's nose** sich dat die Nase putzen; **blow out** *vt* (candle etc) ausblasen; **blow up 1.** *vi* explodieren **2.** *vt* sprengen; (balloon, tyre) aufblasen; PHOT (enlarge) vergrößern; **blow-dry** *vt* föhnen; **blowjob** *n* fam **give sb a ~** jdm einen blasen; **blown** *pp of* **blow**

BLT *n abbr* = **bacon, lettuce and tomato sandwich**; mit Frühstücksspeck, Kopfsalat und Tomaten belegtes Sandwich

blue *adj* blau; fam (unhappy) trübsinnig, niedergeschlagen; (film) pornografisch; (joke) anzüglich; (language) derb; **bluebell** *n* Glockenblume *f*; **blueberry** *n* Blaubeere *f*; **blue cheese** *n* Blauschimmelkäse *m*; **blues** *npl* **the ~** MUS der Blues; **have the ~** fam niedergeschlagen sein

blunder *n* Schnitzer *m*

blunt *adj* (knife) stumpf; fig unverblümt; **bluntly** *adv* geradeheraus

blurred *adj* verschwommen, unklar

blush *vi* erröten

board 1. *n* (of wood) Brett *nt*; (committee) Ausschuss *m*; (of firm) Vorstand *m*; **~ and lodging** Unterkunft und Verpflegung; **on ~** an Bord **2.** *vi* (train, bus) einsteigen in + acc; (ship) an Bord + gen gehen; **boarder** *n* Pensionsgast *m*, Internatsschüler(in) *m(f)*; **board game** *n* Brettspiel *nt*; **boarding card, boarding pass** *n* Bordkarte *f*, Einsteigekarte *f*; **boarding school** *n* Internat *nt*; **board meeting** *n* Vorstandssitzung *f*; **boardroom** *n* Sitzungssaal *m* (des Vorstands)

boast 1. *vi* prahlen (about mit) **2.** *n* Prahlerei *f*

boat *n* Boot *nt*; (ship) Schiff *nt*; **boatman** *n* (hirer) Bootsverleiher *m*; **boat race** *n* Regatta *f*

bob(sleigh) *n* Bob *m*

bodily 1. *adj* körperlich **2.** *adv* (forcibly) gewaltsam; **body** *n* Körper *m*; (dead) Leiche *f*; (of car) Karosserie *f*; **body-building** *nt* Bodybuilding *nt*; **bodyguard** *n* Leibwächter *m*; (group) Leibwache *f*; **body jewellery** *n* Intimschmuck *m*; **body odour** *n*

Körpergeruch *m*; **body piercing** *n* Piercing *nt*; **bodywork** *n* Karosserie *f*

boil 1. *vt, vi* kochen **2.** *n* MED Geschwür *nt*; **boiler** *n* Boiler *m*; **boiling** *adj* (*water etc*) kochend (*heiß*); **I was ~ (***hot***)** mir war fürchterlich heiß; (*with rage*) ich kochte vor Wut; **boiling point** *n* Siedepunkt *m*

bold *adj* kühn, mutig; (*colours*) kräftig; (*type*) fett

Bolivia *n* Bolivien *nt*

bomb 1. *n* Bombe *f* **2.** *vt* bombardieren

bond *n* (*link*) Bindung *f*

bone *n* Knochen *m*; (*of fish*) Gräte *f*

boner *n* (*US*) *fam* Schnitzer *m*; (*erection*) Ständer *m*

bonfire *n* Feuer *nt* (im Freien)

bonnet *n* (*Brit*) AUTO Haube *f*; (*for baby*) Häubchen *nt*

bonny *adj* (*esp Scot*) hübsch

bonus *n* Bonus *m*, Prämie *f*

boo 1. *n* auspfeifen **2.** *vi* buhen **3.** *n* Buhruf *m*

book 1. *n* Buch *nt*; (*of tickets, stamps*) Heft *nt* **2.** *vt* (*ticket etc*) bestellen; (*hotel, flight etc*) buchen; **fully ~ed (up)** ausgebucht; (*performance*) ausverkauft; **be ~ed in** eintragen; **be ~ed in at a hotel** ein Zimmer in einem Hotel bestellt haben; **bookable** *adj* im Vorverkauf erhältlich; **bookcase** *n* Bücherregal *nt*;

booking *n* Buchung *f*; **booking office** *n* RAIL Fahrkartenschalter *m*; THEAT Vorverkaufsstelle *f*; **booklet** *n* Broschüre *f*; **bookmark** *n a.* IT Lesezeichen *nt*; **bookshelf** *n* Bücherbord *nt*; **bookshelves** Bücherregal *nt*; **bookshop**, **bookstore** *n* (*esp US*) Buchhandlung *f*

boom 1. *n* (*of business*) Boom *m*; (*noise*) Dröhnen *nt* **2.** *vi* (*business*) boomen; *fam* florieren

boomerang *n* Bumerang *m*

boost 1. *n* Auftrieb *m* **2.** *vt* (*production, sales*) ankurbeln; (*power, profits etc*) steigern; **booster** (*injection*) *n* Wiederholungsimpfung *f*

boot 1. *n* Stiefel *m*; (*Brit*) AUTO Kofferraum *m* **2.** *vt* IT laden, booten

booth *n* (*at fair etc*) Bude *f*; (*at trade fair etc*) Stand *m*

booze 1. *n fam* Alkohol *m* **2.** *vi fam* saufen

border *n* (*edge*) Rand *m*; **north / south of the Border** (*Brit*) in Schottland / England; **borderline** *n* Grenze *f*

bore 1. *pt of* **bear 2.** *vt* (*hole etc*) bohren; (*person*) langweilen **3.** *n* (*person*) Langweiler(in) *m(f)*; (*thing*) langweilige Sache; **bored** *adj* **be ~** sich langweilen; **boredom** *n* Langeweile *f*; **boring** *adj* langweilig

born adj he was ~ in London er ist in London geboren

borne pp of bear

borough n Stadtbezirk m

borrow vt borgen

Bosnia-Herzegovina n Bosnien-Herzegowina nt; **Bosnian 1.** adj bosnisch **2.** n Bosnier(in) m(f)

boss n Chef(in) m(f), Boss m

botanical adj botanisch; ~ **garden(s)** botanischer Garten

both 1. adj ~ **the books** beide Bücher **2.** pron (people) beide; (things) beides; ~ (**of**) **the boys** beide Jungs; **I like** ~ **of them** ich mag sie (alle) beide **3.** adv ~ **X and Y** sowohl X als auch Y

bother 1. vt ärgern, belästigen; **it doesn't** ~ **me** das stört mich nicht; **he can't be** ~**ed with details** mit Details gibt er sich nicht ab; **I'm not** ~**ed** das ist mir egal **2.** vi kümmern (about um); **don't** ~ (das ist) nicht nötig, lass es! **3.** n (trouble) Mühe f; (annoyance) Ärger m

bottle 1. n (of container) Flasche f **2.** vt (in Flaschen) abfüllen; **bottle bank** n Altglascontainer m; **bottled** adj in Flaschen; ~ **beer** Flaschenbier n; **bottleneck** n fig Engpass m; **bottle opener** n Flaschenöffner m

bottom 1. n (of container) Boden m; (underside) Untersei-

te f; fam (of person) Po m; **at the** ~ **of the sea / table / page** auf dem Meeresgrund / am Tabellenende / unten auf der Seite **2.** adj unterste(r, s); **be** ~ **of the class / league** Klassenletzte(r) / Tabellenletzte(r) sein; ~ **gear** AUTO erster Gang

bought pt, pp of **buy**

bounce vi (ball) springen, aufprallen; ~ **up and down** (person) herumhüpfen

bouncy adj (ball) gut springend; (person) munter; **bouncy castle**® n Hüpfburg f

bound 1. pt, pp of **bind 2.** adj (tied up) gebunden; (obliged) verpflichtet; **be** ~ **to do sth** (sure to) etw bestimmt tun (werden); (have to) etw tun müssen; **it's** ~ **to happen** es muss so kommen; **be** ~ **for ...** auf dem Weg nach ... sein; **boundary** n Grenze f

bouquet n (flowers) Strauß m; (of wine) Blume f

bow 1. n (ribbon) Schleife f; (instrument, weapon) Bogen m **2.** vi sich verbeugen **3.** n (with head) Verbeugung f; (of ship) Bug m

bowels npl Darm m

bowl 1. n (basin) Schüssel f; (shallow) Schale f; (for animal) Napf m **2.** vt, vi (in cricket) werfen

bowling n Kegeln nt; bowling

break

alley n Kegelbahn f; **bowling green** n Rasen m zum Bowling-Spiel; **bowls** nsing (game) Bowling-Spiel n

bow tie n Fliege f

box n Schachtel f; (cardboard) Karton m; (bigger) Kasten m; (space on form) Kästchen nt; THEAT Loge f; **boxer** n Boxer(in) m(f); **boxers, boxer shorts** npl Boxershorts pl; **boxing** n SPORT Boxen nt; **Boxing Day** n zweiter Weihnachtsfeiertag; **boxing gloves** npl Boxhandschuhe pl; **box office** n Kasse f

boy n Junge m

boycott 1. n Boykott m 2. vt boykottieren

boyfriend n (fester) Freund m; **boy scout** n Pfadfinder m

bra n BH m

brace n TECH Strebe f; (on teeth) Spange f

bracelet n Armband nt

braces npl (Brit) Hosenträger pl

bracket 1. n (in text) Klammer f; TECH Träger m 2. vt einklammern

brag vi angeben

brain n ANAT Gehirn nt; (mind) Verstand m; (intelligence) Grips m; **brainy** adj schlau, clever

brake 1. n Bremse f 2. vi bremsen; **brake fluid** n Bremsflüssigkeit f; **brake light** n Bremslicht nt; **brake pedal** n Bremspedal nt

branch n (of tree) Ast m; (of family, subject) Zweig m; (of firm) Filiale f, Zweigstelle f; **branch off** vi (road) abzweigen

brand n COMM Marke f

brand-new adj (funkel)nagelneu

brandy n Weinbrand m

brass n Messing nt; (Brit fam (money) Knete f; **brass band** n Blaskapelle f

brave adj tapfer, mutig

brawn n (strength) Muskelkraft f; GASTR Sülze f; **brawny** adj muskulös

Brazil n Brasilien nt; **Brazilian** 1. adj brasilianisch 2. n Brasilianer(in) m(f); **brazil nut** n Paranuss f

bread n Brot nt; **breadbin** (Brit), **breadbox** (US) n Brotkasten m; **breadcrumbs** npl Brotkrumen pl; GASTR Paniermehl nt; **breaded** adj paniert; **breadknife** n Brotmesser nt

breadth n Breite f

break 1. n (fracture) Bruch m; (rest) Pause f; (short holiday) Kurzurlaub m; *give me a ~* hör auf damit! 2. vt (fracture) brechen; (in pieces) zerbrechen; (toy, device) kaputtmachen; (promise) nicht halten; (silence) brechen; (law) verletzen; (news) mitteilen (to sb jdm); *I broke my leg* ich habe mir das Bein gebrochen; *he broke it to her* *gently* er hat es ihr schonend beigebracht **3.** *vi* (*come apart*) (auseinander) brechen; (*in pieces*) zerbrechen; (*toy, device*) kaputtgehen; (*day, dawn*) anbrechen; (*news*) bekannt werden; **break down** *vi* (*car*) eine Panne haben; (*machine*) versagen; (*person*) zusammenbrechen; **break in** *vi* (*burglar*) einbrechen; **break into** *vt* einbrechen in + *acc*; **break off** *vi*, *vt* abbrechen; **break out** *vi* ausbrechen; **~ in a rash** einen Ausschlag bekommen; **break up 1.** *vi* aufbrechen; (*meeting, organisation*) sich auflösen; (*marriage*) in die Brüche gehen; (*couple*) sich trennen; **school breaks up on Friday** am Freitag beginnen die Ferien **2.** *vt* aufbrechen; (*marriage*) zerstören; (*meeting*) auflösen; **breakable** *adj* zerbrechlich; **breakdown** *n* (*of car*) Panne *f*; (*of machine*) Störung *f*; (*of person, relations, system*) Zusammenbruch *m*; **breakdown service** *n* Pannendienst *m*; **breakdown truck** *n* Abschleppwagen *m*

breakfast *n* Frühstück *nt*; **have ~** frühstücken

break-in *n* Einbruch *m*; **breakup** *n* (*of meeting, organisation*) Auflösung *f*; (*of marriage*) Zerrüttung *f*

breast *n* Brust *f*; **breastfeed** *vt* stillen; **breaststroke** *n* Brustschwimmen *nt*

breath *n* Atem *m*; **out of ~** außer Atem; **breathalyse** *vt* (ins Röhrchen) blasen lassen; **breathalyser** *n* Promillemesser *m*; **breathe** *vt*, *vi* atmen; **breathe in** *vt*, *vi* einatmen; **breathe out** *vt*, *vi* ausatmen; **breathless** *adj* atemlos; **breath-taking** *adj* atemberaubend

bred *pt*, *pp* of **breed**

breed 1. *n* (*race*) Rasse *f* **2.** *vi* sich vermehren **3.** *vt* züchten; **breeder** *n* Züchter(in) *m(f)*; *fam* Hetero *m*; **breeding** *n* (*of animals*) Züchtung *f*

breeze *n* Brise *f*

brevity *n* Kürze *f*

brew 1. *vt* (*beer*) brauen; (*tea*) kochen; **brewery** *n* Brauerei *f*

bribe 1. *n* Bestechungsgeld *nt* **2.** *vt* bestechen; **bribery** *n* Bestechung *f*

brick *n* Backstein *m*; **bricklayer** *n* Maurer(in) *m(f)*

bride *n* Braut *f*; **bridegroom** *n* Bräutigam *m*; **bridesmaid** *n* Brautjungfer *f*

bridge *n* Brücke *f*, Bridge *nt*

brief 1. *adj* kurz **2.** *vt* instruieren (*on* über + *acc*)

briefcase *n* Aktentasche *f*

briefs *npl* Slip *m*

bright *adj* hell; (*colour*) leuchtend; (*cheerful*) heiter; (*intelligent*) intelligent; (*idea*) glänzend; **brighten up 1.** vt aufhellen; (*person*) aufheitern **2.** vi sich aufheitern; (*person*) fröhlicher werden

brilliant adj (*sunshine, colour*) strahlend; (*person*) brillant; (*idea*) glänzend; (*Brit*) fam **it was ~** es war fantastisch

brim n Rand m

bring vt bringen; (*with one*) mitbringen; **bring about** vt herbeiführen, bewirken; **bring back** vt zurückbringen; (*memories*) wecken; **bring down** vt (*reduce*) senken; (*government etc*) zu Fall bringen; **bring in** vt hereinbringen; (*introduce*) einführen; **bring out** vt herausbringen; **bring up** vt (*child*) aufziehen; (*question*) zur Sprache bringen

bristle n Borste f

Brit n fam Brite m, Britin f; **Britain** n Großbritannien nt; **British 1.** adj britisch; **the ~ Isles** pl die Britischen Inseln pl **2.** n **the ~** pl die Briten pl

brittle adj spröde

broad adj breit; (*accent*) stark; **in ~ daylight** am helllichten Tag

B road n (*Brit*) ≈ Landstraße f

broadcast 1. n Sendung f **2.** irr vt, vi senden; (*event*) übertragen

broaden vt **~ the mind** den

Horizont erweitern; **broad- -minded** adj tolerant

broccoli n Brokkoli pl

brochure n Prospekt m, Broschüre f

broke 1. pt of **break 2.** adj (*Brit*) fam pleite; **broken** pp of **break**; **broken-heart- ed** adj untröstlich

broker n Makler(in) m(f)

bronchitis n Bronchitis f

brooch n Brosche f

broom n Besen m

Bros abbr = **brothers**, Gebr.

broth n Fleischbrühe f

brothel n Bordell nt

brother n Bruder m; **~s** pl COMM Gebrüder pl; **broth- er-in-law** n Schwager m

brought pt, pp of **bring**

brow n (*eyebrow*) (Augen-) braue f; (*forehead*) Stirn f

brown adj braun; **brown bread** n Mischbrot nt; (*wholemeal*) Vollkornbrot nt; **brownie** n GASTR Brownie m; (*Brit*) junge Pfadfinderin; **brown paper** n Packpapier nt; **brown rice** n Naturreis m; **brown sugar** n brauner Zucker

browse vi (*in book*) blättern; (*in shop*) herumschauen; **browser** n IT Browser m

bruise 1. n blauer Fleck **2.** vt **~ one's arm** sich dat einen blauen Fleck (am Arm) holen

brush 1. n Bürste f; (*for sweeping*) Handbesen m;

(*for painting*) Pinsel *m* **2.** *vt* bürsten; (*sweep*) fegen; **~ one's teeth** sich *dat* die Zähne putzen; **brush up** (*French etc*) auffrischen

Brussels sprouts *npl* Rosenkohl *m*, Kohlsprossen *pl*

brutality *n* Brutalität *f*

BSc *abbr* = **Bachelor of Science**

BSE *abbr* = **bovine spongiform encephalopathy**; BSE *f*

bubble *n* Blase *f*; **bubble bath** *n* Schaumbad *nt*; **bubbly 1.** *adj* sprudelnd; (*person*) temperamentvoll **2.** *n fam* Schampus *m*

buck *n* (*animal*) Bock *m*; (*US*) *fam* Dollar *m*

bucket *n* Eimer *m*

buckle 1. *n* Schnalle *f* **2.** *vi* TECH sich verbiegen **3.** *vt* zuschnallen

bud *n* Knospe *f*

Buddhism *n* Buddhismus *m*; **Buddhist 1.** *adj* buddhistisch **2.** *n* Buddhist(in) *m(f)*

buddy *n fam* Kumpel *m*

budgie *n fam* Wellensittich *m*

buffalo *n* Büffel *m*

buffet *n* (*food*) (kaltes) Büfett *nt*

bug 1. *n* IT Bug *m*, Programmfehler *m*; (*listening device*) Wanze *f*; (*US*, *insect*) Insekt *nt*; *fam* (*illness*) Infektion *f* **2.** *vt fam* nerven

bugger 1. *n vulg* Scheißkerl *m* **2.** *interj vulg* Scheiße *f*; **bug-**

ger off *vi* (*Brit*) *vulg* abhauen, Leine ziehen

buggy *n* (*for baby*) Buggy® *m*; (*US*, *pram*) Kinderwagen *m*

build *vt* bauen; **build up** *vt* aufbauen; **building** *n* Gebäude *nt*; **building site** *n* Baustelle *f*

built *pt*, *pp of* **build**; **built-in** *adj* (*cupboard*) Einbau-, eingebaut

bulb *n* BOT (Blumen)zwiebel *f*; ELEC Glühbirne *f*

Bulgaria *n* Bulgarien *nt*; **Bulgarian 1.** *adj* bulgarisch **2.** *n* (*person*) Bulgare *m*, Bulgarin *f*; (*language*) Bulgarisch *nt*

bulimia *n* Bulimie *f*

bulk *n* (*size*) Größe *f*; (*greater part*) Großteil *m* (*of* + *gen*); **in ~ en** gros; **bulky** *adj* (*goods*) sperrig; (*person*) stämmig

bull *n* Stier *m*; **bulldog** *n* Bulldogge *f*; **bulldoze** *vt* planieren; **bulldozer** *n* Planierraupe *f*

bullet *n* Kugel *f*

bulletin *n* Bulletin *nt*; (*announcement*) Bekanntmachung *f*; MED Krankenbericht *m*; **bulletin board** *n* (*US*) IT schwarzes Brett

bullshit *n fam* Scheiß *m*

bully *n* Tyrann *m*

bum *n fam* (*Brit*, *backside*) Po *m*; (*US*, *vagrant*) Penner *m*

bumblebee *n* Hummel *f*

bump 1. *n fam* (*swelling*) Beule *f*; (*road*) Unebenheit *f*;

(*blow*) Stoß *m* **2.** *vt* stoßen; **~ one's head** sich *dat* den Kopf anschlagen (*on* an + *dat*); **bump into** stoßen gegen; *fam* (*meet*) (zufällig) begegnen + *dat*; **bumper 1.** *n* AUTO Stoßstange *f* **2.** *adj* (*edition etc*) Riesen-; (*crop etc*) Rekord-; **bumpy** *adj* holp(e)rig

bun *n* süßes Brötchen

bunch *n* (*of flowers*) Strauß *m*; *fam* (*of people*) Haufen *m*; **~ of keys** Schlüsselbund *m*

bundle *n* Bündel *nt*

bungee jumping *n* Bungeejumping *nt*

bunk *n* Koje *f*; **bunk bed(s)** *n*(*pl*) Etagenbett *nt*

bunker *n* Bunker *m*

bunny *n* Häschen *nt*

buoy *n* Boje *f*; **buoyant** *adj* (*floating*) schwimmend

burden *n* Last *f*

bureau *n* Büro *nt*; (*government department*) Amt *nt*; **bureaucracy** *n* Bürokratie *f*; **bureau de change** *n* Wechselstube *f*

burger *n* Hamburger *m*

burglar *n* Einbrecher(in) *m*(*f*); **burglar alarm** *n* Alarmanlage *f*; **burglarize** *vt* (*US*) einbrechen in + *acc*; **burglary** *n* Einbruch *m*; **burgle** *vt* einbrechen in + *acc*

burial *n* Beerdigung *f*

burn 1. *vt* verbrennen; (*food*,

slightly) anbrennen; **~ one's hand** sich *dat* die Hand verbrennen **2.** *vi* brennen **3.** *n* (*injury*) Brandwunde *f*; (*on material*) verbrannte Stelle

burp 1. *vi* rülpsen **2.** *vt* (*baby*) aufstoßen lassen

bursary *n* Stipendium *nt*

burst 1. *vt* platzen lassen **2.** *vi* platzen; **~ into tears** in Tränen ausbrechen

bury *vt* (*in grave*) beerdigen; (*hide*) vergraben

bus *n* Bus *m*; **bus driver** *n* Busfahrer(in) *m*(*f*)

bush *n* Busch *m*

business *n* Geschäft *nt*; (*enterprise*) Unternehmen *nt*; (*concern, affair*) Sache *f*; **I'm here on ~** ich bin geschäftlich hier; **it's none of your ~** das geht dich nichts an; **business card** *n* Visitenkarte *f*; **business class** *n* AVIAT Businessclass *f*; **business hours** *npl* Geschäftsstunden *pl*; **businessman** *n* Geschäftsmann *m*; **business studies** *npl* Betriebswirtschaftslehre *f*; **businesswoman** *n* Geschäftsfrau *f*

bus service *n* Busverbindung *f*; **bus shelter** *n* Wartehäuschen *nt*; **bus station** *n* Busbahnhof *m*; **bus stop** *n* Bushaltestelle *f*

bust 1. *n* Büste *f* **2.** *adj* (*broken*) kaputt; **go ~** Pleite gehen

busy adj beschäftigt; (street, place) belebt; (esp US, telephone) besetzt; ~ **signal** (US) Besetztzeichen nt

but 1. conj aber; (only) nur; **not this ~ that** nicht dies, sondern das **2.** prep (except) außer; **any colour ~ blue** jede Farbe, nur nicht blau; **nothing ~ ...** nichts als ...; **the last/next house ~ one** das vorletzte/übernächste Haus

butcher n Metzger(in) m(f)

butter n Butter f; **buttercup** n Butterblume f; **butterfly** n Schmetterling m

buttocks npl Gesäß nt

button 1. n Knopf m **2.** vt zuknöpfen; **buttonhole** n Knopfloch nt

buy 1. n Kauf m **2.** vt kaufen (from von); **buyer** n Käufer(in) m(f)

buzz 1. n Summen nt; **give sb a ~** fam jdn anrufen **2.** vi summen; **buzzer** n Summer m

by 1. prep (cause, author) von; (means) mit; (beside, near) bei, an; (via) durch; (before)

bis; (according to) nach; **go ~ train/bus/car** mit dem Zug/Bus/Auto fahren; **send ~ post** mit der Post® schicken; **a house ~ the river** ein Haus am or beim Fluss; **her side** neben ihr, an ihrer Seite; **leave ~ the back door** durch die Hintertür rausgehen; **~ day/night** tags/nachts; **they'll be here ~ five** bis fünf Uhr müssten sie hier sein; **judge ~ appearances** nach dem Äußeren urteilen; **rise ~ 10%** um 10% steigen; **it missed me ~ inches** es hat mich um Zentimeter verfehlt; **divided/multiplied ~ 7** dividiert durch/multipliziert mit 7; **~ oneself** allein **2.** adv (past) vorbei; **rush ~** vorbeirasen

bye-bye interj fam Wiedersehen, tschüss

by-election n Nachwahl f; **bypass** n Umgehungsstraße f; MED Bypass m; **byroad** n Nebenstraße f; **bystander** n Zuschauer(in) m(f)

byte n Byte nt

C

C abbr = **Celsius**; C

c abbr = **circa**; ca

cab n Taxi nt

cabbage n Kohl m

cabin n NAUT Kajüte f; AVIAT Passagierraum m; (wooden house) Hütte f; **cabin crew** n Flugbegleitpersonal nt

cabinet n Schrank m; (for display) Vitrine f; POL Kabinett

campus

nt

cable n ELEC Kabel nt; **cable-car** n Seilbahn f; **cable television, cablevision** (US) n Kabelfernsehen nt

cactus n Kaktus m

CAD abbr = **computer-aided design**; CAD nt

Caesarean adj ~ (**section**) Kaiserschnitt m

café n Café nt; **cafeteria** n Cafeteria f; **cafetiere** n Kaffeebereiter m

caffein(e) n Koffein nt

cage n Käfig m

Cairo n Kairo nt

cake n Kuchen m; **cake shop** n Konditorei f

calculate vt berechnen; (estimate) kalkulieren; **calculating** adj berechnend; **calculation** n (estimate) Kalkulation f; **calculator** n Taschenrechner m

calendar n Kalender m

calf n Kalb nt; ANAT Wade f

California n Kalifornien nt

call 1. vt (name, describe as) nennen; (TEL anrufen; IT, AVIAT aufrufen; **what's this ~ed?** wie heißt das? **2.** vi (shout) rufen; (for help um Hilfe); (visit) vorbeikommen; ~ **at the doctor's** beim Arzt vorbeigehen; (of train) ~ **at** in ... halten **3.** n (shout) Ruf m; TEL Anruf m; IT, AVIAT Aufruf m; **make a ~** telefonieren; **give sb a ~** jdn anrufen; **be on ~** Bereit-

schaftsdienst haben; **call back** vt, vi zurückrufen; **call for** vt (come to pick up) abholen; (demand, require) verlangen; **call off** vt absagen

call centre n Callcenter nt; **caller** n Besucher(in) m(f); TEL Anrufer(in) m(f)

calm 1. n Stille f; (also of person) Ruhe f; (of sea) Flaute f **2.** vt beruhigen **3.** adj ruhig; **calm down** vi sich beruhigen

calorie n Kalorie f

calves pl of **calf**

Cambodia n Kambodscha nt

camcorder n Camcorder m

came pt of **come**

camel n Kamel nt

camera n Fotoapparat m, Kamera f

camomile n Kamille f

camouflage n Tarnung f

camp 1. n Lager nt; (camping place) Zeltplatz m **2.** vi zelten, campen **3.** adj fam theatralisch, tuntig

campaign 1. n Kampagne f; POL Wahlkampf m **2.** vi sich einsetzen (for/against für/gegen)

campbed n Campingliege f; **camper** n (person) Camper(in) m(f); (van) Wohnmobil nt; **camping** n Zelten nt, Camping nt; **campsite** n Zeltplatz m, Campingplatz m

campus n (of university) Universitätsgelände nt, Campus m can **1.** vaux (be able) können; (permission) dürfen; I ~not or ~'t see ich kann nichts sehen; ~ I go now? darf ich jetzt gehen? **2.** n (for food, beer) Dose f; (for water, milk) Kanne f

Canada n Kanada nt; Canadian **1.** adj kanadisch **2.** n Kanadier(in) m(f)

canal n Kanal m

canary n Kanarienvogel m

cancel vt (plans) aufgeben; (meeting, event) absagen; COMM (order etc) stornieren; IT löschen; AVIAT streichen; **be ~led** (event, train, bus) ausfallen; cancellation n Absage f; COMM Stornierung f; AVIAT gestrichener Flug

cancer n MED Krebs m; Cancer n ASTR Krebs m

candid adj (person, conversation) offen

candidate n (for post) Bewerber(in) m(f); POL Kandidat(in) m(f)

candle n Kerze f; candlelight n Kerzenlicht nt; candlestick n Kerzenhalter m

candy n (US) Bonbon m; (quantity) Süßigkeiten pl; candy-floss n (Brit) Zuckerwatte f

canned adj Dosen-

cannot contr of **can not**

canoe n Kanu nt; canoeing n Kanufahren nt

can opener n Dosenöffner m

canopy n Baldachin m; (awn-ing) Markise f; (over entrance) Vordach nt

can't contr of **can not**

canteen n (in factory) Kantine f; (in university) Mensa f

canvas n (for sails, shoes) Segeltuch nt; (for tent) Zeltstoff m; (for painting) Leinwand f

canvass vi um Stimmen werben (for für)

canyon n Felsenschlucht f; canyoning n Canyoning nt

cap n Mütze f; (lid) Verschluss m, Deckel m

capability n Fähigkeit f; capable adj fähig; **be ~ of sth** zu etw fähig (or imstande) sein

capacity n (of building, container) Fassungsvermögen nt; (ability) Fähigkeit f; (function) **in his ~ as ...** in seiner Eigenschaft als ...

cape n (garment) Cape nt, Umhang m; GEO Kap nt

caper n (for cooking) Kaper f

capital n FIN (money, letter) Großbuchstabe m; ~ (city) Hauptstadt f; capitalism n Kapitalismus m; capital punishment n die Todesstrafe

Capricorn n ASTR Steinbock m

capsule n Kapsel f

captain n Kapitän m; (army) Hauptmann m

captive n Gefangene(r) mf; capture **1.** vt (person) fassen, gefangen nehmen; (town etc) einnehmen; IT (data) erfassen **2.** n Gefangennahme f; IT Erfassung f

car n Auto nt; (US) RAIL Wagen m

carambola n Sternfrucht f

caravan n Wohnwagen m; **caravan site** n Campingplatz m für Wohnwagen

caraway (seed) n Kümmel m

carbohydrate n Kohle(n)hydrat nt

car bomb n Autobombe f

carbon n Kohlenstoff m

carburettor, carburetor (US) n Vergaser m

card n Karte f; (material) Pappe f; cardboard n Pappe f; ~ **(box)** Karton m; (smaller) Pappschachtel f; **card game** n Kartenspiel m

cardiac adj Herz-

cardigan n Strickjacke f

cardphone n Kartentelefon nt

care 1. n (worry) Sorge f; (carefulness) Sorgfalt f; (looking after things, people) Pflege f; **with ~** sorgfältig; (cautiously) vorsichtig; **take ~** (watch out) vorsichtig sein; (in address) **~ of** bei; **take ~ of** sorgen für, sich kümmern um **2.** vi **I don't ~** es ist mir egal; **~ about** sth Wert auf etw acc legen; **he ~s about her** sie liegt ihm am Herzen; **care for** vt (look after) sorgen für, sich kümmern um; (like) mögen

career n Karriere f, Laufbahn f; **careers adviser** n Berufsberater(in) m(f)

carefree adj sorgenfrei; **careful, carefully** adj, adv sorgfältig; (cautious, cautiously) vorsichtig; **careless, carelessly** adj, adv nachlässig; (driving etc) leichtsinnig; (remark) unvorsichtig; **carer** n Betreuer(in) m(f), Pfleger(in) m(f); **caretaker** n Hausmeister(in) m(f); **careworker** n Pfleger(in) m(f)

car-ferry n Autofähre f

cargo n Ladung f

car hire, car hire company n Autovermietung f

Caribbean 1. n Karibik f **2.** adj karibisch

caring adj mitfühlend; (parent, partner) liebevoll; (looking after sb) fürsorglich

car insurance n Kraftfahrzeugversicherung f

carnation n Nelke f

carnival n Volksfest nt; (before Lent) Karneval m

carol n Weihnachtslied nt

carp n (fish) Karpfen m

car park n (Brit) Parkplatz m; (multi-storey car park) Parkhaus nt

carpenter n Zimmermann m

carpet n Teppich m

car phone n Autotelefon nt; **carpool 1.** n (arrangement) Fahrgemeinschaft f; (vehicles) Fuhrpark m **2.** vi eine Fahrgemeinschaft bilden; **car rental** n

Autovermietung f

carriage n (Brit) RAIL (coach) Wagen m; (compartment) Abteil nt; (horse-drawn) Kutsche f; (transport) Beförderung f; **carriageway** n (Brit, on road) Fahrbahn f

carrier n COMM Spediteur(in) m(f); **carrier bag** n Tragetasche f

carrot n Karotte f

carry vt tragen; (in vehicle) befördern; (have on one) bei sich haben; **carry on 1.** vi (continue) weitermachen **2.** vt (continue) fortführen; ~ **on working** weiter arbeiten; **carry out** vt (orders, plan) ausführen, durchführen

carrycot n Babytragetasche f

carsick adj **he gets** ~ ihm wird beim Autofahren übel

cart n Wagen m, Karren m; (US, shopping trolley) Einkaufswagen m

carton n (Papp)karton m; (of cigarettes) Stange f

cartoon n Cartoon m or nt; (one drawing) Karikatur f; (film) (Zeichen)trickfilm m

cartridge n (for film) Kassette f; (for gun, pen, printer) Patrone f; (for copier) Kartusche f

carve vt, vi (wood) schnitzen; (stone) meißeln; (meat) schneiden, tranchieren; **carving** n (in wood) Schnitzerei f; (in stone) Skulptur f, Carving nt

car wash n Autowaschanlage f

case n (crate) Kiste f; (box) Schachtel f; (for spectacles) Etui nt; LAW Fall m; **in** ~ falls; **in that** ~ in dem Fall; **in** ~ **of fire** bei Brand; **it's a** ~ **of** ... es handelt sich hier um ...

cash 1. n Bargeld nt; **in** ~ bar; ~ **on delivery** per Nachnahme **2.** vt (check / cheque) einlösen; **cash desk** n Kasse f; **cash dispenser** n Geldautomat m; **cashier** n Kassierer(in) m(f); **cash machine** n (Brit) Geldautomat m

cashmere n Kaschmirwolle f

cash payment n Barzahlung f; **cashpoint** n (Brit) Geldautomat m

casing n Gehäuse nt

casino n Kasino nt

cask n Fass nt

casserole n Kasserole f; (food) Schmortopf m

cassette n Kassette f; **cassette recorder** n Kassettenrecorder m

cast 1. vt (throw) werfen; THEAT, FILM besetzen; (roles) verteilen **2.** n THEAT, FILM Besetzung f; MED Gipsverband m

caster n ~ **sugar** Streuzucker m

castle n Burg f

casual adj (arrangement, remark) beiläufig; (attitude, manner) (nach)lässig, zwanglos; (dress) leger; (work, earnings) Gelegenheits-; (look, glance) flüchtig; ~ wear Freizeitkleidung f; ~ sex Gelegenheitssex m; casually adv (remark, say) beiläufig; (meet) zwanglos; (dressed) leger

casualty n Verletzte(r) mf; (dead) Tote(r) mf; (department in hospital) Notaufnahme f

cat n Katze f; (male) Kater m

catalog (US), catalogue n Katalog m

cataract n Wasserfall m; MED grauer Star

catarrh n Katarr(h) m

catastrophe n Katastrophe f

catch 1. n (fish etc) Fang m 2. vt fangen; (thief) fassen; (train, bus etc) nehmen; (not miss) erreichen; ~ a cold sich erkälten; ~ fire Feuer fangen; I didn't ~ that das habe ich nicht mitgekriegt; catch up vt, vi ~ with sb jdn einholen; ~ on sth etw nachholen; catching adj ansteckend

category n Kategorie f

cater vi die Speisen und Getränke liefern (for für); cater for vt (have facilities for) eingestellt sein auf + acc; catering n Versorgung f mit Speisen und Getränken, Gastronomie f; catering service n Partyservice m

caterpillar n Raupe f

cathedral n Kathedrale f, Dom m

Catholic 1. adj katholisch 2. Katholik(in) m(f)

cat nap n (Brit) kurzer Schlaf; cat's eyes npl (in road) Katzenaugen pl, Reflektoren pl

catsup n (US) Ketschup nt or m

cattle npl Vieh nt

caught pt, pp of catch

cauliflower n Blumenkohl m; cauliflower cheese n Blumenkohl m in Käsesoße

cause 1. n (origin) Ursache f (of für); (reason) Grund m (for zu); (purpose) Sache f; for a good ~ für wohltätige Zwecke; no ~ for alarm/complaint kein Grund zur Aufregung/Klage 2. vt verursachen

causeway n Damm m

caution 1. n Vorsicht f; LAW, SPORT Verwarnung f 2. vt (ver)warnen; cautious adj vorsichtig

cave n Höhle f

cavity n Hohlraum m; (in tooth) Loch nt

cayenne (pepper) n Cayennepfeffer m

CCTV abbr = closed circuit television; Videoüberwachungsanlage f

CD abbr = Compact Disc; CD f; CD player n CD-Spieler m; CD-ROM abbr = Compact Disc Read Only Memory; CD-ROM f cease 1. *vi* aufhören 2. *vt* beenden; **~ doing sth** aufhören, etw zu tun; cease fire *n* Waffenstillstand *m*

ceiling *n* Decke *f*

celebrate *vt*, *vi* feiern; celebrated *adj* gefeiert; celebration *n* Feier *f*; celebrity *n* Berühmtheit *f*, Star *m*

celeriac *n* (Knollen)sellerie *m or f*; celery *n* (Stangen)sellerie *m or f*

cell *n* Zelle *f*; (*US*) → **cellphone**

cellar *n* Keller *m*

cello *n* Cello *nt*

cellphone, cellular phone *n* Mobiltelefon *nt*, Handy *nt*

Celt *n* Kelte *m*, Keltin *f*; Celtic 1. *adj* keltisch 2. *n* (*language*) Keltisch *nt*

cement *n* Zement *m*

cemetery *n* Friedhof *m*

cent *n* (*of dollar, euro etc*) Cent *m*

center *n* (*US*) → **centre**

centiliter (*US*), centilitre *n* Zentiliter *m*; centimeter (*US*), centimetre *n* Zentimeter *m*

central *adj* zentral; Central America *n* Mittelamerika *nt*; Central Europe *n* Mitteleuropa *nt*; central heating *n* Zentralheizung *f*; centralize *vt* zentralisieren; central locking *n* AUTO Zentralverriegelung *f*; central reservation *n* (*Brit*) Mittelstreifen *m*; central station *n* Haupt-

bahnhof *m*

centre 1. *n* Mitte *f*; (*building, of city*) Zentrum *nt* 2. *vt* zentrieren; centre forward *n* SPORT Mittelstürmer *m*

century *n* Jahrhundert *nt*

ceramic *adj* keramisch

cereal *n* (*any grain*) Getreide *nt*; (*breakfast cereal*) Frühstücksflocken *pl*

ceremony *n* Feier *f*, Zeremonie *f*

certain *adj* sicher (*of + gen*); (*particular*) bestimmt; **for ~** mit Sicherheit; certainly *adv* sicher; (*without doubt*) bestimmt; **~! aber sicher!; ~ not** ganz bestimmt nicht!

certificate *n* Bescheinigung *f*; (*in school, of qualification*) Zeugnis *nt*; certify *vt*, *vi* bescheinigen

cervical smear *n* Abstrich *m*

CFC *abbr* → **chlorofluorocarbon**; FCKW *nt*

chain 1. *n* Kette *f* 2. *vt* **~ (up)** anketten

chair *n* Stuhl *m*; (*university*) Lehrstuhl *m*; (*armchair*) Sessel *m*; (*chairperson*) Vorsitzende(r) *mf*; chairlift *n* Sessellift *m*; chairman *n* Vorsitzende(r) *m*; (*of firm*) Präsident *m*; chairperson *n* Vorsitzende(r) *mf*; (*of firm*) Präsident(in) *m(f)*; chairwoman *n* Vorsitzende *f*; (*of firm*) Präsidentin *f*

chalet *n* (*in mountains*) Berghütte *f*; (*holiday dwelling*)

Ferienhäuschen nt

chalk n Kreide f

challenge 1. n Herausforderung f 2. vt (person) herausfordern; (statement) bestreiten

chambermaid n Zimmermädchen nt

champagne n Champagner m

champion n SPORT Meister(in) m(f); championship n Meisterschaft f; Champions League n Champions League f

chance n (fate) Zufall m; (possibility) Möglichkeit f; (opportunity) Gelegenheit f; (risk) Risiko nt; by ~ zufällig; he doesn't stand a ~ (of winning) er hat keinerlei Chance(, zu gewinnen)

chancellor n Kanzler(in) m(f)

chandelier n Kronleuchter m

change 1. vt verändern; (alter) ändern; (money, wheel, nappy) wechseln; (exchange) (um)tauschen; ~ one's clothes umziehen; ~ trains umsteigen; ~ gear AUTO schalten 2. vi sich ändern; (esp outwardly) sich verändern; (get changed) sich umziehen 3. n Veränderung f; (alteration) Änderung f; (money) Wechselgeld nt; (coins) Kleingeld nt; for a ~ zur Abwechslung; can you give me ~ for £10? können

Sie mir auf 10 Pfund herausgeben?; change down vi (Brit) AUTO herunterschalten; change over vi sich umstellen (to auf + acc); change up vi (Brit) AUTO hochschalten

changeable adj (weather) veränderlich, wechselhaft; change machine n Geldwechsler m; changing room n Umkleideraum m

channel n Kanal m; RADIO, TV Kanal m, Sender m; the (English) Channel der Ärmelkanal; the Channel Islands die Kanalinseln; channel-hopping n Zappen nt

chaos n Chaos nt; chaotic adj chaotisch

chap n (Brit) fam Bursche m, Kerl m

chapel n Kapelle f

chapped adj (lips) aufgesprungen

chapter n Kapitel nt

character n Charakter m, Wesen nt; (in a play, novel etc) Figur f; TYPO Zeichen nt; he's a real ~ er ist ein echtes Original; characteristic n typisches Merkmal

charcoal n Holzkohle f

charge 1. n (cost) Gebühr f; LAW Anklage f; free of ~ gratis, kostenlos; be ~ verantwortlich sein für 2. vt (money) verlangen; LAW anklagen; (battery) laden

charity n (*institution*) wohltätige Organisation f; *a collection for* ~ eine Sammlung für wohltätige Zwecke; charity shop n Geschäft einer 'charity', in dem freiwillige Helfer gebrauchte Kleidung, Bücher etc verkaufen

charm 1. n Charme m 2. vt bezaubern; charming adj reizend, charmant

chart 1. n Diagramm nt; (*map*) Karte f; *the* ~*s* pl die Charts, die Hitliste

charter 1. n Urkunde f 2. vt NAUT, AVIAT chartern; charter flight n Charterflug m

chase 1. vt jagen, verfolgen 2. n Verfolgungsjagd f; (*hunt*) Jagd f

chassis n AUTO Fahrgestell nt

chat 1. vi plaudern; IT chatten 2. n Plauderei f; chat up vt anmachen, anbaggern; chatroom n IT Chatroom m; chat show n Talkshow f

chauffeur n Chauffeur(in) m(f), Fahrer(in) m(f)

cheap adj billig; (*of poor quality*) minderwertig

cheat vt, vi betrügen; (*in school, game*) mogeln

Chechnya n Tschetschenien nt

check1 1. vt (*examine*) überprüfen (*for* auf + acc); TECH (*adjustment etc*) kontrollieren; (*US, tick*) abhaken; AVIAT (*luggage*) einchecken; (*US, coat*) abgeben 2. n (*examina-*

tion, restraint) Kontrolle f; (*US, restaurant bill*) Rechnung f; (*pattern*) Karo(muster) nt; (*US*) → *cheque*; check in vt, vi AVIAT einchecken; (*into hotel*) sich anmelden; check out vi sich abmelden, auschecken; check up vi nachprüfen; ~ *on sb* Nachforschungen über jdn anstellen

checkers nsing (*US*) Damespiel nt

check-in n (*airport*) Check-in m; (*hotel*) Anmeldung f; check-in desk n Abfertigungsschalter m; checking account n (*US*) Scheckkonto nt; check list n Kontrollliste f; checkout n (*supermarket*) Kasse f; checkout time n (*hotel*) Abreise(zeit) f; checkpoint n Kontrollpunkt m; checkroom n (*US*) Gepäckaufbewahrung f; checkup n MED (ärztliche) Untersuchung

cheddar n Cheddarkäse m

cheek n Backe f, Wange f; (*insolence*) Frechheit f; *what a* ~ so eine Frechheit!; cheekbone n Backenknochen m; cheeky adj frech

cheer 1. n Beifallsruf m; ~*s* (*when drinking*) prost!; (*Brit fam*) (*thanks*) danke; (*Brit, goodbye*) tschüs 2. vt zujubeln + dat 3. vi jubeln; cheer up 1. vt aufmuntern 2. vi fröhlicher werden;

cheerful *adj* fröhlich

cheese *n* Käse *m*; cheeseboard *n* Käsebrett *nt*; (*as course*) (gemischte) Käseplatte; cheesecake *n* Käsekuchen *m*

chef *n* Koch *m*; (*in charge of kitchen*) Küchenchef(in) *m(f)*

chemical 1. *adj* chemisch 2. Chemikalie *f*; chemist *n* (*pharmacist*) Apotheker(in) *m(f)*; (*industrial chemist*) Chemiker(in) *m(f)*; **~'s (shop)** Apotheke *f*; chemistry *n* Chemie *f*

cheque *n* (*Brit*) Scheck *m*; cheque account *n* (*Brit*) Girokonto *nt*; cheque book *n* (*Brit*) Scheckheft *nt*; cheque card *n* (*Brit*) Scheckkarte *f*

chequered *adj* kariert

cherish *vt* (*look after*) liebevoll sorgen für; (*hope*) hegen; (*memory*) bewahren

cherry *n* Kirsche *f*; cherry tomato *n* Kirschtomate *f*

chess *n* Schach *nt*; chessboard *n* Schachbrett *nt*

chest *n* Brust *f*; (*box*) Kiste *f*; **~ of drawers** Kommode *f*

chestnut *n* Kastanie *f*

chew *vt*, *vi* kauen; chewing gum *n* Kaugummi *m*

chick *n* Küken *nt*; chicken *n* Huhn *nt*; (*food: roast*) Hähnchen *nt*; (*coward*) Feigling *m*; chicken breast *n* Hühnerbrust *f*; chicken Kiev *n* paniertes Hähnchen, mit

Knoblauchbutter gefüllt; chickenpox *n* Windpocken *pl*; chickpea *n* Kichererbse *f*

chicory *n* Chicorée *f*

chief 1. *n* (*of department etc*) Leiter(in) *m(f)*; (*boss*) Chef(in) *m(f)*; (*of tribe*) Häuptling *m* 2. *adj* Haupt-; chiefly *adv* hauptsächlich

child *n* Kind *nt*; child allowance, child benefit (*Brit*) *n* Kindergeld *nt*; childhood *n* Kindheit *f*; childish *adj* kindisch; child lock *n* Kindersicherung *f*; childproof *adj* kindersicher; children *pl* of **child**; child seat *n* Kindersitz *m*

Chile *n* Chile *nt*

chill 1. *n* Kühle *f*; MED Erkältung *f* 2. *vt* (*wine*) kühlen; chill out *vi fam* relaxen; chilled *adj* gekühlt

chilli *n* Pepperoni *pl*; (*spice*) Chili *m*; chilli con carne *n* Chili con carne *nt*

chilly *adj* kühl, frostig

chimney *n* Schornstein *m*; chimneysweep *n* Schornsteinfeger(in) *m(f)*

chimpanzee *n* Schimpanse *m*

chin *n* Kinn *nt*

china *n* Porzellan *nt*

China *n* China *nt*; Chinese 1. *adj* chinesisch 2. *n* (*person*) Chinese *m*, Chinesin *f*; (*language*) Chinesisch *nt*; Chinese leaves *npl* Chinakohl *m*

chip 1. *n* (*of wood etc*) Splitter

m; (damage) angeschlagene Stelle; IT Chip m; ~s (Brit, potatoes) Pommes frites pl; (US, crisps) Kartoffelchips pl 2. vt anschlagen, beschädigen; chippie fam, chip shop n Frittenbude f

chiropodist n Fußpfleger(in) m(f)

chirp vi zwitschern

chisel n Meißel m

chives npl Schnittlauch m

chlorine n Chlor nt

chocaholic, chocoholic n Schokoladenfreak m; choc- -ice n Eis nt mit Schokoladenüberzug; chocolate n Schokolade f; (chocolate- -coated sweet) Praline f; **a bar of ~** eine Tafel Schokolade; **a box of ~s** eine Schachtel Pralinen; chocolate cake n Schokoladenkuchen m

choice 1. n Wahl f; (selection) Auswahl f 2. adj auserlesen; (product) Qualitäts-

choir n Chor m

choke 1. vi sich verschlucken; SPORT die Nerven verlieren 2. vt erdrosseln 3. n AUTO Choke m

cholera n Cholera f

cholesterol n Cholesterin nt

choose vt wählen; (pick out) sich aussuchen; **there are three to ~ from** es stehen drei zur Auswahl

chop 1. vt (zer)hacken; (meat etc) klein schneiden 2. n (meat) Kotelett nt; **get the**

~ gefeuert werden; chopsticks npl Essstäbchen pl

chorus n Chor m; (in song) Refrain m

chose, chosen pt, pp of **choose**

chowder n (US) dicke Suppe mit Meeresfrüchten

christen vt taufen; christening n Taufe f; Christian 1. adj christlich 2. n Christ(in) m(f); Christian name n (Brit) Vorname m

Christmas n Weihnachten pl; Christmas card n Weihnachtskarte f; Christmas carol n Weihnachtslied nt; Christmas Day n der erste Weihnachtstag; Christmas Eve n Heiligabend m; Christmas pudding n Plumpudding m; Christmas tree n Weihnachtsbaum m

chronic adj MED chronisch

chubby adj (child) pummelig; (adult) rundlich

chuck vt fam schmeißen; chuck in vt fam (job) hinschmeißen; chuck out vt fam rausschmeißen; chuck up vi fam kotzen

chunk n Klumpen m; (of bread) Brocken m; (of meat) Batzen m; chunky adj (person) stämmig

Chunnel n fam Kanaltunnel m

church n Kirche f; churchyard n Kirchhof m

chute n Rutsche f

clam chowder

chutney n Chutney m
CIA abbr = **Central Intelligence Agency**; (US) CIA f
CID abbr = **Criminal Investigation Department**; (Brit) ≈ Kripo f
cider n ≈ Apfelmost m
cigar n Zigarre f; cigarette n Zigarette f
cinema n Kino nt
cinnamon n Zimt m
circa prep circa
circle 1. n Kreis m 2. vi kreisen; circuit n Rundfahrt f; (on foot) Rundgang m; (for racing) Rennstrecke f; ELEC Stromkreis m; circular 1. adj (kreis)rund, kreisförmig f 2. n Rundschreiben nt; circulation n (of blood) Kreislauf m; (of newspaper) Auflage f
circumstances npl (facts) Umstände pl; (financial condition) Verhältnisse pl; in/ under the ~ unter den Umständen; under no ~ auf keinen Fall
circus n Zirkus m
cissy n fam Weichling m
cistern n Zisterne f; (of WC) Spülkasten m
cite vt zitieren
citizen n Bürger(in) m(f); (of nation) Staatsangehörige(r) mf; citizenship n Staatsangehörigkeit f
city n Stadt f; (large) Großstadt f; the ~ (London's financial centre) die (Londo-

ner) City; city centre n Innenstadt f, Zentrum nt
civil adj (of town) Bürger-; (of state) staatsbürgerlich; (not military) zivil; civil ceremony n standesamtliche Hochzeit; civil engineering n Hoch- und Tiefbau m, Bauingenieurwesen nt; civilian n Zivilist(in) m(f); civilization n Zivilisation f, Kultur f; civilized adj zivilisiert, kultiviert; civil partnership n eingetragene Partnerschaft; civil rights npl Bürgerrechte pl; civil servant n (Staats)beamte(r) m, (Staats)beamtin f; civil service n Staatsdienst m; civil war n Bürgerkrieg m
CJD abbr = **Creutzfeld-Jakob disease**; Creutzfeld-Jakob--Krankheit f
cl abbr = **centilitre(s)**; cl
claim 1. vt beanspruchen; (apply for) beantragen; (demand) fordern; (assert) behaupten (that dass) 2. n (demand) Forderung f (for für); (right) Anspruch m (to auf + acc); ~ for damages Schadensersatzforderung f; make or put in a ~ (insurance) Ansprüche geltend machen; claimant n Antragsteller(in) m(f)
clam n Venusmuschel f; clam chowder n (US) dicke Muschelsuppe (mit Sellerie, Zwiebeln etc)

clap vi (Beifall) klatschen
claret n roter Bordeaux(wein)
clarify vt klären
clash 1. vi (physically) zusammenstoßen (with mit); (argue) sich auseinandersetzen (with mit); fig (colours) sich beißen **2.** n Zusammenstoß m; (argument) Auseinandersetzung f
class 1. n Klasse f **2.** vt einordnen, einstufen
classic 1. adj (mistake, example etc) klassisch **2.** n Klassiker m; (music, ballet etc) klassisch
classification n Klassifizierung f; **classify** vt klassifizieren; **classified advertisement** Kleinanzeige f
classroom n Klassenzimmer nt
classy adj fam nobel, exklusiv
clause n LING Satz m; LAW Klausel f
claw n Kralle f
clay n Lehm m; (for pottery) Ton m
clean 1. adj sauber; **~ driving licence** Führerschein ohne Strafpunkte **2.** adv (completely) glatt **3.** vt sauber machen; (carpet etc) reinigen; (window, shoes, vegetables) putzen; (wound) säubern; **clean up 1.** vt aufräumen **2.** vi aufräumen (person) Putzmann m, Putzfrau f; (substance) Putzmittel nt; **~'s** (firm) Reinigung f

cleanse vt reinigen; (wound) säubern; **cleanser** n Reinigungsmittel nt
clear 1. adj klar; (distinct) deutlich; (conscience) rein; (free, road etc) frei; **be ~ about sth** sich über etw im Klaren sein **2.** adv klar; **stand ~** zurücktreten **3.** vt (road, room etc) räumen; (table) abräumen; LAW (find innocent) freisprechen (of von) **4.** vi (fog, mist) sich verziehen; (weather) aufklaren; **clear away** vt wegräumen; (dishes) abräumen; **clear off** vi fam abhauen; **clear up 1.** vi (tidy up) aufräumen; (weather) sich aufklären **2.** vt (room) aufräumen; (litter) wegräumen; (matter) klären
clearance sale n Räumungsverkauf m; **clearing** n Lichtung f; **clearly** adv klar; (speak, remember) deutlich; (obviously) eindeutig; **clearway** n (Brit) Straße f mit Halteverbot nt
clench vt (fist) ballen; (teeth) zusammenbeißen
clergyman n Geistliche(r) m
clerk n (US) (in office) Büroangestellte(r) m/f; (US, salesperson) Verkäufer(in) m(f)
clever adj schlau, klug
cliché n Klischee nt
click 1. n IT Mausklick m **2.** vi klicken; **~ on sth** IT etw anklicken; **it ~ed** fam ich hab's/er hat's etc ge-

schnallt; *they ~ed* sie haben sich gleich verstanden; **click on** *vt* IT anklicken

client *n* Kunde *m*, Kundin *f*; LAW Mandant(in) *m(f)*

cliff *n* Klippe *f*

climate *n* Klima *nt*

climax *n* Höhepunkt *m*

climb 1. *vi (person)* klettern; *(aircraft, sun)* steigen; *(road)* ansteigen **2.** *vt (mountain)* besteigen; *(tree etc)* klettern auf + *acc* **3.** *n* Aufstieg *m*; **climbing** *n* Klettern *nt*, Bergsteigen *nt*; **climbing frame** *n* Klettergerüst *nt*

cling *vi* sich klammern *(to* an + *acc)*; **cling film®** *n* Frischhaltefolie *f*

clinic *n* Klinik *f*

clip 1. *n* Klammer *f* **2.** *vt (fix)* anklemmen *(to* an + *acc)*; *(fingernails)* schneiden; **clippers** *npl* Schere *f*; *(for nails)* Zwicker *m*

cloak *n* Umhang *m*; **cloakroom** *n (for coats)* Garderobe *f*

clock *n* Uhr *f*; AUTO *fam* Tacho *m*; **round the ~** rund um die Uhr; **clockwise** *adv* im Uhrzeigersinn; **clockwork** *n* Uhrwerk *nt*

cloister *n* Kreuzgang *m*

clone 1. *n* Klon *m* **2.** *vt* klonen

close 1. *adj* nahe *(to* + *dat)*; *(friend, contact)* eng; *(resemblance)* groß; **~ to the beach** in der Nähe des Strandes; **~ win** knapper Sieg; **on ~r ex-**

amination bei näherer *or* genauerer Untersuchung **2.** *adv* dicht; **he lives ~** er wohnt ganz in der Nähe **3.** *vt* schließen; *(road)* sperren; *(discussion, matter)* abschließen **4.** *vi* schließen **5.** *n* Ende *nt*; **close down 1.** *vi* schließen; *(factory)* stillgelegt werden **2.** *vt (shop)* schließen; *(factory)* stilllegen; **closed** *adj* zu; *(shop etc)* geschlossen; *(shop etc)* gesperrt; **closed circuit television** *n* Videoüberwachungsanlage *f*; **closely** *adv (related)* eng, nah; *(packed, follow)* dicht; *(attentively)* genau

closet *n (esp US)* Schrank *m*

close-up *n* Nahaufnahme *f*

closing *adj* **~ date** letzter Termin; *(for competition)* Einsendeschluss *m*; **~ time** *(of shop)* Ladenschluss *m*; *(Brit, of pub)* Polizeistunde *f*

cloth *n (material)* Tuch *nt*; *(for cleaning)* Lappen *m*

clothe *vt* kleiden; **clothes** *npl* Kleider *pl*, Kleidung *f*; **clothes peg**, *(US)* **clothes pin** *n* Wäscheklammer *f*; **clothing** *n* Kleidung *f*

clotted *adj* **~ cream** dicke Sahne (aus erhitzter Milch)

cloud *n* Wolke *f*; **cloudy** *adj (sky)* bewölkt; *(liquid)* trüb

clove *n* Gewürznelke *f*; **~ of**

garlic Knoblauchzehe f

clover n Klee m; cloverleaf n Kleeblatt nt

clown n Clown m

club n (weapon) Knüppel m; (society) Klub m, Verein m; (nightclub) Disko f; (golf club) Golfschläger m; **~s**, Kreuz nt; clubbing n **go ~** in die Disko gehen; club class n AVIAT Businessclass f

clue n Anhaltspunkt m, Hinweis m; **he hasn't a ~** er hat keine Ahnung

clumsy adj unbeholfen, ungeschickt

clung pt, pp of cling

clutch n AUTO Kupplung f

cm abbr = **centimetre(s)**; cm

c / o abbr = **care of**; bei

Co abbr = **company**

coach 1. n (Brit, bus) Reisebus m; RAIL (Personen)wagen m; SPORT (trainer) Trainer(in) m(f) 2. vt Nachhilfeunterricht geben + dat; SPORT trainieren; coach (class) n AVIAT Economyclass f; coach driver n Busfahrer(in) m(f); coach station n Busbahnhof m; coach trip n Busfahrt f; (tour) Busreise f

coal n Kohle f

coalition n POL Koalition f

coast n Küste f; coastguard n Küstenwache f; coastline n Küste f

coat n Mantel m; (jacket) Jacke f; (on animals) Fell nt,

Pelz m; (of paint) Schicht f; **~ of arms** Wappen nt; coathanger n Kleiderbügel m; coating n Überzug m; (layer) Schicht f

cobble(stone)s npl Kopfsteine pl; (surface) Kopfsteinpflaster nt

cobweb n Spinnennetz nt

cocaine n Kokain nt

cock n Hahn m; vulg (penis) Schwanz m

cockle n Herzmuschel f

cockpit n (in plane, racing car) Cockpit nt; cockroach n Kakerlake f; cocksure adj todsicher; cocktail n Cocktail m; cock-up n (Brit) fam **make a ~ of sth** bei etw Mist bauen; cocky adj großspurig, von sich selbst überzeugt

cocoa n Kakao m

coconut n Kokosnuss f

cod n Kabeljau m

COD abbr = **cash on delivery**; per Nachnahme

code n Kode m

coffee n Kaffee m; coffee bar n Café nt; coffee break n Kaffeepause f; coffee maker n Kaffeemaschine f; coffee pot n Kaffeekanne f; coffee shop n Café nt; coffee table n Couchtisch m

coffin n Sarg m

coil n Rolle f; ELEC Spule f; MED Spirale f

coin n Münze f

coincide vi (happen together)

come

zusammenfallen (*with* mit); coincidence *n* Zufall *m*

coke *n* Koks *m*; **Coke®** Cola *f*

cola *n* Cola *f*

cold **1.** *adj* kalt; **I'm ~** mir ist kalt, ich friere **2.** *n* Kälte *f*; (*illness*) Erkältung *f*, Schnupfen *m*; **catch a ~** sich erkälten; cold box *n* Kühlbox *f*; coldness *n* Kälte *f*; cold sore *n* Herpes *m*

coleslaw *n* Krautsalat *m*

collaborate *vi* zusammenarbeiten (*with* mit); collaboration *n* Zusammenarbeit *f*; (*of one party*) Mitarbeit *f*

collapse **1.** *vi* zusammenbrechen; (*building etc*) einstürzen **2.** *n* Zusammenbruch *m*; (*of building*) Einsturz *m*

collar *n* Kragen *m*; (*for dog, cat*) Halsband *nt*; collarbone *n* Schlüsselbein *nt*

colleague *n* Kollege *m*, Kollegin *f*

collect **1.** *vt* sammeln; (*fetch*) abholen **2.** *vi* sich sammeln; collect call *n* (*US*) R-Gespräch *nt*; collected *adj* (*works*) gesammelt; (*person*) gefasst; collector *n* Sammler(in) *m(f)*; collection *n* Sammlung *f*; REL Kollekte *f*; (*from postbox*) Leerung *f*

college *n* (*residential*) College *nt*; (*specialist*) Fachhochschule *f*; (*vocational*) Berufsschule *f*; (*US, university*) Universität *f*; **go to ~** (*US*) studieren

collide *vi* zusammenstoßen; collision *n* Zusammenstoß *m*

colloquial *adj* umgangssprachlich

Cologne *n* Köln *nt*

colon *n* (*punctuation mark*) Doppelpunkt *m*

colonial *adj* Kolonial-; colony *n* Kolonie *f*

color *n* (*US*), colour **1.** *n* Farbe *f*; (*of skin*) Hautfarbe *f* **2.** *vt* anmalen; (*bias*) färben; colour-blind *adj* farbenblind; coloured *adj* farbig; (*biased*) gefärbt; colour film *n* Farbfilm *m*; colourful *adj* lit, fig bunt; (*life, past*) bewegt; colouring *n* (*in food etc*) Farbstoff *m*; (*complexion*) Gesichtsfarbe *f*; colourless *adj* farblos; colour photo(graph) *n* Farbfoto *nt*; colour television *n* Farbfernsehen *nt*

column *n* Säule *f*; (*of print*) Spalte *f*

comb **1.** *n* Kamm *m* **2.** *vt* kämmen; **~ one's hair** sich kämmen

combination *n* Kombination *f*; (*mixture*) Mischung *f* (*of* aus); combine *vt* verbinden (*with* mit); (*two things*) kombinieren

come *vi* kommen; (*arrive*) ankommen; (*on list, in order*) stehen; (*with adjective: become*) werden; **~ and see us** besuchen Sie uns mal!

coming ich komm ja schon!; ~ *first/ second* erster/ zweiter werden; ~ *true* wahr werden; ~ *loose* sich lockern; *the years to* ~ die kommenden Jahre; *there's one more to* ~ es kommt noch eins/ noch einer; *how* ..., *how* ...? *fam* wie kommt es, dass ...?; ~ *to think of it* *fam* wie mir gerade einfällt; come across *vt* (*find*) stoßen auf + *acc*; come back *vi* zurückkommen; *I'll* ~ *to that* ich komme darauf zurück; come down *vi* herunterkommen; (*rain, snow, price*) fallen; come from *vt* (*result*) kommen von; *where do you* ~? wo kommen Sie her?; *I* ~ *London* ich komme aus London; come in *vi* hereinkommen; (*arrive*) ankommen; come off *vi* (*button, handle etc*) abgehen; (*succeed*) gelingen; ~ *well/ badly* gut/ schlecht wegkommen; come on *vi* (*progress*) vorankommen; ~! komm!; (*hurry*) beeil dich!; (*encouraging*) los!; come out *vi* herauskommen; (*photo*) was werden; (*homosexual*) sich outen; come round *vi* (*visit*) vorbeikommen; (*regain consciousness*) wieder zu sich kommen; come to 1. *vi* (*regain consciousness*) wieder zu sich kommen 2. *vt* (*sum*) sich belaufen auf + *acc*;

when it comes to ... wenn es um ... geht; come up *vi* hochkommen; (*sun, moon*) aufgehen; ~ (*for discussion*) zur Sprache kommen; come up to *vt* (*approach*) zukommen auf + *acc*; (*water*) reichen bis zu; (*expectations*) entsprechen + *dat*; come up with *vt* (*idea*) haben; (*solution, answer*) kommen auf + *acc*; ~ *a suggestion* einen Vorschlag machen

comedian *n* Komiker(in) *m(f)*; comedy *n* Komödie *f*

come-on *n give sb the* ~ *fam* jdn anmachen

comfort 1. *n* Komfort *m*; (*consolation*) Trost *m* 2. *vt* trösten; comfortable *adj* bequem; (*income*) ausreichend; (*temperature, life*) angenehm; comfort station *n* (*US*) Toilette *f*; comforting *adj* tröstlich

comic 1. *n* (*magazine*) Comic(heft) *nt*; (*comedian*) Komiker(in) *m(f)* 2. *adj* komisch

coming *adj* kommend; (*event*) bevorstehend

comma *n* Komma *nt*

command 1. *n* Befehl *m*; (*control*) Führung *f*; MIL Kommando *nt* 2. *vt* befehlen + *dat*

commemorate *vt* gedenken + *gen*; commemoration *n in* ~ *of* in Gedenken an + *acc*

comment 1. n (remark) Bemerkung f; (note) Anmerkung f; (official) Kommentar m (on zu); **no ~** kein Kommentar **2.** vi sich äußern (on zu); **commentary** n Kommentar m (on zu); TV, SPORT Livereportage f; **commentator** n Kommentator(in) m(f); TV, SPORT Reporter(in) m(f)

commerce n Handel m; **commercial 1.** adj kommerziell; (training) kaufmännisch; **~ break** Werbepause **2.** n TV Werbespot m

commission 1. n Auftrag m; (fee) Provision f; (reporting body) Kommission f **2.** vt beauftragen

commit 1. vt (crime) begehen **2.** vr **~ oneself** (undertake) sich verpflichten (to zu); **commitment** n Verpflichtung f; POL Engagement nt

committee n Ausschuss m, Komitee nt

common 1. adj (experience) allgemein, alltäglich; (shared) gemeinsam; (widespread, frequent) häufig, pej gewöhnlich, ordinär; **have sth in ~** etw gemein haben **2.** n (Brit, land) Gemeindewiese f; **commonly** adv häufig, allgemein; **commonplace** adj alltäglich; pej banal; **commonroom** n Gemeinschaftsraum m; **Commons** n (Brit) POL **the**

(**House of**) **~** das Unterhaus; **common sense** n gesunder Menschenverstand

communal adj gemeinsam; (of a community) Gemeinschafts-, Gemeinde-

communicate vi kommunizieren (with mit); **communication** n Kommunikation f, Verständigung f; **communicative** adj gesprächig

communion n (Holy) **Communion** Heiliges Abendmahl; (Catholic) Kommunion f

communism n Kommunismus m; **communist 1.** adj kommunistisch **2.** n Kommunist(in) m(f)

community n Gemeinschaft f; **community centre** n Gemeindezentrum nt; **community service** n LAW Sozialdienst m

commutation ticket n (US) Zeitkarte f; **commute** vi pendeln; **commuter** n Pendler(in) m(f)

compact 1. adj kompakt **2.** n (for make-up) Puderdose f; (US, car) ≈ Mittelklassewagen m; **compact camera** n Kompaktkamera f; **compact disc** n Compact Disc f, CD f

companion n Begleiter(in) m(f)

company n Gesellschaft f; COMM Firma f; **keep sb ~** jdm Gesellschaft leisten;

company car n Firmenauto nt

comparable adj vergleichbar (with, to mit); comparatively adv verhältnismäßig; compare vt vergleichen (with, to mit); **~d with** or **to** im Vergleich zu; **beyond ~** unvergleichlich; comparison n Vergleich m; **in ~ with** im Vergleich mit (or zu)

compartment n RAIL Abteil nt; (in desk etc) Fach nt

compass n Kompass m; **~es** pl Zirkel m

compassion n Mitgefühl nt

compatible adj vereinbar (with mit); IT kompatibel; **we're not ~** wir passen nicht zueinander

compensate 1. vt (person) entschädigen (for für) 2. vi **~ for sth** Ersatz für etw leisten; (make up for) etw ausgleichen; compensation n Entschädigung f; (money) Schadenersatz m; LAW Abfindung f

compete vi konkurrieren (for um); SPORT kämpfen (for um); (take part) teilnehmen (in an + dat)

competence n Fähigkeit f; LAW Zuständigkeit f; competent adj fähig; LAW zuständig

competition n (contest) Wettbewerb m; COMM Konkurrenz f (for um); competitive adj (firm, price, product)

konkurrenzfähig; competitor n COMM Konkurrent(in) m(f); SPORT Teilnehmer(in) m(f)

complain vi klagen; (formally) sich beschweren (about über + acc); complaint n Klage f; (formal) Beschwerde f; MED Leiden nt

complement vt ergänzen

complete 1. adj vollständig; (finished) fertig; (failure, disaster) total; (happiness) vollkommen; **are we ~?** sind wir vollzählig? 2. vt vervollständigen; (form) ausfüllen; completely adv völlig; **not ~ ...** nicht ganz ...

complex 1. adj (task, theory etc) kompliziert 2. n Komplex m

complexion n Gesichtsfarbe f, Teint m

complicated adj kompliziert; complication n Komplikation f

compliment n Kompliment nt; complimentary adj lobend; (free of charge) Gratis-; **~ ticket** Freikarte f

component n Bestandteil m

compose vt (music) komponieren; **~ oneself** sich zusammennehmen; composed adj gefasst; **be ~ of** bestehen aus; composition n (of a group) Zusammensetzung f; MUS Komposition f

comprehend vt verstehen; comprehension n Verständnis *nt*

comprehensive *adj* umfassend; **~ school** Gesamtschule *f*

comprise *vt* umfassen, bestehen aus

compromise 1. *n* Kompromiss *m* **2.** *vi* einen Kompromiss schließen

compulsory *adj* obligatorisch

computer *n* Computer *m*; **computer aided** *adj* computergestützt; **computer-controlled** *adj* rechnergesteuert; **computer game** *n* Computerspiel *nt*; **computer-literate** *adj* **be ~** mit dem Computer umgehen können; **computer scientist** *n* Informatiker(in) *m(f)*; **computing** *n* (*subject*) Informatik *f*

con *fam* **1.** *n* Schwindel *m* **2.** *vt* betrügen (*out of* um)

conceal *vt* verbergen (*from* vor + *dat*)

conceive *vt* (*imagine*) sich vorstellen; (*child*) empfangen

concentrate *vi* sich konzentrieren (*on* auf + *acc*); **concentration** *n* Konzentration *f*

concept *n* Begriff *m*

concern 1. *n* (*affair*) Angelegenheit *f*; (*worry*) Sorge *f*; **it's not my ~** das geht mich nichts an; **there's no cause for ~** kein Grund zur Beunruhigung **2.** *vt* (*affect*) angehen; (*have connection with*)

betreffen; (*be about*) handeln von; **those ~ed** die Betroffenen; **as far as I'm ~ed** was mich betrifft; **concerned** *adj* (*anxious*) besorgt; **concerning** *prep* bezüglich, hinsichtlich + *gen*

concert *n* Konzert *nt*; **~ hall** Konzertsaal *m*

concession *n* Zugeständnis *nt*; (*reduction*) Ermäßigung *f*

conclude *vt* (*end*) beenden, (ab)schließen; (*infer*) folgern (*from* aus); **~ that ...** zu dem Schluss kommen, dass ...; **conclusion** *n* Schluss *m*, Schlussfolgerung *f*

concrete 1. *n* Beton *m* **2.** *adj* konkret

concussion *n* Gehirnerschütterung *f*

condition *n* (*state*) Zustand *m*; (*requirement*) Bedingung *f*; **on ~ that ...** unter der Bedingung, dass ...; **~s** *pl* (*circumstances, weather*) Verhältnisse *pl*

conditioner *n* Weichspüler *m*; (*for hair*) Pflegespülung *f*

condo *n* → **condominium**

condolences *npl* Beileid *nt*

condom *n* Kondom *nt*

condominium *n* (*US, apartment*) Eigentumswohnung *f*

conduct 1. *n* (*behaviour*) Verhalten *nt* **2.** *vt* führen, leiten; (*orchestra*) dirigieren

cone *n* Kegel *m*; (*for ice cream*) Waffeltüte *f*; (*fir cone*) (Tannen)zapfen *m*

conference n Konferenz f

confess vt, vi ~ **that ...** gestehen, dass ...; **confession** n Geständnis nt; REL Beichte f

confidence n Vertrauen nt (in zu); (assurance) Selbstvertrauen nt; **confident** adj (sure) zuversichtlich (that ... dass ...), überzeugt (of von); (self-assured) selbstsicher; **confidential** adj vertraulich

confine vt beschränken (to auf + acc)

confirm vt bestätigen; **confirmation** n Bestätigung f; REL Konfirmation f; **confirmed** adj überzeugt; (bachelor) eingefleischt

confuse vt verwirren; (sth with sth) verwechseln (with mit); (several things) durcheinanderbringen; **confused** adj (person) konfus, verwirrt; (account) verworren; **confusing** adj verwirrend; **confusion** n Verwirrung f; (of two things) Verwechslung f; (muddle) Chaos nt

congestion n Stau m

congratulate vt gratulieren (on zu); **congratulations** npl Glückwünsche pl; ~! gratuliere!, herzlichen Glückwunsch!

congregation n REL Gemeinde f

congress n Kongress m; (US) **Congress** der Kongress; **congressman, congresswoman** n (US) Mitglied nt des Repräsentantenhauses

conjunction n LING Konjunktion f; **in ~ with** in Verbindung mit

connect 1. vt verbinden (with, to mit); ELEC (appliance etc) anschließen (to an + acc) **2.** vi (train, plane) Anschluss haben (with an + acc); **~ing flight** Anschlussflug m; **~ing train** Anschlusszug m; **connection** n Verbindung f; (link) Zusammenhang m; (for train, plane, electrical appliance) Anschluss m (with, to an + acc); (business etc) Beziehung f (with zu); **in ~ with** in Zusammenhang mit; **bad ~** TEL schlechte Verbindung; ELEC Wackelkontakt m; **connector** n IT (computer) Stecker m

conscience n Gewissen nt; **conscientious** adj gewissenhaft

conscious adj (act) bewusst; MED bei Bewusstsein

consecutive adj aufeinander folgend

consent 1. n Zustimmung f **2.** vi zustimmen (to dat)

consequence n Folge f, Konsequenz f; **consequently** adv folglich

conservation n Erhaltung f; (of buildings) Denkmalschutz m; (nature conservation) Naturschutz m; **conservation area** n Naturschutzgebiet nt; (in town) unter Denkmalschutz stehendes Gebiet

Conservative *adj* POL konservativ

conservatory *n* (*greenhouse*) Gewächshaus *nt*; (*room*) Wintergarten *m*

consider *vt* (*reflect on*) nachdenken über, sich überlegen; (*take into account*) in Betracht ziehen; (*regard*) halten für; **he is ~ed (to be) ...** er gilt als ...; **considerable** *adj* beträchtlich; **considerate** *adj* aufmerksam, rücksichtsvoll; **consideration** *n* (*thoughtfulness*) Rücksicht *f*; (*thought*) Überlegung *f*; **take sth into ~** etw in Betracht ziehen; **considering 1.** *prep* in Anbetracht + *gen* **2.** *conj* da

consist *vi* **~ of** ... bestehen aus

consistent *adj* (*behaviour, process etc*) konsequent; (*statements*) übereinstimmend; (*argument*) folgerichtig; (*performance, results*) beständig

consolation *n* Trost *m*; **console** *vt* trösten

consonant *n* Konsonant *m*

conspicuous *adj* auffällig, auffallend

conspiracy *n* Komplott *nt*

constable *n* (*Brit*) Polizist(in) *m(f)*

Constance *n* Konstanz *nt*; **Lake ~** der Bodensee

constant *adj* (*continual*) ständig, dauernd; (*unchanging: temperature etc*) gleich bleibend; **constantly** *adv* dauernd

consternation *n* (*dismay*) Bestürzung *f*

constituency *n* Wahlkreis *m*

constitution *n* Verfassung *f*; (*of person*) Konstitution *f*

construct *vt* bauen; **construction** *n* (*process, result*) Bau *m*; (*method*) Bauweise *f*; **under ~** im Bau befindlich; **construction site** *n* Baustelle *f*

consulate *n* Konsulat *nt*

consult *vt* um Rat fragen; (*doctor*) konsultieren; (*book*) nachschlagen in + *dat*; **consultant** *n* MED Facharzt *m*, Fachärztin *f*; **consultation** *n* Beratung *f*; MED Konsultation *f*

consume *vt* verbrauchen; (*food*) konsumieren; **consumer** *n* Verbraucher(in) *m(f)*

contact 1. *n* (*touch*) Berührung *f*; (*communication*) Kontakt *m*; (*person*) Kontaktperson *f*; **be/keep in ~ (with sb)** (mit jdm) in Kontakt sein/bleiben **2.** *vt* sich in Verbindung setzen mit; **contact lenses** *npl* Kontaktlinsen *pl*

contagious *adj* ansteckend

contain *vt* enthalten; **container** *n* Behälter *m*; (*for transport*) Container *m*

contaminate vt verunreinigen; (chemically) verseuchen; **~d by radiation** strahlenverseucht, verstrahlt; **contamination** n Verunreinigung f; (by radiation) Verseuchung f

contemporary adj zeitgenössisch

contempt n Verachtung f; **contemptuous** adj verächtlich

content adj zufrieden

content(s) npl Inhalt m

contest 1. n (Wett)kampf m (for um); (competition) Wettbewerb m **2.** vt kämpfen um + acc; (dispute) bestreiten; **contestant** n Teilnehmer(in) m(f)

context n Zusammenhang m; **out of ~** aus dem Zusammenhang gerissen

continent n Kontinent m, Festland nt; **the Continent** (Brit) das europäische Festland, der Kontinent; **continental** adj kontinental; **~ breakfast** kleines Frühstück mit Brötchen und Marmelade, Kaffee oder Tee

continual adj (endless) ununterbrochen; (constant) dauernd, ständig; **continually** adv dauernd; (again and again) immer wieder; **continuation** n Fortsetzung f; **continue 1.** vi weitermachen (with mit); (esp talking) fortfahren (with mit); (travel-ling) weiterfahren; (state, conditions) fortdauern, anhalten **2.** vt fortsetzen; **to be ~d** Fortsetzung folgt; **continuous** adj (endless) ununterbrochen; (constant) ständig

contraceptive n Verhütungsmittel nt

contract n Vertrag m

contradict vt widersprechen + dat; **contradiction** n Widerspruch m

contrary 1. n Gegenteil nt; **on the ~** im Gegenteil **2.** adj **~ to** entgegen + dat

contrast 1. n Kontrast m, Gegensatz m; **in ~ to** im Gegensatz zu **2.** vt entgegensetzen

contribute vt, vi beitragen (to zu); (money) spenden (to für); **contribution** n Beitrag m

control 1. vt (master) beherrschen; (temper etc) im Griff haben; (esp TECH) steuern; **~ oneself** sich beherrschen **2.** n Kontrolle f; (mastery) Beherrschung f; (of business) Leitung f; (esp TECH) Steuerung f; **~s** pl (knobs, switches etc) Bedienungselemente pl; (collectively) Steuerung f; **be out of ~** außer Kontrolle sein; **control knob** n Bedienungsknopf m; **control panel** n Schalttafel f

controversial adj umstritten

convalesce vi gesund werden; **convalescence** n Genesung f

convenience n (quality, thing) Annehmlichkeit f; **at your ~** wann es Ihnen passt; **with all modern ~s** mit allem Komfort; convenience food n Fertiggericht nt; convenient adj günstig, passend

convent n Kloster nt

convention n (custom) Konvention f; (meeting) Konferenz f; conventional adj herkömmlich, konventionell

conversation n Gespräch nt, Unterhaltung f

conversion n Umwandlung f (into in + acc); (of building) Umbau m (into zu); (calculation) Umrechnung f; conversion table n Umrechnungstabelle f; convert vt umwandeln; (person) bekehren; IT umrechnen; **~ into Euros** in Euro umrechnen; convertible n AUTO Kabrio nt

convey vt (carry) befördern; (feelings) vermitteln; conveyor belt n Förderband nt, Fließband nt

convict 1. vt verurteilen (of wegen) 2. n Strafgefangene(r) mf; conviction n LAW Verurteilung f; (strong belief) Überzeugung f

convince vt überzeugen (of von); convincing adj überzeugend

cook 1. vt, vi kochen 2. n Koch m, Köchin f; cookbook n Kochbuch nt; cooker n Herd m; cookie n (US) Keks m; cooking n Kochen nt; (style of cooking) Küche f

cool 1. adj kühl, gelassen; fam (brilliant) cool, stark 2. vt, vi (ab)kühlen; **~ it** reg dich ab! 3. n **keep/lose one's ~** fam ruhig bleiben/durchdrehen; cool down vi abkühlen; (calm down) sich beruhigen

cooperate vi zusammenarbeiten, kooperieren; cooperation n Zusammenarbeit f, Kooperation f; cooperative 1. adj hilfsbereit 2. n Genossenschaft f

cop n fam (policeman) Bulle m

cope vi zurechtkommen, fertig werden (with mit)

Copenhagen n Kopenhagen nt

copier n Kopierer m

copper n Kupfer nt; (Brit) fam (policeman) Bulle m; fam (coin) Kupfermünze f; **~s** Kleingeld nt

copy 1. n Kopie f; (of book) Exemplar nt 2. vt kopieren; (imitate) nachahmen; copyright n Urheberrecht nt

coral n Koralle f

cord n Schnur f; (material) Kordsamt m

cordial adj freundlich

cordless adj (phone) schnurlos

core n Kern m; (of apple, pear) Kerngehäuse nt; core

business n Kerngeschäft nt;
cork n (material) Kork m;
(stopper) Korken m; cork-
screw n Korkenzieher m
corn n Getreide nt, Korn nt;
(US, maize) Mais m; (on
foot) Hühnerauge nt; ~ on
the cob (gekochter) Mais-
kolben; corned beef n Corn-
edbeef nt
corner 1. n Ecke f; (on road)
Kurve f; SPORT Eckstoß m
2. vt in die Enge treiben;
corner shop n Laden m an
der Ecke
cornflakes npl Cornflakes pl;
cornflour (Brit), cornstarch
(US) n Maismehl nt
Cornish adj kornisch; ~ pasty
mit Fleisch und Kartoffeln
gefüllte Pastete; Cornwall n
Cornwall nt
coronary n MED Herzinfarkt
m
corporation n (US) COMM Aktiengesellschaft f
corpse n Leiche f
correct 1. adj (accurate) richtig; (proper) korrekt 2. vt
korrigieren, verbessern; correction n (esp written) Kor-
rektur f
correspond vi entsprechen
(to dat); (two things) übereinstimmen; corresponding
adj entsprechend
corridor n (in building) Flur
m; (in train) Gang m
corrupt adj korrupt
cosmetic adj kosmetisch;

cosmetics npl Kosmetika
pl; cosmetic surgery n
Schönheitschirurgie f
cosmopolitan adj international; (attitude) weltoffen
cost 1. vt kosten 2. n Kosten
pl; at all ~s, at any ~ um jeden Preis; ~ of living Lebenshaltungskosten pl; costly adj kostspielig
costume n THEAT Kostüm nt
cosy adj gemütlich
cot n (Brit) Kinderbett nt;
(US) Campingliege f
cottage n kleines Haus;
(country cottage) Landhäus-
chen nt; cottage cheese n
Hüttenkäse m; cottage pie
n Hackfleisch mit Kartoffelbrei überbacken
cotton n Baumwolle f; cotton
candy n (US) Zuckerwatte
f; cotton wool n (Brit) Watte
f
couch n Couch f; (sofa) Sofa
nt; couchette n Liegewa-
gen(platz) m
cough 1. vi husten 2. n Husten
m; cough mixture n Hustensaft m; cough sweet n Hustenbonbon nt
could pt of can; konnte conditional könnte; ~ you come
earlier? könntest du früher
kommen?; couldn't contr
of could not
council n POL Rat m; (local ~)
Gemeinderat m; (town ~)
Stadtrat m; council estate
n Siedlung f des sozialen

Wohnungsbaus; **council house** *n* Sozialwohnung *f*; **council tax** *n* Gemeindesteuer *f*

count 1. *vt, vi* zählen; *(include)* mitrechnen **2.** *n* Zählung *f*; *(noble)* Graf *m*; **count on** *vt (rely on)* sich verlassen auf + *acc*; *(expect)* rechnen mit

counter *n (in shop)* Ladentisch *m*; *(in café)* Theke *f*; *(in bank, post office)* Schalter *m*; **counter attack 1.** *n* Gegenangriff *m* **2.** *vi* zurückschlagen; **counter-clockwise** *adv (US)* entgegen dem Uhrzeigersinn

counterfoil *n* (Kontroll)abschnitt *m*

counterpart *n* Gegenstück *nt* *(of* zu*)*

countess *n* Gräfin *f*

countless *adj* zahllos, unzählig

country *n* Land *nt*; *in the ~* auf dem Land(e); *in this ~* hierzulande; **country cousin** *n fam* Landei *nt*; **country dancing** *n* Volkstanz *m*; **countryman** *n (compatriot)* Landsmann *m*; **country music** *n* Countrymusic *f*; **country road** *n* Landstraße *f*; **countryside** *n* Landschaft *f*; *(rural area)* Land *nt*

county *n (Brit)* Grafschaft *f*; *(US)* Verwaltungsbezirk *m*; **county town** *n (Brit)* ≈ Kreisstadt *f*

couple *n* Paar *nt*; *a ~ of* ein paar

coupon *n (voucher)* Gutschein *m*

courage *n* Mut *m*

courgette *n (Brit)* Zucchini *f*

courier *n (for tourists)* Reiseleiter(in) *m(f)*; *(messenger)* Kurier *m*

course *n (of study)* Kurs *m*; *(for race)* Strecke *f*; NAUT, AVIAT Kurs *m*; *(at university)* Studiengang *m*; *(in meal)* Gang *m*; *of ~* natürlich; *in the ~ of* während

court *n* SPORT Platz *m*; LAW Gericht *nt*

courtesy *n* Höflichkeit *f*; *~ bus/coach* (gebührenfreier) Zubringerbus

courthouse *n (US)* Gerichtsgebäude *nt*; **court order** *n* Gerichtsbeschluss *m*; **courtroom** *n* Gerichtssaal *m*

courtyard *n* Hof *m*

cousin *n (male)* Cousin *m*; *(female)* Cousine *f*

cover 1. *vt* bedecken *(in, with* mit*)*; *(distance)* zurücklegen; *(loan, costs)* decken **2.** *n (for bed etc)* Decke *f*; *(of cushion)* Bezug *m*; *(lid)* Deckel *m*; *(of book)* Umschlag *m*; *(insurance)* ~ Versicherungsschutz *m*; **cover up** *vt* zudecken; *(error etc)* vertuschen; **coverage** *n* Berichterstattung *f* *(of* über + *acc*); **cover charge** *n* Kosten *pl* für ein Gedeck; **covering letter** *n*

Begleitbrief *m*; **cover story** *n* (*newspaper*) Titelgeschichte *f*

cow *n* Kuh *f*

coward *n* Feigling *m*; **cowardly** *adj* feig(e)

cowboy *n* Cowboy *m*

cozy *adj* (*US*) gemütlich

CPU *abbr* = **central processing unit**; Zentraleinheit *f*

crab *n* Krabbe *f*

crabby *adj* mürrisch, reizbar

crack 1. *n* Riss *m*; (*in pottery, glass*) Sprung *m*; (*drug*) Crack *nt*; **have a ~ at sth** etw ausprobieren **2.** *vi* (*pottery, glass*) einen Sprung bekommen; (*wood, tree etc*) einen Riss bekommen; **get ~ing** *fam* loslegen **3.** *vt* (*bone*) anbrechen; (*nut, code*) knacken

cracker *n* (*biscuit*) Kräcker *m*; (*Christmas cracker*) Knallbonbon *nt*; **crackers** *adj* *fam* verrückt, bekloppt

crackle *vi* knistern; (*telephone, radio*) knacken; **crackling** *n* GASTR Kruste *f* (*des Schweinebratens*)

cradle *n* Wiege *f*

craft *n* Handwerk *nt*; (*art*) Kunsthandwerk *nt*; **craftsman** *n* Handwerker *m*

cram **1.** *vt* stopfen (*into* in + *acc*); **be ~med with ...** mit ... voll gestopft sein **2.** *vi* (*revise for exam*) pauken (*for* für)

cramp *n* Krampf *m*

cranberry *n* Preiselbeere *f*

crane *n* (*machine*) Kran *m*; (*bird*) Kranich *m*

crap 1. *n* *vulg* Scheiße *f*; (*rubbish*) Mist *m* **2.** *adj* beschissen, Scheiß-

crash 1. *vi* einen Unfall haben; (*two vehicles*) zusammenstoßen; (*plane, computer*) abstürzen; (*economy*) zusammenbrechen; **~ into sth** gegen etw knallen **2.** *vt* einen Unfall haben mit **3.** *n* (*car*) Unfall *m*; (*train*) Unglück *nt*; (*collision*) Zusammenstoß *m*; AVIAT, IT Absturz *m*; (*noise*) Krachen *nt*; **crash barrier** *n* Leitplanke *f*; **crash course** *n* Intensivkurs *m*; **crash helmet** *n* Sturzhelm *m*

crate *n* Kiste *f*; (*of beer*) Kasten *m*

crater *n* Krater *m*

craving *n* starkes Verlangen, Bedürfnis *nt*

crawl 1. *vi* kriechen; (*baby*) krabbeln **2.** *n* (*swimming*) Kraul *nt*; **crawler lane** *n* Kriechspur *f*

crayfish *n* Languste *f*

crayon *n* Buntstift *m*

crazy *adj* verrückt (*about* nach)

cream 1. *n* (*from milk*) Sahne *f*, Rahm *m*; (*polish, cosmetic*) Creme *f* **2.** *adj* cremefarben; **cream cake** *n* (*small*) Sahnetörtchen *nt*; (*big*) Sahnetorte *f*; **cream cheese** *n* Frischkäse *m*; **creamer** *n*

Kaffeeweißer *m*; creamy *adj* sahnig

crease **1.** *n* Falte *f* **2.** *vt* falten; (*untidy*) zerknittern

create *vt* schaffen; (*cause*) verursachen; creative (*person*) kreativ; creature *n* Geschöpf *nt*

crèche *n* Kinderkrippe *f*

credible *adj* (*person*) glaubwürdig; credibility *n* Glaubwürdigkeit *f*

credit *n* FIN (*amount allowed*) Kredit *m*; (*amount possessed*) Guthaben *nt*; (*recognition*) Anerkennung *f*; **~s** (*of film*) Abspann *m*; credit card *n* Kreditkarte *f*

creep *vi* kriechen; you **give me the ~** er ist mir nicht ganz geheuer; creepy *adj* (*frightening*) gruselig, unheimlich

crept *pt*, *pp* of **creep**

cress *n* Kresse *f*

crest *n* Kamm *m*; (*coat of arms*) Wappen *nt*

crew *n* Besatzung *f*, Mannschaft *f*

crib *n* (*US*) Kinderbett *nt*

cricket *n* (*insect*) Grille *f*; (*game*) Kricket *nt*

crime *n* Verbrechen *nt*; criminal **1.** *n* Verbrecher(in) *m(f)* **2.** *adj* kriminell, strafbar

crisis *n* Krise *f*

crisp *adj* knusprig; crisps *npl* (*Brit*) Chips *pl*; crispbread *n* Knäckebrot *nt*

criterion *n* Kriterium *nt*; crit-

ic *n* Kritiker(in) *m(f)*; critical *adj* kritisch; critically *adv* kritisch; **~ ill / injured** schwer krank / verletzt; criticism *n* Kritik *f*; criticize *vt* kritisieren

Croat *n* Kroate *m*, Kroatin *f*; Croatia *n* Kroatien *nt*; Croatian *adj* kroatisch

crockery *n* Geschirr *nt*

crocodile *n* Krokodil *nt*

crocus *n* Krokus *m*

crop *n* (*harvest*) Ernte *f*; crops *npl* Getreide *nt*

croquette *n* Krokette *f*

cross **1.** *n* Kreuz *nt*; **mark sth with a ~** etw ankreuzen **2.** *vt* (*road, river etc*) überqueren; (*legs*) übereinander schlagen; **it ~ed my mind** es fiel mir ein; **~ one's fingers** die Daumen drücken **3.** *adj* ärgerlich, böse; cross out *vt* durchstreichen

crossbar *n* (*of bicycle*) Stange *f*; SPORT Querlatte *f*; cross-country *adj* **~ running** Geländelauf *m*; **~ skiing** Langlauf *m*; cross-eyed *adj* **be ~** schielen; crossing *n* (*crossroads*) (Straßen)kreuzung *f*; (*for pedestrians*) Fußgängerüberweg *m*; (*on ship*) Überfahrt *f*; crossroads *nsing or pl* Straßenkreuzung *f*; cross section *n* Querschnitt *m*; crosswalk *n* (*US*) Fußgängerüberweg *m*; crossword (puzzle) *n* Kreuzworträtsel *nt* crouch *vi* hocken

crouton *n* Croûton *m*

crow *vi* Krähe *f*

crowd 1. *n* Menge *f* 2. *vi* sich drängen (*into* in + *acc*; *round* um); crowded *adj* überfüllt

crown 1. *n* Krone *f* 2. *vt* krönen; crown jewels *npl* Kronjuwelen *pl*

crucial *adj* entscheidend

crude 1. *adj* primitiv; (*humour, behaviour*) derb, ordinär 2. *n* ~ (oil) Rohöl *nt*

cruel *adj* grausam (*to* zu, gegen); (*unfeeling*) gefühllos; cruelty *n* Grausamkeit *f*; ~ to animals Tierquälerei *f*

cruise 1. *n* Kreuzfahrt *f* 2. *vi* (*ship*) kreuzen; (*car*) mit Reisegeschwindigkeit fahren; cruise liner *n* Kreuzfahrtschiff *nt*; cruise missile *n* Marschflugkörper *m*

crumb *n* Krume *f*

crumble 1. *vt, vi* zerbröckeln 2. *n* mit Streuseln überbackenes Kompott

crumpet *n* weiches Hefegebäck zum Toasten (*attractive woman*) *fam* Schnecke *f*

crumple *vt* zerknittern; crumple zone *n* AUTO Knautschzone *f*

crunchy *adj* (*Brit*) knusprig

crusade *n* Kreuzzug *m*

crush 1. *vt* zerdrücken; (*finger etc*) quetschen; (*spices, stone*) zerstoßen 2. *n* have a ~ on sb in jdn verknallt sein; crushing *adj* (*defeat, remark*) ver-

nichtend

crust *n* Kruste *f*; crusty *adj* knusprig

crutch *n* Krücke *f*

cry 1. *vi* (*call*) rufen; (*scream*) schreien; (*weep*) weinen 2. *n* (*call*) Ruf *m*; (*louder*) Schrei *m*

crypt *n* Krypta *f*

cu *abbr* = see you; (*SMS, E-Mail*) ≈ bis bald

cub *n* (*animal*) Junge(s) *nt*

Cuba *n* Kuba *nt*

cube *n* Würfel *m*

cubic *adj* Kubik-

cubicle *n* Kabine *f*

cuckoo *n* Kuckuck *m*

cucumber *n* Salatgurke *f*

cuddle 1. *vt* in den Arm nehmen; (*amorously*) schmusen mit 2. *n* Liebkosung *f*, Umarmung *f*; have a ~ schmusen; cuddly *adj* verschmust; cuddly toy *n* Plüschtier *nt*

cuff *n* Manschette *f*; (*US, trouser cuff*) Aufschlag *m*; cufflink *n* Manschettenknopf *m*

cuisine *n* Kochkunst *f*, Küche *f*

cul-de-sac *n* (*Brit*) Sackgasse *f*

culprit *n* Schuldige(r) *mf*, Übeltäter(in) *m(f)*

cult *n* Kult *m*

cultivate *vt* AGR (*land*) bebauen; (*crop*) anbauen; cultivated *adj* (*person*) kultiviert, gebildet

cultural *adj* kulturell, Kultur-; culture *n* Kultur *f*; cultured *adj* gebildet, kultiviert; **culture vulture** *fam* (*Brit*) *n* Kulturfanatiker(in) *m(f)*

cumbersome *adj* (*object*) unhandlich

cumin *n* Kreuzkümmel *m*

cunning *adj* schlau; (*person a.*) gerissen

cup *n* Tasse *f*; (*prize*) Pokal *m*; *it's not his ~ of tea* das ist nicht sein Fall; **cupboard** *n* Schrank *m*; **cup final** *n* Pokalendspiel *nt*

curable *adj* heilbar

curb *n* (*US*) = **kerb**

curd *n ~ cheese*, *~s* ≈ Quark *m*

cure 1. *n* Heilmittel *nt* (*for* gegen); (*process*) Heilung *f* **2.** *vt* heilen; GASTR (*salt*) pökeln; (*smoke*) räuchern

curious *adj* neugierig; (*strange*) seltsam

curl 1. *n* Locke *f* **2.** *vi* sich kräuseln; **curly** *adj* lockig

currant *n* (*dried*) Korinthe *f*; (*red, black*) Johannisbeere *f*

currency *n* Währung *f*; **foreign ~** Devisen *pl*

current 1. *n* (*in water*) Strömung *f*; (*electric ~*) Strom *m* **2.** *adj* (*issue, affairs*) aktuell, gegenwärtig; (*expression*) gängig; **current account** *n* Girokonto *nt*; **currently** *adv* zur Zeit

curriculum *n* Lehrplan *m*; **curriculum vitae** *n* (*Brit*) Lebenslauf *m*

curry *n* Currygericht *nt*; **curry**

powder *n* Curry(pulver) *nt*

curse 1. *vi* (*swear*) fluchen (*at* auf *+ acc*) **2.** *n* Fluch *m*

cursor *n* IT Cursor *m*

curtain *n* Vorhang *m*; *it was ~s for Benny* für Benny war alles vorbei

curve *n* Kurve *f*; **curved** *adj* gebogen

cushion *n* Kissen *nt*

custard *n* dicke Vanillesoße, die warm oder kalt zu vielen englischen Nachspeisen gegessen wird

custom *n* Brauch *m*; (*habit*) Gewohnheit *f*; **customary** *adj* üblich; **custom-built** *adj* nach Kundenangaben gefertigt; **customer** *n* Kunde *m*, Kundin *f*; **customer loyalty card** *n* Kundenkarte *f*; **customer service** *n* Kundendienst *m*

customs *npl* (*organization, location*) Zoll *m*; *pass through ~* durch den Zoll gehen; **customs officer** *n* Zollbeamte(r) *m*, Zollbeamtin *f*

cut 1. *vt* schneiden; (*cake*) anschneiden; (*wages, benefits*) kürzen; (*prices*) heruntersetzen; *I ~ my finger* ich habe mir in den Finger geschnitten **2.** *n* Schnitt *m*; (*wound*) Schnittwunde *f*; (*reduction*) Kürzung *f* (*in gen*); **price/ tax ~** Preissenkung / Steuersenkung *f*; **cut back** *vt* (*workforce etc*) reduzieren;

cut down vt (tree) fällen; ~ **on sth** etwas einschränken; cut in vi AUTO scharf einscheren; cut off vt abschneiden; (gas, electricity) abdrehen, abstellen; TEL **I was ~** ich wurde unterbrochen

cute adj putzig, niedlich; (US, shrewd) clever

cutlery n Besteck nt

cutlet n (pork) Kotelett nt; (veal) Schnitzel nt

cut-price adj verbilligt

cutting 1. n (from paper) Ausschnitt m (of plant) Ableger m 2. adj (comment) verletzend

CV abbr = **curriculum vitae**

cwt abbr = **hundredweight;** ≈ Zentner, m

cybercafé n Internetcafé nt;

cyberspace n Cyberspace m

cyclamen n Alpenveilchen nt

cycle 1. n Fahrrad nt 2. vi Rad fahren; cycle lane, cycle path n Radweg m; cycling n Radfahren nt; cyclist n Radfahrer(in) m(f)

cylinder n Zylinder m

cynical adj zynisch

cypress n Zypresse f

Cypriot 1. adj zypriotisch 2. n Zypriote m, Zypriotin f; Cyprus n Zypern nt

czar n Zar m; czarina n Zarin f

Czech 1. adj tschechisch 2. n (person) Tscheche m, Tschechin f; (language) Tschechisch nt; Czech Republic n Tschechische Republik, Tschechien nt

D

dab vt (wound, nose etc) betupfen (with mit)

dad(dy) n Papa m, Vati m; daddy-longlegs nsing (Brit) Schnake f; (US) Weberknecht m

daffodil n Osterglocke f

daft adj fam blöd, doof

daily 1. adj, adv täglich 2. n (paper) Tageszeitung f

dairy n (on farm) Molkerei f; dairy products npl Milchprodukte pl

daisy n Gänseblümchen nt

dam 1. n Staudamm m 2. vt

stauen

damage 1. n Schaden m; **~s pl** LAW Schadenersatz m 2. vt beschädigen; (reputation, health) schädigen, schaden + dat

damn 1. adj fam verdammt 2. vt (condemn) verurteilen; ~ (it)! verflucht! 3. n **he doesn't give a ~** es ist ihm völlig egal

damp 1. adj feucht 2. n Feuchtigkeit f; dampen vt befeuchten

dance 1. n Tanz m; (event)

daylight saving time

Tanzveranstaltung f 2. vi tanzen; **dance floor** n Tanzfläche f; **dancer** n Tänzer(in) m(f); **dancing** n Tanzen nt
dandelion n Löwenzahn m
dandruff n Schuppen pl
Dane n Däne m, Dänin f
danger n Gefahr f; **be in ~** in Gefahr sein; **dangerous** adj gefährlich
Danish 1. adj dänisch 2. n (language) dänisch nt; **the ~** pl die Dänen; **Danish pastry** n Plundergebäck nt
Danube n Donau f
dare vi ~ **(to) do sth** es wagen, etw zu tun; **I didn't ~ ask** ich traute mich nicht, zu fragen; **how ~ you** was fällt dir ein!; **daring** adj (person) mutig; (film, clothes etc) gewagt
dark 1. adj dunkel; (gloomy) düster, trübe; (sinister) finster; **~ chocolate** Bitterschokolade f; **~ green/ blue** dunkelgrün/ dunkelblau 2. n Dunkelheit f; **dark glasses** npl Sonnenbrille f; **darkness** n Dunkelheit nt
darling n Schatz m; (also favourite) Liebling m
dart n Wurfpfeil m; **darts** nsing (game) Darts nt
dash 1. vi stürzen, rennen 2. vt ~ **hopes** Hoffnungen zerstören 3. n (in text) Gedankenstrich m; (of liquid) Schuss m; **dashboard** n Armaturenbrett nt
data npl Daten pl; **data bank,**

data base n Datenbank f;
data capture n Datenerfassung f; **data processing** n Datenverarbeitung f; **data protection** n Datenschutz m
date 1. n Datum nt; (for meeting, delivery etc) Termin m; (with person) Verabredung f; (with girlfriend etc) Date nt; (fruit) Dattel f; **what's the ~ (today)?** der Wievielte ist heute?; **out of ~** veraltet; **up to ~** adj (news) aktuell; (fashion) zeitgemäß 2. vt (letter etc) datieren; (person) gehen mit; **dated** adj altmodisch; **date of birth** n Geburtsdatum nt; **dating agency** n Partnervermittlung f
daughter n Tochter f; **daughter-in-law** n Schwiegertochter f
dawn 1. n Morgendämmerung f 2. vi dämmern; **it ~ed on me** mir ging ein Licht auf
day n Tag m; **one ~** eines Tages; **by ~** bei Tag; **~ by ~** Tag für Tag; **the ~ after/ before** am Tag danach/ zuvor; **the ~ before yesterday** vorgestern; **the ~ after tomorrow** übermorgen; **these ~s** heutzutage; **in those ~s** damals; **let's call it a ~** Schluss für heute!; **daydream 1.** n Tagtraum m 2. vi (mit offenen Augen) träumen; **daylight** n Tageslicht nt; **daylight saving time** n

Sommerzeit f; **day nursery** n Kindertagesstätte f; **day return** n (Brit) RAIL Tagesrückfahrkarte f; **daytrip** n Tagesausflug m

dazzle vt blenden

dead 1. adj tot; (limb) abgestorben **2.** adv genau; fam total, völlig; ~ **tired** adj todmüde; ~ **slow** (sign) Schritt fahren; **dead end** n Sackgasse f; **deadline** n Termin m; (period) Frist f; ~ **for applications** Anmeldeschluss m; **deadly 1.** adj tödlich **2.** adv ~ **dull** todlangweilig

deaf adj taub; **deafen** vt taub machen; **deafening** adj ohrenbetäubend

deal 1. vt, vi (cards) geben, austeilen **2.** n (business ~) Geschäft nt; (agreement) Abmachung f; **it's a** ~ abgemacht!; **a good/great** ~ **of** ziemlich/sehr viel; **deal in** vt fus handeln mit vt (matter) sich beschäftigen mit; (book, film) behandeln mit; (successfully: person, problem) fertig werden mit; (matter) erledigen; **dealer** n COMM Händler(in) m(f); (drugs) Dealer(in) m(f)

dealt pt, pp of **deal**

dear 1. adj lieb, teuer; **Dear Sir or Madam** Sehr geehrte Damen und Herren; **Dear David** Lieber David **2.** n Schatz m; (as address) mein Schatz, Liebling; **dearly** adv (love) (heiß und) innig; (pay) teuer

death n Tod m; (of project, hopes) Ende nt; ~**s** pl Todesfälle; (in accident) Todesopfer; **death certificate** n Totenschein m; **death penalty** n Todesstrafe f; **death toll** n Zahl f der Todesopfer

debatable adj fraglich; (question) strittig; **debate 1.** n Debatte f **2.** vt debattieren

debit 1. n Soll nt **2.** vt (account) belasten; **debit card** n Geldkarte f

debris n Trümmer pl

debt n Schuld f; **be in** ~ verschuldet sein

decade n Jahrzehnt nt

decaff n fam koffeinfreier Kaffee; **decaffeinated** adj koffeinfrei

decanter n Dekanter m, Karaffe f

decay 1. n Verfall m; (rotting) Verwesung f; (of tooth) Fäule f **2.** vi verfallen; (rot) verwesen; (wood) vermodern; (teeth) faulen; (leaves) verrotten

deceased n **the** ~ der/die Verstorbene

deceive vt täuschen

December n Dezember m; → **September**

decent adj anständig

decide 1. vt (question) entscheiden; (body of people) beschließen; **I can't** ~ **what to do** ich kann mich nicht entscheiden, was ich tun soll **2.** *vi* sich entscheiden; **~ on sth** (*in favour of sth*) sich für etw entscheiden, sich zu etw entschließen; **decided** *adj* entschieden; (*clear*) deutlich; **decidedly** *adv* entschieden

decimal *adj* Dezimal-; **decimal system** *n* Dezimalsystem *nt*

decipher *vt* entziffern

decision *n* Entscheidung *f* (*on* über + *acc*); (*of committee, jury etc*) Beschluss *m*; **make a ~** eine Entscheidung treffen; **decisive** *adj* entscheidend; (*person*) entscheidungsfreudig

deck *n* NAUT Deck *nt*; (*of cards*) Blatt *nt*; **deckchair** *n* Liegestuhl *m*

declaration *n* Erklärung *f*; **declare** *vt* erklären; (*state*) behaupten (*that* dass); (*at customs*) **have you anything to ~?** haben Sie etwas zu verzollen?

decline 1. *n* Rückgang *m* **2.** *vt* (*invitation, offer*) ablehnen **3.** *vi* (*become less*) sinken, abnehmen; (*health*) sich verschlechtern

decode *vt* entschlüsseln

decorate *vt* (aus)schmücken; (*wallpaper*) tapezieren; (*paint*) anstreichen; **decoration** *n* Schmuck *m*; (*process*) Schmücken *nt*; (*wallpapering*) Tapezieren *nt*; (*paint-*

ing) Anstreichen *nt*; **Christmas ~s** Weihnachtsschmuck *m*; **decorator** *n* Maler(in) *m(f)*

decrease 1. *n* Abnahme *f* **2.** *vi* abnehmen

dedicate *vt* widmen (*to sb* jdm); **dedicated** *adj* (*person*) engagiert; **dedication** *n* Widmung *f*; (*commitment*) Hingabe *f*, Engagement *nt*

deduce *vt* folgern, schließen (*from* aus, *that* dass)

deduct *vt* abziehen (*from* von); **deduction** *n* (*of money*) Abzug *m*; (*conclusion*) (Schluss)folgerung *f*

deed *n* Tat *f*

deep *adj* tief; **deepen** *vt* vertiefen; **deep-freeze** *n* Tiefkühltruhe *f*; (*upright*) Gefrierschrank *m*; **deep-fry** *vt* frittieren

deer *n* Reh *nt*; (*with stag*) Hirsch *m*

defeat 1. *n* Niederlage *f*; **admit ~** sich geschlagen geben **2.** *vt* besiegen

defect *n* Defekt *m*, Fehler *m*; **defective** *adj* fehlerhaft

defence *n* Verteidigung *f*; **defend** *vt* verteidigen; **defendant** *n* LAW Angeklagte(r) *mf*; **defender** *n* SPORT Verteidiger(in) *m(f)*; **defensive** *adj* defensiv

deficiency *n* Mangel *m*; **deficit** *n* Defizit *nt*

define *vt* (*word*) definieren; (*duties, powers*) bestimmen;

definite adj (clear) klar, eindeutig; (certain) sicher; **it's ~** es steht fest; definitely adv bestimmt; definition n Definition f; PHOT Schärfe f

deflate vt die Luft ablassen aus

defrost vt (fridge) abtauen; (food) auftauen

degree n Grad m; (at university) akademischer Grad; **to a certain ~** einigermaßen; **I have a ~ in chemistry** ≈ ich habe Chemie studiert

dehydrated adj (food) getrocknet, Trocken-; (person) ausgetrocknet

de-ice vt enteisen

delay 1. vt (postpone) verschieben, aufschieben; **be ~ed** (event) sich verzögern; **the train/flight was ~ed** der Zug/die Maschine hatte Verspätung 2. vi warten; (hesitate) zögern 3. n Verzögerung f; (of train etc) Verspätung f; **without ~** unverzüglich; delayed adj (train etc) verspätet

delegation n Abordnung f; (foreign) Delegation f

delete vt (aus)streichen; IT löschen; deletion n Streichung f; IT Löschung f

deli n fam Feinkostgeschäft nt

deliberate adj (intentional) absichtlich; deliberately adv mit Absicht, extra

delicate adj (fine) fein; (fragile) zart; a. MED empfindlich;

(situation) heikel

delicatessen nsing Feinkostgeschäft nt

delicious adj köstlich, lecker

delight n Freude f; delighted adj sehr erfreut (with über + acc); delightful adj entzückend; (weather, meal etc) herrlich

deliver vt (goods) liefern (to sb jdm); (letter, parcel) zustellen; (speech) halten; (baby) entbinden; delivery n Lieferung f; (of letter, parcel) Zustellung f; (of baby) Entbindung f; delivery van n Lieferwagen m

delude vt täuschen; **don't ~ yourself** mach dir nichts vor; delusion n Irrglaube m

de luxe adj Luxus-

demand 1. vt verlangen (from von); (time, patience etc) erfordern 2. n (request) Forderung f, Verlangen nt (for nach); COMM (for goods) Nachfrage f; **on ~** auf Wunsch; **very much in ~** sehr gefragt; demanding adj anspruchsvoll

demerara n ~ (sugar) brauner Zucker

demister n Defroster m

demo n fam Demo f

democracy n Demokratie f; democrat, Democrat (US) POL Demokrat(in) m(f); democratic adj demokratisch; **the Democratic Party** (US) POL die Demokratische

Partei

demolish vt abreißen; fig zerstören

demonstrate vt, vi demonstrieren, beweisen; **demonstration** n Demonstration f

denationalization n Privatisierung f

denial n Leugnung f; (official ~) Dementi m

denim n Jeansstoff m; denim jacket n Jeansjacke f; denims npl Bluejeans pl

Denmark n Dänemark n

denomination n REL Konfession f; COMM Nennwert m

dense adj dicht; fam (stupid) schwer von Begriff; density n Dichte f

dent 1. n Beule f, Delle f **2.** vt einbeulen

dental adj Zahn-; ~ **care** Zahnpflege f; ~ **floss** Zahnseide f; **dentist** n Zahnarzt m, Zahnärztin f; **dentures** npl Zahnprothese f; (full) Gebiss nt

deny vt leugnen, bestreiten; (refuse) ablehnen

deodorant n Deo(dorant) nt; ~ **spray** Deospray nt or m

depart vi abreisen; (bus, train) abfahren for nach, from von); (plane) abfliegen (for nach, from von)

department n Abteilung f; (at university) Institut nt; POL (ministry) Ministerium nt; **department store** n Kaufhaus nt

departure n (of person) Weggang m; (on journey) Abreise f (for nach); (of train etc) Abfahrt f (for nach); (of plane) Abflug m (for nach); departure lounge n AVIAT Abflughalle f; departure time n Abfahrtzeit f; AVIAT Abflugzeit f

depend vi it ~s es kommt darauf an (whether, if ob); depend on vt (thing) abhängen von; (person: rely on) sich verlassen auf + acc; (person, area etc) angewiesen sein auf + acc; **it ~s on the weather** es kommt auf das Wetter an; **dependable** adj zuverlässig; **dependent** adj abhängig (on von)

deplorable adj bedauerlich

deport vt ausweisen, abschieben; **deportation** n Abschiebung f

deposit 1. n (down payment) Anzahlung f; (security) Kaution f; (for bottle) Pfand nt; (to bank account) Einzahlung f; (in river etc) Ablagerung f **2.** vt (put down) abstellen; absetzen; (to bank account) einzahlen; (sth valuable) deponieren; **deposit account** n Sparkonto nt

depot n Depot nt

depress vt (in mood) deprimieren; **depressed** adj (person) niedergeschlagen, deprimiert; ~ **area** Notstandsgebiet nt; **depressing** adj deprimierend; **depression** n (*mood*) Depression f; METEO Tief nt

deprive vt **~ sb of sth** jdn einer Sache berauben; **deprived** adj (*child*) (sozial) benachteiligt

dept abbr = **department**; Abt.

depth n Tiefe f

deputy 1. adj stellvertretend; Vize- **2.** n Stellvertreter(in) m(f); US POL Abgeordnete(r) mf

derail vt entgleisen lassen; **be ~ed** entgleisen

dermatitis n Hautentzündung f

derogatory adj abfällig

descend vi hinabsteigen, hinuntergehen; (*person*) ~ or **be ~ed from** abstammen von; **descendant** n Nachkomme m; **descent** n (*coming down*) Abstieg m; (*origin*) Abstammung f

describe vt beschreiben; **description** n Beschreibung f

desert 1. n Wüste f **2.** vt verlassen; (*abandon*) im Stich lassen; **deserted** adj verlassen; (*empty*) menschenleer

deserve vt verdienen

design 1. n (*plan*) Entwurf m; (*of vehicle, machine*) Konstruktion f; (*of object*) Design nt; (*planning*) Gestaltung f **2.** vt entwerfen; (*machine etc*) konstruieren; **~ed for sb/sth** (*intended*) für jdn/etw konzipiert; **designer** n

Designer(in) m(f); TECH Konstrukteur(in) m(f); **designer drug** n Designerdroge f

desirable n wünschenswert; (*person*) begehrenswert; **desire 1.** n Wunsch m (*for* nach); (*esp sexual*) Begierde f (*for* nach) **2.** vt wünschen; (*ask for*) verlangen; **if ~d** auf Wunsch

desk n Schreibtisch m; (*reception ~*) Empfang m; (*at airport etc*) Schalter m; **desktop publishing** n Desktop-publishing nt

despair 1. n Verzweiflung f (*at* über + acc) **2.** vi verzweifeln (*of* an + dat)

despatch → **dispatch**

desperate adj verzweifelt; (*situation*) hoffnungslos; **be ~ for sth** etw dringend brauchen, unbedingt wollen; **desperation** n Verzweiflung f

despicable adj verachtenswert; **despise** vt verachten

despite prep trotz + gen

dessert n Nachtisch m; **dessertspoon** n Dessertlöffel m

destination n (*of person*) (Reise)ziel nt; (*of goods*) Bestimmungsort m; **destine** vt **we're ~d for Hull** wir sind auf dem Weg nach Hull; **destiny** n Schicksal nt

destroy vt zerstören; (*completely*) vernichten; **destruction** n Zerstörung f; (*com-

plete) Vernichtung *f*; **de-structive** *adj* zerstörerisch, destruktiv

detach *vt* abnehmen; (*from form etc*) abtrennen; (*free*) lösen (*from* von); **detachable** *adj* abnehmbar; (*from form etc*) abtrennbar; **detached** *adj* (*attitude*) distanziert, objektiv; **~ house** Einzelhaus *nt*

detail (*US*) *n* Einzelheit *f*, Detail *nt*; (*further*) **~s from ...** Näheres erfahren Sie bei ...; **go into ~** ins Detail gehen; **in ~** ausführlich; **detailed** *adj* detailliert, ausführlich

detain *vt* aufhalten; (*police*) in Haft nehmen

detect *vt* entdecken; (*notice*) wahrnehmen; **detective** *n* Detektiv(in) *m(f)*; **detective story** *n* Detektivroman *m*, Krimi *m*

detergent *n* Reinigungsmittel *nt*; (*soap powder*) Waschmittel *nt*

deteriorate *vi* sich verschlechtern

determination *n* Entschlossenheit *f*; **determine** *vt* bestimmen; **determined** *adj* (*fest*) entschlossen

detest *vt* verabscheuen; **detestable** *adj* abscheulich

detour *n* Umweg *m*; (*of traffic*) Umleitung *f*

deuce *n* TENNIS Einstand *m*

devastate *vt* verwüsten; **devastating** *adj* verheerend

develop 1. *vt* entwickeln; (*illness*) bekommen **2.** *vi* sich entwickeln; **developing country** *n* Entwicklungsland *nt*; **development** *n* (*free*) Entwicklung *f*; (*of land*) Erschließung *f*

device *n* Vorrichtung *f*, Gerät *nt*

devil *n* Teufel *m*

devoted *adj* liebend; (*servant etc*) treu ergeben; **devotion** *n* Hingabe *f*

devour *vt* verschlingen

dew *n* Tau *m*

diabetes *n* Diabetes *m*, Zuckerkrankheit *f*; **diabetic 1.** *adj* zuckerkrank, für Diabetiker **2.** *n* Diabetiker(in) *m(f)*

diagnosis *n* Diagnose *f*

diagonal *adj* diagonal

diagram *n* Diagramm *nt*

dial 1. *n* Skala *f*; (*of clock*) Zifferblatt *nt* **2.** *vt* TEL wählen; **dial code** *n* (*US*) Vorwahl *f*

dialect *n* Dialekt *m*

dialling code *n* (*Brit*) Vorwahl *f*; **dialling tone** *n* (*Brit*) Amtszeichen *nt*

dialogue, dialog (*US*) *n* Dialog *m*

dial tone *n* (*US*) Amtszeichen *nt*

dialysis *n* MED Dialyse *f*

diameter *n* Durchmesser *m*

diamond *n* Diamant *m*, Karo *nt*

diaper *n* (*US*) Windel *f*

diarrhoea *n* Durchfall *m*

diary n (Taschen)kalender m; (account) Tagebuch nt

dice npl Würfel pl

dictation n Diktat nt

dictator n Diktator(in) m(f); dictatorship n Diktatur f

dictionary n Wörterbuch nt

did pt of do

didn't contr of did not

die vi sterben (of an + dat); (plant, animal) eingehen; (engine) absterben; **be dying to do sth** darauf brennen, etw zu tun; **I'm dying for a drink** ich brauche unbedingt was zu trinken; die away vi schwächer werden; (sound) sich legen; die down vi nachlassen; die out vi aussterben

diesel n (fuel, car) Diesel m

diet n Kost f; (special food) Diät f 2. vi eine Diät machen

differ vi (be different) sich unterscheiden; (disagree) anderer Meinung sein; difference n Unterschied m; **it makes no ~ (to me)** es ist (mir) egal; **it makes a big ~** es macht viel aus; different adj andere(r, s); (various) verschieden; **be quite ~** ganz anders sein (from als); (two people, things) völlig verschieden sein; differentiate vt, vi unterscheiden; (differently adv anders (from als); (from one another) unterschiedlich

difficult adj schwierig; **I find it ~** es fällt mir schwer; diffi-

culty n Schwierigkeit f

dig vt, vi (hole) graben; dig in vi fam (to food) reinhauen; **~!** greif(t) zu!; dig up vt ausgraben

digest vt verdauen; digestion n Verdauung f; digestive adj **~ biscuit** (Brit) Vollkornkeks m

digit n Ziffer f; digital adj digital; digital camera n Digitalkamera f

dignified adj würdevoll; dignity n Würde f

dilapidated adj baufällig

dill n Dill m

dilute vt verdünnen

dim 1. adj (light) schwach; (outline) undeutlich; (stupid) schwer von Begriff 2. vt verdunkeln; (US AUTO abblenden; **~med headlights** (US) Abblendlicht nt

dime n (US) Zehncentstück nt

dimension n Dimension f; **~s** pl Maße pl

diminish 1. vt verringern 2. vi sich verringern

dimple n Grübchen nt

dine vi speisen; dine out vi außer Haus essen; diner n Gast m; RAIL Speisewagen m; (US) Speiselokal nt

dinghy n Ding(h)i nt; (inflatable) Schlauchboot nt

dining car n Speisewagen m; dining room n Esszimmer nt; (in hotel) Speiseraum m

dinner n Abendessen nt; (lunch) Mittagessen m

(public) Diner *nt*; **be at ~** beim Essen sein; **have ~** zu Abend/Mittag essen; **dinner jacket** *n* Smoking *m*; **dinnertime** *n* Essenszeit *f*

dinosaur *n* Dinosaurier *m*

dip 1. *vt* tauchen *(in in* + *acc)*; **~ (one's headlights)** *(Brit)* AUTO abblenden; **~ped headlights** Abblendlicht *nt* **2.** *n* *(in ground)* Bodensenke *f*; *(sauce)* Dip *m*

diploma *n* Diplom *nt*

diplomatic *adj* diplomatisch

dipstick *n* Ölmessstab *m*

direct 1. *adj* direkt; *(cause, consequence)* unmittelbar; **~ debit** *(mandate)* Einzugsermächtigung *f*; **~ train** durchgehender Zug **2.** *vt* *(aim, send)* richten *(at, to* an + *acc)*; *(film)* die Regie führen bei; *(traffic)* regeln; **direct current** *n* ELEC Gleichstrom *m*

direction *n* *(course)* Richtung *f*; FILM Regie *f*; **in the ~ of ...** in Richtung ...; **~s** *pl* **for use** *(to a place)* Gebrauchsanweisung *f*; **~s** *pl* **for use** *(to a place)* Wegbeschreibung *f*

directly *adv* direkt; *(at once)* sofort

director *n* Direktor(in) *m(f)*, Leiter(in) *m(f)*; *(of film)* Regisseur(in) *m(f)*

directory *n* Adressbuch *nt*, Telefonbuch *nt*; **~ enquiries** or *(US)* **assistance** TEL Auskunft *f*

dirt *n* Schmutz *m*, Dreck *m*; **dirt cheap** *adj* spottbillig; **dirty** *adj* schmutzig

disability *n* Behinderung *f*; **disabled 1.** *adj* behindert, Behinderten- **2.** *npl* **the ~** die Behinderten

disadvantage *n* Nachteil *m*; **at a ~** benachteiligt; **disadvantageous** *adj* nachteilig, ungünstig

disagree *vi* anderer Meinung sein; *(two people)* sich nicht einig sein; *(two reports etc)* nicht übereinstimmen; **disagreeable** *adj* unangenehm; *(person)* unsympathisch; **disagreement** *n* Meinungsverschiedenheit *f*

disappear *vi* verschwinden

disappoint *vt* enttäuschen; **disappointing** *adj* enttäuschend; **disappointment** *n* Enttäuschung *f*

disapprove *vi* missbilligen *(of acc)*

disarm 1. *vt* entwaffnen **2.** *vi* POL abrüsten; **disarmament** *n* Abrüstung *f*; **disarming** *adj* *(smile, look)* gewinnend

disaster *n* Katastrophe *f*; **disastrous** *adj* katastrophal

disbelief *n* Ungläubigkeit *f*

disc *n* Scheibe *f*, CD *f*; → **disk** ANAT Bandscheibe *f*

discharge 1. *n* MED Ausfluss *m* **2.** *vt* *(person)* entlassen; *(emit)* ausstoßen; MED ausscheiden

discipline *n* Disziplin *f*

disc jockey n Diskjockey m

disclose vt bekannt geben; (secret) enthüllen

disco n Disko f, Diskomusik f

discomfort n (slight pain) leichte Schmerzen pl; (unease) Unbehagen nt

disconnect vt (electricity, gas, phone) abstellen; (unplug) ~ **the TV (from the mains)** den Stecker des Fernsehers herausziehen; TEL **I've been ~ed** das Gespräch ist unterbrochen worden

discontinue vt einstellen; (product) auslaufen lassen

discotheque n Diskothek f

discount n Rabatt m

discover vt entdecken; discovery n Entdeckung f

discredit 1. vt in Verruf bringen **2.** n Misskredit m

discreet adj diskret

discrepancy n Unstimmigkeit f, Diskrepanz f

discriminate vi unterscheiden; ~ **against sb** jdn diskriminieren; discrimination n (different treatment) Diskriminierung f

discus n Diskus m

discuss vt diskutieren, besprechen; discussion n Diskussion f

disease n Krankheit f

disembark vi von Bord gehen

disgrace 1. n Schande f **2.** vt Schande machen + dat; (family etc) Schande bringen über + acc; (less strong) bla-

mieren; **disgraceful** adj skandalös; **it's ~** es ist eine Schande

disguise 1. vt verkleiden; (voice) verstellen **2.** n Verkleidung f

disgust 1. n Abscheu m; (physical) Ekel m **2.** vt anekeln, anwidern; **disgusting** adj widerlich; (physically) ekelhaft

dish n Schüssel f; (food) Gericht nt; **~es** pl (crockery) Geschirr nt; **do/wash the ~es** abwaschen; dishcloth n (for washing) Spültuch nt; (for drying) Geschirrtuch nt

dishearten vt entmutigen; **don't be ~ed** lass den Kopf nicht hängen!

dishonest adj unehrlich

dish towel n (US) Geschirrtuch nt; dish washer n Geschirrspülmaschine f

dishy adj (Brit) fam klasse, attraktiv

disillusioned adj desillusioniert

disinfect vt desinfizieren; disinfectant n Desinfektionsmittel nt

dislike 1. n Abneigung f **2.** vt nicht mögen; ~ **doing sth** etw ungern tun

dislocate vt MED verrenken,

distinguish

ausrenken

dismal adj trostlos

dismantle vt auseinander nehmen; (machine) demontieren

dismay n Bestürzung f; dismayed adj bestürzt

dismiss vt (employee) entlassen; **dismissal** n Entlassung f

disobedience n Ungehorsam m; **disobedient** adj ungehorsam; **disobey** vt nicht gehorchen + dat

disorder n (mess) Unordnung f; (riot) Aufruhr m; MED Störung f, Leiden nt

disorganized adj chaotisch

disparaging adj geringschätzig

dispatch vt abschicken, abfertigen

dispensable adj entbehrlich; **dispense** vt verteilen; dispense with vt verzichten auf + acc; **dispenser** n Automat m

disperse vi sich zerstreuen

display 1. n (exhibition) Ausstellung f, Show f; (of goods) Auslage f; TECH Anzeige f, Display nt 2. vt zeigen; (goods) ausstellen

disposable adj (container, razor etc) Wegwerf-; ~ **nappy** Wegwerfwindel f; **disposal** n Loswerden nt; (of property) Beseitigung f; **be at sb's** ~ jdm zur Verfügung stehen; **dispose of** vt loswerden

(waste etc) beseitigen

dispute 1. n Streit m; (industrial) Auseinandersetzung f 2. vt bestreiten

disqualification n Disqualifikation f; **disqualify** vt disqualifizieren

disregard vt nicht beachten

disreputable adj verrufen

disrespect n Respektlosigkeit f

disrupt vt stören; (interrupt) unterbrechen; **disruption** n Störung f; (interruption) Unterbrechung f

dissatisfied adj unzufrieden

dissent n Widerspruch m

dissolve 1. vt auflösen 2. vi sich auflösen

dissuade vt (davon abbringen) ~ **sb from doing sth** jdn davon abbringen, etw zu tun

distance n Entfernung f; **in the/from a** ~ in / aus der Ferne; **distant** adj (a. in time) fern; (relative etc) entfernt; (person) distanziert

distaste n Abneigung f (for gegen)

distil vt destillieren; **distillery** n Brennerei f

distinct adj verschieden; (clear) klar, deutlich; **distinction** n (difference) Unterschied m; (in exam etc) Auszeichnung f; **distinctive** adj unverkennbar; **distinctly** adv deutlich

distinguish vt unterscheiden

(*sth from sth*) etw von etw)

distort *vt* verzerren; (*truth*) verdrehen

distract *vt* ablenken; **distraction** *n* Ablenkung *f*; (*diversion*) Zerstreuung *f*

distress 1. *n* (*need, danger*) Not *f*; (*suffering*) Leiden *nt*; (*mental*) Qual *f*; (*worry*) Kummer *m* **2.** *vt* mitnehmen, erschüttern; **distressed area** *n* Notstandsgebiet *nt*

distribute *vt* verteilen; COMM (*goods*) vertreiben; **distribution** *n* Verteilung *f*; COMM (*of goods*) Vertrieb *m*; **distributor** *n* AUTO Verteiler *m*; COMM Händler(in) *m(f)*

district *n* Gegend *f*; (*administrative*) Bezirk *m*; **district attorney** *n* (*US*) Staatsanwalt *m*, Staatsanwältin *f*

distrust 1. *vt* misstrauen + *dat* **2.** *n* Misstrauen *nt*

disturb *vt* stören; (*worry*) beunruhigen; **disturbance** *n* Störung *f*; **disturbing** *adj* beunruhigend

ditch 1. *n* Graben *m* **2.** *vt fam* (*person*) den Laufpass geben + *dat*; (*plan etc*) verwerfen

ditto *n* dito, ebenfalls

dive 1. *n* (*into water*) Kopfsprung *m*; AVIAT Sturzflug *m*; *fam* zwielichtiges Lokal *nt* **2.** *vi* (*under water*) tauchen; **diver** *n* Taucher(in) *m(f)*

diverse *adj* verschieden; **diversion** *n* (*of traffic*) Umleitung *f*; (*distraction*) Ablen-

kung *f*; **divert** *vt* ablenken; (*traffic*) umleiten

divide 1. *vt* teilen; (*in several parts, between people*) aufteilen **2.** *vi* sich teilen; **dividend** *n* Dividende *f*

divine *adj* göttlich

diving *n* (Sport)tauchen *nt*; (*jumping*) Springen *nt*; SPORT (*from board*) Kunstspringen *nt*; **diving board** *n* Sprungbrett *nt*; **diving goggles** *npl* Taucherbrille *f*; **diving mask** *n* Tauchmaske *f*

division *n* MATH Division *f*; (*department*) Abteilung *f*; SPORT Liga *f*

divorce 1. *n* Scheidung *f* **2.** *vt* sich scheiden lassen von; **divorced** *adj* geschieden; **get ~** sich scheiden lassen; **divorcee** *n* Geschiedene(r) *mf*

DIY *abbr* = **do-it-yourself**; **DIY centre** *n* Baumarkt *m*

dizzy *adj* schwindlig

DJ 1. *abbr* = **disc jockey**; Diskjockey *m*, DJ *m* **2.** *abbr* = **dinner jacket**; Smoking *m*

do 1. *v aux* (*in negatives*) **I don't know** ich weiß es nicht; **he didn't come** er ist nicht gekommen; (*in questions*) **does she swim?** schwimmt sie?; (*for emphasis*) **he does like talking** er redet sehr gern; (*replacing verb*) **they drink more than we do** sie trinken mehr als wir; **please don't!** bitte tun Sie / tu das nicht!; (*in ques-

tion tags) **you know him, don't you?** du kennst ihn doch, oder? **2.** *vt* tun, machen; (*clean: room etc*) saubermachen; (*study*) studieren; AUTO (*speed*) fahren; (*distance*) zurücklegen; **she has nothing to ~** sie hat nichts zu tun; **~ the dishes** abwaschen; **you can't ~ Cambridge in a day** Cambridge kann man nicht an einem Tag besichtigen **3.** *vi* (*get on*) vorankommen; (*be enough*) reichen; **~ well/ badly** gut/schlecht vorankommen; (*in exam etc*) gut/schlecht abschneiden; **how are you doing?** wie geht's denn so?; **that (much) should ~** das dürfte reichen **4.** *n* (*party*) Party *f*; do away with *vt* abschaffen; do up *vt* (*fasten*) zumachen; (*parcel*) verschnüren; (*renovate*) wieder herrichten; do with *vt* (*need*) brauchen; **I could ~ a drink** ich könnte einen Drink gebrauchen; do without *vt* auskommen ohne; **I can ~ your comments** auf deine Kommentare kann ich verzichten

dock *n* Dock *nt*; LAW Anklagebank *f*; **dockyard** *n* Werft *f*

doctor *n* Arzt *m*, Ärztin *f*; (*in title, also academic*) Doktor *m*

document *n* Dokument *nt*; documentary *n* Dokumentarfilm *m*; documentation *n* Dokumentation *f*

docusoap *n* Reality-Serie *f*, Dokusoap *f*

dodgy *adj* nicht ganz in Ordnung; (*dishonest, unreliable*) zwielichtig; **he has a ~ stomach** er hat sich den Magen verdorben

dog *n* Hund *m*; **doggie bag** *n* Tüte oder Box, in der die Essensreste aus dem Restaurant mit nach Hause genommen werden können

do-it-yourself 1. *n* Heimwerken *nt*, Do-it-yourself *nt* **2.** *adj* Heimwerker-; do--it-yourselfer *n* Bastler(in) *m(f)*, Heimwerker(in) *m(f)*

doll *n* Puppe *f*

dollar *n* Dollar *m*

dolphin *n* Delphin *m*

domain *n* Domäne *f*; IT Domain *f*

dome *n* Kuppel *f*

domestic *adj* häuslich; (*within country*) Innen-, Binnen-; **domesticated** *adj* (*person*) häuslich; (*animal*) zahm; **domestic flight** *n* Inlandsflug *m*

domicile *n* (ständiger) Wohnsitz

dominant *adj* dominierend, vorherrschend

dominoes *npl* Domino(spiel) *nt*

donate *vt* spenden; **donation** *n* Spende *f*

done 1. pp of **do 2.** adj
(cooked) gar; **well ~** durchgebraten

doner (kebab) n Döner (Kebab) m

donkey n Esel m

donor n Spender(in) m(f)

don't contr of **do not**

door n Tür f; **doorbell** n Tür-
klingel f; **door handle** n Tür-
klinke f; **doorknob** n Tür-
knauf m; **doormat** n Fußab-
treter m; **doorstep** n Türstu-
fe f; **right on our ~** direkt vor
unserer Haustür

dope SPORT **1.** n (for athlete)
Aufputschmittel nt **2.** vt dopen; **dopey** adj fam ver-
kloppt; (from drugs) bene-
belt; (sleepy) benommen

dormitory n Schlafsaal m;
(US) Studentenwohnheim nt

dosage n Dosierung f; **dose**
1. n Dosis f **2.** vt dosieren

dot n Punkt m; **on the ~** auf
die Minute genau

double 1. adj, adv doppelt; ~
the quantity die zweifache
Menge, doppelt so viel **2.**
vt verdoppeln **3.** n (person)
Doppelgänger(in) m(f); FILM
Double nt; **double bass** n
Kontrabass m; **double bed**
n Doppelbett nt; **double-**
-click vt IT doppelklicken;
double cream n Sahne mit
hohem Fettgehalt; **double-**
decker n Doppeldecker m;
double glazing n Doppel-
verglasung f; **double-park**

vi in zweiter Reihe parken;
double room n Doppelzimmer nt; **doubles** npl SPORT
(also match) Doppel nt

doubt 1. n Zweifel m; **no ~** ohne Zweifel, zweifellos; wahrscheinlich; **have one's ~s**
Bedenken haben **2.** vt bezweifeln; (statement, word)
anzweifeln; **I ~ it** das bezweif-
le ich; **doubtful** adj zweifelhaft, zweifelnd; **it is ~ wheth-**
er ... es ist fraglich, ob ...;
doubtless adv ohne Zweifel, sicherlich

dough n Teig m; **doughnut** n
Donut m (rundes Hefege-
bäck)

dove n Taube f

down 1. n Daunen pl; (fluff)
Flaum m **2.** adv unten; (motion) nach unten; (towards
speaker) herunter; (away
from speaker) hinunter; ~
here/there hier/dort unten;
(downstairs) **they came ~ for**
breakfast sie kamen zum
Frühstück herunter **3.** prep
(towards speaker) herunter;
(away from speaker) hinunter; **drive ~ the hill/road**
den Berg/die Straße hinunter fahren; (along) **walk ~ the**
street die Straße entlang gehen; **he's ~ the pub** fam er ist
in der Kneipe **4.** vt fam
(drink) runterkippen **5.** adj
niedergeschlagen, depri-
miert

downcast adj niedergeschla-

gen; **downfall** n Sturz m;
down-hearted adj entmutigt; **downhill** adv bergab
download vt downloaden, herunterladen; **down payment** n Anzahlung f; **downs** npl Hügelland nt; **downsize** 1. vt (business) verkleinern 2. vi sich verkleinern
Down's syndrome n MED Downsyndrom nt
downstairs adv unten; (motion) nach unten; **downstream** adv flussabwärts; **downtown** 1. adv (be, work etc) in der Innenstadt; (go) in die Innenstadt 2. adj (US) in der Innenstadt; ~ **Chicago** die Innenstadt von Chicago; **down under** adv fam (in/to Australia) in/nach Australien; (in/to New Zealand) in/nach Neuseeland; **downwards** adv, adj nach unten; (movement, trend) Abwärts-
doze 1. vi dösen 2. n Nickerchen nt
dozen n Dutzend nt
DP abbr = **data processing**; DV f
draft n (outline) Entwurf m; (US) MIL Einberufung f
drag 1. vt schleppen 2. n fam **be a** ~ (boring) stinklangweilig sein; (laborious) ein ziemlicher Schlauch sein; **drag on** vi sich in die Länge ziehen
dragon n Drache m; **dragonfly** n Libelle f
drain 1. n Abfluss m 2. vt (water, oil) ablassen; (vegetables etc) abgießen; (land) entwässern, trockenlegen 3. vi (of water) abfließen; **drainpipe** n Abflussrohr nt
drama n Drama nt; **dramatic** adj dramatisch
drank pt of **drink**
drapes npl (US) Vorhänge pl
drastic adj drastisch
draught n (Luft)zug m; **there's a** ~ es zieht; **on** ~ (beer) vom Fass; **draughts** nsing Damespiel nt; **draughty** adj zugig
draw 1. vt (pull) ziehen; (crowd) anlocken, anziehen; (picture) zeichnen 2. vi SPORT unentschieden spielen 3. n SPORT Unentschieden nt; (attraction) Attraktion f; (for lottery) Ziehung f; **draw out** vt herausziehen; (money) abheben; **draw up** 1. vt (formulate) entwerfen; (list) erstellen 2. vi (car) anhalten
drawback n Nachteil m
drawer n Schublade f
drawing n Zeichnung f; **drawing pin** n Reißzwecke f
drawn pp of **draw**
dread 1. n Furcht f (of vor + dat) 2. vt sich fürchten vor + dat; **dreadful** adj furchtbar; **dreadlocks** npl Rastalocken pl
dream 1. vt, vi träumen (about von) 2. n Traum m; **dreamt**

pt, pp of **dream**

dreary adj (weather, place) trostlos; (book etc) langweilig

drench vt durchnässen

dress 1. n Kleidung f; (garment) Kleid nt **2.** vt anziehen; (wound) verbinden; **get ~ed** sich anziehen; (in costume) sich verkleiden (as als); **dress circle** n THEAT erster Rang; **dresser** n Anrichte f; (US, dressing table) (Frisier)kommode f; **dressing** n GASTR Dressing nt, Soße f; MED Verband m; **dressing gown** n Morgenmantel m; **dressing room** n SPORT Umkleideraum m; THEAT Künstlergarderobe f; **dressing table** n Frisierkommode f; **dress rehearsal** n THEAT Generalprobe f

drew pt of **draw**

dried adj getrocknet; (milk, flowers) Trocken-; **~ fruit** Dörrobst nt; **drier** n → **dryer**

drift 1. vi treiben **2.** n (of snow) Verwehung f; fig Tendenz f; **if you get my ~** wenn du mich richtig verstehst

drill 1. n Bohrer m **2.** vt, vi bohren

drink 1. vt, vi trinken **2.** n Getränk nt; (alcoholic) Drink m; **drink-driving** n (Brit) Trunkenheit f am Steuer; **drinking water** n Trinkwasser nt

drip 1. n Tropfen m **2.** vi tropfen; **dripping 1.** n Bratenfett nt **2.** adj **~ (wet)** tropfnass

drive 1. vt (car, person in car) fahren; (force: person, animal) treiben; TECH antreiben; **~ sb mad** jdn verrückt machen **2.** vi fahren **3.** n Fahrt f; (entrance) Einfahrt f, Auffahrt f; IT Laufwerk nt; **drive away, drive off 1.** vi wegfahren **2.** vt vertreiben; **drive-in** adj Drive-in-; **cinema** (US) Autokino nt; **driven** pp of **drive**

driver n Fahrer(in) m(f); IT Treiber m; **~'s license** (US) Führerschein m; **~'s seat** Fahrersitz m; **driving** n (Auto)fahren nt; **driving lesson** n Fahrstunde f; **driving licence** n (Brit) Führerschein m; **driving school** n Fahrschule f; **driving seat** n (Brit) Fahrersitz m; **driving test** n Fahrprüfung f

drizzle 1. n Nieselregen m **2.** vi nieseln

drop n (of liquid) Tropfen m; (fall in price etc) Rückgang m **2.** vt (give up) fallen lassen **3.** vi (fall) herunterfallen; (figures, temperature) sinken, zurückgehen; **drop by, drop in** vi vorbeikommen; **drop off** vi (to sleep) einnicken; **drop out** vi (withdraw) aussteigen; (university) das Studium abbrechen; **dropout**

Aussteiger(in) m(f)

drove pt of **drive**

drown 1. vi ertrinken **2.** vt ertränken

drowsy adj schläfrig

drug 1. n MED Medikament nt, Arznei f; (addictive) Droge f; (narcotic) Rauschgift nt; **be on ~s** drogensüchtig sein **2.** vt (mit Medikamenten) betäuben; **drug addict** n Rauschgiftsüchtige(r) mf; **drug dealer** n Drogenhändler(in) m(f); **druggist** n (US) Drogist(in) m(f); **drugstore** n (US) Drogerie f

drum n Trommel f; **~s** pl Schlagzeug nt

drunk 1. pp of **drink 2.** adj betrunken; **get ~** sich betrinken **3.** n Betrunkene(r) mf; (alcoholic) Trinker(in) m(f); **drunk-driving** n (US) Trunkenheit f am Steuer; **drunken** adj betrunken, besoffen

dry 1. adj trocken **2.** vt trocknen; (dishes, oneself, one's hands etc) abtrocknen **3.** vi trocknen, trocken werden; **dry out** vi trocknen; **dry-clean** vt chemisch reinigen; **dry-cleaning** n chemische Reinigung; **dryer** n Trockner m; (for hair) Föhn m; (over head) Trockenhaube f

DTP abbr = **desktop publishing**; DTP nt

dual adj doppelt; **~ carriageway** (Brit) zweispurige Schnellstraße f; **~ nationali-**

ty doppelte Staatsangehörigkeit; **dual-purpose** adj Mehrzweck-

dubbed adj (film) synchronisiert

dubious adj zweifelhaft

duchess n Herzogin f

duck n Ente f

dude n (US) fam Typ m; **a cool ~** ein cooler Typ

due 1. adj (time) fällig; (fitting) angemessen; **in ~ course** zu gegebener Zeit; **~ to** infolge + gen, wegen + gen **2.** adv **~ south/north etc** direkt nach Norden/Süden

dug pt, pp of **dig**

duke n Herzog m

dull adj (colour, light, weather) trübe; (boring) langweilig

duly adv ordnungsgemäß; (as expected) wie erwartet

dumb adj stumm; fam (stupid) doof, blöde

dumb-bell n Hantel f

dummy 1. n (sham) Attrappe f; (in shop) Schaufensterpuppe f; (Brit, teat) Schnuller m; fam (person) Dummkopf m **2.** adj unecht, Schein-; **~ run** Testlauf m

dump 1. n Abfallhaufen m; fam (place) Kaff nt **2.** vt lit, fig abladen; fam **he ~ed her** er hat mir ihr Schluss gemacht

dumpling n Kloß m, Knödel m

dune n Düne f

dung n Dung m; (manure) Mist m

dungeon n Kerker m

duplex n zweistöckige Wohnung; (US) Doppelhaushälfte f

duplicate 1. n Duplikat nt **2.** vt (make copies of) kopieren; (repeat) wiederholen

durable adj haltbar; **duration** n Dauer f

during prep (time) während + gen

dusk n Abenddämmerung f

dust 1. n Staub m **2.** vt abstauben; **dustbin** n (Brit) Mülleimer m; **dustcart** n (Brit) Müllwagen m; **duster** n Staubtuch nt; **dustman** n (Brit) Müllmann m; **dustpan** n Kehrschaufel f; **dusty** adj staubig

Dutch 1. adj holländisch **2.** n (language) Holländisch m; **speak/talk double ~** fam Quatsch reden; **the ~** pl die Holländer; **Dutchman** n Holländer m; **Dutchwoman** n Holländerin f

duty n Pflicht f; (task) Aufgabe f; (tax) Zoll m; **on/off ~** im Dienst/nicht im Dienst; **be on ~** Dienst haben; **duty-free** adj zollfrei; **~ shop** Dutyfreeshop m

duvet n Federbett nt

DVD n abbr = **digital versatile disk**; DVD f

dwarf n Zwerg(in) m(f)

dwelling n Wohnung f

dye 1. n Farbstoff m **2.** vt färben

dynamo n Dynamo m

dyslexia n Legasthenie f; **dyslexic** adj legasthenisch; **be ~** Legastheniker(in) sein

dyspepsia n Verdauungsstörung f

E

E111 form n ≈ Auslandskrankenschein m

each 1. adj jeder/jede/jedes **2.** pron jeder/jede/jedes; **I'll have one of ~** ich nehme von jedem eins; **they ~ have a car** jeder von ihnen hat ein Auto; **~ other** einander, sich; **for/against ~ other** füreinander/gegeneinander **3.** adv je; **they cost 10 dollars ~** sie kosten 10 Dollar das Stück

eager adj eifrig; **be ~ to do sth** darauf brennen, etw zu tun

eagle n Adler m

ear n Ohr nt; **earache** n Ohrenschmerzen pl; **eardrum** n Trommelfell nt

earl n Graf m

early adj, adv früh; **be 10 minutes ~** 10 Minuten zu früh kommen; **at the earliest** frühestens; **in ~ June/2008** Anfang Juni / 2008; **~ retirement** vorzeitiger Ruhestand; **~ warning system** Frühwarnsystem nt

earn vt verdienen; earnings npl Verdienst m, Einkommen nt

earphones npl Kopfhörer m; earplug n Ohrenstöpsel m, Ohropax® nt; earring n Ohrring m

earth 1. n Erde f; **what on ~ ...?** was in aller Welt ...? 2. vt erden; earthquake n Erdbeben nt

ease 1. vt (pain) lindern 2. n (easiness) Leichtigkeit f; **feel at ~** sich wohl fühlen; **feel ill at ~** sich nicht wohl fühlen; easily adv leicht; **he is ~ the best** er ist mit Abstand der Beste

east 1. n Osten m; **to the ~ of** östlich von 2. adv (go, face) nach Osten 3. adj Ost-; **~ wind** Ostwind m; eastbound adj (in) Richtung Osten

Easter n Ostern nt; **at ~** zu Ostern; Easter egg n Osterei nt; Easter Sunday n Ostersonntag m

eastern adj Ost-, östlich; **Eastern Europe** Osteuropa nt; East Germany n Ostdeutschland nt; eastwards adv nach Osten

easy adj leicht; (task, solution) einfach; (life) bequem; (manner) ungezwungen

easy-care adj pflegeleicht; easy-going adj gelassen

eat vt essen; (animal) fressen; eat out vi zum Essen ausgehen; eat up vt aufessen

eaten pp of **eat**

eavesdrop vi (heimlich) lauschen; **~ on sb** jdn belauschen

eccentric adj exzentrisch

echo 1. n Echo nt 2. vi widerhallen

ecological adj ökologisch; **~ disaster** Umweltkatastrophe f; ecology n Ökologie f

economic adj wirtschaftlich, Wirtschafts-; economical adj wirtschaftlich; (person) sparsam; economics nsing or pl Wirtschaftswissenschaft f; economist n Wirtschaftswissenschaftler(in) m(f); economize vi sparen (on an + dat); economy n (of state) Wirtschaft f; (thrift) Sparsamkeit f; economy class n AVIAT Economyclass f

ecstasy n Ekstase f; (drug) Ecstasy f

eczema n Ekzem nt

edge n Rand m; (of knife) Schneide f; **on ~** nervös; edgy adj nervös

edible adj essbar

Edinburgh n Edinburg nt

edit vt (series, newspaper etc) herausgeben; (text) redigieren; (film) schneiden; IT editieren; edition n Ausgabe f; editor n Redakteur(in) m(f);

(of series etc) Herausgeber(in) m(f)

educate vt (child) erziehen; (at school, university) ausbilden; (public) aufklären; educated adj gebildet; education n Erziehung f; (studies, training) Ausbildung f; (subject of study) Pädagogik f; (system) Schulwesen nt; (knowledge) Bildung f; educational adj pädagogisch; ~ **television** Schulfernsehen nt

eel n Aal m

eerie adj unheimlich

effect n Wirkung f (on auf + acc); **come into** ~ in Kraft treten; **effective** adj wirksam, effektiv

efficiency n Leistungsfähigkeit f; (of method) Wirksamkeit f; **efficient** adj TECH leistungsfähig; (method) wirksam, effizient

effort n Anstrengung f; (attempt) Versuch m; **make an** ~ sich anstrengen; **effortless** adj mühelos

eg abbr = **exempli gratia (for example)**; z. B.

egg n Ei nt; **eggcup** n Eierbecher m; **eggplant** n (US) Aubergine f; **eggshell** n Eierschale f

ego n Ich nt; (self-esteem) Selbstbewusstsein nt

Egypt n Ägypten nt; **Egyptian** 1. adj ägyptisch 2. n Ägypter(in) m(f)

eiderdown n Daunendecke f

eight 1. num acht; **at the age of** ~ im Alter von acht Jahren; **it's** ~ **(o'clock)** es ist acht Uhr 2. n (a. bus etc) Acht f; (boat) Achter m; **eighteen** 1. num achtzehn 2. n Achtzehn f; → **eight**; **eighteenth** adj achtzehnte(r, s); → **eighth**; **eighth** 1. adj achte(r, s); **the** ~ **of June** der achte Juni 2. n (fraction) Achtel nt; **an** ~ **of a litre** ein Achtelliter; **eightieth** adj achtzigste(r, s); → **eighth**; **eighty** 1. num achtzig 2. n Achtzig f; → **eight**

Eire n die Republik Irland

either 1. conj ~ ... **or** entweder ... oder 2. pron ~ **of the two** eine(r, s) von beiden 3. adj **on** ~ **side** auf beiden Seiten 4. adv **I won't go** ~ ich gehe auch nicht

elaborate 1. adj (complex) kompliziert; (plan) ausgeklügelt; (decoration) kunstvoll 2. vi **could you** ~ **on that?** könntest du mehr darüber sagen?

elastic adj elastisch; ~ **band** Gummiband nt

elbow n Ellbogen m

elder 1. adj (of two) älter 2. n Ältere(r) m; bot Holunder m; elderly adj älter(e, r, s) 2. **the** ~ die älteren Leute; **eldest** adj älteste(r, s)

elect vt wählen; **he was** ~**ed chairman** er wurde zum Vorsitzenden gewählt; **election**

n Wahl *f*; election campaign *n* Wahlkampf *m*
electric *adj* elektrisch; (*car, motor, razor etc*) Elektro-; ~ **blanket** Heizdecke *f*; ~ **cooker** Elektroherd *m*; ~ **current** elektrischer Strom; ~ **shock** Stromschlag *m*; **electrical** *adj* elektrisch; ~ **goods/ appliances** Elektrogeräte; **electrician** *n* Elektriker(in) *m(f)*; **electricity** *n* Elektrizität *f*; **electronic** *adj* elektronisch
elegant *adj* elegant
element *n* Element *nt*; **an ~ of truth** ein Körnchen Wahrheit; **elementary** *adj* einfach; (*basic*) grundlegend; ~ **stage** Anfangsstadium *nt*; ~ **school** (*US*) Grundschule *f*; ~ **maths/ French** Grundkenntnisse in Mathematik / Französisch
elephant *n* Elefant *m*
elevator *n* (*US*) Fahrstuhl *m*
eleven 1. *num* elf **2.** (*team, bus etc*) Elf *f* → **eight**; **eleventh 1.** *adj* elfte(r, s) **2.** (*fraction*) Elftel *nt* → **eighth**
eligible *adj* in Frage kommend; (*for grant etc*) berechtigt; ~ **bachelor** begehrter Junggeselle
eliminate *vt* ausschließen (*from* aus), ausschalten; (*problem etc*) beseitigen
elm *n* Ulme *f*
elope *vi* durchbrennen (*with sb* mit jdm)

eloquent *adj* redegewandt
else *adv* **anybody/ anything** ~ (*in addition*) sonst (noch) jemand/etwas; (*other*) ein anderer/etwas anderes; **somebody** ~ jemand anders; **everyone** ~ alle anderen; **or** ~ sonst; **elsewhere** *adv* anderswo, woanders; (*direction*) woandershin
ELT *abbr* = **English Language Teaching**
e-mail, E-mail 1. *vi, vt* mailen (*sth to sb* jdm etw) **2.** *n* E-Mail *f*; **e-mail address** *n* E-Mail-Adresse *f*
embankment *n* Böschung *f*; (*for railway*) Bahndamm *m*
embargo *n* Embargo *nt*
embark *vi* an Bord gehen
embarrass *vt* in Verlegenheit bringen; **embarrassed** *adj* verlegen; **embarrassing** *adj* peinlich
embassy *n* Botschaft *f*
embrace 1. *vt* umarmen **2.** *n* Umarmung *f*
embroider *vt* besticken; **embroidery** *n* Stickerei *f*
embryo *n* Embryo *m*
emerge *vi* auftauchen; **it ~d that ...** es stellte sich heraus, dass ...
emergency 1. *n* Notfall *m* **2.** *adj* Not-; ~ **exit** Notausgang *m*; ~ **room** (*US*) Notaufnahme *f*; ~ **service** Notdienst *m*; ~ **stop** Vollbremsung *f*
emigrate *vi* auswandern
emotion *n* Emotion *f*, Gefühl

nt; **emotional** adj (person) emotional; (experience, moment, scene) ergreifend

emperor n Kaiser m

emphasis n Betonung f; **emphasize** vt betonen; **emphatic, emphatically** adj, adv nachdrücklich

empire n Reich nt

employ vt beschäftigen; (hire) anstellen; (use) anwenden; **employee** n Angestellte(r) mf; **employer** n Arbeitgeber(in) m(f); **employment** n Beschäftigung f; (position) Stellung f

empress n Kaiserin f

empty 1. adj leer 2. vt (contents) leeren; (container) ausleeren

enable vt ~ **sb to do sth** es jdm ermöglichen, etw zu tun

enamel n Email nt; (of teeth) Zahnschmelz m

enchanting adj bezaubernd

enclose vt einschließen; (in letter) beilegen (in, with dat); **enclosure** n (for animals) Gehege nt; (in letter) Anlage f

encore n Zugabe f

encounter 1. n Begegnung f 2. vt (person) begegnen + dat; (difficulties) stoßen auf + acc

encourage vt ermutigen; **encouragement** n Ermutigung f

encyclopaedia n Lexikon nt, Enzyklopädie f

end 1. n Ende nt; (of film, play

etc) Schluss m; (purpose) Zweck m; **at the ~ of May** Ende Mai; **come to an ~** zu Ende sein; **in the ~** schließlich; **come to an ~** zu Ende gehen 2. vt beenden 3. vi enden; **end up** vi enden

endanger vt gefährden; ~**ed species** vom Aussterben bedrohte Art

ending n (of book) Ausgang m; (last part) Schluss m; (of word) Endung f

endive n Endiviensalat m

endless adj endlos; (possibilities) unendlich

endurance n Ausdauer f; **endure** vt ertragen

enemy 1. n Feind(in) m(f) 2. adj feindlich

energetic adj energiegeladen; (active) aktiv; **energy** n Energie f

enforce vt durchsetzen; (obedience) erzwingen

engage vt (employ) einstellen; (singer, performer) engagieren; **engaged** adj verlobt; (toilet, telephone line) besetzt; **get ~** sich verloben (to mit); **engaged tone** n (Brit) TEL Belegzeichen nt; **engagement** n (marry) Verlobung f

engine n AUTO Motor m; RAIL Lokomotive f; ~ **failure** AUTO Motorschaden m; ~ **trouble** AUTO Defekt am Motor; **engineer** n Ingenieur(in) m(f); (US) RAIL Lokomotivführer(in) m(f); **engineering**

n Technik *f*; (*mechanical engineering*) Maschinenbau *m*; (*subject*) Ingenieurwesen *nt*; **engine immobilizer** *n* AUTO Wegfahrsperre *f*

England *n* England *nt*; **English 1.** *adj* englisch; **he's ~** er ist Engländer; **the ~ Channel** der Ärmelkanal **2.** *n* (*language*) Englisch *nt*; **in ~** auf Englisch; **translate into ~** ins Englische übersetzen; (*people*) **the ~** *pl* die Engländer; **Englishman** *n* Engländer *m*; **Englishwoman** *n* Engländerin *f*

engrave *vt* eingravieren; **engraving** *n* Stich *m*

engrossed *adj* vertieft (*in sth* in etw *acc*)

enjoy *vt* genießen; **I ~ reading** ich lese gern; **he ~s teasing her** es macht ihm Spaß, sie aufzuziehen; **did you ~ the film?** hat dir der Film gefallen?; **enjoyable** *adj* angenehm; (*entertaining*) unterhaltsam; **enjoyment** *n* Vergnügen *nt*; (*stronger*) Freude *f* (*of* an + *dat*)

enlarge *vt* vergrößern; (*expand*) erweitern; **enlargement** *n* Vergrößerung *f*

enormous, enormously *adj*, *adv* riesig, ungeheuer

enough 1. *adj* genug; **that's ~** das reicht!; (*stop it*) Schluss damit!; **I've had ~** das hat mir gereicht!; (*eat*) ich bin satt **2.** *adv* genug, genügend

enquire *vi* sich erkundigen (*about* nach); **enquiry** *n* (*question*) Anfrage *f*; (*for information*) Erkundigung *f* (*about* über + *acc*); (*investigation*) Untersuchung *f*; **'Enquiries'** „Auskunft"

enrol *vi* sich einschreiben; (*for course, school*) sich anmelden; **enrolment** *n* Einschreibung *f*, Anmeldung *f*

en suite *adj*, *n* **room with ~** (**bathroom**) Zimmer *nt* mit eigenem Bad

ensure *vt* sicherstellen

enter 1. *vt* eintreten in + *acc*, betreten; (*drive into*) einfahren in + *acc*; (*country*) einreisen in + *acc*; (*in list*) eintragen; IT eingeben; (*race, contest*) teilnehmen an + *dat* **2.** *vi* (*towards speaker*) hereinkommen; (*away from speaker*) hineingehen

enterprise *n* COMM Unternehmen *nt*

entertain *vt* (*guest*) bewirten; (*amuse*) unterhalten; **entertaining** *adj* unterhaltsam; **entertainment** *n* (*amusement*) Unterhaltung *f*

enthusiasm *n* Begeisterung *f*; **enthusiastic** *adj* begeistert (*about* von)

entire, entirely *adj*, *adv* ganz

entitle *vt* (*qualify*) berechtigen (*to* zu); (*name*) betiteln

entrance *n* Eingang *m*; (*for vehicles*) Einfahrt *f*; (*entering*) Eintritt *m*; THEAT Auftritt m; **entrance exam** n Aufnahmeprüfung f; **entrance fee** n Eintrittsgeld nt

entrust vt ~ **sb with sth** jdm etw anvertrauen

entry n (way in) Eingang m; (entering) Eintritt m; (in vehicle) Einreise f; (into country) Einreise f; (admission) Zutritt m; (in diary, accounts) Eintrag m; **'no ~'** „Eintritt verboten"; (for vehicles) „Einfahrt verboten"; **entry phone** n Türsprechanlage f

envelope n (Brief)umschlag m

enviable adj beneidenswert; **envious** adj neidisch

environment n Umgebung f; (ecology) Umwelt f; **environmental** adj Umwelt-; **environmentalist** n Umweltschützer(in) m(f)

envy 1. n Neid m (of auf + acc) 2. vt beneiden (sb sth jdn um etw)

epidemic n Epidemie f

epilepsy n Epilepsie f; **epileptic** adj epileptisch

episode n Episode f; TV Fortsetzung f, Folge f

epoch n Zeitalter nt, Epoche f

equal 1. adj gleich (to + dat) 2. n Gleichgestellte(r) mf 3. vt gleichen; (match) gleichkommen + dat; **two times two ~s four** zwei mal zwei ist gleich vier; **equality** n Gleichheit f; (equal rights) Gleichbe-

rechtigung f; **equalize** vi SPORT ausgleichen; **equalizer** n SPORT Ausgleichstreffer m; **equally** adv gleich; (on the other hand) andererseits; **equation** n MATH Gleichung f

equator n Äquator m

equilibrium n Gleichgewicht nt

equip vt ausrüsten; (kitchen) ausstatten; **equipment** n Ausrüstung f; (for kitchen) Ausstattung f; **electrical ~** Elektrogeräte pl

equivalent 1. adj gleichwertig (to dat); (corresponding) entsprechend (to dat) 2. n Äquivalent nt; (amount) gleiche Menge; (in money) Gegenwert m

era n Ära f, Zeitalter nt

erase vt ausradieren; (tape, disk) löschen; **eraser** n Radiergummi m

erect 1. adj aufrecht 2. vt (building, monument) errichten; (tent) aufstellen; **erection** n Errichtung f; ANAT Erektion f

erotic adj erotisch

err vi sich irren

erratic adj (behaviour) unberechenbar; (bus link etc) unregelmäßig; (performance) unbeständig

error n Fehler m; **error message** n IT Fehlermeldung f

erupt vi ausbrechen

escalator n Rolltreppe f

escalope n Schnitzel nt

escape 1. n Flucht f; (from prison etc) Ausbruch m; **there's no ~** es gibt keinen Ausweg; **have a narrow ~** gerade noch davonkommen 2. vt (pursuers) entkommen + dat; (punishment etc) entgehen + dat 3. vi (from pursuers) entkommen (from dat); (from prison etc) ausbrechen (from dat); (leak: gas) ausströmen; (water) auslaufen

escort 1. n (companion) Begleiter(in) m(f); (guard) Eskorte f 2. vt (lady) begleiten

especially adv besonders

espionage n Spionage f

essay n Aufsatz m; (literary) Essay m

essential 1. adj (necessary) unentbehrlich, unverzichtbar; (basic) wesentlich 2. n the ~s pl das Wesentliche; essentially adv im Wesentlichen

establish vt (set up) gründen; (introduce) einführen; (relations) aufnehmen; (prove) nachweisen; ~ that ... feststellen, dass ...; establishment n Institution f; (business) Unternehmen nt

estate n Gut nt; (housing ~) Siedlung f; (country house) Landsitz m; estate agent n (Brit) Grundstücksmakler(in) m(f), Immobilienmakler(in) m(f); estate car

n (Brit) Kombiwagen m

estimate 1. n Schätzung f; COMM (of price) Kostenvoranschlag m 2. vt schätzen

estuary n Mündung f

etching n Radierung f

eternal, eternally adj, adv ewig; eternity n Ewigkeit f

ethical adj ethisch; ethics npl Ethik f

Ethiopia n Äthiopien nt

ethnic adj ethnisch; (clothes etc) landesüblich; ~ minority ethnische Minderheit

EU abbr = European Union; EU f

euro n FIN Euro m; Eurocheque n Euroscheck m; Europe n Europa nt; European 1. adj europäisch; ~ Parliament Europäisches Parlament; ~ Union Europäische Union 2. n Europäer(in) m(f); Eurosceptic n Euroskeptiker(in) m(f); Eurotunnel n Eurotunnel m

evacuate vt (place) räumen; (people) evakuieren

evaluate vt auswerten

evaporate vi verdampfen; fig verschwinden; ~d milk Kondensmilch f

even 1. adj (flat) eben; (regular) gleichmäßig; (equal) gleich; (number) gerade; the score is ~ es steht unentschieden 2. adv sogar; ~u selbst (or sogar) du; ~ if selbst wenn, wenn auch; ~ though obwohl; not ~ nicht

einmal; **~ better** noch besser;
even out vi (*prices*) sich einpendeln

evening n Abend m; **in the ~** abends, am Abend; **this ~** heute Abend; **evening class** n Abendkurs m; **evening dress** n (*generally*) Abendkleidung f; (*woman's*) Abendkleid nt

evenly adv gleichmäßig

event n Ereignis nt; (*organized*) Veranstaltung f; SPORT (*discipline*) Disziplin f; **in the ~** im Falle + gen

eventual adj (*final*) letztendlich; **eventually** adv (*at last*) am Ende; (*given time*) schließlich

ever adv (*at any time*) je(mals); **don't ~ do that again** tu das ja nie wieder; **he's the best ~** er ist der Beste, den es je gegeben hat; **have you ~ been to the States?** bist du schon einmal in den Staaten gewesen?; **for ~** (für) immer; **for ~ and ~** auf immer und ewig; **~ so ...** fam äußerst ...; **~ so drunk** ganz schön betrunken

every adj jeder / jede / jedes; **~ day** jeden Tag; **~ other day** jeden zweiten Tag; **~ five days** alle fünf Tage; **I have ~ reason to believe that ...** ich habe allen Grund anzunehmen, dass ...; **everybody** pron jeder, alle pl; **everyday** adj (*commonplace*) alltäglich; (*clothes, language etc*)

Alltags-; **everyone** pron jeder, alle pl; **everything** pron alles; **everywhere** adv überall; (*with direction*) überallhin

evidence n Beweise pl; (*single piece*) Beweis m; (*testimony*) Aussage f; **evident, evidently** adj, adv offensichtlich

evil 1. adj böse **2.** Böse(s) nt

evolution n Entwicklung f; (*of life*) Evolution f; **evolve** vi sich entwickeln

ex- pref Ex-, ehemalig; **~-wife** frühere Frau, Exfrau f; **ex** n fam Verflossene(r) mf, Ex mf

exact adj genau; **exactly** adv genau; **not ~ fast** nicht gerade schnell

exaggerate vt, vi übertreiben; **exaggerated** adj übertrieben; **exaggeration** n Übertreibung f

exam n Prüfung f; **examination** n MED (etc) Untersuchung f, Prüfung f; (*at university*) Examen nt; (*at customs etc*) Kontrolle f; **examine** vt untersuchen (*for* + acc); (*check*) kontrollieren, prüfen; **examiner** n Prüfer(in) m(f)

example n Beispiel nt; **for ~** zum Beispiel

excavation n Ausgrabung f

exceed vt überschreiten, übertreffen; **exceedingly** adv äußerst

excel 1. vt übertreffen **2.** vi

sich auszeichnen (*in* in + *dat*, *at* bei); **excellent, excellently** *adj, adv* ausgezeichnet

except 1. *prep* ~ außer + *dat*; ~ **for** abgesehen von **2.** *vt* ausnehmen; **exception** *n* Ausnahme *f*; **exceptional, exceptionally** *adj, adv* außergewöhnlich

excess *n* Übermaß *nt* (*of* an + *dat*); **excess baggage** *n* Übergepäck *nt*; **excess fare** *n* Nachlösegebühr *f*; **excessive, excessively** *adj, adv* übermäßig; **excess weight** *n* Übergewicht *nt*

exchange 1. *n* Austausch *m* (*for* gegen); (*of bought items*) Umtausch *m* (*for* gegen); FIN Wechsel *m*; TEL Vermittlung *f*, Zentrale *f* **2.** *vt* austauschen; (*goods*) tauschen; (*bought items*) umtauschen (*for* gegen); (*money, blows*) wechseln; **exchange rate** *n* Wechselkurs *m*

excited *adj* aufgeregt; **exciting** *adj* aufregend; (*book, film*) spannend

exclamation *n* Ausruf *m*; **exclamation mark, exclamation point** (*US*) *n* Ausrufezeichen *nt*

exclude *vt* ausschließen; **exclusion** *n* Ausschluss *m*; **exclusive** *adj* (*select*) exklusiv; (*sole*) alleinig; **exclusively** *adv* ausschließlich

excruciating *adj* fürchterlich, entsetzlich

excursion *n* Ausflug *m*

excuse 1. *vt* entschuldigen; ~ **me** Entschuldigung! **2.** *n* Entschuldigung *f*, Ausrede *f*

ex-directory *adj* **be** ~ (*Brit*) TEL nicht im Telefonbuch stehen

execution *n* (*killing*) Hinrichtung *f*; **executive** *n* leitender Angestellter, leitende Angestellte

exemplary *adj* beispielhaft

exercise *n* (*in school, sports*) Übung *f*; (*movement*) Bewegung *f*; **get more** ~ mehr Sport treiben

exert *vt* (*influence*) ausüben

exhaust *vt* (*fumes*) Abgase *pl*; AUTO Auspuff *m*; **exhausted** *adj* erschöpft; **exhausting** *adj* anstrengend

exhibit *n* (*in exhibition*) Ausstellungsstück *nt*; **exhibition** *n* Ausstellung *f*

exhilarating *adj* belebend, erregend

exile 1. *n* Exil *nt*; (*person*) Verbannte(r) *mf* **2.** *vt* verbannen

exist *vi* existieren; (*live*) leben (*on* von); **existence** *n* Existenz *f*; **come into** ~ entstehen; **existing** *adj* bestehend

exit *n* Ausgang *m*; (*for vehicles*) Ausfahrt *f*

exotic *adj* exotisch

expand 1. *vt* ausdehnen, erweitern **2.** *vi* sich ausdehnen; **expansion** *n* Expansion *f*, Erweiterung *f*

expect 1. *vt* erwarten; (*sup-*

pose) annehmen; **he ~s me to do it** er erwartet, dass ich es mache; **I ~ it'll rain** es wird wohl regnen; **I ~** ich denke schon **2.** *vi* **be ~ing** ein Kind erwarten

expenditure *n* Ausgaben *pl*

expense *n* Kosten *pl*; (*single cost*) Ausgabe *f*; (**business**) **~s** *pl* Spesen *pl*; **at sb's ~** auf jds Kosten; **expensive** *adj* teuer

experience 1. *n* Erfahrung *f*; (*particular incident*) Erlebnis *nt*; **by/ from ~** aus Erfahrung **2.** *vt* erfahren, erleben; (*hardship*) durchmachen; **experienced** *adj* erfahren

experiment 1. *n* Versuch *m*, Experiment *nt* **2.** *vi* experimentieren

expert 1. *n* Experte *m*, Expertin *f*; (*professional*) Fachmann *m*, Fachfrau *f*; LAW Sachverständige(r) *mf* & **2.** *adj* fachmännisch; **expertise** *n* Sachkenntnis *f*

expire *vi* (*end*) ablaufen; **expiry date** *n* Verfallsdatum *nt*

explain *vt* erklären (*sth to sb* jdm etw); **explanation** *n* Erklärung *f*

explicit *adj* ausdrücklich, deutlich

explode *vi* explodieren

exploit *vt* ausbeuten

explore *vt* erforschen

explosion *n* Explosion *f*; **explosive 1.** *adj* explosiv **2.** *n* Sprengstoff *m*

export 1. *vt*, *vi* exportieren **2.** *n* Export *m* **3.** *adj* (*trade*) Export-

expose *vt* (*to danger etc*) aussetzen (*to dat*); (*uncover*) freilegen; (*imposter*) entlarven; **exposed** *adj* (*position*) ungeschützt; MED Unterkühlung *f*; PHOT (*time*) Belichtung(szeit) *f*; **24 ~s** 24 Aufnahmen

express 1. *adj* (*speedy*) Express-, Schnell-; **~ delivery** Eilzustellung *f* **2.** *n* RAIL Schnellzug *m* **3.** *vt* ausdrücken **4.** *vr* **~ oneself** sich ausdrücken; **expression** *n* (*phrase*) Ausdruck *m*; (*look*) Gesichtsausdruck *m*; **expressway** *n* (*US*) Schnellstraße *f*

extend 1. *vt* (*arms*) ausstrecken; (*lengthen*) verlängern; (*building*) vergrößern, ausbauen; (*business, limits*) erweitern; **extension** *n* (*lengthening*) Verlängerung *f*; (*of building*) Anbau *m*; TEL Anschluss *m*; **extensive** *adj* (*knowledge*) umfangreich; **extent** *n* (*length*) Länge *f*; (*size*) Ausdehnung *f*; (*scope*) Umfang *m*, Ausmaß *nt*; **to a certain/ large ~** in gewissem/ hohem Maße

exterior *n* Äußere(s) *nt*

external *adj* äußere(r, s), Außen-; **externally** *adv* äußerlich

factor

extinct *adj* (*species*) ausgestorben

extinguish *vt* löschen; extinguisher *n* Löschgerät *nt*

extra **1.** *adj* zusätzlich; *~* ***charge*** Zuschlag *m*; *~* ***time*** SPORT Verlängerung *f* **2.** *adv* besonders; *~* ***large*** (*clothing*) übergroß **3.** *npl* ~**s** zusätzliche Kosten *pl*; (*food*) Beilagen *pl*; (*accessories*) Zubehör *nt*; (*for car etc*) Extras *pl*

extract **1.** *vt* herausziehen (*from* aus); (*tooth*) ziehen **2.** *n* (*from book etc*) Auszug *m*

extraordinary *adj* außerordentlich; (*unusual*) ungewöhnlich; (*amazing*) erstaunlich

extreme **1.** *adj* äußerste(r, s);

(*drastic*) extrem **2.** *n* Extrem *nt*; extremely *adv* äußerst, höchst; extreme sports *npl* Extremsportarten *pl*; extremist **1.** *adj* extremistisch **2.** *n* Extremist *m*

extrovert *adj* extrovertiert

exultation *n* Jubel *m*

eye **1.** *n* Auge *nt*; ***keep an ~ on sb/sth*** auf jdn/etw aufpassen **2.** *vt* mustern; eyebrow *n* Augenbraue *f*; eyelash *n* Wimper *f*; eyelid *n* Augenlid *nt*; eyeliner *n* Eyeliner *m*; eyeopener *n* ***that was an ~*** das hat mir die Augen geöffnet; eyeshadow *n* Lidschatten *m*; eyesight *n* Sehkraft *f*; eyesore *n* Schandfleck *m*; eye witness *n* Augenzeuge *m*, Augenzeugin *f*

F

fabric *n* Stoff *m*

fabulous *adj* sagenhaft

façade *n* Fassade *f*

face **1.** *n* Gesicht *nt*; (*of clock*) Zifferblatt *nt*; (*of mountain*) Wand *f*; ***in the ~ of*** trotz + *gen*; ***be ~ to ~*** (*people*) einander gegenüberstehen **2.** *vt, vi* (*person*) gegenüberstehen + *dat*; (*at table*) gegenübersitzen + *dat*; *~* ***north*** (*room*) nach Norden sein; ***~ (up to) the facts*** den Tatsachen ins Auge sehen; ***be ~d with sth*** mit etw konfrontiert

sein; face cream *n* Gesichtscreme *f*

facet *n* *fig* Aspekt *m*

face value *n* Nennwert *m*

facial **1.** *adj* Gesichts- **2.** *n* *fam* (kosmetische) Gesichtsbehandlung

facilitate *vt* erleichtern

facility *n* (*building etc to be used*) Einrichtung *f*, Möglichkeit *f*

fact *n* Tatsache *f*; ***as a matter of ~***, ***in ~*** eigentlich, tatsächlich

factor *n* Faktor *m*

factory n Fabrik f; **factory outlet** n Fabrikverkauf m
factual adj sachlich
faculty n Fähigkeit f; (at university) Fakultät f; (US, teaching staff) Lehrkörper m
fade vi verblassen
fag n (Brit) fam (cigarette) Kippe f; (US) fam pej Schwule(r) m
Fahrenheit n Fahrenheit
fail 1. vt (exam) nicht bestehen **2.** vi versagen; (plan, marriage) scheitern; (student) durchfallen; (eyesight) nachlassen; **words ~ me** ich bin sprachlos; **failure** n (person) Versager(in) m(f); (act) Versagen nt; (of engine etc) Ausfall m; (of plan, marriage) Scheitern nt
faint 1. adj schwach; (sound) leise; fam **I haven't a ~est (idea)** ich habe keine Ahnung **2.** vi ohnmächtig werden (with vor + dat); **faintness** n MED Schwächegefühl nt
fair 1. adj (hair) blond; (skin) hell; (just) gerecht; fair; (reasonable) ganz ordentlich; (in school) befriedigend; (weather) schön; (wind) günstig; **a ~ number/amount of** ziemlich viele/ viel **2.** adv (play) fair spielen; fig fair sein; **~ enough** in Ordnung! **3.** n (fun~) Jahrmarkt m; COMM Messe f; **fair-haired** adj blond; **fairly** adv (honestly) fair; (rather) ziemlich
fairy n Fee f; **fairy tale** n Märchen nt
faith n (trust) Vertrauen nt (in sb zu jdm); REL Glaube m; **faithful, faithfully** adj, adv treu; **Yours ~ly** Hochachtungsvoll
fake 1. n (thing) Fälschung f **2.** adj vorgetäuscht **3.** vt fälschen
fall 1. vi fallen; (from a height, badly) stürzen; **~ ill** krank werden; **~ asleep** einschlafen; **~ in love** sich verlieben **2.** n (person) Fall m; (accident) Sturz m; (decrease) Sinken nt (in + gen); (US, autumn) Herbst m; **fall apart** vi auseinanderfallen; **fall behind** vi zurückbleiben; (with work, rent) in Rückstand geraten; **fall down** vi (person) hinfallen; **fall off** vi herunterfallen; (decrease) zurückgehen; **fall out** vi herausfallen; (quarrel) sich streiten; **fall over** vi hinfallen; **fall through** vi (plan etc) ins Wasser fallen
fallen pp of **fall**
false adj falsch; (artificial) künstlich; **false alarm** n blinder Alarm; **false start** n SPORT Fehlstart m; **false teeth** npl (künstliches) Gebiss
fame n Ruhm m
familiar adj vertraut, bekannt; **be ~ with** vertraut sein mit,

gut kennen; **familiarity** n Vertrautheit f

family n Familie f; *(including relations)* Verwandtschaft f; **family man** n Familienvater m; **family name** n Familienname m, Nachname m

famine n Hungersnot f

famous adj berühmt

fan n *(hand-held)* Fächer m; ELEC Ventilator m; *(admirer)* Fan m

fanatic n Fanatiker(in) m(f)

fancy 1. adj *(elaborate)* kunstvoll; *(unusual)* ausgefallen **2.** vt *(like)* gern haben; **he fancies her** er steht auf sie; ~ **that** stell dir vor!, so was!; **fancy dress** n Kostüm nt, Verkleidung f

fan heater n Heizlüfter m

fantasise vi träumen *(about* von); **fantastic** adj fantastisch; **that's** ~ *fam* das ist ja toll!; **fantasy** n Fantasie f

far 1. adj weit; **the ~ end of the room** das andere Ende des Zimmers; **the Far East** der Ferne Osten **2.** adv weit; ~ **better** viel besser; **by ~ the best** bei weitem der/die/ das Beste; **as ~ as ...** bis zum *or* zur ...; *(with place name)* bis nach ...; **as ~ as I'm concerned** was mich betrifft, von mir aus; **so ~** soweit, bisher; **faraway** adj weit entfernt; *(look)* verträumt

fare n Fahrpreis m

farm n Bauernhof m, Farm f; **farmer** n Bauer m, Bäuerin f, Landwirt(in) m(f); **farmhouse** n Bauernhaus nt; **farming** n Landwirtschaft f; **farmland** n Ackerland nt; **farmyard** n Hof m

far-reaching adj weit reichend; **far-sighted** adj weitsichtig

fart 1. n fam Furz m; **old-** fam *(person)* alter Sack m **2.** vi fam furzen

farther adj, adv comparative of **far**; → **further**; **farthest** adj, adv superlative of **far**; → **furthest**

fascinating adj faszinierend; **fascination** n Faszination f

fashion n *(clothes)* Mode f; *(manner)* Art und Weise f; **be in** ~ (in) Mode sein; **out of** ~ unmodisch; **fashionable, fashionably** adj, adv *(clothes, person)* modisch

fast 1. adj schnell; *(dye)* waschecht; **be** ~ *(clock)* vorgehen **2.** adv schnell; *(firmly)* fest; **be** ~ **asleep** fest schlafen **3.** n Fasten nt **4.** vi fasten

fasten vt *(attach)* befestigen *(to* an + dat*)*; *(do up)* zumachen; ~ **your seatbelts** bitte anschnallen; **fastener, fastening** n Verschluss m

fast food n Fast Food nt; **fast forward** n *(for tape)* Schnellvorlauf m; **fast lane** n Überholspur f

fat 1. *adj* dick; *(meat)* fett **2.** *n* Fett *nt*

fatal *adj* tödlich

fate *n* Schicksal *nt*

fat-free *adj* fettfrei

father 1. *n* Vater *m*; *(priest)* Pfarrer *m* **2.** *vt* *(child)* zeugen; **Father Christmas** *n* der Weihnachtsmann; **father-in-law** *n* Schwiegervater *m*

fatigue *n* Ermüdung *f*

fattening *adj* **be ~** dick machen; **fatty** *adj* *(food)* fettig

faucet *n* *(US)* Wasserhahn *m*

fault *n* Fehler *m*; TECH Defekt *m*; ELEC Störung *f*; *(blame)* Schuld *f*; **it's your ~** du bist daran schuld; **faulty** *adj* fehlerhaft; TECH defekt

favor *(US)*, **favour 1.** *n* *(approval)* Gunst *f*; *(kindness)* Gefallen *m*; **in ~ of** für; **I'm in ~ (of going)** ich bin dafür, dass wir gehen); **do sb a ~** jdm einen Gefallen tun **2.** *vt* *(prefer)* vorziehen; **favourite 1.** *n* Liebling *m*, Favorit(in) *m(f)* **2.** *adj* Lieblings-

fax 1. *vt* faxen **2.** *n* Fax *nt*; **fax number** *n* Faxnummer *f*

FBI *abbr* = **Federal Bureau of Investigation**; FBI *nt*

fear 1. *n* Angst *f* *(of* + *dat)* **2.** *vt* befürchten; **I ~ that most** hast du am meisten Angst; **fearful** *adj* *(timid)* ängstlich, furchtsam; *(terrible)* fürchterlich

feasible *adj* machbar

feast *n* Festessen *nt*

feather *n* Feder *f*

feature 1. *n* *(facial)* (Gesichts)zug *m*; *(characteristic)* Merkmal *nt*; *(of car etc)* Ausstattungsmerkmal *nt*; *(in the press)* Feature *nt* **2.** *vt* bringen, (als Besonderheit) zeigen; **feature film** *n* Spielfilm *m*

February *n* Februar *m*; → **September**

fed *pt, pp of* **feed**

federal *adj* Bundes-; **the Federal Republic of Germany** die Bundesrepublik Deutschland

fed-up *adj* **be ~ with sth** etw satt haben; **I'm ~** ich habe die Nase voll

fee *n* Gebühr *f*; *(of doctor, lawyer)* Honorar *nt*

feeble *adj* schwach

feed 1. *vt* *(baby, animal)* füttern; *(support)* ernähren **2.** *n* *(for baby)* Mahlzeit *f*; *(for animals)* Futter *nt*; IT *(paper ~)* Zufuhr *f*; **feed in** *vt* *(information)* eingeben; **feedback** *n* *(information)* Feed-back *nt*

feel 1. *vt* *(sense)* fühlen; *(pain)* empfinden; *(think)* meinen **2.** *vi* *(person)* sich fühlen; **I ~ cold** mir ist kalt; **do you ~ like a walk?** hast du Lust, spazieren zu gehen?; **feeling** *n* Gefühl *nt*

feet *pl of* **foot**

fell 1. pt of fall 2. vt (tree) fällen

fellow n Kerl m, Typ m; ~ citizen Mitbürger(in) m(f)

felt 1. pt, pp of feel 2. n Filz m; felt tip, felt-tip pen n Filzstift m

female n (of animals) Weibchen nt 2. adj weiblich; ~ doctor Ärztin f; ~ dog Hündin f; feminine adj weiblich

fence n Zaun m

fencing n sport Fechten nt

fender n (US) auto Kotflügel m

fennel n Fenchel m

fern n Farn m

ferocious adj wild

ferry 1. n Fähre f 2. vt übersetzen

festival n rel Fest nt; art, mus Festspiele pl; (pop music) Festival nt; festive adj festlich; festivities n Feierlichkeiten pl

fetch vt holen; (collect) abholen; (in sale, money) einbringen; fetching adj reizend

fetish n Fetisch m

fetus n (US) Fötus m

fever n Fieber nt; feverish adj med fiebrig; fig fieberhaft

few adj, pron a/ wenige pl; a ~ pl ein paar; fewer adj weniger; fewest adj wenigste(r, s)

fiancé n Verlobte(r) m; fiancée n Verlobte f

fiber (US), fibre n Faser f; (material) Faserstoff m

fiction n (novels) Prosaliteratur f; fictional, fictitious adj erfunden

fiddle 1. n Geige f; (trick) Betrug m 2. vt (accounts, results) frisieren; fiddle with vt herumfummeln an + dat

fidelity n Treue f

fidget vi zappeln; fidgety adj zappelig

field n Feld nt; (grass-covered) Wiese f; fig (of work) (Arbeits)gebiet nt

fierce adj heftig; (animal, appearance) wild; (criticism, competition) scharf

fifteen 1. num fünfzehn 2. n Fünfzehn f; → eight; fifteenth adj fünfzehnte(r, s); → eighth; fifth 1. adj fünfte(r, s) 2. n (fraction) Fünftel nt; → eighth; fifty 1. num fünfzig 2. n Fünfzig f; → eight; fiftieth adj fünfzigste(r, s); → eighth

fig n Feige f

fight 1. vi kämpfen (with, against gegen, for, over um) 2. vt (person) kämpfen mit; fig (disease, fire etc) bekämpfen 3. n Kampf m; (brawl) Schlägerei f; (argument) Streit m; fight back vi zurückschlagen; fight off vt abwehren

figurative adj übertragen

figure 1. n (person) Gestalt f; (of person) Figur f; (number) Zahl f, Ziffer f; (amount) Betrag m; a four-figure sum eine vierstellige Summe 2. vt (US, think) glauben 3. vi (ap-

pear) erscheinen; **figure out** vt (_work out_) herausbekommen; **I can't figure him out** ich werde aus ihm nicht schlau; **figure skating** n Eiskunstlauf m

file 1. n (_tool_) Feile f; (_dossier_) Akte f; IT Datei f; (_folder_) Aktenordner m; **on ~** in den Akten **2.** vt (_metal, nails_) feilen; (_papers_) ablegen (_under_ unter)

fill vt füllen; (_tooth_) plombieren; (_post_) besetzen; **fill in** vt (_hole_) auffüllen; (_form_) ausfüllen; (_tell_) informieren (_on_ über); **fill out** vt (_form_) ausfüllen; **fill up** vi AUTO voll tanken

fillet n Filet nt

filling n GASTR Füllung f; (_for tooth_) Plombe f; **filling station** n Tankstelle f

film 1. n Film m **2.** vt (_scene_) filmen; **film star** n Filmstar m; **film studio** n Filmstudio nt

filter n Filter m; (_traffic lane_) Abbiegespur f **2.** vt filtern

filth n Dreck m; **filthy** adj dreckig

fin n Flosse f

final 1. adj letzte(r, s); (_stage, round_) End-; (_decision, version_) endgültig; **~ score** n SPORT Schlussstand m **2.** n SPORT Endspiel nt; (_competition_) Finale nt; **~s** pl, Abschlussexamen nt; **finalize** vt die endgültige Form geben

+ dat; finally adv (_lastly_) zuletzt; (_eventually_) schließlich, endlich

finance 1. n Finanzwesen nt; **~s** pl Finanzen pl **2.** vt finanzieren; **financial** adj finanziell; (_adviser, crisis, policy etc_) Finanz-

find vt finden; **he was found dead** er wurde tot aufgefunden; **I ~ myself in difficulties** ich befinde mich in Schwierigkeiten; **she ~s it difficult/easy** es fällt ihr schwer/leicht; **find out** vt herausfinden; **findings** npl LAW Ermittlungsergebnis nt; MED Befund m

fine 1. adj (_thin_) dünn, fein; (_good_) gut; (_splendid_) herrlich; schön; **I'm ~** es geht mir gut; **that's ~** das ist OK **2.** adv (_well_) gut **3.** n LAW Geldstrafe f **4.** vt LAW mit einer Geldstrafe belegen; **fine arts** npl **the ~** die schönen Künste pl

finger 1. n Finger m **2.** vt herumfingern an + dat; **fingernail** n Fingernagel m; **fingerprint** n Fingerabdruck m; **fingertip** n Fingerspitze f

finicky adj (_person_) pingelig; (_work_) knifflig

finish 1. n Ende nt; SPORT Finish nt; (_line_) Ziel nt; (_of product_) Verarbeitung f **2.** vt beenden; (_book etc_) zu Ende lesen; (_food_) aufessen; (_drink_) austrinken **3.** vi zu

Ende gehen; (*song, story*) enden; (*person*) fertig sein; (*stop*) aufhören; **have you ~ed?** bist du fertig?; ~ **first/second** SPORT als erster/zweiter durchs Ziel gehen; **finishing line** *n* Ziellinie *f*

Finland *n* Finnland *nt*; **Finn** *n* Finne *m*, Finnin *f*; **Finnish 1.** *adj* finnisch **2.** *n* (*language*) Finnisch *nt*

fir *n* Tanne *f*

fire 1. *n* Feuer *nt*; (*house etc*) Brand *m*; **set ~ to sth** etw in Brand stecken; **be on ~** brennen **2.** *vt* (*bullets, rockets*) abfeuern; *fam* (*dismiss*) feuern **3.** *vi* AUTO (*engine*) zünden; **~ at sb** auf jdn schießen; **fire alarm** *n* Feuermelder *m*; **fire brigade** *n* Feuerwehr *f*; **fire engine** *n* Feuerwehrauto *nt*; **fire escape** *n* Feuerleiter *f*; **fire extinguisher** *n* Feuerlöscher *m*; **firefighter** *n* Feuerwehrmann *m*, Feuerwehrfrau *f*; **fireman** *n* Feuerwehrmann *m*; **fireplace** *n* (offener) Kamin; **fireproof** *adj* feuerfest; **fire station** *n* Feuerwache *f*; **fireworks** *npl* Feuerwerk *nt*

firm 1. *adj* fest; (*person*) **be ~** entschlossen auftreten **2.** *n* Firma *f*

first 1. *adj* erste(r, s) **2.** *adv* (*at first*) zuerst; (*firstly*) erstens; (*arrive, finish*) als erste(r); (*happen*) zum ersten Mal; **~**

of all zuallererst **3.** *n* (*person*) Erste(r) *mf*; AUTO (*gear*) erster Gang; **~** *adv* zuerst, anfangs; **first aid** *n* erste Hilfe; **first-class 1.** *adj* erstklassig; (*compartment, ticket*) erster Klasse; **~ mail** (*Brit*) bevorzugt beförderte Post **2.** *adv* (*travel*) erster Klasse; **first floor** *n* (*Brit*) erster Stock; (*US*) Erdgeschoss *nt*; **first lady** *n* (*US*) Frau *f* des Präsidenten; **firstly** *adv* erstens; **first name** *n* Vorname *m*; **first night** *n* THEAT Premiere *f*; **first-rate** *adj* erstklassig

fir tree *n* Tannenbaum *m*

fish 1. *n* Fisch *m* **2.** *vi* fischen; (*with rod*) angeln; **go ~ing** fischen/angeln gehen

fishbone *n* Gräte *f*; **fish farm** *n* Fischzucht *f*; **fish finger** *n* (*Brit*) Fischstäbchen *nt*; **fishing** *n* Fischen *nt*; (*with rod*) Angeln *nt*; **fishing boat** *n* Fischerboot *nt*; **fishing line** *n* Angelschnur *f*; **fishing rod** *n* Angelrute *f*; **fishmonger** *n* Fischhändler(in) *m(f)*; **fish stick** *n* (*US*) Fischstäbchen *nt*; **fish tank** *n* Aquarium *nt*; **fishy** *adj fam* (*suspicious*) faul

fist *n* Faust *f*

fit 1. *adj* MED gesund; SPORT in Form, fit; **keep ~** sich in Form halten **2.** *vt* passen + *dat*; (*attach*) anbringen (*to* an + *dat*); (*install*) einbauen (*in* in + *acc*) **3.** *vi* passen; (*in space, gap*) hineinpassen

4. n (of clothes) Sitz m; MED Anfall m; **it's a good ~** es passt gut; **fit in 1.** vt (accommodate) unterbringen; (find time for) einschieben **2.** vi (in space) hineinpassen; (plans, ideas) passen; **he doesn't ~ (here)** er passt nicht hierher; **~ with sb's plans** sich mit jds Plänen vereinbaren lassen; fitness n MED Gesundheit f; SPORT Fitness f; fitted carpet n Teppichboden m; fitted kitchen n Einbauküche f; fitting **1.** adj passend **2.** n (of dress) Anprobe f; **~s** pl Ausstattung f

five 1. num fünf **2.** n Fünf f; → **eight**; fiver n (Brit) fam Fünfpfundschein m

fix vt befestigen (to an + dat); (settle) festsetzen; (place, time) ausmachen; (repair) reparieren; fixer n (drug addict) Fixer(in) m(f); fixture n **~s (and fittings)** pl Ausstattung f

fizzy adj sprudelnd; **~ drink** Limo f

flabbergasted adj fam platt

flabby adj (fat) wabbelig

flag n Fahne f

flake 1. n Flocke f **2.** vi **~ (off)** abblättern

flamboyant adj extravagant

flame n Flamme f; (person) **an old ~** eine alte Liebe

flan n (fruit ~) Obstkuchen m

flannel 1. n Flanell m; (Brit,

face ~) Waschlappen m **2.** vi herumlabern

flap 1. n Klappe f; fam **be in a ~** rotieren **2.** vt (wings) schlagen mit **3.** vi flattern

flared adj (trousers) mit Schlag; flares npl Schlaghose f

flash 1. n Blitz m; (news ~) Kurzmeldung f; PHOT Blitzlicht nt; **in a ~** in Nu **2.** vt **~ one's (head)lights** die Lichthupe betätigen **3.** vi aufblinken; (brightly) aufblitzen; flashback n Rückblende f; flashlight n PHOTO Blitzlicht nt; (US, torch) Taschenlampe f; flashy adj grell, protzig; fam protzig

flat 1. adj flach; (surface) eben; (drink) abgestanden; (tyre) platt; (battery) leer; (refusal) glatt **2.** n (Brit, rooms) Wohnung f; AUTO Reifenpanne f; **flat screen** n IT Flachbildschirm m; flatten vt platt machen, einebnen

flatter vt schmeicheln + dat; flattering adj schmeichelhaft

flatware n (US) Besteck nt

flavor (US), **flavour 1.** n Geschmack m **2.** vt Geschmack geben + dat; (with spices) würzen; flavouring n Aroma nt

flaw n Fehler m; flawless adj fehlerlos; (complexion) makellos

flea n Floh m

fled pt, pp of **flee**
flee vi fliehen
fleece n (of sheep) Vlies nt; (soft material) Fleece m; (jacket) Fleecejacke f
fleet n Flotte f
flesh n Fleisch nt
flew pt of **fly**
flex n (Brit) ELEC Schnur f
flexibility n Biegsamkeit f; fig Flexibilität f; **flexible** adj biegsam; (plans, person) flexibel; flexitime n gleitende Arbeitszeit, Gleitzeit f
flicker vi flackern; TV flimmern
flies pl of **fly 2**
flight n Flug m; (escape) Flucht f; ~ **of stairs** Treppe f; flight attendant n Flugbegleiter(in) m(f); flight recorder n Flugschreiber m
flimsy adj leicht gebaut, nicht stabil; (thin) hauchdünn; (excuse) fadenscheinig
fling 1. vt schleudern **2.** n **have a ~** eine (kurze) Affäre haben
flint n Feuerstein m
flip vt schnippen; ~ **a coin** eine Münze werfen; **flip through** vt (book) durchblättern; flipchart n Flipchart nt
flipper n Flosse f
flirt vi flirten
float vi schwimmen; (in air) schweben
flock n (of sheep) Herde f; (of birds) Schwarm m; (of people) Schar f

flood 1. n Hochwasser nt, Überschwemmung f; fig Flut f **2.** vt überschwemmen;
floodlight n Flutlicht nt; floodlit adj (building) angestrahlt
floor n Fußboden m; (storey) Stock m; **ground ~** (Brit), **first ~** (US) Erdgeschoss nt; **first ~** (Brit), **second ~** (US) erster Stock
flop 1. n fam (failure) Reinfall m, Flop m **2.** vi misslingen, floppen
floppy disk n Diskette f
Florence n Florenz nt
flounder n (fish) Flunder f
flour n Mehl nt
flourish 1. vi gedeihen; (business) gut laufen; (boom) florieren **2.** vt (wave about) schwenken; **flourishing** adj blühend
flow 1. n Fluss m; **go with the ~** mit dem Strom schwimmen **2.** vi fließen
flower 1. n Blume f **2.** vi blühen; flower bed n Blumenbeet nt; flowerpot n Blumentopf m
flown pp of **fly**
flu n fam Grippe f
fluent adj (Italian etc) fließend; **be ~ in German** fließend Deutsch sprechen
fluid 1. n Flüssigkeit f **2.** adj flüssig
flung pt, pp of **fling**
flush 1. n (lavatory) Wasserspülung f; (blush) Röte f **2.**

vi (*lavatory*) spülen

flute n Flöte f

fly 1. vt, vi fliegen; **how time flies** wie die Zeit vergeht! **2.** n (*insect*) Fliege f; **~/flies** pl (*on trousers*) Hosenschlitz m; **fly-drive** n Urlaub m mit Flug und Mietwagen; **flyover** n (*Brit*) Straßenüberführung f, Eisenbahnüberführung f; **flysheet** n Überzelt nt

foal n Fohlen nt

foam 1. n Schaum m **2.** vi schäumen

focus 1. n Brennpunkt m; **in/out of ~** (*photo*) scharf/unscharf **2.** vt (*camera*) scharf stellen **3.** vi sich konzentrieren (*on* auf + *acc*)

foetus n Fötus m

fog n Nebel m; **foggy** adj neblig; **fog light** n AUTO (*at rear*) Nebelschlussleuchte f

foil n Folie f

fold 1. vt falten **2.** vi fam (*business*) eingehen **3.** n Falte f; **fold up 1.** vt (*map etc*) zusammenfalten; (*chair etc*) zusammenklappen **2.** vi (*business*) fam eingehen; **folder** n (*portfolio*) Aktenmappe f; (*pamphlet*) Broschüre f; IT Ordner m; **folding** adj zusammenklappbar; (*bicycle, chair*) Klapp-

folk n Leute pl; MUS Folk m; **my ~s** pl fam meine Leute **2.** adj Volks-

follow 1. vt folgen + dat; (*pur-*

sue) verfolgen; (*understand*) folgen können + dat; (*career, news etc*) verfolgen; **as ~s** wie folgt **2.** vi folgen; (*result*) sich ergeben (*from* aus); **follow up** vt (*request, rumour*) nachgehen + dat, weiter verfolgen; **follower** n Anhänger(in) m(f); **following 1.** adj folgend; **the ~ day** am (darauf) folgenden Tag **2.** prep nach

fond adj **be ~ of** gern haben; **fondly** adv (*with love*) liebevoll; **fondness** n Vorliebe f; (*for people*) Zuneigung f

fondue n Fondue nt

font n Taufbecken nt; TYPO Schriftart f

food n Essen nt, Lebensmittel pl; (*for animals*) Futter nt; **food poisoning** n Lebensmittelvergiftung f; **food processor** n Küchenmaschine f; **foodstuff** n Lebensmittel nt

fool 1. n Idiot m, Narr m; **make a ~ of oneself** sich blamieren **2.** vt (*deceive*) hereinlegen **3.** vi **~ around** herumalbern; (*waste time*) herumtrödeln; **foolish** adj dumm; **foolproof** adj idiotensicher

foot 1. n Fuß m; (*measure*) Fuß m (30,48 cm); **on ~** zu Fuß **2.** vt (*bill*) bezahlen; **foot-and-mouth disease** n Maulund Klauenseuche f; **football** n Fußball m; (*US*) Football m; **footballer** n Fußball-

spieler(in) *m(f)*; **footbridge**
n Fußgängerbrücke *f*; **foot-
ing** *n* (*hold*) Halt *m*; **foot-
note** *n* Fußnote *f*; **footpath**
n Fußweg *m*; **footprint** *n*
Fußabdruck *m*; **footwear** *n*
Schuhwerk *nt*

for 1. *prep* für; **I'm all ~ it** ich
bin ganz dafür; (*purpose*)
what ~? wozu?; **~ pleasure**
zum Vergnügen; **what's ~
lunch?** was gibt es zum Mittagessen?; (*destination*) **the
train ~ London** der Zug nach
London; (*because of*) **~ this
reason** aus diesem Grund;
famous ~ bekannt für, berühmt wegen; (*with time*)
we talked ~ two hours wir
redeten zwei Stunden lang;
(*up to now*) **we have been
talking ~** wir reden seit zwei
den seit zwei Stunden; (*with
distance*) **~ miles (and miles)**
meilenweit; **bends ~ 2 miles**
kurvenreich auf 2 Meilen; **as
~ ...** was ... betrifft **2.** *conj*
denn

forbade *pt of* **forbid**
forbid *vt* verbieten

force 1. *n* Kraft *f*, Gewalt *f*;
come into ~ in Kraft treten;
the Forces *pl* die Streitkräf-
te **2.** *vt* zwingen; **forced** *adj*
(*smile*) gezwungen
forceps *npl* Zange *f*
forearm *n* Unterarm *m*
forecast 1. *vt* voraussagen;
(*weather*) vorhersagen **2.** *n*
Vorhersage *f*

forefinger *n* Zeigefinger *m*
foreground *n* Vordergrund *m*
forehand *n* SPORT Vorhand *f*
forehead *n* Stirn *f*
foreign *adj* ausländisch; **foreigner** *n* Ausländer(in)
m(f); **foreign exchange** *n*
Devisen *pl*; **foreign language** *n* Fremdsprache *f*;
foreign minister, **foreign
secretary** *n* Außenminis-
ter(in) *m(f)*
foremost *adj* erste(r, s); (*leading*) führend
forerunner *n* Vorläufer(in)
m(f)
foresee *irr vt* vorhersehen;
foreseeable *adj* absehbar
forest *n* Wald *m*; **forestry** *n*
Forstwirtschaft *f*
forever *adv* für immer
forgave *pt of* **forgive**
forge 1. *n* Schmiede *f* **2.** *vt*
schmieden; (*fake*) fälschen;
forgery *n* Fälschung *f*
forget *vt*, *vi* vergessen; **~
about sth** etw vergessen;
forgetful *adj* vergesslich;
forget-me-not *n* Vergissmeinnicht *nt*
forgive *vt*, *vi* verzeihen; **~ sb
for sth** jdm etw verzeihen
forgot *pt of* **forget**
forgotten *pp of* **forget**
fork 1. *n* Gabel *f*; (*in road*) Gabelung *f* **2.** *vi* (*road*) sich ga-
beln
form 1. *n* (*shape*) Form *f*,
Klasse *f*; (*document*) Formular *nt*; (*person*) **be in** (**good**)

~ in Form sein 2. vt bilden

formal adj förmlich, formell; **formality** n Formalität f

format 1. n Format nt 2. vt IT formatieren

former adj frühere(r, s); (opposite of latter) erstere(r, s); **formerly** adv früher

formula n Formel f

forth adv **and so ~** und so weiter; **forthcoming** adj kommend, bevorstehend

fortieth adj vierzigste(r, s); → **eighth**

fortnight n vierzehn Tage pl

fortress n Festung f

fortunate adj glücklich; **I was ~** ich hatte Glück; **fortunately** adv zum Glück; **fortune** n (money) Vermögen nt; **good ~** Glück nt; **fortune-teller** n Wahrsager(in) m(f)

forty 1. num vierzig 2. n Vierzig f; → **eight**

forward 1. adv vorwärts 2. n SPORT Stürmer(in) m(f) 3. vt (send on) nachsenden; IT weiterleiten; **forwards** adv vorwärts

foster child n Pflegekind nt; **foster parents** npl Pflegeeltern pl

fought pt, pp of **fight**

foul 1. adj (weather) schlecht; (smell) übel 2. n SPORT Foul nt

found 1. pt, pp of **find** 2. vt (establish) gründen; **foundations** npl Fundament nt

fountain n Springbrunnen m;

fountain pen n Füller m

four 1. num vier 2. n Vier f; → **eight**; **fourteen** 1. num vierzehn 2. n Vierzehn f; → **eight**; **fourteenth** adj vierzehnte(r, s); → **eighth**; **fourth** adj vierte(r, s); → **eighth**

fowl n Geflügel nt

fox n Fuchs m

fraction n MATH Bruch m; (part) Bruchteil m; **fracture** 1. n MED Bruch m 2. vt brechen

fragile adj zerbrechlich

fragment n Bruchstück nt

fragrance n Duft m; **fragrant** adj duftend

frail adj gebrechlich

frame 1. n Rahmen m; (of spectacles) Gestell nt; **~ of mind** Verfassung f 2. vt einrahmen; **framework** n Rahmen m, Struktur f

France n Frankreich nt

frank adj offen

frankfurter n (Frankfurter) Würstchen nt

frankly adv offen gesagt; **quite ~** ganz ehrlich

frantic adj (activity) hektisch; (effort) verzweifelt; **~ with worry** außer sich vor Sorge

fraud n (trickery) Betrug m; (person) Schwindler(in) m(f)

freak 1. n Anomalie f; (ani-

mal, person) Missgeburt *f*; **fam** (*fan*) Fan *m*, Freak *m* **2.** *adj* (*conditions*) außergewöhnlich, seltsam; **freak out** *vi fam* ausflippen

freckle *n* Sommersprosse *f*

free 1. *adj, adv* frei; (*without payment*) gratis, kostenlos; **for ~** umsonst **2.** *vt* befreien; **freebie** *n* fam Werbegeschenk *nt*; **freedom** *n* Freiheit *f*; **freefone** *adj* **a ~ number** eine gebührenfreie Nummer; **free kick** *n* SPORT Freistoß *m*

freelance 1. *adj* freiberuflich tätig; *vi* freischaffend **2.** *n* Freiberufler(in) *m(f)*

free-range *adj* (*hen*) frei laufend; **~ eggs** *pl* Freilandeier *pl*

freeway *n* (*US*) (gebührenfreie) Autobahn

freeze 1. *vi* (*feel cold*) frieren; (*of lake etc*) zufrieren; (*water etc*) gefrieren **2.** *vt* einfrieren; **freezer** *n* Tiefkühltruhe *f*; (*in fridge*) Gefrierfach *nt*; **freezing** *adj* eiskalt; **I'm ~** mir ist eiskalt; **freezing point** *n* Gefrierpunkt *m*

freight *n* (*goods*) Fracht *f*; (*money charged*) Frachtgebühr *f*; **freight car** *n* (*US*) Güterwagen *m*; **freight train** *n* (*US*) Güterzug *m*

French 1. *adj* französisch **2.** *n* (*language*) Französisch *nt*; **the ~** *pl* die Franzosen; **French bean** *n* grüne Boh-

ne; **French bread** *n* Baguette *f*; **French dressing** *n* Vinaigrette *f*; **French fries** (*US*) *npl* Pommes frites *pl*; **French kiss** *n* Zungenkuss *m*; **Frenchman** *n* Franzose *m*; **French toast** *n* (*US*) in Ei und Milch getunktes gebratenes Brot; **French window(s)** *n(pl)* Balkontür *f*, Terrassentür *f*; **Frenchwoman** *n* Französin *f*

frequency *n* Häufigkeit *f*; PHYS Frequenz *f*; **frequent** *adj* häufig; **frequently** *adv* häufig

fresco *n* Fresko *nt*

fresh *adj* frisch; (*new*) neu; **freshen** *vi* ~ (**up**) (*person*) sich frisch machen; **freshman** *n* Erstsemester *nt*; **freshwater fish** *n* Süßwasserfisch *m*

Fri *abbr* = **Friday**; Fr

friction *n* Reibung *f*

Friday *n* Freitag *m*; → **Tuesday**

fridge *n* Kühlschrank *m*

fried *adj* gebraten; **~ potatoes** Bratkartoffeln *pl*; **~ egg** Spiegelei *nt*; **~ rice** gebratener Reis

friend *n* Freund(in) *m(f)*; (*less close*) Bekannte(r) *mf*; **make ~s with sb** sich mit jdm anfreunden; **we're good ~s** wir sind gut befreundet; **friendly 1.** *adj* freundlich **2.** *n* SPORT Freundschaftsspiel *nt*; **friendship** *n* Freundschaft f

fright n Schrecken m; **frighten** vt erschrecken; **be ~ed** Angst haben; **frightening** adj beängstigend

frill n Rüsche f; **~s** fam Schnickschnack

fringe n (edge) Rand m; (on shawl etc) Fransen pl; (hair) Pony m

frizzy adj kraus

frog n Frosch m

from prep von; (place, out of) aus; (with date, time) ab; **travel ~ A to B** von A nach B fahren; **the train ~ Bath** der Zug aus Bath; **where does she come ~?** woher kommt sie?; **it's ten miles ~ here** es ist zehn Meilen von hier (entfernt); **~ May 5th (onwards)** ab dem 5. Mai

front 1. n Vorderseite f; (of house) Fassade f; (Mil, of weather) Front f; (at seaside) Promenade f; **in ~, at the ~** vorne; **in ~ of** vor; **up ~** (in advance) vorher, im Voraus **2.** adj vordere(r, s), Vorder-; (first) vorderste(r, s); **~ door** Haustür f; **~ page** n Titelseite f; **~ seat** Vordersitz m; **~ wheel** Vorderrad m

frontier n Grenze f

front-wheel drive n AUTO Frontantrieb m

frost n Frost m; (white ~) Reif m; **frosting** n (US) Zuckerguss m; **frosty** adj frostig

froth n Schaum m

frown vi die Stirn runzeln

froze pt of **freeze**

frozen 1. pp of **freeze 2.** adj (food) tiefgekühlt, Tiefkühl-; (single ~) Frucht f

fruit n (as collective, a. type) Obst nt; (single ~) Frucht f; **fruit machine** n Spielautomat m; **fruit salad** n Obstsalat m

frustrated adj frustriert; **frustration** n Frustration f, Frust m

fry vt braten; **frying pan** n Bratpfanne f

fuchsia n Fuchsie f

fuck vt vulg ficken; **~ off** verpiss dich!; **fucking** adj vulg Scheiß-

fudge n ≈ weiche Karamellsüßigkeit

fuel n (for heating) Brennstoff m; (for driving) Kraftstoff m; **fuel consumption** n Kraftstoffverbrauch m; **fuel gauge** n Benzinuhr f

fugitive n Flüchtling m

fulfil vt erfüllen

full adj voll; (person: satisfied) satt; (member, employment) Voll(zeit)-; (complete) vollständig; **~ of** voller ...; gen; **full beam** n AUTO Fernlicht nt; **full moon** n Vollmond m; **full stop** n Punkt m; **full-time** adj Ganztagsarbeit f; **full-time** n job n Ganztagsarbeit f; **fully** adv völlig; (recover) voll und ganz; (discuss) ausführlich

fumble vi herumfummeln (with, at an + dat)

gallop

fumes *npl* Dämpfe *pl*; *(of car)* Abgase *pl*

fun *n* Spaß *m*; **for ~** zum Spaß; **it's ~** es macht Spaß; **make ~ of** sich lustig machen über + *acc*

function 1. *n* Funktion *f*; *(event)* Feier *f*; *(reception)* Empfang *m* **2.** *vi* funktionieren

fund *n* Fonds *m*; **~s** *pl* Geldmittel *pl*

fundamental *adj* grundlegend; **fundamentally** *adv* im Grunde

funding *n* finanzielle Unterstützung

funeral *n* Beerdigung *f*

funfair *n* Jahrmarkt *m*

fungus *n* Pilz *m*

funnel *n* Trichter *m*; *(of steamer)* Schornstein *m*

funny *adj (amusing)* komisch, lustig; *(strange)* seltsam

fur *n* Pelz *m*; *(of animal)* Fell *nt*

furious *adj* wütend *(with sb* auf jdn*)*

furnished *adj* möbliert; **furniture** *n* Möbel *pl*; **piece of ~** Möbelstück *nt*

further *comparative of* **far 1.** *adj* weitere(r, s); **~ education** Weiterbildung *f*; **until ~ notice** bis auf weiteres **2.** *adv* weiter; **furthest** *adv* am weitesten entfernt **2.** *adv* am weitesten

fury *n* Wut *f*

fuse 1. *n* ELEC Sicherung *f* **2.** *vi* ELEC durchbrennen; **fuse box** *n* Sicherungskasten *m*

fuss *n* Theater *nt*; **make a ~** ein Theater machen; **fussy** *adj (difficult)* schwierig, kompliziert; *(attentive to detail)* pingelig

future 1. *adj* künftig **2.** *n* Zukunft *f*

fuze *(US)* → **fuse**

fuzzy *adj (indistinct)* verschwommen; *(hair)* kraus

G

gable *n* Giebel *m*

gadget *n* Vorrichtung *f*, Gerät *nt*

Gaelic 1. *adj* gälisch **2.** *n (language)* Gälisch *nt*

gain 1. *vt (obtain, win)* gewinnen; *(advantage, respect)* sich verschaffen; *(wealth)* erwerben; *(weight)* zunehmen **2.** *vi (improve)* gewinnen *(in*

an + *dat*); *(clock)* vorgehen **3.** *n* Gewinn *m* (*in* an + *dat*)

gale *n* Sturm *m*

gall bladder *n* Gallenblase *f*

gallery *n* Galerie *f*, Museum *nt*

gallon *n* Gallone *f*; *(Brit)* 4,546 l *(US)* 3,79 l

gallop 1. *n* Galopp *m* **2.** *vi* galoppieren

gallstone n Gallenstein m
Gambia n Gambia nt
gamble 1. vi um Geld spielen, wetten 2. n it's a ~ es ist riskant; gambling n Glücksspiel nt
game n Spiel nt; (animals) Wild nt; ~s (in school) Sport m
gammon n geräucherter Schinken
gang n (of criminals, youths) Bande f, Gang f, Clique f
gangster n Gangster m
gangway n (Brit, aisle) Gang m, Gangway f
gap n (hole) Lücke f; (in time) Pause f; (in age) Unterschied m
gape vi (mit offenem Mund) starren
gap year n Jahr zwischen Schulabschluss und Studium, das oft zu Auslandsaufenthalten genutzt wird
garage n Garage f; (for repair) (Auto)werkstatt f
garbage n (US) Müll m; fam (nonsense) Quatsch m; garbage can n (US) Mülleimer m; (outside) Mülltonne f; garbage truck n (US) Müllwagen m
garbled adj (story) verdreht
garden n Garten m; (public) ~s Park m; garden centre n Gartencenter nt; gardener n Gärtner(in) m(f); gardening n Gartenarbeit f
gargle vi gurgeln

gargoyle n Wasserspeier m
garlic n Knoblauch m; garlic bread n Knoblauchbrot nt; garlic butter n Knoblauchbutter f
gas n Gas nt; (US, petrol) Benzin nt; step on the ~ Gas geben; gas cooker n Gasherd m; gas cylinder n Gasflasche f; gas fire n Gasofen m
gasket n Dichtung f
gas lighter n (for cigarettes) Gasfeuerzeug nt; gas mask n Gasmaske f; gas meter n Gaszähler m
gasoline n (US) Benzin nt
gasp vi keuchen; (in surprise) nach Luft schnappen
gas pedal n (US) Gaspedal nt; gas pump n (US) Zapfsäule f; gas station n (US) Tankstelle f; gas tank n (US) Benzintank m
gastric adj Magen-; ~ flu Magen-Darm-Grippe f; ~ ulcer Magengeschwür nt
gasworks n Gaswerk nt
gate n Tor nt; (barrier) Schranke f; AVIAT Gate nt, Flugsteig m
gateau n Torte f
gateway n Tor nt
gather 1. vt (collect) sammeln; ~ speed beschleunigen 2. vi (assemble) sich versammeln; (understand) schließen (from aus); gathering n Versammlung f
gauge n Meßgerät nt

gauze *n* Gaze *f*; (*for bandages*) Mull *m*

gave *pt of* **give**

gay *adj* (*homosexual*) schwul

gaze 1. *n* Blick *m* 2. *vi* starren

GCSE *abbr* = **general certificate of secondary education**, Abschlussprüfung *f* der Sekundarstufe, ≈ mittlere Reife

gear *n* AUTO Gang *m*; (*equipment*) Ausrüstung *f*; (*clothes*) Klamotten *pl*; **change ~** schalten; **gearbox** *n* Getriebe *nt*; **gear change**, **gear shift** (*US*) *n* Gangschaltung *f*; **gear lever**, **gear stick** (*US*) *n* Schalthebel *m*

geese *pl of* **goose**

gel 1. *n* Gel *nt* 2. *vi* gelieren; **they really ~led** sie verstanden sich auf Anhieb

gelatine *n* Gelatine *f*

gem *n* Edelstein *m*; *fig* Juwel *nt*

Gemini *nsing* ASTR Zwillinge *pl*

gender *n* Geschlecht *nt*

gene *n* Gen *nt*

general *adj* allgemein; **~ knowledge** Allgemeinbildung *f*; **~ election** Parlamentswahlen *pl*; **generalize** *vi* verallgemeinern; **generally** *adv* im Allgemeinen

generation *n* Generation *f*; **generation gap** *n* Generationsunterschied *m*

generosity *n* Großzügigkeit *f*; **generous** *adj* großzügig;

(*portion*) reichlich

genetic *adj* genetisch; **genetically modified** *adj* gentechnisch verändert, genmanipuliert; → **GM**

Geneva *n* Genf *nt*; **Lake ~** der Genfer See

genitals *npl* Geschlechtsteile *pl*

genius *n* Genie *nt*

gentle *adj* sanft; (*touch*) zart; **gentleman** *n* Herr *m*; (*polite man*) Gentleman *m*

gents *n* '~' (*lavatory*) „Herren"; **the ~** *pl* die Herrentoilette

genuine *adj* echt

geographical *adj* geografisch; **geography** *n* Geografie *f*; (*at school*) Erdkunde *f*

geometry *n* Geometrie *f*

geranium *n* Geranie *f*

germ *n* Keim *m*; MED Bazillus *m*

German 1. *adj* deutsch; **she's ~** sie ist Deutsche; **~ shepherd** Deutscher Schäferhund 2. *n* (*person*) Deutsche(r) *mf*; (*language*) Deutsch *nt*; **in ~** auf Deutsch; **German measles** *n sg* Röteln *pl*; **Germany** *n* Deutschland *nt*

gesture *n* Geste *f*

get 1. *vt* (*receive*) bekommen, kriegen; **~ a cold/flu** sich erkälten/die Grippe bekommen; (*buy*) kaufen; (*obtain*) sich besorgen; (*to keep*) sich anschaffen; **~ sb sth** jdm etw besorgen; (*fetch*) jdm etw holen; *where did you ~ that (from)?* woher hast du das?; *~ a taxi* ein Taxi nehmen; (*persuade*) *~ sb to do sth* jdn dazu bringen, etw zu tun; (*manage*) *~ sth to work* etw zum Laufen bringen; *~ sth done* (oneself) etw machen; (*by sb else*) etw machen lassen; (*bring*) *this isn't ~ting us anywhere* so kommen wir nicht weiter; (*understand*) *don't ~ me wrong* versteh mich nicht falsch! **2.** *vi* (*become*) werden; *~ sth* alt werden; *it's ~ting dark* es wird dunkel; *~ dressed/washed* sich anziehen/waschen; *I'll ~ ready* ich mache mich fertig; *~ lost* sich verirren; (*arrive*) *we got to Dover at 5* wir kamen um 5 in Dover an; *~ somewhere/nowhere* fig (in career) es zu etwas/nichts bringen; (with task, discussion) weiterkommen/nicht weiterkommen; **get across** vt *~ sth* über etw acc kommen; **get sth across** (communicate) etw klarmachen; **get along** vi (manage) zurechtkommen; (people) gut auskommen (with mit); **get at** vt (reach) herankommen an + acc; *what are you getting at?* worauf wollen Sie hinaus?, was meinst du damit?; **get away** vi (leave)

wegkommen; (*escape*) entkommen (from dat); *he got away with it* er kam ungeschoren davon; **get back 1.** vi zurückkommen; TEL *~ to s.o.* jdn zurückrufen; **2.** vt *get sth back* etw zurückbekommen; **get by** vi (manage) auskommen (on mit); **get down 1.** vi heruntersteigen; *~ to business* zur Sache kommen **2.** vt *get sth down* (write) etw aufschreiben; *it gets me down* fam es macht mich fertig; **get in** vi (arrive home) heimkommen; (into car etc) einsteigen; **get into** vt (car, bus etc) einsteigen in + acc; (rage, panic etc) geraten in + acc; *~ trouble* in Schwierigkeiten kommen; **get off** vi, vt (train etc) aussteigen (aus); (horse) absteigen; **get on 1.** vi (progress) vorankommen; (be friends) auskommen (with mit); *be getting ~* alt werden **2.** vi, vt (train etc) einsteigen in + acc; (horse) aufsteigen (auf + acc); **get out 1.** vi herauskommen; (of vehicle) aussteigen (of aus); *~!* raus! **2.** vt (take out) herausholen; (stain, nail) herausbekommen; **get over** vt (recover from) hinwegkommen über + acc; (illness) sich erholen von; (loss) sich abfinden mit; **get through** *vi* durchkommen; **get up** *vi* aufstehen; **get-together** *n* Treffen *nt*

Ghana *n* Ghana *nt*

gherkin *n* Gewürzgurke *f*

ghetto *n* Ghetto *nt*

ghost *n* Gespenst *nt*; (*of sb*) Geist *m*

giant 1. *n* Riese *m* **2.** *adj* riesig

giblets *npl* Geflügelinnereien *pl*

Gibraltar *n* Gibraltar *nt*

giddy *adj* schwindlig

gift *n* Geschenk *nt*; (*talent*) Begabung *f*; **gifted** *adj* begabt; **giftwrap** *vt* als Geschenk verpacken

gigantic *adj* riesig

giggle 1. *vi* kichern **2.** *n* Gekicher *nt*

gill *n* (*of fish*) Kieme *f*

gimmick *n* (*for sales, publicity*) Gag *m*

gin *n* Gin *m*

ginger 1. *n* Ingwer *m* **2.** *adj* (*colour*) kupferrot; (*cat*) rötlichgelb; **ginger ale** *n* Gingerale *nt*; **ginger beer** *n* Ingwerlimonade *f*; **gingerbread** *n* Lebkuchen *m* (*mit Ingwergeschmack*); **ginger(-haired)** *adj* rotblond; **gingerly** *adv* (*move*) vorsichtig

giraffe *n* Giraffe *f*

girl *n* Mädchen *nt*; **girlfriend** *n* (*feste*) Freundin *f*; **girl guide** *n* (*Brit*), **girl scout** (*US*) Pfadfinderin *f*

gist *n* **get the ~** (*of it*) das Wesentliche verstehen

give 1. *vt* geben; (*as present*) schenken (*to sb* jdm); (*state: name etc*) angeben; (*speech*) halten; (*blood*) spenden; **~ sb sth** jdm etw geben / schenken **2.** *vi* (*yield*) nachgeben; **give away** *vt* (*give free*) verschenken; (*secret*) verraten; **give back** *vt* zurückgeben; **give in** *vi* aufgeben; **give up** *vt, vi* aufgeben; **give way** *vi* (*collapse, yield*) nachgeben; (*traffic*) die Vorfahrt beachten

given 1. *pp of* **give 2.** *adj* (*fixed*) festgesetzt; (*certain*) bestimmt; **~ name** (*US*) Vorname *m* **3.** *conj* **~ that ...** angesichts der Tatsache, dass ...

glacier *n* Gletscher *m*

glad *adj* froh (*about* über); **I was ~** (*to hear*) **that ...** es hat mich gefreut, dass ...; **gladly** *adv* gerne

glance 1. *n* Blick *m* **2.** *vi* einen Blick werfen (*at* auf + *acc*)

gland *n* Drüse *f*; **glandular fever** *n* Drüsenfieber *nt*

glare 1. *n* grelles Licht; (*stare*) stechender Blick **2.** *vi* (*angrily*) **~ at sb** jdn böse anstarren

glass *n* Glas *nt*; **~es** *pl* Brille *f*

glen *n* (*Scot*) (enges) Bergtal *nt*

glide *vi* gleiten; (*hover*) schweben; **glider** *n* Segelflugzeug *nt*; **gliding** *n* Segelfliegen *nt*

glimpse *n* flüchtiger Blick

glitter *vi* glitzern; *(eyes)* funkeln

glitzy *adj fam* glanzvoll, Schickimicki-

global *adj* global, Welt-; ~ **warming** die Erwärmung der Erdatmosphäre; **globe** *n (sphere)* Kugel *f; (world)* Erdball *m; (map)* Globus *m*

gloomily, gloomy *adv, adj* düster

glorious *adj (victory, past)* ruhmreich; *(weather, day etc)* herrlich; **glory** *n* Herrlichkeit *f*

gloss *n (shine)* Glanz *m*

glossary *n* Glossar *n*

glossy 1. *adj (surface)* glänzend **2.** *n (magazine)* Hochglanzmagazin *nt*

glove *n* Handschuh *m;* **glove compartment** *n* Handschuhfach *nt*

glow *vi* glühen

glucose *n* Traubenzucker *m*

glue 1. *n* Klebstoff *m* **2.** *vt* kleben

glutton *n* Vielfraß *m;* **a ~ for punishment** *fam* Masochist *m*

GM *abbr* = **genetically modified**; Gen-; ~ **foods** gentechnisch veränderte Lebensmittel

GMT *abbr* = **Greenwich Mean Time**; WEZ *f*

go 1. *vi* gehen; *(in vehicle, travel)* fahren; *(plane)* fliegen;

(road) führen *(to* nach); *(depart: train, bus)* (ab)fahren; *(person)* (fort)gehen; *(disappear)* verschwinden; *(time)* vergehen; *(function)* gehen, funktionieren; *(machine, engine)* laufen; *(fit, suit)* passen *(with* zu); *(fail)* nachlassen; **I have to ~ to the doctor/to London** ich muss zum Arzt/nach London; **~ shopping** einkaufen gehen; **~ for a walk/swim** spazieren/schwimmen gehen; **has he gone yet?** ist er schon weg?; **the wine ~es in the cupboard** kommt in den Schrank; **get sth ~ing** etw in Gang setzen; **keep ~ing** weitermachen; *(machine etc)* weiterlaufen; **how's the job ~ing?** was macht der Job?; **~ deaf/mad/grey** taub/verrückt/grau werden **2.** *v aux* **be ~ing to do sth** etw tun werden; **I was ~ing to do it** ich wollte es tun **3.** *n (attempt)* Versuch *m;* **can I have another ~?** darf ich noch mal (probieren)?; **it's my ~** ich bin dran; **in one ~** auf einen Schlag; *(drink)* in einem Zug; **go after** *vt* nachlaufen + *dat;* **go ahead** *vi (in front)* vorausgehen; *(start)* anfangen; **go away** *vi* weggehen; *(on holiday, business)* verreisen; **go back** *vi (return)* zu-

rückgehen; **go by 1.** vi vorbeigehen; (vehicle) vorbeifahren; (years, time) vergehen **2.** vt (judge by) vorgehen nach; **go down** vi (sun, ship) untergehen; (flood, temperature) zurückgehen; (price) sinken; **~ well/badly** gut/schlecht ankommen; **go in** vi hineingehen; **go into** vt (enter) hineingehen in + acc; (crash) fahren gegen, hineinfahren in + acc; **~ teaching/politics/the army** Lehrer werden/in die Politik gehen/zum Militär gehen; **go off 1.** vi (depart) weggehen; (in vehicle) wegfahren; (lights) ausgehen; (milk etc) sauer werden; (gun, bomb, alarm) losgehen **2.** vt (dislike) nicht mehr mögen; **go on** vi (continue) weitergehen; (lights) angehen; **~ with or doing sth** etw weitermachen; **go out** vi (leave house) hinausgehen; (fire, light, person socially) ausgehen; **~ for a meal** essen gehen; **go up** vi (temperature, price) steigen; (lift) hochfahren; **go without** vt verzichten auf + acc; (food, sleep) auskommen ohne

go-ahead 1. adj (progressive) fortschrittlich **2.** n grünes Licht

goal n (aim) Ziel nt; SPORT Tor nt; **goalie, goalkeeper** n Torwart m; **goalpost** n Torpfos-

ten m

goat n Ziege f

gob 1. n (Brit) fam Maul nt; **shut your ~** halt's Maul! **2.** vi spucken; **gobsmacked** fam (surprised) platt

god n Gott m; **thank God** Gott sei Dank; **godchild** n Patenkind nt; **goddaughter** n Patentochter f; **goddess** n Göttin f; **godfather** n Pate m; **godmother** n Patin f; **godson** n Patensohn m

goggles npl Schutzbrille f; (for skiing) Skibrille f; (for diving) Taucherbrille f

going adj (rate) üblich; **goings-on** npl Vorgänge pl

go-kart n Gokart m

gold 1. n Gold nt **2.** adj golden; **goldfish** n Goldfisch m; **gold-plated** adj vergoldet

golf n Golf nt; **golf ball** n Golfball m; **golf club** n Golfschläger m; (association) Golfklub m; **golf course** n Golfplatz m

gone 1. pp of **go**; **he's ~** er ist weg **2.** prep **just ~ three** gerade drei Uhr vorbei

good 1. n (benefit) Wohl nt; (morally good things) Gute(s) nt; **it's for your own ~** es ist zu deinem Besten or Vorteil; **it's no ~** (doing sth) es hat keinen Sinn or Zweck; (thing) für immer **2.** adj gut; (suitable) passend; (thorough) gründlich; (well-behaved) brav; (*kind*) nett, lieb; **be ~ at sport/maths** gut in Sport/Mathe sein; **be no ~ at sport/maths** schlecht in Sport/Mathe sein; **too ~ to be true** zu schön, um wahr zu sein; **this is just not ~ enough** so geht das nicht; **a ~ three hours** gute drei Stunden; **~ morning/evening** guten Morgen/Abend; **~ night** gute Nacht; **have a ~ time** sich gut amüsieren

goodbye *interj* auf Wiedersehen

Good Friday *n* Karfreitag *m*

good-looking *adj* gut aussehend

goods *npl* Waren *pl*, Güter *pl*; goods train *n* (*Brit*) Güterzug *m*

goose *n* Gans *f*; gooseberry *n* Stachelbeere *f*; goose bumps *n*, goose pimples *npl* Gänsehaut *f*

gorge *n* Schlucht *f*

gorgeous *adj* wunderschön; **he's ~** er sieht toll aus

gorilla *n* Gorilla *m*

gossip 1. *n* (*talk*) Klatsch *m*; (*person*) Klatschtante *f* 2. *vi* klatschen, tratschen

got *pt, pp of* get

gotten (*US*) *pp of* get

govern *vt* regieren; (*province etc*) verwalten; government *n* Regierung *f*; governor *n* Gouverneur(in) *m(f)*; govt *abbr* = **government**; Regierung *f*

gown *n* Abendkleid *nt*; (*academic*) Robe *f*

GP *abbr* = **General Practitioner**; praktischer Arzt

GPS *n abbr* = **global positioning system**; GPS *nt*

grab *vt* packen; (*person*) schnappen

graceful *adj* anmutig

grade *n* Niveau *nt*; (*of goods*) Güteklasse *f*; (*mark*) Note *f*; (*US, year*) Klasse *f*; **make the ~** es schaffen; grade crossing *n* (*US*) Bahnübergang *m*; grade school *n* (*US*) Grundschule *f*

gradient *n* (*upward*) Steigung *f*; (*downward*) Gefälle *nt*

gradual, gradually *adj, adv* allmählich

graduate 1. *n* Uniabsolvent(in) *m(f)*, Akademiker(in) *m(f)* 2. *vi* einen akademischen Grad erwerben

grain *n* (*cereals*) Getreide *nt*; (*of corn, sand*) Korn *nt*

gram *n* Gramm *nt*

grammar *n* Grammatik *f*; grammar school *n* (*Brit*) ≈ Gymnasium *nt*

gran *n fam* Oma *f*

grand 1. *adj pej* hochnäsig; (*posh*) vornehm 2. *n fam* 1000 Pfund bzw. 1000 Dollar

grand(d)ad *n fam* Opa *m*; granddaughter *n* Enkelin *f*; grandfather *n* Großvater *m*; grandma *n fam* Oma *f*; grandmother *n* Großmutter *f*; grandpa *n fam* Opa *m*;

grandparents *npl* Großeltern *pl*; **grandson** *n* Enkel *m*

grandstand *n* SPORT Tribüne *f*

granny *n fam* Oma *f*

grant 1. *vt* gewähren (*sb sth* jdm etw); **take sb/ sth for ~ed** jdn/etw als selbstverständlich hinnehmen **2.** *n* Subvention *f*, finanzielle Unterstützung *f*; (*for university*) Stipendium *nt*

grape *n* Weintraube *f*; **grapefruit** *n* Grapefruit *f*; **grape juice** *n* Traubensaft *m*

graph *n* Diagramm *nt*; **graphic** *adj* grafisch; (*description*) anschaulich

grasp *vt* ergreifen; (*understand*) begreifen

grass *n* Gras *nt*; (*lawn*) Rasen *m*; **grasshopper** *n* Heuschrecke *f*

grate 1. *n* Feuerrost *m* **2.** *vi* kratzen **3.** *vt* (*cheese*) reiben

grateful, gratefully *adj, adv* dankbar

grater *n* Reibe *f*

gratifying *adj* erfreulich

gratitude *n* Dankbarkeit *f*

grave 1. *n* Grab *nt* **2.** *adj* ernst; (*mistake*) schwer

gravel *n* Kies *m*

graveyard *n* Friedhof *m*

gravity *n* Schwerkraft *f*; (*seriousness*) Ernst *m*

gravy *n* Bratensoße *f*

gray *adj* (*US*) grau

graze 1. *vi* (*of animals*) grasen **2.** *vt* (*touch*) streifen; MED abschürfen **3.** *n* MED Abschür-

fung *f*

grease 1. *n* (*fat*) Fett *nt*; (*lubricant*) Schmiere *f* **2.** *vt* einfetten; TECH schmieren

greasy *adj* fettig; (*hands, tools*) schmierig; *fam* (*person*) schleimig

great *adj* groß; *fam* (*good*) großartig, super; **a ~ deal of** viel; **Great Britain** *n* Großbritannien *nt*; **great--grandfather** *n* Urgroßvater *m*; **great-grandmother** *n* Urgroßmutter *f*; **greatly** *adv* sehr; **~ disappointed** zutiefst enttäuscht

Greece *n* Griechenland *nt*

greed *n* Gier *f* (*for* nach); (*for food*) Gefräßigkeit *f*; **greedy** *adj* gierig; (*for food*) gefräßig

Greek 1. *adj* griechisch **2.** *n* (*person*) Grieche *m*, Griechin *f*; (*language*) Griechisch *nt*

green 1. *adj* grün **2.** *n* (*colour, for golf*) Grün *nt*; (*village ~*) Dorfwiese *f*; **~s** (*vegetables*) grünes Gemüse; **the Greens, the Green Party** POL die Grünen; **green card** *n* (*US, work permit*) Arbeitserlaubnis *f*; (*Brit, for car*) grüne Versicherungskarte; **greengage** *n* Reneklode *f*; **greengrocer** *n* Obst- und Gemüsehändler(in) *f*; **greenhouse** *n* Gewächshaus *nt*; **~ effect** Treibhauseffekt *m*; **Greenland** *n* Grönland

nt; **green pepper** n grüner
Paprika; **green salad** n grüner Salat
greet vt grüßen; **greeting** n
Gruß m
grew pt of **grow**
grey adj grau; **grey-haired** adj
grauhaarig; **greyhound** n
Windhund m
grid n Gitter nt; **gridlock** n
Verkehrsinfarkt m; **grid-
locked** adj (roads) völlig ver-
stopft; (talks) festgefahren
grief n Kummer m; (over loss)
Trauer f
grievance n Beschwerde f
grieve vi trauern (for um)
grill 1. n (on cooker) Grill m **2.**
vt grillen
grim adj (face, humour) grim-
mig; (situation, prospects)
trostlos
grin 1. n Grinsen nt **2.** vi grinsen
grind vt mahlen; (sharpen)
schleifen; (US, meat) durchdrehen
grip 1. n Griff m; **get a ~** reiß
dich zusammen!; **get to ~s
with sth** etw in den Griff bekommen **2.** vt packen
gristle n Knorpel m
groan vi stöhnen (with vor
+ dat)
grocer n Lebensmittelhänd-
ler(in) m(f); **groceries** npl
Lebensmittel pl
groin n ANAT Leiste f; **groin
strain** n MED Leistenbruch m
groom 1. n Bräutigam m **2.** vt

well ~ed gepflegt
groovy adj fam cool
grope 1. vi tasten **2.** vt (sexually harrass) befummeln
gross adj (coarse) derb; (extreme: negligence, error)
grob; (disgusting) ekelhaft;
COMM brutto; ~ **salary** Brut-
togehalt nt
grotty adj fam mies, vergammelt
ground 1. pt, pp of **grind 2.** n
Boden m, Erde f; SPORT Platz
m; ~**s** pl (around house)
(Garten)anlagen pl; (rea-
sons) Gründe pl; (of coffee)
Satz m; **on (the) ~s of** aufgrund +gen; **ground floor** n
(Brit) Erdgeschoss nt;
ground meat n (US) Hackfleisch nt
group n Gruppe f
grouse n (bird) Schottisches
Moorhuhn; (complaint) Nörgelei f
grow 1. vi wachsen; (increase)
zunehmen (in an); (become)
werden; ~ **old** alt werden; ~
into ... sich entwickeln zu
... **2.** vt (crop, plant) ziehen;
(commercially) anbauen;
I'm ~ing a beard ich lasse
mir einen Bart wachsen;
grow up vi aufwachsen;
(mature) erwachsen werden;
growing adj wachsend; **a ~
number of people** immer
mehr Leute
growl vi knurren
grown pp of **grow**

gutter

grown-up 1. *adj* erwachsen **2.**
n Erwachsene(r) *mf*; **growth**
n Wachstum *nt*; (*increase*)
Zunahme *f*; MED Wucherung
f

grubby *adj* schmuddelig

grudge 1. *n* Abneigung *f*
(*against gegen +* acc); **have ~ sb
sth** jdm etw nicht gönnen

gruelling *adj* aufreibend; (*pace*) mörderisch

gruesome *adj* grausig

grumble *vi* murren (*about*
über + *acc*)

grumpy *adj fam* mürrisch,
grantig

grunt *vi* grunzen

G-string *n* ≈ Tanga *m*

guarantee 1. *n* Garantie *f* (*of*
für) **2.** *vt* garantieren

guard 1. *n* (*sentry*) Wache *f*;
(*in prison*) Wärter(in) *m(f)*;
(*Brit*) RAIL Schaffner(in)
m(f) **2.** *vt* bewachen

guardian *n* Vormund *m*; **~ angel**
Schutzengel *m*

guess 1. *n* Vermutung *f*; (*estimate*) Schätzung *f*; **have a ~**
rate mal! **2.** *vt, vi* raten; (*estimate*) schätzen; **I ~ you're
right** du hast wohl recht; **I
~ so** ich glaube schon;
guesstimate *n fam* grobe
Schätzung

guest *n* Gast *m*; **be my ~**
nur zu!; **guest-house** *n* Pension
f; **guest room** *n* Gästezimmer *nt*

guidance *n* (*direction*) Leitung *f*; (*advice*) Rat *m*;

(*counselling*) Beratung *f*;
for your ~ zu Ihrer Orientierung; **guide 1.** *n* (*person*)
Führer(in) *m(f)*; (*tour*) Reiseleiter(in) *m(f)*; (*book*)
Führer *m* **2.** *vt* führen;
guidebook *n* Reiseführer
m; **guide dog** *n* Blindenhund *m*; **guided tour** *n* Führung *f* (*of* durch); **guidelines**
npl Richtlinien *pl*

guilt *n* Schuld *f*; **guilty** *adj*
schuldig (*of* gen); (*look*)
schuldbewusst; ***have a ~
conscience*** ein schlechtes
Gewissen haben

guinea pig *n* Meerschweinchen *nt*; (*person*) Versuchskaninchen *nt*

guitar *n* Gitarre *f*

gulf *n* Golf *m*; **Gulf States** *npl*
Golfstaaten *pl*

gull *n* Möwe *f*

gullible *adj* leichtgläubig

gulp 1. *n* (kräftiger) Schluck **2.**
vi schlucken

gum *n* (*around teeth, usu pl*)
Zahnfleisch *nt*; (*chewing ~*)
Kaugummi *m*

gun *n* Schusswaffe *f*; (*rifle*)
Gewehr *nt*; (*pistol*) Pistole
f; **gunfire** *n* Schüsse *pl*; **gunpowder** *n* Schießpulver *nt*

gush *vi* (heraus)strömen
(*from* aus)

gut *n* Darm *m*; **~s** *pl* (*intestines*) Eingeweide; (*courage*)
Mumm *m*

gutter *n* (*for roof*) Dachrinne
f; (*in street*) Rinnstein *m*,

Gosse f

guy n (man) Typ m, Kerl m; **~s** pl (US) Leute pl

gym n Turnhalle f; (for working out) Fitnesscenter nt; **gymnasium** n Turnhalle f; **gymnastics** nsing Turnen

nt; **gym-toned** adj durchtrainiert

gynaecologist n Frauenarzt m, Frauenärztin f, Gynäkologe m, Gynäkologin f; **gynaecology** n Gynäkologie f

H

habit n Gewohnheit f; **habitual** adj gewohnt; (drinker, liar) gewohnheitsmäßig

hack vt hacken; **hacker** n IT Hacker(in) m(f)

had pt, pp of **have**

haddock n Schellfisch m

hadn't contr of **had not**

haemophiliac, hemophiliac (US) n Bluter(in) m(f); **haemorrhage, hemorrhage** (US) 1. n Blutung f 2. vi bluten; **haemorrhoids, hemorrhoids** (US) npl Hämorrhoiden pl

haggis n (Scot) mit gehackten Schafsinnereien und Haferschrot gefüllter Schafsmagen

hail 1. n Hagel m 2. vi hageln 3. vt ~ **sb as sth** jdn als etw feiern; **hailstone** n Hagelkorn nt; **hailstorm** n Hagelschauer m

hair n Haar nt, Haare pl; **get one's ~ cut** sich dat die Haare schneiden lassen; **hairbrush** n Haarbürste f; **hair conditioner** n Haarspülung f; **haircut** n Haarschnitt m;

hairdo n Frisur f; **hairdresser** n Friseur m, Friseuse f; **hairdryer** n Haartrockner m; (hand-held) Fön® m; (over head) Trockenhaube f; **hair gel** n Haargel nt; **hair remover** n Enthaarungsmittel nt; **hair spray** n Haarspray nt; **hair style** n Frisur f; **hairy** adj haarig, behaart; fam (dangerous) brenzlig

hake n Seehecht m

half 1. n Hälfte f; SPORT (of game) Halbzeit f; **cut in ~** halbieren 2. adj halb; **three and a ~ pounds** dreieinhalb Pfund; **~ an hour, a ~ hour** eine halbe Stunde; **one and a ~** eineinhalb, anderthalb 3. adv halb, zur Hälfte; **~ asleep** fast eingeschlafen; **~ as big (as)** halb so groß (wie); **half board** n Halbpension f; **half fare** n halber Fahrpreis; **half-hearted** adj halbherzig; **half-hour** n halbe Stunde; **half moon** n Halbmond m; **half pint** n ≈ Viertelliter m or nt; **half**

price n (at) ~ zum halben Preis; **half-term** n (at school) Ferien pl in der Mitte des Trimesters; **half-time** n Halbzeit f; **halfway** adv auf halbem Wege; **halfwit** n fam Trottel m

halibut n Heilbutt m

hall n (building) Halle f; (for audience) Saal m; (entrance hall) Flur m; (large) Diele f; **~ of residence** (Brit) Studentenwohnheim nt

hallo interj hallo

halt 1. n Pause f, Halt m; **come to a ~** zum Stillstand kommen **2.** vt, vi anhalten

halve vt halbieren

ham n Schinken m

hamburger n GASTR Hamburger m

hammer 1. n Hammer m **2.** vt, vi hämmern

hammock n Hängematte f

hamper 1. vt behindern **2.** n (as gift) Geschenkkorb m; (for picnic) Picknickkorb m

hamster n Hamster m

hand 1. n Hand f; (of clock, instrument) Zeiger m; (in card game) Blatt nt; **~s off!** Finger weg!; **on the one ~ ..., on the other ~...** einerseits ..., andererseits ...; **give sb a ~** jdm helfen (with bei); **it's in his ~s** er hat es in der Hand; **be in good ~s** gut aufgehoben sein; **get out of ~** außer Kontrolle geraten **2.** vt (pass) reichen (to sb jdm); hand

down vt (tradition) überliefern; (heirloom) vererben; **hand in** vt einreichen; (at school, university etc) abgeben; **hand out** vt verteilen; **hand over** vt übergeben

handbag n Handtasche f; **handbook** n Handbuch nt; **handbrake** n (Brit) Handbremse f; **hand cream** n Handcreme f; **handcuffs** npl Handschellen pl; **handheld PC** n Handheld m

handicap 1. n Behinderung f, Handikap nt **2.** vt benachteiligen; **handicapped** adj behindert; **the ~** die Behinderten

handicraft n Kunsthandwerk nt

handkerchief n Taschentuch nt

handle 1. n Griff m; (of door) Klinke f; (of cup etc) Henkel m; (for winding) Kurbel f **2.** vt (touch) anfassen; (deal with: matter) sich befassen mit; (people, machine etc) umgehen mit; (situation, problem) fertig werden mit; **handlebars** npl Lenkstange f

hand luggage n Handgepäck nt; **handmade** adj handgefertigt; **be ~** Handarbeit sein; **handout** n (sheet) Handout nt, Thesenpapier nt; **handset** n Hörer m; **please replace the ~** bitte legen Sie auf; **hands-free phone**

Freisprechanlage f; **hand-shake** n Händedruck m

handsome adj (man) gut aussehend

hands-on adj praxisorientiert; ~ *experience* praktische Erfahrung

handwriting n Handschrift f

handy adj (useful) praktisch

hang 1. vt (auf)hängen; (execute: hanged, hanged) hängen 2. vi hängen 3. n **he's got the ~ of it** er hat den Dreh raus; **hang about** vi sich herumtreiben, rumhängen; **hang on** vi sich festhalten (to an + dat); fam (wait) warten; ~ **to sth** etw behalten; **hang up** 1. vi TEL auflegen 2. vt aufhängen

hanger n Kleiderbügel m

hang glider n (Flug)drachen m; (person) Drachenflieger(in) m(f); **hang-gliding** n Drachenfliegen nt

hangover n (bad head) Kater m; (relic) Überbleibsel nt

hankie n fam Taschentuch nt

happen vi geschehen; (sth strange, unpleasant) passieren; *if anything should ~ to me* wenn mir etwas passieren sollte; *it won't ~ again* es wird nicht wieder vorkommen; *I ~ed to be passing* ich kam zufällig vorbei; **happening** n Ereignis nt

happily adv fröhlich, glücklich; (luckily) glücklicherweise; **happiness** n Glück

nt; **happy** adj glücklich; (satisfied) ~ **with sth** mit etw zufrieden; (willing) **be ~ to do sth** etw gerne tun; **Happy Christmas** fröhliche Weihnachten!; **Happy New Year** ein glückliches Neues Jahr!; **Happy Birthday** herzlichen Glückwunsch zum Geburtstag!; **happy hour** n Happy Hour f

harass vt (ständig) belästigen; **harassment** n Belästigung f; (at work) Mobbing nt; **sexual ~** sexuelle Belästigung

harbor (US), **harbour** n Hafen m

hard 1. adj hart; (difficult) schwer, schwierig; (harsh) hart(herzig); *don't be ~ on him* sei nicht zu streng zu ihm; *it's ~ to believe* es ist kaum zu glauben 2. adv (work) schwer; (run) schnell; (rain, snow) stark; *try ~/~er* sich dat große/mehr Mühe geben; **hardback** n gebundene Ausgabe; **hard-boiled** adj (egg) hart gekocht; **hard copy** n IT Ausdruck m; **hard disk** n IT Festplatte f; **harden** 1. vt härten 2. vi hart werden; **hardly** adv kaum; ~ **ever** fast nie; **hardship** n Not f; **hard shoulder** n (Brit) Standspur f; **hardware** n IT Hardware f; Haushalts- und Eisenwaren pl; **hard-working** adj fleißig, tüchtig

hare n Hase m

harm 1. n Schaden m; (bodily) Verletzung f; **it wouldn't do any ~** es würde nicht schaden **2.** vt schaden + dat; (person) verletzen; **harmful** adj schädlich; **harmless** adj harmlos

harp n Harfe f

harsh adj (climate, voice) rau; (light, sound) grell; (severe) hart, streng f

harvest 1. n Ernte f; (time) Erntezeit f **2.** vt ernten

has pres of **have**

hash n GASTR Haschee nt; fam (hashish) Haschisch m; **make a ~ of sth** etw vermasseln; hash browns npl (US) ≈ Kartoffelpuffer pl

hassle n **1.** fam (fuss) Theater nt; **no ~** kein Problem **2.** vt bedrängen

hasn't abbr of **has not**

haste n Eile f; hastily, hasty adv, adj hastig; (rash) vorschnell

hat n Hut m

hatch n NAUT Luke f; (in house) Durchreiche f; **hatchback** n (car) Wagen m mit Hecktür

hate 1. vt hassen; **I ~ doing this** ich mache das sehr ungern **2.** n Hass m (of auf + acc)

haul 1. vt ziehen, schleppen **2.** n (booty) Beute f; haulage n Transport m; (trade) Spedition f

haunted adj **a ~ house** ein Haus, in dem es spukt

have **1.** vt haben; (possess) **you got** or **do you ~ a light?** haben Sie Feuer?; (receive) **I've just had a letter from** ... ich habe soeben einen Brief von ... erhalten; **~ a baby** ein Kind bekommen; (~ to eat/drink) **what are you having?** was möchten Sie (essen/trinken)?; **I had too much wine** ich habe zu viel Wein getrunken; **~ lunch/dinner** zu Mittag/Abend essen; (hold) **~ a party** eine Party geben; (take) **~ a bath/shower** ein Bad nehmen/duschen; (causative) **~ sth done** etw machen lassen; **they had a good time** sie haben sich gut amüsiert; (phrases with 'it') **I won't ~ it** das lasse ich mir nicht bieten!; **we've had it** fam wir sind geliefert **2.** v aux (forming perfect tenses) haben/sein; **he has seen it** er hat es gesehen; **she has come** sie ist gekommen; (expressing compulsion) **~ (got) to do sth** etw tun müssen; **you don't ~ to go** du musst nicht gehen; (in tag questions) **you've been there, ~n't you?** du bist mal dort gewesen, nicht wahr?; have on vt (be wearing) anhaben; (have arranged) vorhaben; (Brit) **you're having me on**

das meinst du nicht ernst

Hawaii n Hawaii nt

hawk n Habicht m

hay n Heu nt; **hay fever** n Heuschnupfen m

hazard n Gefahr f; (risk) Risiko nt; **hazardous** adj gefährlich; **~ waste** Sondermüll m; **hazard warning lights** npl Warnblinkanlage f

haze n Dunst m

hazelnut n Haselnuss f

hazy adj (misty) dunstig; (vague) verschwommen

he pron er

head 1. n Kopf m; (leader) Leiter(in) m(f); (at school) Schulleiter(in) m(f); **~ of state** Staatsoberhaupt nt; (tossing coin) **~s or tails?** Kopf oder Zahl? **2.** adj (leading) Ober-; **~ boy** Schulsprecher m; **~ girl** Schulsprecherin f **3.** vt anführen; (organization) leiten; **head for** vt zusteuern auf + acc; **he's heading for trouble** er wird Ärger bekommen

headache n Kopfschmerzen pl, Kopfweh nt; **header** n (soccer) Kopfball m; (dive) Kopfsprung m; **headfirst** adj kopfüber; **headhunt** vt COMM abwerben; **heading** n Überschrift f; **headlamp**, **headlight** n Scheinwerfer m; **headline** n Schlagzeile f; **headmaster** n Schulleiter m; **headmistress** n Schulleiterin f; **headphones** npl

Kopfhörer m; **headquarters** npl (of firm) Zentrale f; **headrest**, **head restraint** n Kopfstütze f; **headscarf** n Kopftuch nt; **head teacher** n Schulleiter(in) m(f)

heal vt, vi heilen

health n Gesundheit f; **good/ bad for one's ~** gesund/ungesund; **health centre** n Ärztezentrum nt; **health club** n Fitnesscenter nt; **health food** n Reformkost f; **~ store** Bioladen m; **health insurance** n Krankenversicherung f; **health service** n Gesundheitswesen nt; **healthy** adj gesund

heap n Haufen m; **~s of** fam jede Menge **2.** vt, vi häufen

hear vt, vi hören; **~ about sth** von etw erfahren; **I've ~d of it/ him** ich habe schon davon/von ihm gehört; **hearing** n Gehör nt; LAW Verhandlung f; **hearing aid** n Hörgerät nt; **hearsay** n from ~ vom Hörensagen

heart n Herz nt; **lose/ take ~** den Mut verlieren/Mut fassen; **learn by ~** auswendig lernen; (cards) **~s** Herz nt; **queen of ~s** Herzdame f; **heart attack** n Herzanfall m; **heartbeat** n Herzschlag m; **heartbreaking** adj herzzerreißend; **heartbroken** adj todunglücklich, untröstlich; **heartburn** n Sodbrennen nt; **heart failure** n Herzversagen *nt*; **heartfelt** *adj* tief empfunden; **heart-throb** *n fam* Schwarm *m*; **heart-to--heart** *n* offene Aussprache; **hearty** *adj* (*meal, appetite*) herzhaft; (*welcome*) herzlich

heat 1. *n* Hitze *f*; (*pleasant*) Wärme *f*; (*temperature*) Temperatur *f*; SPORT Vorlauf *m* **2.** *vt* (*house, room*) heizen; **heat up 1.** *vi* warm werden **2.** *vt* aufwärmen; **heated** *adj* beheizt; *fig* hitzig; **heater** *n* Heizofen *m*; AUTO Heizung *f*

heath *n* (*Brit*) Heide *f*; **heather** *n* Heidekraut *m*

heating *n* Heizung *f*; **heatstroke** *n* Hitzschlag *m*

heaven *n* Himmel *m*; **heavenly** *adj* himmlisch

heavily *adv* (*rain, drink etc*) stark; **heavy** *adj* schwer; (*rain, traffic, smoker etc*) stark

Hebrew 1. *adj* hebräisch **2.** *n* (*language*) Hebräisch *nt*

hectic *adj* hektisch

he'd *contr* of **he had; he would**

hedge *n* Hecke *f*

hedgehog *n* Igel *m*

heel *n* ANAT Ferse *f*; (*of shoe*) Absatz *m*

hefty *adj* schwer; (*person*) stämmig; (*fine, amount*) saftig

height *n* Höhe *f*; (*of person*) Größe *f*

heir *n* Erbe *m*; **heiress** *n* Er-

bin *f*

held *pt, pp* of **hold**

helicopter *n* Hubschrauber *m*; **heliport** *n* Hubschrauberlandeplatz *m*

hell 1. *n* Hölle *f*; **go to ~** scher dich zum Teufel; **that's a ~ of a lot of money** das ist verdammt viel Geld **2.** *interj* verdammt

he'll *contr* of **he will; he shall**

he'll *interj* hallo

helmet *n* Helm *m*

help 1. *n* Hilfe *f* **2.** *vt, vi* helfen + *dat* (*with* bei); **~ sb (to) do sth** jdm helfen, etw zu tun; **can I ~?** kann ich (Ihnen) behilflich sein?; **I couldn't ~ laughing** ich musste einfach lachen; **I can't ~ it** ich kann nichts dafür; **~ yourself** bedienen Sie sich; **helpful** *adj* (*person*) hilfsbereit; (*useful*) nützlich; **helping** *n* Portion *f*; **helpless** *adj* hilflos

hem *n* Saum *m*

hemophiliac *n* (*US*) Bluter *m*; **hemorrhage** *n* (*US*) Blutung *f*; **hemorrhoids** *npl* (*US*) Hämorrhoiden *pl*

hen *n* Henne *f*

hen night *n* (*Brit*) Junggesellinnenabschied *m*

hence *adv* (*reason*) daher

hepatitis *n* Hepatitis *f*

her 1. *adj* ihr; **she's hurt ~ leg** sie hat sich das Bein verletzt **2.** *pron* (*direct object*) sie; (*indirect object*) ihr; **do you know ~?** kennst du

sie?; *can you help ~?* kannst du ihr helfen?; *it's ~* sie ist's
herb n Kraut nt
herd n Herde f
here adv hier; *(to this place)* hierher; *come ~* komm her; *I won't be ~ for lunch* ich bin zum Mittagessen nicht da
hereditary adj erblich; *hereditary disease* n Erbkrankheit f; *heritage* n Erbe nt
hernia n Leistenbruch m, Eingeweidebruch m
hero n Held m
heroin n Heroin nt
heroine n Heldin f
herring n Hering m
hers pron ihr(r, s); *this is ~* das gehört ihr; *a friend of ~* ein Freund von ihr
herself pron *(reflexive)* sich; *she's bought ~ a flat* sie hat sich eine Wohnung gekauft; *(emphatic)* *she did it ~* sie hat es selbst gemacht; *(all) by ~* allein
he's contr of *he is; he has*
hesitate vi zögern; *don't ~ to ask* fragen Sie ruhig; *hesitation* n Zögern nt; *without ~* ohne zu zögern
heterosexual adj heterosexuell
hi interj hi, hallo
hiccup n Schluckauf m
hid pt of *hide*
hidden pp of *hide*
hide 1. vt verstecken *(from* vor *+ dat)*; *(feelings, truth)* ver-

bergen; *(cover)* verdecken 2. vi sich verstecken *(from* vor *+ dat)*
hideous adj scheußlich
hiding n *(beating)* Tracht f Prügel; *(concealment)* *be in ~* sich versteckt halten; *hiding place* n Versteck nt
hi-fi n Hi-Fi nt; *(system)* Hi-Fi-Anlage f
high 1. adj hoch; *(wind)* stark; *(on drugs)* high 2. adv hoch 3. n METEO Hoch nt; *highchair* n Hochstuhl m; *higher* adj höher; *higher education* n Hochschulbildung f; *high heels* npl Stöckelschuhe pl; *high jump* n Hochsprung m; *Highlands* npl *(schottisches)* Hochland nt; *highlight* 1. n *(in hair)* Strähnchen nt; fig Höhepunkt m 2. vt *(with pen)* hervorheben; *highlighter* n Textmarker m; *highly* adv hoch, sehr; *~ paid* hoch bezahlt; *I think ~ of him* ich habe eine hohe Meinung von ihm; *high pressure* n Hochdruck m; *high school* n *(US)* Highschool f, ≈ Gymnasium nt; *high-speed* adj Schnell-; *high-speed train* n Hochgeschwindigkeitszug m; *high street* n Hauptstraße f; *high tech* 1. adj Hightech-. 2. n Hightech nt; *high tide* n Flut f; *highway* n *(US)* ≈ Autobahn f; *(Brit)* Landstraße f
hijack vt entführen, hijacken;

hijacker n Entführer(in) m(f), Hijacker m

hike 1. vi wandern **2.** n Wanderung f; **hiker** n Wanderer m, Wanderin f; **hiking** n Wandern nt

hilarious adj zum Schreien komisch

hill n Hügel m; (higher) Berg m; **hilly** adj hügelig

him pron (direct object) ihn; (indirect object) ihm; **do you know ~?** kennst du ihn?; **can you help ~?** kannst du ihm helfen?; **it's ~** er ist's; **~ too** er auch

himself pron (reflexive) sich; **he's bought ~ a flat** er hat sich eine Wohnung gekauft; (emphatic) **he did it ~** er hat es selbst gemacht; **(all) by ~** allein

hinder vt behindern; **hindrance** n Behinderung f

Hindu 1. adj hinduistisch **2.** n Hindu m; **Hinduism** n Hinduismus m

hinge n Scharnier nt; (on door) Angel f

hint 1. n Wink m, Andeutung f **2.** vi andeuten (at acc)

hip 1. n Hüfte f **2.** adj (trend) hip, trendy

hippopotamus n Nilpferd nt

hire 1. vt (worker) anstellen; (car, bike etc) mieten **2.** n Miete f; **for ~** (taxi) frei; **hire(d) car** n Mietwagen m; **hire purchase** n Ratenkauf m

his 1. adj sein; **he's hurt ~ leg** er hat sich dat das Bein verletzt **2.** pron seine(r, s); **it's ~** es gehört ihm; **a friend of ~** ein Freund von ihm

historic adj (significant) historisch; **historical** adj (monument etc) historisch; (studies etc) geschichtlich; **history** n Geschichte f

hit 1. n (blow) Schlag m; (on target) Treffer m; (success) Erfolg m; mus Hit m **2.** vt schlagen; (bullet, stone etc) treffen; **the car ~ the tree** das Auto fuhr gegen einen Baum; **~ one's head on sth** sich dat den Kopf an etw dat stoßen; hit (up)on vt stoßen auf +acc; **hit-and-run** adj ~ **accident** Unfall m mit Fahrerflucht

hitch-hike vi trampen; **hitch-hiker** n Tramper(in) m(f); **hitchhiking** n Trampen nt

HIV abbr = **human immunodeficiency virus**; HIV nt; ~ **positive/negative** HIV-positiv/negativ

hive n Bienenstock m

HM abbr = **His/Her Majesty**

HMS abbr = **His/Her Majesty's Ship**

hoarse adj heiser

hoax n Streich m, Jux m; (false alarm) blinder Alarm

hob n (of cooker) Kochfeld nt

hobble vi humpeln

hobby n Hobby nt

hobo n (US) Penner(in) m(f)

hockey *n* Hockey *nt*; (*US*) Eishockey *nt*

hold 1. *vt* halten; (*contain*) enthalten; (*be able to contain*) fassen; (*post, office*) innehaben; (*value*) behalten; (*meeting*) abhalten; (*person as prisoner*) gefangen halten; ~ one's breath den Atem anhalten; ~ hands Händchen halten; ~ the line TEL bleiben Sie am Apparat 2. *vi* halten; (*weather*) sich halten 3. *n* (*grasp*) Halt *m*; (*of ship, aircraft*) Laderaum *m*; hold back *vt* zurückhalten; (*keep secret*) verheimlichen; hold on *vi* sich festhalten; TEL dranbleiben; ~ to sth etw festhalten; hold out 1. *vt* ausstrecken; (*offer*) bieten 2. *vi* durchhalten; hold up *vt* hochhalten; (*support*) stützen; (*delay*) aufhalten; holdall *n* Reisetasche *f*; holder *n* (*person*) Inhaber(in) *m(f)*; holdup *n* (*in traffic*) Stau *m*; (*robbery*) Überfall *m*

hole *n* Loch *nt*; (*of fox, rabbit*) Bau *m*; ~ in the wall (*cash dispenser*) Geldautomat *m*

holiday *n* (*day off*) freier Tag; (*public ~*) Feiertag *m*; (*vacation*) Urlaub *m*; (*at school*) Ferien *pl*; on ~ im Urlaub; go on ~ Urlaub machen; holiday camp *n* Ferienlager *nt*; holiday home *n* Ferienhaus *nt*; (*flat*) Ferienwohnung *f*; holidaymaker *n* Urlau-

ber(in) *m(f)*; holiday resort *n* Ferienort *m*

Holland *n* Holland *nt*

hollow 1. *adj* hohl; (*words*) leer 2. *n* Vertiefung *f*

holly *n* Stechpalme *f*

holy *adj* heilig; Holy Week *n* Karwoche *f*

home 1. *n* Zuhause *nt*; (*area, country*) Heimat *f*; (*institution*) Heim *nt*; at ~ zu Hause; make oneself at ~ es sich bequem machen; away from ~ verreist 2. *adv* go ~ nach Hause gehen / fahren; home address *n* Heimatadresse *f*; home country *n* Heimatland *nt*; home game *n* SPORT Heimspiel *nt*; homeless *adj* obdachlos; homely *adj* häuslich; (*US, ugly*) unscheinbar; home-made *adj* selbst gemacht; Home Office *nt* (*Brit*) Innenministerium *nt*

homeopathic *adj* (*US*) → homoeopathic

home page *n* IT Homepage *f*; Home Secretary *n* (*Brit*) Innenminister(in) *m(f)*; homesick *adj* be ~ Heimweh haben; homework *n* Hausaufgaben *pl*

homicide *n* (*US*) Totschlag *m*

homoeopathic *adj* homöopathisch

homosexual *adj* homosexuell

Honduras *n* Honduras *nt*

honest *adj* ehrlich; honesty *n* Ehrlichkeit *f*

honey *n* Honig *m*; honeydew

melon n Honigmelone f; honeymoon n Flitterwochen pl

Hong Kong n Hongkong nt

honor (US) → honour; honorary adj (member, title etc) Ehren-, ehrenamtlich; honour 1. vt ehren; (cheque) einlösen; (contract) einhalten 2. n Ehre f; in ~ of zu Ehren von; honourable adj ehrenhaft; honours degree n akademischer Grad mit Prüfung im Spezialfach

hood n Kapuze f; AUTO Verdeck nt; (US) AUTO Kühlerhaube f

hoof n Huf m

hook n Haken m; hooked adj (keen) besessen (on von); (drugs) abhängig (on von)

hooligan n Hooligan m

hoot vi AUTO hupen

Hoover® n Staubsauger m; hoover vi, vt staubsaugen

hop 1. vi hüpfen 2. n BOT Hopfen m

hope 1. vi, vt hoffen (for auf + acc); I ~ so/~ not hoffentlich/hoffentlich nicht; I ~ (that) we'll meet ich hoffe, dass wir uns sehen werden 2. n Hoffnung f; there's no ~ es ist aussichtslos; hopeful adj hoffnungsvoll; hopefully adv (full of hope) hoffnungsvoll; (I hope so) hoffentlich; hopeless adj hoffnungslos; (incompetent) miserabel

horizon n Horizont m; horizontal adj horizontal

hormone n Hormon nt

horn n Horn nt; AUTO Hupe f

hornet n Hornisse f

horny adj fam geil

horoscope n Horoskop nt

horrible, horribly adj, adv schrecklich; horrid, horribly adj, adv abscheulich; horrify vt entsetzen; horror n Entsetzen nt; ~s (things) Schrecken pl

hors d'oeuvre n Vorspeise f

horse n Pferd nt; horse chestnut n Rosskastanie f; horsepower n Pferdestärke f, PS nt; horse racing n Pferderennen nt; horseradish n Meerrettich m; horse riding n Reiten nt; horseshoe n Hufeisen nt

hose, hosepipe n Schlauch m

hospitable adj gastfreundlich

hospital n Krankenhaus nt

hospitality n Gastfreundschaft f

host 1. n Gastgeber m; TV (of show) Moderator(in) m(f), Talkmaster(in) m(f) 2. vt (party) geben; TV (TV show) moderieren

hostage n Geisel f

hostel n Wohnheim nt; (youth hostel) Jugendherberge f

hostess n (of a party) Gastgeberin f

hostile adj feindlich; hostility n Feindseligkeit f

hot adj heiß; (drink, food, wa-

ter) warm; (spiced) scharf;
I'm (feeling) ~ mir ist heiß;
hot dog n Hotdog nt

hotel n Hotel nt; **hotel room** n
Hotelzimmer nt

hothouse n Treibhaus nt;
hotline n Hotline f; **hotplate**
n Kochplatte f; **hotpot** n
Fleischeintopf mit Kartoffeleinlage; **hot-water bottle** n
Wärmflasche f

hour n Stunde f; **wait for ~s**
stundenlang warten; **~s** pl
(of shops etc) Geschäftszeiten pl; **hourly** adj stündlich

house 1. n Haus nt; **at my ~**
bei mir (zu Hause); **to my**
~ zu mir (nach Hause); **on**
the ~ auf Kosten des Hauses;
the House of Commons/
Lords das britische Unterhaus/Oberhaus; **the Houses**
of Parliament das britische
Parlamentsgebäude 2. vt unterbringen; **houseboat** n
Hausboot nt; **household** n
Haushalt m; **~ appliance**
Haushaltsgerät nt; **house-**
husband n Hausmann m;
housekeeping n (money) Haushaltung f; (money) Haushaltsgeld nt; **house-trained** adj
stubenrein; **house-warming**
(party) n Einzugsparty f;
housewife n Hausfrau f;
house wine n Hauswein m;
housework n Hausarbeit f

housing n (houses) Wohnungen pl; (house building)
Wohnungsbau m; **housing**

benefit n Wohngeld nt;
housing development,
housing estate (Brit) n
Wohnsiedlung f

hover vi schweben; **hover-**
craft n Luftkissenboot nt

how adv wie; **~ many** wie viele; **~ much** wie viel; **~ are**
you? wie geht es Ihnen?; **~**
are things? wie geht's?; **~'s**
work? was macht die Arbeit?; **~ about ...?** wie wäre
es mit ...?; **however 1.** conj
(but) jedoch, aber **2.** adv
(no matter how) wie ... auch;
~ much it costs wie viel es
auch kostet

howl vi heulen; **howler** n fam
grober Schnitzer

HQ abbr = **headquarters**

hubcap n Radkappe f

hug 1. vt umarmen 2. n Umarmung f

huge adj riesig

hum vi, vt summen

human 1. adj menschlich; **~**
rights Menschenrechte pl
2. ~ (being) Mensch m; **hu-**
manitarian adj humanitär; **hu-**
manity n Menschheit f;
(kindliness) Menschlichkeit
f; **humanities** Geisteswissenschaften pl

humble adj demütig; (modest) bescheiden

humid adj feucht; **humidity** n
(Luft)feuchtigkeit f

humiliate vt demütigen; **hu-**
miliation n Erniedrigung f,
Demütigung f

humor (US) → **humour**; **humorous** adj humorvoll; (story) lustig, witzig; **humour** n Humor m; **sense of ~** Sinn m für Humor

hump n Buckel m

hundred num **one ~, a~** (ein)hundert; **a ~ and one** hundert(und)eins; **two ~** zweihundert; **hundredth 1.** adj hundertste(r, s) **2.** n (fraction) Hundertstel nt; **hundredweight** ≈ Zentner m (50,8 kg)

hung pt, pp of **hang**

Hungarian 1. adj ungarisch **2.** n (person) Ungar(in) m(f); (language) Ungarisch nt; **Hungary** n Ungarn nt

hunger n Hunger m; **hungry** adj hungrig; **be ~** Hunger haben

hunk n fam gut aussehender Mann

hunt 1. n Jagd f; (search) Suche f (for nach) **2.** vt, vi jagen; (search) suchen (for nach); **hunting** n Jagen nt, Jagd f

hurdle n a. fig Hürde f; **the 400m ~s** der 400m-Hürdenlauf

hurl vt schleudern

hurray interj hurra

hurricane n Orkan m

hurried adj eilig; **hurry 1.** n Eile f; **be in a ~** in Eile f; **there's no ~** es eilt nicht **2.** vi sich beeilen; **~ (up)** mach

schnell! **3.** vt antreiben

hurt 1. vt wehtun + dat; (wound: person, feelings) verletzen; **I've ~ my arm** ich habe mir am Arm wehgetan **2.** vi wehtun; **my arm ~s** mir tut der Arm weh

husband n Ehemann m

husky 1. adj rau **2.** n Schlittenhund m

hut n Hütte f

hyacinth n Hyazinthe f

hybrid n Kreuzung f

hydroelectric adj ~ **power station** Wasserkraftwerk nt

hydrofoil n Tragflächenboot nt

hydrogen n Wasserstoff m

hygiene n Hygiene f; **hygienic** adj hygienisch

hymn n Kirchenlied nt

hypermarket n Großmarkt m; **hypersensitive** adj überempfindlich

hyphen n Bindestrich m

hypnosis n Hypnose f; **hypnotize** vt hypnotisieren

hypochondriac n eingebildete(r) Kranke(r)

hypocrisy n Heuchelei f; **hypocrite** n Heuchler(in) m(f)

hypodermic adj, n ~ (**needle**) Spritze f

hypothetical adj hypothetisch

hysteria n Hysterie f; **hysterical** adj hysterisch; (amusing) zum Totlachen

I

I *pron* ich

ice 1. *n* Eis *nt* **2.** *vt* (*cake*) glasieren; **iceberg** *n* Eisberg *m*; **icebox** *n* (*US*) Kühlschrank *m*; **icecold** *adj* eiskalt; **ice cream** *n* Eis *nt*; **ice cube** *n* Eiswürfel *m*; **iced** *adj* eisgekühlt; (*coffee, tea*) Eis-; (*cake*) glasiert; **ice hockey** *n* Eishockey *nt*

Iceland *n* Island *nt*; **Icelander** *n* Isländer(in) *m(f)*; **Icelandic 1.** *adj* isländisch **2.** *n* (*language*) Isländisch *nt*

ice lolly *n* (*Brit*) Eis *nt* am Stiel; **ice rink** *n* Kunsteisbahn *f*; **ice skating** *n* Schlittschuhlaufen *nt*

icing *n* (*on cake*) Zuckerguss *m*

icon *n* Ikone *f*; IT Icon *nt*, Programmsymbol *nt*

icy *adj* (*slippery*) vereist; (*cold*) eisig

I'd *contr of* **I would**; **I had**

ID *abbr* = **identification**; Ausweis *m*

idea *n* Idee *f*; (**I've**) **no ~** (ich habe) keine Ahnung; **that's my ~ of ...** so stelle ich mir ... vor

ideal 1. *n* Ideal *nt* **2.** *adj* ideal; **ideally** *adv* ideal; (*before statement*) idealerweise

identical *adj* identisch; **~ twins** eineiige Zwillinge

identify *vt* identifizieren; **identity** *n* Identität *f*; **identity card** *n* Personalausweis *m*

idiom *n* Redewendung *f*; **idiomatic** *adj* idiomatisch

idiot *n* Idiot(in) *m(f)*

idle *adj* (*doing nothing*) untätig; (*lazy*) faul; (*promise, threat*) leer

idol *n* Idol *nt*; **idolize** *vt* vergöttern

idyllic *adj* idyllisch

i.e. *abbr* = **id est**; d. h.

if *conj* wenn, falls; (*whether*) ob; **~ so** wenn ja; **~ I were you** wenn ich du wäre; **I don't know ~ he's coming** ich weiß nicht, ob er kommt

ignition *n* Zündung *f*; **ignition key** *n* AUTO Zündschlüssel *m*

ignorance *n* Unwissenheit *f*; **ignorant** *adj* unwissend; **ignore** *vt* ignorieren, nicht beachten

I'll *contr of* **I will**; **I shall**

ill *adj* krank; **~ at ease** unbehaglich

illegal *adj* illegal

illegitimate *adj* unzulässig; (*child*) unehelich

illiterate *adj* **be ~** Analphabet(in) sein

illness *n* Krankheit *f*

illuminate *vt* beleuchten; **illuminating** *adj* (*remark*) aufschlussreich

illusion n Illusion f; **be under the ~ that ...** sich einbilden, dass ...

illustrate vt illustrieren; **illustration** n Abbildung f, Bild nt

I'm contr of **I am**

image n Bild nt; (public ~) Image nt; (imagination n Fantasie f; (mistaken) Einbildung f; **imaginative** adj fantasievoll; **imagine** vt sich vorstellen; (wrongly) sich einbilden; **~!** stell dir vor!

imitate vt nachahmen, nach-machen; **imitation 1.** n Nachahmung f **2.** adj imitiert; **~ leather** Kunstleder nt

immaculate adj tadellos; (spotless) makellos

immature adj unreif

immediate adj unmittelbar; (instant) sofortig; (reply) umgehend; **immediately** adv sofort

immense, immensely adj, adv riesig, enorm

immersion heater n Boiler m

immigrant n Einwanderer m, Einwanderin f; **immigration** n Einwanderung f; (facility) Einwanderungskontrolle f

immobilize vt stillen; **immobilizer** n AUTO Wegfahrsperre f

immoral adj unmoralisch

immortal adj unsterblich

immune adj MED immun (from, to gegen); **immune**

system n Immunsystem nt

impact n Aufprall m; (effect) Auswirkung f (on auf + acc)

impatience n Ungeduld f; **impatient, impatiently** adj, adv ungeduldig

impede vt behindern

imperfect adj unvollkommen; (goods) fehlerhaft

imperial adj kaiserlich, Reichs-; **imperialism** n Imperialismus m

impertinence n Unver-schämtheit f, Zumutung f; **impertinent** adj unver-schämt

implant n MED Implantat nt

implausible adj unglaubwür-dig

implement 1. n Werkzeug nt, Gerät nt **2.** vt durchführen

implication n Folge f, Auswir-kung f; (logical) Schlussfol-gerung f; **implicit** adj implizit, unausgesprochen; **imply** vt (indicate) andeuten; (mean) bedeuten; **are you ~ing that ...** wollen Sie damit sagen, dass ...

impolite adj unhöflich

import 1. vt einführen, impor-tieren **2.** n Einfuhr f, Import m

importance n Bedeutung f; **of no ~** unwichtig; **important** adj wichtig (to sb für jdn); (significant) bedeutend; (in-fluential) einflussreich

import duty n Einfuhrzoll m; **import licence** n Einfuhrgenehmigung f

impose vt (conditions) auferlegen (on dat); (penalty, sanctions) verhängen (on gegen); **imposing** adj eindrucksvoll, imposant

impossible adj unmöglich

impotence n Machtlosigkeit f; (sexual) Impotenz f; **impotent** adj machtlos; (sexually) impotent

impractical adj unpraktisch; (plan) undurchführbar

impress vt beeindrucken; **impression** n Eindruck m; **impressive** adj eindrucksvoll

imprison vt inhaftieren; **imprisonment** n Inhaftierung f

improper adj (indecent) unanständig; (use) unsachgemäß

improve 1. vt verbessern **2.** vi sich verbessern, besser werden; (patient) Fortschritte machen; **improvement** n Verbesserung f (in + gen; on gegenüber); (in appearance) Verschönerung f

improvise vt, vi improvisieren

impulse n Impuls m; **impulsive** adj impulsiv

in 1. prep in + dat; (expressing motion) in + acc; (in the case of) bei; **put it ~ the drawer** es in die Schublade; **~ the army** beim Militär; **~ itself** an sich; (time) **~ the morning/afternoon/evening** am Morgen / Nachmittag / Abend; **at three ~ the afternoon** um drei Uhr nachmit-

tags; **~ 2007** (im Jahre) 2007; **~ July** im Juli; **~ a week** in einer Woche; **~ writing** schriftlich; **~ German** auf Deutsch; **one ~ ten** einer von zehn, jeder zehnte; **~ all** insgesamt **2.** adv (go) hinein; (come) herein; **be ~** zu Hause sein; (in fashion) in sein, modisch sein; (arrived) angekommen sein; **sb is ~ for sth** jdm steht etw bevor; (sth unpleasant) jmd kann sich auf etw acc gefasst machen; **be ~ on sth** an etw dat beteiligt sein

inability n Unfähigkeit f

inaccessible adj a. fig unzugänglich

inaccurate adj ungenau

inadequate adj unzulänglich

inappropriate adj unpassend; (clothing) ungeeignet; (remark) unangebracht

incapable adj unfähig (of zu); **be ~ of doing sth** nicht imstande sein, etw zu tun

incense n Weihrauch m

incentive n Anreiz m

incessant, incessantly adj, adv unaufhörlich

incest n Inzest m

inch n Zoll m (2,54 cm)

incident n Vorfall m; (disturbance) Zwischenfall m; **incidentally** adv nebenbei bemerkt, übrigens

inclination n Neigung f; **inclined** adj **be ~ to do sth** dazu neigen, etw zu tun

include vt einschließen; (on list, in group) aufnehmen; **including** prep einschließlich (+ gen); **not ~ service** Bedienung nicht inbegriffen; **inclusive** adj einschließlich (of + gen); (price) Pauschal-

incoherent adj zusammenhanglos

income n Einkommen nt; (from business) Einkünfte pl; **income tax** n Einkommensteuer f; (on wages, salary) Lohnsteuer f; **incoming** adj ankommend; (mail) eingehend

incompatible adj unvereinbar; (people) unverträglich; IT nicht kompatibel

incompetent adj unfähig

incomplete adj unvollständig

incomprehensible adj unverständlich

inconceivable adj unvorstellbar

inconsiderate adj rücksichtslos

inconsistency n Inkonsequenz f; (contradictory) Widersprüchlichkeit f; **inconsistent** adj inkonsequent; (contradictory) widersprüchlich; (work) unbeständig

inconvenience n Unannehmlichkeit f; (trouble) Umstände pl; **inconvenient** adj ungünstig, unbequem; (time) **it's ~ for me** es kommt mir ungelegen; **if it's not too**

~ for you wenn es dir passt

incorporate vt aufnehmen (into in + acc); (include) enthalten

incorrect adj falsch; (improper) inkorrekt

increase 1. n Zunahme f (in an + dat); (in amount, speed) Erhöhung f (in + gen); **~ in size** Vergrößerung f **2.** vt (price, taxes, salary, speed etc) erhöhen; (wealth) vermehren; (number) vergrößern **3.** vi zunehmen (in an + dat); (prices) steigen; (in size) größer werden; (in number) sich vermehren; **increasingly** adv zunehmend

incredible, incredibly adj, adv unglaublich; (very good) fantastisch

incredulous adj ungläubig, skeptisch

incriminate vt belasten

incubator n Brutkasten m

incurable adj unheilbar

indecent adj unanständig

indecisive adj (person) unentschlossen; (result) nicht entscheidend

indeed adv tatsächlich; (as answer) allerdings; **very hot ~** wirklich sehr heiß

indefinite adj unbestimmt; **indefinitely** adv endlos; (postpone) auf unbestimmte Zeit

independence n Unabhängigkeit f; **independent** adj unabhängig (of von); (person) selbstständig

indescribable *adj* unbeschreiblich

index *n* Index *m*, Verzeichnis *nt*; **index finger** *n* Zeigefinger *m*

India *n* Indien *nt*; **Indian 1.** *adj* indisch; (*Native American*) indianisch **2.** *n* Inder(in) *m(f)*; (*Native American*) Indianer(in) *m(f)*; **Indian Ocean** *n* Indischer Ozean; **Indian summer** *n* Spätsommer *m*, Altweibersommer *m*

indicate 1. *vt* (*show*) zeigen; (*instrument*) anzeigen; (*suggest*) hinweisen auf + *acc* **2.** *vi* AUTO blinken; **indication** *n* (*sign*) Anzeichen *nt* (*of* für); **indicator** *n* AUTO Blinker *m*

indifferent *adj* (*not caring*) gleichgültig (*to, towards* gegenüber); (*mediocre*) mittelmäßig

indigestible *adj* unverdaulich; **indigestion** *n* Verdauungsstörung *f*

indignity *n* Demütigung *f*

indirect, indirectly *adj, adv* indirekt

indiscreet *adj* indiskret

indispensable *adj* unentbehrlich

indisposed *adj* unwohl

indisputable *adj* unbestreitbar; (*evidence*) unanfechtbar

individual 1. *n* Einzelne(r) *mf* **2.** *adj* einzeln; (*distinctive*) eigen, individuell; **~ case**

Einzelfall *m*; **individually** *adv* (*separately*) einzeln

Indonesia *n* Indonesien *nt*

indoor *adj* (*shoes*) Haus-; (*plant, games*) Zimmer-; SPORT (*soccer, championship, record etc*) Hallen-; **indoors** *adv* drinnen, im Haus

indulge *vi* **~ in sth** sich *dat* etw gönnen; **indulgence** *n* Nachsicht *f*; (*enjoyment*) (übermäßiger) Genuss *m*; (*luxury*) Luxus *m*; **indulgent** *adj* nachsichtig (*with* gegenüber)

industrial *adj* Industrie-, industriell; **~ estate** Industriegebiet *nt*; **industry** *n* Industrie *f*

inedible *adj* nicht essbar, ungenießbar

ineffective *adj* unwirksam, wirkungslos; **inefficient** *adj* unwirksam; (*use, machine*) unwirtschaftlich; (*method etc*) unrationell

inequality *n* Ungleichheit *f*

inevitable *adj* unvermeidlich; **inevitably** *adv* zwangsläufig

inexcusable *adj* unverzeihlich

inexpensive *adj* preisgünstig

inexperience *n* Unerfahrenheit *f*; **inexperienced** *adj* unerfahren

inexplicable *adj* unerklärlich

infallible *adj* unfehlbar

infamous *adj* (*person*) berüchtigt (*for* wegen); (*deed*) niederträchtig

infancy n frühe Kindheit; **infant** n Säugling m; (*small child*) Kleinkind nt; **infant school** n Vorschule f

infatuated adj verrannt or verknallt (*with* in + acc)

infect vt (*person*) anstecken; (*wound*) infizieren; **infection** n Infektion f; **infectious** adj ansteckend

inferior adj (*in quality*) minderwertig; (*in rank*) untergeordnet; **inferiority** n Minderwertigkeit f

infertile adj unfruchtbar

inflame vt MED entzünden; **inflammation** n MED Entzündung f

inflatable adj aufblasbar; **inflate** vt aufpumpen; (*by blowing*) aufblasen; (*prices*) hochtreiben

inflation n Inflation f

inflexible adj unflexibel

in-flight adj (*catering, magazine*) Bord-

influence 1. n Einfluss m (*on* auf + acc) **2.** vt beeinflussen; **influential** adj einflussreich

influenza n Grippe f

inform vt informieren (*of, about* über + acc); **keep sb ~ed** jdn auf dem Laufenden halten

informal adj zwanglos, ungezwungen

information n Auskunft f, Informationen pl; **for your ~** zu Ihrer Information; **further ~** weitere Informationen, weiteres; **information desk** n Auskunftsschalter m; **information technology** n Informationstechnik f; **informative** adj aufschlussreich

infra-red adj infrarot

infrastructure n Infrastruktur f

infuriate vt wütend machen; **infuriating** adj äußerst ärgerlich

infusion n (*herbal tea*) Aufguss m; MED Infusion f

ingenious adj (*person*) erfinderisch; (*device*) raffiniert; (*idea*) genial

ingredient n GASTR Zutat f

inhabit vt bewohnen; **inhabitant** n Einwohner(in) m(f)

inhale vt einatmen; (*cigarettes*) mit Inhalieren; **inhaler** n Inhalationsgerät nt

inherit vt erben; **inheritance** n Erbe nt

in-house adj intern

inhuman adj unmenschlich

initial 1. adj anfänglich; **~ stage** Anfangsstadium nt **2.** vt mit Initialen unterschreiben; **initially** adv anfangs; **initials** npl Initialen pl

initiative n Initiative f

inject vt (*drug etc*) einspritzen; **~ sb with sth** jdm etw (ein)spritzen; **injection** n Spritze f, Injektion f

injure vt verletzen; **~ one's leg** sich dat das Bein verletzen; **injury** n Verletzung f

injustice n Ungerechtigkeit f

ink n Tinte f; **ink-jet printer** n Tintenstrahldrucker m

inland 1. adj Binnen- **2.** adv landeinwärts; **inland revenue** n (Brit) Finanzamt nt

in-laws npl fam Schwiegereltern pl

inline skates npl Inlineskates pl, Inliner pl

inmate n Insasse m

inn n Gasthaus nt

inner adj innere(r, s); ~ **city** Innenstadt f

innocence n Unschuld f; **innocent** adj unschuldig

innovation n Neuerung f

innumerable adj unzählig

inoculate vt impfen (against gegen); **inoculation** n Impfung f

in-patient n stationärer Patient, stationäre Patientin

input n (contribution) Beitrag m; IT Eingabe f

inquire → **enquire**; **inquiry** → **enquiry**

insane adj wahnsinnig; MED geisteskrank; **insanity** n Wahnsinn m

insatiable adj unersättlich

inscription n (on stone etc) Inschrift f

insect n Insekt nt

insecure adj (person) unsicher; (shelves) instabil

insensitive adj unempfindlich (to gegen); (unfeeling) gefühllos

inseparable adj unzertrennlich

insert 1. vt einfügen; (coin) einwerfen; (key etc) hineinstecken **2.** n (in magazine) Beilage f; **insertion** n (in text) Einfügen nt

inside 1. n **the** ~ das Innere; (surface) die Innenseite; **from the** ~ von innen **2.** adj innere(r, s), Innen-; ~ **lane** AUTO Innenspur f; SPORT Innenbahn f **3.** adv (place) innen; (direction) hinein; **go** ~ hineingehen **4.** prep (place) in + dat; (into) in + acc ... hinein; (time, within) innerhalb + gen; **inside out** adv verkehrt herum; (know) in- und auswendig; **insider** n Eingeweihte(r) mf, Insider(in) m(f)

insight n Einblick m (into in + acc)

insincere adj unaufrichtig, falsch

insinuation n Andeutung f

insist vi darauf bestehen; ~ **on sth** auf etw dat bestehen; **insistent** adj hartnäckig

insomnia n Schlaflosigkeit f

inspect vt prüfen, kontrollieren; **inspection** n Prüfung f; (check) Kontrolle f; **inspector** n (police) Inspektor(in) m(f); (senior) Kommissar(in) m(f); (on bus etc) Kontrolleur(in) m(f)

inspiration n Inspiration f; **inspire** vt (respect) einflößen (in dat); (person) inspirieren

install vt (software) installieren

installment, instalment n Rate f; (of story) Folge f; **pay in ~s** auf Raten zahlen; **installment plan** n (US) Ratenkauf m

instance n (of discrimination) Fall m; (example) Beispiel nt; **for ~** zum Beispiel

instant 1. n Augenblick m **2.** adj sofortig; **instant coffee** n Instantkaffee m; **instantly** adv sofort

instead adv stattdessen; **instead of** prep (an)statt + gen

instinct n Instinkt m; **instinctive, instinctively** adj, adv instinktiv

institute n Institut nt; **institution** n (organisation) Institution f, Einrichtung f; (home) Anstalt f

instruct vt anweisen; **instruction** n (teaching) Unterricht m; (command) Anweisung f; **~s for use** Gebrauchsanweisung f; **instructor** n Lehrer(in) m(f); (US) Dozent(in) m(f)

instrument n Instrument nt; **instrument panel** n Armaturenbrett nt

insufficient adj ungenügend

insulate vt ELEC isolieren; **insulating tape** n Isolierband nt; **insulation** n Isolierung f

insulin n Insulin nt

insult 1. n Beleidigung f **2.** vt beleidigen; **insulting** adj beleidigend

insurance n Versicherung f; **~ company** Versicherungsgesellschaft f; **~ policy** Versicherungspolice f; **insure** vt versichern (against gegen)

intake n Aufnahme f

integrate vt integrieren (into in + acc)

integrity n Integrität f, Ehrlichkeit f

intellect n Intellekt m; **intellectual** adj intellektuell; (interests etc) geistig

intelligence n (understanding) Intelligenz f; **intelligent** adj intelligent

intend vt beabsichtigen; **~ to do sth** vorhaben, etw zu tun

intense adj intensiv; (pressure) enorm; (competition) heftig; **intensity** n Intensität f; **intensive** adj intensiv; **intensive care unit** n Intensivstation f

intention n Absicht f; **intentional, intentionally** adj, adv absichtlich

interact vi aufeinander einwirken; **interaction** n Interaktion f, Wechselwirkung f; **interactive** adj interaktiv

interchange n (of motorways) Autobahnkreuz nt; **interchangeable** adj austauschbar

intercity n Intercityzug m, IC m

intercom n (Gegen)sprechanlage f

intercourse n (sexual) Geschlechtsverkehr *m*

interest 1. *n* Interesse *nt*; FIN (*on money*) Zinsen *pl*; COMM (*share*) Anteil *m*; **be of ~** von Interesse sein (*to für*) **2.** *vt* interessieren; **interested** *adj* interessiert (*in* an + *dat*); **be ~ed in** sich interessieren für; **are you ~ in coming?** hast du Lust, mitzukommen?; **interesting** *adj* interessant; **interest rate** *n* Zinssatz *m*

interface *n* IT Schnittstelle *f*

interfere *vi* (*meddle*) sich einmischen (*with, in* in + *acc*); **interference** *n* Einmischung *f*; TV, RAD Störung *f*

interior 1. *adj* Innen- **2.** *n* Innere(r, s) *nt*; (*of car*) Innenraum *m*; (*of house*) Innenausstattung *f*

intermediate *adj* Zwischen-

intermission *n* Pause *f*

intern *n* Assistent(in) *m(f)*

internal *adj* innere(r, s); (*flight*) Inlands-; **~ revenue** (*US*) Finanzamt *nt*; **internally** *adv* innen; (*in body*) innerlich

international 1. *adj* international; **~ match** Länderspiel *nt*; **~ flight** Auslandsflug *m* **2.** *n* SPORT (*player*) Nationalspieler(in) *m(f)*

Internet *n* IT Internet *nt*; **Internet banking** *n* Onlinebanking *nt*; **Internet café** *n* Internetcafé *nt*; **Internet provider** *n* Internetprovider *m*

interpret *vi, vt* (*translate*) dolmetschen; (*explain*) interpretieren; **interpretation** *n* Interpretation *f*; **interpreter** *n* Dolmetscher(in) *m(f)*

interrogate *vt* verhören; **interrogation** *n* Verhör *nt*

interrupt *vt* unterbrechen; **interruption** *n* Unterbrechung *f*

intersection *n* (*of roads*) Kreuzung *f*

interstate *n* (*US*) zwischenstaatlich; **~ highway** ≈ Bundesautobahn *f*

interval *n* (*space, time*) Abstand *m*; (*theatre etc*) Pause *f*

intervene *vi* eingreifen (*in* in); **intervention** *n* Eingreifen *nt*; POL Intervention *f*

interview 1. *n* Interview *nt*; (*for job*) Vorstellungsgespräch *nt* **2.** *vt* interviewen; (*job applicant*) ein Vorstellungsgespräch führen mit; **interviewer** *n* Interviewer(in) *m(f)*

intestine *n* Darm *m*; **~s** *pl* Eingeweide *pl*

intimate *adj* (*friends*) vertraut, eng; (*atmosphere*) gemütlich; (*sexually*) intim

intimidate *vt* einschüchtern; **intimidation** *n* Einschüchterung *f*

into *prep* in + *acc*; (*crash*) gegen; **translate ~ French** ins Französische übersetzen; **be ~ sth** *fam* auf etw *acc* stehen

intolerable *adj* unerträglich
intolerant *adj* intolerant
intoxicated *adj* betrunken; *fig* berauscht
intricate *adj* kompliziert
intrigue *vt* faszinieren; **intriguing** *adj* faszinierend, fesselnd
introduce *vt* (*person*) vorstellen (*to sb* jdm); (*sth new*) einführen (*to* in + *acc*); **introduction** *n* Einführung *f* (*to* in + *acc*); (*to book*) Einleitung *f* (*to* zu); (*to person*) Vorstellung *f*
introvert *n* Introvertierte(r) *mf*
intuition *n* Intuition *f*
invade *vt* einfallen in + *acc*
invalid 1. *n* Kranke(r) *mf*; (*disabled*) Invalide *m* **2.** *adj* (*not valid*) ungültig
invaluable *adj* äußerst wertvoll, unschätzbar
invariably *adv* ständig; (*every time*) jedes Mal, ohne Ausnahme
invasion *n* Invasion *f* (*of* in + *acc*)
invent *vt* erfinden; **invention** *n* Erfindung *f*; **inventor** *n* Erfinder(in) *m(f)*
inverted commas *npl* Anführungszeichen *pl*
invest *vt, vi* investieren (*in* in + *acc*)
investigate *vt* untersuchen; **investigation** *n* Untersuchung *f* (*into* + *gen*)
investment *n* Investition *f*;

it's a good ~ es ist eine gute Anlage
invigorating *adj* erfrischend, belebend; (*tonic*) stärkend
invisible *adj* unsichtbar
invitation *n* Einladung *f*; **invite** *vt* einladen
invoice *n* (*bill*) Rechnung *f*
involuntary *adj* unbeabsichtigt
involve *vt* verwickeln (*in sth* in etw *acc*); (*entail*) zur Folge haben; **be ~d in sth** (*participate in*) an etw *dat* beteiligt sein; **I'm not ~d** (*affected*) ich bin nicht betroffen
inward *adj* innere(r, s); **inwardly** *adv* innerlich; **inwards** *adv* nach innen
iodine *n* Jod *nt*
IOU *abbr* = **I owe you**; Schuldschein *m*
IQ *abbr* = **intelligence quotient**; IQ *m*
Iran *n* der Iran
Iraq *n* der Irak
Ireland *n* Irland *nt*
iris *n* (*flower*) Schwertlilie *f*; (*of eye*) Iris *f*
Irish 1. *adj* irisch; **~ coffee** Irishcoffee *m*; **~ Sea** die Irische See **2.** *n* (*language*) Irisch *nt*; **the ~** *pl* die Iren *pl*; **Irishman** *n* Ire *m*; **Irishwoman** *n* Irin *f*
iron 1. *n* Eisen *nt*; (*for ironing*) Bügeleisen *nt* **2.** *adj* eisern **3.** *vt* bügeln
ironic(al) *adj* ironisch
ironing board *n* Bügelbrett *nt*

irony n Ironie f

irrational adj irrational

irregular adj unregelmäßig

irrelevant adj belanglos, irrelevant

irreplaceable adj unersetzlich

irresistible adj unwiderstehlich

irresponsible adj verantwortungslos

irretrievable adv unwiederbringlich; (loss) unersetzlich

irritable adj reizbar; **irritate** vt (annoy) ärgern; (deliberately) reizen; **irritation** n (anger) Ärger m; MED Reizung f

is present of **be**: ist

Islam n Islam m; **Islamic** adj islamisch

island n Insel f; **Isle** n (in names) **the ~ of Man** die Insel Man; **the British ~s** die Britischen Inseln

isn't contr of **is not**

isolate vt isolieren; **isolated** adj (remote) abgelegen; **isolation** n Isolierung f

Israel n Israel nt; **Israeli** 1. adj israelisch 2. n Israeli m or f

issue 1. n (matter) Frage f; (problem) Problem nt; (subject) Thema nt; (of newspaper etc) Ausgabe f; **that's not the ~** darum geht es nicht 2. vt ausgeben; (document) ausstellen; (orders) erteilen; (book) herausgeben

it pron (as subject) er / sie / es;

(as direct object) ihn / sie / es; (as indirect object) ihm / ihr / ihm; **the worst thing about ~** das Schlimmste daran; **who is ~?** ~'s me / ~'s him wer ist da? ich bin's / er ist's; ~'s **your turn** du bist dran; **that's ~** ja genau!; ~'s **raining** es regnet; ~'s **Charlie here**, hier spricht Charlie

IT abbr = **information technology**; IT f

Italian 1. adj italienisch 2. n Italiener(in) m(f); (language) Italienisch nt

italic 1. adj kursiv 2. npl in ~s kursiv

Italy n Italien nt

itch 1. n Juckreiz m; **I have an ~** mich juckt es 2. vi jucken; **he is ~ing to ...** es juckt ihn, zu ...; **itchy** adj juckend

it'd contr of **it would**; **it had**

item n (article) Gegenstand m; (in catalogue) Artikel m; (on list, in accounts) Posten m; (on agenda) Punkt m; (in news) Bericht m; TV (radio) Meldung f

itinerary n Reiseroute f

it'll contr of **it will**; **it shall**

its pron sein; (feminine form) ihr

it's contr of **it is**; **it has**

itself pron (reflexive) sich; (emphatic) **the house ~ is OK** das Haus selbst or an sich ist in Ordnung; **by ~** allein; **the door closes (by) ~** die

Tür schließt sich von selbst
I've contr of **I have**

ivory n Elfenbein nt
ivy n Efeu nt

J

jab 1. vt (needle, knife) stechen (into in + acc) **2.** n fam Spritze f
jack n AUTO Wagenheber m, Bube m; **jack in** vt fam aufgeben, hinschmeißen; **jack up** vt (car etc) aufbocken
jacket n Jacke f; (of man's suit) Jackett nt; (of book) Schutzumschlag m; **jacket potato** n (in der Schale) gebackene Kartoffel
jack-knife 1. n Klappmesser nt **2.** vi (truck) sich quer stellen
jacuzzi® n (bath) Whirlpool m
jail 1. n Gefängnis nt **2.** vt einsperren
jam 1. n Konfitüre f, Marmelade f; (traffic ~) Stau m **2.** vt (street) verstopfen; **be ~med** (stuck) klemmen; **~ on the brakes** eine Vollbremsung machen
Jamaica n Jamaika nt
jam-packed adj proppenvoll
janitor n (US) Hausmeister(in) m(f)
January n Januar m
Japan n Japan nt; **Japanese 1.** adj japanisch **2.** n (person) Japaner(in) m(f); (language) Japanisch nt

jar n Glas nt
jaundice n Gelbsucht f
javelin n Speer m; SPORT Speerwerfen nt
jaw n Kiefer m
jazz n Jazz m
jealous adj eifersüchtig (of auf + acc); **don't make me ~** mach mich nicht neidisch; **jealousy** n Eifersucht f
jeans npl Jeans pl
jelly n Gelee nt; (dessert) Götterspeise f; (US, jam) Marmelade f; **jelly baby** n (sweet) Gummibärchen nt; **jellyfish** n Qualle f
jeopardize vt gefährden
jerk 1. n Ruck m; fam (idiot) Trottel m **2.** vt ruckartig bewegen **3.** vi (rope) rucken; (muscles) zucken
Jerusalem n Jerusalem nt
jet n (of water etc) Strahl m; (nozzle) Düse f; (aircraft) Düsenflugzeug nt; **jet foil** n Tragflächenboot nt; **jetlag** n Jetlag m (Müdigkeit nach langem Flug)
jetty n Landesteg m; (larger) Landungsbrücke f
Jew n Jude m, Jüdin f
jewel n Edelstein m; (esp) fig Juwel nt; **jeweller, jeweler** (US) n Juwelier(in) m(f);

jewellery, jewelery (*US*) *n* Schmuck *m*

Jewish *adj* jüdisch; **she's ~** sie ist Jüdin

jigsaw (*puzzle*) *n* Puzzle *nt*

jilt *vt* laufen lassen + *dat*

jitters *npl fam* **have the ~** Bammel haben; **jittery** *adj fam* ganz nervös

job *n* (*piece of work*) Arbeit *f*; (*task*) Aufgabe *f*; (*occupation*) Stellung *f*, Job *m*; **what's your ~?** was machen Sie beruflich?; **jobcentre** *n* Arbeitsvermittlungsstelle *f*, Arbeitsamt *nt*; **job-hunting** *n* **go ~** auf Arbeitssuche gehen; **jobless** *adj* arbeitslos; **job seeker** *n* Arbeitssuchende(r) *m/f*; **jobseeker's allowance** *n* Arbeitslosengeld *nt*; **job-sharing** *n* Arbeitsplatzteilung *f*

jockey *n* Jockey *m*

jog 1. *n* (*of person*) anstoßen **2.** *vi* (*run*) joggen; **jogging** *n* Jogging *nt*; **go ~** joggen gehen

john *n* (*US*) *fam* Klo *nt*

join 1. *vt* (*put together*) verbinden (*to* mit); (*club etc*) beitreten + *dat*; **~ sb** sich anschließen; (*sit with*) sich zu jdm setzen **2.** *vi* (*unite*) sich vereinigen; (*rivers*) zusammenfließen; **join in** *vi*, *vt* mitmachen (*with* bei)

joinery *n* Schreinerei *f*

joint 1. *n* (*of bones*) Gelenk *nt*;

(*in pipe etc*) Verbindungsstelle *f*; (*of meat*) Braten *m*; (*of marijuana*) Joint *m* **2.** *adj* gemeinsam; **joint account** *n* Gemeinschaftskonto *nt*; **jointly** *adv* gemeinsam

joke 1. *n* Witz *m*; (*prank*) Streich *m*; **for a ~** aus Spaß; **it's no ~** das ist nicht zum Lachen **2.** *vi* Witze machen; **you must be joking** das ist ja wohl nicht dein Ernst!

jolly *adj* lustig, vergnügt

Jordan *n* (*country*) Jordanien *nt*; (*river*) Jordan *m*

jot down *vt* sich notieren; **jotter** *n* Notizbuch *nt*

journal *n* (*diary*) Tagebuch *nt*; (*magazine*) Zeitschrift *f*; **journalism** *n* Journalismus *m*; **journalist** *n* Journalist(in) *m(f)*

journey *n* Reise *f*; (*esp on stage, by car, train*) Fahrt *f*

joy *n* Freude *f* (*at* über + *acc*); **joystick** *n* IT Joystick *m*; AVIAT Steuerknüppel *m*

judge 1. *n* Richter(in) *m(f)*; SPORT Punktrichter(in) *m(f)* **2.** *vt* beurteilen (*by* nach) **3.** *vi* urteilen (*by* nach); **judg(e)ment** *n* LAW Urteil *nt*; (*opinion*) Ansicht *f*; **an error of ~** Fehleinschätzung *f*

judo *n* Judo *nt*

jug *n* Krug *m*

juggle *vi* jonglieren (*with* mit)

juice *n* Saft *m*; **juicy** *adj* saftig

July *n* Juli *m*; → **September**

jumble 1. *n* Durcheinander *nt*

2. vt ~ **(up)** durcheinander werfen; (facts) durcheinanderbringen; **jumble sale** n (for charity) Wohltätigkeitsbasar m

jump 1. vi springen; (nervously) zusammenzucken; ~ **to conclusions** voreilige Schlüsse ziehen **2.** vt (omit) überspringen; ~ **the lights** bei Rot über die Kreuzung fahren; ~ **the queue** sich vordrängen **3.** n Sprung m; (for horses) Hindernis nt; **jumper** n Pullover m; (US, dress) Trägerkleid nt; (person, horse) Springer(in) m(f); **jumper cables** npl (US), **jump leads** npl (Brit) AUTO Starthilfekabel nt

junction n (of roads) Kreuzung f; RAIL Knotenpunkt m

June n Juni m; → **September**

jungle n Dschungel m

junior 1. adj (younger) jünger; (lower position) untergeordnet (to sb jdm) **2.** n she's two years my ~ sie ist zwei Jahre jünger als ich; **junior high (school)** n (US) ≈ Mittelschule f; **junior school** n (Brit) Grundschule f

junk n (trash) Plunder m; **junkfood** n Nahrungsmittel pl mit geringem Nährwert,

Junkfood nt; **junkie** n fam Junkie m, Fixer(in) m(f); fig (fan) Freak m; **junk mail** n Reklame f; IT Junkmail f; **junk shop** n Trödelladen m

jury n Geschworene pl; (in competition) Jury f

just 1. adj gerecht **2.** adv (recently) gerade; (exactly) genau; ~ **as expected** wie erwartet; ~ **as nice** genauso nett; (barely) ~ **in time** gerade noch rechtzeitig; (immediately) ~ **before/after** ... gleich vor/nach ...; (small distance) ~ **round the corner** gleich um die Ecke; (a little) ~ **over an hour** etwas mehr als eine Stunde; (only) ~ **the two of us** nur wir beide; ~ **a moment** Moment mal; (absolutely, simply) **it was ~ fantastic** es war einfach klasse; (more or less) mehr oder weniger; ~ **about ready** fast fertig

justice n Gerechtigkeit f; **justifiable** adj berechtigt; **justifiably** adv zu Recht; **justify** vt rechtfertigen

juvenile n **1.** adj Jugend-, jugendlich **2.** n Jugendliche(r) mf

K

k *abbr* = **thousand**; **15k** 15 000
K *abbr* = **kilobyte**; KB
kangaroo *n* Känguru *nt*
karaoke *n* Karaoke *nt*
karate *n* Karate *nt*
kart *n* Gokart *m*
kayak *n* Kajak *m or nt*
Kazakhstan *n* Kasachstan *nt*
kebab *n* (*shish ~*) Schaschlik *nt or m*; (*doner ~*) Kebab *m*
keel *n* NAUT Kiel *m*; **keel over** *vi* (*boat*) kentern; (*person*) umkippen
keen *adj* begeistert (*on* von); (*hardworking*) eifrig; (*mind, wind*) scharf; (*interest, feeling etc*) stark; **be ~ on sb** von jdm angetan sein; **she's ~ on riding** sie reitet gern; **be ~ to do sth** darauf erpicht sein, etw zu tun
keep 1. *vt* (*retain*) behalten; (*secret*) für sich behalten; (*observe*) einhalten; (*promise*) halten; (*run: shop, diary, accounts*) führen; (*animals*) halten; (*support, family etc*) unterhalten, versorgen; (*store*) aufbewahren; **~ sb waiting** jdn warten lassen; **~ sb from doing sth** jdn davon abhalten, etw zu tun; **~ sth clean/secret** etw sauber/geheim halten; '**~ clear**' „(bitte) freihalten"; **~ this to yourself** behalten Sie das für

sich **2.** *vi* (*food*) sich halten; (*remain, with adj*) bleiben; **~ quiet** sei ruhig!; **~ left** links fahren; **~ doing sth** (*repeatedly*) etw immer wieder tun; **~ at it** mach weiter so!; **it ~s happening** es passiert immer wieder; **keep back 1.** *vi* zurückbleiben **2.** *vt* zurückhalten; (*information*) verschweigen (*from sb* jdm); **keep off** *vt* (*person, animal*) fernhalten; '**~ off the grass**' „Betreten des Rasens verboten"; **keep on 1.** *vi* weitermachen; (*walking*) weitergehen; (*in car*) weiterfahren; **~ doing sth** (*persistently*) etw immer wieder tun **2.** *vt* (*coat etc*) anbehalten; **keep out 1.** *vt* nicht hereinlassen **2.** *vi* draußen bleiben; '**~ (on sign)** Eintritt verboten; **keep to** *vt* (*road, path*) bleiben auf + *dat*; (*plan etc*) sich halten an + *acc*; **~ the point** bei der Sache bleiben; **keep up 1.** *vi* Schritt halten (*with* mit) **2.** *vt* (*maintain*) aufrechterhalten; (*speed*) halten; **~ appearances** den Schein wahren; **keep it up!** *fam* weiter so!

keeper *n* (*museum etc*) Aufseher(in) *m(f)*; (*goalkeeper*)

Torwart *m*; (*zoo keeper*) Tierpfleger(in) *m(f)*; **keep-fit** *n* Fitnesstraining *nt*; **~ exercises** Gymnastik *f*

kennel *n* Hundehütte *f*; **kennels** *n* Hundepension *f*

Kenya *n* Kenia *nt*

kept *pt, pp of* **keep**

kerb *n* Randstein *m*

kerosene *n* (*US*) Petroleum *nt*

ketchup *n* Ket(s)chup *nt or m*

kettle *n* Kessel *m*

key 1. *n* Schlüssel *m*; (*of piano, computer*) Taste *f*; MUS Tonart *f*; (*for map etc*) Zeichenerklärung *f* **2.** *vt* **~ (in)** IT eingeben **3.** *adj* entscheidend; **keyboard** *n* (*of piano, computer*) Tastatur *f*; **keyhole** *n* Schlüsselloch *nt*; **keypad** *n* IT Nummernblock *m*; **keyring** *n* Schlüsselring *m*

kick 1. *n* Tritt *m*; SPORT Stoß *m* **2.** *vt, vi* treten; **kick out** *vt fam* rausschmeißen (*of* aus); **kick-off** *n* SPORT Anstoß *m*

kid 1. *n* (*child*) Kind *nt* **2.** *vt* (*tease*) auf den Arm nehmen **3.** *vi* Witze machen; **you're ~ding** das ist doch nicht dein Ernst!; **no ~ding** aber echt!

kidnap *vt* entführen; **kidnapper** *n* Entführer(in) *m(f)*; **kidnapping** *n* Entführung *f*

kidney *n* Niere *f*; **kidney machine** *n* künstliche Niere

kill *vt* töten; (*esp intentionally*) umbringen; (*weeds*) vernich-

ten; **killer** *n* Mörder(in) *m(f)*

kilo *n* Kilo *nt*; **kilobyte** *n* Kilobyte *nt*; **kilogramme** *n* Kilogramm *nt*; **kilometer** (*US*), **kilometre** *n* Kilometer *m*; **~s per hour** Stundenkilometer *pl*; **kilowatt** *n* Kilowatt *nt*

kilt *n* Schottenrock *m*

kind 1. *adj* nett, freundlich (*to* zu) **2.** *n* Art *f*; (*of coffee, cheese etc*) Sorte *f*; **what ~ of...?** was für ein(e) ...?; **this ~ of ...** so ein(e) ...; **~ of** (+ *adj*) *fam* irgendwie

kindergarten *n* Kindergarten *m*

kindly 1. *adj* nett, freundlich **2.** *adv* liebenswürdigerweise

king *n* König *m*; **kingdom** *n* Königreich *nt*; **king-size** *adj* im Großformat; (*bed*) extra groß

kipper *n* Räucherhering *m*

kiss 1. *n* Kuss *m*; **~ of life** Mund-zu-Mund-Beatmung *f* **2.** *vt* küssen

kit *n* (*equipment*) Ausrüstung *f*; *fam* Sachen *pl*; (*sports kit*) Sportsachen *pl*; (*for building sth*) Bausatz *m*

kitchen *n* Küche *f*; **kitchen foil** *n* Alufolie *f*; **kitchen scales** *n* Küchenwaage *f*; **kitchenware** *n* Küchengeschirr *nt*

kite *n* Drachen *m*

kitten *n* Kätzchen *nt*

kiwi *n* (*fruit*) Kiwi *f*

km *abbr* = **kilometres**; km

knack *n* Dreh *m*, Trick *m*;

get/ have got the ~ den Dreh herauskriegen/ heraushaben; **knackered** *adj* (*Brit*) *fam* fix und fertig, kaputt

knee *n* Knie *nt*; **kneecap** *n* Kniescheibe *f*; **knee-jerk** *adj* (*reaction*) reflexartig; **kneel** *vi* knien; (*action, kneel down*) sich hinknien

knelt *pt, pp of* **kneel**

knew *pt of* **know**

knickers *npl* (*Brit*) Schlüpfer *m*

knife *n* Messer *nt*

knight *n* Ritter *m*; (*in chess*) Pferd *nt*, Springer *m*

knit *vt, vi* stricken; **knitting** *n* (*piece of work*) Strickarbeit *f*; (*activity*) Stricken *nt*; **knitwear** *n* Strickwaren *pl*

knob *n* (*on door*) Knauf *m*; (*on radio etc*) Knopf *m*

knock **1.** *vt* (*with hammer etc*) schlagen; (*accidentally*) stoßen; ***~ one's head*** sich *dat* den Kopf anschlagen **2.** *vi* klopfen (*on, at an + acc*) **3.** *n* (*blow*) Schlag *m*; (*on door*) Klopfen *nt*; ***there was a ~*** (***at the door***) es klopfte; **knock down** *vt* (*object*) umstoßen; (*person*) niederschlagen; (*with car*) anfahren; (*building*) abreißen; **knock out** *vt* (*stun*) bewusstlos schlagen; (*boxer*) k.o.

schlagen

knot *n* Knoten *m*

know *n, vi* wissen; (*be acquainted with: people, places*) kennen; (*recognize*) erkennen; (*language*) können; ***I'll let you ~*** ich sage dir Bescheid; ***I ~ some French*** ich kann etwas Französisch; ***get to ~ sb*** jdn kennen lernen; ***be ~n as*** bekannt sein als; **know of** *vt* kennen; ***not that I ~*** nicht dass ich wüsste; **know-all** *n fam* Klugscheißer *m*; **know-how** *n* Kenntnis *f*, Know-how *nt*; **knowing** *adj* (*look, smile*) vielsagend; **knowledge** *n* Wissen *nt*; (*of a subject*) Kenntnisse *pl*; ***to (the best of) my ~*** meines Wissens

known *pp of* **know**

knuckle *n* (Finger)knöchel *m*; GASTR Hachse *f*; **knuckle down** *vi* sich an die Arbeit machen

Koran *n* Koran *m*

Korea *n* Korea *nt*

Kosovo *n* der Kosovo

kph *abbr* = **kilometres per hour**; km/h

Kremlin *n* **the ~** der Kreml

Kurd *n* Kurde *m*, Kurdin *f*; **Kurdish** *adj* kurdisch

Kuwait *n* Kuwait *nt*

L

L abbr (Brit) AUTO = **learner**

LA abbr of **Los Angeles**

lab n fam Labor nt

label n Etikett nt; (tied) Anhänger m; (adhesive) Aufkleber m; (record ~) Label nt **2.** vt etikettieren; pej abstempeln

laboratory n Labor nt

laborious adj mühsam; **labor** (US), **labour 1.** n Arbeit f; MED Wehen pl; **be in ~** Wehen haben **2.** adj POL Labour-; **~ Party** Labour Party f; **labor union** n (US) Gewerkschaft f; **labourer** n Arbeiter(in) m(f)

lace 1. n (fabric) Spitze f; (of shoe) Schnürsenkel m **2.** vt **~ (up)** zuschnüren

lack 1. vt, vi **be ~ing** fehlen; **we ~ the time** uns fehlt die Zeit **2.** n Mangel m; **for ~ of** aus Mangel an + dat

lacquer n Lack m; (Brit, hair lacquer) Haarspray nt

lad n Junge m

ladder n Leiter f; (in tight) Laufmasche f

laddish adj (Brit) machohaft

laden adj beladen (with mit)

ladies, ladies' room n Damentoilette f; (as title) Lady f; **ladybird, ladybug** (US) n Marienkäfer m

lag 1. vi **~ (behind)** zurückliegen **2.** vt (pipes) isolieren

lager n helles Bier; **~ lout** betrunkener Rowdy

laid pt, pp of **lay**; **laid-back** adj fam cool, gelassen

lain pp of **lie**

lake n See m

lamb n Lamm nt; (meat) Lammfleisch nt; **lamb chop** n Lammkotelett nt

lame adj lahm; (excuse) faul; (argument) schwach

lament 1. n Klage f **2.** vt beklagen

laminated adj beschichtet

lamp n Lampe f; (in street) Laterne f; (in car) Licht nt, Scheinwerfer m

land 1. n Land nt **2.** vi (from ship) an Land gehen; AVIAT landen; **landing** n Landung f; (on stairs) Treppenabsatz m; **landing stage** n Landesteg m; **landing strip** n Landebahn f

landlady n Hauswirtin f, Vermieterin f; **landlord** n (of house) Hauswirt m, Vermieter m; (of pub) Gastwirt m; **landowner** n Grundbesitzer(in) m(f); **landscape** n Landschaft f; (format) Querformat nt; **landslide** n GEO Erdrutsch m

lane n (in country) enge Landstraße, Weg m; (in town) Gasse f; (of motorway) Spur f; SPORT Bahn f; **get in ~** (in car) sich einordnen

language n Sprache f

lantern n Laterne f

lap n **1.** Schoß m; (in race) Runde f **2.** vt (in race) überholen

lapse n **1.** (mistake) Irrtum m; (moral) Fehltritt m **2.** vi ablaufen

laptop n Laptop m

large adj groß; **by and ~** im Großen und Ganzen; **largely** adv zum größten Teil; **large--scale** adj groß angelegt, Groß-

lark n (bird) Lerche f

larynx n Kehlkopf m

laser n Laser m; **laser printer** n Laserdrucker m

lash vt peitschen; **lash out** vi (with fists) um sich schlagen; (spend money) sich in Unkosten stürzen (on mit)

lass n Mädchen nt

last 1. adj letzte(r, s); **the ~ but one** der/die/das vorletzte; **~ night** gestern Abend; **~ but not least** nicht zuletzt **2.** adv zuletzt; (last time) das letzte Mal; **at ~** endlich **3.** n (person) Letzte(r) mf; (thing) Letzte nt; **he was the ~ to leave** er ging als Letzter **4.** vi (continue) dauern; (remain in good condition) durchhalten; (remain good) sich halten; (money)

ausreichen; **lasting** adj dauerhaft; (impression) nachhaltig; **lastly** adv schließlich; **last-minute** adj in letzter Minute; **last name** n Nachname m

late 1. adj spät; (after proper time) zu spät; (train etc) verspätet; (dead) verstorben; **be ~ zu spät kommen**; (train etc) Verspätung haben **2.** adv spät; (after proper time) zu spät; **late availibility flight** n Last-Minute-Flug m; **lately** adv in letzter Zeit; **late opening** n verlängerte Öffnungszeiten pl; **later** adj, adv später; **see you ~** bis später; **latest 1.** adj späteste(r, s) (most recent) neueste(r, s) **2.** n (news) das Neueste; **at the ~** spätestens

Latin 1. n Latein nt **2.** adj lateinisch; **Latin America** n Lateinamerika nt; **Latin-American 1.** adj lateinamerikanisch **2.** n Lateinamerikaner(in) m(f)

latitude n GEO Breite f

latter adj (second of two) letztere(r, s) (last: part, years) letzte(r, s, späte)

Latvia n Lettland nt

laugh 1. n Lachen nt; **for a ~** aus Spaß **2.** vi lachen (at, about über + acc); **~ at sb** sich über jdn lustig machen; **it's no ~ing matter** es ist nicht zum Lachen; **laughter**

n Gelächter *nt*

launch 1. *n* (*launching*, *of ship*) Stapellauf *m*; (*of rocket*) Abschuss *m*; (*of product*) Markteinführung *f*; (*event*) Eröffnungsfeier *f* **2.** *vt* (*ship*) vom Stapel lassen; (*rocket*) abschießen; (*product*) einführen; (*project*) in Gang setzen

laundrette *n* (*Brit*), **laundromat** *n* (*US*) Waschsalon *m*; **laundry** *n* (*place*) Wäscherei *f*; (*clothes*) Wäsche *f*

lavatory *n* Toilette *f*

lavender *n* Lavendel *m*

lavish *adj* verschwenderisch; (*furnishings etc*) üppig; (*gift*) großzügig

law *n* Gesetz *nt*; (*system*) Recht *nt*; (*for study*) Jura; (*of sport*) Regel *f*; **against the ~** gesetzwidrig; **law-abiding** *adj* gesetzestreu; **law court** *n* Gerichtshof *m*; **lawful** *adj* rechtmäßig

lawn *n* Rasen *m*; **lawnmower** *n* Rasenmäher *m*

lawsuit *n* Prozess *m*; **lawyer** *n* Rechtsanwalt *m*, Rechtsanwältin *f*

laxative *n* Abführmittel *nt*

lay 1. *pt* of **lie 2.** *vt* legen; (*table*) decken; *vulg* legen, poppen, bumsen; (*egg*) legen **3.** *adj* Laien-; **lay down** *vt* hinlegen; **lay on** *vt* (*provide*) anbieten; (*organize*) veranstalten, bereitstellen; **layabout** *n* Faulenzer(in) *m*(*f*)

layer *n* Schicht *f*

layman *n* Laie *m*

layout *n* Gestaltung *f*; (*of book etc*) Lay-out *nt*

laze *vi* faulenzen; **laziness** *n* Faulheit *f*; **lazy** *adj* faul; (*day*, *time*) gemütlich

lb *abbr* = **pound**; Pfd.

lead 1. *n* Blei *nt* **2.** *vt*, *vi* führen; (*group etc*) leiten; **~ the way** vorangehen **3.** *n* (*race*) Führung *f*; (*distance*, *time ahead*) Vorsprung *m* (*over* vor + *dat*); THEAT Hauptrolle *f*; (*dog's*) Leine *f*; ELEC (*flex*) Leitung *f*; **lead astray** *vt* irreführen; **lead away** *vt* wegführen; **lead back** *vi* zurückführen; **lead to** *vt* (*street*) hinführen nach; (*result in*) führen zu; **lead up to** *vt* (*drive*) führen zu

leaded *adj* (*petrol*) verbleit

leader *n* Führer(in) *m*(*f*); (*of party*) Vorsitzende(r) *m*(*f*); (*of project*, *expedition*) Leiter(in) *m*(*f*); SPORT (*in race*) der/die Erste; (*in league*) Tabellenführer *m*; **leadership** *n* Führung *f*

lead-free *adj* (*petrol*) bleifrei

leading *adj* führend, wichtig

leaf *n* Blatt *nt*; **leaflet** *n* Prospekt *m*; (*pamphlet*) Flugblatt *nt*; (*with instructions*) Merkblatt *nt*

league *n* Bund *m*; SPORT Liga *f*

leak 1. *n* (*gap*) undichte Stelle; (*escape*) Leck *nt* **2.** *vi* (*pipe etc*) undicht sein; (*liquid* *etc)* auslaufen; **leaky** *adj* undicht

lean 1. *adj (meat)* mager **2.** *vi (not vertical)* sich neigen; *(rest)* ~ **against sth** sich an etw *acc* lehnen; *(support oneself)* ~ **on sth** sich auf etw *acc* stützen **3.** *vt* lehnen *(on, against* an + *acc)*; **lean back** *vi* sich zurücklehnen; **lean towards** *vt* tendieren zu

leant *pt, pp of* **lean**

leap 1. *n* Sprung *m* **2.** *vi* springen; **leap year** *n* Schaltjahr *nt*

learn *vt, vi* lernen; *(find out)* erfahren; ~ *(how) to swim* schwimmen lernen; **learned** *adj* gelehrt; **learner** *n* Anfänger(in) *m(f)*; *(Brit, driver)* Fahrschüler(in) *m(f)*

learnt *pt, pp of* **learn**

lease 1. *n (of land, premises etc)* Pacht *f; (contract)* Pachtvertrag *m; (of house, car etc)* Miete *f; (contract)* Mietvertrag *m* **2.** *vt* pachten; *(house, car etc)* mieten; **lease out** *vt* vermieten; **leasing** *n* Leasing *nt*

least 1. *adj* wenigste(r, s); *(slightest)* geringste(r, s) **2.** *adv* am wenigsten; ~ *expensive* billigste(r, s) **3.** *n* **the ~** das Mindeste; *not in the ~* nicht im geringsten; **at ~** wenigstens; *(with number)* mindestens

leather 1. *n* Leder *nt* **2.** *adj* ledern, Leder-

leave 1. *n (time off)* Urlaub *m;* **on ~** auf Urlaub; *take one's ~* Abschied nehmen *(of* von*)* **2.** *vt (place, person)* verlassen; *(~ behind: message, scar etc)* hinterlassen; *(after death)* hinterlassen *(to sb* jdm*); (entrust)* überlassen *(to sb* jdm*);* **be left** *(remain)* übrig bleiben; ~ *me alone* lass mich in Ruhe!; *don't ~ it to the last minute* warte nicht bis zur letzten Minute **3.** *vi* (weg)gehen, (weg)fahren; *(on journey)* abreisen; *(bus, train)* abfahren *(for* nach*);* **leave behind** *vt* zurücklassen; *(scar etc)* hinterlassen; **leave out** *vt* auslassen; *(person)* ausschließen *(of* von*)*

leaves *pl of* **leaf**

leaving do *n* Abschiedsfeier *f*

Lebanon *n* **the ~** der Libanon

lecture *n* Vortrag *m; (at university)* Vorlesung *f;* **give a ~** einen Vortrag / eine Vorlesung halten; **lecturer** *n* Dozent(in) *m(f)*; **lecture theatre** *n* Hörsaal *m*

led *pt, pp of* **lead**

LED *abbr =* **light-emitting diode**; Leuchtdiode *f*

leek *n* Lauch *m*

left 1. *pt, pp of* **leave 2.** *adj* linke(r, s) **3.** *adv (position)* links; *(movement)* nach links **4.** *n (side)* linke Seite; *the Left* POL die Linke; *on / to the ~* links *(of* von*);* left-

-hand *adj* linke(r, s); **~ bend** Linkskurve *f*; **~ drive** Linkssteuerung *f*; **left-handed** *adj* linkshändig; **left-hand side** *n* linke Seite

left-luggage locker *n* Gepäckschließfach *nt*; **left-luggage office** *n* Gepäckaufbewahrung *f*

left-overs *npl* Reste *pl*

left wing *n* linker Flügel; **left-wing** *adj* POL linksgerichtet

leg *n* Bein *nt*; (*of meat*) Keule *f*

legacy *n* Erbe *nt*, Erbschaft *f*

legal *adj* Rechts-, rechtlich; (*allowed*) (*limit, age*) gesetzlich; **~ aid** Rechtshilfe *f*; **legalize** *vt* legalisieren; **legally** *adv* legal

legible, legibly *adj, adv* leserlich

legislation *n* Gesetze *pl*

legitimate *adj* rechtmäßig, legitim

legroom *n* Platz *m* für die Beine

leisure 1. *n* (*time*) Freizeit *f* **2.** *adj* Freizeit-; **~ centre** Freizeitzentrum *nt*; **leisurely** *adj* gemächlich

lemon *n* Zitrone *f*; **lemonade** *n* Limonade *f*; **lemon curd** *n* Brotaufstrich *aus Zitronen, Butter, Eiern und Zucker*; **lemon juice** *n* Zitronensaft *m*; **lemon sole** *n* Seezunge *f*

lend *vt* leihen; **~ sb sth** jdm etw leihen

length *n* Länge *f*; **4 metres in**

~ 4 Meter lang; **what ~ is it?** wie lange ist es?; **lengthy** *adj* sehr lange; (*dragging*) langwierig

lenient *adj* nachsichtig

lens *n* Linse *f*; PHOT Objektiv *nt*

lent *pt, pp of* **lend**

Lent *n* Fastenzeit *f*

lentil *n* BOT Linse *f*

Leo *n* ASTR Löwe *m*

leopard *n* Leopard *m*

lept *pt, pp of* **leap**

lesbian 1. *adj* lesbisch **2.** *n* Lesbe *f*

less *adj, adv n* weniger; **~ and ~** immer weniger; (**~ often**) immer seltener; **lessen 1.** *vi* abnehmen, nachlassen **2.** *vt* verringern; (*pain*) lindern; **lesser** *adj* geringer; (*amount*) kleiner

lesson *n* (*at school*) Stunde *f*; (*unit of study*) Lektion *f*; *fig* Lehre *f*; REL Lesung *f*; **~s start at 9** der Unterricht beginnt um 9

let *vt* lassen; (*lease*) vermieten; **~ sb have sth** jdm etw geben; **~'s go** gehen wir; **~ go (of sth)** (etw) loslassen; **let down** *vt* herunterlassen; (*fail to help*) im Stich lassen; (*disappoint*) enttäuschen; **let in** *vt* hereinlassen; **let out** *vt* hinauslassen; (*secret*) verraten; (*scream etc*) ausstoßen

lethal *adj* tödlich

let's *abbr* = **let us**

letter *n* (*of alphabet*) Buchstabe m; (message) Brief m; (official letter) Schreiben nt; (letterbox n Briefkasten m

lettuce n Kopfsalat m

leukaemia, leukemia (US) n Leukämie f

level 1. adj (horizontal) waagerecht; (ground) eben; (two things, two runners) auf selber Höhe; **~ on points** punktgleich **2.** adv (run etc) auf gleicher Höhe, gleich auf; **draw ~** (in race) gleichziehen (with mit); (in game) ausgleichen **3.** n (altitude) Höhe f; (standard) Niveau nt; (on the ~ with **4.** vt (ground) einebnen; **level crossing** n (Brit) (schienengleicher) Bahnübergang m; **level-headed** adj vernünftig

lever (US) n Hebel m; fig Druckmittel nt; lever up vt hochstemmen

liability n Haftung f; (burden) Belastung f; (obligation) Verpflichtung f; **liable** adj **be ~ for sth** (responsible) für etw haften

liar n Lügner(in) m(f)

liberal adj (generous) großzügig; (broad-minded) liberal; **Liberal Democrat 1.** n (Brit) POL Liberaldemokrat(in) m(f) **2.** adj liberaldemokratisch; **the ~ Party** die Liberaldemokratische Partei

liberate vt befreien; **liberation** n Befreiung f

liberty n Freiheit f

Libra n ASTR Waage f

library n Bibliothek f; (lending library) Bücherei f

Libya n Libyen nt

lice pl of **louse**

licence n (permit) Genehmigung f; COMM Lizenz f; (driving ~) Führerschein m; **license 1.** n (US) → **licence 2.** vt genehmigen; **licensed** adj (restaurant etc) mit Schankerlaubnis; **license plate** n (US) AUTO Nummernschild nt; **licensing hours** npl Ausschankzeiten pl

lick 1. vt lecken **2.** n Lecken nt

licorice n Lakritze f

lid n Deckel m; (eye~) Lid nt

lie 1. n Lüge f; **~ detector** Lügendetektor m **2.** vi lügen; **~ to sb** jdn belügen **3.** vi (rest, be situated) liegen; (lie down) sich legen; (snow) liegen bleiben; **be lying third** an dritter Stelle liegen; **lie about** vi herumliegen; **lie down** vi sich hinlegen

lie in vi **have a ~** ausschlafen

life n Leben nt; **get ~** lebenslänglich bekommen; **life assurance** n Lebensversicherung f; **lifebelt** n Rettungsring m; **lifeboat** n Rettungsboot nt; **lifeguard** n Bademeister(in) m(f), Rettungsschwimmer(in) m(f); **life insurance** n Lebensversicherung f; **life jacket** n

Schwimmweste *f*; **lifeless** *adj* (*dead*) leblos; **lifelong** *adj* lebenslang; **life preserver** *n* (*US*) Rettungsring *m*; **life-saving** *adj* lebensrettend; **life-size(d)** *adj* in Lebensgröße; **life span** *n* Lebensspanne *f*; **life style** *n* Lebensstil *m*; **lifetime** *n* Lebenszeit *f*

lift 1. *vt* (hoch)heben; (*ban*) aufheben **2.** *n* (*Brit, elevator*) Aufzug *m*, Lift *m*; **give sb a ~** jdn im Auto mitnehmen; **lift up** *vt* hochheben

ligament *n* Band *nt*

light 1. *vt* beleuchten; (*fire, cigarette*) anzünden **2.** *n* Licht *nt*; (*lamp*) Lampe *f*; **~s** *pl* AUTO Beleuchtung *f*; (*traffic lights*) Ampel *f*; **in the ~ of** angesichts + *gen* **3.** *adj* (*bright*) hell; (*not heavy, easy*) leicht; (*punishment*) milde; (*taxes*) niedrig; **~ blue/green** hellblau/hellgrün; **light up 1.** *vt* (*illuminate*) beleuchten **2.** *vi* (*a. eyes*) aufleuchten

light bulb *n* Glühbirne *f*

lighten 1. *vi* hell werden **2.** *vt* (*give light to*) erhellen; (*make less heavy*) leichter machen; *fig* erleichtern

lighter *n* (*cigarette lighter*) Feuerzeug *nt*

light-hearted *adj* unbeschwert; **lighthouse** *n* Leuchtturm *m*; **lighting** *n* Beleuchtung *f*; **lightly** *adv*

leicht; **light meter** *n* PHOT Belichtungsmesser *m*

lightning *n* Blitz *m*

like 1. *vt* mögen, gern haben; **he ~s swimming** er schwimmt gern; **would you ~ ...?** hätten Sie gern ...?; **I'd ~ to go home** ich möchte nach Hause (gehen); **I don't ~ the film** der Film gefällt mir nicht **2.** *prep* wie; **what's it/he ~?** wie ist es/er?; **he looks ~ you** er sieht dir ähnlich; **~ that/this** so; **likeable** *adj* sympathisch

likelihood *n* Wahrscheinlichkeit *f*; **likely** *adj* wahrscheinlich; **the bus is ~ to be late** der Bus wird wahrscheinlich Verspätung haben

like-minded *adj* gleich gesinnt

likewise *adv* ebenfalls; **do ~** das Gleiche tun

liking *n* (*for person*) Zuneigung *f*; (*for type, things*) Vorliebe *f* (*for* für)

lilac 1. *n* Flieder *m* **2.** *adj* fliederfarben

lily *n* Lilie *f*; **~ of the valley** Maiglöckchen *nt*

limb *n* Glied *nt*

limbo *n* **in ~** (*plans*) auf Eis gelegt

lime *n* (*tree*) Linde *f*; (*fruit*) Limone *f*; (*substance*) Kalk *m*; **lime juice** *n* Limonensaft *m*; **limelight** *n* *fig* Rampenlicht *nt*; **limestone** *n* Kalkstein *m*

limit 1. *n* Grenze *f*; (*for pollu-*

tion etc) Grenzwert *m*; **drive over the ~** das Tempolimit überschreiten; **that's the ~** jetzt reicht's!, das ist die Höhe! **2.** *vt* beschränken (*to* auf + *acc*); (*freedom, spending*) einschränken; **limitation** *n* Beschränkung *f*; (*of freedom, spending*) Einschränkung *f*; **limited** *adj* begrenzt; **~ liability company** Gesellschaft *f* mit beschränkter Haftung, GmbH *f*; **public ~ company** Aktiengesellschaft *f*

limp 1. *vi* hinken **2.** *adj* schlaff
line 1. *n* Linie *f*; (*written*) Zeile *f*; (*on face*) Falte *f*; (*row*) Reihe *f*; (*US, queue*) Schlange *f*; RAIL Bahnlinie *f*; TEL Leitung *f*; (*range of items*) Kollektion *f*; **hold the ~** bleiben Sie am Apparat; **stand in ~** Schlange stehen; **something along those ~s** etwas in dieser Art; **drop me a ~** schreib mir ein paar Zeilen; **~s** THEAT Text *m* **2.** *vt* (*clothes*) füttern; (*streets*) säumen; **lined** *adj* (*paper*) liniert; (*face*) faltig; **line up** *vi* sich aufstellen; (*US, form queue*) sich anstellen

linen *n* Leinen *nt*; (*sheets etc*) Wäsche *f*
liner *n* Überseedampfer *m*, Passagierschiff *nt*
linesman *n* SPORT Linienrichter *m*
lingerie *n* Damenunterwä-

sche *f*
lining *n* (*of clothes*) Futter *nt*; (*brake ~*) Bremsbelag *m*
link 1. *n* (*connection*) Verbindung *f*; (*of chain*) Glied *nt*; (*relationship*) Beziehung *f* (*with* zu); (*between events*) Zusammenhang *m*; (*Internet*) Link *m* **2.** *vt* verbinden
lion *n* Löwe *m*
lip *n* Lippe *f*; **lipstick** *n* Lippenstift *m*
liqueur *n* Likör *m*
liquid 1. *n* Flüssigkeit *f* **2.** *adj* flüssig
liquor *n* Spirituosen *pl*
liquorice *n* Lakritze *f*
Lisbon *n* Lissabon *nt*
lisp *vi, n* lispeln
list 1. *n* Liste *f* **2.** *vt* auflisten, aufzählen; **~ed** *adj* unter Denkmalschutz stehend; **~ed building** unter Denkmalschutz stehendes Gebäude
listen *vi* zuhören; **listen to** *vt* (*person*) zuhören + *dat*; (*radio*) hören auf; (*advice*) hören auf; **listener** *n* Zuhörer(in) *m(f)*; (*to radio*) Hörer(in) *m(f)*
lit *pt, pp of* **light**
liter *n* (*US*) Liter *m*
literacy *n* Fähigkeit *f* zu lesen und zu schreiben; **literal** *adj* (*translation, meaning*) wörtlich; (*actual*) buchstäblich; **literally** *adv* (*translate, take sth*) wörtlich; (*literary*) literarisch; **literary** *adj* (*critic, journal etc*) Literatur-; **literature** *n* Literatur *f*; (*brochures etc*)

Informationsmaterial *nt*

Lithuania *n* Litauen *nt*

litre *n* Liter *m*

litter 1. *n* Abfälle *pl*; *(of animals)* Wurf *m* **2.** *vt* **be ~ed with** übersät sein mit; **litter bin** *n* Abfalleimer *m*

little 1. *adj* klein; *(in quantity)* wenig; **a ~ while ago** vor kurzer Zeit **2.** *adv*, *n* wenig; **a ~** ein bisschen, ein wenig; **as ~ as possible** so wenig wie möglich; **for as ~ as £5** ab nur 5 Pfund; **I see very ~ of them** ich sehe sie sehr selten; **~ by ~** nach und nach; **little finger** *n* kleiner Finger

live 1. *adj* lebendig; ELEC geladen, unter Strom; TV *(radio, event)* live; **~ broadcast** Direktübertragung *f* **2.** *vi* leben; *(not die)* überleben; *(dwell)* wohnen; **you ~ and learn** man lernt nie aus **3.** *vt* (*life*) führen; **live on 1.** *vi* weiterleben **2.** *vt* **~ sth** von etw leben; *(feed)* sich von etw ernähren; **earn enough to ~** genug verdienen, um davon zu leben; **live together** *vi* zusammenleben; **live up to** *vt* (*reputation*) gerecht werden + *dat*; *(expectations)* entsprechen + *dat*; **live with** *vt* (*parents etc*) wohnen bei; *(partner)* zusammenleben mit; *(difficulty)* **you'll just have to ~ it** du musst dich eben damit abfinden

liveliness *n* Lebhaftigkeit *f*;

lively *adj* lebhaft

liver *n* Leber *f*

lives *pl of* **life**

livestock *n* Vieh *nt*

living 1. *n* Lebensunterhalt *m*; **what do you do for a ~?** was machen Sie beruflich? **2.** *adj* lebend; **living room** *n* Wohnzimmer *nt*

lizard *n* Eidechse *f*

load 1. *n* Last *f*; *(cargo)* Ladung *f*; TECH *fig* Belastung *f*; **~s of rubbish** *fam* massenhaft; **it was a ~ of rubbish** *fam* es war grottenschlecht **2.** *vt* (*vehicle*) beladen; IT laden; *(film)* einlegen

loaf *n* ~ (**of bread**) Brot *nt*

loaf about *vi* faulenzen

loan 1. *n* (*item leant*) Leihgabe *f*; FIN Darlehen *nt*, geliehen **2.** *vt* leihen (*to sb* jdm)

loathe *vt* verabscheuen

loaves *pl of* **loaf**

lobby *n* Vorhalle *f*; POL Lobby *f*

lobster *n* Hummer *m*

local 1. *adj* (*traffic, time etc*) Orts-; *(radio, news, paper)* Lokal-; *(government, authority)* Kommunal-; *(anaesthetic)* örtlich; **~ call** TEL Ortsgespräch *nt*; **~ elections** Kommunalwahlen *pl*; **~ time** Ortszeit *f*; **~ train** Nahverkehrszug *m*; **the ~ shops** die Geschäfte am Ort **2.** *n* (*pub*) Stammlokal *nt*; **the ~s** *pl* die Ortsansässigen *pl*;

locally *adv* örtlich, am Ort

locate vt (find) ausfindig machen; (establish) errichten; **be ~d** sich befinden (in, at in + dat); **location** n (position) Lage f; FILM Drehort m

loch n (Scot) See m

lock 1. n Schloss nt; NAUT Schleuse f; (of hair) Locke f **2.** vt (door etc) abschließen **3.** vi (door etc) sich abschließen lassen; (wheels) blockieren; **lock in** vt einschließen, einsperren; **lock out** vt aussperren; **lock up** vt (house) abschließen; (person) einsperren

locker n Schließfach nt; **locker room** n (US) Umkleideraum m

locksmith n Schlosser(in) m(f)

locust n Heuschrecke f

lodge 1. n (small house) Pförtnerhaus nt; (porter's lodge) Pförtnerloge f **2.** vi in Untermiete wohnen (with bei); **lodger** n Untermieter(in) m(f); **lodging** n Unterkunft f

loft n Dachboden m

log n Klotz m; NAUT Log nt; **keep a ~ of sth** Buch führen; **log in** vi IT sich einloggen; **log off** vi IT sich ausloggen; **log on** vi IT sich einloggen; **log out** vi IT sich ausloggen

logic n Logik f; **logical** adj logisch

logo n Logo nt

loin n Lende f

loiter vi sich herumtreiben

lollipop n Lutscher m; **~ man/lady** (Brit) Schülerlotse m, Schülerlotsin f

lolly n Lutscher m; fam (money) Knete f

London n London nt

loneliness n Einsamkeit f; **lonely, lonesome** (esp US) adj einsam

long 1. adj lang; (distance) weit; **it's a ~ way** es ist weit (to nach); **for a ~ time** lange; **how ~ is the film?** wie lange dauert der Film?; **in the ~ run** auf die Dauer lange; **not for ~** nicht lange; **~ ago** vor langer Zeit; **before ~** bald; **all day ~** den ganzen Tag; **no ~er** nicht mehr; **as ~ as** solange **3.** vi sich sehnen (for nach); (be waiting) sehnsüchtig warten (for auf); **long-distance call** n Ferngespräch nt; **long drink** n Longdrink m; **long-haul flight** n Langstreckenflug m; **longing** n Sehnsucht f (for nach); **longingly** adv sehnsüchtig; **longitude** n Länge f; **long jump** n Weitsprung m; **long-life milk** n H-Milch f; **long-range** adj Langstrecken-, Fern-; **~ missile** Langstreckenrakete f; **long-sighted** adj weitsichtig; **long-standing** adj alt, langjährig; **long-term** adj langfristig; (car park, effect

lout

etc) Langzeit-; ~ **unemployment** Langzeitarbeitslosig-
keit *f*

loo *n (Brit) fam* Klo *nt*

look 1. *n* Blick *m; (appearance)* ~**(s)** *pl* Aussehen *nt;
I'll have a* ~ ich schau mal
nach; *have a* ~ *at sth* sich
dat etw ansehen; *can I have
a* ~*?* darf ich mal sehen? **2.** *vi*
schauen, gucken; *(search)*
nachsehen; *(appear)* aussehen; *(I'm) just* ~*ing* ich
schau nur; *it* ~*s like rain*
es sieht nach Regen aus **3.**
vt ~ *what you've done* sieh
dir mal an, was du da angestellt hast; *(appear) he* ~*s his
age* man sieht ihm sein Alter
an; ~ *one's best* sehr vorteilhaft aussehen; **look after** *vt
(care for)* sorgen für; *(keep
an eye on)* aufpassen auf
+ *acc*; **look at** *vt* ansehen; anschauen; **look back** *vi* sich
umsehen; *fig* zurückblicken;
look down on *vt fig* herabsehen auf + *acc*; **look for** *vt* suchen; **look forward to** *vt* sich
freuen auf + *acc*; **look into** *vt
(investigate)* untersuchen;
look out *vi* hinaussehen *(of
the window* zum Fenster);
(watch out) Ausschau halten
(for nach); ~*!* Vorsicht!;
look up 1. *vi* aufsehen **2.** *vt (word
etc)* nachschlagen; **look up
to** *vt* aufsehen zu

loop *n* Schleife *f*

loose *adj* locker; *(knot, but-*

ton) lose; **loosen** *vt* lockern;
(knot) lösen

loot *n* Beute *f*

lop-sided *adj* schief

lord *n (ruler)* Herr *m; (Brit, title)* Lord *m; the Lord (God)*
Gott der Herr; *the (House
of) Lords* das Ober-
haus

lorry *n (Brit)* Lastwagen *m*

lose 1. *vt* verlieren; ~ *weight*
abnehmen; ~ *one's life* umkommen **2.** *vi* verlieren;
(clock, watch) nachgehen;
loser *n* Verlierer(in) *m(f)*;
loss *n* Verlust *m;* **lost 1.** *pt,
pp of* **lose;** *we're* ~ wir haben
uns verlaufen **2.** *adj* verloren; **lost-and-found** *(US)*,
lost property (office) *n*
Fundbüro *nt*

lot *n (batch) fam* Menge *f,*
Haufen *m; a* ~ viel(e); *a* ~
of money viel Geld; ~*s of
people* viele Leute; *the
(whole)* ~ alles; *(people)* alle;
(parking) ~ *(US)* Parkplatz
m

lotion *n* Lotion *f*

lottery *n* Lotterie *f*

loud *adj* laut; *(colour)* schrei-
end; **loudspeaker** *n* Lautsprecher *m; (of stereo)* Box *f*

lounge 1. *n* Wohnzimmer *nt;
(in hotel)* Aufenthaltsraum
m; (at airport) Warteraum
m **2.** *vi* sich herumlümmeln

louse *n* Laus *f;* **lousy** *adj fam*
lausig

lout *n* Rüpel *m*

lovable adj liebenswert

love 1. n Liebe f (of zu); (person, address) Liebling m, Schatz m; SPORT null; **be in ~** verliebt sein (with sb in jdn); **fall in ~** sich verlieben (with sb in jdn); **make ~** (sexually) sich lieben; **make ~ to** (or with) **sb** mit jdm schlafen; **give her my ~** grüße sie von mir; **~, Tom** liebe Grüße, Tom **2.** vt (person) lieben; (activity) lieber mögen; **~ to do sth** etw für sein Leben gerne tun; **I'd ~ a cup of tea** ich hätte liebend gern eine Tasse Tee; **love affair** n (Liebes)verhältnis nt; **love letter** n Liebesbrief m; **love life** n Liebesleben nt; **lovely** adj schön, wunderschön; (charming) reizend; **we had a ~ time** es war sehr schön; **lover** n Liebhaber(in) m(f); **loving** adj liebevoll

low 1. adj niedrig; (level, note, neckline) tief; (quality, standard) schlecht; (not loud) leise; (depressed) niedergeschlagen; **we're ~ on petrol** wir haben kaum noch Benzin **2.** n METEO Tief nt; **low-calorie** adj kalorienarm; **low-emission** adj schadstoffarm; **lower 1.** adj niedriger; (storey, class etc) untere(r, s) **2.** vt herunterlassen; (eyes, price) senken; (pressure) verringern; **low-fat** adj fettarm; **low tide** n

Ebbe f

loyal adj treu; **loyalty** n Treue f

lozenge n Pastille f

Ltd abbr = **limited**; ≈ GmbH f

luck n Glück nt; **bad ~** Pech nt; **luckily** adv glücklicherweise, zum Glück; **lucky** adj (number, day etc) Glücks-; **be ~** Glück haben

ludicrous adj grotesk

luggage n Gepäck nt; **luggage compartment** n Gepäckraum m; **luggage rack** n Gepäcknetz nt

lukewarm adj lauwarm

lullaby n Schlaflied nt

lumbago n Hexenschuss m

luminous adj leuchtend

lump n Klumpen m; MED Schwellung f; (in breast) Knoten m; (of sugar) Stück nt; **lump sum** n Pauschalsumme f

lunacy n Wahnsinn m; **lunatic 1.** adj wahnsinnig **2.** n Wahnsinnige(r) mf

lunch, luncheon n Mittagessen nt; **have ~** zu Mittag essen; **lunch break, lunch hour** n Mittagspause f; **lunchtime** n Mittagszeit f

lung n Lunge f

lurk vi lauern

lust n (sinnliche) Begierde f (for nach)

luster (US), **lustre** n Glanz m

Luxembourg n Luxemburg nt

luxurious adj luxuriös, Lu-

xus-; luxury n (a. *luxuries* pl)
Luxus m; ~ **goods** Luxusgüter pl

lynx n Luchs m

lyrics npl (*words for song*)
Liedtext m

M

m abbr = *metre*; m
M abbr = **Motorway**; A; (*size*)
= **medium**; M
ma n fam Mutti f
mac n (Brit) fam Regenmantel m
Macedonia n Mazedonien nt
machine n Maschine f; machine gun n Maschinengewehr nt; machinery n Maschinen pl; fig Apparat m
mackerel n Makrele f
macro n IT Makro nt
mad adj wahnsinnig, verrückt; (dog) tollwütig; (angry) wütend, sauer (at auf + acc); fam ~ **about** (fond of) verrückt nach; **work like** ~ wie verrückt arbeiten; **are you** ~? spinnst du?
madam n gnädige Frau
mad cow disease n Rinderwahnsinn m; **maddening** adj zum Verrücktwerden
made pt, pp of **make**
made-to-measure adj nach Maß; ~ **suit** Maßanzug m
madly adv wie verrückt; (with adj) wahnsinnig; madman n Verrückte(r) m f; madwoman n Verrückte f; madness n Wahnsinn m
magazine n Zeitschrift f

maggot n Made f
magic 1. n Magie f; (activity) Zauberei f; fig (effect) Zauber m; **as if by** ~ wie durch Zauberei 2. adj Zauber-; (powers) magisch; magician n Zauberer m, Zaub(r)erin f
magnet n Magnet m; magnetic adj magnetisch
magnificent, magnificently adj, adv herrlich, großartig
magnify vt vergrößern; magnifying glass n Vergrößerungsglas nt, Lupe f
magpie n Elster f
maid n Dienstmädchen nt; maiden name n Mädchenname m; maiden voyage n Jungfernfahrt f
mail 1. n Post f; (e-mail) Mail f 2. vt (post) aufgeben; (send) mit der Post® schicken (to an + acc); mailbox n (US) Briefkasten m; IT Mailbox f; mailing list n Adressenliste f; mailman n (US) Briefträger m; mail order n Bestellung f per Post; mail order firm n Versandhaus n
main 1. adj Haupt-; ~ **course** Hauptgericht nt; **the** ~ **thing** die Hauptsache 2. n (pipe) Hauptleitung f; mainframe

n Großrechner m; **mainland**
n Festland nt; **mainly** adv
hauptsächlich; **main road** n
Hauptverkehrsstraße f;
main street n (US) Hauptstraße f

maintain vt (keep up) aufrechterhalten; (machine,
roads) instand halten; (service) warten; **maintenance**
n Instandhaltung f; TECH
Wartung f

maize n Mais m

majestic adj majestätisch;
majesty n Majestät f; **his/
her Majesty** seine/ihre Majestät

major 1. adj (bigger) größer;
(important) bedeutend; ~
part Großteil m; (role) wichtige Rolle; ~ **road** Hauptverkehrsstraße f; MUS **A** ~
A-Dur nt **2.** vi (US) ~ **in
sth** etw als Hauptfach studieren

Majorca n Mallorca nt

majority n Mehrheit f; **be in
the** ~ in der Mehrzahl sein

make 1. vt (manufacture) machen; (manufacture) herstellen; (clothes) anfertigen;
(dress) nähen; (soup) zubereiten; (bread, cake) backen;
(tea, coffee) kochen; (speech)
halten; (earn) verdienen;
(decision) treffen; **it's made
of gold** es ist aus Gold; ~
sb do sth jdn dazu bringen,
etw zu tun; (force) jdn zwingen, etw zu tun; **she made**

us wait sie ließ uns warten;
what ~s you think that?
wie kommen Sie darauf?;
he never really made it er
hat es nie zu etwas gebracht;
**she didn't ~ it through the
night** sie hat die Nacht nicht
überlebt; (calculate) **I ~ it
£5/a quarter to six** nach
meiner Rechnung kommt
es auf 5 Pfund/nach meiner
Uhr ist es dreiviertel sechs;
he's just made for this job
er ist für diese Arbeit wie geschaffen; **make for** vt zusteuern auf + acc; **make of** vt
(think of) halten von; **I
couldn't ~ anything of it**
ich wurde daraus nicht
schlau; **make off** vi sich davonmachen (with mit); **make
out** vt (cheque) ausstellen;
(list) aufstellen; (understand) verstehen; (discern)
ausmachen; ~ (that) ... es so
hinstellen, als ob ...; **make
up 1.** vt (team etc) bilden;
(face) schminken; (invent:
story etc) erfinden; ~ **one's
mind** sich entscheiden;
make it up with sb sich
mit jdm aussöhnen **2.** vi sich
versöhnen; **make up for** vt
ausgleichen; (time) aufholen
make-believe adj Fantasie-;
makeover n gründliche Veränderung, Verschönerung f;
maker n (COMM Hersteller(in)
m(f); **makeshift** adj behelfsmäßig; **make-up** n Make-up

nt, Schminke *f*; **making** *n* Herstellung *f*

malaria *n* Malaria *f*

Malaysia *n* Malaysia *nt*

male 1. *n* Mann *m*; *(animal)* Männchen *nt* **2.** *adj* männlich; **~ chauvinist** Chauvi *m*, Macho *m*; **~ nurse** Krankenpfleger *m*

malfunction 1. *vi* nicht richtig funktionieren **2.** *n* Defekt *m*

malice *n* Bosheit *f*; **malicious** *adj* boshaft; *(damage)* mutwillig

malignant *adj* bösartig

mall *n* *(US)* Einkaufszentrum *nt*

malnutrition *n* Unterernährung *f*

malt *n* Malz *nt*

Malta *n* Malta *nt*; **Maltese 1.** *adj* maltesisch **2.** *n* *(person)* Malteser(in) *m(f)*; *(language)* Maltesisch *nt*

maltreat *vt* schlecht behandeln; *(violently)* misshandeln

mammal *n* Säugetier *nt*

mammoth *adj* Mammut-, Riesen-

man 1. *n* *(male)* Mann *m*; *(human race)* Mann *m*, der Mensch, die Menschen *pl*; *(in chess)* Figur *f* **2.** *vt* besetzen

manage 1. *vi* zurechtkommen; **can you ~?** schaffst du es?; **~ without sth** ohne etw auskommen, auf etw verzichten können **2.** *vt* *(control)* leiten; *(musician, sportsman)* managen; *(cope with)* fertig werden mit; *(task, portion, climb etc)* schaffen; **~ to do sth** es schaffen, etw zu tun; **manageable** *adj* *(object)* handlich; *(task)* zu bewältigen; **management** *nt* Leitung *f*; *(directors)* Direktion *f*; *(subject)* Management *nt*, Betriebswirtschaft *f*; **management consultant** *n* Unternehmensberater(in) *m(f)*; **manager** *n* Geschäftsführer(in) *m(f)*; *(departmental manager)* Abteilungsleiter(in) *m(f)*; *(of branch, bank)* Filialleiter(in) *m(f)*; *(of musician, sportsman)* Manager(in) *m(f)*; **managing director** *n* Geschäftsführer(in) *m(f)*

mane *n* Mähne *f*

maneuver *(US)* → **manoeuvre**

mango *n* Mango *f*

man-hour *n* Arbeitsstunde *f*

manhunt *n* Fahndung *f*

mania *n* Manie *f*; **maniac** *n* Wahnsinnige(r) *mf*; *(fan)* Fanatiker(in) *m(f)*

manicure *n* Maniküre *f*

manipulate *vt* manipulieren

mankind *n* Menschheit *f*

manly *adj* männlich

man-made *adj* *(product)* künstlich

manner *n* Art *f*; **in this ~** auf diese Art und Weise; **~s** *pl* Manieren *pl*

manoeuvre 1. *n* Manöver *nt* **2.** *vt, vi* manövrieren

manor n ~ (*house*) Herrenhaus nt

manpower n Arbeitskräfte pl

mansion n Villa f; (*of old
family*) Herrenhaus nt

manslaughter n Totschlag m

manual 1. adj manuell, Hand-
2. n Handbuch nt

manufacture 1. vt herstellen
2. n Herstellung f; manufacturer n Hersteller m

manure n Dung m; (*esp artificial*) Dünger m

many adj, pron viele; ~ times
oft; not ~ people nicht viele
Leute; too ~ problems zu
viele Probleme

map n Landkarte f; (*of town*)
Stadtplan m

maple n Ahorn m

marathon n Marathon m

marble n Marmor m; (*for
playing*) Murmel f

march 1. vi marschieren 2. n
Marsch m; (*protest*) De-
monstration f

March n März m; → **September**

mare n Stute f

margarine n Margarine f

margin n Rand m; (*extra
amount*) Spielraum m; COMM
Gewinnspanne f; marginal
adj (*difference etc*) geringfü-
gig

marijuana n Marihuana nt

marinade n GASTR Marinade
f; marinated adj mariniert

marine adj Meeres-

marital adj ehelich; ~ status

Familienstand m

maritime adj See-

marjoram n Majoran m

mark 1. n (*spot*) Fleck m; (*at
school*) Note f; (*sign*) Zeichen nt 2. vt (*indicate*) markieren; (*schoolwork*) beno-
ten, korrigieren, Flecken
machen or + acc; marker
n (*in book*) Lesezeichen nt;
(*pen*) Marker m

market 1. n Markt m 2. vt
COMM (*new product*) auf
den Markt bringen; (*goods*)
vertreiben; marketing n
Marketing nt; market leader
n Marktführer m; market
place n Marktplatz m; market research n Marktfor-
schung f

marmalade n Orangenmar-
melade f

maroon adj rötlich braun

marquee n großes Zelt

marriage n Ehe f; (*wedding*)
Heirat f (*to* mit); married
adj (*person*) verheiratet

marrow n (*bone marrow*)
Knochenmark nt; (*vegeta-
ble*) Kürbis m

marry 1. vt heiraten; (*join*)
trauen 2. vi ~ / get married
heiraten

marsh n Marsch f, Sumpf m

marshal n (*at rally etc*) Ordner
m; (*US, police*) Bezirkspoli-
zeichef m

martial arts npl Kampfsport-
arten pl

martyr n Märtyrer(in) m(f)

marvel **1.** n Wunder nt **2.** vi staunen (at über + acc); marvellous, marvelous (US) adj wunderbar

mascara n Wimperntusche f

mascot n Maskottchen nt

masculine adj männlich

mashed adj ~ **potatoes** pl Kartoffelbrei m, Kartoffelpüree nt

mask **1.** n Maske f **2.** vt (feelings) verbergen

masochist n Masochist(in) m(f)

mason n (stonemason) Steinmetz(in) m(f); masonry n Mauerwerk nt

mass n Masse f; (of people) Menge f; REL Messe f; ~**es of** massenhaft

massacre n Blutbad nt

massage **1.** n Massage f **2.** vt massieren

massive adj (powerful) gewaltig; (very large) riesig

mass media n (stonemason) Massenmedien pl; mass production n Massenproduktion f

master **1.** n Herr m; (of dog) Besitzer m, Herrchen nt; (artist) Meister m **2.** vt meistern; (language etc) beherrschen; masterly adj meisterhaft; masterpiece n Meisterwerk nt

masturbate vi masturbieren

mat n Matte f; (for table) Untersetzer m

match **1.** n Streichholz nt; SPORT Wettkampf m; (ball games) Spiel nt; (tennis) Match nt **2.** vt (be like, suit) passen zu; (equal) gleichkommen + dat **3.** vi zusammenpassen; matchbox n Streichholzschachtel f; matching adj (one item) passend; (two items) zusammenpassend

mate **1.** n (companion) Kumpel m; (of animal) Weibchen nt/Männchen nt **2.** vi sich paaren

material n Material nt; (for book etc, cloth) Stoff m; materialistic adj materialistisch; materialize vi zustande kommen; (hope) wahr werden

maternal adj mütterlich; maternity adj ~ **dress** Umstandskleid nt; ~ **leave** Elternzeit f (der Mutter); ~ **ward** Entbindungsstation f

math n (US) fam Mathe f; mathematical adj mathematisch; mathematics nsing Mathematik f; maths nsing (Brit) fam Mathe f

matter **1.** n (substance) Materie f; (affair) Sache f; **a per-sonal** ~ eine persönliche Angelegenheit; **a** ~ **of taste** eine Frage des Geschmacks; **no** ~ **how!** egal wie!; **what is the** ~? was ist los?; **as a** ~ **of fact** eigentlich; **a** ~ **of time** eine Frage der Zeit **2.** vi darauf ankommen, wichtig sein; **it doesn't** ~ es macht nichts; **matter-of-fact** *adj* sachlich, nüchtern

mattress n Matratze f

mature 1. *adj* reif **2.** *vi* reif werden; **maturity** n Reife f

maximum 1. *adj* Höchst-, höchste(r, s); **~ speed** Höchstgeschwindigkeit f **2.** n Maximum nt

may vaux (be possible) können; (have permission) dürfen; **it ~ rain** es könnte regnen; **~ I smoke?** darf ich rauchen?; **we ~ as well go** wir können ruhig gehen

May n Mai m; → **September**

maybe *adv* vielleicht

mayo (US) fam. mayonnaise n Mayo f, Mayonnaise f, Majonäse f

mayor n Bürgermeister m

maze n Irrgarten m; fig Wirrwarr nt

MB abbr = **megabyte**; MB nt

me pron (direct object) mich; (indirect object) mir; **it's ~** ich bin's

meadow n Wiese f

meal n Essen nt, Mahlzeit f; **go out for a ~** essen gehen; **meal pack** nt (US) tiefgekühltes Fertiggericht; **meal time** n Essenszeit f

mean 1. *vt* (signify) bedeuten; (have in mind) meinen; (intend) vorhaben; **I~ it** ich meine das ernst; **what do you ~ (by that)?** was willst du damit sagen?; **~ to do sth** etw tun wollen; **it was ~t for**

you es war für dich bestimmt (or gedacht); **it was ~t to be a joke** es sollte ein Witz sein **2.** *vi* **he ~s well** er meint es gut **3.** *adj* (stingy) geizig; (spiteful) gemein (zu zu); **meaning** n Bedeutung f; (of life, poem) Sinn m; **meaningful** *adj* sinnvoll; **meaningless** *adj* (text) ohne Sinn

means n Mittel nt; (pl, funds) Mittel pl; **by ~ of** durch, mittels; **by all ~** selbstverständlich; **by no ~** keineswegs; **~ of transport** Beförderungsmittel

meant pp, pp of **mean**

meantime *adv* **in the ~** inzwischen; **meanwhile** *adv* inzwischen

measles nsing Masern pl; **German ~** Röteln pl

measure 1. *vt, vi* messen **2.** n (unit, device for measuring) Maß nt; (step) Maßnahme f; **take ~s** Maßnahmen ergreifen; **measurement** n (amount measured) Maß nt

meat n Fleisch nt; **meatball** n Fleischbällchen nt

mechanic n Mechaniker(in) m(f); **mechanical** *adj* mechanisch; **mechanics** nsing Mechanik f; **mechanism** n Mechanismus m

medal n Medaille f; (decoration) Orden m; **medalist** (US), **medallist** n Medaillengewinner(in) m(f)

media npl Medien pl

median strip n (US) Mittelstreifen m

mediate vi vermitteln

medical 1. adj medizinisch; (treatment etc) ärztlich; ~ **student** Medizinstudent(in) m(f) 2. n Untersuchung f; **Medicare** n (US) Krankenkasse f für ältere Leute; **medication** n Medikamente pl; **be on** ~ Medikamente nehmen; **medicinal** adj Heil-; ~ **herbs** Heilkräuter pl; **medicine** n Arznei f; (science) Medizin f

medieval adj mittelalterlich

mediocre adj mittelmäßig

meditate vi meditieren; fig nachdenken (on über + acc)

Mediterranean n (sea) Mittelmeer nt; (region) Mittelmeerraum m

medium 1. adj (quality, size) mittlere(r, s); (steak) halbdurch; ~ (**dry**) (wine) halbtrocken; ~ **sized** mittelgroß; ~ **wave** Mittelwelle f 2. n Medium nt; (means) Mittel nt

meet 1. vt treffen; (by arrangement) sich treffen mit; (difficulties) stoßen auf + acc; (get to know) kennen lernen; (requirement, demand) gerecht werden + dat; (deadline) einhalten; **pleased to ~ you** sehr angenehm!; ~ **sb at the station** jdn vom Bahnhof abholen 2. vi sich treffen; (become acquainted) sich kennen lernen; **we've met**

(**before**) wir kennen uns schon; **meet up** vt sich treffen (**with** mit); **meet with** vt (group) zusammenkommen mit; (difficulties, resistance etc) stoßen auf + acc; **meeting** n Treffen nt; (business meeting) Besprechung f; (of committee) Sitzung f; (assembly) Versammlung f; **meeting place**, **meeting point** n Treffpunkt m

megabyte n Megabyte nt

melody n Melodie f

melon n Melone f

melt vt, vi schmelzen

member n Mitglied nt; (of tribe, species) Angehörige(r) mf; **Member of Parliament** Parlamentsabgeordnete(r) mf; **membership** n Mitgliedschaft f; **membership card** n Mitgliedskarte f

memo n Mitteilung f, Memo nt; **memo pad** n Notizblock m

memorable adj unvergesslich; **memorial** n Denkmal nt (**to** für); **memorize** vt sich einprägen, auswendig lernen; **memory** n Gedächtnis nt; IT (of computer) Speicher m; (sth recalled) Erinnerung f; **in ~ of** zur Erinnerung an + acc

men pl of **man**

menace n Bedrohung f; (danger) Gefahr f

mend 1. vt reparieren; (clothes) flicken 2. n **be on**

the ~ auf dem Wege der Besserung sein
meningitis n Hirnhautentzündung f
menopause n Wechseljahre pl
mental adj geistig; *~ hospital* psychiatrische Klinik; **mentality** n Mentalität f; **mentally** adv geistig; *~ handicapped* geistig behindert; *~ ill* geisteskrank
mention **1.** n Erwähnung f **2.** vt erwähnen (*to sb* jdm gegenüber); *don't ~ it* bitte sehr, gern geschehen
menu n Speisekarte f; IT Menü nt
merchandise n Handelsware f; **merchant** adj Handels-
merciful adj gnädig; **mercifully** adv glücklicherweise
mercury n Quecksilber nt
mercy n Gnade f
mere adj bloß; **merely** adv bloß, lediglich
merge vi verschmelzen; AUTO sich einfädeln; COMM fusionieren; **merger** n COMM Fusion f
meringue n Baiser nt
merit n Verdienst nt; (*advantage*) Vorzug m
merry adj fröhlich; *fam* (*tipsy*) angeheitert; *Merry Christmas* Fröhliche Weihnachten!; **merry-go-round** n Karussell nt
mess n Unordnung f; (*muddle*) Durcheinander nt; (*dirty*) Schweinerei f; (*trouble*) Schwierigkeiten pl; *in a ~* (*muddled*) durcheinander; (*untidy*) unordentlich; *fig* (*person*) in der Klemme; *make a ~ of sth* etw verpfuschen; **mess about** vi (*tinker with*) herummurksen (*with* an + dat); (*play the fool*) herumalbern; (*do nothing in particular*) herumgammeln; **mess up** vt verpfuschen; (*make untidy*) in Unordnung bringen; (*dirty*) schmutzig machen
message n Mitteilung f, Nachricht f; *can I give him a ~?* kann ich ihm etwas ausrichten?; *please leave a ~* (*on answerphones*) bitte hinterlassen Sie eine Nachricht; *I get the ~* ich hab's verstanden
messenger n Bote m
messy adj (*untidy*) unordentlich; (*situation etc*) verfahren
met pt, pp of **meet**
metal n Metall nt; **metallic** adj metallisch
meteorology n Meteorologie f
meter n Zähler m; (*parking meter*) Parkuhr f; (*US*) → **metre**
method n Methode f
meticulous adj (*painful*) genau
metre n Meter m or nt; **metric** adj metrisch; *~ system* Dezimalsystem nt

Mexico n Mexiko nt

mice pl of **mouse**

mickey n **take the ~ (out of sb)** fam (jdn) auf den Arm nehmen

microchip n IT Mikrochip m; **microphone** n Mikrofon nt; **microscope** n Mikroskop nt; **microwave (oven)** n Mikrowelle(nherd) f(m)

mid adj **in ~ January** Mitte Januar; **he's in his ~ forties** er ist Mitte vierzig

midday n Mittag m; **at ~** mittags

middle 1. n Mitte f; **in the ~ of** mitten in + dat; **be in the ~ of doing sth** gerade dabei sein, etw zu tun 2. adj mittlere(r, s), Mittel-; **middle-aged** adj mittleren Alters; **Middle Ages** npl **the ~** das Mittelalter; **middle-class** adj mittelständisch; (bourgeois) bürgerlich; **middle classes** npl **the ~** der Mittelstand; **Middle East** n **the ~** der Nahe Osten; **middle name** n zweiter Vorname

Midlands npl **the ~** Mittelengland nt

midnight n Mitternacht f

midst n **in the ~ of** mitten in + dat

midsummer n Hochsommer m; **Midsummer's Day** Sommersonnenwende f

midway adv **at** halbem Wege; **~ through the film** nach der Hälfte des Films;

midweek adj, adv in der Mitte der Woche

midwife n Hebamme f

midwinter n tiefster Winter

might 1. pt of **may**; (possibility) könnte; (permission) dürfte; (would) würde; **they ~ still come** sie könnten noch kommen; **I thought she ~ change her mind** ich dachte schon, sie würde sich anders entscheiden 2. n Macht f, Kraft f

mighty adj gewaltig; (powerful) mächtig

migraine n Migräne f

migrant n (bird) Zugvogel m; **~ worker** Gastarbeiter(in) m(f); migrate vi abwandern; (birds) nach Süden ziehen

mike n fam Mikro nt

Milan n Mailand nt

mild adj mild; (person) sanft; **mildly** adv **put it ~** gelinde gesagt; mildness n Milde f

mile n Meile f (= 1,609 km); **for ~s (and ~s)** kilometerweit; **~s per hour** Meilen pro Stunde; **~s better than** hundertmal besser als; mileage n Meilen pl, Meilenzahl f; mileometer n ≈ Kilometerzähler m; milestone n a. fig Meilenstein m

militant adj militant; military adj Militär-, militärisch

milk 1. n Milch f 2. vt melken; milk chocolate n Vollmilchschokolade f; milkman n Milchmann m; milk shake

mill

n Milkshake *m*, Milchmixgetränk *nt*

mill *n* Mühle *f*; (*factory*) Fabrik *f*

millennium *n* Jahrtausend *nt*

millet *n* Hirse *f*

milligramme *n* Milligramm *nt*; **milliliter** (*US*), **millilitre** *n* Milliliter *m*; **millimeter** (*US*), **millimetre** *n* Millimeter *m*

million *n* Million *f*; **five ~** fünf Millionen; **~s of people** Millionen von Menschen; **millionaire** *n* Millionär(in) *m(f)*

mime 1. *n* Pantomime *f* **2.** *vt*, *vi* mimen; **mimic 1.** *n* Imitator(in) *m(f)* **2.** *vt*, *vi* nachahmen; **mimicry** *n* Nachahmung *f*

mince 1. *vt* (zer)hacken **2.** *n* (*meat*) Hackfleisch *nt*; **mincemeat** *n* süße Gebäckfüllung aus Rosinen, Äpfeln, Zucker, Gewürzen und Talg; **mince pie** *n mit 'mincemeat' gefülltes süßes Weihnachtsgebäck*

mind 1. *n* (*intellect*) Verstand *m*; (*also person*) Geist *m*; **out of sight, out of ~** aus den Augen, aus dem Sinn; **he is out of his ~** er ist nicht bei Verstand; **keep sth in ~** etw im Auge behalten; **I've a lot on my ~** mich beschäftigt so vieles im Moment; **change one's ~** es sich *dat* anders überlegen **2.** *vt* (*look after*) aufpassen auf + *acc*;

(*object to*) etwas haben gegen; **~ you, ...** allerdings ...; **I wouldn't ~ ...** ich hätte nichts gegen ...; **'~ the step'** „Vorsicht Stufe!" **3.** *vi* etwas dagegen haben; **do you ~ if I ...** macht es Ihnen etwas aus, wenn ich ...; **I don't ~** es ist mir egal, meinetwegen; **never ~** macht nichts

mine 1. *pron* meine(r, s); **this is ~** das gehört mir; **a friend of ~** ein Freund von mir **2.** *n* (*coalmine*) Bergwerk *nt*; MIL Mine *f*

miner *n* Bergarbeiter *m*

mineral *n* Mineral *nt*; **mineral water** *n* Mineralwasser *nt*

mingle *vi* sich mischen (*with* unter + *acc*)

minibar *n* Minibar *f*; **minibus** *n* Kleinbus *m*; **minicab** *n* Kleintaxi *nt*

minimal *adj* minimal; **minimize** *vt* auf ein Minimum reduzieren; **minimum 1.** *n* Minimum *nt* **2.** *adj* Mindest-

mining *n* Bergbau *m*

miniskirt *n* Minirock *m*

minister *n* POL Minister(in) *m(f)*; REL Pastor(in) *m(f)*, Pfarrer(in) *m(f)*; **ministry** *n* POL Ministerium *nt*

minor 1. *adj* kleiner; (*insignificant*) unbedeutend; (*operation, offence*) harmlos; **~ road** Nebenstraße *f*; MUS **A ~** a-Moll *nt* **2.** *n* (*Brit, under 18*) Minderjährige(r) *mf*; **minority** *n* Minderheit *f*

mint n Minze f; (sweet) Pfefferminz(bonbon) nt; **mint sauce** n Minzsoße f

minus prep minus; (without) ohne

minute 1. adj winzig; **in ~ detail** genauestens **2.** n Minute f; **just a** ~ Moment mal!; **any** ~ jeden Augenblick; ~**s** pl (of meeting) Protokoll nt

miracle n Wunder nt; **miraculous** adj unglaublich

mirage n Fata Morgana f, Luftspiegelung f

mirror n Spiegel m

misbehave vi sich schlecht benehmen

miscalculation n Fehlkalkulation f; (misjudgement) Fehleinschätzung f

miscarriage n MED Fehlgeburt f

miscellaneous adj verschieden

mischief n Unfug m; **mischievous** adj (person) durchtrieben; (glance) verschmitzt

misconception n falsche Vorstellung

misconduct n Vergehen nt

miser n Geizhals m

miserable adj (person) todunglücklich; (conditions, life) elend; (pay, weather) miserabel

miserly adj geizig

misery n Elend nt; (suffering) Qualen pl

misfit n Außenseiter(in) m(f)

misfortune n Pech nt

misguided adj irrig; (optimism) unangebracht

misinform vt falsch informieren

misinterpret vt falsch auslegen

misjudge vt falsch beurteilen

mislay irr vt verlegen

mislead irr vt irreführen; **misleading** adj irreführend

misprint n Druckfehler m

mispronounce vt falsch aussprechen

miss 1. vt (fail to hit, catch) verfehlen; (not notice, hear) nicht mitbekommen; (be too late to) verpassen; (chance) versäumen; (regret the absence of) vermissen; **I** ~ **you** du fehlst mir **2.** vi nicht treffen; (shooting) danebenschießen; (ball, shot etc) danebengehen; **miss out 1.** vt auslassen **2.** vi ~ **on sth** etw verpassen

Miss n (unmarried woman) Fräulein nt

missile n Geschoss nt; (rocket) Rakete f

missing adj (person) vermisst; (thing) fehlend; **be/ go** ~ vermisst werden, fehlen

mission n POL, MIL, REL Auftrag m, Mission f; **missionary** n Missionar(in) m(f)

mist n (feiner) Nebel m; (haze) Dunst m; **mist over, mist up** vi sich beschlagen

mistake 1. n Fehler m; **by** ~

aus Versehen **2.** *irr vt* (*misunderstand*) falsch verstehen; (*mix up*) verwechseln (*for* mit); mistaken *adj* (*idea, identity*) falsch; **be ~** sich irren, falsch liegen

mistletoe *n* Mistel *f*

mistreat *vt* schlecht behandeln

mistress *n* (*lover*) Geliebte *f*

mistrust **1.** *n* Misstrauen *nt* (*of* gegen) **2.** *vt* misstrauen + *dat*

misty *adj* neblig; (*hazy*) dunstig

misunderstand *irr vt, vi* falsch verstehen; misunderstanding *n* Missverständnis *nt*; (*disagreement*) Differenz *f*

mitten *n* Fausthandschuh *m*

mix **1.** *n* (*mixture*) Mischung *f* **2.** *vt* mischen; (*blend*) vermischen (*with* mit); (*drinks, music*) mixen; **~ business with pleasure** das Angenehme mit dem Nützlichen verbinden **3.** *vi* (*liquids*) sich vermischen lassen; mix up *vt* (*mix*) zusammenmischen; (*confuse*) verwechseln (*with* mit); mixed *adj* gemischt; **a ~ bunch** eine bunt gemischte Truppe; **~ grill** Mixedgrill *m*; **~ vegetables** Mischgemüse *nt*; mixer *n* (*for food*) Mixer *m*; mixture *n* Mischung *f*; MED Saft *m*; mix-up *n* Durcheinander *nt*

ml *abbr* = **millilitre**; ml

mm *abbr* = **millimetre**; mm

moan **1.** *n* Stöhnen *nt*; (*complaint*) Gejammer *nt* **2.** *vi* stöhnen; (*complain*) jammern, meckern (*about* über + *acc*)

mobile **1.** *adj* beweglich; (*on wheels*) fahrbar **2.** *n* (*phone*) Handy *nt*; mobile phone *n* Mobiltelefon *nt*, Handy *nt*

mobility *n* Beweglichkeit *f*

mock **1.** *vt* verspotten **2.** *adj* Schein-; mockery *n* Spott *m*

mod cons *abbr* = **modern conveniences**; (moderner) Komfort

mode *n* Art *f*; IT Modus *m*

model **1.** *n* Modell *nt*; (*example*) Vorbild *nt*; (*fashion*) Model *nt* **2.** *adj* (*miniature*) Modell-; (*perfect*) Muster- **3.** *vt* (*make*) formen **4.** *vi* **she ~s for Versace** sie arbeitet als Model bei Versace

modem *n* Modem *nt*

moderate **1.** *adj* mäßig; (*views, politics*) gemäßigt; (*income, success*) mittelmäßig **2.** *n* POL Gemäßigte(r) *mf* **3.** *vt* mäßigen

modern *adj* modern; **~ history** neuere Geschichte; **~ Greek** Neugriechisch *nt*; modernize *vt* modernisieren

modest *adj* bescheiden; modesty *n* Bescheidenheit *f*

modification *n* Abänderung *f*; modify *vt* abändern

moist *adj* feucht; moisten *vt* befeuchten; moisture *n* Feuchtigkeit *f*; moisturizer n Feuchtigkeitscreme f

molar n Backenzahn m

mold (US) → **mould**

mole n (spot) Leberfleck m; (animal) Maulwurf m

molecule n Molekül nt

molest vt belästigen

molt (US) → **moult**

molten adj geschmolzen

mom n (US) Mutti f

moment n Moment m, Augenblick m; **just a ~** Moment mal!; **at** (or for) **the ~** im Augenblick; **in a ~** gleich

momentous adj bedeutsam

Monaco n Monaco nt

monarch n Monarchie f

monastery n (for monks) Kloster nt

Monday n Montag m; → **Tuesday**

monetary adj (reform, policy, union) Währungs-; **~ unit** Geldeinheit f

money n Geld nt

monitor 1. n (screen) Monitor m 2. vt (progress etc) überwachen

monk n Mönch m

monkey n Affe m; **~ business** Unfug m

monsoon n Monsun m

monster 1. n (animal, thing) Monstrum nt 2. adj Riesen-; monstrosity n Monstrosität f; (thing) Ungetüm nt

month n Monat m; monthly 1. adj monatlich; (ticket, salary) Monats- 2. adv monatlich 3. n (magazine) Monats-

(zeit)schrift f

monty n **go the full ~** fam (strip) alle Hüllen fallen lassen; (go the whole hog) aufs Ganze gehen

monument n Denkmal nt (to für); monumental adj (huge) gewaltig

mood n (of person) Laune f; (a. general) Stimmung f; **be in a good/bad ~** gute/ schlechte Laune haben, gut/schlecht drauf sein; **be in the ~ for sth** zu etw aufgelegt sein; moody adj launisch

moon n Mond m; **be over the ~** fam überglücklich sein; moonlight 1. n Mondlicht nt 2. vi schwarzarbeiten; moonlit adj (night, landscape) mondhell

moor 1. n Moor m 2. vt, vi festmachen; moorings npl Liegeplatz m; moorland n Moorland nt, Heideland nt

moose n Elch m

mop n Mopp m; mop up vt aufwischen

moped n (Brit) Moped nt

moral 1. adj moralisch; (values) sittlich 2. n Moral f; **~s** pl Moral f; morale n Stimmung f, Moral f; morality n Moral f, Ethik f

more adj, pron adv mehr; (additional) noch; **three ~** noch drei; **some ~ tea?** ist etwas Tee?; **are there any ~?** gibt es noch welche?; **I don't** *go there any* ~ ich gehe nicht mehr hin; (*forming comparative*) ~ *important* wichtiger; ~ *slowly* langsamer; ~ *and* ~ immer mehr; ~ *and* ~ *beautiful* immer schöner; ~ *or less* mehr oder weniger; **moreish** *adj* (*food*) *these crisps are really* ~ ich kann mit diesen Chips nicht aufhören; **moreover** *adv* außerdem

morgue *n* Leichenschauhaus *nt*

morning *n* Morgen *m*; *in the* ~ am Morgen, morgens; (*tomorrow*) morgen früh; *this* ~ heute morgen **2.** *adj* Morgen-; (*early*) Früh-; (*walk etc*) morgendlich; **morning after pill** *n* die Pille danach; **morning sickness** *n* Schwangerschaftsübelkeit *f*

Morocco *n* Marokko *nt*
moron *n* Idiot(in) *m(f)*
morphine *n* Morphium *nt*
morsel *n* Bissen *m*
mortal 1. *adj* sterblich; (*wound*) tödlich **2.** *n* Sterbliche(r) *mf*; **mortality** *n* (*death rate*) Sterblichkeitsziffer *f*
mortgage *n* Hypothek *f* **2.** *vt* mit einer Hypothek belasten
mosaic *n* Mosaik *nt*
Moscow *n* Moskau *nt*
Moslem *adj*, *n* → **Muslim**
mosque *n* Moschee *f*
mosquito *n* (Stech)mücke *f*;

(*tropical*) Moskito *m*; ~ *net* Moskitonetz *nt*

moss *n* Moos *nt*

most 1. *adj* meiste *pl*, die meisten; *in* ~ *cases* in den meisten Fällen **2.** *adv* (*with verbs*) am meisten; (*with adj*) ...ste; (*with adv*) am ...sten; (*very*) äußerst, höchst; *he ate* *the* (~) hat am meisten gegessen; *the* ~ *beautiful/interesting* der/die/das schönste/interessanteste; ~ *interesting* hochinteressant! **3.** *n* das meiste, der größte Teil; (*people*) die meisten; ~ *of the money/players* das meiste Geld/die meisten Spieler; *for the* ~ *part* zum größten Teil; *five at the* ~ höchstens fünf; *make the* ~ *of sth* etw voll ausnützen; **mostly** *adv* (*most of the time*) meistens; (*mainly*) hauptsächlich; (*for the most part*) größtenteils

MOT *abbr* = *Ministry of Transport*; ~ (*test*) ≈ TÜV *m*
motel *n* Motel *nt*
moth *n* Nachtfalter *m*; (*wool-eating*) Motte *f*; **mothball** *n* Mottenkugel *f*
mother 1. *n* Mutter *f* **2.** *vt* bemuttern; **mother-in-law** *n* Schwiegermutter *f*; **mother-to-be** *n* werdende Mutter
motion *n* Bewegung *f*; (*in meeting*) Antrag *m*
motivate *vt* motivieren

motor 1. n Motor m; fam (car) Auto nt **2.** adj Motor-; **Motorail train®** n (Brit) Autoreisezug m; **motorbike** n Motorrad nt; **motorboat** n Motorboot m; **motorcycle** n Motorrad nt; **motorist** n Autofahrer(in) m(f); **motor oil** n Motorenöl nt; **motor racing** n Autorennsport m; **motor scooter** n Motorroller m; **motor vehicle** n Kraftfahrzeug nt; **motorway** n (Brit) Autobahn f

mould 1. n Form f; (mildew) Schimmel m **2.** vt formen; **mouldy** adj formbar

mount 1. vt (horse) steigen auf + acc; (exhibition etc) organisieren; (painting) mit einem Passepartout versehen **2.** vi (up) (an)steigen **3.** n Passepartout nt

mountain n Berg m; **mountaineer** n Bergsteiger(in) m(f); **mountaineering** n Bergsteigen nt; **mountainside** n Berghang m

mourn 1. vt betrauern **2.** vi trauern (for um); **mourning** n Trauer f; **be in ~** trauern (for um)

mouse n Maus f; IT Maus f; **mouse mat, mouse pad** (US) n Mauspad nt; **mouse trap** n Mausefalle f

mousse n GASTR Creme f; (styling ~) Schaumfestiger m

moustache n Schnurrbart m

mouth n Mund m; (of animal) Maul nt; (of cave) Eingang m; (of bottle etc) Öffnung f; (of river) Mündung f; **keep one's ~ shut** fam den Mund halten; **mouthful** n (of drink) Schluck m; (of food) Bissen m; **mouth organ** n Mundharmonika f; **mouthwash** n Mundwasser nt; **mouthwatering** adj appetitlich, lecker

move 1. n (movement) Bewegung f; (in game) Zug m; (step) Schritt m; (moving house) Umzug m; **make a ~** (in game) ziehen; (leave) sich auf den Weg machen; **get a ~ on (with sth)** sich (mit etw) beeilen **2.** vt bewegen; (object) rücken; (car) wegfahren; (transport: goods) befördern; (people) transportieren; (in job) versetzen; (emotionally) bewegen, rühren; **I can't ~ it** (stuck, too heavy) ich bringe es nicht von der Stelle; **~ house** umziehen **3.** vi sich bewegen; (change place) gehen; (vehicle, ship) fahren; (move house, town etc) umziehen; (in game) ziehen; **move about** vi sich bewegen; (travel) unterwegs sein; **move away** vi weggehen; (move town) wegziehen; **move in** vi (to house) einziehen; **move on** vi weitergehen; (vehicle) weiterfahren; **move out** vi ausziehen; **move up** vi (in queue) *etc*) aufrücken; **movement** *n* Bewegung *f*

movie *n* Film *m*; **the ~s** (*the cinema*) das Kino

moving *adj* (*emotionally*) ergreifend, berührend

mow *vt* mähen; **mower** *n* (*lawn~*) Rasenmäher *m*

mown *pp* of **mow**

Mozambique *n* Mosambik *nt*

MP *abbr* = **Member of Parliament**; Parlamentsabgeordnete(r) *mf*

mph *abbr* = **miles per hour**; Meilen pro Stunde

Mr *n* (*form of address*) Herr

Mrs *n* (*form of address*) Frau

Ms *n* (*form of address for any woman, married or unmarried*) Frau

Mt *abbr* = **Mount**; Berg *m*

much 1. *adj* viel; **we haven't got ~ time** wir haben nicht viel Zeit **2.** *adv* viel; (*with verb*) sehr; **~ better** viel besser; **I like it very ~** es gefällt mir sehr gut; **I don't like it ~** ich mag es nicht besonders; **thank you very ~** danke sehr; **~ as I like him** so sehr ich ihn mag; **we don't see them ~** wir sehen sie nicht sehr oft; **~ the same** fast gleich **3.** *n* viel; **as ~ as you want** so viel du willst; **he's not ~ of a cook** er ist kein großer Koch

muck *n* Dreck *m*; **muck about** *vi* fam herumalbern; **muck up** *vt* fam dreckig ma-

chen; (*spoil*) vermasseln; **mucky** *adj* dreckig

mucus *n* Schleim *m*

mud *n* Schlamm *m*

muddle 1. *n* Durcheinander *nt*; **be in a ~** ganz durcheinander sein **2.** *vt* ~ (*up*) durcheinander bringen; **muddled** *adj* konfus

muddy *adj* schlammig; (*shoes*) schmutzig; **mudguard** *n* Schutzblech *nt*

muesli *n* Müsli *nt*

muffin *n* Muffin *m*; (*Brit*) weiches, flaches Milchbrötchen aus Hefeteig, das meist getoastet und mit Butter gegessen wird

muffle *vt* (*sound*) dämpfen; **muffler** *n* (*US*) Schalldämpfer *m*

mug 1. *n* (*cup*) Becher *m*; fam (*fool*) Trottel *m* **2.** *vt* (*attack and rob*) überfallen; **mugging** *n* Raubüberfall *m*

mule *n* Maulesel *m*

mulled *adj* **~ wine** Glühwein *m*

multicolored (*US*), **multicoloured** *adj* bunt; **multicultural** *adj* multikulturell; **multigrade** *adj* **~ oil** Mehrbereichsöl *nt*; **multilingual** *adj* mehrsprachig

multiple 1. *n* Vielfache(s) *nt* **2.** *adj* mehrfach; (*several*) mehrere; **multiple-choice** (**method**) *n* Multiple-Choice-Verfahren *nt*

multiplex *adj*, *n* **~** (**cinema**)

Multiplexkino nt

multiply 1. vt multiplizieren (by mit) **2.** vi sich vermehren

multi-purpose adj Mehrzweck-; **multistorey** (car park) n Parkhaus nt

mum n fam (mother) Mutti f, Mami f

mumble vt, vi murmeln

mummy n (dead body) Mumie f; fam (mother) Mutti f, Mami f

mumps nsing Mumps m

Munich n München nt

municipal adj städtisch

murder 1. n Mord m; **the traffic was ~** der Verkehr war die Hölle **2.** vt ermorden; **murderer** n Mörder(in) m(f)

murky adj düster; (water) trüb

murmur vt, vi murmeln

muscle n Muskel m; **muscular** adj (strong) muskulös; (cramp, pain etc) Muskel-

museum n Museum nt

mushroom n (essbarer) Pilz; (button ~) Champignon m

mushy adj breiig

music n Musik f; **musical 1.** adj (sound) melodisch; (person) musikalisch; **~ instrument** Musikinstrument nt **2.** n (show) Musical nt; **musically** adv musikalisch; **musician** n Musiker(in) m(f)

Muslim 1. adj moslemisch **2.** n Moslem m, Muslime f

mussel n Miesmuschel f

must 1. vaux (need to) müs-

sen; (in negation) dürfen; **I ~n't forget that** ich darf das nicht vergessen; (certainty) **he ~ be there by now** er ist inzwischen bestimmt schon da; (assumption) **I ~ have lost it** ich habe es wohl verloren; **~ you?** muss das sein? **2.** n Muss nt

mustache n (US) Schnurrbart m

mustard n Senf m

mustn't contr of **must not**

mute adj stumm

mutter vt, vi murmeln

mutton n Hammelfleisch nt

mutual adj gegenseitig; **by ~ consent** in gegenseitigem Einverständnis

my adj mein; **I've hurt ~ leg** ich habe mir das Bein verletzt

Myanmar n Myanmar nt

myself pron (reflexive) acc, mir dat; **I've hurt ~** ich habe mich verletzt; **I've bought ~ a flat** ich habe mir eine Wohnung gekauft; (emphatic) **I did it ~** ich habe es selbst gemacht; (all) **by ~** allein

mysterious adj geheimnisvoll, mysteriös; (inexplicable) rätselhaft; **mystery** n Geheimnis nt; (puzzle) Rätsel nt

myth n Mythos m; fig (untrue story) Märchen nt; **mythology** n Mythologie f

N

nag *vt, vi* herumnörgeln (*sb* an jdm); **nagging** *n* Nörgelei *f*

nail 1. *n* Nagel *m* **2.** *vt* nageln (*to* an); nailbrush *n* Nagelbürste *f*; nail clippers *npl* Nagelknipser *m*; nailfile *n* Nagelfeile *f*; nail polish *n* Nagellack *m*; nail polish remover *n* Nagellackentferner *m*; nail scissors *npl* Nagelschere *f*; nail varnish *n* Nagellack *m*

naive *adj* naiv

naked *adj* nackt

name 1. *n* Name *m*; **his ~ is ...** er heißt ...; **what's your ~?** wie heißen Sie?; (*reputation*) **have a good/bad ~** einen guten/schlechten Ruf haben **2.** *vt* nennen (*after* nach); (*sth new*) benennen; (*nominate*) ernennen (*as* als/zu); **a boy ~d ...** ein Junge namens ...; **namely** *adv* nämlich; name plate *n* Namensschild *nt*

nan bread *n* (*warm serviertes*) indisches Fladenbrot

nanny *n* Kindermädchen *nt*

nap *n* **have a ~** ein Nickerchen machen

napkin *n* (*at table*) Serviette *f*

Naples *n* Neapel *nt*

nappy *n* (Brit) Windel *f*

narrow 1. *adj* eng, schmal; (*victory, majority*) knapp; **have a ~ escape** mit knap-

per Not davonkommen **2.** *vi* sich verengen; **narrow down** *vt* einschränken (*to* sth auf etw *acc*); **narrow -minded** *adj* engstirnig

nasty *adj* ekelhaft; (*person*) fies; (*remark*) gehässig; (*accident, wound etc*) schlimm

nation *n* Nation *f*; national **1.** *adj* national; **~ anthem** Nationalhymne *f*; **National Health Service** (Brit) staatlicher Gesundheitsdienst; **~ insurance** (Brit) Sozialversicherung *f*; **~ park** Nationalpark *m* **2.** *n* Staatsbürger(in) *m(f)*; **nationality** *n* Staatsangehörigkeit *f*, Nationalität *f*; **nationwide** *adj, adv* landesweit

native 1. *adj* einheimisch; (*inborn*) angeboren, natürlich; **Native American** Indianer(in) *m(f)*; **~ country** Heimatland *nt*; **a ~ German** ein gebürtiger Deutscher, eine gebürtige Deutsche; **~ language** Muttersprache *f*; **~ speaker** Muttersprachler(in) *m(f)* **2.** *n* Einheimische(r) *mf*; (*in colonial context*) Eingeborene(r) *mf*

nativity play *n* Krippenspiel *nt*

NATO *acr* = **North Atlantic Treaty Organization**; Nato *f*

natural *adj* natürlich; (*law, science, forces etc*) Natur-; (*inborn*) angeboren; **~ resources** Bodenschätze *pl*; **naturally** *adv* natürlich; (*by nature*) von Natur aus
nature *n* Natur *f*; (*type*) Art *f*; **by ~** von Natur aus; **nature reserve** *n* Naturschutzgebiet *nt*
naughty *adj* (*child*) ungezogen; (*cheeky*) frech
nausea *n* Übelkeit *f*
nautical *adj* nautisch; **~ mile** Seemeile *f*
nave *n* Hauptschiff *nt*
navel *n* Nabel *m*
navigate *vi* navigieren; (*in car*) lotsen, dirigieren; **navigation** *n* Navigation *f*; (*in car*) Lotsen *nt*
navy *n* Marine *f*
near 1. *adj* nahe; **my ~est relations** meine nächsten Verwandten; **in the ~ future** in nächster Zukunft; **that was a ~ miss** (*or thing*) das war knapp; (*with price*) **... or ~est offer** Verhandlungsbasis ... **2.** *adv* in der Nähe; **come ~er** näher kommen; (*event*) näher rücken **3.** *prep* **~ (to)** (*space*) nahe an + *dat*; (*vicinity*) in der Nähe + *gen*; **~ the station** in der Nähe des Bahnhofs, in Bahnhofsnähe; **nearby 1.** *adj* nahe gelegen **2.** *adv* in der Nähe; **nearly** *adv* fast; **near-sighted** *adj* kurzsichtig

neat *adj* ordentlich; (*work, writing*) sauber; (*undiluted*) pur
necessarily *adv* notwendigerweise; **not ~** nicht unbedingt; **necessary** *adj* notwendig, nötig; **it's ~ to ...** man muss ...; **it's not ~ for him to come** er braucht nicht mitzukommen; **necessity** *n* Notwendigkeit *f*; **the bare necessities** das absolut Notwendigste
neck *n* Hals *m*; (*size*) Halsweite *f*; **necklace** *n* Halskette *f*; **necktie** *n* (*US*) Krawatte *f*
nectarine *n* Nektarine *f*
née *adj* geborene
need 1. *n* (*requirement*) Bedürfnis *nt* (*for* für); (*necessity*) Notwendigkeit *f*; (*poverty*) Not *f*; **be in ~ of sth** etw brauchen; **if ~(s) be** wenn nötig **2.** *vt* brauchen; **I ~ to speak to you** ich muss mit dir reden; **you ~n't go** du brauchst nicht (zu) gehen, du musst nicht gehen
needle *n* Nadel *f*
needless, needlessly *adj, adv* unnötig; **~ to say** selbstverständlich
negative 1. *n* LING Verneinung *f*; PHOT Negativ *nt* **2.** *adj* negativ; (*answer*) verneinend
neglect 1. *n* Vernachlässigung *f* **2.** *vt* vernachlässigen; **negligence** *n* Nachlässigkeit *f*; **negligent** *adj* nachlässig
negotiate *vi* verhandeln; ne-

gotiation n Verhandlung f
neigh vi (horse) wiehern
neighbor (US), **neighbour** n Nachbar(in) m(f); **neighbo(u)rhood** n Nachbarschaft f
neighbo(u)ring adj benachbart
neither 1. adj, pron keine(r, s) von beiden; ~ **of you/us** keiner von euch/uns beiden 2. adv ~ ... **nor** ... weder ... noch ... 3. conj **I'm not going - ~ am I** ich gehe nicht - ich auch nicht
nephew n Neffe m
nerd n fam Schwachkopf m; **he's a real computer ~** er ist ein totaler Computerfreak
nerve n Nerv m; **he gets on my ~s** er geht mir auf die Nerven; (courage) **keep/lose one's ~** die Nerven behalten/verlieren; (cheek) **have the ~ to do sth** die Frechheit besitzen, etw zu tun; **nerve-racking** adj nervenaufreibend; **nervous** adj (apprehensive) ängstlich; (on edge) nervös; **nervous breakdown** n Nervenzusammenbruch m
nest 1. n Nest nt 2. vi nisten
net 1. n Netz nt; **the Net** (Internet) das Internet; **on the ~** im Netz 2. adj (price, weight) Netto-; ~ **profit** Reingewinn m
Netherlands npl **the** ~ die

Niederlande pl
network n Netz nt; TV, RADIO Sendenetz nt; IT Netzwerk nt
neurosis n Neurose f; **neurotic** adj neurotisch
neuter adj BIO geschlechtslos; LING sächlich
neutral 1. adj neutral 2. n (gear in car) Leerlauf m
never adv nie(mals); ~ **before** noch nie; ~ **mind** macht nichts!; **never-ending** adj endlos; **nevertheless** adv trotzdem
new adj neu; **this is all ~ to me** das ist für mich noch ungewohnt
New England n Neuengland nt
Newfoundland n Neufundland nt
newly adv neu; ~ **made** (cake) frisch gebacken; **newly-weds** npl Frischvermählte pl; **new moon** n Neumond m
news nsing (item of ~) Nachricht f; RADIO, TV Nachrichten pl; **good** ~ eine erfreuliche Nachricht; **what's the** ~? was gibt's Neues?; **have you heard the** ~? hast du das Neueste gehört?; **news-agent**, **news dealer** (US) n Zeitungshändler(in) m(f); **news bulletin** n Nachrichtensendung f; **news flash** n Kurzmeldung f; **newsgroup** n IT Diskussionsforum n, Newsgroup f; **newsletter** n Mitteilungsblatt nt; **news-**

paper n Zeitung f
New Year n das neue Jahr; **Happy ~** (ein) frohes Neues Jahr!; (*toast*) Prosit Neujahr!; **~'s Day** Neujahr nt, Neujahrstag m; **~'s Eve** Silvesterabend m; **~'s resolution** guter Vorsatz fürs neue Jahr

New York n New York nt
New Zealand 1. n Neuseeland nt 2. adj neuseeländisch; New Zealander n Neuseeländer(in) m(f)
next 1. adj nächste(r, s); **the week after ~** übernächste Woche; **~ time I see him** wenn ich ihn das nächste Mal sehe; **you're ~** du bist jetzt dran 2. adv als Nächstes; (*then*) dann, darauf; **to ~** neben + dat; **to last** vorletzte(r, s); **~ to impossible** nahezu unmöglich; **the ~ best thing** das Nächstbeste; **~ door** nebenan
NHS abbr = **National Health Service**
Niagara Falls npl Niagarafälle pl
nibble vt knabbern an + dat; nibbles npl Knabberzeug nt
Nicaragua n Nicaragua nt
nice adj nett, sympathisch; (*taste, food, drink*) gut; (*weather*) schön; **have a ~ day** (US) schönen Tag noch!; nicely adv nett; (*well*) gut; **that'll do ~** das genügt vollauf

nick vt fam (*steal*) klauen
nickel n CHEM Nickel nt; (US, coin) Nickel m
nickname n Spitzname m
nicotine n Nikotin nt; nicotine patch n Nikotinpflaster nt
niece n Nichte f
Nigeria n Nigeria nt
Nigerian n Nigerianer nt
night n Nacht f; (*before bed*) Abend m; **good ~** gute Nacht!; **at (or by) ~** nachts; **have an early ~** früh schlafen gehen; nightcap n Schlummertrunk m; nightclub n Nachtklub m; nightdress n Nachthemd nt; nightie n fam Nachthemd nt
nightingale n Nachtigall f
night life n Nachtleben nt; nightly adv (*every evening*) jeden Abend; (*every night*) jede Nacht; nightmare n Albtraum m; nighttime n Nacht f; **at ~** nachts
nil n SPORT null
Nile n Nil m
nine 1. num neun; **~ times out of ten** so gut wie immer 2. n (a. bus etc) Neun f; → **eight**; nineteen 1. num neunzehn 2. n (a. bus etc) Neunzehn f; → **eight**; nineteenth adj neunzehnte(r, s); → **eighth**; ninetieth adj neunzigste(r, s); → **eighth**; ninety 1. num neunzig 2. n Neunzig f; → **eight**; ninth 1. adj neunte(r, s) 2. n (*fraction*) Neuntel nt; → **eighth**

nipple n Brustwarze f
nitrogen n Stickstoff m
no 1. adv nein; (after comparative) nicht; **I can wait ~ longer** ich kann nicht länger warten; **I have ~ more money** ich habe kein Geld mehr **2.** adj kein; **in ~ time** im Nu; **~ way** fam keinesfalls; **it's ~ use** (or **good**) es hat keinen Zweck; **~ smoking** Rauchen verboten **3.** n Nein nt
nobody 1. pron niemand; (emphatic) keiner; **~ knows** keiner weiß es; **~ else** sonst niemand, kein anderer **2.** n Niemand m
no-claims bonus n Schadenfreiheitsrabatt m
nod vi, vt nicken; **nod off** vi einnicken
noise n (loud) Lärm m; (sound) Geräusch nt; **noisy** adj laut; (crowd) lärmend
nominate vt (in election) aufstellen; (appoint) ernennen
non- pref Nicht-; (with adj) nicht-, un-; **non-alcoholic** adj alkoholfrei
none pron keine(r, s); **~ of them** keiner von ihnen; **~ of it is any use** nichts davon ist brauchbar; **there are ~ left** es sind keine mehr da; (with comparative) **be ~ the wiser** auch nicht schlauer sein
nonetheless adv nichtsdestoweniger
non-fiction n Sachbücher pl;

non-resident n 'open to ~s'' „auch für Nichthotelgäste"; **non-returnable** adj **~ bottle** Einwegflasche f
nonsense n Unsinn m
non-smoker n Nichtraucher(in) m(f); **non-smoking** adj Nichtraucher-; **non-standard** adj nicht serienmäßig; **nonstop 1.** adj (train) durchgehend; (flight) Nonstop- **2.** adv (travel) ununterbrochen; (fly) ohne Zwischenlandung
noodles npl Nudeln pl
noon n Mittag m; **at ~** um 12 Uhr mittags
no one pron niemand; (emphatic) keiner; **~ else** sonst niemand, kein anderer
nor conj **neither ... ~ ...** weder ... noch ...; **~ does he** ich rauche nicht, er auch nicht
normal adj normal; **get back to ~** sich wieder normalisieren; **normally** adv (usually) normalerweise
north 1. n Norden m; **to the ~ of** nördlich von **2.** adv (go, face) nach Norden **3.** adj Nord-; **North America** n Nordamerika nt; **northbound** adj (in) Richtung Norden; **northeast 1.** n Nordosten m; **to the ~ of** nordöstlich von **2.** adv (go, face) nach Nordosten **3.** adj Nordost-; **northern** adj nördlich; **~ France** Nordfrank-

reich nt; **Northern Ireland** n Nordirland nt; **North Pole** n Nordpol m; **North Sea** n Nordsee f; **northwards** adv nach Norden; **northwest 1.** n Nordwesten m; **to the ~ of** nordwestlich von **2.** adv (go, face) nach Nordwesten **3.** adj Nordwest-

Norway n Norwegen nt; **Norwegian 1.** adj norwegisch **2.** n (person) Norweger(in) m(f); (language) Norwegisch nt

nose n Nase f; **nosebleed** n Nasenbluten nt; **nose-dive** n Sturzflug m

nosey → **nosy**

nostril n Nasenloch nt

nosy adj neugierig

not adv nicht; **~ one of them** kein einziger von ihnen; **I told him ~ to (do it)** ich sagte ihm, er solle es nicht tun; **~ at all** überhaupt nicht, keineswegs; (don't mention it) gern geschehen; **~ yet** noch nicht

notable adj bemerkenswert; **note 1.** n (written) Notiz f; (short letter) paar Zeilen pl; (comment in book etc) Anmerkung f; (bank-) Schein m; MUS (sign) Note f; (sound) Ton m; **make a ~ of sth** sich dat etw notieren; (of lecture etc) Aufzeichnungen pl; **take ~s** sich dat Notizen machen (of über + acc) **2.** vt (notice) bemerken (that dass); (write down) notieren;

notebook n Notizbuch nt; IT Notebook nt; **notepad** n Notizblock m; **notepaper** n Briefpapier nt

nothing n nichts; **~ but ...** lauter ...; **for ~** umsonst; **he thinks ~ of it** er macht sich nichts daraus

notice 1. n (announcement) Bekanntmachung f; (on ~ board) Anschlag m; (attention) Beachtung f; (advance warning) Ankündigung f; (to leave job, flat etc) Kündigung f; **at short ~** kurzfristig; **until further ~** bis auf weiteres; **give sb ~** jdm kündigen; **hand in one's ~** kündigen; **take (no) ~ of (sth)** etw (nicht) beachten **2.** vt bemerken; **noticeable** adj erkennbar; (visible) sichtbar; **be ~** auffallen; **notice board** n Anschlagtafel f

notification n Benachrichtigung f (of von); **notify** vt benachrichtigen (of von)

notorious adj berüchtigt

nought n Null f

noun n Substantiv nt

novel 1. n Roman m **2.** adj neuartig; **novelty** n Neuheit f

November n November m; → **September**

novice n Neuling m

now adv (at the moment) jetzt; (introductory phrase) also; **right ~** jetzt gleich; **just ~** gerade; **by ~** inzwischen; **from**

~ **on** ab jetzt; ~ **and again** (or **then**) ab und zu; nowadays *adv* heutzutage

nowhere *adv* nirgends; **we're getting** ~ wir kommen nicht weiter; ~ **near** noch lange nicht

nozzle *n* Düse *f*

nuclear *adj* (*energy etc*) Kern-; ~ **power station** Kernkraftwerk *nt*

nude 1. *adj* nackt **2.** *n* (*person*) Nackte(r) *mf*; (*painting etc*) Akt *m*; **nudist** *n* Nudist(in) *m(f)*, FKK-Anhänger(in) *m(f)*; **nudist beach** *n* FKK-Strand *m*

nuisance *n* Ärgernis *nt*; (*person*) Plage *f*; **what a** ~ wie ärgerlich!

numb 1. *adj* taub, gefühllos **2.** *vt* betäuben

number 1. *n* Nummer *f*; MATH Zahl *f*; (*quantity*) (An)zahl *f*; **in small/large** ~**s** in kleinen/großen Mengen; **a** ~ **of times** mehrmals **2.** *vt* (*give a number to*) nummerieren; (*count*) zählen (*among* zu); **his days are** ~**ed** seine Tage sind gezählt; **number plate** *n* (*Brit*) AUTO Nummernschild *nt*

numeral *n* Ziffer *f*; **numerical** *adj* numerisch; (*superiority*) zahlenmäßig; **numerous**

adj zahlreich

nun *n* Nonne *f*

Nuremberg *n* Nürnberg *nt*

nurse 1. *n* Krankenschwester *f*; (*male* ~) Krankenpfleger *m* **2.** *vt* (*patient*) pflegen; (*baby*) stillen; **nursery** *n* Kinderzimmer *nt*; (*for plants*) Gärtnerei *f*; (*tree*) Baumschule *f*; **nursery rhyme** *n* Kinderreim *m*; **nursery school** *n* Kindergarten *m*; ~ **teacher** Kindergärtner(in) *m(f)*, Erzieher(in) *m(f)*; **nursing** *n* (*profession*) Krankenpflege *f*; ~ **home** *n* Privatklinik *f*

nut *n* Nuss *f*; TECH (*for bolt*) Mutter *f*; **nutcase** *n* *fam* Spinner(in) *m(f)*; **nutcracker** *n*, **nutcrackers** *npl* Nussknacker *m*

nutmeg *n* Muskat *m*, Muskatnuss *f*

nutrition *n* Ernährung *f*; **nutritious** *adj* nahrhaft

nuts *fam* **1.** *adj* verrückt; **be** ~ **about sth** nach etw verrückt sein **2.** *npl* (*testicles*) Eier *pl*

nutshell *n* Nussschale *f*; **in a** ~ kurz gesagt

nutter *n* *fam* Spinner(in) *m(f)*; **nutty** *adj* verrückt

nylon® **1.** *n* Nylon® *nt* **2.** *adj* Nylon-

O

O *n* TEL Null *f*

oak 1. *n* Eiche *f* **2.** *adj* Eichen-

OAP *abbr* = **old-age pensioner**; Rentner(in) *m(f)*

oar *n* Ruder *nt*

oasis *n* Oase *f*

oath *n* (*statement*) Eid *m*

oats *npl* Hafer *m*; GASTR Haferflocken *pl*

obedience *n* Gehorsam *m*; **obedient** *adj* gehorsam; **obey** *vt, vi* gehorchen + *dat*

object 1. *n* Gegenstand *m*; (*abstract*) Objekt *nt*; (*purpose*) Ziel *nt* **2.** *vi* dagegen sein; (*raise objection*) Einwände erheben (*to* gegen); (*morally*) Anstoß nehmen (*to* an + *dat*); **do you ~ to my smoking?** haben Sie etwas dagegen, wenn ich rauche?; **objection** *n* Einwand *m*

objective 1. *n* Ziel *nt* **2.** *adj* objektiv; **objectivity** *n* Objektivität *f*

obligation *n* (*duty*) Pflicht *f*; (*commitment*) Verpflichtung *f*; **no ~** unverbindlich; **obligatory** *adj* obligatorisch; **oblige** *vt* **~ sb to do sth** jdn (dazu) zwingen, etw zu tun; **he felt ~d to accept the offer** er fühlte sich verpflichtet, das Angebot anzunehmen

oblong 1. *n* Rechteck *nt* **2.** *adj* rechteckig

oboe *n* Oboe *f*

obscene *adj* obszön

observation *n* (*watching*) Beobachtung *f*; (*remark*) Bemerkung *f*; **observe** *vt* (*notice*) bemerken; (*watch*) beobachten; (*customs*) einhalten

obsessed *adj* besessen (*with an idea etc* von einem Gedanken etc); **obsession** *n* Manie *f*

obsolete *adj* veraltet

obstacle *n* Hindernis *nt* (*to* für)

obstinate *adj* hartnäckig

obstruct *vt* versperren; (*pipe*) verstopfen; (*hinder*) behindern, aufhalten; **obstruction** *n* Blockierung *f*; (*of pipe*) Verstopfung *f*; (*obstacle*) Hindernis *nt*

obtain *vt* erhalten; **obtainable** *adj* erhältlich

obvious *adj* offensichtlich; **it was ~ to me that ...** es war mir klar, dass ...; **obviously** *adv* offensichtlich

occasion *n* Gelegenheit *f*; (*special event*) (großes) Ereignis; **on the ~ of** anlässlich + *gen*; **special ~** besonderer Anlass; **occasional, occasionally** *adj, adv* gelegentlich

occupant *n* (*of house*) Bewohner(in) *m(f)*; (*of vehicle*) Insasse *m*, Insassin *f*; **occupation** *n* Beruf *m*; (*pastime*) Beschäftigung *f*; (*of country etc*) Besetzung *f*; **occupied** *adj* (*country, seat, toilet*) besetzt; (*person*) beschäftigt; **keep sb/oneself ~** jdn/sich beschäftigen; **occupy** *vt* (*country*) besetzen; (*time*) beanspruchen; (*mind, person*) beschäftigen

occur *vi* vorkommen; **~ to sb** jdm einfallen

ocean *n* Ozean *m*; (*US, sea*) das Meer *nt*

o'clock *adv* **5 ~** 5 Uhr; **at 10 ~** um 10 Uhr

octagon *n* Achteck *nt*

October *n* Oktober *m*; → **September**

octopus *n* Tintenfisch *m*

odd *adj* (*strange*) sonderbar; (*not even*) ungerade; (*one missing*) einzeln; **be the ~ one out** nicht dazugehören; **odds** *npl* Chancen *pl*; **against all ~** entgegen allen Erwartungen

odometer *n* (*US*) AUTO Meilenzähler *m*

odor (*US*), **odour** *n* Geruch *m*

of *prep gen* von; (*material, origin*) aus; **the name ~ the hotel** der Name des Hotels; **the works ~ Shakespeare** Shakespeares Werke; **a friend ~ mine** ein Freund von mir; **the fourth ~ June**

der vierte Juni; (*quantity*) **a glass ~ water** ein Glas Wasser; **a litre ~ wine** ein Liter Wein; **a girl ~ ten** ein zehnjähriges Mädchen; (*US, in time*) **it's five ~ three** es ist fünf vor drei; (*cause*) **die ~ cancer** an Krebs sterben

off 1. *adv* (*away*) weg, fort; (*free*) frei; (*switch*) ausgeschaltet; (*milk*) sauer; **a mile ~** eine Meile entfernt; **I'll be ~ now** ich gehe jetzt; **have the day/Monday ~** heute/Montag freihaben; **the lights are ~** die Lichter sind aus; **the concert is ~** das Konzert fällt aus; **I got 10% ~** ich habe 10% Nachlass bekommen **2.** *prep* (*away from*) von; **jump/fall ~ the roof** vom Dach springen/fallen; **get ~ the bus** aus dem Bus aussteigen; **he's ~ work/school** er hat frei/schulfrei; **take £20 ~ the price** den Preis um 20 Pfund herabsetzen

offence *n* (*crime*) Straftat *f*; (*minor*) Vergehen *nt*; (*to feelings*) Kränkung *f*; **cause/take ~** Anstoß erregen/nehmen; **offend** *vt* kränken; (*eye, ear*) beleidigen; **offender** *n* Straffällige(r) *mf*; **offense** (*US*) → **offence**; **offensive 1.** *adj* anstößig; (*insulting*) beleidigend; (*smell*) übel, abstoßend **2.** *n* MIL Offensive *f*

on

offer 1. n Angebot nt; **on ~** COMM im Angebot **2.** vt anbieten (*to sb* jdm); (*money, a chance etc*) bieten

offhand 1. adj lässig **2.** adv (*say*) auf Anhieb

office n Büro nt; (*position*) Amt nt; **doctor's ~** (*US*) Arztpraxis f; **office block** n Bürogebäude nt; **office hours** npl Dienstzeit f; (*notice*) Geschäftszeiten pl; **officer** n MIL Offizier(in) m(f); (*official*) Polizeibeamte(r) m, Polizeibeamtin f; **office worker** n Büroangestellte(r) mf; **official 1.** adj offiziell; (*report etc*) amtlich; **~ language** Amtssprache f **2.** n Beamte(r) m, Beamtin f, Repräsentant(in) m(f)

off-licence n (*Brit*) Wein- und Spirituosenhandlung f; **off-line** adj IT offline; **off-peak** adj außerhalb der Stoßzeiten; (*rate, ticket*) verbilligt; **off-putting** adj, abstoßend; **off-season** adj außerhalb der Saison

offshore adj küstennah, Küsten-; (*oil rig*) im Meer; **offside** n AUTO Fahrerseite f; SPORT Abseits nt

often adv oft; **every so ~** von Zeit zu Zeit

oil 1. n Öl nt **2.** vt ölen; **oil level** n Ölstand m; **oil painting** n Ölgemälde nt; **oil-rig** n (Öl)bohrinsel f; **oil slick** n Ölteppich m; **oil tanker** n

Öltanker m; (*truck*) Tankwagen m; **oily** adj ölig; (*skin, hair*) fettig

ointment n Salbe f

OK, okay adj fam okay, in Ordnung; **that's ~ by** (or **with**) **me** das ist mir recht

old adj alt; **old age** n Alter nt; **~ pensioner** Rentner(in) m(f); **old-fashioned** adj altmodisch; **old people's home** n Altersheim nt

olive n Olive f; **olive oil** n Olivenöl nt

Olympic adj olympisch; **the ~ Games, the ~s** pl die Olympischen Spiele pl, die Olympiade

omelette n Omelett nt

omit vt auslassen

on 1. prep (*position*) auf + dat; (*with motion*) auf + acc; (*vertical surface, day*) an + dat; (*with motion*) an + acc; **it's ~ the table** es ist auf dem Tisch; **hang it ~ the wall** häng es an die Wand; **I haven't got it ~ me** ich habe es nicht bei mir; **~ TV** im Fernsehen; **~ the left** links; **~ the right** rechts; **~ the train/ bus** im Zug/Bus; **~ the twelfth** am zwölften; **~ Sunday** am Sonntag; **~ Sundays** sonntags **2.** adj, adv (*light etc*) TV, ELEC an; **what's ~ at the cinema?** was läuft im Kino?; **I've nothing ~** (*nothing arranged*) ich habe nichts vor; (*no clothes*) ich habe nichts an; *leave the light* ~ das Licht brennen lassen

once 1. *adv* (*one time, in the past*) einmal; *at* ~ sofort; (*at the same time*) gleichzeitig; ~ *more* noch einmal; *for* ~ ausnahmsweise (einmal); ~ *in a while* ab und zu mal **2.** *conj* wenn ... einmal; *you've got used to it* sobald Sie sich daran gewöhnt haben

oncoming *adj* entgegenkommend; ~ *traffic* Gegenverkehr *m*

one 1. *num* eins **2.** *adj* ein, eine, ein; (*only*) einzige(r, s); ~ *day* eines Tages; *the* ~ *and only* ~ der/die unvergleichliche ... **3.** *pron* eine(r, s); (*people, you*) man; *the* ~ *who/that* ... der(jenige), der/die(jenige), das/das(jenige), das ...; *this* ~, *that* ~ dieser/diese/dieses; *the blue* ~ der/die/das Blaue; *which* ~? welcher/welche/welches?; ~ *another* einander; **one-off 1.** *adj* einmalig **2.** *n* a ~ etwas Einmaliges; **one-parent family** *n* Einelternfamilie *f*; **one-piece** *adj* einteilig; **oneself** *pron* (*reflexive*) sich; *cut* ~ sich schneiden; **one-way** *adj* ~ *street* Einbahnstraße *f*; ~ *ticket* (*US*) einfache Fahrkarte

onion *n* Zwiebel *f*

on-line *adj* IT online; ~ *banking* Homebanking *nt*

only 1. *adv* nur; (*with time*) erst; ~ *yesterday* erst gestern; *he's* ~ *four* er ist erst vier; ~ *just arrived* gerade erst angekommen **2.** *adj* einzige(r, s); ~ *child* Einzelkind *nt*

o.n.o. *abbr* = *or nearest offer*; VB

onside *adv* SPORT nicht im Abseits

onto *prep* auf + *acc*; (*vertical surface*) an + *acc*

onwards *adv* voran, vorwärts; *from today* ~ von heute an, ab heute

opaque *adj* undurchsichtig

open 1. *adj* offen; *in the* ~ *air* im Freien; ~ *to the public* für die Öffentlichkeit zugänglich; *the shop is* ~ *all day* das Geschäft hat den ganzen Tag offen **2.** *vt* öffnen, aufmachen; (*meeting, account, new building*) eröffnen; (*road*) dem Verkehr übergeben **3.** *vi* (*door, window etc*) aufgehen, sich öffnen; (*shop, bank*) öffnen, aufmachen; (*begin*) anfangen (*with* mit); **open day** *n* Tag *m* der offenen Tür; **opening** *n* Öffnung *f*; (*beginning*) Anfang *m*; (*official, of exhibition etc*) Eröffnung *f*; ~ *hours* (*or times*) Öffnungszeiten *pl*; **openly** *adv* offen; **open-minded** *adj* aufgeschlossen; **open-**

-plan *adj* ~ **office** Groß-
raumbüro *nt*

opera *n* Oper *f*; **opera glasses** *npl* Opernglas *nt*; **opera
house** *n* Oper *f*, Opernhaus
nt

operate 1. *vt* (*machine*) bedienen; (*brakes, lights*) betätigen 2. *vi* (*machine*) laufen;
(*bus etc*) verkehren (*between
zwischen*); ~ (**on sb**) MED
(jdn) operieren; **operating
theatre** *n* Operationssaal
m; **operation** *n* (*of machine*)
Bedienung *f* (*on an* + *dat*);
(*undertaking*) Unternehmen *nt*; **in** ~ (*machine*) in Betrieb; **have an**
~ operiert werden (*for wegen*)

opinion *n* Meinung *f* (*on* zu);
in my ~ meiner Meinung
nach

opponent *n* Gegner(in) *m(f)*

opportunity *n* Gelegenheit *f*

oppose *vt* sich widersetzen
+ *dat*; (*idea*) ablehnen; opposed *adj* **be** ~ **to sth** gegen
etw sein; **as** ~ **to** im Gegensatz zu; **opposing** *adj* (*team*)
gegnerisch; (*points of view*)
entgegengesetzt

opposite 1. *adj* (*house*) gegen-
überliegend; (*direction*) entgegengesetzt; **the** ~ **sex** das
andere Geschlecht 2. *adv* gegenüber 3. *prep* gegenüber;
~ **me** mir gegenüber 4. *n* Gegenteil *nt*

opposition *n* Widerstand *m*

(*to* gegen); POL Opposition *f*

oppress *vt* unterdrücken

opt *vi* ~ **for sth** sich für etw
entscheiden

optician *n* Optiker(in) *m(f)*

optimist *n* Optimist(in) *m(f)*;
optimistic *adj* optimistisch

optimum *adj* optimal

option *n* Möglichkeit *f*, COMM
Option *f*; **have no** ~ keine
Wahl haben; **optional** *adj*
freiwillig; ~ **extras** AUTO Extras *pl*

or *conj* oder; (*otherwise*)
sonst; **hurry up,** ~ (**else**) **we'll
be late** beeil dich, sonst
kommen wir zu spät

oral 1. *adj* mündlich; ~ **sex**
Oralverkehr *m* 2. *n* (*exam*)
Mündliche(s) *nt*

orange 1. *n* Orange *f* 2. *adj*
orangefarben; **orange juice**
n Orangensaft *m*

orbit 1. *n* Umlaufbahn *f* 2. *vt*
umkreisen

orchard *n* Obstgarten *m*

orchestra *n* Orchester *nt*;
(*US*) THEAT Parkett *nt*

orchid *n* Orchidee *f*

ordeal *n* Tortur *f*; (*emotional*)
Qual *f*

order 1. *n* (*sequence*) Reihenfolge *f*; (*good arrangement*)
Ordnung *f*; (*command*) Befehl *m*; LAW Anordnung *f*;
(*condition*) Zustand *m*, Bestellung *f*; **out of** ~ (*not func-
tioning*) außer Betrieb; (*unsuitable*) nicht angebracht;
in ~ (*items*) richtig geordnet

(all right) in Ordnung; **in ~ to do sth** um etw zu tun **2.** vt *(arrange)* ordnen; *(command)* befehlen; **~ sb to do sth** jdm befehlen, etw zu tun; *(food, product)* bestellen; **order form** n Bestellschein m

ordinary adj gewöhnlich, normal

ore n Erz nt

organ n MUS Orgel f; ANAT Organ nt

organic adj organisch; *(farming, vegetables)* Bio-, Öko-; **~ farmer** Biobauer m, Biobäuerin f; **~ food** Biokost f

organization n Organisation f; *(arrangement)* Ordnung f; **organize** vt organisieren; **organizer** n (elektronisches) Notizbuch

orgasm n Orgasmus m

oriental adj orientalisch

orientation n Orientierung f

origin n Ursprung m; *(of person)* Herkunft f; **original 1.** adj *(first)* ursprünglich; *(painting)* original; *(idea)* originell **2.** n Original nt; **originally** adv ursprünglich

Orkneys npl, **Orkney Islands** npl Orkneyinseln pl

ornamental adj dekorativ

orphan n Waise f, Waisenkind nt; **orphanage** n Waisenhaus nt

orthodox adj orthodox

orthopaedic, **orthopedic** *(US)* adj orthopädisch

ostrich n ZOOL Strauß m

other adj, pron andere(r, s); **any ~ questions?** sonst noch Fragen?; **the ~ day** neulich; **every ~ day** jeden zweiten Tag; *(someone)* **some-one/something or ~** irgend jemand/irgend etwas; **otherwise** adv sonst; *(differently)* anders

OTT adj abbr = **over the top**; übertrieben

otter n Otter m

ought vt *(obligation)* sollte; *(probability)* dürfte; *(stronger)* müsste; **you ~ to do that** Sie sollten das tun; **that ~ to do** das müsste *(or* dürfte) reichen

ounce n Unze f *(28,35 g)*

our adj unser; **ours** pron unsere(r, s); **this is ~** das gehört uns; **a friend of ~** ein Freund von uns; **ourselves** pron *(reflexive)* uns; **we enjoyed ~** wir haben uns amüsiert; **we've got the house to ~** wir haben das Haus für uns; *(emphatic)* **we did it ~** wir haben es selbst gemacht; *(all)* **by ~** allein

out adv hinaus/heraus; *(not indoors)* draußen; *(not at home)* nicht zu Hause; *(not alight)* aus; *(unconscious)* bewusstlos; *(published)* herausgekommen; *(results)* bekannt gegeben; **have you been ~ yet?** waren Sie schon draußen?; **I was ~ when they called** ich war nicht da, als

oval

sie vorbeikamen; *be ~ and about* unterwegs sein; *the fire is ~* das Feuer ist ausgegangen

outback n *(in Australia) the ~* das Hinterland

outboard adj *~ motor* Außenbordmotor m

outbreak n Ausbruch m

outcome n Ergebnis nt

outcry n *(public protest)* Protestwelle f *(against* gegen)

outdo irr vt übertreffen

outdoor adj Außen-; SPORT im Freien; *~ swimming pool* Freibad nt; **outdoors** adv draußen, im Freien

outer adj äußere(r, s); **outer space** n Weltraum m

outfit n Ausrüstung f; *(clothes)* Kleidung f

outgoing adj kontaktfreudig

outgrow irr vt *(clothes)* herauswachsen aus

outing n Ausflug m

outlet n Auslass m, Abfluss m; *(US)* Steckdose f; *(shop)* Verkaufsstelle f

outline n Umriss m; *(summary)* Abriss m

outlive vt überleben

outlook n Aussicht(en) f(pl); *(attitude)* Einstellung f *(on* zu)

outnumber vt zahlenmäßig überlegen sein + dat; *~ed* zahlenmäßig unterlegen

out of prep *(motion, motive, origin)* aus; *(position, away from)* außerhalb + gen; *~*

danger/ sight/ breath außer Gefahr/ Sicht/ Atem; *made ~ wood* aus Holz gemacht; *we are ~ bread* wir haben kein Brot mehr; **out-of-date** adj veraltet; **out-of-the-way** adj abgelegen

outpatient n ambulanter Patient, ambulante Patientin

output n Produktion f; *(of engine)* Leistung f; IT Ausgabe f

outrage n *(great anger)* Empörung f *(at* über); *(wicked deed)* Schandtat f; *(crime)* Verbrechen nt; *(indecency)* Skandal m; **outrageous** adj unerhört; *(clothes, behaviour etc)* unmöglich, schrill

outright 1. adv *(killed)* sofort **2.** adj total; *(denial)* völlig; *(winner)* unbestritten

outside 1. n Außenseite f; *on the ~* außen **2.** adj äußere(r, s), Außen-; *(chance)* sehr gering **3.** adv außen; *go ~* nach draußen gehen **4.** prep außerhalb + gen; **outsider** n Außenseiter(in) m(f)

outsize adj übergroß; *(clothes)* in Übergröße

outskirts npl *(of town)* Stadtrand m

outstanding adj hervorragend; *(debts etc)* ausstehend

outward adj äußere(r, s); *~ journey* Hinfahrt f; **outwardly** adv nach außen hin; **outwards** adv nach außen

oval adj oval

ovary n Eierstock m

ovation n Ovation f, Applaus m

oven n Backofen m; **ovenproof** adj feuerfest

over 1. prep (position) über + dat; (motion) über + acc; **they spent a long time ~** sie haben lange dazu gebraucht; **from all ~ England** aus ganz England; **~ £20** mehr als 20 Pfund; **~ the phone/radio** am Telefon/im Radio; **talk ~ a glass of wine** sich bei einem Glas Wein unterhalten; **~ the summer** während des Sommers **2.** adv (across) hinüber/herüber; (finished) vorbei; (match, play etc) zu Ende; (left) übrig; **~ there/in America** da drüben/drüben in Amerika; **~ to you** Sie sind dran; **it's (all) ~ between us** es ist aus zwischen uns; **~ and ~ again** immer wieder; **start (all) ~ again** noch einmal von vorn anfangen; **children of 8 and ~** Kinder von 8 Jahren und darüber

over- pref über-

overall 1. n (Brit) Kittel m **2.** adj (situation) allgemein; (length) Gesamt-; **~ majority** absolute Mehrheit **3.** adv insgesamt; **overalls** npl Overall m

overboard adv über Bord

overbooked adj überbucht

overcharge vt zu viel verlangen von

overcome irr vt überwinden; **~ by sleep/emotion** von Schlaf/Rührung übermannt

overcooked adj zu lange gekocht; (meat) zu lange gebraten

overcrowded adj überfüllt

overdo irr vt übertreiben; **you're ~ing it** du übertreibst es; **overdone** adj übertrieben; (food) zu lange gekocht; (meat) zu lange gebraten

overdose n Überdosis f

overdraft n Kontoüberziehung f; **overdrawn** adj überzogen

overdue adj überfällig

overestimate vt überschätzen

overexpose vt PHOT überbelichten

overflow vi überlaufen

overhead 1. adj AVIAT **~ locker** Gepäckfach nt; **~ projector** Overheadprojektor m; **~ railway** Hochbahn f **2.** adv oben

overhear irr vt zufällig mit anhören

overheat vi (engine) heiß laufen

overjoyed adj überglücklich (at über)

overland 1. adj Überland- **2.** adv (travel) über Land

overlap vi (dates etc) sich überschneiden; (objects) sich teilweise decken

overload vt überladen

overlook vt (view from above)

überblicken; (*not notice*) übersehen; (*pardon*) hinwegsehen über + *acc*

overnight 1. *adj* (*journey, train*) Nacht-; **~ bag** Reisetasche *f*; **~ stay** Übernachtung *f* **2.** *adv* über Nacht

overpass *n* Überführung *f*

overpay *vt* überbezahlen

overrule *vt* verwerfen; (*decision*) aufheben

overseas 1. *adj* Übersee-; *fam* Auslands-; **~ students** Studenten aus Übersee **2.** *adv* (*go*) nach Übersee; (*live, work*) in Übersee

oversee *irr vt* beaufsichtigen

overshadow *vt* überschatten

oversight *n* Versehen *nt*

oversimplify *vt* zu sehr vereinfachen

oversleep *irr vi* verschlafen

overtake *irr vt, vi* überholen

overtime *n* Überstunden *pl*

overturn *vt, vi* umkippen

overweight *adj* **be ~** Übergewicht haben

overwhelm *vt* überwältigen; **overwhelming** *adj* überwäl-

tigend

overwork 1. *n* Überarbeitung *f* **2.** *vi* sich überarbeiten; **overworked** *adj* überarbeitet

owe *vt* schulden; **~ sth to sb** (*money*) jdm etw schulden; (*favour etc*) jdm etw verdanken; **how much do I ~ you?** was bin ich Ihnen schuldig?; **owing to** *prep* wegen + *gen*

owl *n* Eule *f*

own 1. *vt* besitzen **2.** *adj* eigen; **on one's ~** allein; **he has a flat of his ~** er hat eine eigene Wohung; **~ owner** *n* Besitzer(in) *m(f)*; (*of business*) Inhaber(in) *m(f)*; **ownership** *n* Besitz *m*; **under new ~** unter neuer Leitung

ox *n* Ochse *m*; **oxtail** *n* Ochsenschwanz *m*; **~ soup** Ochsenschwanzsuppe *f*

oxygen *n* Sauerstoff *m*

oyster *n* Auster *f*

oz *abbr* = **ounces**, Unzen *pl*

Oz *n fam* Australien *nt*

ozone *n* Ozon *nt*; **~ layer** Ozonschicht *f*

P

p 1. *abbr* = **page**; S. **2.** *n abbr* = **penny, pence**

p.a. *abbr* = **per annum**

pace 1. *n* (*speed*) Tempo *nt*; (*step*) Schritt *m*; **pacemaker** *n* MED Schrittmacher *m*

Pacific *n* **the ~** (**Ocean**) der

Pazifik

pacifier *n* (*US, for baby*) Schnuller *m*

pack 1. *n* (*of cards*) Spiel *nt*; (*esp US, of cigarettes*) Schachtel *f*; (*gang*) Bande *f*; (*US, backpack*) Rucksack *m* **2.** *vt* (*case*) packen; (*clothes*) einpacken **3.** *vi* (*for holiday*) packen; **pack in** *vt* (*Brit*) *fam* (*job*) hinschmeißen; **package** *n* Paket *nt*; **package deal** *n* Pauschalangebot *nt*; **package holiday, package tour** *n* Pauschalreise *f*; **packaging** *n* (*material*) Verpackung *f*; **packed lunch** *n* (*Brit*) Lunchpaket *nt*; **packet** *n* Päckchen *nt*; (*of cigarettes*) Schachtel *f*

pad *n* (*of paper*) Schreibblock *m*; (*padding*) Polster *nt*; **padded envelope** *n* wattierter Umschlag; **padding** *n* (*material*) Polsterung *f*

paddle 1. *n* (*for boat*) Paddel *nt* **2.** *vi* (*in boat*) paddeln; **paddling pool** *n* (*Brit*) Planschbecken *nt*

padlock *n* Vorhängeschloss *nt*

page *n* (*of book etc*) Seite *f*

pager *n* Piepser *m*

paid 1. *pt, pp* of **pay 2.** *adj* bezahlt

pain *n* Schmerz *m*; **be in ~** Schmerzen haben; **she's a** (*real*) **~** sie nervt; **painful** *adj* (*physically*) schmerzhaft; **painkiller** *n* schmerzstillendes Mittel

painstaking *adj* sorgfältig

paint 1. *n* Farbe *f* **2.** *vt* anstreichen; (*picture*) malen; **paintbrush** *n* Pinsel *m*; **painter** *n* Maler(in) *m(f)*; **painting** *n* (*picture*) Bild *nt*, Gemälde *n*

pair *n* Paar *nt*; **a ~ of shoes** ein Paar Schuhe; **a ~ of scissors** eine Schere; **a ~ of trousers** eine Hose

pajamas *npl* (*US*) Schlafanzug *m*

Pakistan *n* Pakistan *nt*

pal *n* *fam* Kumpel *m*

palace *n* Palast *m*

pale *adj* (*face*) blass, bleich; (*colour*) hell

palm (*of hand*) Handfläche *f*; **~** (*tree*) Palme *f*; **palmtop** (computer) *n* Palmtop(computer) *m*

pamper *vt* verhätscheln

pan *n* (*saucepan*) Topf *m*; (*frying pan*) Pfanne *f*; **pancake** *n* Pfannkuchen *m*; **Pancake Day** *n* (*Brit*) Fastnachtsdienstag *m*

panda *n* Panda *m*

pane *n* Scheibe *f*

panel *n* (*of wood*) Tafel *f*; (*in discussion*) Diskussionsteilnehmer *m*

panic 1. *n* Panik *f* **2.** *vi* in Panik geraten; **panicky** *adj* panisch

pansy *n* (*flower*) Stiefmütterchen *nt*

panties *npl* (Damen)slip *m*

pantomime *n* (*Brit*) um die Weihnachtszeit aufgeführte Märchenkomödie

pants *npl* Unterhose *f*; (*esp US, trousers*) Hose *f*

pantyhose *npl* (*US*) Strumpfhose *f*; **panty-liner** *n* Slipeinlage *f*

paper 1. *n* Papier *nt*; (*newspa-*

per) Zeitung f; (exam) Klausur f; (for reading at conference) Referat nt; ~s pl (identity papers) Papiere pl; ~ bag Papiertüte f; ~ cup Pappbecher m 2. vt (wall) tapezieren; paperback n Taschenbuch nt; paper clip n Büroklammer f; paper feed n (of printer) Papiereinzug m; paperwork n Schreibarbeit f
parachute 1. n Fallschirm m 2. vi abspringen
paracetamol n (tablet) Paracetamoltablette f
parade 1. n (procession) Umzug m; MIL Parade f 2. vi vorbeimarschieren
paradise n Paradies nt
paragliding n Gleitschirmfliegen nt
paragraph n Absatz m
parallel 1. adj parallel 2. n MATH Parallele f
paralyze vt lähmen; fig lahm legen
paranoid adj paranoid
paraphrase vt umschreiben; (sth spoken) anders ausdrücken
parasailing n Parasailing nt
parasol n Sonnenschirm m
parcel n Paket m
pardon n LAW Begnadigung f; ~ me/ I beg your ~ verzeihen Sie bitte; (objection) aber ich bitte Sie; I beg your ~?/~ me? wie bitte?
parent n Elternteil m; ~s pl Eltern pl; ~s-in-law pl

Schwiegereltern pl; parental adj elterlich, Eltern-
parish n Gemeinde f
park 1. n Park m 2. vt, vi parken; parking n Parken nt; 'no ~' „Parken verboten"; parking brake n (US) Handbremse f; parking disc n Parkscheibe f; parking fine n Geldbuße f für falsches Parken; parking lights npl (US) Standlicht nt; parking lot n (US) Parkplatz m; parking meter n Parkuhr f; parking place n, parking space n Parkplatz m; parking ticket n Strafzettel m
parliament n Parlament nt
parrot n Papagei m
parsley n Petersilie f
parsnip n Pastinake f (längliches, weißes Wurzelgemüse)
part 1. n Teil m; (of machine) Teil nt; THEAT Rolle f; (US, in hair) Scheitel m; take ~ teilnehmen (in an + dat); for the most ~ zum größten Teil 2. adj Teil- 3. vt (separate) trennen; (hair) scheiteln 4. vi (people) sich trennen
partial adj (incomplete) teilweise, Teil-; (biased) parteiisch
participant n Teilnehmer(in) m(f); participate vi teilnehmen (in an + dat)
particular 1. adj (specific) bestimmt; (exact) genau; (fussy) eigen; in ~ insbeson-

dere 2. n ~s pl (details) Einzelheiten pl; (about person) Personalien pl; **particularly** adv besonders

parting n (farewell) Abschied m; (Brit, in hair) Scheitel m

partly adv teilweise

partner n Partner(in) m(f); **partnership** n Partnerschaft f

partridge n Rebhuhn nt

part-time 1. adj Teilzeit- 2. adv **work ~** Teilzeit arbeiten

party 1. n (celebration) Party f; POL, LAW Partei f; (group) Gruppe f 2. vi feiern

pass 1. n (on foot) vorbeigehen an + dat; (in car etc) vorbeifahren an + dat; (time) verbringen; (exam) bestehen; (law) verabschieden; **~ sth to sb**, **~ sb sth** jdm etw reichen; **~ the ball to sb** jdm den Ball zuspielen 2. vi (on foot) vorbeigehen; (in car etc) vorbeifahren; (years) vergehen; (in exam) bestehen 3. n (document) Ausweis m; SPORT Pass m; **pass away** vi (die) verscheiden; **pass by 1.** vi (on foot) vorbeigehen; (in car etc) vorbeifahren 2. vt (on foot) vorbeigehen an + dat; (in car etc) vorbeifahren an + dat; **pass on** vt weitergeben (to an + acc); (disease) übertragen (to auf + acc); **pass out** vi (faint) ohnmächtig werden; **pass round** vt he-

rumreichen

passage n (corridor) Gang m; (in book, music) Passage f; **passageway** n Durchgang m

passenger n Passagier(in) m(f); (on bus) Fahrgast m; (on train) Reisende(r) m(f); (in car) Mitfahrer(in) m(f)

passer-by n Passant(in) m(f)

passion n Leidenschaft f; **passionate** adj leidenschaftlich; **passion fruit** n Passionsfrucht f

passive 1. adj passiv 2. n **(voice)** LING Passiv nt

passport n (Reise)pass m; **passport control** n Passkontrolle f

password n IT Passwort nt

past 1. n Vergangenheit f 2. adv (by) vorbei; **it's five ~** es ist fünf nach 3. adj (years) vergangen; (president etc) ehemalig; **in the ~ two months** in den letzten zwei Monaten 4. prep (telling time) nach; **it's half ~ 10** es ist halb 11; **go ~ sth** an etw dat vorbeigehen/-fahren

pasta n Nudeln pl

paste 1. vt (stick) kleben; IT einfügen 2. n (glue) Kleister m

pastime n Zeitvertreib m

pastry n Teig m; (cake) Stückchen nt

pasty n (Brit) Pastete f

patch 1. n (area) Fleck m; (for mending) Flicken m 2. vt flicken

pâté n Pastete f

paternal adj väterlich; **~ grandmother** Großmutter f väterlicherseits; **paternity leave** n Elternzeit f (des Vaters)

path n a. ɪт Pfad m; a. fig Weg m

pathetic adj (bad) kläglich, erbärmlich; **it's ~** es ist zum Heulen

patience n Geduld f; (Brit,) Patience f; **patient 1.** adj geduldig **2.** n Patient(in) m(f)

patio n Terrasse f

patriotic adj patriotisch

patrol car n Streifenwagen m; **patrolman** n (US) Streifenpolizist m

patron n (sponsor) Förderer m, Förderin f; (in shop) Kunde m, Kundin f

patronize vt (treat condescendingly) von oben herab behandeln; **patronizing** adj (attitude) herablassend

pattern n Muster nt

pause 1. n Pause f **2.** vi (speaker) innehalten

pavement n (Brit) Bürgersteig m; (US) Pflaster nt

pay 1. vt bezahlen; **he paid (me) £20 for it** er hat (mir) 20 Pfund dafür gezahlt; **~ attention** Acht geben (to auf + acc); **~ sb a visit** jdn besuchen **2.** vi zahlen; (be profitable) sich bezahlt machen; **~ for sth** etw bezahlen **3.** n Be-

zahlung f, Lohn m; **pay back** vt (money) zurückzahlen; **pay in** vt (into account) einzahlen; **payable** adj zahlbar; (due) fällig; **payday** n Zahltag m; **payee** n Zahlungsempfänger(in) m(f); **payment** n Bezahlung f; (money) Zahlung f; **pay phone** n Münzfernsprecher m

PC 1. abbr = **personal computer**; PC m **2.** abbr = **politically correct**; politisch korrekt

PDA abbr = **personal digital assistant**; PDA m

PE abbr = **physical education**, ; Sport m

pea n Erbse f

peace n Frieden m; **peaceful** adj friedlich

peach n Pfirsich m

peacock n Pfau m

peak n (of mountain) Gipfel m; fig Höhepunkt m; **peak period** n Stoßzeit f; (season) Hochsaison f

peanut n Erdnuss f; **peanut butter** n Erdnussbutter f

pear n Birne f

pearl n Perle f

pebble n Kiesel m

pecan n Pekannuss f

peck vt, vi picken; **peckish** adj (Brit) fam ein bisschen hungrig

peculiar adj (odd) seltsam; **~ to** charakteristisch für; **peculiarity** n (singular quality) Besonderheit f; (strangeness)

Eigenartigkeit f

pedal n Pedal nt

pedestrian n Fußgänger(in) m(f); **pedestrian crossing** n Fußgängerüberweg m

pee vi fam pinkeln

peel 1. n Schale f 2. vt schälen 3. vi (paint etc) abblättern; (skin etc) sich schälen

peer 1. n Gleichaltrige(r) mf 2. vi starren

peg n (for coat etc) Haken m; (for tent) Hering m; (clothes) ~ (Wäsche)klammer f

pelvis n Becken nt

pen n (ball-point) Kuli m, Kugelschreiber m; (fountain pen) Füller m

penalize vt (punish) bestrafen; **penalty** n (punishment) Strafe f; (in soccer) Elfmeter m

pence pl of **penny**

pencil n Bleistift m; **pencil sharpener** n (Bleistift)spitzer m

penetrate vt durchdringen; (enter into) eindringen in + acc

penfriend n Brieffreund(in) m(f)

penguin n Pinguin m

penicillin n Penizillin nt

peninsula n Halbinsel f

penis n Penis m

penknife n Taschenmesser nt

penny n (Brit) Penny m; (US) Centstück nt

pension n Rente f; (for civil servants, executives etc) Pension f; **pensioner** n Rentner(in) m(f); **pension plan, pension scheme** n Rentenversicherung f

penultimate adj vorletzte(r, s)

people npl (persons) Leute pl; (von Staat) Volk nt; (inhabitants) Bevölkerung f; **people carrier** n Minivan m

pepper n Pfeffer m; (vegetable) Paprika m; **peppermint** n (sweet) Pfefferminz m

per prep pro; ~ **annum** pro Jahr; ~ **cent** Prozent m

percentage n Prozentsatz m

percolator n Kaffeemaschine f

percussion n MUS Schlagzeug nt

perfect 1. adj perfekt; (utter) völlig 2. vt vervollkommnen; **perfectly** adv perfekt; (utterly) völlig

perform 1. vt (task) ausführen; (play) aufführen; MED (operation) durchführen 2. vi THEAT auftreten; **performance** n (show) Vorstellung f; (efficiency) Leistung f

perfume n Duft m; (substance) Parfüm nt

perhaps adv vielleicht

peril n Gefahr f

period n (length of time) Zeit f; (in history) Zeitalter nt, Stunde f; MED Periode f; (US, full stop) Punkt m; **for a ~ of three years** für einen Zeitraum von drei Jahren;

periodical *n* Zeitschrift *f*
peripheral *n* IT Peripheriegerät *nt*
perish *vi* (*die*) umkommen; (*material*) verderben
perjury *n* Meineid *m*
perm *n* Dauerwelle *f*
permanent, permanently *adj, adv* ständig
permission *n* Erlaubnis *f*; permit **1.** *n* Genehmigung *f* **2.** *vt* erlauben, zulassen; ~ **sb to do sth** jdm erlauben, etw zu tun
persecute *vt* verfolgen
perseverance *n* Ausdauer *f*
Persian *adj* persisch
persist *vi* (*in belief etc*) bleiben (*in* bei); (*rain, smell*) andauern; persistent *adj* beharrlich
person *n* Mensch *m*; (*in official context*) Person *f*; **in** ~ persönlich; **personal** *adj* persönlich; (*private*) privat; personality *n* Persönlichkeit *f*; **personal organizer** *n* Organizer *m*; **personal stereo** *n* Walkman® *m*; personnel *n* Personal *nt*
perspective *n* Perspektive *f*
perspire *vi* schwitzen
persuade *vt* überreden; (*convince*) überzeugen; persuasive *adj* überzeugend
perverse *adj* pervers; (*obstinate*) eigensinnig; pervert **1.** *n* Perverse(r) *mf* **2.** *vt* (*morally*) verderben
pessimist *n* Pessimist(in

m(f)); pessimistic *adj* pessimistisch
pest *n* (*insect*) Schädling *m*; *fig* (*person*) Nervensäge *f*; (*thing*) Plage *f*; pester *vt* plagen; pesticide *n* Schädlingsbekämpfungsmittel *nt*
pet **1.** *n* (*animal*) Haustier *nt*; (*person*) Liebling *m*
petition *n* Petition *f*
petrol *n* (*Brit*) Benzin *nt*; **petrol pump** *n* (*at garage*) Zapfsäule *f*; **petrol station** *n* Tankstelle *f*; **petrol tank** *n* Benzintank *m*
pharmacy *n* (*shop*) Apotheke *f*
phase *n* Phase *f*
PhD *abbr* = **Doctor of Philosophy**; Dr. phil; (*dissertation*) Doktorarbeit *f*; **do one's** ~ promovieren
pheasant *n* Fasan *m*
phenomenon *n* Phänomen *nt*
Philippines *npl* Philippinen *pl*
philosophical *adj* philosophisch; *fig* gelassen; philosophy *n* Philosophie *f*
phone *n* **1.** *n* Telefon *nt* **2.** *vt, vi* anrufen; **phone book** *n* Telefonbuch *nt*; **phone bill** *n* Telefonrechnung *f*; **phone booth, phone box** (*Brit*) *n* Telefonzelle *f*; **phonecall** *n* Telefonanruf *m*; **phonecard** *n* Telefonkarte *f*; **phone number** *n* Telefonnummer *f*
photo *n* Foto *nt*; **photo booth** *n* Fotoautomat *m*; photo-

copier n Kopiergerät nt; **photocopy 1.** n Fotokopie f **2.** vt fotokopieren; **photograph 1.** n Fotografie f, Aufnahme f **2.** vt fotografieren; **photographer** n Fotograf(in) m(f); **photography** n Fotografie f

phrase n (expression) Redewendung f, Ausdruck m; **phrase book** n Sprachführer m

physical 1. adj (bodily) körperlich, physisch **2.** n ärztliche Untersuchung; **physically** adv (bodily) körperlich, physisch; **~ handicapped** körperbehindert

physician n Arzt m, Ärztin f

physics nsing Physik f

physiotherapy n Physiotherapie f

physique n Körperbau m

piano n Klavier m

pick vt (flowers, fruit) pflücken; (choose) auswählen; (team) aufstellen; **pick out** vt auswählen; **pick up** vt (lift up) aufheben; (collect) abholen; (learn) lernen

pickle 1. n (food) (Mixed) Pickles pl **2.** vt einlegen

pickpocket n Taschendieb(in) m(f)

picnic n Picknick nt

picture 1. n Bild nt; **go to the ~s** (Brit) ins Kino gehen **2.** vt (visualize) sich vorstellen; **picture book** n Bilderbuch nt; **picturesque** adj male-

risch

pie n (meat) Pastete f; (fruit) Kuchen m

piece n Stück nt; (part) Teil nt; (in chess) Figur f; (in draughts) Stein m; **a ~ of cake** ein Stück Kuchen; **fall to ~s** auseinanderfallen

pier n Pier m

pierce vt durchstechen, durchbohren; (cold, sound) durchdringen; **pierced** adj (part of body) gepierct; **piercing** adj durchdringend

pig n Schwein nt

pigeon n Taube f

piggy adj fam verfressen; **pigheaded** adj dickköpfig; **piglet** n Ferkel nt; **pigsty** n Schweinestall m; **pigtail** n Zopf m

pile n (heap) Haufen m; (one on top of another) Stapel m; **pile up** vi (accumulate) sich anhäufen

pile-up n AUTO Massenkarambolage f

pill n Tablette f; **the ~** die (Antibaby)pille; **be on the ~** die Pille nehmen

pillar n Pfeiler m

pillow n (Kopf)kissen nt; **pillowcase** n (Kopf)kissenbezug m

pilot n AVIAT Pilot(in) m(f)

pimple n Pickel m

pin 1. n (for fixing) Nadel f; (in sewing) Stecknadel f; TECH Stift m; **I've got ~s and needles in my leg** mein Bein ist mir eingeschlafen **2.** *vt* (*fix with pin*) heften (*to* an + *acc*)

PIN *acr* = **personal identification number**; **~** (**number**) PIN *f*, Geheimzahl *f*

pincers *npl* (*tool*) Kneifzange *f*

pinch 1. *n* (*of salt*) Prise *f* **2.** *vt* zwicken; *fam* (*steal*) klauen **3.** *vi* (*shoe*) drücken

pine *n* Kiefer *f*

pineapple *n* Ananas *f*

pink *adj* rosa

pint *n* Pint *nt* (*Brit: 0,57 l, US: 0,473l*); (*Brit, glass of beer*) Bier *nt*

pious *adj* fromm

pip *n* (*of fruit*) Kern *m*

pipe *n* (*for smoking*) Pfeife *f*; (*for water, gas*) Rohrleitung *f*

pirate *n* Pirat(in) *m(f)*; (*pirated copy* *n* Raubkopie *f*)

Pisces *nsing* ASTR Fische *pl*; **she's a ~** sie ist Fisch

piss 1. *vi vulg* pissen **2.** *n vulg* Pisse *f*; **take the ~ out of sb** jdn verarschen; **piss off** *vi vulg* sich verpissen; **pissed** *adj* (*Brit, fam, drunk*) sturzbesoffen; (*US, fam, annoyed*) stocksauer

pistachio *n* Pistazie *f*

piste *n*, Piste *f*

pistol *n* Pistole *f*

pit *n* (*hole*) Grube *f*; (*coalmine*) Zeche *f*; **the ~s** (*in motor racing*) die Box; **be the ~s** *fam* grottenschlecht sein

pitch 1. *n* SPORT Spielfeld *nt*; MUS (*of instrument*) Tonlage *f*; (*of voice*) Stimmlage *f* **2.** *vt* (*tent*) aufschlagen; (*throw*) werfen; **pitch-black** *adj* pechschwarz

pitcher *n* (*US, jug*) Krug *m*

pitiful *adj* (*contemptible*) jämmerlich

pitta bread *n* Pittabrot *nt*

pity 1. *n* Mitleid *nt*; **what a ~** wie schade; **it's a ~** es ist schade **2.** *vt* Mitleid haben mit

pizza *n* Pizza *f*

place 1. *n* (*spot, in text*) Stelle *f*; (*town etc*) Ort; (*house*) Haus *nt*; (*position, seat, on course*) Platz *m*; **~ of birth** Geburtsort *m*; **at my ~** bei mir; **in third ~** auf den dritten Platz; **out of ~** nicht an der richtigen Stelle; (*remark*) unangebracht; **in ~ of** anstelle von; **in the first ~** (*firstly*) erstens; (*immediately*) gleich; (*in any case*) überhaupt **2.** *vt* (*put*) stellen, setzen; (*lay flat*) legen; (*advertisement*) setzen (*in* in + *acc*); COMM (*order*) aufgeben; **place mat** *n* Set *nt*

plague *n* Pest *f*

plaice *n* Scholle *f*

plain 1. *adj* (*clear*) klar, deutlich; (*simple*) einfach; (*not beautiful*) unattraktiv; (*yoghurt*) Natur-; (*Brit, chocolate*) (Zart)bitter- **2.** *n* Ebene *f*; **plainly** *adv* (*frankly*) offen; (*simply*) einfach; (*obviously*) eindeutig plait 1. n Zopf m 2. vt flechten

plan 1. n Plan m; (for essay etc) Konzept nt 2. vt planen; ~ to do sth, ~ on doing sth vorhaben, etw zu tun 3. vi planen

plane n Pflanze f; (aircraft) Flugzeug nt; (tool) Hobel m; MATH Ebene f

planet n Planet m

plank n Brett nt

plant 1. n Pflanze f; (factory) Werk nt 2. vt (tree etc) pflanzen; plantation n Plantage f

plaque n Gedenktafel f; (on teeth) Zahnbelag m

plaster n (Brit) MED (sticking plaster) Pflaster nt; (on wall) Verputz m; to have one's arm in ~ den Arm in Gips haben

plastered adj fam besoffen; get (absolutely) ~ sich besaufen

plastic 1. n Kunststoff m; pay with ~ mit Kreditkarte bezahlen 2. adj Plastik-; plastic bag n Plastiktüte f; plastic surgery n plastische Chirurgie f

plate n (for food) Teller m; (flat sheet) Platte f; (plaque) Schild nt

platform n RAIL Bahnsteig m

platinum n Platin nt

play 1. n Spiel nt; THEAT (Theater)stück nt 2. vt spielen; (another player or team) spielen gegen; ~ the piano Klavier spielen 3. vi spielen; play at vt what are you

~ing at? was soll das?; play back vt abspielen; play down vt herunterspielen

playacting n Schauspielerei f; playback n Wiedergabe f; player n Spieler(in) m(f); playful adj (person) verspielt; (remark) scherzhaft; playground n Spielplatz m; (in school) Schulhof m; playgroup n Spielgruppe f; playing card n Spielkarte f; playing field n Sportplatz m; playmate n Spielkamerad(in) m(f); playwright n Dramatiker(in) m(f)

plc abbr = public limited company; AG f

plea n Bitte f (for um)

plead vi dringend bitten (with sb jdn); LAW ~ guilty sich schuldig bekennen

pleasant, pleasantly adj, adv angenehm

please 1. adv bitte; more tea? - yes, ~ noch Tee? - ja, bitte 2. vt (be agreeable to) gefallen + dat; ~ yourself wie du willst; pleased adj zufrieden; (glad) erfreut; ~ to meet you freut mich, angenehm; pleasing adj erfreulich; pleasure n Vergnügen nt, Freude f; it's a ~ gern geschehen

pledge 1. n (promise) Versprechen nt 2. vt (promise) versprechen

plenty 1. n ~ of eine Menge, viel(e); be ~ genug sein, reichen; **I've got ~** ich habe mehr als genug **2.** adv (US) fam ganz schön

plimsolls npl (Brit) Turnschuhe pl

plonk 1. n (Brit) fam (wine) billiger Wein **2.** vt **~ sth (down)** hin hinknallen

plot 1. n (of story) Handlung f; (conspiracy) Komplott nt; (of land) Stück nt Land, Grundstück nt **2.** vi ein Komplott schmieden

plough, plow (US) **1.** n Pflug m **2.** vt, vi AGR pflügen; **ploughman's lunch** n (Brit) in einer Kneipe serviertes Gericht aus Käse, Brot, Mixed Pickles etc

pluck vt (eyebrows, guitar) zupfen; (chicken) rupfen; **pluck up (one's) courage** Mut aufbringen

plug 1. n (for sink, bath) Stöpsel m; ELEC Stecker m; AUTO (Zünd)kerze f; (publicity) Schleichwerbung f **2.** vt fam (advertise) Reklame machen für; **plug in** vt anschließen

plum 1. n Pflaume f **2.** adj fam (job etc) Super-

plumber n Klempner(in) m(f)

plump adj rundlich

plunge 1. vt (knife) stoßen; (into water) tauchen **2.** vi stürzen; (into water) tauchen

plural n Plural m

plus 1. prep plus; (as well as) und **2.** adj Plus-; **20 ~** mehr

als 20 **3.** n fig Plus nt

plywood n Sperrholz nt

pm abbr = **post meridiem; at 3 ~** um 3 Uhr nachmittags; **at 8 ~** um 8 Uhr abends

pneumonia n Lungenentzündung f

poached adj (egg) pochiert, verloren

PO Box abbr = **post office box,** Postfach nt

pocket 1. n Tasche f **2.** vt (put in ~) einstecken; **pocketbook** n (US, wallet) Brieftasche f; **pocket calculator** n Taschenrechner m; **pocket money** n Taschengeld nt

poem n Gedicht nt; **poet** n Dichter(in) m(f); **poetic** adj poetisch; **poetry** n (art) Dichtung f; (poems) Gedichte pl

point 1. n Punkt m; (spot) Stelle f; (sharp tip) Spitze f; (moment) Zeitpunkt m; (purpose) Zweck m; (idea) Argument nt; (decimal) Dezimalstelle f; **~s** pl RAIL Weiche f; **~ of view** Standpunkt m; **three ~ two** drei Komma zwei; **at some ~** irgendwann (mal); **get to the ~** zur Sache kommen; **there's no ~** es hat keinen Sinn; **I was on the ~ of leaving** ich wollte gerade gehen **2.** vt (gun etc) richten (at auf + acc); **~ one's finger at** mit dem Finger zeigen auf + acc **3.** vi (with finger etc) zeigen (at, to auf + acc);

point out vt (*indicate*) aufzeigen; (*mention*) hinweisen auf + acc; **pointed** adj spitz; (*question*) gezielt; **pointer** n (*on dial*) Zeiger m; (*tip*) Hinweis m; **pointless** adj sinnlos

poison 1. n Gift nt **2.** vt vergiften; **poisonous** adj giftig

poke vt (*with stick, finger*) stoßen, stupsen; (*put*) stecken

Poland n Polen nt

polar adj Polar-, polar; **~ bear** Eisbär m

pole n Stange f; GEO, ELEC Pol m

Pole n Pole m, Polin f

pole vault n Stabhochsprung m

police n Polizei f; **police car** n Polizeiwagen m; **policeman** n Polizist m; **police station** n (Polizei)wache f; **policewoman** n Polizistin f

policy n (*plan*) Politik f; (*principle*) Grundsatz m; (*insurance policy*) (Versicherungs)police f

polio n Kinderlähmung f

polish 1. n (*for furniture*) Politur f; (*for floor*) Wachs nt; (*for shoes*) Creme f; (*shine*) Glanz m; fig Schliff m **2.** vt polieren; (*shoes*) putzen; fig den letzten Schliff geben + dat

Polish 1. adj polnisch **2.** n Polnisch nt

polite adj höflich; **politeness** n Höflichkeit f

political, politically adj, adv politisch; **~ly correct** politisch korrekt; **politician** n Politiker(in) m(f); **politics** nsing or pl Politik f

poll n (*election*) Wahl f; (*opinion poll*) Umfrage f

pollen n Pollen m, Blütenstaub m; **pollen count** n Pollenflug m

polling station n Wahllokal nt

pollute vt verschmutzen; **pollution** n Verschmutzung f

pompous adj aufgeblasen; (*language*) geschwollen

pond n Teich m

ponder vt nachdenken über + acc

pony n Pony nt; **ponytail** n Pferdeschwanz m

pool 1. n (*swimming pool*) Schwimmbad nt; (*private*) Swimmingpool m; (*game*) Poolbillard nt **2.** vt (*money etc*) zusammenlegen

poor 1. adj arm; (*not good*) schlecht **2.** npl **the ~** die Armen pl; **poorly 1.** adv (*badly*) schlecht **2.** adj (*Brit*) krank

pop 1. n (*music*) Pop m; (*noise*) Knall m **2.** vt (*put*) stecken; (*balloon*) platzen lassen **3.** vi (*balloon*) platzen; (*cork*) knallen; **~ in** (*person*) vorbeischauen; **popcorn** n Popcorn nt

Pope n Papst m

poppy n Mohn m

Popsicle® n (*US*) Eis nt am

Stiel

popular adj (well-liked) beliebt (with bei); (widespread) weit verbreitet

population n Bevölkerung f; (of town) Einwohner pl

porcelain n Porzellan nt

porch n Vorbau m; (US, verandah) Veranda f

porcupine n Stachelschwein nt

pork n Schweinefleisch nt; **pork chop** n Schweinekotelett nt; **pork pie** n Schweinefleischpastete f

porn n Porno m; **pornographic** adj pornografisch; **pornography** n Pornografie f

porridge n Haferbrei m

port n (harbour) Hafen m; NAUT (left side) Backbord nt; (wine) Portwein m; IT Anschluss m

portable adj tragbar; (radio) Koffer-

portal n IT Portal nt

porter n Pförtner(in) m(f); (for luggage) Gepäckträger m

porthole n Bullauge nt

portion n Teil m; (of food) Portion f

portrait n Porträt nt

Portugal n Portugal nt; **Portuguese 1.** adj portugiesisch **2.** n Portugiese m, Portugiesin f; (language) Portugiesisch nt

pose 1. n Haltung f **2.** vi posieren **3.** vt (threat, problem)

darstellen

posh adj fam piekfein

position 1. n Stellung f; (place) Position f, Lage f; (job) Stelle f; (opinion) Standpunkt m; **be in a ~ to do sth** in der Lage sein, etw zu tun **2.** vt aufstellen; IT (cursor) positionieren

positive adj positiv; (convinced) sicher; (definite) eindeutig

possess vt besitzen; **possession** n ~(s pl) Besitz m

possibility n Möglichkeit f; **possible** adj möglich; **if ~** wenn möglich; **as big/ soon as ~** so groß/bald wie möglich; **possibly** adv (perhaps) vielleicht; **I've done all I can** ich habe mein Möglichstes getan

post 1. n (mail) Post f; (pole) Pfosten m; (job) Stelle f **2.** vt (letters) aufgeben; **keep sb ~ed** jdn auf dem Laufenden halten; **postage** n Porto nt; **postal** adj Post-; **postbox** n Briefkasten m; **postcard** n Postkarte f; **postcode** n (Brit) Postleitzahl f

poster n Plakat nt, Poster m

postgraduate n jmd, der nach dem seine Studien nach dem ersten akademischen Grad weiterführt

postman n Briefträger m; **postmark** n Poststempel m

postmortem n Autopsie f

post office n Post® f; **post of-**

fice box n Postfach nt

postpone vt verschieben (till auf + acc)

posture n Haltung f

pot 1. n Topf m; (teapot, coffee pot) Kanne f **2.** vt (plant) eintopfen

potato n Kartoffel f

potential 1. adj potenziell **2.** n Potenzial nt; **potentially** adv potenziell

pottery n (objects) Töpferwaren pl

potty 1. adj (Brit) fam verrückt **2.** n Töpfchen nt

poultry n Geflügel nt

pound 1. n (money) Pfund nt; (weight) Pfund nt (0,454 kg); **a ~ of cherries** ein Pfund Kirschen; **ten~ note** Zehnpfundschein m

pour 1. n (liquid) gießen; (rice, sugar etc) schütten; **~ sb sth** (drink) jdm etw eingießen; **pouring** adj (rain) strömend

poverty n Armut f

powder n Pulver nt; (cosmetic) Puder m; **powder room** n Damentoilette f

power 1. n Macht f; (ability) Fähigkeit f; (strength) Stärke f; ELEC Strom m; **be in ~** an der Macht sein **2.** vt betreiben, antreiben; **power-assisted steering** n Servolenkung f; **power cut** n Stromausfall m; **powerful** adj (politician etc) mächtig; (engine, government) stark; (argument) durchschlagend; pow-

erless adj machtlos; **power station** n Kraftwerk nt

p&p abbr = **postage and packing**

PR 1. abbr = **public relations 2.** abbr = **proportional representation**

practical, practically adj, adv praktisch; **practice 1.** n (training) Übung f; (custom) Gewohnheit f; (doctor's, lawyer's) Praxis f; **in ~** (in reality) in der Praxis; **out of ~** außer Übung; **put sth into ~** etw in die Praxis umsetzen **2.** vt, vi (US) → **practise**; **practise 1.** vt (instrument, movement) üben; (profession) ausüben **2.** vi üben; (doctor, lawyer) praktizieren

Prague n Prag nt

praise 1. n Lob nt **2.** vt loben

pram n (Brit) Kinderwagen m

prawn n Garnele f, Krabbe f; **prawn crackers** npl Krabbenchips pl

pray vi beten; **prayer** n Gebet nt

pre- pref vor-, prä-

preach vi predigen

precaution n Vorsichtsmaßnahme f

precede vt vorausgehen + dat; **preceding** adj vorhergehend

precinct n (Brit, pedestrian precinct) Fußgängerzone f; (Brit, shopping precinct) Einkaufsviertel nt; (US, district) Bezirk m

precious adj kostbar; ~ **stone** Edelstein m

précis n Zusammenfassung f

precise, precisely adj, adv genau

precondition n Vorbedingung f

predecessor n Vorgänger(in) m(f)

predict vt voraussagen; **predictable** adj vorhersehbar; (person) berechenbar

predominant adj vorherrschend; **predominantly** adv überwiegend

preface n Vorwort nt

prefer vt vorziehen (to dat), lieber mögen (to als); ~ **to do sth** etw lieber tun; **preferably** adv vorzugsweise, am liebsten; **preference** n (liking) Vorliebe f; **preferential** adj **get** ~ **treatment** bevorzugt behandelt werden

prefix n (US) TEL Vorwahl f

pregnancy n Schwangerschaft f; **pregnant** adj schwanger; **two months** ~ im zweiten Monat schwanger

prejudice n Vorurteil nt; **prejudiced** adj (person) voreingenommen

preliminary adj (measures) vorbereitend; (results) vorläufig; (remarks) einleitend

premature adj vorzeitig; (hasty) voreilig

premiere n Premiere f

premises npl (offices) Räumlichkeiten pl; (of factory, school) Gelände nt

premium-rate adj TEL zum Höchsttarif

preoccupied adj **be** ~ **with sth** mit etw sehr beschäftigt sein

prepaid adj vorausbezahlt; (envelope) frankiert

preparation n Vorbereitung f; **prepare 1.** vt vorbereiten (for auf + acc); (food) zubereiten; **be** ~ **to do sth** bereit sein, etw zu tun **2.** vi sich vorbereiten (for auf + acc)

prerequisite n Voraussetzung f

prescribe vt vorschreiben; MED verschreiben; **prescription** n Rezept nt

presence n Gegenwart f; **present 1.** adj (in attendance) anwesend (at bei); (current) gegenwärtig; ~ **tense** Gegenwart f, Präsens nt **2.** n Gegenwart f; (gift) Geschenk nt; **at** ~ zurzeit **3.** vt TV, RADIO präsentieren; (problem) darstellen; (report etc) vorlegen; **present-day** adj heutig; **presently** adv bald; (at present) zurzeit

preservative n Konservierungsmittel nt; **preserve** vt erhalten; (food) einmachen, konservieren

president n Präsident(in) m(f); **presidential** adj Präsidenten-; (election) Präsidentschafts-

press 1. n (newspapers, machine) Presse f **2.** vt (push) drücken; **~ a button** auf einen Knopf drücken **3.** vi (push) drücken; **pressing** adj dringend; **press-stud** n Druckknopf m; **press-up** n (Brit) Liegestütz m; **pressure** n Druck m; **be under ~** unter Druck stehen; **put ~ on sb** jdn unter Druck setzen; **pressure cooker** n Schnellkochtopf m; **pressurize** vt (person) unter Druck setzen

presumably adv vermutlich; **presume** vt, vi annehmen

presumptuous adj anmaßend

presuppose vt voraussetzen

pretend 1. vt **~ that** so tun als ob; **~ to do sth** vorgeben, etw zu tun **2.** vi **she's ~ing** sie tut nur so

pretentious adj anmaßend; (person) wichtigtuerisch

pretty 1. adj hübsch **2.** adv ziemlich

prevent vt verhindern; **~ sb from doing sth** jdn daran hindern, etw zu tun

preview n FILM Voraufführung f; (trailer) Vorschau f

previous, previously adj, adv früher

prey n Beute f

price 1. n Preis m **2.** vt **it's ~d at £10** es ist mit 10 Pfund ausgezeichnet; **priceless** adj unbezahlbar; **price list** n Preisliste f; **price tag** n Preisschild nt

prick 1. n Stich m; vulg (penis) Schwanz m; vulg (person) Arsch m **2.** vt stechen in + acc; **~ one's finger** sich dat in den Finger stechen; **prickly** adj stachelig

pride 1. n Stolz m; (arrogance) Hochmut m **2.** vt **~ oneself on sth** auf etw acc stolz sein

priest n Priester m

primarily adv vorwiegend; **primary** adj Haupt-; **~ school** Grundschule f

prime 1. adj Haupt-; (excellent) erstklassig **2.** n **in one's ~** in den besten Jahren; **prime minister** n Premierminister(in) m(f); **prime time** n TV Hauptsendezeit f

primitive adj primitiv

prince n Prinz m; (ruler) Fürst m; **princess** n Prinzessin f; (wife of ruler) Fürstin f

principal 1. adj Haupt-, wichtigste(r, s) **2.** n, Rektor(in) m(f)

principle n Prinzip nt; **in ~** im Prinzip; **on ~** aus Prinzip

print 1. n (picture) Druck m; PHOT Abzug m; (made by feet, fingers) Abdruck m; **out of ~** vergriffen **2.** vt drucken; (photo) abziehen; **print out** vt IT ausdrucken; **printed matter** n Drucksache f; **printer** n Drucker m; **printout** n IT Ausdruck m

prior adj früher; **a ~ engage-**

ment eine vorher getroffene Verabredung

priority *n* (*thing having precedence*) Priorität *f*

prison *n* Gefängnis *nt*; **prisoner** *n* Gefangene(r) *mf*

privacy *n* Privatleben *nt*; **private 1.** *adj* privat; (*confidential*) vertraulich **2.** *n* einfacher Soldat; **in ~** privat; (*confidentially*) vertraulich; **privatize** *vt* privatisieren

privilege *n* Privileg *nt*; **privileged** *adj* privilegiert

prize *n* Preis *m*; **prize money** *n* Preisgeld *nt*; **prizewinner** *n* Gewinner(in) *m(f)*; **prizewinning** *adj* preisgekrönt

pro *n* (*professional*) Profi *m*; **the ~s and cons** *pl* das Für und Wider

pro- *pref* pro-

probability *n* Wahrscheinlichkeit *f*; **probable, probably** *adj*, *adv* wahrscheinlich

probation *n* Probezeit *f*; LAW Bewährung *f*

probe 1. *n* (*investigation*) Untersuchung *f* **2.** *vt* untersuchen

problem *n* Problem *nt*; **no ~** kein Problem!

procedure *n* Verfahren *nt*

proceed 1. *vi* (*continue*) fortfahren; (*set about sth*) vorgehen **2.** *vt* **~ to do sth** anfangen, etw zu tun; **proceedings** *npl* LAW Verfahren *nt*; **proceeds** *npl* Erlös *m*

process 1. *n* Prozess *m*, Vorgang *m*; (*method*) Verfahren *nt* **2.** *vt* (*application etc*) bearbeiten; (*food, data*) verarbeiten; (*film*) entwickeln

procession *n* Umzug *m*

processor *n* IT Prozessor *m*; GASTR Küchenmaschine *f*

produce 1. *n* AGR Produkte *pl*, Erzeugnisse *pl* **2.** *vt* (*manufacture*) herstellen, produzieren; (*on farm*) erzeugen; (*film*, *play*, *record*) produzieren; (*cause*) hervorrufen; **producer** *n* (*manufacturer*) Hersteller(in) *m(f)*; (*of film, play, record*) Produzent(in) *m(f)*; **product** *n* Produkt *nt*, Erzeugnis *nt*; **production** *n* Produktion *f*; THEAT Inszenierung *f*; **productive** *adj* produktiv; (*land*) ertragreich

prof *n* *fam* Professor(in) *m(f)*

profession *n* Beruf *m*; **professional 1.** *n* Profi *m* **2.** *adj* beruflich; (*expert*) fachlich; (*sportsman, actor etc*) Berufs-

professor *n* Professor(in) *m(f)*; (*US, lecturer*) Dozent(in) *m(f)*

proficient *adj* kompetent (*in* in + *dat*)

profile *n* Profil *nt*; **keep a low ~** sich rar machen

profit 1. *n* Gewinn *m* **2.** *vi* profitieren (*by*, *from* von); **profitable** *adj* rentabel

profound *adj* tief; (*idea, thinker*) tiefgründig; (*knowl-*

edge) profund

program 1. *n* IT Programm *nt*;
(*US*) → **programme** 2. *vt* IT
programmieren; (*US*) →
programme

programme 1. *n* Programm
nt; TV, RADIO Sendung *f* 2.
vt programmieren; **programmer** *n* Programmie-
rer(in) *m(f)*; **programming**
n IT Programmieren *nt*; ~
language Programmier-
sprache *f*

progress 1. *n* Fortschritt *m*;
make ~ Fortschritte machen
2. *vi* (*work, illness etc*) fort-
schreiten; (*improve*) Fortschritte machen; **progressive** *adj* (*person, policy*) fortschrittlich; **progressively**
adv zunehmend

prohibit *vt* verbieten

project *n* Projekt *nt*

prolong *vt* verlängern

prom *n* (*at seaside*) Promenade *f*; (*Brit, concert*) Konzert
nt (*bei dem ein Großteil
des Publikums im Parkett
Stehplätze hat*); (*US, dance*)
Ball für die Schüler und Studenten von Highschools oder
Colleges

prominent *adj* (*politician, actor etc*) prominent; (*easily
seen*) auffallend

promiscuous *adj* promisk

promise 1. *n* Versprechen *nt*
2. *vt* versprechen; ~ **sb sth**
jdm etw versprechen; ~ **to
do sth** versprechen, etw zu

tun 3. *vi* versprechen; **promising** *adj* viel versprechend

promote *vt* (*in rank*) befördern; (*help on*) fördern;
COMM werben für; **promo-
tion** *n* (*in rank*) Beförderung
f; COMM Werbung *f* (*of* für)

prompt 1. *adj* prompt; (*punctual*) pünktlich 2. *adv* **at two
o'clock** ~ Punkt zwei Uhr 3.
vt THEAT (*actor*) soufflieren
+ *dat*

prone *adj* **be** ~ **to sth** zu etw
neigen

pronounce *vt* (*word*) aussprechen; **pronunciation** *n*
Aussprache *f*

proof *n* Beweis *m*; (*of alcohol*)
Alkoholgehalt *m*

prop 1. *n* Stütze *f*; THEAT Re-
quisit *nt* 2. *vt* ~ **sth against
sth** etw gegen etw lehnen;
prop up *vt* stützen; *fig* unterstützen

proper *adj* richtig; (*morally
correct*) anständig

property *n* (*possession*) Eigentum *nt*; (*characteristic*)
Eigenschaft *f*

proportion *n* Verhältnis *nt*;
(*share*) Teil *m*; ~**s** *pl* (*size*)
Proportionen *pl*; **in** ~ **to** im
Verhältnis zu; **proportional**
adj proportional; ~ **representation** Verhältniswahl-
recht *nt*

proposal *n* Vorschlag *m*; ~ (**of
marriage**) (Heirats)antrag
m; **propose** 1. *vt* vorschlagen
2. *vi* (*offer marriage*) einen

Heiratsantrag machen (*to sb* jdm)

proprietor *n* Besitzer(in) *m(f)*; (*of pub, hotel*) Inhaber(in) *m(f)*

prose *n* Prosa *f*

prosecute *vt* verfolgen (*for* wegen)

prospect *n* Aussicht *f*

prosperity *n* Wohlstand *m*; **prosperous** *adj* wohlhabend; (*business*) gut gehend

prostitute *n* Prostituierte(r) *mf*

protect *vt* schützen (*from, against* vor + *dat,* gegen); **protection** *n* Schutz *m* (*from, against* vor + *dat,* gegen); **protective** *adj* schützend; (*clothing etc*) Schutz-

protein *n* Protein *nt,* Eiweiß *nt*

protest 1. *n* Protest *m*; (*demonstration*) Protestkundgebung *f* **2.** *vi* protestieren (*against* gegen); (*demonstrate*) demonstrieren

Protestant 1. *adj* protestantisch **2.** *n* Protestant(in) *m(f)*

proud, proudly *adj, adv* stolz (*of* auf + *acc*)

prove *vt* beweisen; (*turn out to be*) sich erweisen als

proverb *n* Sprichwort *nt*

provide *vt* zur Verfügung stellen; (*drinks, music etc*) sorgen für; (*person*) versorgen (*with* mit); **provide for** *vt* (*family etc*) sorgen für; **provided** *conj* ~ (**that**) vorausge-

setzt, dass; **provider** *n* IT Provider *m*

provision *n* (*condition*) Bestimmung *f;* **~s** *pl* (*food*) Proviant *m*

provoke *vt* provozieren; (*cause*) hervorrufen

proximity *n* Nähe *f*

prudent *adj* klug; (*person*) umsichtig

prudish *adj* prüde

prune *n* Backpflaume *f* **2.** *vt* (*tree etc*) zurechtstutzen

PS *abbr* = **postscript**; PS *nt*

pseudo *adj* pseudo-, Pseudo-; **pseudonym** *n* Pseudonym *nt*

psychiatric *adj* psychiatrisch; (*illness*) psychisch; **psychiatrist** *n* Psychiater(in) *m(f)*; **psychiatry** *n* Psychiatrie *f;* **psychic** *adj* übersinnlich; **I'm not ~** ich kann keine Gedanken lesen; **psychoanalysis** *n* Psychoanalyse *f;* **psychoanalyst** *n* Psychoanalytiker(in) *m(f)*; **psychological** *adj* psychologisch; **psychology** *n* Psychologie *f;* **psychopath** *n* Psychopath(in) *m(f)*

pto *abbr* = **please turn over**; b.w.

pub *n* (*Brit*) Kneipe *f*

puberty *n* Pubertät *f*

public 1. *n the* (**general**) ~ die (breite) Öffentlichkeit; **in ~** in der Öffentlichkeit **2.** *adj* öffentlich; (*relating to the state*) Staats- *f;* **~ conveni-**

ence (*Brit*) öffentliche Toilette; ~ *holiday* gesetzlicher Feiertag; ~ *opinion* die öffentliche Meinung; ~ *relations pl* Öffentlichkeitsarbeit f; Public Relations *pl*; ~ *school* (*Brit*) Privatschule f; **publication** *n* Veröffentlichung f; **publicity** *n* Publicity f; (*advertisements*) Werbung f; **publish** *vt* veröffentlichen; **publisher** *n* Verleger(in) *m(f)*; (*company*) Verlag *m*; **publishing** *n* Verlagswesen *nt*

pudding *n* (*course*) Nachtisch *m*

puddle *n* Pfütze f

puff *vi* (*pant*) schnaufen

puffin *n* Papageientaucher *m*

puff paste (*US*), **puff pastry** *n* Blätterteig *m*

pull 1. *n* Ziehen *nt*; **give sth a ~** an etw *dat* ziehen **2.** *vt* (*cart, tooth*) ziehen; (*rope, handle*) ziehen an + *dat*; *fam* (*date*) abschleppen; ~ *a muscle* sich *dat* einen Muskel zerren; ~ *sb's leg* jdn auf den Arm nehmen **3.** *vi* ziehen; **pull apart** *vt* (*separate*) auseinander ziehen; **pull down** *vt* (*blind*) herunterziehen; (*house*) abreißen; **pull in** *vi* hineinfahren; (*stop*) anhalten; **pull off** *vt* (*clothes*) ausziehen; (*deal etc*) zuwege bringen; **pull on** *vt* (*clothes*) anziehen; **pull out 1.** *vi* (*car from lane*) aus-

scheren; (*train*) abfahren; (*withdraw*) aussteigen (*of aus*) **2.** *vt* herausziehen; (*tooth*) ziehen; (*troops*) abziehen; **pull up 1.** *vt* (*raise*) hochziehen; (*chair*) heranziehen **2.** *vi* anhalten

pullover *n* Pullover *m*

pulp *n* Brei *m*; (*of fruit*) Fruchtfleisch *nt*

pulpit *n* Kanzel f

pulse *n* Puls *m*

pump *n* Pumpe f; (*in petrol station*) Zapfsäule f; **pump up** *vt* (*tyre etc*) aufpumpen

pumpkin *n* Kürbis *m*

pun *n* Wortspiel *nt*

punch 1. *n* (*blow*) (Faust-)schlag *m*; (*tool*) Locher *m*; (*hot drink*) Punsch *m*; (*cold drink*) Bowle f **2.** *vt* (*strike*) schlagen; (*ticket, paper*) lochen

punctual, punctually *adj, adv* pünktlich

punctuation *n* Interpunktion f; **punctuation mark** *n* Satzzeichen *nt*

puncture *n* (*flat tyre*) Reifenpanne f

punish *vt* bestrafen; **punishment** *n* Strafe f; (*action*) Bestrafung f

pupil *n*, Schüler(in) *m(f)*

puppet *n* Puppe f; (*string puppet*) Marionette f

puppy *n* junger Hund

purchase 1. *n* Kauf *m* **2.** *vt* kaufen

pure *adj* rein; (*clean*) sauber;

(*utter*) pur; **purely** *adv* rein;
purify *vt* reinigen; **purity** *n*
Reinheit *f*

purple *adj* violett

purpose *n* Zweck *m*; (*of person*) Absicht *f*; **on ~** absichtlich

purr *vi* (*cat*) schnurren

purse *n* Geldbeutel *m*; (*US, handbag*) Handtasche *f*

pursue *vt* (*person, car*) verfolgen; (*hobby, studies*) nachgehen + *dat*

pus *n* Eiter *m*

push 1. *n* Stoß *m* **2.** *vt* (*person*) stoßen; (*car, chair etc*) schieben; (*button*) drücken; (*drugs*) dealen **3.** *vi* (*in crowd*) drängeln; **push in** *vi* (*in queue*) sich vordrängeln; **push off** *vi fam* (*leave*) abhauen; **push on** *vi* (*with job*) weitermachen; **push up** *vt* (*prices*) hochtreiben; **pushchair** *n* (*Brit*) Sportwagen *m*; **pusher** *n* (*of drugs*) Dealer(in) *m(f)*; **push-up** *n* (*US*) Liegestütz *m*; **pushy** *adj fam* aufdringlich, penetrant

put *vt* tun; (*upright*) stellen; (*flat*) legen; (*express*) ausdrücken; (*write*) schreiben; **he ~ his hand in his pocket** er steckte die Hand in die Tasche; **he ~ his hand on her shoulder** er legte ihr die Hand auf die Schulter; **~ money into one's account** Geld auf sein Konto einzah-

len; **put aside** *vt* (*money*) zurücklegen; **put away** *vt* (*tidy away*) wegräumen; **put back** *vt* zurücklegen; (*clock*) zurückstellen; **put down** *vt* (*in writing*) aufschreiben; (*Brit, animal*) einschläfern; (*rebellion*) niederschlagen; **put the phone down** (den Hörer) auflegen; **put one's name down for sth** sich für etw eintragen; **put forward** *vt* (*idea*) vorbringen; (*name*) vorschlagen; (*clock*) vorstellen; **put off** *vt* (*switch off*) ausschalten; (*postpone*) verschieben; **put sb off doing sth** jdn davon abbringen, etw zu tun; **put on** *vt* (*switch on*) anmachen; (*clothes*) anziehen; (*hat, glasses*) aufsetzen; (*make-up, CD*) auflegen; **put the kettle on** Wasser aufsetzen; **put weight on** zunehmen; **put out** *vt* (*hand, foot*) ausstrecken; (*light, cigarette*) ausmachen; **put up** *vt* (*picture*) aufhängen; (*tent*) aufstellen; (*building*) errichten; (*price*) erhöhen; (*person*) unterbringen; **~ with** sich abfinden mit; **I won't ~ with it** das lasse ich mir nicht gefallen

putt *vt, vi* SPORT putten

puzzle 1. *n* Rätsel *nt*; (*toy*) Geduldsspiel *nt*; (*jigsaw*) ~ Puzzle *nt* **2.** *vt* vor ein Rätsel stellen; **it ~s me** es ist mir ein

Rätsel; **puzzling** adj rätselhaft
pyjamas npl Schlafanzug m

pylon n Mast m
pyramid n Pyramide f

Q

quack vi quaken
quaint adj (idea, tradition) kurios; (picturesque) malerisch
qualification n (for job) Qualifikation f; (from school, university) Abschluss m; **qualified** adj (for job) qualifiziert; **qualify 1.** vt (limit) einschränken; **be qualified to do sth** berechtigt sein, etw zu tun **2.** vi (finish training) seine Ausbildung abschließen; SPORT sich qualifizieren
quality n Qualität f; (characteristic) Eigenschaft f
quantity n Menge f, Quantität f
quarantine n Quarantäne f
quarrel 1. n Streit m **2.** vi sich streiten; **quarrelsome** adj streitsüchtig
quarter 1. n (fourth) (of year) Vierteljahr nt; (US, coin) Vierteldollar m; **a ~ of an hour** eine Viertelstunde **2.** vt vierteln
quarter final n Viertelfinale nt
quartet n Quartett nt
quay n Kai m
queen n Königin f; (in cards, chess) Dame f

queer 1. adj (strange) seltsam, sonderbar; pej (homosexual) schwul **2.** n pej Schwule(r) m
quench vt (thirst) löschen
query 1. n Frage f **2.** vt in Frage stellen; (bill) reklamieren
question 1. n Frage f; **that's out of the ~** das kommt nicht in Frage **2.** vt (person) befragen; (suspect) verhören; (express doubt about) bezweifeln; **questionable** adj zweifelhaft; (improper) fragwürdig; **question mark** n Fragezeichen nt; **questionnaire** n Fragebogen m
queue 1. n (Brit) Schlange f; **jump the ~** sich vordrängeln **2.** vi ~ (up) Schlange stehen
quibble vi kleinlich sein; (argue) streiten
quiche n Quiche f
quick adj schnell; (short) kurz; **be ~** mach schnell!; **quickly** adv schnell
quid n (Brit) fam Pfund nt
quiet 1. adj (not noisy) leise; (peaceful, calm) still, ruhig; **be ~** sei still!; **keep ~ about sth** etw acc nichts sagen **2.** n Stille f, Ruhe f; **quietly** adv leise; (calmly) ruhig
quilt n (Stepp)decke f

quit 1. vt (leave) verlassen; (job) aufgeben; ~ **doing sth** aufhören, etw zu tun 2. vi aufhören; (resign) kündigen

quite adv (fairly) ziemlich; (completely) ganz, völlig; **I don't ~ understand** ich verstehe das nicht ganz; ~ **a few** ziemlich viele; ~ **so** richtig!

quits adj **be ~ with sb** mit jdm quitt sein

quiver vi zittern

quiz n (competition) Quiz nt

quota n Anteil m; COMM, POL Quote f

quotation n Zitat nt; (price) Kostenvoranschlag m; quotation marks npl Anführungszeichen pl; quote 1. vt (text, author) zitieren; (price) nennen 2. n Zitat nt; (price) Kostenvoranschlag m; **in ~s** in Anführungszeichen

R

rabbi n Rabbiner m

rabbit n Kaninchen nt

rabies nsing Tollwut f

raccoon n Waschbär m

race 1. n (competition) Rennen nt; (people) Rasse f 2. vt um die Wette laufen/fahren 3. vi (rush) rennen; racecourse n Rennbahn f; racetrack n Rennbahn f

racial adj Rassen-; ~ **discrimination** Rassendiskriminierung f

racing n (horse) ~ Pferderennen nt; (motor) ~ Autorennen nt; racing car n Rennwagen m

racism n Rassismus m; racist 1. n Rassist(in) m(f) 2. adj rassistisch

rack 1. n Ständer m, Gestell nt 2. vt ~ **one's brains** sich dat den Kopf zerbrechen

racket n SPORT Schläger m;

(noise) Krach m

radar n Radar nt or m

radiation n (radioactive) Strahlung f

radiator n Heizkörper m; AUTO Kühler m

radical adj radikal

radio n Rundfunk m, Radio nt

radioactivity n Radioaktivität f

radio alarm n Radiowecker m; radio station n Rundfunkstation f

radiotherapy n Strahlenbehandlung f

radish n Radieschen nt

radius n Radius m; **within a five-mile** ~ im Umkreis von fünf Meilen (of um)

raffle n Tombola f; raffle ticket n Los nt

raft n Floß nt

rag n Lumpen m; (for cleaning) Lappen m

rage 1. n Wut f; **be all the ~** der letzte Schrei sein **2.** vi toben; (disease) wüten

raid 1. n Überfall m (on auf + acc); (by police) Razzia f (on gegen) **2.** vt (bank etc) überfallen; (by police) eine Razzia machen in + dat

rail n (on stairs, balcony etc) Geländer nt; (of ship) Reling f; RAIL Schiene f; **railcard** n (Brit) ≈ Bahncard® f; **railing** n Geländer nt; **~s** pl (fence) Zaun m; **railroad** n (US) Eisenbahn f; **railroad station** n (US) Bahnhof m; **railway** n (Brit) Eisenbahn f; **railway station** n Bahnhof m

rain 1. n Regen m **2.** vi regnen; **it's ~ing** es regnet; **rainbow** n Regenbogen m; **raincoat** n Regenmantel m; **rainforest** n Regenwald m; **rainy** adj regnerisch

raise 1. n (US, of wages / salary) Gehalts- / Lohnerhöhung f **2.** vt (lift) hochheben; (increase) erhöhen; (family) großziehen; (livestock) züchten; (money) aufbringen; (objection) erheben; **~ one's voice** (in anger) laut werden

raisin n Rosine f

rally 1. n POL Kundgebung f; AUTO Rallye f

RAM acr = **random access memory**; RAM m

ramble 1. n Wanderung f **2.** vi (walk) wandern; (talk) schwafeln

ramp n Rampe f

ran pt of **run**

ranch n Ranch f

rancid adj ranzig

random 1. adj willkürlich **2.** at ~ (choose) willkürlich; (fire) ziellos

randy adj (Brit) fam geil, scharf

rang pt of **ring**

range 1. n (selection) Auswahl f (of an + dat); COMM Sortiment nt (of an + dat); (of missile, telescope) Reichweite f; (of mountains) Kette f; **in this price ~** in dieser Preisklasse **2.** vi **~ from ... to ...** (temperature, sizes, prices) liegen zwischen ... und ...

rank 1. n Rang m; (social position) Stand m **2.** vt einstufen **3.** vi **~ among** zählen zu

ransom n Lösegeld nt

rap n MUS Rap m

rape 1. n Vergewaltigung f **2.** vt vergewaltigen

rapid, rapidly adj, adv schnell

rapist n Vergewaltiger m

rare adj selten, rar; (especially good) vortrefflich; (steak) blutig; **rarely** adv selten; **rarity** n Seltenheit f

rash 1. adj unbesonnen **2.** n MED (Haut)ausschlag m

rasher n ~ (of bacon) (Speck-) scheibe f

raspberry n Himbeere f

rat n Ratte f

rate 1. n (proportion, frequency) Rate f; (speed) Tempo nt;

~ **(of exchange)** (Wechsel-)kurs m; ~ **of interest** Zinssatz m; **at any** ~ auf jeden Fall 2. vt (evaluate) einschätzen (as als)

rather adv (in preference) lieber; (fairly) ziemlich; **I'd** ~ **stay here** ich würde lieber hier bleiben; **I'd** ~ **not** lieber nicht; **or** ~ (more accurately) vielmehr

ratio n Verhältnis nt

rational adj rational; **rationalize** vt rationalisieren

rattle 1. n (toy) Rassel f 2. vt (keys, coins) klimpern mit; (person) durcheinander bringen 2. vi (window) klappern; (bottles) klirren; rattle off vi herunterrasseln; **rattlesnake** n Klapperschlange f

rave 1. vi (talk wildly) fantasieren; (rage) toben; (enthuse) schwärmen (about von) 2. n (Brit, event) Raveparty f

raven n Rabe m

raving adv ~ **mad** total verrückt

ravishing adj hinreißend

raw adj (food) roh; (skin) wund; (climate) rau

ray n (of light) Strahl m; ~ **of hope** Hoffnungsschimmer m

razor n Rasierapparat m; **razor blade** n Rasierklinge f

Rd n abbr = **road**; Str.

re prep betreffs + gen

reach 1. n **within/out of** (sb's) ~ in/außer (jds)

Reichweite; **within easy** ~ **of the shops** nicht weit von den Geschäften 2. vt (arrive at, contact) erreichen; (come down/up as far as) reichen bis zu; (contact) **can you** ~ **it?** kommen Sie dran?; reach for vt greifen nach; reach out vi die Hand ausstrecken; ~ **for** greifen nach

react vi reagieren (to auf + acc); **reaction** n Reaktion f (to auf + acc); **reactor** n Reaktor m

read 1. vt lesen; (meter) ablesen; ~ **sth to sb** jdm vorlesen 2. vi lesen; ~ **to sb** jdm vorlesen; **it** ~**s well** es liest sich gut; **it** ~**s as follows** es lautet folgendermaßen; read out vt vorlesen; read through vt durchlesen; read up on vt nachlesen über + acc; **readable** adj (book) lesenswert; (handwriting) lesbar; **reader** n Leser(in) m(f)

readily adv (willingly) bereitwillig; ~ **available** leicht erhältlich

reading n (action) Lesen nt; (from meter) Zählerstand m; **reading glasses** npl Lesebrille f; **reading lamp** n Leselampe f; **reading matter** n Lektüre f

readjust 1. vt (mechanism etc) neu einstellen 2. vi sich wieder anpassen (to an + acc) ready *adj* fertig, bereit; **be ~ to do sth** (*willing*) bereit sein, etw zu tun; **are you ~ to go?** bist du so weit?; **get sth ~** etw fertig machen; **get** (**oneself**) **~** sich fertig machen; **ready cash** *n* Bargeld *nt*; **ready-made** *adj* (*product*) Fertig-; (*clothes*) Konfektions-; **~ meal** Fertiggericht *nt*

real **1.** *adj* wirklich; (*actual*) eigentlich; (*genuine*) echt; (*idiot etc*) richtig; **for ~** echt; **this time it's for ~** diesmal ist es ernst; **get ~** sei realistisch! **2.** *adv fam* (*esp US*) echt

real estate *n* Immobilien *pl*

realistic, realistically *adj, adv* realistisch; reality *n* Wirklichkeit *f*; **in ~** in Wirklichkeit; realization *n* (*awareness*) Erkenntnis *f*; realize *vt* (*understand*) begreifen; (*plan, idea*) realisieren; **I ~d** (**that**) ... mir wurde klar, dass ...

really *adv* wirklich

real time *n* IT **in ~** in Echtzeit

realtor *n* (*US*) Grundstücksmakler(in) *m(f)*

reappear *vi* wieder erscheinen

rear **1.** *adj* hintere(r,s), Hinter- **2.** *n* (*of building, vehicle*) hinterer Teil; **at the ~ of** hinter + *dat*; (*inside*) hinten in + *dat*; **rear light** *n* AUTO Rücklicht *nt*

rearm *vi* wieder aufrüsten

rearrange *vt* (*furniture, system*) umstellen; (*meeting*) verlegen (**for** auf + *acc*)

rear-view mirror *n* Rückspiegel *m*; rear window *n* AUTO Heckscheibe *f*

reason **1.** *n* (*cause*) Grund *m* (**for** für); (*ability to think*) Verstand *m*; (*common sense*) Vernunft *f*; **for some ~** aus irgendeinem Grund **2.** *vi* **~ with sb** mit jdm vernünftig reden; reasonable *adj* (*person, price*) vernünftig; (*offer*) akzeptabel; (*chance*) reell; (*food, weather*) ganz gut; reasonably *adv* vernünftig; (*fairly*) ziemlich

reassure *vt* beruhigen; **she ~d me that** ... sie versicherte mir, dass ...

rebel **1.** *n* Rebell(in) *m(f)* **2.** *vi* rebellieren; rebellion *n* Aufstand *m*

reboot *vt, vi* IT rebooten

rebuild *irr vt* wieder aufbauen

recall *vt* (*remember*) sich erinnern an + *acc*; (*call back*) zurückrufen

recap *vt, vi* rekapitulieren

receipt *n* (*document*) Quittung *f*; (*receiving*) Empfang *m*; **~s** *pl* (*money*) Einnahmen *pl*

receive *vt* (*news etc*) erhalten, bekommen; (*visitor*) empfangen; receiver *n* TEL Hörer *m*; RADIO Empfänger *m*

recent *adj* (*event*) vor kurzem

stattgefunden; (*photo*) neueste(r,s); (*invention*) neu; **in ~ years** in den letzten Jahren; **recently** *adv* vor kurzem; (*in the last few days or weeks*) in letzter Zeit

reception *n* Empfang *m*; **receptionist** *n* (*in hotel*) Empfangschef *m*, Empfangsdame *f*; (*woman in firm*) Empfangsdame *f*; MED Sprechstundenhilfe *f*

recess *n* (*in wall*) Nische *f*; (*US, in school*) Pause *f*

recession *n* Rezession *f*

recharge *vt* (*battery*) aufladen; **rechargeable** *adj* wieder aufladbar

recipe *n* Rezept *nt* (*for* für)

recipient *n* Empfänger(in) *m(f)*

reciprocal *adj* gegenseitig

recite *vt* vortragen

reckless *adj* leichtsinnig; (*driving*) gefährlich

reckon 1. *vt* (*calculate*) schätzen; (*think*) glauben **2.** *vi* ~ **with** rechnen mit

reclaim *vt* (*baggage*) abholen; (*expenses, tax*) zurückverlangen

recline *vi* (*person*) sich zurücklehnen; **reclining seat** *n* Liegesitz *m*

recognition *n* (*acknowledgement*) Anerkennung *f*; **in ~ of** in Anerkennung + *gen*; **recognize** *vt* erkennen; (*approve officially*) anerkennen

recommend *vt* empfehlen;

recommendation *n* Empfehlung *f*

reconcile *vt* (*people*) versöhnen; (*facts*) (miteinander) vereinbaren

reconsider *vt* noch einmal überdenken

reconstruct *vt* wieder aufbauen; (*crime*) rekonstruieren

record 1. *n* MUS (Schall)platte *f*; (*best performance*) Rekord *m*; **keep a ~ of** Buch führen über + *acc* **2.** *adj* (*time etc*) Rekord- **3.** *vt* (*write down*) aufzeichnen; (*on tape etc*) aufnehmen; **~ed message** Ansage *f*; **recorded delivery** (*Brit*) **by ~** per Einschreiben

recorder *n* (*instrument*) Blockflöte *f*; (**cassette**) ~ (Kassetten)rekorder *m*; **recording** *n* (*on tape etc*) Aufnahme *f*

recover 1. *vt* (*money, item*) zurückbekommen; (*appetite, strength*) wiedergewinnen **2.** *vi* sich erholen

recreation *n* Erholung *f*; **recreational** *adj* Freizeit-; **~ vehicle** (*US*) Wohnmobil *nt*

recruit 1. *n* MIL Rekrut(in) *m(f)*; (*in firm, organization*) neues Mitglied **2.** *vt* MIL rekrutieren; (*members*) anwerben; (*staff*) einstellen; **recruitment agency** *n* Personalagentur *f*

rectangle *n* Rechteck *nt*; **rectangular** *adj* rechteckig

recuperate *vi* sich erholen

recyclable *adj* recycelbar, wieder verwertbar; **recycle** *vt* recyceln, wieder verwerten; **~d paper** Recyclingpapier *nt*; **recycling** *n* Recycling *nt*, Wiederverwertung *f*

red 1. *adj* rot **2.** *n* **in the ~** in den roten Zahlen; **red cabbage** *n* Rotkohl *m*; **redcurrant** *n* (rote) Johannisbeere

redeem *vt* COMM einlösen

red-handed *adj* **catch sb ~** jdn auf frischer Tat ertappen

redhead *n* Rothaarige(r) *mf*

redial *vt, vi* nochmals wählen

redirect *vt* (*traffic*) umleiten; (*forward*) nachsenden

red light *n* (*traffic signal*) rotes Licht; **go through the ~** bei Rot über die Ampel fahren

red meat *n* Rind-, Lamm-, Rehfleisch

redo *irr vt* nochmals machen

reduce *vt* reduzieren (*to* auf + *acc, by* um); **reduction** *n* Reduzierung *f*; (*in price*) Ermäßigung *f*

redundant *adj* überflüssig; **be made ~** entlassen werden

red wine *n* Rotwein *m*

reef *n* Riff *nt*

reel *n* Spule *f*; (*on fishing rod*) Rolle *f*; **reel off** *vt* herunterrasseln

ref *n* (*referee*) Schiri *m*

refectory *n* (*at college*) Mensa *f*

refer 1. *vt* **~ sb to sb/sth** jdn

an jdn / etw verweisen; **~ sth to sb** (*query, problem*) etw an jdn weiterleiten **2.** *vi* **~ to** (*mention, allude to*) sich beziehen auf + *acc*; (*book*) nachschlagen in + *dat*

referee *n* Schiedsrichter(in) *m(f)*; (*in boxing*) Ringrichter *m*; (*Brit, for job*) Referenz *f*

reference *n* (*allusion*) Anspielung *f* (*to* auf + *acc*); (*for job*) Referenz *f*; (*in book*) Verweis *m*; **~ (number)** (*in document*) Aktenzeichen *nt*; **with ~ to** mit Bezug auf + *acc*; **reference book** *n* Nachschlagewerk *nt*

referendum *n* Referendum *nt*

refill 1. *vt* nachfüllen **2.** *n* (*for ballpoint pen*) Ersatzmine *f*

refine *vt* (*purify*) raffinieren; (*improve*) verfeinern; **refined** *adj* (*genteel*) fein

reflect 1. *vt* reflektieren; *fig* widerspiegeln **2.** *vi* nachdenken (*on* über + *acc*); **reflection** *n* (*image*) Spiegelbild *nt*; (*thought*) Überlegung *f*

reflex *n* Reflex *m*

reform 1. *n* Reform *f* **2.** *vt* reformieren; (*person*) bessern

refrain *vi* **~ from doing sth** es unterlassen, etw zu tun

refresh *vt* erfrischen; **refreshing** *adj* erfrischend; **refreshments** *npl* Erfrischungen *pl*

refrigerator *n* Kühlschrank *m*

refuel *vt, vi* auftanken

refuge *n* Zuflucht *f* (*from* vor

+ *dat*); **take ~** sich flüchten (*from* vor + *dat*, *in* in + *acc*); **refugee** *n* Flüchtling *m*

refund 1. *n* (*of money*) Rückerstattung *f*; **get a ~ (on sth)** sein Geld (für etw) zurückbekommen *2*. *vt* zurückerstatten

refusal *n* (*to do sth*) Weigerung *f*; **refuse 1.** *n* Müll *m*, Abfall *m* 2. *vt* ablehnen; **~ sb sth** jdm etw verweigern; **~ to do sth** sich weigern, etw zu tun 3. *vi* sich weigern

regain *vt* wiedergewinnen, wiedererlangen

regard 1. *n* **with ~ to** in Bezug auf + *acc*; **in this ~** in dieser Hinsicht; **~s** (*at end of letter*) mit freundlichen Grüßen; **give my ~s to ...** viele Grüße an ... + *acc* 2. *vt* **~ sb/ sth as sth** jdn/etw als etw betrachten; **as ~s ...** was ... betrifft; **regarding** *prep* bezüglich + *gen*; **regardless 1.** *adj* **~ of** ohne Rücksicht auf + *acc* 2. *adv* trotzdem; **carry on ~** einfach weitermachen

regime *n* POL Regime *nt*

region *n* (*of country*) Region *f*, Gebiet *nt*; **regional** *adj* regional

register 1. *n* Register *nt*, Namensliste *f* 2. *vt* (*with an authority*) registrieren lassen; (*birth, death, vehicle*) anmelden 3. *vi* (*at hotel, for course*) sich anmelden; (*at universi-*

ty) sich einschreiben; **registered** *adj* eingetragen; (*letter*) eingeschrieben; **by ~ post** per Einschreiben; **registration** *n* (*for course*) Anmeldung *f*; (*at university*) Einschreibung *f*; AUTO (*number*) (polizeiliches) Kennzeichen; **registration form** *n* Anmeldeformular *nt*; **registration number** *n* AUTO (polizeiliches) Kennzeichen; **registry office** *n* Standesamt *nt*

regret 1. *n* Bedauern *nt* 2. *vt* bedauern; **regrettable** *adj* bedauerlich

regular 1. *adj* regelmäßig; (*size*) normal 2. *n* (*client*) Stammkunde *m*, Stammkundin *f*; (*in bar*) Stammgast *m*; (*petrol*) Normalbenzin *nt*; **regularly** *adv* regelmäßig

regulate *vt* regulieren; (*using rules*) regeln; **regulation** *n* (*rule*) Vorschrift *f*

rehabilitation *n* Rehabilitation *f*

rehearsal *n* Probe *f*; **rehearse** *vt*, *vi* proben

reign 1. *n* Herrschaft *f* 2. *vi* herrschen (*over* über + *acc*)

reimburse *vt* (*person*) entschädigen; (*expenses*) zurückerstatten

reindeer *n* Rentier *nt*

reinforce *vt* verstärken

reinstate *vt* (*employee*) wieder einstellen

reject 1. *n* COMM Ausschussartikel *m* 2. *vt* ablehnen; **rejec-**

tion n Ablehnung f
relapse n Rückfall m
relate 1. vt (story) erzählen; (connect) in Verbindung bringen (to mit) **2.** v ~ to (refer) sich beziehen auf + acc; **related** adj verwandt (to mit); **relation** n (relative) Verwandte(r) mf; (connection) Beziehung f; **relationship** n (connection) Beziehung f; (between people) Verhältnis nt

relative 1. n Verwandte(r) mf **2.** adj relativ; **relatively** adv relativ, verhältnismäßig

relax 1. vi sich entspannen; ~! reg dich nicht auf! **2.** vt (grip, conditions) lockern; **relaxation** n (rest) Entspannung f; **relaxed** adj entspannt

release 1. n (from prison) Entlassung f; **new/recent ~** (film, CD) Neuerscheinung f **2.** vt (animal, hostage) freilassen; (prisoner) entlassen; (handbrake) lösen; (news) veröffentlichen; (film, CD) herausbringen

relent vi nachgeben; **relentless**, **relentlessly** adj, adv (merciless) erbarmungslos; (neverending) unaufhörlich

relevance n Relevanz f (to für); **relevant** adj relevant (to für)

reliable, **reliably** adj, adv zuverlässig; **reliant** adj ~ **on** abhängig von

relic n (from past) Relikt nt

relief n (from anxiety, pain) Erleichterung f; (assistance) Hilfe f; **relieve** vt (pain) lindern; (boredom) überwinden; (take over from) ablösen; **I'm ~d** ich bin erleichtert

religion n Religion f; **religious** adj religiös

relish 1. n (for food) würzige Soße f **2.** vt (enjoy) genießen; **I don't ~ the thought of getting up early** der Gedanke, früh aufzustehen, behagt mir gar nicht

reluctant adj widerwillig; **be ~ to do sth** etw nur ungern tun; **reluctantly** adv widerwillig

rely on vt sich verlassen auf + acc; (depend on) abhängig sein von

remain vi bleiben; (be left over) übrig bleiben; **remainder** n a. MATH Rest m; **remaining** adj übrig; **remains** npl Überreste pl

remark 1. n Bemerkung f **2.** vt ~ bemerken, dass; **remarkable**, **remarkably** adj, adv bemerkenswert

remedy n Mittel nt (for gegen)

remember 1. vt sich erinnern an + acc; ~ **to do sth** daran denken, etw zu tun; **I must ~ that** das muss ich mir merken **2.** vi sich erinnern

remind vt ~ **sb of/about sb/sth** jdn an jdn/etw erinnern; ~ **sb to do sth** jdn daran erinnern, etw zu tun; **that ~s me** dabei fällt mir ein ...; **reminder** n (to pay) Mahnung f

remnant n Rest m

remote 1. adj (place) abgelegen; (slight) gering **2.** n TV Fernbedienung f; **remote control** n Fernsteuerung f; (device) Fernbedienung f

removal n Entfernung f; (Brit, move from house) Umzug m; **removal firm** n (Brit) Spedition f; **remove** vt entfernen; (lid) abnehmen; (doubt, suspicion) zerstreuen

rename vt umbenennen

renew vt erneuern; (licence, passport, library book) verlängern lassen

renovate vt renovieren

renowned adj berühmt (for für)

rent 1. n Miete f; **for ~** (US) zu vermieten **2.** vt (as hirer, tenant) mieten; (as owner) vermieten; **~ed car** Mietwagen m; **rent out** vt vermieten; **rental 1.** n (as hirer, TV etc) Leihgebühr f **2.** adj Miet-

reorganize vt umorganisieren

rep n COMM Vertreter(in) m(f)

repair 1. n Reparatur f **2.** vt reparieren; (damage) wieder gutmachen

repay irr vt (money) zurückzahlen; **~ sb for sth** fig sich bei jdm für etw revanchieren

repeat 1. n RADIO, TV Wiederholung f **2.** vt wiederholen;

repetition n Wiederholung f

replace vt ersetzen (with durch); (put back) zurückstellen; zurücklegen; **replacement** n (thing, person) Ersatz m; (temporarily in job) Vertretung f

replay 1. n (action) m(f) Wiederholung f **2.** vt (game) wiederholen

replica n Kopie f

reply 1. n Antwort f **2.** vi antworten; **~ to sb/sth** jdm/auf etw acc antworten **3.** vt **~ that** antworten, dass

report 1. n Bericht m, Zeugnis nt **2.** vt (tell) berichten; (give information against) melden; (to police) anzeigen **3.** vi (present oneself) sich melden; **~ sick** sich krankmelden; **report card** n (US, in school) Zeugnis nt; **reporter** n Reporter(in) m(f)

represent vt darstellen; (speak for) vertreten; **representation** n (picture etc) Darstellung f; **representative 1.** n Vertreter(in) m(f); (US) POL Abgeordnete(r) mf **2.** adj repräsentativ (for für)

reproduce vt (copy) reproduzieren **2.** vi BIO sich fortpflanzen; **reproduction** n (copy) Reproduktion f; BIO Fortpflanzung f

reptile n Reptil nt

republic n Republik f; **republican 1.** adj republikanisch **2.**

n Republikaner(in) m(f)

repulsive adj abstoßend

reputation n Ruf m

request 1. n Bitte f (for um); **on ~** auf Wunsch **2.** vt bitten um

require vt (need) brauchen; (desire) verlangen; **required** adj erforderlich; **requirement** n (condition) Anforderung f; (need) Bedingung f

rerun n Wiederholung f

rescue 1. n Rettung f; **come to sb's ~** jdm zu Hilfe kommen **2.** vt retten

research 1. n Forschung f **2.** vi forschen (into über + acc) **3.** vt erforschen; **researcher** n Forscher(in) m(f)

resemblance n Ähnlichkeit f (to mit); **resemble** vt ähneln + dat

resent vt übel nehmen

reservation n (booking) Reservierung f; (doubt) Vorbehalt m; **I have a ~** (in hotel, restaurant) ich habe reserviert; **reserve 1.** n (store) Vorrat m (of an + dat); (manner) Zurückhaltung f; sport Reservespieler(in) m(f); (game ~) Naturschutzgebiet nt **2.** vt (book in advance) reservieren; **reserved** adj reserviert

residence n Wohnsitz m; (living) Aufenthalt m; **~ permit** Aufenthaltsgenehmigung f; **~ hall** Studentenwohnheim nt; **resident** n (in house) Bewohner(in) m(f); (in town,

area) Einwohner(in) m(f)

resign 1. vt (post) zurücktreten von; (job) kündigen **2.** vi (from post) zurücktreten; (from job) kündigen; **resignation** n (from post) Rücktritt m; (from job) Kündigung f

resist vt widerstehen + dat; **resistance** n Widerstand m (to gegen)

resit (Brit) **1.** vt irr vi wiederholen **2.** n Wiederholungsprüfung f

resolution n (intention) Vorsatz m; (decision) Beschluss m

resolve vt (problem) lösen

resort 1. n (holiday resort) Urlaubsort m; **as a last ~** als letzter Ausweg **2.** vi **~ to** greifen zu; (violence) anwenden

resources npl (money) (Geld)mittel pl; (mineral resources) Bodenschätze pl

respect 1. n Respekt m (for vor + dat); (consideration) Rücksicht f (for auf + acc); **with ~ to** in Bezug auf + acc; **in this ~** in dieser Hinsicht; **in all due ~** bei allem Respekt **2.** vt respektieren; **respectable** adj (person, family) angesehen; (district) anständig; (achievement, result) beachtlich; **respected** adj angesehen

respective adj jeweilig; **respectively** adv **5% and 10% ~** 5% beziehungsweise

10%

respond vi antworten (to auf + acc); (react) reagieren (to auf + acc); (to treatment) ansprechen (to auf + acc); **response** n Antwort f; (reaction) Reaktion f; **in ~ to** als Antwort auf + acc

responsibility n Verantwortung f; **that's her ~** dafür ist sie verantwortlich; **responsible** adj verantwortlich (for für); (trustworthy) verantwortungsbewusst; (job) verantwortungsvoll

rest 1. n (relaxation) Ruhe f; (break) Pause f; (remainder) Rest m; **have** (or **take**) **a ~** sich ausruhen; (break) Pause machen **2.** vi (relax) sich ausruhen; (lean) lehnen (on, against an + dat, gegen)

restaurant n Restaurant nt; **restaurant car** n (Brit) Speisewagen m

restful adj (holiday etc) erholsam, ruhig; **restless** adj unruhig

restore vt (painting, building) restaurieren; (order) wiederherstellen; (give back) zurückgeben

restrain vt (person, feelings) zurückhalten; **~ oneself** sich beherrschen

restrict vt beschränken (to auf + acc); **restricted** adj beschränkt; **restriction** n Einschränkung f (on + gen)

rest room n (US) Toilette f

result 1. n Ergebnis nt; (consequence) Folge f; **as a ~ of** infolge + gen **2.** vi **~ in** führen zu; **~ from** sich ergeben aus

resume vt (work, negotiations) wieder aufnehmen; (journey) fortsetzen

résumé n Zusammenfassung f; (US, curriculum vitae) Lebenslauf m

resuscitate vt wiederbeleben

retail adv im Einzelhandel; **retailer** n Einzelhändler(in) m(f)

retain vt behalten; (heat) halten

rethink irr vt noch einmal überdenken

retire vi (from work) in den Ruhestand treten; (withdraw) sich zurückziehen; **retired** adj (person) pensioniert; **retirement** n (time of life) Ruhestand m; **retirement age** n Rentenalter nt

retrain vi sich umschulen lassen

retreat 1. n Rückzug m (from aus); (refuge) Zufluchtsort m **2.** vi sich zurückziehen

retrieve vt (recover) wiederbekommen; (rescue) retten; (data) abrufen

retrospect n **in ~** rückblickend

return 1. n (going back) Rückkehr f; (giving back) Rückgabe f; (profit) Gewinn m; (Brit, retunr ticket) Rückfahrkarte f; (plane ticket)

Rückflugticket *nt*, Return *m*; **in ~ als** Gegenleistung (*for* für); ***many happy ~s*** (*of the day*) herzlichen Glückwunsch zum Geburtstag! **2.** *vi* (*person*) zurückkehren; (*doubts, symptoms*) wieder auftreten **3.** *vt* (*give back*) zurückgeben; ***I ~ed his call*** ich habe ihn zurückgerufen; **returnable** *adj* (*bottle*) Pfand-; **return flight** *n* (*Brit*) Rückflug *m*; (*both ways*) Hin- und Rückflug *m*; **return key** *n* IT Eingabetaste *f*; **return ticket** *n* (*Brit*) Rückfahrkarte *f*; (*for plane*) Rückflugticket *nt*

reunification *n* Wiedervereinigung *f*; **reunion** *n* (*party*) Treffen *nt*; **reunite** *vt* *vi* wieder vereinigen

reveal *vt* (*make known*) enthüllen; (*secret*) verraten; **revealing** *adj* aufschlussreich; (*dress*) freizügig

revenge *n* Rache *f*; (*in game*) Revanche *f*; ***take ~ on sb (for sth)*** sich an jdm (für etw) rächen

revenue *n* Einnahmen *pl*

reverse 1. *n* (*back*) Rückseite *f*; (*opposite*) Gegenteil *nt*; AUTO ~ (**gear**) Rückwärtsgang *m* **2.** *adj* **in ~ order** in umgekehrter Reihenfolge **3.** *vt* (*order*) umkehren; (*decision*) umstoßen; (*car*) zurücksetzen **4.** *vi* rückwärts fahren

review 1. *n* (*of book, film etc*) Rezension *f*; **be under ~** überprüft werden **2.** *vt* (*book, film etc*) rezensieren; (*re-examine*) überprüfen

revise 1. *vt* revidieren; (*text*) überarbeiten; (*Brit, in school*) wiederholen **2.** *vi* (*Brit, in school*) den Stoff wiederholen; **revision** *n* (*of text*) Überarbeitung *f*; (*Brit*) Wiederholung *f*

revitalize *vt* neu beleben

revive *vt* (*person*) wieder beleben; (*tradition, interest*) wieder aufleben lassen

revolt *n* Aufstand *m*; **revolting** *adj* widerlich

revolution *n* POL *fig* Revolution *f*; **revolutionary 1.** *adj* revolutionär **2.** *n* Revolutionär(in) *m(f)*

revolve *vi* sich drehen (*around* um); **revolver** *n* Revolver *m*; **revolving door** *n* Drehtür *f*

reward 1. *n* Belohnung *f* **2.** *vt* belohnen; **rewarding** *adj* lohnend

rewind *irr vt* (*tape*) zurückspulen

rheumatism *n* Rheuma *nt*

rhinoceros *n* Nashorn *nt*

Rhodes *n* Rhodos *nt*

rhubarb *n* Rhabarber *m*

rhyme 1. *n* Reim *m* **2.** *vi* sich reimen (*with* auf + *acc*)

rhythm *n* Rhythmus *m*

rib *n* Rippe *f*

ribbon *n* Band *nt*

rice n Reis m; **rice pudding** n Milchreis m

rich 1. adj reich; (food) schwer **2.** npl **the ~** die Reichen pl

rickety adj wackelig

rid vt **get ~ of sb/sth** jdn/etw loswerden

ridden pp of **ride**

riddle n Rätsel nt

ride 1. vt (horse) reiten; (bicycle) fahren **2.** vi (on horse) reiten; (on bike) fahren **3.** n (in vehicle, on bike) Fahrt f; (on horse) (Aus)ritt m; **go for a ~** (in car, on bike) spazieren fahren; (on horse) reiten gehen; **take sb for a ~** fam jdn verarschen; **rider** n (on horse) Reiter(in) m(f)

ridiculous adj lächerlich; **don't be ~** red keinen Unsinn!

riding 1. n Reiten nt **2.** adj Reit-

rifle n Gewehr nt

right 1. adj (correct, just) richtig; (opposite of left) rechte(r, s); (clothes, job etc) passend; **be ~** (person) Recht haben; (clock) richtig gehen; **that's ~** das stimmt! **2.** n Recht nt (to auf + acc); (side) rechte Seite; **the Right** POL die Rechte; **take a ~** AUTO rechts abbiegen; **on the ~** rechts (of von); **to the ~** nach rechts (of von) **3.** adv (towards the ~) nach rechts; (directly) direkt; (exactly) genau; **turn ~** AUTO rechts ab-

biegen; **~ away** sofort; **~ now** im Moment; (immediately) sofort; **right angle** n rechter Winkel; **right-hand drive 1.** n Rechtssteuerung f **2.** adj rechtsgesteuert; **right-handed** adj **he is ~** er ist Rechtshänder; **right-hand side** n rechte Seite; **on the ~** auf der rechten Seite; **rightly** adv zu Recht; **right of way** n **have ~** AUTO Vorfahrt haben; **right wing** n POL, SPORT rechter Flügel; **right-wing** adj Rechts-; **~ extremist** Rechtsradikale(r) mf

rigid adj (stiff) starr; (strict) streng

rim n (of cup etc) Rand m; (of wheel) Felge f

rind n (of cheese) Rinde f; (of bacon) Schwarte f; (of fruit) Schale f

ring 1. vt, vi (bell) läuten; TEL anrufen **2.** n (on finger, in boxing) Ring m; (circle) Kreis m; (at circus) Manege f; **give sb a ~** TEL jdn anrufen; **ring back** vt, vi zurückrufen; **ring up** vt, vi anrufen

ringing tone n TEL Rufzeichen nt

ring road n (Brit) Umgehungsstraße f

ringtone n Klingelton m

rink n (ice rink) Eisbahn f; (for roller-skating) Rollschuhbahn f

rinse vt spülen

riot n Aufruhr m

rip 1. n Riss m **2.** vt zerreißen; **~ sth open** etw aufreißen **3.** vi reißen; **rip off** vt fam (person) übers Ohr hauen; **rip up** vt zerreißen

ripe adj (fruit) reif; **ripen** vi reifen

rip-off n **that's a ~** fam (too expensive) das ist Wucher

rise 1. vi (from sitting, lying) aufstehen; (sun) aufgehen; (prices, temperature) steigen; (ground) ansteigen **2.** n (increase) Anstieg m (in + gen); (pay rise) Gehaltserhöhung f; (to power, fame) Aufstieg m (to zu); (slope) Steigung f; **risen** pp of **rise**

risk 1. n Risiko nt **2.** vt riskieren; **risky** adj riskant

ritual n Ritual nt

rival n Rivale m, Rivalin f (for um); COMM Konkurrent(in) m(f); **rivalry** n Rivalität f; COMM, SPORT Konkurrenz f

river n Fluss m; **the River Thames** (Brit), **the Thames River** (US) die Themse; **riverside** n Flussufer nt **2.** adj am Flussufer

road n Straße f; fig Weg m; **on the ~** (travelling) unterwegs; **roadblock** n Straßensperre f; **roadmap** n Straßenkarte f; **road rage** n aggressives Verhalten im Straßenverkehr; **roadside** n **at** (or **by**) **the ~** am Straßenrand; **roadsign** n Verkehrsschild nt; **road tax** n Kraftfahrzeugsteuer f; **roadworks** npl Straßenarbeiten pl; **roadworthy** adj fahrtüchtig

roar 1. n (of person, lion) Brüllen nt; (von Verkehr) Donnern nt **2.** vi (person, lion) brüllen (with vor + dat)

roast vt Braten m **2.** adj **~ beef** Rinderbraten m; **~ chicken** Brathähnchen nt; **~ pork** Schweinebraten m; **~ potatoes** pl im Backofen gebratene Kartoffeln **3.** vt (meat) braten

rob vt bestehlen; (bank, shop) ausrauben; **robbery** n Raub m

robe n (US, dressing gown) Morgenrock m; (of judge, priest etc) Robe f, Talar m

robin n Rotkehlchen nt

robot n Roboter m

rock 1. n (substance) Stein m; (boulder) Felsbrocken m; MUS Rock m; **on the ~s** (drink) mit Eis; (marriage) gescheitert **2.** vt, vi (swing) schaukeln; (dance) rocken; **rock climbing** n Klettern nt

rocket n Rakete f; (in salad) Rucola f

rocking chair n Schaukelstuhl m

rocky adj (landscape) felsig; (path) steinig

rod n (bar) Stange f; (fishing rod) Rute f

rode pt of **ride**

rogue n Schurke m

round

role n Rolle f; **role model** n Vorbild nt

roll 1. n (of film, paper etc) Rolle f; (bread ∼) Brötchen nt 2. vt (move by ∼ing) rollen; (cigarette) drehen 3. vi (move by ∼ing) rollen; **roll out** vt (pastry) ausrollen; **roll over** vi (person) sich umdrehen; **roll up 1.** vi fam (arrive) antanzen 2. vt (carpet) aufrollen; **roll one's sleeves up** die Ärmel hochkrempeln

roller n (hair∼) (Locken)wickler m; **roller coaster** n Achterbahn f; **roller skates** npl Rollschuhe pl; **roller-skating** n Rollschuhlaufen nt; **rolling pin** n Nudelholz nt; **roll-on** (deodorant) n Deoroller m

ROM acr = **read only memory**; ROM m

Roman 1. adj römisch 2. n Römer(in) m(f); **Roman Catholic 1.** adj römisch-katholisch 2. n Katholik(in) m(f)

romance n Romantik f; (love affair) Romanze f

Romania n Rumänien nt; **Romanian 1.** adj rumänisch 2. n Rumäne m, Rumänin f; (language) Rumänisch nt

romantic adj romantisch

roof n Dach nt; **roof rack** n Dachgepäckträger m

rook n (in chess) Turm m

room n Zimmer nt, Raum m; (large, for gatherings etc) Saal m; (space) Platz m; fig

Spielraum m; **make ∼ for** Platz machen für; **room-mate** n Zimmergenosse m, Zimmergenossin f; (US, sharing apartment) Mitbewohner(in) m(f); **room service** n Zimmerservice m

root n Wurzel f; **root out** vt ausrotten; **root vegetable** n Wurzelgemüse nt

rope n Seil nt; **know the ∼s** fam sich auskennen

rose 1. pt of **rise** 2. n Rose f

rosé n Rosé(wein) m

rotate 1. vt (turn) rotieren lassen 2. vi rotieren; **rotation** n (turning) Rotation f; **in ∼** abwechselnd

rotten adj (decayed) faul; (mean) gemein; (unpleasant) scheußlich; (ill) elend

rough 1. adj (not smooth) rau; (path) uneben; (coarse, violent) grob; (crossing) stürmisch; (without comforts) hart; (unfinished, makeshift) grob; (approximate) ungefähr; **∼ draft** Rohentwurf m; **I have a ∼ idea** ich habe eine ungefähre Vorstellung 2. adv **sleep ∼** im Freien schlafen 3. vt ∼ **it** primitiv leben; **roughly** adv grob; (approximately) ungefähr

round 1. adj rund 2. adv **all ∼** (on all sides) rundherum; **I'll be ∼ at 8** ich werde um acht Uhr da sein; **the other way ∼** umgekehrt 3. prep (sur-

rounding) um (... herum); ~ (**about**) (*approximately*) ungefähr; ~ **the corner** um die Ecke; **go ~ the world** um die Welt reisen; **she lives ~ here** sie wohnt hier in der Gegend **4.** *n* Runde *f*; (*of bread, toast*) Scheibe *f*; **it's my ~** (*of drinks*) die Runde geht auf mich **5.** *vt* (*corner*) biegen um; **round off** *vt* abrunden; **round up** *vt* (*number, price*) aufrunden

roundabout 1. *n* (*Brit*) AUTO Kreisverkehr *m*; (*Brit, merry-go-round*) Karussell *nt* **2.** *adj* umständlich; **round-the-clock** *adj* rund um die Uhr; **round trip** *n* Rundreise *f*; **round-trip ticket** *n* (*US*) Rückfahrkarte *f*; (*for plane*) Rückflugticket *nt*

route *n* Route *f*; (*bus, plane etc service*) Linie *f*; *fig* Weg *m*

routine 1. *n* Routine *f* **2.** *adj* Routine-

row **1.** *n* (*line*) Reihe *f*; ***three times in a ~**** dreimal hintereinander **2.** *vt, vi* (*boat*) rudern **3.** *n* (*noise*) Krach *m*; (*dispute*) Streit *m*

rowboat *n* (*US*) Ruderboot *nt*

row house *n* (*US*) Reihenhaus *nt*

rowing *n* Rudern *nt*; **rowing boat** *n* (*Brit*) Ruderboot *nt*; **rowing machine** *n* Rudergerät *nt*

royal *adj* königlich; **royalty** *n* (*family*) Mitglieder *pl* der königlichen Familie; **royalties** *pl* (*from book, music*) Tantiemen *pl*

RSPCA *abbr* = **Royal Society for the Prevention of Cruelty to Animals**; britischer Tierschutzverein

RSVP *abbr* = **répondez s'il vous plaît**; u. A. w. g.

rub *vt* reiben; *vi* hin *in* einmassieren; **rub out** *vt* (*with eraser*) ausradieren

rubber *n* Gummi *m*; (*Brit, eraser*) Radiergummi *m*; (*US*) *fam* (*contraceptive*) Gummi *m*; **rubber stamp** *n* Stempel *m*

rubbish *n* Abfall *m*; (*nonsense*) Quatsch *m*; (*poor-quality thing*) Mist *m*; **don't talk ~** red keinen Unsinn!; **rubbish bin** *n* Mülleimer *m*; **rubbish dump** *n* Müllabladeplatz *m*

rubble *n* Schutt *m*

ruby *n* (*stone*) Rubin *m*

rucksack *n* Rucksack *m*

rude *adj* (*impolite*) unhöflich; (*indecent*) unanständig

rug *n* Teppich *m*; (*next to bed*) Bettvorleger *m*; (*for knees*) Wolldecke *f*

rugby *n* Rugby *nt*

rugged *adj* (*coastline*) zerklüftet; (*features*) markant

ruin 1. *n* Ruine *f*; (*financial, social*) Ruin *m* **2.** *vt* ruinieren

rule 1. *n* Regel *f*; (*governing*) Herrschaft *f*; **as a ~** in der

Regel **2.** *vt, vi* (*govern*) regieren; (*decide*) entscheiden; **ruler** *n* Lineal *nt*; (*person*) Herrscher(in) *m(f)*

rum *n* Rum *m*

rumble *vi* (*stomach*) knurren; (*train, truck*) rumpeln

rummage *vi* ~ (**around**) herumstöbern

rumor (*US*), **rumour** *n* Gerücht *nt*

run 1. *vt* (*race, distance*) laufen; (*machine, engine, computer program, water*) laufen lassen; (*manage*) leiten, führen; (*car*) unterhalten; *I ran her home* ich habe sie nach Hause gefahren **2.** *vi* laufen; (*move quickly*) rennen; (*bus, train*) fahren; (*path etc*) verlaufen; (*machine, engine, computer program*) laufen; (*flow*) fließen; (*colours, make-up*) verlaufen; ~ *for President* für die Präsidentschaft kandidieren; *be ~ning low* knapp werden; *my nose is ~ning* mir läuft die Nase; *it ~s in the family* es liegt in der Familie **3.** *n* (*on foot*) Lauf *m*; (*in car*) Spazierfahrt *f*; (*series*) Reihe *f*; (*sudden demand*) Ansturm *m* (*on* auf + *acc*); (*in tights*) Laufmasche *f*; (*in cricket, baseball*) Lauf *m*; *go for a* ~ laufen gehen; (*in car*) eine Spazierfahrt machen; *in the long* ~ auf die Dauer; *on the* ~ auf der Flucht; (*from*

vor + *dat*); **run about** *vi* herumlaufen; **run away** *vi* weglaufen; **run down** *vt* (*with car*) umfahren; (*criticize*) heruntermachen; *be* ~ (*tired*) abgespannt sein; **run into** *vt* (*meet*) zufällig treffen; (*problem*) stoßen auf + *acc*; **run off** *vi* weglaufen; **run out** *vi* (*person*) hinausrennen; (*liquid*) auslaufen; (*lease,time*) ablaufen; (*money, supplies*) ausgehen; *he ran* ~ *of money* ihm ging das Geld aus; **run over** *vt* (*with car*) überfahren; **run up** *vt* (*debt, bill*) machen

rung *pp of* **ring**

runner *n* (*athlete*) Läufer(in) *m(f)*; *do a* ~ *fam* wegrennen; **runner beans** *npl* (*Brit*) Stangenbohnen *pl*

running 1. *n* SPORT Laufen *nt*; (*management*) Leitung *f*, Führung *f* **2.** *adj* (*water*) fließend; ~ *costs* Betriebskosten *pl*; (*for car*) Unterhaltskosten *pl*; *3 days* ~ 3 Tage hintereinander

runny *adj* (*food*) flüssig; (*nose*) laufend

runway *n* Start- und Landebahn *f*

rural *adj* ländlich

rush 1. *n* Eile *f*; (*for tickets etc*) Ansturm *m* (*for* auf + *acc*); *be in a* ~ es eilig haben; *there's no* ~ es eilt nicht **2.** *vt* (*do too quickly*) hastig machen; (*meal*) hastig essen; ~

sb to hospital jdn auf dem schnellsten Weg ins Krankenhaus bringen; **don't ~ me** dräng nich nicht 3. vi (*hurry*) eilen; **rush hour** n Hauptverkehrszeit f

rusk n Zwieback m

Russia n Russland nt; **Russian 1.** adj russisch **2.** n Russe m, Russin f; (*language*) Russisch nt

rust 1. n Rost m **2.** vi rosten; **rustproof** adj rostfrei; **rusty** adj rostig

ruthless adj rücksichtslos; (*treatment, criticism*) schonungslos

rye n Roggen m

S

sabotage vt sabotieren

sachet n Päckchen nt

sack 1. n (*bag*) Sack m; **get the ~** fam rausgeschmissen werden **2.** vt fam rausschmeißen

sacred adj heilig

sacrifice 1. n Opfer nt **2.** vt opfern

sad adj traurig

saddle n Sattel m

sadistic adj sadistisch

sadly adv (*unfortunately*) leider

safe 1. adj (*free from danger*) sicher; (*out of danger*) in Sicherheit; (*careful*) vorsichtig; **have a ~ journey** gute Fahrt! **2.** n Safe m; **safeguard 1.** n Schutz m **2.** vt schützen (*against* vor + dat); **safely** adv sicher; (*arrive*) wohlbehalten; (*drive*) vorsichtig; **safety** n Sicherheit f; **safety belt** n Sicherheitsgurt m; **safety pin** n Sicherheitsnadel f

Sagittarius n ASTR Schütze m

Sahara n **the ~** (*Desert*) die (Wüste) Sahara

said pt, pp of **say**

sail 1. n Segel nt; **set ~** losfahren (*for* nach) **2.** vi (*in yacht*) segeln; (*on ship*) mit dem Schiff fahren; (*ship*) auslaufen (*for* nach) **3.** vt (*yacht*) segeln mit; (*ship*) steuern; **sailboat** n (*US*) Segelboot nt; **sailing** n **go ~** segeln gehen; **sailing boat** n (*Brit*) Segelboot nt; **sailor** n Seemann m; (*in navy*) Matrose m

saint n Heilige(r) mf

sake n **for the ~ of** um + gen ... willen; **for your ~** deinetwegen, dir zuliebe

salad n Salat m; **salad cream** n (*Brit*) majonäseartige Salatsoße; **salad dressing** n Salatsoße f

salary n Gehalt nt

sale n Verkauf m; (*at reduced prices*) Ausverkauf m; **for ~** zu verkaufen; **sales clerk** n

(US) Verkäufer(in) *m(f)*;
salesman *n* Verkäufer *m*;
(rep) Vertreter *m*; **sales rep**
n Vertreter(in) *m(f)*; **sales-woman** *n* Verkäuferin *f*;
(rep) Vertreterin *f*

saliva *n* Speichel *m*

salmon *n* Lachs *m*

saloon *n (ship's lounge)* Salon
m; *(US, bar)* Kneipe *f*

salt 1. *n* Salz *nt* **2.** *vt (flavour)*
salzen; *(roads)* mit Salz
streuen; **salt cellar, salt
shaker** *(US)* *n* Salzstreuer
m; **salty** *adj* salzig

same 1. *adj* **the ~** *(similar)*
der / die / das gleiche, die
gleichen *pl*; *(identical)* der-/
/die-dasselbe, dieselben *pl*;
they live in the ~ house
sie wohnen im selben Haus
2. *pron* **the ~** *(similar)* der /
die / das Gleiche, die Glei-
chen *pl*; *(identical)* der-/
/die-dasselbe, dieselben *pl*;
I'll have the ~ again ich
möchte noch mal das Glei-
che; **all the ~** trotzdem; **the
~ to you** gleichfalls; **it's all
the ~ to me** es ist mir egal
3. *adv* **the ~** gleich

sample 1. *n* Probe *f*; *(of fab-ric)* Muster *nt* **2.** *vt* probieren

sanctions *npl* POL Sanktio-
nen *pl*

sanctuary *n (refuge)* Zuflucht
f; *(for animals)* Schutzgebiet
nt

sand *n* Sand *m*

sandal *n* Sandale *f*

sandwich *n* Sandwich *nt*

sandy *adj (full of sand)* sandig; **~ beach** Sandstrand *m*

sane *adj* geistig gesund, normal; *(sensible)* vernünftig

sang *pt of* **sing**

sanitary *adj* hygienisch; **sanitary napkin** *(US)*, **sanitary
towel** *n* Damenbinde *f*

sank *pt of* **sink**

Santa (Claus) *n* der Weihnachtsmann

sarcastic *adj* sarkastisch

sardine *n* Sardine *f*

sari *n* Sari *m (von indischen
Frauen getragenes Gewand)*

sat *pt, pp of* **sit**

Sat *abbr = Saturday;* Sa.

satellite *n* Satellit *m*; **satellite
dish** *n* Satellitenschüssel *f*

satin *n* Satin *m*

satisfaction *n (contentment)*
Zufriedenheit *f*; **is that to
your ~?** sind Sie damit zufrieden?; **satisfactory** *adj*
zufrieden stellend; **satisfied**
adj zufrieden *(with* mit*)*; **satisfy** *vt* zufrieden stellen;
(conditions) erfüllen; *(need,
demand)* befriedigen; **satis-
fying** *adj* befriedigend

Saturday *n* Samstag *m*, Sonnabend *m*; → **Tuesday**

sauce *n* Soße *f*; **saucepan** *n*
Kochtopf *m*; **saucer** *n* Unter-
tertasse *f*

Saudi Arabia *n* Saudi-Arabi-
en *nt*

sauna *n* Sauna *f*

sausage *n* Wurst *f*; **sausage**

roll *n* mit Wurst gefülltes Blätterteigröllchen

savage *adj* (*person, attack*) brutal; (*animal*) wild

save 1. *vt* (*rescue*) retten (*from* vor + *dat*); (*money, time, electricity etc*) sparen; (*strength*) schonen; IT speichern; **~ sb's life** jdm das Leben retten **2.** *vi* sparen **3.** *n* (*in soccer*) Parade *f*; **save up** *vi* sparen (*for* auf + *acc*); **saving** *n* (*of money*) Sparen *nt*; **~s** *pl* Ersparnisse *pl*; **~s account** Sparkonto *nt*

savory (*US*), **savoury** *adj* (*not sweet*) pikant

saw 1. *vt* sägen **2.** *n* (*tool*) Säge *f* **3.** *pt of* **see**; **sawdust** *n* Sägemehl *nt*

saxophone *n* Saxophon *nt*

say 1. *vt* sagen (*to sb* jdm); (*prayer*) sprechen; **what does the letter ~?** was steht im Brief?; **the rules ... that ...** in den Regeln heißt es, dass ...; **he's said to be rich** er soll reich sein **2.** *n* **have a ~ in sth** bei etw ein Mitspracherecht haben **3.** *adv* zum Beispiel; **saying** *n* Sprichwort *nt*

scab *n* (*on cut*) Schorf *m*

scaffolding *n* (Bau)gerüst *nt*

scale *n* (*of map etc*) Maßstab *m*; (*on thermometer etc*) Skala *f*; (*of pay*) Tarifsystem *nt*; MUS Tonleiter *f*; (*of fish, snake*) Schuppe *f*; **to ~** maßstabsgerecht; **on a large/small ~** in großem/kleinem

Umfang; **scales** *npl* (*for weighing*) Waage *f*

scalp *n* Kopfhaut *f*

scan 1. *vt* (*examine*) genau prüfen; (*read quickly*) überfliegen; IT scannen **2.** *n* MED Ultraschall *m*; **scan in** *vt* IT einscannen

scandal *n* Skandal *m*

Scandinavia *n* Skandinavien *nt*; **Scandinavian 1.** *adj* skandinavisch **2.** *n* Skandinavier(in) *m(f)*

scanner *n* Scanner *m*

scapegoat *n* Sündenbock *m*

scar *n* Narbe *f*

scarce *adj* selten; (*in short supply*) knapp; **scarcely** *adv* kaum

scare 1. *n* (*general alarm*) Panik *f* **2.** *vt* erschrecken; **be ~d** Angst haben (*of* vor + *dat*)

scarf *n* Schal *m*; (*on head*) Kopftuch *nt*

scarlet *adj* scharlachrot; **scarlet fever** *n* Scharlach *m*

scary *adj* (*film, story*) gruselig

scatter *vt* verstreuen; (*seed, gravel*) streuen; (*disperse*) auseinander treiben

scene *n* (*location*) Ort *m*; (*division of play*) THEAT Szene *f*; (*view*) Anblick *m*; **make a ~** eine Szene machen; **scenery** *n* (*landscape*) Landschaft *f*; THEAT Kulissen *pl*; **scenic** *adj* (*landscape*) malerisch; **~ route** landschaftlich schöne Strecke

scent *n* (*perfume*) Parfüm *nt*;

(*smell*) Duft *m*

sceptical *adj* (*Brit*) skeptisch

schedule 1. *n* (*plan*) Programm *nt*; (*of work*) Zeitplan *m*; (*list*) Liste *f*; (*US, of trains, buses, air traffic*) Fahr-, Flugplan *m*; **on** ~ planmäßig; **be behind** ~ **with** sth mit etw in Verzug sein **2.** *vt* **the meeting is ..d for next Monday** die Besprechung ist für nächsten Montag angesetzt; **scheduled** *adj* (*departure, arrival*) planmäßig; ~ **flight** Linienflug *m*

scheme 1. *n* (*plan*) Plan *m*; (*project*) Projekt *nt*; (*dishonest*) Intrige *f* **2.** *vi* intrigieren

scholar *n* Gelehrte(r) *mf*; **scholarship** *n* (*grant*) Stipendium *nt*

school *n* Schule *f*; (*university department*) Fachbereich *m*; (*US, university*) Universität *f*; **school bag** *n* Schultasche *f*; **schoolbook** *n* Schulbuch *nt*; **schoolboy** *n* Schüler *m*; **schoolgirl** *n* Schülerin *f*; **schoolteacher** *n* Lehrer(in) *m(f)*; **schoolwork** *n* Schularbeiten *pl*

sciatica *n* Ischias *m*

science *n* Wissenschaft *f*; (*natural science*) Naturwissenschaft *f*; **science fiction** *n* Sciencefiction *f*; **scientific** *adj* wissenschaftlich; **scientist** *n* Wissenschaftler(in) *m(f)*; (*natural sciences*) Naturwissenschaftler(in) *m(f)*

scissors *npl* Schere *f*

scone *n* kleines süßes Hefebrötchen mit oder ohne Rosinen, das mit Butter oder Dickrahm und Marmelade gegessen wird

scoop 1. *n* (*exclusive story*) Exklusivbericht *m*; **a** ~ **of ice-cream** eine Kugel Eis **2.** *vt* ~ (**up**) schaufeln

scooter *n* (*Motor*)roller *m*; (*toy*) (Tret)roller *m*

scope *n* Umfang *m*; (*opportunity*) Möglichkeit *f*

score *n* SPORT Spielstand *m*; (*final result*) Spielergebnis *nt*; (*in quiz etc*) Punktestand *m*; MUS Partitur *f*; **keep** (**the**) ~ mitzählen **2.** *vt* (*goal*) schießen; (*points*) machen **3.** *vi* (*keep score*) mitzählen; **scoreboard** *n* Anzeigetafel *f*

scorn *n* Verachtung *f*; **scornful** *adj* verächtlich

Scorpio *n* ASTR Skorpion *m*

scorpion *n* Skorpion *m*

Scot *n* Schotte *m*, Schottin *f*; **Scotch 1.** *adj* schottisch **2.** *n* (*whisky*) schottischer Whisky, Scotch *m*

Scotch tape® *n* (*US*) Tesafilm® *m*

Scotland *n* Schottland *nt*; **Scotsman** *n* Schotte *m*; **Scotswoman** *n* Schottin *f*; **Scottish** *adj* schottisch

scout *n* (*boy scout*) Pfadfinder *m*

scrambled eggs *npl* Rührei *nt*

scrap 1. n (bit) Stückchen nt, Fetzen m; (metal) Schrott m **2.** vt (car) verschrotten; (plan) verwerfen

scrape 1. n (scratch) Kratzer m **2.** vt (car) schrammen; (wall) streifen; **~ one's knee** sich das Knie schürfen; **scrape through** vi (exam) mit knapper Not bestehen

scrap heap n Schrotthaufen m; **scrap metal** n Schrott m; **scrap paper** n Schmierpapier nt

scratch 1. n (mark) Kratzer m; **start from ~** von vorne anfangen **2.** vt kratzen; (car) zerkratzen; **~ one's arm** sich am Arm kratzen

scream 1. n Schrei m **2.** vi schreien (with vor + dat); **~ at sb** jdn anschreien

screen 1. n TV, IT Bildschirm m; FILM Leinwand f **2.** vt (film) zeigen; (applicants, luggage) überprüfen; **screenplay** n Drehbuch nt; **screen saver** n IT Bildschirmschoner m

screw 1. n Schraube f **2.** vt vulg (have sex with) poppen; **~ sth to sth** etw an etw acc schrauben; **~ off/on** (lid) ab-/aufschrauben; **screw up** vt (paper) zusammenknüllen; (make a mess of) vermasseln; **screwdriver** n Schraubenzieher m

scribble vt, vi kritzeln

script n (of play) Text m; (of film) Drehbuch nt; (style of writing) Schrift f

scroll down vi IT runterscrollen; **scroll up** vi IT raufscrollen; **scroll bar** n IT Scrollbar f

scrub vt schrubben

scruffy adj vergammelt

scuba-diving n Sporttauchen nt

sculptor n Bildhauer(in) m(f); **sculpture** n ART Bildhauerei f; (statue) Skulptur f

sea n Meer nt. See f; **seafood** n Meeresfrüchte pl; **sea front** n Strandpromenade f; **seagull** n Möwe f

seal 1. n (animal) Robbe f; (stamp, impression) Siegel nt; TECH Verschluss m; (ring etc) Dichtung f **2.** vt versiegeln; (envelope) zukleben

seam n Naht f

seaport n Seehafen m

search 1. n Suche f (for nach); **do a ~ for** IT suchen nach; **in ~ of** auf der Suche nach **2.** vi suchen (for nach) **3.** vt durchsuchen; **search engine** n IT Suchmaschine f

seashell n Muschel f; **seashore** n Strand m; **seasick** adj seekrank; **seaside** n **at the ~** am Meer; **seaside resort** n Seebad nt

season 1. n Jahreszeit f, Saison f; **high/low** ~ Hoch-/Nebensaison f **2.** vt (flavour) würzen

seasoning n Gewürz nt

season ticket n RAIL Zeitkar-

te f; THEAT Abonnement nt;
SPORT Dauerkarte f

seat 1. n (place) Platz m;
(chair) Sitz m; **take a ~** setzen Sie sich **2.** vt **the hall
~s 300** der Saal hat 300 Sitz-
plätze; **please be ~ed** bitte
setzen Sie sich; **remain ~ed**
sitzen bleiben; **seat belt** n Sicherheitsgurt m

sea view n Seeblick m; **seaweed** n Seetang m

secluded adj abgelegen

second 1. adj zweite(r, s); **the~
of June** der zweite Juni **2.**
adv (in second position) an
zweiter Stelle; (secondly)
zweitens; **he came ~** er ist
Zweiter geworden **3.** n (of
time) Sekunde f; (moment)
Augenblick m; ~ (**gear**) der
zweite Gang; (second helping) zweite Portion; **just a ~**
(einen) Augenblick!; **secondary** adj zweitrangig; **~**
(less important)
zweitrangig; **~
education** hö-
here Schulbildung f; **~
school** weiterführende
Schule; **second-class 1.** adj
(ticket) zweiter Klasse; **~
stamp** Briefmarke für nicht
bevorzugt beförderte Sen-
dungen **2.** adv (travel) zweiter Klasse; **secondhand**
adj,adv gebraucht; (information) aus zweiter Hand; **secondly** adv zweitens; **second-
rate** adj pej zweitklassig

secret 1. n Geheimnis nt **2.** adj
geheim; (admirer) heimlich

secretary n Sekretär(in) m(f);
(minister) Minister(in) m(f);
Secretary of State n (US)
Außenminister(in) m(f)

secretive adj geheimnistue-
risch; **secretly** adv heimlich

sect n Sekte f

section n (part) Teil m; (of
document) Abschnitt m; (department) Abteilung f

secure 1. adj (safe) sicher
(from + vor + dat); (firmly
fixed) fest **2.** vt (make firm)
befestigen; (window, door)
fest verschließen; (obtain)
sich sichern; **securely** adv
fest; (safely) sicher; **security**
n Sicherheit f

sedative n Beruhigungsmittel
nt

seduce vt verführen; **seductive** adj verführerisch

see 1. vt sehen; (understand)
verstehen; (check) nachsehen; (accompany) begleiten;
(visit) besuchen; (talk to)
sprechen; **~ the doctor** zum
Arzt gehen; **~ sb home** jdn
nach Hause begleiten; **~
you tschüs!; ~ you on Friday**
bis Freitag! **2.** vi sehen; (understand) verstehen; (check)
nachsehen; (you) **~** siehst
du!; **we'll ~** mal sehen; **see
about** vt (attend to) sich
kümmern um; **see off** vt
(say goodbye to) verabschieden; **see out** vt (show out)
zur Tür bringen; **see
through** vt **see sth through**

etw zu Ende bringen; **~ sb/ sth** jdn/etw durchschauen; **see to** vi sich kümmern um; **~ it that ...** sieh zu, dass ...

seed n (*of plant*) Samen m; (*in fruit*) Kern m; **seedless** adj kernlos

seek vt suchen; (*fame*) streben nach; **~ sb's advice** jdn um Rat fragen

seem vi scheinen; **he ~s (to be) honest** er scheint ehrlich zu sein

seen pp of **see**

seesaw n Wippe f

segment n Teil m

seize vt packen; (*confiscate*) beschlagnahmen; (*opportunity, power*) ergreifen

seldom adv selten

select 1. adj (*exclusive*) exklusiv **2.** vt auswählen; **selection** n Auswahl f (*of* an + *dat*)

self n Selbst nt, Ich nt; **he's his old ~ again** er ist wieder ganz der Alte; **self-adhesive** adj selbstklebend; **self-assured** n selbstsicher; **self-catering** adj für Selbstversorger; **self-centred** adj egozentrisch; **self-confidence** n Selbstbewusstsein nt; **self-confident** adj selbstbewusst; **self-conscious** adj befangen, verklemmt; **self-contained** adj (*flat*) separat; **self-control** n Selbstbeherrschung f; **self-defence** n Selbstverteidigung f; **self-**

-**employed** adj selbstständig

selfish, selfishly adj, adv egoistisch, selbstsüchtig

self-pity n Selbstmitleid nt; **self-respect** n Selbstachtung f; **self-service 1.** n Selbstbedienung f **2.** adj Selbstbedienungs-

sell 1. vt verkaufen; **~ sb sth, ~ sth to sb** jdm etw verkaufen; **do you ~ postcards?** haben Sie Postkarten? **2.** vi (*product*) sich verkaufen; **sell out** vi **be sold ~** ausverkauft sein; **sell-by date** n Haltbarkeitsdatum nt

Sellotape® n (*Brit*) Tesafilm® m

semi n (*Brit, house*) Doppelhaushälfte f; **semicircle** n Halbkreis m; **semicolon** n Semikolon nt; **semidetached** (*house*) n (*Brit*) Doppelhaushälfte f; **semifinal** n Halbfinale nt

seminar n Seminar nt

senate n Senat m; **senator** n Senator(in) m(f)

send vt schicken; **~ sb sth, ~ sth to sb** jdm etw schicken; **~ her my best wishes** grüße sie von mir; **send away 1.** vt wegschicken **2.** vi **~ for** anfordern; **send back** vt zurückschicken; **send for** vt (*person*) holen lassen; (*by post*) anfordern; **send off** vt (*by post*) abschicken

sender n Absender(in) m(f)

senior 1. adj (*older*) älter;

(*high-ranking*) höher; (*pupils*) älter; **he is ~ to me** er ist mir übergeordnet **2.** *n* **he's eight years my ~** er ist acht Jahre älter als ich; **senior citizen** *n* Senior(in) *m(f)*

sensation *n* Gefühl *nt*; (*excitement, person, thing*) Sensation *f*; **sensational** *adj* sensationell

sense 1. *n* (*faculty, meaning*) Sinn *m*; (*feeling*) Gefühl *nt*; (*understanding*) Verstand *m*; **~ of smell/taste** Geruchs-/Geschmackssinn *m*; **have a ~ of humour** Humor haben; **make ~** (*sentence etc*) einen Sinn ergeben; (*be sensible*) Sinn machen; **in a ~** gewissermaßen **2.** *vt* spüren; **senseless** *adj* (*stupid*) sinnlos

sensible, sensibly *adj, adv* vernünftig

sensitive *adj* empfindlich (*to* gegen); (*easily hurt*) sensibel; (*subject*) heikel

sent *pt, pp of* **send**

sentence 1. *n* LING Satz *m*; LAW Strafe *f* **2.** *vt* verurteilen (*to* zu)

sentiment *n* (*sentimentality*) Sentimentalität *f*; (*opinion*) Ansicht *f*; **sentimental** *adj* sentimental

separate 1. *adj* verschieden, separat; (*individual*) einzeln **2.** *vt* trennen (*from* von); **they are ~d** (*couple*) sie leben getrennt **3.** *vi* sich trennen; **separately** *adv* getrennt; (*singly*) einzeln

September *n* September *m*; **in ~** im September; **on the 2nd of ~** am 2. September; **at the beginning/in the middle/at the end of ~** Anfang/Mitte/Ende September; **last/next ~** letzten/nächsten September

septic *adj* vereitert

sequel *n* (*to film, book*) Fortsetzung *f* (*to* von)

sequence *n* (*order*) Reihenfolge *f*

Serb *n* Serbe *m*, Serbin *f*; **Serbia** *n* Serbien *nt*

sergeant *n* Polizeimeister(in) *m(f)*; MIL Feldwebel(in) *m(f)*

serial 1. *n* TV Serie *f*; (*in newspaper etc*) Fortsetzungsroman *m* **2.** *adj* IT seriell; **~ number** Seriennummer *f*

series *nsing* Reihe *f*; TV, RADIO Serie *f*

serious *adj* ernst; (*injury, illness, mistake*) schwer; (*discussion*) ernsthaft; **are you ~?** ist das dein Ernst?; **seriously** *adv* ernsthaft; (*hurt*) schwer; **~?** im Ernst?; **take sb ~** jdn ernst nehmen

sermon *n* REL Predigt *f*

servant *n* Diener(in) *m(f)*; **serve 1.** *vt* (*customer*) bedienen; (*food*) servieren; (*one's country etc*) dienen + *dat*; (*sentence*) verbüßen; **I'm be-**

ing *~d* ich werde schon bedient; *it ~s him right* es geschieht ihm recht **2.** *vi* dienen *(as* als), aufschlagen **3.** *n*, Aufschlag *m*

server *n* IT Server *m*

service 1. *n (in shop, hotel)* Bedienung *f; (activity, amenity)* Dienstleistung *f; (set of dishes)* Service *nt;* AUTO Inspektion *f;* TECH Wartung *f;* REL Gottesdienst *m*, Aufschlag *m;* *train-/bus* Zug-/Busverbindung *f;* *~ not included'* „Bedienung nicht inbegriffen" **2.** *vt* AUTO, TECH warten; **service area** *n (on motorway)* Raststätte *f (mit Tankstelle);* **service charge** *n* Bedienung *f;* **service provider** *n* IT Provider *m;* **service station** *n* Tankstelle *f*

serving *n (portion)* Portion *f*

session *n (of court, assembly)* Sitzung *f*

set 1. *vt (place)* stellen; *(lay flat)* legen; *(arrange)* anordnen; *(table)* decken; *(trap, record)* aufstellen; *(time, price)* festsetzen; *(watch, alarm)* stellen *(for* auf + *acc);* *~ sb a task* jdm eine Aufgabe stellen; *~ free* freilassen; *~ a good example* ein gutes Beispiel geben; *the novel is ~ in London* spielt in London **2.** *vi (sun)* untergehen; *(become hard)* fest werden; *(bone)* zusam-

menwachsen **3.** *n (collection of things)* Satz *m; (of cutlery, furniture)* Garnitur *f; (group of people)* Kreis *m;* RADIO, TV Apparat *m*, Satz *m;* THEAT Bühnenbild *nt;* FILM (Film-)kulisse *f* **4.** *adj (agreed, prescribed)* festgelegt; *(ready)* bereit; *~ meal* Menü *nt;* **set aside** *vt (money)* beiseite legen; *(time)* einplanen; **set off 1.** *vi* aufbrechen *(for* nach) **2.** *vt (alarm)* auslösen; *(enhance)* hervorheben; **set out 1.** *vi* aufbrechen *(for* nach) **2.** *vt (chairs, chesspieces etc)* aufstellen; *(state)* darlegen; *~ to do sth (intend)* beabsichtigen, etw zu tun; **set up 1.** *vt (firm, organization)* gründen; *(stall, tent, camera)* aufbauen; *(meeting)* vereinbaren **2.** *vi* *~ as a doctor* sich als Arzt niederlassen

setback *n* Rückschlag *m*

settee *n* Sofa *nt*, Couch *f*

setting *n (of novel, film)* Schauplatz *m; (surroundings)* Umgebung *f*

settle 1. *vt (bill, debt)* begleichen; *(dispute)* beilegen; *(question)* klären; *(stomach)* beruhigen **2.** *vi* *~ (down) (feel at home)* sich einleben; *(calm down)* sich beruhigen; **settle in** *vi (in new place)* sich einleben; *(in job)* sich eingewöhnen; **settlement** *n (of bill, debt)* Begleichung *f;*

(colony) Siedlung *f*; **reach a ~** sich einigen

setup *n (organization)* Organisation *f*; *(situation)* Situation *f*

seven 1. *num* sieben **2.** *n* Sieben *f*; → **eight**; **seventeen 1.** *num* siebzehn **2.** *n* Siebzehn *f*; → **eight**; **seventeenth** *adj* siebzehnte(r, s); → **eighth**; **seventh 1.** *adj* siebte(r, s) **2.** *n (fraction)* Siebtel *nt*; → **eighth**; **seventieth** *adj* siebzigste(r, s); → **eighth**; **seventy 1.** *num* siebzig; **~-one** einundsiebzig **2.** *n* Siebzig *f*; **be in one's seventies** in den Siebzigern sein; → **eight**

several *adj, pron* mehrere

severe *adj (strict)* streng; *(serious)* schwer; *(pain)* stark; *(winter)* hart; **severely** *adv (harshly)* hart; *(seriously)* schwer

sew *vt, vi* nähen

sewage *n* Abwasser *nt*; **sewer** *n* Abwasserkanal *m*

sewing *n* Nähen *nt*; **sewing machine** *n* Nähmaschine *f*

sewn *pp of* **sew**

sex *n* Sex *m*; *(gender)* Geschlecht *nt*; **have ~** Sex haben *(with mit)*; **sexism** *n* Sexismus *m*; **sexist 1.** *adj* sexistisch **2.** *n* Sexist(in) *m(f)*; **sex life** *n* Sex(ual)leben *nt*

sexual *adj* sexuell; **~ discrimination/ harassment** sexuelle Diskriminierung / Belästigung; **~ intercourse** Geschlechtsverkehr *m*; **sexuality** *n* Sexualität *f*

sexy *adj* sexy

Seychelles *npl* Seychellen *pl*

shack *n* Hütte *f*

shade 1. *n (shadow)* Schatten *m*; *(for lamp)* (Lampen-) schirm *m*; *(colour)* Farbton *m*; **~s** *(US, sunglasses)* Sonnenbrille *f* **2.** *vt (from sun)* abschirmen; *(in drawing)* schattieren

shadow *n* Schatten *m*

shady *adj* schattig; *fig* zwielichtig

shake 1. *vt* schütteln; *(shock)* erschüttern; **~ do with sb** jdm die Hand geben; **~ one's head** den Kopf schütteln **2.** *vi (tremble)* zittern; *(building, ground)* schwanken; **shake off** *vt* abschütteln; **shaken** *pp of* **shake**; **shaky** *adj (trembling)* zittrig; *(table, chair, position)* wackelig

shall *vaux* werden; *(in questions)* sollen; **I ~ do my best** ich werde mein Bestes tun; **I come too?** soll ich mitkommen?; **where ~ we go?** wo gehen wir hin?

shallow *adj* seicht; *(person)* oberflächlich

shame *n (feeling of ~)* Scham *f*; *(disgrace)* Schande *f*; **what a ~** wie schade!; **~ on you** schäm dich!; **it's a ~ that ...** schade, dass ...

shampoo 1. *n* Shampoo *nt*;

have a ~ and set sich die Haare waschen und legen lassen; **2.** vt (hair) waschen; (carpet) schamponieren

shandy n Radler m, Alsterwasser nt

shan't contr of **shall not**

shape 1. n Form f; (unidentified figure) Gestalt f; **in the ~ of** in Form + gen; **be in good ~** (healthwise) in guter Verfassung sein; **take ~** (plan, idea) Gestalt annehmen **2.** vt (clay, person) formen; **-shaped** suf -förmig; **heart~** herzförmig

share 1. n Anteil + dat (in, of an m); FIN Aktie f **2.** vt, vi teilen; **shareholder** n Aktionär(in) m(f)

shark n Haifisch m

sharp 1. adj scharf; (pin) spitz; (person) scharfsinnig; (pain) heftig; (increase, fall) abrupt; **C/F ~** MUS Cis/Dis nt **2.** adv **at 2 o'clock ~** Punkt 2 Uhr; **sharpen** vt (knife) schärfen; (pencil) spitzen; **sharpener** n (pencil sharpener) Spitzer m

shatter 1. vt zerschmettern; fig zerstören **2.** vi zerspringen; **shattered** adj (exhausted) kaputt

shave 1. vt rasieren **2.** vi sich rasieren **3.** n Rasur f; **that was a close ~** fig das war knapp; **shave off** vt **shave one's beard off** sich den Bart abrasieren; **shaven 1.**

pp of **shave 2.** adj (head) kahl geschoren; **shaver** n ELEC Rasierapparat m; **shaving brush** n Rasierpinsel m; **shaving foam** n Rasierschaum m

shawl n Tuch nt

she pron sie f

shed 1. n Schuppen m **2.** vt (tears, blood) vergießen; (hair, leaves) verlieren

she'd contr of **she had; she would**

sheep n Schaf nt; **sheepdog** n Schäferhund m; **sheepskin** n Schaffell nt

sheer adj (madness) rein; (steep) steil; (transparent) hauchdünn; **by ~ chance** rein zufällig

sheet n (on bed) Betttuch nt; (of paper) Blatt nt; (of metal) Platte f; (of glass) Scheibe f

shelf n Bücherbord nt, Regal nt; **shelves** pl (item of furniture) Regal nt

she'll contr of **she will; she shall**

shell 1. n (of egg, nut) Schale f; (sea~) Muschel f **2.** vt (peas, nuts) schälen; **shellfish** n (as food) Meeresfrüchte pl

shelter 1. n (protection) Schutz m; (accommodation) Unterkunft f; (bus shelter) Wartehäuschen nt **2.** vt schützen (from vor + dat) **3.** vi sich unterstellen; **sheltered** adj (spot) geschützt; (life) behütet

shelve vt fig aufschieben;
shelves pl of **shelf**
shepherd n Schäfer m; shepherd's pie n Hackfleischauflauf mit Decke aus Kartoffelpüree
sherry n Sherry m
she's contr of **she is**; **she has**
shield 1. n Schild m; fig Schutz m 2. vt schützen (from vor + dat)
shift 1. n (change) Veränderung f; (period at work, workers) Schicht f; (on keyboard) Umschalttaste f 2. vt (furniture etc) verrücken; ~ gear(s) (US) AUTO schalten 3. vi (move) sich bewegen; (move up) rutschen; shift key n Umschalttaste f
shin n Schienbein nt
shine 1. vi (be shiny) glänzen; (sun) scheinen; (lamp) leuchten 2. vt (polish) polieren 3. n Glanz m
shingles nsing MED Gürtelrose f
shiny adj glänzend
ship 1. n Schiff nt 2. vt (send) versenden; (by ship) verschiffen; shipment n (goods) Sendung f; (sent by ship) Ladung f; shipwreck n Schiffbruch m; shipyard n Werft f
shirt n Hemd nt
shit n vulg Scheiße f; ~! Scheiße!; shitty adj fam beschissen
shiver vi zittern (with vor

+ dat)

shock 1. n (mental, emotional) Schock m; be in ~ unter Schock stehen; get a ~ ELEC einen Schlag bekommen 2. vt schockieren; shock absorber n Stoßdämpfer m; shocked adj schockiert (by über + acc); shocking adj schockierend
shoe n Schuh m; shoelace n Schnürsenkel m; shoe polish n Schuhcreme f
shone pt, pp of **shine**
shook pt of **shake**
shoot 1. vt (wound) anschießen; (kill) erschießen; FILM drehen; fam (heroin) drücken 2. vi (with gun, move quickly) schießen; ~ at sb auf jdn schießen 3. n (of plant) Trieb m; shooting n (exchange of gunfire) Schießerei f; (killing) Erschießung f
shop 1. n Geschäft nt, Laden m 2. vi einkaufen; shop assistant n Verkäufer(in) m(f); shopkeeper n Geschäftsinhaber(in) m(f); shoplifting n Ladendiebstahl m; shopping n (activity) Einkaufen nt; (goods) Einkäufe pl; do the ~ einkaufen; go ~ einkaufen gehen; shopping bag n Einkaufstasche f; shopping cart n (US) Einkaufswagen m; shopping center (US), shopping centre n Einkaufszentrum nt;

shopping list n Einkaufszettel m; shopping trolley n (Brit) Einkaufswagen m; shop window n Schaufenster nt

shore n Ufer nt; on ~ an Land

short adj sehr kurz; (person) klein; be ~ of money knapp bei Kasse sein; be ~ of time wenig Zeit haben; ~ of breath kurzatmig; cut ~ (holiday) abbrechen; we are two ~ wir haben zwei zu wenig; it's ~ for ... das ist die Kurzform von ...; shortage n Knappheit f (of an + dat); shortbread n Buttergebäck nt; short circuit n Kurzschluss m; shortcoming n Unzulänglichkeit f; (of person) Fehler m; shortcut n (quicker route) Abkürzung f; IT Shortcut m; shorten vt kürzen; (in time) verkürzen; shortlist n be on the ~ in der engeren Wahl sein; short-lived adj kurzlebig; shortly adv bald; shorts npl Shorts pl; short-sighted adj kurzsichtig; short-sleeved adj kurzärmelig; short-stay car park n Kurzzeitparkplatz m; short story n Kurzgeschichte f; short-term adj kurzfristig

shot 1. pt, pp of shoot 2. n (from gun, in soccer) Schuss m; PHOT, FILM Aufnahme f; (injection) Spritze f; (of alcohol) Schuss m

should 1. pt of shall 2. vaux I ~ go now ich sollte jetzt gehen; you ~n't have said that das hättest du nicht sagen sollen; that ~ be enough das müsste reichen

shoulder n Schulter f

shouldn't contr of should not

should've contr of should have

shout 1. n Schrei m; (call) Ruf m 2. vt rufen; (order) brüllen 3. vi schreien; ~ at anschreien

shove 1. vt (person) schubsen; (car, table etc) schieben 2. vi (in crowd) drängeln

shovel 1. n Schaufel f 2. vt schaufeln

show 1. vt zeigen; ~ sb sth, ~ sth to sb jdm etw zeigen; ~ sb in jdn hereinführen; ~ sb out jdn zur Tür bringen 2. n FILM, THEAT Vorstellung f; TV Show f; (exhibition) Ausstellung f; show off vi pej angeben; show round vt herumführen; show sb round the house / the town jdm das Haus / die Stadt zeigen; show up vi (arrive) auftauchen

shower 1. n Dusche f; (rain) Schauer m; have (or take) a ~ duschen 2. vi (wash) duschen

showing n FILM Vorstellung f

shown pp of show

showroom n Ausstellungsraum m

shrank *pt of* **shrink**

shred 1. *n (of paper, fabric)* Fetzen *m* **2.** *vt (in shredder)* (im Reißwolf) zerkleinern; **shredder** *n (for paper)* Reißwolf *m*

shrimp *n* Garnele *f*

shrink *vi* schrumpfen; *(clothes)* eingehen

shrivel *vi* ~ **(up)** schrumpfen; *(skin)* runzlig werden

Shrove Tuesday *n* Fastnachtsdienstag *m*

shrub *n* Busch *m*, Strauch *m*

shrug *vt, vi* ~ **(one's shoulders)** mit den Achseln zucken

shrunk *pp of* **shrink**

shudder *vi* schaudern; *(ground, building)* beben

shuffle *vt, vi* mischen

shut **1.** *vt* zumachen, schließen; ~ **your mouth** *fam* halt den Mund! **2.** *vi* schließen **3.** *adj* geschlossen; **we're** ~ wir haben geschlossen; **shut down 1.** *vt* schließen; *(computer)* ausschalten **2.** *vi* schließen; *(computer)* sich ausschalten **in** *vt* einsperren; **shut out** *vt (lock out)* aussperren; **shut oneself out** *vt* sich aussperren; **shut up 1.** *vt (lock up)* abschließen; *(silence)* zum Schweigen bringen **2.** *vi* *(keep quiet)* den Mund halten; ~! halt den Mund!; **shutter** *n (on window)* (Fenster-)laden *m*; **shutter release** *n*

Auslöser *m*

shuttle bus *n* Shuttlebus *m*

shuttlecock *n* Federball *m*

shuttle service *n* Pendelverkehr *m*

shy *adj* schüchtern; *(animal)* scheu

Sicily *n* Sizilien *nt*

sick *adj* krank; *(joke)* makaber; **be** ~ *(Brit, vomit)* sich übergeben; **be off** ~ wegen Krankheit fehlen; **I feel** ~ mir ist schlecht!; **be** ~ **of sb/sth** jdn/etw satt haben; **it makes me** ~ *fig* es ekelt mich an; **sickbag** *n* Spucktüte *f*; **sick leave** *n* **be on** ~ krankgeschrieben sein; **sickness** *n* Krankheit *f*; *(Brit, nausea)* Übelkeit *f*

side 1. *n* Seite *f*; *(of road)* Rand *m*; *(of mountain)* Hang *m*; SPORT Mannschaft *f*; **by my** ~ neben mir; ~ **by** ~ nebeneinander **2.** *adj (door, entrance)* Seiten-; **sideboard** *n* Anrichte *f*, **sideboards**, **sideburns** *(US)* *npl* Koteletten *pl*; **side dish** *n* Beilage *f*; **side effect** *n* Nebenwirkung *f*; **side order** *n* Beilage *f*; **side road** *n* Nebenstraße *f*; **side street** *n* Seitenstraße *f*; **sidewalk** *n (US)* Bürgersteig *m*; **sideways** *adv* seitwärts

sieve *n* Sieb *nt*

sift *vt (flour etc)* sieben

sigh *vi* seufzen

sight *n (power of seeing)* Sehvermögen nt; (view, thing seen) Anblick m; **~s** pl (of city etc) Sehenswürdigkeiten pl; **have bad ~** schlecht sehen; **lose~ of** aus den Augen verlieren; **out of ~** außer Sicht; sightseeing n go **~** Sehenswürdigkeiten besichtigen; **~ tour** Rundfahrt f

sign 1. n Zeichen nt; (notice, road **~**) Schild nt 2. vt unterschreiben 3. vi unterschreiben; **~ for sth** den Empfang einer Sache gen bestätigen; **~ in/out** sich ein-/austragen; sign up vi (for course) sich einschreiben; MIL sich verpflichten

signal 1. n Signal nt 2. vi (car driver) blinken

signature n Unterschrift f

significant adj (important) bedeutend, wichtig; (meaning sth) bedeutsam

sign language n Zeichensprache f; signpost n Wegweiser m

silence 1. n Stille f; (of person) Schweigen nt; **~!** Ruhe! 2. vt zum Schweigen bringen; silent adj still; (taciturn) schweigsam; **she remained ~** sie schwieg

silk 1. n Seide f 2. adj Seidenseiden-

silly adj dumm, albern; **don't do anything ~** mach keine Dummheiten

silver 1. n Silber nt; (coins) Silbermünzen pl 2. adj Silber-, silbern; silver wedding n silberne Hochzeit

similar adj ähnlich (to dat); similarity n Ähnlichkeit f (to mit); similarly adv (equally) ebenso

simple adj einfach; (unsophisticated) schlicht; simplify vt vereinfachen; simply adv einfach; (merely) bloß; (dress) schlicht

simulate vt simulieren

simultaneous, simultaneously adj, adv gleichzeitig

sin 1. n Sünde f 2. vi sündigen

since 1. adv seitdem; (in the meantime) inzwischen 2. prep seit + dat; **ever ~ 1995** schon seit 1995 3. conj (time) seit, seitdem; (because) da, weil; **ever ~ I've known her** seit ich sie kenne; **it's ages ~ I've seen him** ich habe ihn seit langem nicht mehr gesehen

sincere adj aufrichtig; sincerely adv aufrichtig; **Yours ~** mit freundlichen Grüßen

sing vt, vi singen

Singapore n Singapur nt

singer n Sänger(in) m(f)

single 1. adj (one only) einzig; (not double) einzeln; (bed, room) Einzel-; (unmarried) ledig; (Brit, ticket) einfach 2. n (Brit, ticket) einfache Fahrkarte; MUS Single f; single out vt (choose) auswählen; single-handed, single-handedly adv im Alleingang; **single parent** *n* Alleinerziehende(r) *mf*

singular *adj* Singular *m*

sinister *adj* unheimlich

sink 1. *vt* (*ship*) versenken **2.** *vi* sinken **1.** *n* Spülbecken *nt*; (*in bathroom*) Waschbecken *nt*

sip *vt* nippen an + *dat*

sir *n* **yes,** ~ ja(, mein Herr); **can I help you,** ~? kann ich Ihnen helfen?; *Sir James* (*title*) Sir James

sister *n* Schwester *f*; (*Brit, nurse*) Schwester *f*; **sister-in-law** *n* Schwägerin *f*

sit 1. *vi* (*be sitting*) sitzen; (~ *down*) sich setzen; (*committee, court*) tagen **2.** *vt* (*Brit, exam*) machen; **sit down** *vi* sich hinsetzen; **sit up** *vi* (*from lying position*) sich aufsetzen

site *n* Platz *m*; (*building site*) Baustelle *f*; (*website*) Site *f*

sitting *n* (*meeting, for portrait*) Sitzung *f*; **sitting room** *n* Wohnzimmer *nt*

situated *adj* **be** ~ liegen

situation *n* (*circumstances*) Situation *f*, Lage *f*; (*job*) Stelle *f*; **'~s vacant/ wanted'** (*Brit*) „Stellenangebote/ Stellengesuche"

six 1. *num* sechs **2.** *n* Sechs *f*; → **eight**; **sixpack** *n* (*of beer etc*) Sechserpack *nt*; **sixteen 1.** *num* sechzehn **2.** *n* Sechzehn *f*; → **eight**; **sixteenth** *adj* sechzehnte(r, s); →

eighth; **sixth 1.** *adj* sechste(r, s); ~ **form** (*Brit*) ≈ Oberstufe *f* **2.** *n* (*fraction*) Sechstel *nt*; → **eighth**; **sixtieth** *adj* sechzigste(r, s); → **eighth**; **sixty 1.** *num* sechzig; ~-**one** einundsechzig **2.** *n* Sechzig *f*; **be in one's sixties** in den Sechzigern sein; → **eight**

size *n* Größe *f*; **what** ~ **are you?** welche Größe haben Sie?; **a** ~ **too big** eine Nummer zu groß

sizzle *vi* brutzeln

skate 1. *n* Schlittschuh *m*; (*roller skate*) Rollschuh *m* **2.** *vi* Schlittschuh laufen; (*roller-skate*) Rollschuh laufen; **skateboard** *n* Skateboard *nt*; **skating** *n* Eislauf *m*; (*roller-skate*) Rollschuhlauf *m*; **skating rink** *n* Eisbahn *f*; (*for roller-skating*) Rollschuhbahn *f*

skeleton *n* Skelett *nt*

skeptical *n* (*US*) → **sceptical**

sketch 1. *n* Skizze *f*; THEAT Sketch *m* **2.** *vt* skizzieren

ski *n* Ski *m* **2.** *vi* Ski laufen; **ski boot** *n* Skistiefel *m*

skid *vi* AUTO schleudern

skier *n* Skiläufer(in) *m(f)*; **skiing** *n* Skilaufen *nt*; **go** ~ **Ski** laufen gehen; ~ **holiday** Skiurlaub *m*; **skiing instructor** *n* Skilehrer(in) *m(f)*

ski-lift *n* Skilift *m*

skill *n* Geschick *nt*; (*acquired*

technique) Fertigkeit *f*;
skilled *adj* geschickt (*at*, *in* in + *dat*); (*worker*) Fach-; (*work*) fachmännisch

skim *vt* ~ **(off)** (*fat etc*) abschöpfen; ~ **(through)** (*read*) überfliegen; **skimmed milk** *n* Magermilch *f*

skin *n* Haut *f*; (*fur*) Fell *nt*; (*peel*) Schale *f*; **skinny** *adj* dünn

skip 1. *vi* hüpfen; (*with rope*) Seil springen **2.** *vt* (*miss out*) überspringen; (*meal*) ausfallen lassen; (*school*, *lesson*) schwänzen

ski pants *npl* Skihose *f*; **ski pass** *n* Skipass *m*; **ski pole** *n* Skistock *m*; **ski resort** *n* Skiort *m*

skirt *n* Rock *m*

ski run *n* (Ski)abfahrt *f*; **ski stick** *n* Skistock *m*; **ski tow** *n* Schlepplift *m*

skittle *n* Kegel *m*; ~**s** (*game*) Kegeln *nt*

skive *vi* ~ **(off)** (*Brit*) *fam* sich drücken; (*from school*) schwänzen; (*from work*) blaumachen

skull *n* Schädel *m*

sky *n* Himmel *m*; **skydiving** *n* Fallschirmspringen *nt*; **skylight** *n* Dachfenster *nt*; **skyscraper** *n* Wolkenkratzer *m*

slam *vt* zuschlagen; **slam on** *vt* **slam the brakes on** voll auf die Bremse treten

slander 1. *n* Verleumdung *f* **2.** *vt* verleumden

slang *n* Slang *m*

slap 1. *n* Klaps *m*; (*across face*) Ohrfeige *f* **2.** *vt* schlagen; ~ **sb's face** jdn ohrfeigen

slash 1. *n* (*punctuation mark*) Schrägstrich *m* **2.** *vt* (*face*, *tyre*) aufschlitzen; (*prices*) stark herabsetzen

slate *n* (*rock*) Schiefer *m*; (*roof slate*) Schieferplatte *f*

slaughter *vt* (*animals*) schlachten; (*people*) abschlachten

Slav 1. *adj* slawisch **2.** *n* Slawe *m*, Slawin *f*

slave *n* Sklave *m*, Sklavin *f*; **slave away** *vi* schuften; **slave-driver** *n* *fam* Sklaventreiber(in) *m(f)*; **slavery** *n* Sklaverei *f*

sleaze *n* (*corruption*) Korruption *f*; **sleazy** *adj* (*bar*, *district*) zwielichtig

sledge *n* Schlitten *m*

sleep 1. *vi* schlafen **2.** *n* Schlaf *m*; **put to** ~ (*animal*) einschläfern; **sleep in** *vi* (*lie in*) ausschlafen; **sleeper** *n* RAIL (*train*) Schlafwagenzug *m*; (*carriage*) Schlafwagen *m*; **sleeping bag** *n* Schlafsack *m*; **sleeping car** *n* Schlafwagen *m*; **sleeping pill** *n* Schlaftablette *f*; **sleepless** *adj* schlaflos; **sleepy** *adj* schläfrig; (*place*) verschlafen

sleet *n* Schneeregen *m*

sleeve *n* Ärmel *m*; **sleeveless** *adj* ärmellos

sleigh *n* (Pferde)schlitten *m*

slender *adj* schlank; *fig* gering
slept *pt, pp of* **sleep**
slice 1. *n* Scheibe *f*; (*of cake, tart, pizza*) Stück *nt* **2.** *vt* ~ (**up**) in Scheiben schneiden
slid *pt, pp of* **slide**
slide 1. *vt* gleiten lassen; (*push*) schieben **2.** *vi* gleiten; (*slip*) rutschen **3.** *n* PHOT Dia *nt*; (*in playground*) Rutschbahn *f*; (*Brit, for hair*) Spange *f*
slight *adj* leicht; (*problem, difference*) klein; **not in the ~est** nicht im Geringsten; **slightly** *adv* etwas; (*injured*) leicht
slim 1. *adj* (*person*) schlank; (*book*) dünn; (*chance, hope*) gering **2.** *vi* abnehmen
slime *n* Schleim *m*; **slimy** *adj* schleimig
sling 1. *vt* werfen **2.** *n* (*for arm*) Schlinge *f*
slip 1. *n* (*mistake*) Flüchtigkeitsfehler *m*; ~ **of paper** Zettel *m* **2.** *vt* (*put*) stecken; ~ **on/off** (*garment*) an-/ausziehen; **it ~ped my mind** ich habe es vergessen **3.** *vi* (*lose balance*) (aus)rutschen; (*slip*) rutschen
slipper *n* Hausschuh *m*; **slippery** *adj* (*path, road*) glatt; (*soap, fish*) glitschig; **slip-road** *n* (*Brit, onto motorway*) Auffahrt *f*; (*off motorway*) Ausfahrt *f*
slit 1. *vt* aufschlitzen **2.** *n* Schlitz *m*
slope 1. *n* Neigung *f*; (*side of*

hill) Hang *m* **2.** *vi* (*be sloping*) schräg sein; **slope down** *vi* (*land, road*) abfallen; **sloping** *adj* (*floor, roof*) schräg
sloppy *adj* (*careless*) schlampig
slot *n* (*opening*) Schlitz *m*; IT Steckplatz *m*; **we have a ~ free at 2** (*free time*) um 2 ist noch ein Termin frei; **slot machine** *n* Automat *m*; (*for gambling*) Spielautomat *m*
Slovak 1. *adj* slowakisch **2.** *n* (*person*) Slowake *m*, Slowakin *f*; (*language*) Slowakisch *nt*; **Slovakia** *n* Slowakei *f*
Slovene, Slovenian 1. *adj* slowenisch **2.** *n* (*person*) Slowene *m*, Slowenin *f*; (*language*) Slowenisch *nt*; **Slovenia** *n* Slowenien *nt*
slow *adj* langsam; (*business*) flau; **be ~** (*clock*) nachgehen; (*stupid*) begriffsstutzig sein; **slow down** *vi* langsamer werden; (*when driving/ walking*) langsamer fahren/gehen; **slowly** *adv* langsam; **slow motion** *n* **in ~** in Zeitlupe
slug *n* ZOOL Nacktschnecke *f*
slums *n* Slums *pl*
slump 1. *n* Rückgang *m* (*in an + dat*) **2.** *vi* (*onto chair etc*) sich fallen lassen; (*prices*) stürzen
slung *pt, pp of* **sling**
slur *n* (*insult*) Verleumdung *f*; **slurred** *adj* undeutlich

slush n (snow) Schneematsch m; **slushy** adj matschig; fig schmalzig

slut n pej Schlampe f

smack 1. n Klaps m **2.** vt ~ **sb** jdm einen Klaps geben

small adj klein; **small ads** npl (Brit) Kleinanzeigen pl; **small change** n Kleingeld nt; **small letters** npl **in ~** in Kleinbuchstaben; **smallpox** n Pocken pl; **small print** n **the ~** das Kleingedruckte; **small-scale** adj (map) in kleinem Maßstab; **small talk** n Konversation f, Smalltalk m

smart adj (elegant) schick; (clever) clever; **smart card** n Chipkarte f; **smartly** adv (dressed) schick

smash 1. n (car crash) Zusammenstoß m, Schmetterball m **2.** vt (break) zerschlagen; fig (record) brechen, deutlich übertreffen **3.** vi (break) zerbrechen; ~ **into** (car) krachen gegen; **smashing** adj fam toll

smear 1. n (mark) Fleck m; MED Abstrich m; fig Verleumdung f **2.** vt (spread) schmieren; (make dirty) beschmieren; fig verleumden

smell 1. vt riechen **2.** vi riechen (of nach); (unpleasantly) stinken **3.** n Geruch m; (unpleasant) Gestank m; **smelly** adj übel riechend; **smelt** pt, pp of **smell**

smile 1. n Lächeln nt **2.** vi lächeln; ~ **at sb** jdn anlächeln

smog n Smog m

smoke 1. n Rauch m **2.** vt rauchen; (food) räuchern **3.** vi rauchen; **smoke alarm** n Rauchmelder m; **smoked** adj (food) geräuchert; **smoke-free** adj (zone, building) rauchfrei; **smoker** n Raucher(in) m(f); **smoking** n Rauchen nt; **'no ~'** „Rauchen verboten"

smooth 1. adj glatt; (flight, crossing) ruhig; (movement) geschmeidig; (without problems) reibungslos; pej (person) aalglatt **2.** vt (hair, dress) glatt streichen; (surface) glätten; **smoothly** adv, reibungslos; **run ~** (engine) ruhig laufen

smudge vt (writing, lipstick) verschmieren

smug adj selbstgefällig

smuggle vt schmuggeln; ~ **in/out** herein-/herausschmuggeln

smutty adj (obscene) schmutzig

snack n Imbiss m; **have a ~** eine Kleinigkeit essen

snail n Schnecke f; **snail mail** n fam Schneckenpost f

snake n Schlange f

snap 1. n (photo) Schnappschuss m **2.** adj (decision) spontan **3.** vt (break) zerbrechen; (rope) zerreißen **4.** vi (break) brechen; (rope) reißen; (*bite*) schnappen (*at* nach); **snap fastener** *n* (*US*) Druckknopf *m*; **snapshot** *n* Schnappschuss *m*

snatch *vt* (*grab*) schnappen

sneak *vi* (*move*) schleichen; **sneakers** *npl* (*US*) Turnschuhe *pl*

sneeze *vi* niesen

sniff 1. *vi* schniefen; (*smell*) schnüffeln (*at* an + *dat*) **2.** *vt* schnuppern an + *dat*; (*glue*) schnüffeln

snob *n* Snob *m*; **snobbish** *adj* versnobt

snog *vi*, *vt* knutschen

snooker *n* Snooker *nt*

snoop *vi* ~ (**around**) (herum-)schnüffeln

snooze *n*, *vi* (**have a**) ~ ein Nickerchen machen

snore *vi* schnarchen

snorkel *n* Schnorchel *m*; **snorkelling** *n* Schnorcheln *nt*

snout *n* Schnauze *f*

snow 1. *n* Schnee *m* **2.** *vi* schneien; **snowball** *n* Schneeball *m*; **snowboard** *n* Snowboard *nt*; **snowboarding** *n* Snowboarding *nt*; **snowdrift** *n* Schneewehe *f*; **snowflake** *n* Schneeflocke *f*; **snowman** *n* Schneemann *m*; **snowplough, snowplow** (*US*) *n* Schneepflug *m*; **snowstorm** *n* Schneesturm *m*; **snowy** *adj* (*region*) schneereich; (*landscape*) verschneit

snug *adj* (*person*, *place*) gemütlich

snuggle up *vi* ~ **to sb** sich an jdn ankuscheln

so 1. *adv* so; ~ **many** / **much** so viele / viel; ~ **do I** ich auch; *I* **hope** ~ hoffentlich; *30 or* ~ etwa 30; ~ **what?** na und?; **and** ~ **on** und so weiter **2.** *conj* (*therefore*) also, deshalb

soak *vt* durchnässen; (*leave in liquid*) einweichen; *I'm* ~**ed** ich bin durchnässt; **soaking** *adj* ~ (**wet**) durchnässt

soap *n* Seife *f*; **soap (opera)** *n* Seifenoper *f*

sob *vi* schluchzen

sober *adj* nüchtern; **sober up** *vi* nüchtern werden

so-called *adj* so genannt

soccer *n* Fußball *m*

sociable *adj* gesellig

social *adj* sozial; (*sociable*) gesellig; **socialist 1.** *adj* sozialistisch **2.** *n* Sozialist(in) *m(f)*; **socialize** *vi* unter die Leute gehen; **social security** *n* (*Brit*) Sozialhilfe *f*; (*US*) Sozialversicherung *f*

society *n* Gesellschaft *f*; (*club*) Verein *m*

sock *n* Socke *f*

socket *n* ELEC Steckdose *f*

soda *n* (*soda water*) Soda *f*; (*US*, *pop*) Limo *f*

sofa *n* Sofa *nt*; **sofa bed** *n* Schlafcouch *f*

soft *adj* weich; (*quiet*) leise; (*lighting*) gedämpft; (*kind*) gutmütig; (*weak*) nachgiebig; **~ drink** alkoholfreies Getränk; **softly** adv sanft; (quietly) leise; **software** n IT Software f

soil n Erde f; (ground) Boden m

solar adj Sonnen-, Solar-

solarium n Solarium nt

sold pt, pp of **sell**

soldier n Soldat(in) m(f)

sole 1. n Sohle f; (fish) Seezunge f 2. vt besohlen 3. adj einzig; (owner, responsibility) alleinig; **solely** adv nur

solemn adj feierlich; (person) ernst

solicitor n (Brit) Rechtsanwalt m, Rechtsanwältin f

solid adj (hard) fest; (gold, oak etc) massiv; (solidly built) solide; (meal) kräftig; **three hours ~** drei volle Stunden

solitary adj einsam; (single) einzeln; **solitude** n Einsamkeit f

soluble adj löslich; (problem) lösbar; **solution** n Lösung f (to + gen); **solve** vt lösen

somber (US), **sombre** adj düster

some 1. adj etwas; (with plural nouns) einige; ~ **woman (or other)** irgendeine Frau; **would you like ~ more (wine)?** möchten Sie noch etwas (Wein)? 2. pron etwas; (plural) einige; ~ **of the team** einige (aus) der Mannschaft 3. adv ~ **50 people (or so)** et-

wa 50 Leute

somebody pron jemand; ~ **(or other)** irgendjemand; ~ **else** jemand anders; **someday** adv irgendwann; **somehow** adv irgendwie; **someone** pron → **somebody**; **someplace** adv (US) → **somewhere**; **something** 1. pron etwas; ~ **(or other)** irgendetwas; ~ **else** etwas anderes; ~ **nice** etwas Nettes; **would you like ~ to drink?** möchten Sie etwas zu trinken? 2. adv ~ **like 20** ungefähr 20; **sometime** adv irgendwann; **sometimes** adv manchmal; **somewhat** adv ein wenig; **somewhere** adv irgendwo; (to a place) irgendwohin; ~ **else** irgendwo anders; (to another place) irgendwo anders hin; ~ **around 6** ungefähr 6

son n Sohn m

song n Lied nt

son-in-law n Schwiegersohn m

soon adv bald; (early) früh; **too ~** zu früh; **as ~ as I ...** sobald ich ...; **as ~ as possible** so bald wie möglich; **sooner** adv (time) früher; (for preference) lieber

soot n Ruß m

soothe vt beruhigen; (pain) lindern

sophisticated adj (person) kultiviert; (machine) hoch entwickelt; (plan) ausgeklügelt

soppy *adj fam* rührselig

soprano *n* Sopran *m*

sore 1. *adj be* ~ weh tun; *have a* ~ *throat* Halsschmerzen haben **2.** *n* wunde Stelle

sorrow *n* Kummer *m*

sorry *adj* (*sight, figure*) traurig; (*I'm*) ~ (*excusing*) Entschuldigung!; *I'm* ~ (*regretful*) es tut mir leid!; ~? wie bitte?; *I feel* ~ *for him* er tut mir leid

sort 1. *n* Art *f*; *what* ~ *of film is it?* was für ein Film ist das?; *a* ~ *of* eine Art + *gen*; *all* ~ *s of things* alles Mögliche **2.** *adv* ~ *of fam* irgendwie **3.** *vt* sortieren; *everything's* ~*ed* (*dealt with*) alles ist geregelt; **sort out** *vt* (*classify etc*) sortieren; (*problems*) lösen

sought *pt, pp of* **seek**

soul *n* Seele *f*

sound 1. *adj* (*healthy*) gesund; (*safe*) sicher; (*sensible*) vernünftig; (*theory*) stichhaltig; (*thrashing*) tüchtig **2.** *adv be* ~ *asleep* fest schlafen. **3.** *n* (*noise*) Geräusch *nt*; MUS Klang *m*; TV Ton *m* **4.** *vt* ~ *one's horn* hupen **5.** *vi* (*seem*) klingen (*like* wie); **soundcard** *n* IT Soundkarte *f*; **soundproof** *adj* schalldicht

soup *n* Suppe *f*

sour *adj* sauer; *fig* mürrisch

source *n* Quelle *f*; *fig* Ursprung *m*

sour cream *n* saure Sahne

south 1. *n* Süden *m*; *to the* ~ *of* südlich von **2.** *adv* (*go, face*) nach Süden **3.** *adj* Süd-; **South Africa** *n* Südafrika *nt*; **South African 1.** *adj* südafrikanisch **2.** *n* Südafrikaner(in) *m(f)*; **South America** *n* Südamerika *nt*; **South American 1.** *adj* südamerikanisch **2.** *n* Südamerikaner(in) *m(f)*; **southbound** *adj* (in) Richtung Süden; **southern** *adj* Süd-, südlich; **southwards** *adv* nach Süden

souvenir *n* Andenken *nt* (*of* an + *acc*)

sow 1. *vt* säen; (*field*) besäen **2.** *n* (*pig*) Sau *f*

soya bean *n* Sojabohne *f*

soy sauce *n* Sojasoße *f*

spa *n* (*place*) Kurort *m*

space 1. *n* (*room*) Platz *m*, Raum *m*; (*outer space*) Weltraum *m*; (*gap*) Zwischenraum *m*; (*for parking*) Lücke *f*; **space bar** *n* Leertaste *f*; **spacecraft** *n* Raumschiff *nt*; **space shuttle** *n* Raumfähre *f*

spacing *n* (*in text*) Zeilenabstand *m*; *double* ~ zweizeiliger Abstand

spacious *adj* geräumig

spade *n* Spaten *m*; ~*s* Pik *nt*

spaghetti *nsing* Spaghetti *pl*

Spain *n* Spanien *nt*

spam *n* IT Spam *m*

Spaniard *n* Spanier(in) *m(f)*; **Spanish 1.** *adj* spanisch **2.** *n* (*language*) Spanisch *nt*

spanner n (Brit) Schraubenschlüssel m

spare 1. adj (as replacement)
Ersatz-; ~ part Ersatzteil
nt; ~ room Gästezimmer
nt; ~ time Freizeit f; ~ tyre
Ersatzreifen m 2. n (spare
part) Ersatzteil nt 3. vt (lives,
feelings) verschenen; can
you ~ (me) a moment? hät-
ten Sie einen Moment Zeit?

spark n Funke m; sparkle vi
funkeln; sparkling wine n
Schaumwein m, Sekt m;
spark plug n Zündkerze f

sparrow n Spatz m

sparse adj spärlich; sparsely
adv ~ populated dünn besie-
delt

spasm n MED Krampf m

spat pt, pp of spit

speak 1. vt sprechen; can you
~ French? sprechen Sie
Französisch?; ~ one's mind
seine Meinung sagen 2. vi
sprechen (to mit, zu); (make
speech) reden; ~ing TEL am
Apparat; so to ~ sozusagen;
speak up vi (louder) lauter
sprechen; speaker n Spre-
cher(in) m(f); (public speaker) Redner(in) m(f); (loudspeaker) Lautsprecher m

spear n Speer m

special 1. adj besondere(r, s),
speziell 2. n (on menu) Tagesgericht nt; (in shop) Sonderangebot nt; special delivery n Eilzustellung f; specialist n Spezialist(in) m(f);

TECH Fachmann m, Fachfrau
f; MED Facharzt m, Fachärztin f; speciality n Spezialität
f; specialize vi sich spezialisieren (in auf + acc); specially adv besonders; (specifi-
cally) extra; special offer n
Sonderangebot nt; specialty
n (US) → speciality

species nsing Art f

specific adj spezifisch; (precise) genau; specify vt genau
angeben

specimen n (sample) Probe f;
(example) Exemplar nt

spectacle n Schauspiel nt

spectacles npl Brille f

spectacular adj spektaku-
lär

spectator n Zuschauer(in)
m(f)

sped pt, pp of speed

speech n (address) Rede f;
(faculty) Sprache f; make a
~ eine Rede halten; speech-
less adj sprachlos (with or
+ dat)

speed 1. vi rasen; exceed ~
limit zu schnell fahren 2. n
Geschwindigkeit f; (of film)
Lichtempfindlichkeit f;
speed up 1. vt beschleunigen 2. vi schneller werden/
fahren; speedboat n Renn-
boot nt; speed bump n Bo-
denschwelle f; speed limit n
Geschwindigkeitsbegren-
zung f; speedometer n Ta-
chometer m; speed trap n
Radarfalle f; speedy adj

schnell

spell 1. vt buchstabieren; **how do you ~ ...?** wie schreibt man ...? **2.** n (period) Weile f; **a cold/ hot ~** (weather) ein Kälteeinbruch / eine Hitzewelle; (enchantment) Zauber m; **spellchecker** n IT Rechtschreibprüfung f; **spelling** n Rechtschreibung f; **~ mistake** Schreibfehler m

spelt pt, pp of **spell**

spend vt (money) ausgeben (on für); (time) verbringen

spent pt, pp of **spend**

sperm n Sperma nt

sphere n (globe) Kugel f; fig Sphäre f

spice 1. n (food) Gewürz nt; fig Würze f **2.** vt würzen; **spicy** adj würzig

spider n Spinne f

spike n (on railing etc) Spitze f; (on shoe, tyre) Spike m

spill vt verschütten

spin 1. vi (turn) sich drehen; (washing) schleudern; **my head is ...ning** mir dreht sich alles **2.** vt (turn) drehen; (coin) hochwerfen **3.** n (turn) Drehung f

spinach n Spinat m

spin-drier n Wäscheschleuder f

spine n Rückgrat nt; (of animal, plant) Stachel m; (of book) Rücken m

spiral 1. n Spirale f **2.** adj spiralförmig; **spiral staircase** n Wendeltreppe f

spire n Turmspitze f

spirit n (essence, soul) Geist m; (humour, mood) Stimmung f; (courage) Mut m; (verve) Elan m; **~s** pl (drinks) Spirituosen pl

spiritual adj geistig; REL geistlich

spit 1. vi spucken **2.** n (for roasting) (Brat)spieß m; (saliva) Spucke f; **spit out** vt ausspucken

spite n Boshaftigkeit f; **in ~ of** trotz + gen; **spiteful** adj boshaft

spitting image n **he's the ~ of you** er ist dir wie aus dem Gesicht geschnitten

splash 1. vt (person, object) bespritzen **2.** vi (liquid) spritzen; (play in water) planschen

splendid adj herrlich

splinter n Splitter m

split 1. vt (stone, wood) spalten; (share) teilen **2.** vi (stone, wood) sich spalten **3.** n (in stone, wood) Spalt m; (in clothing) Riss m; fig Spaltung f; **split up 1.** vi (couple) sich trennen **2.** vt (divide up) aufteilen; **split ends** npl (Haar)spliss m; **splitting** adj (headache) rasend

spoil 1. vt verderben; (child) verwöhnen **2.** vi (food) verderben

spoilt pt, pp of **spoil**

spoke 1. pt of **speak 2.** n Speiche f

spoken pp of **speak**

spokesperson n Sprecher(in) m(f)

sponge n (for washing) Schwamm m; **sponge cake** n Biskuitkuchen m

sponsor 1. n (of event, programme) Sponsor(in) m(f) 2. vt unterstützen; (event, programme) sponsern

spontaneous, spontaneously adj, adv spontan

spool n Spule f

spoon n Löffel m

sport n Sport m; **sports car** n Sportwagen m; **sports centre** n Sportzentrum nt; **sportsman** n Sportler m; **sportswear** n Sportkleidung f; **sportswoman** n Sportlerin f; **sporty** adj sportlich

spot 1. n (dot) Punkt m; (of paint, blood etc) Fleck m; (place) Stelle f; (pimple) Pickel m; **on the ~** vor Ort; (at once) auf der Stelle 2. vt (notice) entdecken; (difference) erkennen; **spotless** adj (clean) blitzsauber; **spotlight** n (lamp) Scheinwerfer m; **spotty** adj (pimply) pickelig

spouse n Gatte m, Gattin f

spout n Schnabel m

sprain vt ~ **one's ankle** sich den Knöchel verstauchen

sprang pt of **spring**

spray 1. n (liquid in can) Spray nt or m; (spray (can)) Spraydose f 2. vt (plant, insects)

besprühen; (car) spritzen

spread 1. vt (open out) ausbreiten; (news, disease) verbreiten; (butter, jam) streichen 2. vi (news, disease, fire) sich verbreiten 3. n (of disease, religion etc) Verbreitung f; (for bread) Aufstrich m; **spreadsheet** n IT Tabellenkalkulation f

spring 1. vi (leap) springen 2. n (season) Frühling m; (coil) Feder f; (water) Quelle f; **springboard** n Sprungbrett nt; **spring onion** n (Brit) Frühlingszwiebel f; **spring roll** n (Brit) Frühlingsrolle f

sprinkle vt streuen; (liquid) sprengen; **~ sth with sth** etw mit etw bestreuen; **sprinkler** n (for lawn) Rasensprenger m; (for fire) Sprinkler m

sprint vi rennen; SPORT sprinten

sprout 1. n (of plant) Trieb m; (from seed) Keim m; (**Brussels**) **~s** pl Rosenkohl m 2. vi sprießen

sprung pp of **spring**

spun pt, pp of **spin**

spy 1. n Spion(in) m(f) 2. vt spionieren; **~ on sb** jdm nachspionieren

squad n SPORT Mannschaft f

square 1. n (shape) Quadrat nt; (open space) Platz m; (on chessboard etc) Feld $nt 2. adj (in shape) quadratisch; **2 ~ metres** 2 Quadratmeter;

2 metres ~ 2 Meter im Quadrat **3.** vt **3** ~d √3 hoch 2

squash 1. n (*drink*) Fruchtsaftgetränk nt; SPORT Squash nt; (*US, vegetable*) Kürbis m **2.** vt zerquetschen

squeak vi (*door, shoes etc*) quietschen; (*animal*) quieken

squeal vi (*person*) kreischen (*with* vor + *dat*)

squeeze 1. vt drücken; (*orange*) auspressen **2.** vi ~ **into the car** sich in den Wagen hineinzwängen

squid n Tintenfisch m

squirrel n Eichhörnchen nt

St 1. abbr = *saint*; SPORT **St. 2.** abbr = *street*; Str.

stab vt (*person*) einstechen auf + acc; (*to death*) erstechen; **stabbing** adj (*pain*) stechend

stabilize 1. vt stabilisieren **2.** vi sich stabilisieren

stable 1. n Stall m **2.** adj stabil

stack 1. n (*pile*) Stapel m **2.** vt ~ (**up**) (auf)stapeln

stadium n Stadion nt

staff n (*personnel*) Personal nt, Lehrkräfte pl

stag n Hirsch m; **stag night** n (*Brit*) Junggesellenabschied m

stage 1. n (*theatre*) Bühne f; (*of project, life etc*) Stadium nt; (*of journey*) Etappe f; **at this** ~ zu diesem Zeitpunkt **2.** vt THEAT aufführen, inszenieren; (*demonstration*) veranstalten

stagger 1. vi wanken **2.** vt (*amaze*) verblüffen; **staggering** adj (*amazing*) umwerfend; (*amount, price*) Schwindel erregend

stagnant adj (*water*) stehend; **stagnate** vi stagnieren

stain n Fleck m; **stained-glass window** n Buntglasfenster nt; **stainless steel** n rostfreier Stahl; **stain remover** n Fleck(en)entferner m

stair n (Treppen)stufe f; ~**s** pl Treppe f; **staircase** n Treppe f

stake n (*post*) Pfahl m; (*in betting*) Einsatz m; FIN Anteil m (*in* an + *dat*); **be at** ~ auf dem Spiel stehen

stale adj (*bread*) alt; (*beer*) schal

stalk 1. n Stiel m **2.** vt (*wild animal*) sich anpirschen an + acc; (*person*) nachstellen + dat

stall 1. n (*in market*) (Verkaufs)stand m; (*in stable*) Box f; ~**s** pl THEAT Parkett nt **2.** vt (*engine*) den Motor abwürgen; (*car*) stehen bleiben **3.** vi (*driver*) den Motor abwürgen

stamina n Durchhaltevermögen nt

stammer vi, vt stottern

stamp 1. n (*postage stamp*) Briefmarke f; (*for document*) Stempel m **2.** vt (*passport etc*) stempeln; (*mail*) frankieren

stand 1. *vi* stehen; (*as candidate*) kandidieren **2.** *vt* (*place*) stellen; (*endure*) aushalten; **I can't ~ her** ich kann sie nicht ausstehen **3.** *n* (*stall*) Stand *m*; (*seats in stadium*) Tribüne *f*; (*for coats, bicycles*) Ständer *m*; (*for small objects*) Gestell *nt*; **stand around** *vi* herumstehen; **stand by 1.** *vi* (*be ready*) sich bereithalten; (*be inactive*) danebenstehen **2.** *vt* (*person*) halten zu; (*decision, promise*) stehen zu; **stand for** *vt* (*represent*) stehen für; (*tolerate*) hinnehmen; **stand in for** *vt* einspringen für; **stand out** *vi* (*be noticeable*) auffallen; **stand up 1.** *vi* (*get up*) aufstehen **2.** *vt* (*girlfriend, boyfriend*) versetzen; **stand up for** *vt* sich einsetzen für

standard 1. *n* (*norm*) Norm *f*; **~ of living** Lebensstandard *m* **2.** *adj* Standard-

standardize *vt* vereinheitlichen

stand-by 1. *n* (*thing in reserve*) Reserve *f*; **on ~** in Bereitschaft **2.** *adj* (*flight, ticket*) Standby-; **standing order** *n* (*at bank*) Dauerauftrag *m*; **standpoint** *n* Standpunkt *m*; **standstill** *n* Stillstand *m*; **come to a ~** stehen bleiben; *fig* zum Erliegen kommen

stank *pt of* **stink**

staple 1. *n* (*for paper*) Heftklammer *f* **2.** *vt* heften (*to* an + *acc*); **stapler** *n* Hefter *m*

star 1. *n* Stern *m*; (*person*) Star *m* **2.** *vt* **the film ~s Hugh Grant** der Film zeigt Hugh Grant in der Hauptrolle **3.** *vi* die Hauptrolle spielen

starch *n* Stärke *f*

stare *vi* starren; **~ at** anstarren

starfish *n* Seestern *m*

star sign *n* Sternzeichen *nt*

start 1. *n* (*beginning*) Anfang *m*, Beginn *m*; SPORT Start *m*; (*lead*) Vorsprung *m*; **from the ~** von Anfang an **2.** *vt* anfangen; (*car, engine*) starten; (*business, family*) gründen; **~ to do sth, ~ doing sth** anfangen, etw zu tun **3.** *vi* (*begin*) anfangen; (*car*) anspringen; (*on journey*) aufbrechen; SPORT starten; (*jump*) zusammenfahren; **~ing from Monday** ab Montag; **start off 1.** *vi* (*discussion, process etc*) anfangen, beginnen **2.** *vi* (*begin*) anfangen, beginnen; (*on journey*) aufbrechen; **start up 1.** *vi* (*in business*) anfangen **2.** *vt* (*car, engine*) starten; (*business*) gründen; **starter** *n* (*Brit, first course*) Vorspeise *f*; AUTO Anlasser *m*; **starting point** *n* Ausgangspunkt *m*

startle *vt* erschrecken; **startling** *adj* überraschend

starve *vi* hungern; (*to death*) verhungern; **I'm ~ing** ich habe einen Riesenhunger

state 1. n (condition) Zustand m; POL Staat m; **~ of health/mind** Gesundheits-/Geisteszustand m; **the (United) States** die (Vereinigten) Staaten f pl **2.** adj States-; (control, education) staatlich **3.** vt erklären; (facts, name etc) angeben; **stated** adj (fixed) festgesetzt; **statement** n (official declaration) Erklärung f; (to police) Aussage f; (from bank) Kontoauszug m; **state-of-the-art** adj hochmodern, auf dem neuesten Stand der Technik

static adj (unchanging) konstant

station 1. n (for trains, buses) Bahnhof m; (underground station) Station f; (police station, fire station) Wache f; TV, RADIO Sender m **2.** vt MIL stationieren

stationer's n ~ **(shop)** Schreibwarengeschäft nt; **stationery** n Schreibwaren pl

station wagon n (US) Kombiwagen m

statistics nsing (science) Statistik f; (figures) Statistiken pl

statue n Statue f

status n Status m; (prestige) Ansehen nt

stay 1. n Aufenthalt m **2.** vi bleiben; (with friends, in hotel) wohnen (with bei); **~ the night** übernachten; **stay away** vi wegbleiben; **~ from sb** sich von jdm fern halten; **stay behind** vi zurückbleiben; (at work) länger bleiben; **stay in** vi (at home) zu Hause bleiben; **stay out** vi (not come home) wegbleiben; **stay up** vi (at night) aufbleiben

steady 1. adj (speed) gleichmäßig; (progress, increase) stetig; (job, income, girlfriend) fest; (worker) zuverlässig; (hand) ruhig; **they've been going ~ for two years** sie sind seit zwei Jahren fest zusammen **2.** vt (nerves) beruhigen

steak n Steak nt; (of fish) Filet nt

steal vt stehlen

steam 1. n Dampf m **2.** vt GASTR dämpfen; **steam up** vi (window) beschlagen; **steamer** n GASTR Dampfkochtopf m; (ship) Dampfer m

steel n Stahl m **2.** adj Stahl-

steep adj steil

steeple n Kirchturm m

steer vt, vi steuern; (car, bike etc) lenken; **steering** n AUTO Lenkung f; **steering wheel** n Steuer nt, Lenkrad nt

stem n (of plant, glass) Stiel m

step 1. n Schritt m; (stair) Stufe f; (measure) Maßnahme f; **~ by ~** Schritt für Schritt **2.** vi treten; **~ this way, please** hier entlang, bitte; **step**

down vi (resign) zurücktreten

stepbrother n Stiefbruder m; **stepchild** n Stiefkind nt; **stepfather** n Stiefvater m; **stepmother** n Stiefmutter f; **stepsister** n Stiefschwester f

stereo n ~ (*system*) Stereoanlage f

sterile adj steril; **sterilize** vt sterilisieren

sterling n FIN das Pfund Sterling

stern 1. adj streng 2. n Heck nt

stew n Eintopf m

steward n (on plane, ship) Steward m; **stewardess** n Stewardess f

stick 1. vt (with glue etc) kleben; (pin etc) stecken; fam (put) tun 2. vi (get jammed) klemmen; (hold fast) haften 3. n Stock m; (hockey stick) Schläger m; (of chalk) Stück nt; (of celery, rhubarb) Stange f; **stick out** 1. vt **stick one's tongue out (at sb)** (jdm) die Zunge herausstrecken 2. vi (protrude) vorstehen; (ears) abstehen; (be noticeable) auffallen; **stick to** vt (rules, plan etc) sich halten an + dat; **sticker** n Aufkleber m; **sticky** adj klebrig; (weather) schwül; ~ **label** Aufkleber m; ~ **tape** Klebeband nt

stiff adj steif

stifle vt (yawn etc, opposition) unterdrücken; **stifling** adj drückend

still 1. adj still; (drink) ohne Kohlensäure 2. adv (yet, even now) (immer) noch; (all the same) immerhin; (sit, stand) still; **he doesn't believe me** er glaubt mir immer noch nicht; **keep** ~ halt still!; **bigger/better** ~ noch größer/besser

stimulate vt anregen, stimulieren; **stimulating** adj anregend; **stimulus** n (incentive) Anreiz m

sting 1. vt (wound with sting) stechen 2. vi (eyes, ointment etc) brennen 3. n (insect wound) Stich m

stingy adj fam geizig

stink 1. vi stinken (of nach) 2. n Gestank m

stir 1. vt (mix) (um)rühren; **stir up** vt (mob) aufhetzen; (memories) wachrufen; ~ **trouble** Unruhe stiften; **stir-fry** vt (unter Rühren) kurz anbraten

stitch 1. n (in sewing) Stich m; (in knitting) Masche f; **have a** ~ (pain) Seitenstechen haben; **he had to have** ~**es** er musste genäht werden; **she had her** ~**es out** ihr wurden die Fäden gezogen; **be in** ~**es** fam sich kaputtlachen 2. vt nähen; **stitch up** vt (hole, wound) nähen

stock 1. n (supply) Vorrat m (of an + dat); (of shop) Bestand m; (for soup etc) Brühe f; **~s and shares** pl Aktien und Wertpapiere pl; **be in/out of ~** vorrätig/nicht vorrätig sein; **take ~** Inventur machen; fig Bilanz ziehen **2.** vt (keep in shop) führen; **stock up** vi sich eindecken (on, with stoff)

stockbroker n Börsenmakler(in) m(f)

stock cube n Brühwürfel m

stock exchange n Börse f

stocking n Strumpf m

stock market n Börse f

stole pt of **steal**, **stolen** pp of **steal**

stomach n Magen m; (belly) Bauch m; **on an empty ~** auf leeren Magen; **stomach-ache** n Magenschmerzen pl; **stomach upset** n Magenverstimmung f

stone 1. n Stein m; (seed) Kern m, Stein m; (weight) britische Gewichtseinheit (6,35 kg) **2.** adj Stein-, aus Stein

stony adj (ground) steinig

stood pt, pp of **stand**

stool n Hocker m

stop 1. n Halt m; (for bus, tram, train) Haltestelle f; **come to a ~** anhalten **2.** vt (vehicle, passer-by) anhalten; (put an end to) ein Ende machen + dat; (cease) aufhören mit; (prevent from happening) verhindern; (bleeding) stillen; (engine, machine) abstellen; (payments)

einstellen; (cheque) sperren; **~ doing sth** aufhören, etw zu tun; **~ sb (from) doing sth** jdn daran hindern, etw zu tun; **~ it** hör auf (damit)! **3.** vi (vehicle) anhalten; (during journey) Halt machen; (pedestrian, passer-by) stehen bleiben; (rain, noise) aufhören; (stay) bleiben; **stop by** vi vorbeischauen; **stop over** vi Halt machen; (overnight) übernachten; **stopover** n (on journey) Zwischenstation f; **stopper** n Stöpsel m; **stop sign** n Stoppschild nt; **stopwatch** n Stoppuhr f

storage n Lagerung f; **store 1.** n (supply) Vorrat m (of an + dat); (place for storage) Lager nt; (large shop) Kaufhaus nt; (US, shop) Geschäft nt **2.** vt lagern; IT speichern; **storeroom** n Lagerraum m

storey n (Brit) Stock m, Stockwerk nt

storm 1. n Sturm m; (thunderstorm) Gewitter nt **2.** vt, vi (with movement) stürmen; **stormy** adj stürmisch

story n Geschichte f; (plot) Handlung f; (US, of building) Stock m, Stockwerk nt

stout adj (fat) korpulent; (shoes) fest

stove n Herd m; (for heating) Ofen m

stow vt verstauen; **stowaway** n blinder Passagier

straight 1. adj (not curved) gerade; (hair) glatt; (honest) ehrlich (with zu); fam (heterosexual) hetero 2. adv (directly) direkt; (immediately) sofort; (drink) pur; (think) klar; **~ ahead** geradeaus; **go ~ on** geradeaus weitergehen/weiterfahren; **straightaway** adv sofort; **straightforward** adj einfach; (person) aufrichtig

strain 1. n Belastung f **2.** vt (eyes) überanstrengen; (rope, relationship) belasten; (vegetables) abgießen; **~ a muscle** sich einen Muskel zerren; **strained** adj (relations) gespannt; **~ muscle** Muskelzerrung f; **strainer** n Sieb nt

strand 1. n (of wool) Faden m; (of hair) Strähne f **2.** vt **be (left) ~ed** (person) festsitzen

strange adj seltsam; (unfamiliar) fremd; **strangely** adv seltsam; **~ enough** seltsamerweise; **stranger** n Fremde(r) mf

strangle vt (kill) erdrosseln

strap n Riemen m; (on dress etc) Träger m; (on watch) Band nt **2.** vt (fasten) festschnallen (to an + dat); **strapless** adj trägerlos

strategy n Strategie f

straw n Stroh nt; (drinking ~) Strohhalm m

strawberry n Erdbeere f

stray 1. n streunendes Tier **2.** adj (cat, dog) streunend **3.** vi streunen

streak n (of colour, dirt) Streifen m; (in hair) Strähne f; (in character) Zug m

stream 1. n (flow of liquid) Strom m; (brook) Bach m **2.** vi strömen

street n Straße f; **streetcar** n (US) Straßenbahn f; **street lamp, street light** n Straßenlaterne f; **street map** n Stadtplan m

strength n Kraft f, Stärke f; **strengthen** vt verstärken; fig stärken

strenuous adj anstrengend

stress 1. n Stress m; (on word) Betonung f **2.** vt betonen; (put under stress) stressen; **stressed** adj **~ (out)** gestresst

stretch 1. n (of land) Stück nt; (of road) Strecke f **2.** vt (material, shoes) dehnen; (rope, canvas) spannen; (person in job etc) fordern; **~ one's legs** (walk) sich die Beine vertreten **3.** vi (person) sich strecken; (area) sich erstrecken (to bis zu); **stretch out 1.** vt ausstrecken **2.** vi (reach) sich strecken; (lie down) sich ausstrecken; **stretcher** n Tragbahre f

strict, strictly adj, adv (severe(ly)) streng; (exact(ly)) genau

strike 1. n (match) anzünden; (hit) schlagen; (find) finden; **it struck me as strange** es kam mir seltsam vor **2.** vi (*stop work*) streiken; (*attack*) zuschlagen; (*clock*) schlagen **3.** *n* (*by workers*) Streik *m*; **be on ~** streiken; **strike up** *vt* (*conversation*) anfangen; (*friendship*) schließen; **striking** *adj* auffallend; (*resemblance*) verblüffend

string *n* (*for tying*) Schnur *f*; MUS, TENNIS Saite *f*; **the ~s** *pl* (*section of orchestra*) die Streicher *pl*

strip 1. *n* Streifen *m*; (*Brit, of soccer player*) Trikot *nt* **2.** *vt* (*undress*) ausziehen **3.** *vi* (*undress*) sich ausziehen, strippen

stripe *n* Streifen *m*; **striped** *adj* gestreift

stripper *n* Stripper(in) *m(f)*; (*paint stripper*) Farbentferner *m*

strive *vi* **~ to do sth** bemüht sein, etw zu tun; **~ for sth** nach etw streben

stroke 1. *n* MED, TENNIS *etc* Schlag *m*; (*of pen, brush*) Strich *m* **2.** *vt* streicheln

stroll 1. *n* Spaziergang *m* **2.** *vi* spazieren; **stroller** *n* (*US, for baby*) Buggy *m*

strong *adj* stark; (*healthy*) robust; (*wall, table*) stabil; (*shoes*) fest; (*influence, chance*) groß; **strongly** *adv* stark; (*believe*) fest; (*constructed*) stabil

strove *pt of* **strive**

struck *pt, pp of* **strike**

structural, structurally *adj*

strukturell; **structure** *n* Struktur *f*; (*building, bridge*) Konstruktion *f*, Bau *m*

struggle 1. *n* Kampf *m* (*for* um) **2.** *vi* (*fight*) kämpfen (*for* um); (*do sth with difficulty*) sich abmühen; **~ to do sth** sich abmühen, etw zu tun

stub 1. *n* (*of cigarette*) Kippe *f*; (*of ticket, cheque*) Abschnitt *m*

stubble *n* Stoppeln *pl*

stubborn *adj* (*person*) stur

stuck 1. *pt, pp of* **stick 2.** *adj* **be ~** (*jammed*) klemmen; (*at a loss*) nicht mehr weiterwissen; **get ~** (*car in snow etc*) stecken bleiben

student *n* Student(in) *m(f)*, Schüler(in) *m(f)*

studio *n* Studio *nt*

study 1. *n* (*investigation*) Untersuchung *f*; (*studying*) Studium *nt*; (*room*) Arbeitszimmer *nt* **2.** *vt, vi* studieren; **~ for an exam** sich auf eine Prüfung vorbereiten

stuff 1. *n* Zeug *nt*, Sachen *pl* **2.** *vt* (*push*) stopfen; GASTR füllen; **~ oneself** *fam* sich voll stopfen; **stuffing** *n* GASTR Füllung *f*

stuffy *adj* (*room*) stickig; (*person*) spießig

stumble *vi* stolpern; (*when speaking*) stocken

stun *vt* (*shock*) fassungslos machen; **I was ~ned** ich war fassungslos (*or* völlig überrascht)

stung pt, pp of **sting**

stunk pp of **stink**

stunning adj (marvellous) fantastisch; (beautiful) atemberaubend; (very surprising, shocking) überwältigend; unfassbar

stupid adj dumm; **stupidity** n Dummheit f

sturdy adj robust; (building, car) stabil

stutter vi, vt stottern

stye n MED Gerstenkorn nt

style 1. n Stil m 2. vt (hair) stylen; **styling mousse** n Schaumfestiger m; **stylish** adj elegant

subconscious 1. adj unterbewusst 2. n **the ~** das Unterbewusstsein

subject 1. n (topic) Thema nt; (in school) Fach nt; (citizen) Staatsangehörige(r) mf; (of kingdom) Untertan(in) m(f); LING Subjekt nt; **change the ~** das Thema wechseln 2. adj **be ~ to** (dependent on) abhängen von; (under control of) unterworfen sein + dat

subjective adj subjektiv

sublet irr vt untervermieten (to an + acc)

submarine n U-Boot nt

submerge 1. vt (put in water) eintauchen 2. vi tauchen

submit 1. vt (application, claim) einreichen 2. vi (surrender) sich ergeben

subordinate 1. adj untergeordnet (to + dat) 2. n Untergebene(r) mf

subscribe vi **~ to** (magazine etc) abonnieren; **subscription** n (to magazine etc) Abonnement nt; (to club etc) (Mitglieds)beitrag m

subsequent adj nach(folgend); **subsequently** adv später, anschließend

subside vi (floods) zurückgehen; (storm) sich legen; (building) sich senken

substance n Substanz f

substantial adj beträchtlich; (improvement) wesentlich; (meal) reichhaltig

substitute 1. n Ersatz m; SPORT Ersatzspieler(in) m(f) 2. vt **~ A for B** B durch A ersetzen

subtitle n Untertitel m

subtle adj (difference, taste) fein; (plan) raffiniert

subtract vt abziehen (from von)

suburb n Vorort m; **suburban** adj vorstädtisch, Vorstadt-

subway n (Brit) Unterführung f; (US) RAIL U-Bahn f

succeed 1. vi erfolgreich sein; **he ~ed (in doing it)** es gelang ihm(, es zu tun) 2. vt nachfolgen + dat; **succeeding** adj nachfolgend; **success** n Erfolg m; **successful** adj, adv erfolgreich

successive adj aufeinander folgend; **successor** n Nachfolger(in) *m(f)*

such 1. *adj* solche(r, s); **~ a book** so ein Buch, ein solches Buch; **it was ~ a success that ...** es war solch ein Erfolg, dass ...; **~ as** wie **2.** *adv* so; **~ a hot day** so ein heißer Tag **3.** *pron* **as ~** als solche(r, s); **suchlike 1.** *adj* derartig **2.** *pron* dergleichen

suck *vt* (*toffee etc*) lutschen; (*liquid*) saugen; **it ~s** *fam* das ist beschissen

Sudan *n* (*the*) ~ der Sudan

sudden *adj* plötzlich; **all of a ~** ganz plötzlich; **suddenly** *adv* plötzlich

sue *vt* verklagen

suede *n* Wildleder *nt*

suffer 1. *vt* erleiden **2.** *vi* leiden; **~ from** MED leiden an + *dat*

sufficient, sufficiently *adj*, *adv* ausreichend

suffocate *vt, vi* ersticken

sugar 1. *n* Zucker *m* **2.** *vt* zuckern; **sugary** *adj* (*sweet*) süß

suggest *vt* vorschlagen; (*imply*) andeuten; **I ~ saying nothing** ich schlage vor, nichts zu sagen; **suggestion** *n* (*proposal*) Vorschlag *m*; **suggestive** *adj* vielsagend; (*sexually*) anzüglich

suicide *n* (*act*) Selbstmord *m*

suit 1. *n* (*man's clothes*) Anzug *m*; (*lady's clothes*) Kostüm *nt*; (*cards*) Farbe *f* **2.** *vt* (*be*

convenient for*) passen + *dat*; (*clothes, colour*) stehen + *dat*; (*climate, food*) bekommen + *dat*; **suitable** *adj* geeignet (*for* für)

suitcase *n* Koffer *m*

suite *n* (*of rooms*) Suite *f*; (*sofa and chairs*) Sitzgarnitur *f*

sulk *vi* schmollen; **sulky** *adj* eingeschnappt

sultana *n* (*raisin*) Sultanine *f*

sum *n* Summe *f*; (*money*) Betrag *m*; (*calculation*) Rechenaufgabe *f*

summarize *vt, vi* zusammenfassen; **summary** *n* Zusammenfassung *f*

summer *n* Sommer *m*; **summer camp** *n* (*US*) Ferienlager *nt*; **summertime** *n* **in** (*the*) ~ im Sommer

summit *n a.* POL Gipfel *m*

summon *vt* (*doctor, fire brigade etc*) rufen; (*to one's office*) zitieren; **summon up** *vt* (*courage, strength*) zusammennehmen

summons *nsing* LAW Vorladung *f*

sumptuous *adj* luxuriös; (*meal*) üppig

sun 1. *n* Sonne *f* **2.** *vt* ~ **oneself** sich sonnen

Sun *abbr* = **Sunday**; So.

sunbathe *vi* sich sonnen; **sunbed** *n* Sonnenbank *f*; **sunblock** *n* Sunblocker *m*; **sunburn** *n* Sonnenbrand *m*; **sunburnt** *adj* **be/ get ~** einen Sonnenbrand haben/

bekommen

sundae n Eisbecher m

Sunday n Sonntag m; → **Tuesday**

sung pp of **sing**

sunglasses npl Sonnenbrille f; **sunhat** n Sonnenhut m

sunk pp of **sink**

sunlamp n Höhensonne f; **sunlight** n Sonnenlicht nt; **sunny** adj sonnig; **sun protection factor** n Lichtschutzfaktor m; **sunrise** n Sonnenaufgang m; **sunroof** n AUTO Schiebedach nt; **sunscreen** n Sonnenschutzmittel nt; **sunset** n Sonnenuntergang m; **sunshade** n Sonnenschirm m; **sunshine** n Sonnenschein m; **sunstroke** n Sonnenstich m; **suntan** n (Sonnen)bräune f; ~ **lotion** (or **oil**) Sonnenöl n

super adj fam toll

superb, **superbly** adj, adv ausgezeichnet

superficial, **superficially** adj, adv oberflächlich

superfluous adj überflüssig

superior 1. adj (better) besser (to als); (higher in rank) höher gestellt (to als), höher 2. n (in rank) Vorgesetzte(r) mf

supermarket n Supermarkt m

supersonic adj Überschall-

superstitious adj abergläubisch

supervise vt beaufsichtigen; **supervisor** n Aufsicht f; (at university) Doktorvater m

supper n Abendessen nt; (late-night snack) Imbiss m

supplement 1. n (extra payment) Zuschlag m; (of newspaper) Beilage f 2. vt ergänzen; **supplementary** adj zusätzlich

supplier n Lieferant(in) m(f); **supply** 1. vt (deliver) liefern; (drinks, music etc) sorgen für; ~ **sb with sth** (provide) jdn mit etw versorgen 2. n (stock) Vorrat m (of an + dat)

support 1. n Unterstützung f; TECH Stütze f 2. vt (hold up) tragen, stützen; (provide for) ernähren, unterhalten; (speak in favour of) unterstützen; **he ~s Manchester United** er ist Manchester-United-Fan

suppose vt (assume) annehmen; **I ~ so** ich denke schon; **I ~ not** wahrscheinlich nicht; **you're not ~d to smoke here** du darfst hier nicht rauchen; **supposedly** adv angeblich

suppress vt unterdrücken

surcharge n Zuschlag m

sure 1. adj sicher; **I'm (not)** ~ ich bin mir (nicht) sicher; **make** ~ **you lock up** vergiss nicht abzuschließen 2. adv ~**!** klar!; **surely** adv ~ **you don't mean it?** das ist nicht dein Ernst, oder?

surf 1. n Brandung f 2. vi SPORT surfen 3. vt ~ **the net** im Internet surfen

surface 1. n Oberfläche f **2.** vi auftauchen

surfboard n Surfbrett nt; **surfer** n Surfer(in) m(f); **surfing** n Surfen nt

surgeon n Chirurg(in) m(f); **surgery** n (operation) Operation f; (room) Praxis f, Sprechzimmer nt; (consulting time) Sprechstunde f; **have ~** operiert werden

surname n Nachname m

surpass vt übertreffen

surprise 1. n Überraschung f **2.** vt überraschen; **surprising** adj überraschend; **surprisingly** adv überraschenderweise, erstaunlicherweise

surrender 1. vi sich ergeben (to + dat) **2.** vt (weapon, passport) abgeben

surround vt umgeben; (stand all round) umringen; **surrounding 1.** adj (countryside) umliegend **2.** n ~s pl Umgebung f

survey 1. n (opinion poll) Umfrage f; (of literature etc) Überblick m (of über + acc); (of land) Vermessung f **2.** vt (look out over) überblicken; (land) vermessen

survive vt, vi überleben

suspect 1. n Verdächtige(r) mf & adj **2.** adj verdächtig **3.** vt verdächtigen (of + gen); (think likely) vermuten

suspend vt (from work) suspendieren; (payment) vorübergehend einstellen; (player) sperren; (hang up) aufhängen; **suspender** n (Brit) Strumpfhalter m; ~s pl (US, for trousers) Hosenträger pl

suspense n Spannung f

suspicious adj misstrauisch (of sb/sth jdm/etw gegenüber); (causing suspicion) verdächtig

swallow 1. n (bird) Schwalbe f **2.** vt, vi schlucken

swam pt of **swim**

swamp n Sumpf m

swan n Schwan m

swap vt, vi tauschen; ~ **sth for sth** etw gegen etw eintauschen

sway vi schwanken

swear vi (promise) schwören; (curse) fluchen; ~ **at sb** jdn beschimpfen; **swear by** vt (have faith in) schwören auf + acc

sweat 1. n Schweiß m **2.** vi schwitzen; **sweater** n Pullover m; **sweaty** adj verschwitzt

swede n Steckrübe f

Swede n Schwede m, Schwedin f; **Sweden** n Schweden nt; **Swedish 1.** adj schwedisch **2.** n (language) Schwedisch nt

sweep vt, vi (with brush) kehren, fegen

sweet 1. n (Brit, candy) Bonbon nt; (dessert) Nachtisch m **2.** adj süß; (kind) lieb; **sweet-and-sour** adj süßsau-

er; **sweetcorn** n Mais m;
sweeten vt (tea etc) süßen;
sweetener n (substance)
Süßstoff m

swell 1. vi **(up)** (an)schwellen
2. adj (US) fam toll; **swelling** n MED Schwellung f

sweltering adj (heat) drückend

swept pt, pp of **sweep**

swift, swiftly adj, adv schnell

swim 1. vi schwimmen **2.** n **go for a ~** schwimmen gehen;
swimmer n Schwimmer(in) m(f); **swimming** n Schwimmen nt; **go ~** schwimmen gehen; **swimming cap** n (Brit) Badekappe f; **swimming costume** n (Brit) Badeanzug m; **swimming pool** n Schwimmbad nt; (private, in hotel) Swimmingpool m; **swimming trunks** npl (Brit) Badehose f; **swimsuit** n Badeanzug m

swindle vt betrügen (out of um)

swine n Schwein nt

swing 1. vt, vi (object) schwingen **2.** n (for child) Schaukel f

swipe vt (credit card etc) durchziehen; fam (steal) klauen; **swipe card** n Magnetkarte f

Swiss 1. adj schweizerisch **2.** n Schweizer(in) m(f)

switch 1. n ELEC Schalter m **2.** vt (change) wechseln; **~ sth for sth** etw gegen etw eintau-

schen **3.** vi (change) wechseln (to zu); **switch off** vt abschalten, ausschalten;
switch on vt anschalten, einschalten; **switchboard** n TEL Vermittlung f

Switzerland n die Schweiz

swivel 1. vi sich drehen **2.** vt drehen

swollen 1. pp of **swell 2.** adj MED geschwollen; (stomach) aufgebläht

swop → **swap**

sword n Schwert nt

swore pt of **swear**

sworn pp of **swear**

swum pp of **swim**

swung pt, pp of **swing**

syllable n Silbe f

symbol n Symbol nt; **symbolic** adj symbolisch; **symbolize** vt symbolisieren

symmetrical adj symmetrisch

sympathetic adj mitfühlend; (understanding) verständnisvoll; **sympathize** vi mitfühlen (with sb mit jdm); **sympathy** n Mitleid nt; (after death) Beileid nt; (understanding) Verständnis nt

symphony n Sinfonie f

symptom n Symptom nt

synagogue n Synagoge f

synthetic adj (material) synthetisch

Syria n Syrien nt

syringe n Spritze f

system n System nt; **systematic** adj systematisch

T

tab n (for hanging up coat etc) Aufhänger m; IT Tabulator m; **pick up the ~** fam die Rechnung übernehmen

table n Tisch m; (list) Tabelle f; **~ of contents** Inhaltsverzeichnis nt; **tablecloth** n Tischdecke f; **tablespoon** n Servierlöffel m; (in recipes) Esslöffel m

tablet n Tablette f

table tennis n Tischtennis nt; **table wine** n Tafelwein m

tabloid n Boulevardzeitung f

taboo 1. n Tabu nt **2.** adj tabu

tack n (small nail) Stift m; (US, thumbtack) Reißzwecke f

tackle 1. n SPORT Angriff m; (equipment) Ausrüstung f **2.** vt (deal with) in Angriff nehmen; SPORT angreifen; (verbally) zur Rede stellen (about wegen)

tact n Takt m; **tactful, tactfully** adj, adv taktvoll; **tactic(s)** n(pl) Taktik f; **tactless, tactlessly** adj, adv taktlos

tag n (label) Schild nt; (with maker's name) Etikett nt

tail n Schwanz m; **heads or ~s?** Kopf oder Zahl?; **tailback** n (Brit) Rückstau m; **taillight** n AUTO Rücklicht nt

tailor n Schneider(in) m(f)

tailpipe n (US) AUTO Auspuffrohr nt

Taiwan n Taiwan nt

take vt nehmen; (take along with one) mitnehmen; (take to a place) bringen; (subtract) abziehen (from von); (capture: person) fassen; (gain, obtain) bekommen; FIN, COMM einnehmen; (train, taxi) nehmen, fahren mit; (trip, walk, holiday, exam, course, photo) machen; (bath) nehmen; (phone call) entgegennehmen; (decision, precautions) treffen; (risk) eingehen; (advice, job) annehmen; (tablets) ertragen; (heat, pain) ertragen; (react to) aufnehmen; (have room for) Platz haben für; **I'll ~ it** (item in shop) ich nehme es; **how long does it ~?** wie lange dauert es?; **it ~s 4 hours** man braucht 4 Stunden; **I ~ it that ...** ich nehme an, dass ...; **~ place** stattfinden; **take after** vt nachschlagen + dat; **take along** vt mitnehmen; **take apart** vt auseinander nehmen; **take away** vt (remove) wegnehmen (from sb jdm); (subtract) abziehen (from von); **take back** vt (return) zurückbringen; (retract) zurücknehmen; **take down** vt (picture, cur-

tains) abnehmen; (*write down*) aufschreiben; **take in** *vt* (*understand*) begreifen; (*give accommodation to*) aufnehmen; (*deceive*) hereinlegen; (*include*) einschließen; (*show, film etc*) mitnehmen; **take off 1.** *vi* (*plane*) starten **2.** *vt* (*clothing*) ausziehen; (*hat, lid*) abnehmen; (*deduct*) abziehen; **take a day off** einen Tag freinehmen; **take on** *vt* (*undertake*) übernehmen; (*employ*) einstellen; SPORT antreten gegen; **take out** *vt* (*wallet etc*) herausnehmen; (*person, dog*) ausführen; (*insurance*) abschließen; (*money from bank*) abheben; (*book from library*) ausleihen; **take over 1.** *vt* übernehmen **2.** *vi* **he took over (from me)** er hat mich abgelöst; **take to** *vt* **I've taken to her/it** ich mag sie/es; **~ doing sth** (*begin*) anfangen, etw zu tun; **take up** *vt* (*carpet*) hochnehmen; (*space*) einnehmen; (*time*) in Anspruch nehmen; (*hobby*) anfangen mit; (*new job*) antreten; (*offer*) annehmen

taken 1. *pp* of **take 2.** *adj* (*seat*) besetzt; **be ~ with** angetan sein von

takeoff *n* AVIAT Start *m*; **take-out** (US) → **takeaway**; **take-over** *n* COMM Übernahme *f*

tale *n* Geschichte *f*

talent *n* Talent *nt*; **talented** *adj* begabt

talk 1. *n* (*conversation*) Gespräch *nt*; (*rumour*) Gerede *nt*; (*to audience*) Vortrag *m* **2.** *vi* sprechen, reden; (*have conversation*) sich unterhalten; **~ to** (*or* **with**) **sb** (*about sth*) mit jdm (über etw *acc*) sprechen **3.** *vt* (*language*) sprechen; (*nonsense*) reden; (*politics, business*) reden über + *acc*; **~ sb into doing/out of doing sth** jdn überreden/jdm ausreden, etw zu tun; **talk over** *vt* besprechen

talkative *adj* gesprächig

tall *adj* groß; (*building, tree*) hoch

tame 1. *adj* zahm **2.** *vt* (*animal*) zähmen

tampon *n* Tampon *m*

tan 1. *n* (*on skin*) (Sonnen-)bräune *f*; **get/have a ~** braun werden/sein **2.** *vi* braun werden

tangerine *n* Mandarine *f*

tango *n* Tango *m*

tank *n* Tank *m*; (*for fish*) Aquarium *nt*; MIL Panzer *m*

tanker *n* (*ship*) Tanker *m*; (*vehicle*) Tankwagen *m*

tanned *adj* (*by sun*) braun

Tanzania *n* Tansania *f*

tap 1. *n* (*for water*) Hahn *m* **2.** *vt, vi* (*strike*) klopfen; **~ sb on the shoulder** jdm auf die Schulter klopfen; **tap-dance** *vi* steppen

tape 1. n (adhesive tape) Klebeband nt; (for tape recorder) Tonband nt; (cassette) Kassette f; (video) Video nt **2.** vt (record) aufnehmen; **tape up** vt (parcel) zukleben; **tape measure** n Maßband nt; **tape recorder** n Tonbandgerät nt

tapestry n Wandteppich nt

tap water n Leitungswasser nt

tar n Teer m

target n Ziel nt; (board) Zielscheibe f

tariff n (price list) Preisliste f; (tax) Zoll m

tart n (fruit tart) (Obst)kuchen m; (small) (Obst)törtchen nt; fam, pej (prostitute) Nutte f, Schlampe f

tartan n Schottenkaro nt

tartar(e) sauce n Remouladensoße f

task n Aufgabe f; (duty) Pflicht f

Tasmania n Tasmanien nt

taste 1. n Geschmack m; (sense of taste) Geschmackssinn m; (small quantity) Kostprobe f; **it has a strange ~** es schmeckt komisch **2.** vt schmecken; (try) probieren **3.** vi (food) schmecken (of nach); **tasteful, tastefully** adj, adv geschmackvoll; **tasteless, tastelessly** adj, adv geschmacklos; **tasty** adj schmackhaft

taught pt, pp of **teach**

Taurus n ASTR Stier m

tax 1. n Steuer f (on auf + acc) **2.** vt besteuern; **taxation** n Besteuerung f; **tax bracket** n Steuerklasse f; **tax-free** adj steuerfrei

taxi 1. n Taxi nt **2.** vi (plane) rollen; **taxi rank** (Brit), **taxi stand** n Taxistand m

tax return n Steuererklärung f

tea n Tee m; (afternoon tea) ≈ Kaffee und Kuchen; (meal) frühes Abendessen; **teabag** n Teebeutel m; **tea break** n (Tee)pause f

teach 1. vt (person, subject) unterrichten; **~ sb (how) to dance** jdm das Tanzen beibringen **2.** vi unterrichten; **teacher** n Lehrer(in) m(f)

team n SPORT Mannschaft f, Team nt; **teamwork** n Teamarbeit f

teapot n Teekanne f

tear n (in eye) Träne f

tear 1. vt zerreißen; **~ a muscle** (in material etc) Riss m; **tear down** vt (building) abreißen; **tear up** vt (paper) zerreißen

tearoom n Café, in dem in erster Linie Tee serviert wird

tease vt (person) necken (about wegen)

teaspoon n Teelöffel m; **tea towel** n Geschirrtuch nt

technical adj technisch; (knowledge, term, dictionary) Fach-; **technically** adv technisch; **technique** n

Technik f
techno n Techno m
technology n Technologie f
tedious adj langweilig
teen(age) adj (fashions etc) Teenager-; **teenager** n Teenager m; **teens** npl **in one's ~** im Teenageralter
teeth pl of **tooth**
teetotal adj abstinent
telephone 1. n Telefon nt 2. vi telefonieren 3. vt anrufen; **telephone book** n Telefonbuch nt; **telephone booth**, **telephone box** (Brit) n Telefonzelle f; **telephone call** n Telefonanruf m; **telephone directory** n Telefonbuch nt; **telephone number** n Telefonnummer f
telephoto lens n Teleobjektiv nt
telescope n Teleskop nt
television n Fernsehen nt; **television set** n Fernsehapparat m
tell 1. vt (say, inform) sagen (sb sth jdm etw); (story) erzählen; (truth) sagen; (difference) erkennen; (reveal secret) verraten; **~ sb about sth** jdm von etw erzählen; **~ sth from sth** etw von etw unterscheiden 2. vi (be sure) wissen; **tell apart** vt unterscheiden; **tell off** vt schimpfen
telling adj aufschlussreich
telly n (Brit fam) Glotze f; **on (the) ~** in der Glotze

temp 1. n Aushilfskraft f 2. vi als Aushilfskraft arbeiten
temper n (anger) Wut f; (mood) Laune f; **lose one's ~** die Beherrschung verlieren; **temperamental** adj (moody) launisch
temperature n Temperatur f; MED (high temperature) Fieber nt; **have a ~** Fieber haben
temple n Tempel m; ANAT Schläfe f
tempo n Tempo nt
temporarily adv vorübergehend; **temporary** adj vorübergehend; (road, building) provisorisch
tempt vt in Versuchung führen; **temptation** n Versuchung f; **tempting** adj verlockend
ten 1. num zehn 2. n Zehn f; → **eight**
tenant n Mieter(in) m(f); (of land) Pächter(in) m(f)
tend vi **~ to do sth** (person) dazu neigen, etw zu tun; **~ towards** neigen zu; **tendency** n Tendenz f
tender adj (loving) zärtlich; (sore) empfindlich; (meat) zart
tendon n Sehne f
Tenerife n Teneriffa f
tenner n (Brit fam (note) Zehnpfundschein m
tennis n Tennis nt; **tennis court** n Tennisplatz m; **tennis racket** n Tennisschläger m

tenor n Tenor m

tense adj angespannt; (stretched tight) gespannt; **tension** n Spannung f; (strain) Anspannung f

tent n Zelt nt

tenth 1. adj zehnte(r, s) 2. n (fraction) Zehntel nt; → **eighth**

tent peg n Hering m; **tent pole** n Zeltstange f

term n (in school, at university) Trimester nt; (expression) Ausdruck m; **~s** pl (conditions) Bedingungen pl; **be on good ~s with sb** mit jdm gut auskommen; **come to ~s with sth** sich mit etw abfinden; **in the long/short ~** langfristig/kurzfristig; **in ~s of ...** was ... betrifft

terminal 1. n (bus terminal etc) Endstation f; AVIAT Terminal m; IT Terminal nt; ELEC Pol m 2. adj MED unheilbar; **terminally** adv (ill) unheilbar

terminate 1. vt (contract) lösen; (pregnancy) abbrechen 2. vi (train, bus) enden

terrace n (of houses) Häuserreihe f; (in garden etc) Terrasse f; **terraced** adj (garden) terrassenförmig angelegt; **terraced house** n (Brit) Reihenhaus nt

terrible adj schrecklich

terrific adj (very good) fantastisch

terrify vt erschrecken; **be terrified** schreckliche Angst ha-

ben (of vor + dat)

territory n Gebiet nt

terror n Schrecken m; POL Terror m; **terrorism** n Terrorismus m; **terrorist** n Terrorist(in) m(f)

test 1. n Test m, Klassenarbeit f; (driving test) Prüfung f; **put to the ~** auf die Probe stellen 2. vt testen, prüfen

Testament n **The Old/New ~** das Alte/Neue Testament

test-drive vt Probe fahren

testicle n Hoden m

testify vi LAW aussagen

test tube n Reagenzglas nt

tetanus n Tetanus m

text 1. n Text m; (of document) Wortlaut m; (sent by mobile phone) SMS f 2. vt (message) simsen, SMSen; **~ sb** jdm simsen, jdm eine SMS schicken; **I'll ~ it to you** ich schicke es dir per SMS

textbook n Lehrbuch nt

texting n SMS-Messaging nt; **text message** n SMS f

texture n Beschaffenheit f

Thailand n Thailand nt

Thames n Themse f

than prep, conj als; **bigger/faster ~ me** größer/schneller als ich

thank vt danken + dat; **~ you** danke; **~ you very much** vielen Dank; **thankful** adj dankbar; **thankfully** adv (luckily) zum Glück; **thankless** adj undankbar; **thanks** npl Dank m; **~ danke!**; **~ to** dank

+ gen

that **1.** adj der/die/das; (opposed to this) jene(r, s); who's ~ woman? wer ist die Frau?; **I like ~ one** ich mag das da **2.** pron das; (in relative clauses) der/die/das, die pl; ~ **is very good** das ist sehr gut; **the wine ~ I drank** der Wein, den ich getrunken habe; ~ **is (to say)** das heißt **3.** conj dass; **I think ~ ...** ich denke, dass ... **4.** adv so; ~ **good** so gut

that's contr of that is; that has

thaw **1.** vi tauen; (frozen food) auftauen **2.** vt auftauen lassen

the art der/die/das, die pl; **Henry ~ Eighth** Heinrich der Achte; **by ~ hour** pro Stunde; ~ **... ~ better** je ..., desto besser

theater (US), theatre n Theater nt; (for lectures etc) Saal m

theft n Diebstahl m

their adj ihr; **they cleaned ~ teeth** sie putzten sich die Zähne; **someone has left ~ umbrella here** jemand hat seinen Schirm hier vergessen; theirs pron ihre(r, s); **it's ~** es gehört ihnen; **a friend of ~** ein Freund von ihnen; **someone has left ~ here** jemand hat seins hier liegen lassen

them pron (direct object) sie;

(indirect object) ihnen; **do you know ~?** kennst du sie?; (can you help ~?** kannst du ihnen helfen?; **it's ~** sie sind's; **if anyone has a problem you should help ~** wenn jemand ein Problem hat, solltest du ihnen helfen

theme n Thema nt; MUS Motiv nt; ~ **song** Titelmelodie f

themselves pron sich; **they hurt ~** sie haben sich verletzt; **they ~ were not there** sie selbst waren nicht da; **they did it ~** sie haben es selbst gemacht; **(all) by ~** allein

then **1.** adv (at that time) damals; (next) dann; (therefore) also; (furthermore) ferner; **from ~ on** von da an; **by ~** bis dahin **2.** adj damalig; **our ~ boss** unser damaliger Chef

theoretical, theoretically adj, adv theoretisch

theory n Theorie f; **in ~** theoretisch

therapy n Therapie f

there adv dort; (to a place) dorthin; ~ **is/~ are** (exists/exist) es gibt; **it's over ~** es ist da drüben; ~ **you are** (when giving) bitte schön; thereabouts (approximately) so ungefähr; therefore adv daher, deshalb

thermometer n Thermometer nt

Thermos® n ~ (flask) Ther-

thought

mosflasche® f

these pron, adj diese; **~ are not my books** das sind nicht meine Bücher

thesis n (for PhD) Doktorarbeit f

they pron pl sie; (people in general) man; (unidentified person) er/sie; **~ are rich** sie sind reich; **~ say that ...** man sagt, dass ...; **if anyone looks at this, ~ will see** that ... wenn sich jemand dies ansieht, wird er erkennen, dass ...

they'd contr of **they had; they would**

they'll contr of **they will; they shall**

they've contr of **they have**

thick adj dick; (fog) dicht; (liquid) dickflüssig; fam (stupid) dumm; **thicken** vi (fog) dichter werden; (sauce) dick werden

thief n Dieb(in) m(f)

thigh n Oberschenkel m

thimble n Fingerhut m

thin adj dünn

thing n Ding nt; (affair) Sache f; **how are ~s?** wie geht's?; **I can't see a ~** ich kann nichts sehen

think vt, vi denken; (believe) meinen; **I ~ so** ich denke schon; **I don't ~ so** ich glaube nicht; (think about) nachdenken an + acc; (reflect on) nachdenken über + acc; (have opinion of) halten von; **think**

of vt denken an + acc; (devise) sich ausdenken; (have opinion of) halten von; (remember) sich erinnern an + acc; **think over** vt überdenken; **think up** vt sich ausdenken

third 1. adj dritte(r, s) **2.** n (fraction) Drittel nt; **in ~** (gear) im dritten Gang; → **eighth**; thirdly adv drittens; **third-party insurance** n Haftpflichtversicherung f

thirst n Durst m (for nach); **thirsty** adj **be ~** Durst haben

thirteen 1. num dreizehn **2.** n Dreizehn f; → **eight**; **thirteenth** adj dreizehnte(r, s); → **eighth**; **thirtieth** adj dreißigste(r, s); → **eighth**; **thirty 1.** num dreißig; **~one** einunddreißig **2.** n Dreißig f; **be in one's thirties** in den Dreißigern sein; → **eight**

this 1. adj diese(r, s); **~ morning** heute Morgen **2.** pron das, dies; **~ is Mark** (on the phone) hier spricht Mark

thistle n Distel f

thorn n Dorn m, Stachel m

thorough adj gründlich; **thoroughly** adv gründlich; (agree etc) völlig

those 1. pron die da, jene; **~ who** diejenigen, die **2.** adj die, jene

though 1. conj obwohl; **as ~** als ob **2.** adv aber

thought 1. pt, pp of **think 2.** n Gedanke m; (thinking)

Überlegung f; **thoughtful** adj (kind) rücksichtsvoll; (attentive) aufmerksam; (in Gedanken versunken) nachdenklich; **thoughtless** adj (unkind) rücksichtslos, gedankenlos

thousand num (one) ~, a ~ tausend; **five** ~ fünftausend; **~s of** Tausende von

thrash vt (hit) verprügeln; (defeat) vernichtend schlagen

thread 1. n Faden m 2. vt (needle) einfädeln; (beads) auffädeln

threat n Drohung f; (danger) Bedrohung f (to für); **threaten** vt bedrohen; **threatening** adj bedrohlich

three 1. num drei 2. n Drei f; → **eight**; **three-dimensional** adj dreidimensional; **three-quarters** npl drei Viertel pl

threshold n Schwelle f

threw pt of **throw**

thrifty adj sparsam

thrilled adj **be ~ (with sth)** sich (über etw acc) riesig freuen; **thrilling** adj aufregend

thrive vi gedeihen (on bei); (business) fig florieren

throat n Hals m, Kehle f

throbbing adj (pain, headache) pochend

thrombosis n Thrombose f

throne n Thron m

through 1. prep durch; (time) während + gen; (because of) aus, durch; (US, up to and including) bis 2. adv durch; **put sb ~** TEL jdn verbinden (to mit) 3. adj (ticket, train) durchgehend; **~ flight** Direktflug m; **be ~ with sb/sth** mit jdm / etw fertig sein; **throughout** 1. prep (place) überall in 2. adv (time) während + gen; **~ the night** die ganze Nacht hindurch 3. adv überall; (time) die ganze Zeit

throw 1. vt werfen; (rider) abwerfen; (party) geben 2. n Wurf m; **throw away** vt wegwerfen; **throw in** vt (include) dazugeben; **throw out** vt (unwanted object) wegwerfen; (person) hinauswerfen (of aus); **throw up** vt, vi fam (vomit) sich übergeben

thrown pp of **throw**

thru (US) → **through**

thrush n Drossel f

thrust vt, vi (push) stoßen

thruway n (US) Schnellstraße f

thumb 1. n Daumen m 2. vt **~ a lift** per Anhalter fahren; **thumbtack** n (US) Reißzwecke f

thunder 1. n Donner m 2. vi donnern; **thunderstorm** n Gewitter nt

Thur(s) abbr → **Thursday**; Do.

Thursday n Donnerstag m; → **Tuesday**

thus adv (in this way) so; (therefore) somit, also

thyme n Thymian m

Tibet n Tibet nt

tick 1. n (for train, bus) (Fahr-) karte f; (plane ticket) Flugschein m, Ticket nt; (price ticket) (Preis)schild nt; (raffle ticket) Los nt; (for car park) Parkschein m; (for traffic offence) Strafzettel m; **ticket collector, ticket inspector** (Brit) n Fahrkartenkontrolleur(in) m(f); **ticket machine** n (for public transport) Fahrscheinautomat m, (in car park) Parkscheinautomat m; **ticket office** n RAIL Fahrkartenschalter m; THEAT Kasse f

tickle vt kitzeln; **ticklish** adj kitzlig

tide n Gezeiten pl; **the ~ is in/ out** es ist Flut/Ebbe

tidy 1. adj ordentlich 2. vt aufräumen; **tidy up** vt, vi aufräumen

tie 1. n (necktie) Krawatte f; SPORT Unentschieden nt; (bond) Bindung f 2. vt (attach, do up) binden (to an + acc); (tie together) zusammenbinden; (knot) machen; **tie down** vt festbinden (to an + dat); fig binden; **tie up** vt (dog) anbinden; (parcel) verschnüren; (shoelace) bin-

den; (boat) festmachen

tiger n Tiger m

tight 1. adj (clothes) eng; (knot) fest; (screw, lid) fest sitzend; (control, security measures) streng; (timewise) knapp; (schedule) eng 2. adv (shut) fest; (pull) stramm; **hold ~** festhalten!; **tighten** vt (knot, rope, screw) anziehen; (belt) enger machen; (restrictions, control) verschärfen; **tights** npl (Brit) Strumpfhose f

tile n (on roof) Dachziegel m; (on wall, floor) Fliese f

till 1. n Kasse f **2.** prep, conj → **until**

tilt 1. vt kippen; (head) neigen **2.** vi sich neigen

time 1. n (on occasion) Zeit f; Mal nt; MUS Takt m; **local ~** Ortszeit; **what ~ is it?, what's the ~?** wie spät ist es?, wie viel Uhr ist es?; **take one's ~** (over sth) sich (bei etw) Zeit lassen; **have a good ~** Spaß haben; **in two weeks' ~** in zwei Wochen; **at ~s** manchmal; **at the same ~** gleichzeitig; **all the ~** die ganze Zeit; **by the ~ he ...** bis er ...; (in past) als er ...; **for the ~ being** vorläufig; **in ~** (not late) rechtzeitig; **on ~** pünktlich; **the first ~** das erste Mal; **this ~** diesmal; **five ~s** fünfmal; **five ~s six** fünf mal sechs; **four ~s a year** viermal im Jahr; **three**

at a ~ drei auf einmal **2.** vt (*with stopwatch*) stoppen; **you ~d that well** das hast du gut getimt; **time difference** n Zeitunterschied m; **timer** n Timer m; (*switch*) Schaltuhr f; **time-saving** adj Zeit sparend; **time switch** n Schaltuhr f; **timetable** n (*for public transport*) Fahrplan m; (*school*) Stundenplan m; **time zone** n Zeitzone f

timid adj ängstlich

timing n (*coordination*) Timing nt

tin n (*metal*) Blech nt; (*Brit, can*) Dose f; **tinfoil** n Alufolie f; **tinned** adj (*Brit*) aus der Dose; **tin opener** n (*Brit*) Dosenöffner m

tinsel n ≈ Lametta nt

tint n (Farb)ton m; (*in hair*) Tönung f; **tinted** adj getönt

tiny adj winzig

tip 1. n (*money*) Trinkgeld nt; (*hint*) Tipp m; (*end*) Spitze f; (*of cigarette*) Filter m; (*Brit, rubbish tip*) Müllkippe f **2.** vt (*waiter*) Trinkgeld geben + dat; **tip over** vt, vi (*overturn*) umkippen

tipsy adj beschwipst

tiptoe n **on ~** auf Zehenspitzen

tire 1. n (*US*) → **tyre 2.** vt müde machen **3.** vi müde werden; **tired** adj müde; **be ~ of doing sth** es satt haben, etw zu tun; **tireless, tirelessly**

adv unermüdlich; **tiresome** adj lästig; **tiring** adj ermüdend

tissue n ANAT Gewebe nt; (*paper handkerchief*) Papier(taschen)tuch nt; **tissue paper** n Seidenpapier nt

tit n (*bird*) Meise f; fam (*breast*) Titte f

title n Titel m

to prep (*towards*) zu; (*with countries, towns*) nach; (*as far as*) bis; (*with infinitive of verb*) zu; **~ Rome/ Switzerland** nach Rom/ in die Schweiz; **I've been ~ London** ich war schon mal in London; **go ~ town/~ the theatre** in die Stadt/ ins Theater gehen; **from Monday ~ Thursday** von Montag bis Donnerstag; **he came ~ say sorry** er kam, um sich zu entschuldigen; **20 minutes ~ 4** 20 Minuten vor 4; **they won by 4 goals ~ 3** sie haben mit 4 zu 3 Toren gewonnen

toad n Kröte f; **toadstool** n Giftpilz m

toast 1. n (*bread, drink*) Toast m; **a piece** (*or* **slice**) **of ~** eine Scheibe Toast; **propose a ~ to sb** einen Toast auf jdn ausbringen **2.** vt (*bread*) toasten; (*person*) trinken auf + acc; **toaster** n Toaster m

tobacco n Tabak m; **tobacconist's** n ~ (*shop*) Tabakladen *m*

toboggan *n* Schlitten *m*

today *adv* heute; **a week ~** heute in einer Woche; **~'s newspaper** die Zeitung von heute

toddler *n* Kleinkind *nt*

toe *n* Zehe *f*, Zeh *m*; **toenail** *n* Zehennagel *m*

toffee *n* (*sweet*) Karamellbonbon *nt*

tofu *n* Tofu *m*

together *adv* zusammen; **I tied them ~** ich habe sie zusammengebunden

toilet *n* Toilette *f*; **go to the ~** auf die Toilette gehen; **toilet bag** *n* Kulturbeutel *m*; **toilet paper** *n* Toilettenpapier *nt*; **toiletries** *npl* Toilettenartikel *pl*; **toilet roll** *n* Rolle *f* Toilettenpapier

token *n* Marke *f*; (*in casino*) Spielmarke *f*; (*voucher, gift token*) Gutschein *m*; (*sign*) Zeichen *nt*

Tokyo *n* Tokio *nt*

told *pt, pp of* **tell**

tolerant *adj* tolerant (*of gegenüber*); **tolerate** *vt* tolerieren; (*noise, pain, heat*) ertragen

toll *n* (*charge*) Gebühr *f*; **toll-free** *adj, adv* (*US*) TEL gebührenfrei; **toll road** *n* gebührenpflichtige Straße

tomato *n* Tomate *f*; **tomato juice** *n* Tomatensaft *m*; **tomato sauce** *n* Tomatensoße *f*; (*Brit, ketchup*) Tomaten-

ket(s)chup *m or nt*

tomb *n* Grabmal *nt*; **tombstone** *n* Grabstein *m*

tomorrow *adv* morgen; **~ morning** morgen früh; **~ evening** morgen Abend; **the day after ~** übermorgen; **a ~ week (from) ~/~ week** morgen in einer Woche

ton *n* (*Brit*) Tonne *f* (*1016 kg*); (*US*) Tonne *f* (*907 kg*); **~s of books** *fam* eine Menge Bücher

tone *n* Ton *m*; **toner** *n* (*for printer*) Toner *m*; **toner cartridge** *n* Tonerpatrone *f*

tongs *npl* Zange *f*; (*curling tongs*) Lockenstab *m*

tongue *n* Zunge *f*

tonic *n* MED Stärkungsmittel *nt*; **~ (water)** Tonic *nt*

tonight *adv* heute Abend; (*during night*) heute Nacht

tonsils *n* Mandeln *pl*; **tonsillitis** *n* Mandelentzündung *f*

too *adv* zu; (*also*) auch; **~ fast** zu schnell; **~ much/many** zu viel/viele; **me ~** ich auch; **she liked it ~** ihr gefiel es auch

took *pt of* **take**

tool *n* Werkzeug *nt*; **toolbar** *n* IT Symbolleiste *f*; **toolbox** *n* Werkzeugkasten *m*

tooth *n* Zahn *m*; **toothache** *n* Zahnschmerzen *pl*; **toothbrush** *n* Zahnbürste *f*; **toothpaste** *n* Zahnpasta *f*; **toothpick** *n* Zahnstocher *m*

top 1. *n* (*of tower, class, com-*

pany etc) Spitze f; (of mountain) Gipfel m; (of tree) Krone f; (of street) oberes Ende; (of tube, pen) Kappe f; (of box) Oberteil nt; (of bikini) Oberteil nt; (sleeveless) Top nt; **at the ~ of the page** oben auf der Seite; **at the ~ of the league** an der Spitze der Liga; **on ~** oben; **on ~ of** auf + dat; (in addition to) zusätzlich zu; **over the ~** übertrieben 2. adj (floor, shelf) oberste(r, s); (best) Spitzen-; (pupil, school) beste(r, s) 3. vt (exceed) übersteigen; (be better than) übertreffen; (league) an erster Stelle liegen in + dat; **~ped with cream** mit Sahne obendrauf; **top up** vt auffüllen; **can I top you up?** darf ich dir nachschenken?

topic n Thema nt; **topical** adj aktuell

topless adj, adv oben ohne

topping n (on top of pizza, ice-cream etc) Belag m, Garnierung f

torch n (Brit) Taschenlampe f

tore pt of **tear**

torment vt quälen

torn pp of **tear**

tornado n Tornado m

torrential adj (rain) sintflutartig

tortoise n Schildkröte f

torture 1. n Folter f; fig Qual f **2.** vt foltern

Tory (Brit) n Tory m, Konservative(r) mf

toss 1. vt (throw) werfen; (salad) anmachen; **~ a coin** eine Münze werfen 2. n **I don't give a ~** fam es ist mir scheißegal

total 1. n (of figures, money) Gesamtsumme f; **a ~ of 30** insgesamt 30; **in ~** insgesamt 2. adj total; (sum etc) Gesamt- 3. vt (amount to) sich belaufen auf + acc; **totally** adv total

touch 1. n (act of ~ing) Berührung f; (sense of ~) Tastsinn m; (trace) Spur f; **be/keep in ~ with sb** mit jdm in Verbindung bleiben; **get in ~ with sb** sich mit jdm in Verbindung setzen 2. vt (feel) berühren; (emotionally) bewegen; **touch on** vt (topic) berühren; **touchdown** n AVIAT Landung f; **touching** adj (moving) rührend; **touch screen** n Touchscreen m; **touchy** adj empfindlich, zickig

tough adj hart; (material) robust; (meat) zäh

tour 1. n Tour f (of durch); (of town, building) Rundgang m (of durch); (of pop group etc) Tournee f 2. vt eine Tour/einen Rundgang/eine Tournee machen durch 3. vi (on holiday) umherreisen; **tour guide** n Reiseleiter(in) m(f)

tourism n Tourismus m,

Fremdenverkehr m; **tourist** n Tourist(in) m(f); **tourist guide** n (book) Reiseführer m; (person) Fremdenführer(in) m(f); **tourist office** n Fremdenverkehrsamt nt

tournament n Turnier nt

tour operator n Reiseveranstalter m

tow vt abschleppen; (caravan, trailer) ziehen

towards prep ~ **me** mir entgegen, auf mich zu; **we walked ~ the station** wir gingen in Richtung Bahnhof; **my feelings ~ him** meine Gefühle ihm gegenüber

towel n Handtuch nt

tower n Turm m; **tower block** n (Brit) Hochhaus nt

town n Stadt f; **town center** (US), **town centre** n Stadtmitte f, Stadtzentrum nt; **town hall** n Rathaus nt

towrope n Abschleppseil nt; **tow truck** n (US) Abschleppwagen m

toxic adj giftig, Gift-

toy n Spielzeug nt; **toy with** vt spielen mit; **toyshop** n Spielwarengeschäft nt

trace 1. n (mark) Spur f; **without ~** spurlos 2. vt (find) ausfindig machen; **tracing paper** n Pauspapier nt

track n (mark) Spur f; (path) Weg m; RAIL Gleis nt; (on CD, record) Stück nt; **keep / lose ~ of sb / sth** jdn / etw im Auge behal-

ten / aus den Augen verlieren; **track down** vt ausfindig machen; **tracksuit** n Trainingsanzug m

tractor n Traktor m

trade 1. n (commerce) Handel m; (business) Geschäft nt; (skilled job) Handwerk nt 2. vi handeln (in mit) 3. vt (exchange) tauschen (for gegen); **trademark** n Warenzeichen nt; **tradesman** n (shopkeeper) Geschäftsmann m; (workman) Handwerker m; **trade(s) union** n (Brit) Gewerkschaft f

tradition n Tradition f; **traditional, traditionally** adj, adv traditionell

traffic n Verkehr m; pej (trading) Handel m (in mit); **traffic circle** n (US) Kreisverkehr m; **traffic jam** n Stau m; **traffic lights** npl Verkehrsampel f; **traffic warden** n (Brit) ≈ Politesse f

tragedy n Tragödie f; **tragic** adj tragisch

trail 1. n (track) Spur f; (path) Weg m 2. vt (follow) verfolgen; (drag) schleppen; (drag behind) hinter sich herziehen; SPORT zurückliegen hinter + dat 3. vi (hang loosely) schleifen; SPORT weit zurückliegen; **trailer** n Anhänger m; (US, caravan) Wohnwagen m; FILM Trailer m

train 1. n RAIL Zug m 2. vt (teach) ausbilden; SPORT trainieren **3.** vi SPORT trainieren; **~ as** (or **to be**) **a teacher** eine Ausbildung als Lehrer machen; **trained** adj (person, voice) ausgebildet; **trainee** n Auszubildende(r) mf; (academic, practical) Praktikant(in) m(f); **trainer** n SPORT Trainer(in) m(f); **~s** (Brit, shoes) Turnschuhe pl; **training** n Ausbildung f; SPORT Training nt; **train station** n Bahnhof m

tram n (Brit) Straßenbahn f

tramp n Landstreicher(in) m(f)

tranquillizer n Beruhigungsmittel nt

transaction n (piece of business) Geschäft nt

transatlantic adj transatlantisch; **~ flight** Transatlantikflug m

transfer 1. n (of money) Überweisung f **2.** n (US, ticket) Umsteigekarte f **2.** vt (money) überweisen (to sb an jdn); (patient) verlegen; (employee) versetzen; SPORT transferieren **3.** vi (on journey) umsteigen; **transferable** adj übertragbar

transform vt umwandeln; **transformation** n Umwandlung f

transfusion n Transfusion f

transistor n Transistor m

transition n Übergang m (from ... to von ... zu)

translate vt, vi übersetzen;

translation n Übersetzung f; **translator** n Übersetzer(in) m(f)

transmission n TV, RADIO Übertragung f; AUTO Getriebe nt

transparent adj durchsichtig

transplant MED **1.** vt transplantieren **2.** n (operation) Transplantation f

transport 1. n (of goods, people) Beförderung f; **public ~** öffentliche Verkehrsmittel pl **2.** vt befördern, transportieren; **transportation** n → **transport**

trap 1. n Falle f **2.** vt **be ~ped** (in snow, job etc) festsitzen

trash n (book, film etc) Schund m; (US, refuse) Abfall m; **trash can** n (US) Abfalleimer m; **trashy** adj (novel) Schund-

traumatic adj traumatisch

travel 1. n Reisen nt **2.** vi (journey) reisen **3.** vt (distance) zurücklegen; (country) bereisen; **travel agency**, **travel agent** n (company) Reisebüro nt; **traveler** (US) → **traveller**; **traveler's check** (US) → **traveller's cheque**; **traveller** n Reisende(r) mf; **traveller's cheque** n (Brit) Reisescheck m

tray n Tablett nt; (for mail etc) Ablage f; (of printer, photocopier) Fach nt

tread n (on tyre) Profil nt; **tread on** vt treten auf + acc

treasure 1. n Schatz m **2.** vt schätzen

treat 1. n besondere Freude; **it's my ~** das geht auf meine Kosten **2.** vt behandeln; **~ sb (to sth)** jdn (zu etw) einladen; **~ oneself to sth** sich etw leisten; **treatment** n Behandlung f

treaty n Vertrag m

tree n Baum m

tremble vi zittern

tremendous adj gewaltig; fam (very good) toll

trench n Graben m

trend n Tendenz f; (fashion) Mode f, Trend m; **trendy** adj trendy

trespass sign **'no ~ing'** „Betreten verboten"

trial n LAW Prozess m; (test) Versuch m; **trial period** n (for employee) Probezeit f

triangle n Dreieck nt; MUS Triangel m; **triangular** adj dreieckig

tribe n Stamm m

trick 1. n Trick m; (mischief) Streich m **2.** vt hereinlegen

tricky adj (difficult) schwierig; (situation) verzwickt

trifle n Kleinigkeit f; (Brit) GASTR Trifle nt (Nachspeise aus Biskuit, Wackelpudding, Obst, Vanillesoße und Sahne)

trigger 1. n (of gun) Abzug m **2.** vt **~ (off)** auslösen

trim 1. vt (hair, beard) nachschneiden; (nails) schneiden; (hedge) stutzen **2.** n just

a ~, please nur etwas nachschneiden, bitte; **trimmings** npl (decorations) Verzierungen pl; (extras) Zubehör nt; GASTR Beilagen pl

trip 1. n Reise f; (outing) Ausflug m **2.** vi stolpern (over über + acc)

triple 1. adj dreifach **2.** adv **~ the price** dreimal so teuer **3.** vi sich verdreifachen; **triplets** npl Drillinge pl

tripod n Stativ nt

trite adj banal

triumph n Triumph m

trivial adj trivial

trod pt of **tread**

trodden pp of **tread**

trolley n (Brit, in shop) Einkaufswagen m; (for luggage) Kofferkuli m; (serving trolley) Teewagen m

trombone n Posaune f

troops npl MIL Truppen pl

trophy n Trophäe f

tropical adj tropisch

trouble 1. n (problems) Schwierigkeiten pl; (worry) Sorgen pl; (effort) Mühe f; (unrest) Unruhen pl; MED Beschwerden pl; **be in ~** in Schwierigkeiten sein; **get into ~** (with authority) Ärger bekommen; **make ~** Schwierigkeiten machen **2.** vt (worry) beunruhigen; (disturb) stören; **sorry to ~ you** ich muss dich leider kurz stören; **troubled** adj (worried) beunruhigt; **trouble-free** adj problemlos; **troublemaker** *n* Unruhestifter(in) *m(f)*; **troublesome** *adj* lästig

trousers *npl* Hose *f*; **trouser suit** *n* (*Brit*) Hosenanzug *m*

trout *n* Forelle *f*

truck *n* Lastwagen *m*; (*Brit*) RAIL Güterwagen *m*; **trucker** *n* (*US, driver*) Lastwagenfahrer(in) *m(f)*

true *adj* (*factually correct*) wahr; (*genuine*) echt; **come ~** wahr werden

truly *adv* wirklich; **Yours ~** (*in letter*) mit freundlichen Grüßen

trump *n* Trumpf *m*

trumpet *n* Trompete *f*

trunk *n* (*of tree*) Stamm *m*; ANAT Rumpf *m*; (*of elephant*) Rüssel *m*; (*piece of luggage*) Überseekoffer *m*; (*US*) AUTO Kofferraum *m*; **trunks** *npl* (*swimming*) ~ Badehose *f*

trust 1. *n* (*confidence*) Vertrauen *nt* (*in zu*) **2.** *vt* vertrauen + *dat*; **trusting** *adj* vertrauensvoll; **trustworthy** *adj* vertrauenswürdig

truth *n* Wahrheit *f*; **truthful** *adj* ehrlich; (*statement*) wahrheitsgemäß

try 1. *n* Versuch *m* **2.** *vt* (*attempt*) versuchen; (*try out*) ausprobieren; (*sample*) probieren; LAW (*person*) vor Gericht stellen; (*courage, patience*) auf die Probe stellen **3.** *vi* versuchen; (*make effort*) sich bemühen; **try on**

vt (*clothes*) anprobieren; **try out** *vt* ausprobieren

T-shirt *n* T-Shirt *nt*

tub *n* (*for ice-cream, margarine*) Becher *m*

tube *n* (*pipe*) Rohr *nt*; (*of rubber, plastic*) Schlauch *m*; (*for toothpaste, glue etc*) Tube *f*; **the Tube** (*in London*) die U-Bahn; **tube station** *n* U-Bahn-Station *f*

tuck *vt* (*put*) stecken; **tuck in 1.** *vt* (*shirt*) in die Hose stecken; (*person*) zudecken **2.** *vi* (*eat*) zulangen

Tue(s) *abbr* = **Tuesday**; Di.

Tuesday *n* Dienstag *m*; **on ~** (am) Dienstag; **on ~s** dienstags; **this / last / next ~** diesen / letzten / nächsten Dienstag; **(on) ~ morning / afternoon / evening** (am) Dienstag Morgen / Nachmittag / Abend; **every ~** jeden Dienstag; **a week on ~ / ~ week** Dienstag in einer Woche

tug 1. *vt* ziehen **2.** *vi* ziehen (*at an + dat*)

tuition *n* Unterricht *m*; (*US, fees*) Studiengebühren *pl*; **~ fees** *pl* Studiengebühren *pl*

tulip *n* Tulpe *f*

tumble *vi* (*person, prices*) fallen; **tumble dryer** *n* Wäschetrockner *m*

tummy *n fam* Bauch *m*

tumor (*US*), **tumour** *n* Tumor *m*

tuna n Thunfisch m

tune 1. n Melodie f; *be in/ out of ~ (instrument)* gestimmt / verstimmt sein; *(singer)* richtig / falsch singen **2.** vt *(instrument)* stimmen; *(radio)* einstellen *(to* auf + acc)

Tunisia n Tunesien nt

tunnel n Tunnel m; *(under road, railway)* Unterführung f

turbulence n AVIAT Turbulenzen pl; **turbulent** adj stürmisch

Turk n Türke m, Türkin f

turkey n Truthahn m

Turkey n die Türkei; **Turkish 1.** adj türkisch **2.** n *(language)* Türkisch nt

turmoil n Aufruhr m

turn 1. n *(rotation)* Drehung f; *(performance)* Nummer f; *make a left ~* nach links abbiegen; *at the ~ of the century* um die Jahrhundertwende; *it's your ~* du bist dran; *in ~, by ~s* abwechselnd; *take ~s* sich abwechseln **2.** vt *(wheel, key, screw)* drehen; *(to face other way)* umdrehen; *(corner)* biegen um; *(page)* umblättern; *(transform)* verwandeln *(into* in + acc) **3.** vi *(rotate)* sich drehen; *(to face other way)* sich umdrehen; *(change direction: driver, car)* abbiegen; *(become)* werden; *(weather)* umschlagen; *~ into sth (become)* sich in etw acc ver-

wandeln; *~ cold/ green* kalt / grün werden; *~ left/ right* links / rechts abbiegen; **turn away** vt *(person)* abweisen; **turn back 1.** vt *(person)* zurückweisen **2.** vi *(go back)* umkehren; **turn down** vt *(refuse)* ablehnen; *(radio, TV)* leiser stellen; *(heating)* kleiner stellen; **turn off 1.** vi abbiegen **2.** vt *(switch off)* ausschalten; *(tap)* zudrehen; *(engine, electricity)* abstellen; **turn on** vt *(switch on)* einschalten; *(tap)* aufdrehen; *(engine, electricity)* anstellen; *fam (person)* anmachen, antörnen; **turn out 1.** vt *(light)* ausmachen; *(pockets)* leeren **2.** vi *(develop)* sich entwickeln; *as it turned out* wie sich herausstellte; **turn over 1.** vt *onto other side,* umdrehen; *(page)* umblättern **2.** vi *(person)* sich umdrehen; *(car)* sich überschlagen; TV umschalten *(to* auf + acc); **turn round 1.** vt *(to face other way)* umdrehen **2.** vi *(person)* sich umdrehen; *(go back)* umkehren; **turn to** vt sich zuwenden + dat; **turn up 1.** vi *(person, lost object)* auftauchen **2.** vt *(radio, TV)* lauter stellen; *(heating)* höher stellen; **turning** n *(in road)* Abzweigung f; **turning point** n Wendepunkt m

turnip n Rübe f

turnover n FIN Umsatz m

turnpike n (US) gebührenpflichtige Autobahn

turquoise adj türkis

turtle n (Brit) Wasserschild-
kröte f; (US) Schildkröte f

tutor n (private) Privatleh-
rer(in) m(f); (Brit, at university) Tutor(in) m(f)

tuxedo n (US) Smoking m

TV 1. n Fernsehen nt; (~ set)
Fernseher m; **watch** ~ fernsehen; **on** ~ im Fernsehen
2. adj Fernseh-; ~ **pro-
gramme** Fernsehsendung f

tweed n Tweed m

tweezers npl Pinzette f

twelfth adj zwölfte(r, s); →
eighth; **twelve** 1. num zwölf
2. n Zwölf f; → **eight**

twentieth adj zwanzigste(r, s);
→ **eighth**; **twenty** 1. num
zwanzig; **~one** einundzwan-
zig 2. n Zwanzig f; **be in
one's twenties** in den Zwan-
zigern sein; → **eight**

twice adv zweimal; ~ **as
much/many** doppelt so
viel/viele

twig n Zweig m

twilight n (in evening) Dämmerung f

twin 1. n Zwilling m 2. adj

(brother etc) Zwillings-; ~
beds zwei Einzelbetten

twinkle vi funkeln

twin room n Zweibettzimmer
nt; **twin town** n Partnerstadt
f

twist vt (turn) drehen, winden;
(distort) verdrehen; **I've ~ed
my ankle** ich bin mit dem
Fuß umgeknickt

two 1. num zwei; **break sth in**
~ etw in zwei Teile brechen 2.
n Zwei f; **the ~ of them** die
beiden; → **eight**; **two-dimensional** adj zweidimensi-
onal; fig oberflächlich; **two-
piece** adj zweiteilig; **two-
way** adj ~ **traffic** Gegenverkehr

type n (sort) Art f; (typeface)
Schrift(art) f; **he's not my** ~
er ist nicht mein Typ; **typeface** n Schrift(art) f; **type-
writer** n Schreibmaschine f

typhoid n Typhus m

typhoon n Taifun m

typical adj typisch (of für)

typing error n Tippfehler m

tyre n (Brit) Reifen m; **tyre
pressure** n Reifendruck m

Tyrol n **the ~** Tirol nt

U

UFO acr = **unidentified flying
object**; Ufo nt

Uganda n Uganda nt

ugly adj hässlich; (bad)

schlimm

UHT adj abbr = **ultra-heat
treated**; ~ **milk** H-Milch f

UK abbr = **United Kingdom**;

Vereinigtes Königreich *nt*
Ukraine *n the* ~ die Ukraine
ulcer *n* Geschwür *nt*
ultimate *adj* (*final*) letzte(r, s); (*authority*) höchste(r, s); **ultimately** *adv* letzten Endes; (*eventually*) schließlich; **ultimatum** *n* Ultimatum *nt*
ultra- *pref* ultra-
ultrasound *n* MED Ultraschall *m*
umbrella *n* Schirm *m*
umpire *n* Schiedsrichter(in) *m(f)*
umpteen *num fam* zig; ~ **times** zigmal
un- *pref* un-
UN *nsing abbr* = *United Nations*; UNO *f*
unable *adj be* ~ *to do sth* etw nicht tun können
unacceptable *adj* unannehmbar
unaccustomed *adj be* ~ *to sth* etw nicht gewohnt sein
unanimous, **unanimously** *adj, adv* einmütig
unattached *adj* (*without partner*) ungebunden
unattended *adj* (*luggage, car*) unbeaufsichtigt
unauthorized *adj* unbefugt
unavailable *adj* nicht erhältlich; (*person*) nicht erreichbar
unavoidable *adj* unvermeidlich
unaware *adj be* ~ *of sth* sich einer Sache *gen* nicht bewusst sein; *I was* ~ *that ...* ich wusste nicht, dass ...

unbalanced *adj* unausgewogen
unbearable *adj* unerträglich
unbeatable *adj* unschlagbar
unbelievable *adj* unglaublich
uncertain *adj* unsicher
uncle *n* Onkel *m*
uncomfortable *adj* unbequem
unconditional *adj* bedingungslos
unconscious *adj* MED bewusstlos; *be* ~ *of sth* sich einer Sache *gen* nicht bewusst sein; **unconsciously** *adv* unbewusst
uncover *vt* aufdecken
undecided *adj* unschlüssig
undeniable *adj* unbestreitbar
under **1.** *prep* (*beneath*) unter + *dat*; (*with motion*) unter + *acc*; ~ *an hour* weniger als eine Stunde **2.** *adv* (*beneath*) unten; (*with motion*) darunter; *children aged eight and* ~ Kinder bis zu acht Jahren; **under-age** *adj* minderjährig
undercarriage *n* Fahrgestell *nt*
underdog *n* Unterlegene(r) *mf*; (*outsider*) Außenseiter(in) *m(f)*
underdone *adj* GASTR nicht gar, durch
underestimate *vt* unterschätzen
underexposed *adj* PHOT unterbelichtet
undergo *irr vt* (*experience*)

durchmachen; (operation, test) sich unterziehen + dat

undergraduate n Student(in) m(f)

underground 1. adj unterirdisch **2.** n (Brit) U-Bahn f; **underground station** n U-Bahn-Station f

underlie irr vt zugrunde liegen + dat

underline vt unterstreichen

underlying adj zugrunde liegend

underneath 1. prep unter + dat; (with motion) unter + acc **2.** adv darunter

underpants npl Unterhose f; **undershirt** n (US) Unterhemd nt; (woman's) **underpants** npl (US) Unterhose f

understand irr vt, vi verstehen; **I ~ that …** (been told) ich habe gehört, dass …; (sympathize) ich habe Verständnis dafür, dass …; **make oneself understood** sich verständlich machen; **understanding** adj verständnisvoll

undertake irr vt (task) übernehmen; **~ to do sth** sich verpflichten, etw zu tun; **undertaker** n Leichenbestatter(in) m(f); **~'s** (firm) Bestattungsinstitut nt

underwater 1. adv unter Wasser **2.** adj Unterwasser-

underwear n Unterwäsche f

undo irr vt (unfasten) aufmachen; (work) zunichte machen; ɪɪ rückgängig machen

undoubtedly adv zweifellos

undress 1. vt ausziehen **2.** vi sich ausziehen

unearth vt (dig up) ausgraben; (find) aufstöbern

unease n Unbehagen nt; **uneasy** adj (person) unbehaglich; **I'm ~ about it** mir ist nicht wohl dabei

unemployed 1. adj arbeitslos **2.** npl **the ~** die Arbeitslosen pl; **unemployment** n Arbeitslosigkeit f; **unemployment benefit** n Arbeitslosengeld nt

unequal adj ungleich

uneven adj (surface, road) uneben; (contest) ungleich

unexpected adj unerwartet

unfamiliar adj **be ~ with sb/sth** jdn/etw nicht kennen

unfasten vt aufmachen

unfit adj ungeeignet (for für); (in bad health) nicht fit

unforeseen adj unvorhergesehen

unforgettable adj unvergesslich

unforgivable adj unverzeihlich

unfortunate adj (unlucky) unglücklich; **it is ~ that …** es ist bedauerlich, dass …; **unfortunately** adv leider

unfounded adj unbegründet

unhappy adj (sad) unglücklich, unzufrieden

unhealthy adj ungesund

unheard-of adj (unknown) gänzlich unbekannt; (outra-

geous) unerhört

unhitch vt (*caravan, trailer*) abkoppeln

unhurt adj unverletzt

uniform 1. n Uniform f **2.** adj einheitlich

unify vt vereinigen

unimportant adj unwichtig

uninhabited adj unbewohnt

uninstall vt тт deinstallieren

unintentional adj unabsichtlich

union n (*uniting*) Vereinigung f; (*alliance*) Union f

unique adj einzigartig

unit n Einheit f; (*of system, machine*) Teil nt; (*in school*) Lektion f

unite 1. vt vereinigen; **the United Kingdom** das Vereinigte Königreich; **the United Nations** pl die Vereinten Nationen pl; **the United States (of America)** pl die Vereinigten Staaten (von Amerika) pl **2.** vi sich vereinigen

universe n Universum nt

university n Universität f

unkind adj unfreundlich (*to* zu)

unknown adj unbekannt (*to + dat*)

unleaded adj bleifrei

unless conj es sei denn, wenn ... nicht; **don't do it ~ I tell you to** mach das nicht, es sei denn, ich sage es dir; **~ I'm mistaken ...** wenn ich mich nicht irre ...

unlicensed adj (*to sell alcohol*) ohne Lizenz

unlike prep (*in contrast to*) im Gegensatz zu; **it's ~ her to be late** es sieht ihr gar nicht ähnlich, zu spät zu kommen; **unlikely** adj unwahrscheinlich

unload vt ausladen

unlock vt aufschließen

unlucky adj unglücklich; **be ~** Pech haben

unmistakable adj unverkennbar

unnecessary adj unnötig

unoccupied adj (*seat*) frei; (*building, room*) leer stehend

unpack vt, vi auspacken

unpleasant adj unangenehm

unplug vt **~ sth** den Stecker von etw herausziehen

unprecedented adj beispiellos

unpredictable adj (*person, weather*) unberechenbar

unreasonable adj unvernünftig; (*demand*) übertrieben

unreliable adj unzuverlässig

unsafe adj nicht sicher; (*dangerous*) gefährlich

unscrew vt abschrauben

unskilled adj (*worker*) ungelernt

unsuccessful adj erfolglos

unsuitable adj ungeeignet (*for* für)

until 1. prep bis; **not ~** erst; **from Monday ~ Friday** von Montag bis Freitag; **he didn't come home ~ midnight**

er kam erst um Mitternacht nach Hause; ~ **then** bis dahin **2.** *conj* bis; **she won't come ~ you invite her** sie kommt erst, wenn du sie einlädst

unusual, unusually *adj, adv* ungewöhnlich

unwanted *adj* unerwünscht, ungewollt

unwell *adj* krank; **feel ~** sich nicht wohl fühlen

unwilling *adj* **be ~ to do sth** nicht bereit sein, etw zu tun

unwind *irr* **1.** *vt* abwickeln **2.** *vi* (*relax*) sich entspannen

unwrap *vt* auspacken

unzip *vt* am Reißverschluss aufmachen an + *dat*; *rr* entzippen

up 1. *prep* **climb ~ a tree** einen Baum hinaufklettern; **go ~ the street/ the stairs** die Straße entlanggehen/ die Treppe hinaufgehen; **further ~ the hill** weiter oben auf dem Berg **2.** *adv* (*in higher position*) oben; (*to higher position*) nach oben; (*out of bed*) auf; **~ there** dort oben; **~ and down** (*walk, jump*) auf und ab; **what's ~?** *fam* was ist los?; **~ to £100** bis zu 100 Pfund; **what's she ~ to?** was macht sie da?; (*planning*) was hat sie vor?; **it's ~ to you** das liegt bei dir; **I don't feel ~ to it** ich fühle mich dem nicht gewachsen

upbringing *n* Erziehung *f*

update 1. *n* (*list etc*) Aktuali-

sierung *f*; (*software*) Update *nt* **2.** *vt* (*list etc, person*) aktualisieren

upgrade *vt* (*computer*) aufrüsten; **we were ~d** das Hotel hat uns ein besseres Zimmer gegeben

upheaval *n* Aufruhr *m*; POL Umbruch *m*

uphill *adv* bergauf

upon *prep* → **on**

upper *adj* obere(r, s); (*arm, deck*) Ober-

upright *adj, adv* aufrecht

uprising *n* Aufstand *m*

uproar *n* Aufruhr *m*

upset 1. *irr vt* (*overturn*) umkippen; (*disturb*) aufregen; (*sadden*) bestürzen; (*offend*) kränken; (*plans*) durcheinander bringen *2. adj* (*disturbed*) aufgeregt; (*sad*) bestürzt; (*offended*) gekränkt; **~ stomach** Magenverstimmung *f*

upside down *adv* verkehrt herum; *fig* drunter und drüber; **turn sth ~** (*box etc*) etw umdrehen/ durchwühlen

upstairs *adv* (*go, take*) nach oben

up-to-date *adj* modern; (*fashion, information*) aktuell; **keep sb ~** jdn auf dem Laufenden halten

upwards *adv* nach oben

urban *adj* städtisch, Stadt-

urge 1. *n* Drang *m* **2.** *vt* **~ sb to do sth** jdn drängen, etw zu tun; urgent, urgently *adj,* *adv* dringend

urine *n* Urin *m*

us *pron* uns; **can he help ~?** kann er uns helfen?; **it's ~** wir sind's; **both of ~** wir beide

US, USA *nsing abbr* = *United States (of America)*; USA *pl*

use 1. *n* (*using*) Gebrauch *m*; (*for specific purpose*) Verwendung *f*; **in/out of ~** in/außer Gebrauch; **it's no ~** (*doing that*) es hat keinen Zweck(, das zu tun); **it's (of) no ~ to me** das kann ich nicht brauchen **2.** *vt* benutzen, gebrauchen; (*for specific purpose*) verwenden; (*method*) anwenden; **use up** *vt* aufbrauchen

used 1. *adj* (*secondhand*) gebraucht **2.** *vaux* **be ~d to**

sb/sth an jdn/etw gewöhnt sein; **get ~d to sb/sth** sich **~d to live here** sie hat früher mal hier gewohnt; **useful** *adj* nützlich; **useless** *adj* nutzlos; (*unusable*) unbrauchbar; (*pointless*) zwecklos; **user** *n* Benutzer(in) *m(f)*; **user-friendly** *adj* benutzerfreundlich

usual *adj* üblich, gewöhnlich; **as ~** wie üblich; **usually** *adv* normalerweise

utensil *n* Gerät *nt*

uterus *n* Gebärmutter *f*

utilize *vt* verwenden

utmost *adj* äußerst

utter 1. *adj* völlig **2.** *vt* von sich geben; **utterly** *adv* völlig

U-turn *n* AUTO Wende *f*; **do a ~** wenden

V

vacancy *n* (*job*) offene Stelle; (*room*) freies Zimmer; **vacant** *adj* (*room, seat*) frei; (*post*) offen; (*building*) leer stehend; **vacate** *vt* (*room, building*) räumen; (*seat*) frei machen

vacation *n* (*US*) Ferien *pl*, Urlaub *m*; (*at university*) (Semester)ferien *pl*; **go on ~** in Urlaub fahren

vaccinate *vt* impfen; **vaccination** *n* Impfung *f*; **~ card** Impfpass *m*

vacuum 1. *n* Vakuum *nt* **2.** *vt, vi* (staub)saugen; **vacuum cleaner** *n* Staubsauger *m*

vagina *n* Scheide *f*

vague *adj* (*imprecise*) vage; (*resemblance*) entfernt; **vaguely** *adv* in etwa, irgendwie

vain *adj* (*attempt*) vergeblich; (*conceited*) eitel; **vainly** *adv* (*in vain*) vergeblich

valid *adj* (*ticket, passport etc*) gültig; (*argument*) stichhaltig

valley *n* Tal *nt*

valuable *adj* wertvoll; (*time*)

kostbar; **valuables** npl Wertsachen pl

value 1. n Wert m **2.** vt (appreciate) schätzen; **value added tax** n Mehrwertsteuer f

valve n Ventil nt

van n AUTO Lieferwagen m

vanilla n Vanille f

vanish vi verschwinden

vanity n Eitelkeit f; **vanity case** n Schminkkoffer m

vapor (US), **vapour** n (mist) Dunst m; (steam) Dampf m

variable adj (weather, mood) unbeständig; (quality) unterschiedlich; (speed, height) regulierbar; varied adj (interests, selection) vielseitig; (career) bewegt; (work, diet) abwechslungsreich; **variety** n (diversity) Abwechslung f; (assortment) Vielfalt f (of an + dat); (type) Art f; **various** adj verschieden

varnish 1. n Lack m **2.** vt lackieren

vary 1. vt (alter) verändern **2.** vi (be different) unterschiedlich sein; (fluctuate) sich verändern; (prices) schwanken

vase (US) n Vase f

vast adj riesig; (area) weit

VAT abbr = **value added tax**; Mehrwertsteuer f, MwSt.

Vatican n **the ~** der Vatikan

VCR abbr = **video cassette recorder**; Videorekorder m

veal n Kalbfleisch nt

vegan n Veganer(in) m(f)

vegetable n Gemüse nt

vegetarian 1. n Vegetarier(in) m(f) **2.** adj vegetarisch

vehicle n Fahrzeug nt

veil n Schleier m

vein n Ader f

Velcro® n Klettband nt

velvet n Samt m

vending machine n Automat m

venereal disease n Geschlechtskrankheit f

venetian blind n Jalousie f

Venezuela n Venezuela nt

vengeance n Rache f

Venice n Venedig nt

venison n Rehfleisch nt

vent n Öffnung f

ventilate vt lüften; **ventilation** n Belüftung f; **ventilator** n (in room) Ventilator m; **be on a ~** MED künstlich beatmet werden

venture 1. n (project) Unternehmung f; COMM Unternehmen nt **2.** vi (go) (sich) wagen

venue n (for concert etc) Veranstaltungsort m

verb n Verb nt

verdict n Urteil nt

verge 1. n (of road) (Straßen-)rand m; **be on the ~ of doing sth** im Begriff sein, etw zu tun **2.** vi **~ on** grenzen an + acc

verification n (confirmation) Bestätigung f; (check) Überprüfung f; **verify** vt (confirm) bestätigen; (check) überprüfen

vermin npl Schädlinge pl; (insects) Ungeziefer nt
verruca n Warze f
versatile adj vielseitig
verse n (poetry) Poesie f; (stanza) Strophe f
version n Version f
versus prep gegen; (in contrast to) im Gegensatz zu
vertical adj senkrecht, vertikal
very 1. adv sehr; ~ **much** sehr 2. adj the ~ **book I need** genau das Buch, das ich brauche; **at that ~ moment** gerade in dem Augenblick; **at the ~ top** ganz oben; the ~ **best** der/die/das Allerbeste
vest n (Brit) Unterhemd nt; (US, waistcoat) Weste f
vet n Tierarzt m, Tierärztin f
veto 1. n Veto nt 2. vt sein Veto einlegen gegen
via prep über + acc
vibrate vi vibrieren; **vibration** n Vibration f
vicar n Pfarrer(in) m(f)
vice 1. n (evil) Laster nt 2. pref Vize-; **~chairman** stellvertretender Vorsitzender; **~president** Vizepräsident(in) m(f)
vice versa adv umgekehrt
vicinity n **in the** ~ in der Nähe (of + gen)
vicious adj (violent) brutal; (malicious) gemein; **vicious circle** n Teufelskreis m
victim n Opfer nt

victory n Sieg m
video 1. adj Video- 2. n Video nt; (recorder) Videorekorder m 3. vt (auf Video) aufnehmen; **video camera** n Videokamera f; **video cassette** n Videokassette f; **video clip** n Videoclip m; **video recorder** n Videorekorder m; **videotape** 1. n Videoband nt 2. vt (auf Video) aufnehmen
Vienna n Wien nt
Vietnam n Vietnam nt
view 1. n (sight) Blick m (of auf + acc); (vista) Aussicht f; (opinion) Meinung f; **in ~ of** angesichts + gen 2. vt (situation, event) betrachten; (house) besichtigen; **viewer** n (for slides) Diabetrachter m; TV Zuschauer(in) m(f); **viewpoint** n fig Standpunkt m
village n Dorf nt
villain n Schurke m; (in film, story) Bösewicht m
vinegar n Essig m
vineyard n Weinberg m
vintage n (of wine) Jahrgang m
violate vt (treaty) brechen; (rights, rule) verletzen
violence n (brutality) Gewalt f; (of person) Gewalttätigkeit f; **violent** adj brutal; (death) gewaltsam
violet n Veilchen n; (colour) Violett nt
violin n Geige f, Violine f

virgin n Jungfrau f

Virgo n ASTR Jungfrau f

virtual adj IT virtuell; virtually adv praktisch

virtue n Tugend f; **by** ~ **of** aufgrund + gen; virtuous adj tugendhaft

virus n MED, IT Virus nt

visa n Visum nt

visibility n METEO Sichtweite f; **good/poor** ~ gute/schlechte Sicht; visible adj sichtbar; (evident) sichtlich; visibly adv sichtlich

vision n (power of sight) Sehvermögen nt; (foresight) Weitblick m; (dream, image) Vision f

visit 1. n Besuch m; (stay) Aufenthalt m 2. vt besuchen; visiting hours npl Besuchszeiten pl; visitor n Besucher(in) m(f); ~**s' book** Gästebuch nt

visual adj Seh-; (image, joke) visuell; visualize vt sich vorstelle; visually adv visuell; ~ **impaired** sehbehindert

vital adj (essential) unerlässlich, wesentlich; (argument, moment) entscheidend; vitality n Vitalität f; vitally adv äußerst

vitamin n Vitamin nt

vivid adj (description) anschaulich; (memory) lebhaft

V-neck n V-Ausschnitt m

vocabulary n Wortschatz m, Vokabular nt

vocal adj (of the voice) Stimm-; (group) Gesangs-; (protest, person) lautstark

vocation n Berufung f; vocational adj Berufs-

vodka n Wodka m

voice 1. n Stimme f 2. vt äußern; voice mail n Voicemail f

void 1. n Leere f 2. adj LAW ungültig

volcano n Vulkan m

volt n Volt nt; voltage n Spannung f

volume n (of sound) Lautstärke f; (space occupied by sth) Volumen nt; (size, amount) Umfang m; (book) Band m; volume control n Lautstärkeregler m

voluntary, voluntarily adj, adv freiwillig; (unpaid) ehrenamtlich; volunteer 1. n Freiwillige(r) mf 2. vi sich freiwillig melden

voluptuous adj sinnlich

vomit vi sich übergeben

vote 1. n Stimme f; (ballot) Wahl f; (result) Abstimmungsergebnis nt; (right to vote) Wahlrecht nt 2. vt (elect) wählen; **they** ~**d him chairman** sie wählten ihn zum Vorsitzenden 3. vi wählen; ~ **for/against sth** für/gegen etw stimmen; voter n Wähler(in) m(f)

voucher n Gutschein m

vow n Gelöbnis f

vowel n Vokal m

voyage n Reise f

vulgar *adj* vulgär, ordinär

vulnerable *adj* verwundbar; *(sensitive)* verletzlich

vulture *n* Geier *m*

W

wade *vi (in water)* waten

wafer *n* Waffel *f*; REL Hostie *f*; **wafer-thin** *adj* hauchdünn

waffle *n* Waffel *f*; *(Brit) fam (empty talk)* Geschwafel *nt*

wag *vt (tail)* wedeln mit

wage *n* Lohn *m*

waggon *(Brit)*, **wagon** *n (horse-drawn)* Fuhrwerk *nt*; *(Brit)* RAIL Waggon *m*; *(US)* AUTO Wagen *m*

waist *n* Taille *f*; **waistcoat** *n (Brit)* Weste *f*; **waistline** *n* Taille *f*

wait 1. *n* Wartezeit *f* **2.** *vi* warten *(for* auf + *acc)*; *~ and see* abwarten; *~ a minute* Moment mal!; **wait up** *vi* aufbleiben

waiter *n* Kellner *m*

waiting *n* **'no ~'** "Halteverbot"; **waiting list** *n* Warteliste *f*; **waiting room** *n* MED Wartezimmer *nt*; RAIL Wartesaal *m*

waitress *n* Kellnerin *f*

wake 1. *vt* wecken **2.** *vi* aufwachen; **wake up 1.** *vt* aufwecken **2.** *vi* aufwachen; **wake-up call** *n* TEL Weckruf *m*

Wales *n* Wales *nt*

walk 1. *n* Spaziergang *m*; *(ramble)* Wanderung *f*; *(route)* Weg *m*; *go for a ~* spazieren gehen; *it's only a five-minute ~* es sind nur fünf Minuten zu Fuß **2.** *vi* gehen; *(stroll)* spazieren gehen; *(ramble)* wandern **3.** *vt (dog)* ausführen; **walking** *n* **go ~** wandern; **walking shoes** *npl* Wanderschuhe *pl*

wall *n (inside)* Wand *f*; *(outside)* Mauer *f*

wallet *n* Brieftasche *f*

wallpaper 1. *n* Tapete *f*; IT Bildschirmhintergrund *m* **2.** *vt* tapezieren

walnut *n (nut)* Walnuss *f*

waltz *n* Walzer *m*

wander *vi (person)* herumwandern

want 1. *n (lack)* Mangel *m (of* an + *dat)*; *(need)* Bedürfnis *nt*; *for ~ of* aus Mangel an + *dat* **2.** *vt (desire)* wollen; *(need)* brauchen; *he doesn't ~ to* er will nicht

WAP phone *n* WAP-Handy *nt*

war *n* Krieg *m*

ward *n (in hospital)* Station *f*; *(child)* Mündel *nt*

warden *n* Aufseher(in) *m(f)*; *(in youth hostel)* Herbergsvater *m*, Herbergsmutter *f*

wardrobe *n* Kleiderschrank *m*

warehouse n Lagerhaus nt
warfare n Krieg m; (techniques) Kriegsführung f
warm 1. adj warm; (welcome) herzlich; **I'm ~** mir ist warm **2.** vt wärmen; (food) aufwärmen; **warm over** vi (US, food) aufwärmen; **warm up 1.** vt (food) aufwärmen; (room) erwärmen **2.** vi (food, room) warm werden; SPORT sich aufwärmen; **warmly** adv warm; (welcome) herzlich; **warmth** n Wärme f; (of welcome) Herzlichkeit f
warn vt warnen (of, against vor + dat); **~ sb not to do sth** jdn davor warnen, etw zu tun; **warning** n Warnung f; **warning light** n Warnlicht nt; **warning triangle** n AUTO Warndreieck nt
warranty n Garantie f
wart n Warze f
wary adj vorsichtig; (suspicious) misstrauisch
was pt of **be**
wash 1. n **have a ~** sich waschen; **it's in the ~** es ist in der Wäsche **2.** vt waschen; (plates, glasses etc) abwaschen; **~ the dishes** (das Geschirr) abwaschen **3.** vi (clean oneself) sich waschen; **wash off** vt abwaschen; **wash up** vi (Brit, wash dishes) abwaschen; (US, clean oneself) sich waschen; **washable** adj waschbar;

washbag n (US) Kulturbeutel m; **washbasin** n Waschbecken nt; **washcloth** n (US) Waschlappen m; **washer** n TECH Dichtungsring m; (washing machine) Waschmaschine f; **washing** n (laundry) Wäsche f; **washing machine** n Waschmaschine f; **washing powder** n Waschpulver nt; **washing-up** n (Brit) Abwasch m; **do the ~** abwaschen; **washing-up liquid** n (Brit) Spülmittel m; **washroom** n (US) Toilette f
wasn't contr of **was not**
wasp n Wespe f
waste 1. n (materials) Abfall m; (wasting) Verschwendung f; **it's a ~ of time** das ist Zeitverschwendung **2.** adj (superfluous) überschüssig **3.** vt verschwenden (on an + acc); (opportunity) vertun; **waste bin** n Abfalleimer m; **wastepaper basket** n Papierkorb m
watch 1. n (timepiece) (Armband)uhr f **2.** vt (observe) beobachten; (guard) aufpassen auf + acc; (film, play, programme) sich dat ansehen; **~ TV** fernsehen **3.** vi zusehen; (guard) Wache halten; **~ for sb/sth** nach jdm/etw Ausschau halten; **~ out** pass auf!; **watchdog** n Wachhund m; **watchful** adj wachsam
water 1. n Wasser nt; **~ spl** (ter-

ritory) Gewässer *pl* **2.** *vt* (*plant*) gießen **3.** *vi* (*eye*) tränen; *my mouth is ~ing* mir läuft das Wasser im Mund zusammen; *water down vt* verdünnen; **watercolor** (*US*), **watercolour** *n* (*painting*) Aquarell *nt*; (*paint*) Wasserfarbe *f*; **watercress** *n* (*Brunnen*)*kresse f*; **waterfall** *n* Wasserfall *m*; **watering can** *n* Gießkanne *f*; **water level** *n* Wasserstand *m*; **watermelon** *n* Wassermelone *f*; **waterproof** *adj* wasserdicht; **water-skiing** *n* Wasserskilaufen *nt*; **water sports** *npl* Wassersport *m*; **watertight** *adj* wasserdicht; **water wings** *npl* Schwimmflügel *pl*; **watery** *adj* wässrig

wave 1. *n* Welle *f* **2.** *vt* (*move to and fro*) schwenken; (*hand, flag*) winken mit **3.** *vi* (*person*) winken; (*flag*) wehen; **wavelength** *n* Wellenlänge *f*; **wavy** *adj* wellig

wax *n* Wachs *nt*; (*in ear*) Ohrenschmalz *m*

way *n* Weg *m*; (*direction*) Richtung *f*; (*manner*) Art *f*; *can you tell me the ~ to ...* ? wie komme ich (am besten) zu ... ?; *we went the wrong ~* wir sind in die falsche Richtung gefahren/gegangen; *lose one's ~* sich verirren; *make ~ for sb/ sth* jdm/etw Platz machen; *get one's own ~* seinen Wil-

len durchsetzen; *'give ~'* AUTO „Vorfahrt achten"; *the other ~ round* andersherum; *one ~ or another* irgendwie; *in a ~* in gewisser Weise; *in the ~* im Weg; *by the ~* übrigens; *'~ in'* „Eingang"; *'~ out'* „Ausgang"; *no ~ fam* kommt nicht infrage!

we *pron* wir

weak *adj* schwach; **weaken 1.** *vt* schwächen **2.** *vi* schwächer werden

wealth *n* Reichtum *m*; **wealthy** *adj* reich

weapon *n* Waffe *f*

wear 1. *vt* (*have on*) tragen **2.** *vi* (*become worn*) sich abnutzen **3.** *n ~* (*and tear*) Abnutzung *f*; **wear off** *vi* (*diminish*) nachlassen; **wear out 1.** *vt* abnutzen; (*person*) erschöpfen **2.** *vi* sich abnutzen

weary *adj* müde

weather *n* Wetter *nt*; **weather forecast** *n* Wettervorhersage *f*

weave *vt* (*cloth*) weben; (*basket etc*) flechten

web *n a.* fig Netz *nt*; **the Web** das Web, das Internet; **webcam** *n* Webcam *f*; **web page** *n* Webseite *f*; **website** *n* Website *f*

we'd *contr* of *we had*; *we would*

Wed *abbr* = **Wednesday**; Mi.

wedding *n* Hochzeit *f*; **wedding anniversary** *n* Hochzeitstag *m*; **wedding dress**

n Hochzeitskleid *nt*; wedding ring *n* Ehering *m*; wedding shower *n* (*US*) Party für die zukünftige Braut

wedge *n* (*under door etc*) Keil *m*; (*of cheese etc*) Stück *nt*, Ecke *f*

Wednesday *n* Mittwoch *m*; → **Tuesday**

wee *adj*, klein

weed 1. *n* Unkraut *nt* 2. *vt* jäten

week *n* Woche *f*; **twice a ~** zweimal in der Woche; **a ~ on Friday/Friday ~** Freitag in einer Woche; **in two ~s' time, in two ~s** in zwei Wochen; **weekday** *n* Wochentag *m*; **weekend** *n* Wochenende *nt*; **weekly** *adj*, *adv* wöchentlich; (*magazine*) Wochen-

weep *vi* weinen

weigh *vt*, *vi* wiegen; weigh up *vt* abwägen; (*person*) einschätzen; **weight** *n* Gewicht *nt*; **lose/put on ~** abnehmen/zunehmen; **weightlifting** *n* Gewichtheben *nt*; **weight training** *n* Krafttraining *nt*

weird *adj* seltsam; **weirdo** *n* Spinner(in) *m*(*f*)

welcome 1. *n* Empfang *m* 2. *adj* willkommen; (*news*) angenehm; **~ to London** willkommen in London! 3. *vt* begrüßen; **welcoming** *adj* freundlich

welfare *n* Wohl *nt*; (*US*, *social security*) Sozialhilfe *f*; welfare state *n* Wohlfahrtsstaat *m*

well 1. *n* Brunnen *m* 2. *adj* (*in good health*) gesund; **are you ~?** geht es dir gut?; **feel ~, I don't know** nun, ich weiß nicht 4. *adv* gut; **~ done** gut gemacht!; **it may ~ be** das kann wohl sein; **as ~** (*in addition*) auch; **~ over 60** weit über 60

we'll *contr of* **we will; we shall**

well-behaved *adj* brav; **well--done** *adj* (*steak*) durchgebraten

wellingtons *npl* Gummistiefel *pl*

well-known *adj* bekannt; **well-off** *adj* (*wealthy*) wohlhabend; **well-paid** *adj* gut bezahlt

Welsh 1. *adj* walisisch 2. *n* (*language*) Walisisch *nt*; **the ~ pl** die Waliser *pl*; **Welshman** *n* Waliser *m*; **Welshwoman** *n* Waliserin *f*

went *pt of* **go**

wept *pt*, *pp of* **weep**

were *pt of* **be**

we're *contr of* **we are**

weren't *contr of* **were not**

west 1. *n* Westen *m* 2. *adv* (*go*, *face*) nach Westen 3. *adj* West-; **westbound** *adj* (*in*) Richtung Westen; **western** 1. *adj* West-, westlich; **Western Europe** Westeuropa *nt* 2. *n* FILM Western *m*; **West Germany** *n* Westdeutschland *nt*;

whistle

westwards *adv* nach Westen

wet 1. *vt* ~ **oneself** in die Hose machen 2. *adj* nass, feucht; '~ **paint**' „frisch gestrichen"; wet suit *n* Taucheranzug *m*

we've *contr of* **we have**

whale *n* Wal *m*

wharf *n* Kai *m*

what 1. *pron, interj* was; ~**'s your name?** wie heißt du?; ~ **is the letter about?** worum geht es in dem Brief?; ~ **are they talking about?** worüber reden sie?; ~ **for?** wozu? 2. *adj* welche(r, s); ~ **colour is it?** welche Farbe hat es?; *whatever pron* **I'll do** ~ **you want** ich tue alles, was du willst; ~ **he says** egal, was er sagt

what's *contr of* **what is; what has**

wheat *n* Weizen *m*

wheel 1. *n* Rad *nt*; (*steering wheel*) Lenkrad *nt* 2. *vt* (*bicycle, trolley*) schieben; wheelchair *n* Rollstuhl *m*; wheel clamp *n* Parkkralle *f*

when 1. *adv* (*in questions*) wann; ~ **on the day** ~ an dem Tag, als 2. *conj* wenn; (*in past*) als; ~ **I was younger** als ich jünger war; *whenever adv* (*every time*) immer wenn; **come** ~ **you like** komm wann immer du willst

where 1. *adv* wo; ~ **are you going?** wohin gehst du?; ~ **are you from?** woher kommst du? 2. *conj* wo; **that's I**

used to live da habe ich früher gewohnt; *whereabouts* 1. *adv* wo 2. *npl* Aufenthaltsort *m*; *whereas conj* während, wohingegen; *wherever conj* wo immer; ~ **that may be** wo immer das sein mag

whether *conj* ob

which 1. *adj* welche(r, s); ~ **car is yours?** welches Auto gehört dir?; ~ **one?** welche(r, s)? 2. *pron* (*in questions*) welche(r, s); (*in relative clauses*) der/die/das, *pl* die; **it rained,** ~ **upset his plans** es regnete, was seine Pläne durcheinander brachte; *whichever adj, pron* welche(r, s) auch immer

while 1. *n a* ~ eine Weile; **for a** ~ eine Zeit lang; **a short** ~ **ago** vor kurzem 2. *conj* während; (*although*) obwohl

whine *vi* (*person*) jammern

whip 1. *n* Peitsche *f* 2. *vt* (*beat*) peitschen; ~**ped cream** Schlagsahne *f*

whirl *vt, vi* herumwirbeln; *whirlpool n* (*in river, sea*) Strudel *m*; (*pool*) Whirlpool *m*

whisk 1. *n* Schneebesen *m* 2. *vt* (*cream etc*) schlagen

whisker *n* (*of animal*) Schnurrhaar *nt*; ~**s** *pl* (*of man*) Backenbart *m*

whisk(e)y *n* Whisky *m*

whisper *vi, vt* flüstern

whistle 1. *n* Pfiff *m*, Pfeife *f* 2. *vt, vi* pfeifen

white 1. n (of egg) Eiweiß nt; (of eye) Weiße n **2.** adj weiß; (with fear) blass; (coffee) mit Milch

white lie n Notlüge f; **white meat** n helles Fleisch; **white water rafting** n Rafting nt; **white wine** n Weißwein m

Whitsun n Pfingsten nt

who pron (in questions) wer; (in relative clauses) der/ die/ das, die pl; **do you see?** wen hast du gesehen?; **~ does that belong to?** wem gehört das?; **the people ~ live next door** die Leute, die nebenan wohnen; **whoever** pron wer auch immer; **~ you choose** wen auch immer du wählst

whole 1. adj ganz **2.** n Ganze(s) nt; **the ~ of my family** meine ganze Familie; **on the ~** im Großen und Ganzen; **wholefood** n (Brit) Vollwertkost f; **wholeheartedly** adv voll und ganz; **wholemeal** adj (Brit) Vollkorn-; **wholesale** adv (buy, sell) im Großhandel; **wholesome** adj gesund; **wholewheat** adj Vollkorn-; **wholly** adv völlig

whom pron (in questions) wen; (in relative clauses) den/ die/ das, die pl; **with ~ did you speak?** mit wem haben Sie gesprochen?

whooping cough n Keuchhusten m

whose 1. adj (in questions)

wessen; (in relative clauses) dessen/ deren/ dessen, deren pl **2.** pron (in questions) wessen; **~ is this?** wem gehört das?

why adv, conj warum; **that's ~** deshalb

wicked adj böse; fam (great) geil

wide 1. adj breit; (skirt, trousers) weit; (selection) groß **2.** adv wide-angle **lens** n Weitwinkelobjektiv nt; **wide-awake** adj hellwach; **widely** adv weit; **~ known** allgemein bekannt; **widen** vt verbreitern; fig erweitern; **wide-open** adj weit offen; **widescreen TV** n Breitbildfernseher m; **widespread** adj weit verbreitet

widow n Witwe f; **widowed** adj verwitwet; **widower** n Witwer m

width n Breite f

wife n (Ehe)frau f

wig n Perücke f

wild 1. adj wild; (violent) heftig; (plan, idea) verrückt **2.** n **in the ~** in freier Wildbahn; **wildlife** n Tier- und Pflanzenwelt f; **wildly** adv wild; (enthusiastic, exaggerated) maßlos

will 1. vaux he/ they **~ come** er wird/ sie werden kommen; **I won't be back until late** ich komme erst spät zurück; **the car won't start** das Auto will nicht anspringen; **~ you**

have some coffee? möchten Sie eine Tasse Kaffee? **2.** n Wille m; (wish) Wunsch m; (document) Testament nt; **willing** adj bereitwillig; **be ~ to do sth** bereit sein, etw zu tun; **willingly** adv gern(e)

willow n Weide f

wimp n Weichei nt

win 1. vt, vi gewinnen **2.** n Sieg m; **win over, win round** vt für sich gewinnen

wind (rope, bandage) wickeln; **wind down** vt (car window) herunterkurbeln; **wind up** vt (clock) aufziehen; (car window) hochkurbeln; (meeting, speech) abschließen; (person) aufziehen, ärgern

wind n Wind m; MED Blähungen pl

wind instrument n Blasinstrument nt; **windmill** n Windmühle f

window n Fenster nt; (counter) Schalter m; **windowpane** n Fensterscheibe f; **window-shopping** n **go ~** einen Schaufensterbummel machen; **windowsill** n Fensterbrett nt

windpipe n Luftröhre f; **windscreen** n (Brit) Windschutzscheibe f; **windscreen wiper** n (Brit) Scheibenwischer m; **windshield** n (US) Windschutzscheibe f; **windshield wiper** n (US) Scheibenwischer m; **wind-**

surfer n Windsurfer(in) m(f); (board) Surfbrett nt; **windsurfing** n Windsurfen nt

windy adj windig

wine n Wein m; **wine list** n Weinkarte f; **wine tasting** n (event) Weinprobe f

wing n Flügel m; (Brit) AUTO Kotflügel m

wink vi zwinkern; **~ at sb** jdm zuzwinkern

winner n Gewinner(in) m(f), Sieger(in) m(f); **winning 1.** adj (team, horse etc) siegreich **2. ~s** pl Gewinn m

winter n Winter m; **winter sports** npl Wintersport m; **wint(e)ry** adj winterlich

wipe vt abwischen; **~ one's nose** sich dat die Nase putzen; **wipe off** vt abwischen; **wipe out** vt (destroy) vernichten; (data, debt) löschen

wire 1. n Draht m; ELEC Leitung f; (US, telegram) Telegramm nt **2.** vt (plug in) anschließen; (US) TEL telegrafieren (sb sth jdm etw); **wireless** adj drahtlos

wisdom n Weisheit f; **wisdom tooth** n Weisheitszahn m

wise, wisely adj, adv weise

wish 1. n Wunsch m (for nach); **with best ~es** (in letter) herzliche Grüße **2.** vt wünschen, wollen; **~ sb good luck/Merry Christmas** jdm viel Glück/frohe

Weihnachten wünschen; **I ~ I'd never seen him** ich wünschte, ich hätte ihn nie gesehen

witch n Hexe f

with prep mit; (cause) vor + dat; **I'm pleased ~ it** ich bin damit zufrieden; **shiver ~ cold** vor Kälte zittern; **he lives ~ his aunt** er wohnt bei seiner Tante

withdraw irr **1.** vt zurückziehen; (money) abheben; (comment) zurücknehmen **2.** vi sich zurückziehen

wither vi (plant) verwelken

withhold irr vt vorenthalten (from sb jdm)

within prep innerhalb + gen; **~ walking distance** zu Fuß erreichbar

without prep ohne; **~ asking** ohne zu fragen

withstand irr vt standhalten + dat

witness 1. n Zeuge m, Zeugin f **2.** vt Zeuge sein

witty adj geistreich

wives pl of **wife**

wobble vi wackeln; **wobbly** adj wackelig

wok n Wok m

woke pt of **wake**

woken pp of **wake**

wolf n Wolf m

woman n Frau f

womb n Gebärmutter f

women pl of **woman**

won pt, pp of **win**

wonder 1. n (marvel) Wunder nt; (surprise) Staunen nt **2.** vt, vi (speculate) sich fragen; **I ~ what/if ...** ich frage mich, was/ob ...; **wonderful, wonderfully** adj, adv wunderbar

won't contr of **will not**

wood n Holz nt; **~s** Wald m; **wooden** adj Holz-; fig hölzern; **woodpecker** n Specht m

wool n Wolle f; **woollen, woolen** (US) adj Woll-

word 1. n Wort nt; (promise) Ehrenwort nt; **~s** pl (of song) Text m; **have a ~ with sb** mit jdm sprechen; **in other ~s** mit anderen Worten **2.** vt formulieren; **word processor** n (program) Textverarbeitungsprogramm nt

wore pt of **wear**

work 1. n Arbeit f; (of art, literature) Werk nt; **~ of art** Kunstwerk nt; **he's at ~** er ist in/auf der Arbeit; **out of ~** arbeitslos **2.** vi arbeiten (at, on an + dat); (machine, plan) funktionieren; (medicine, plan) wirken; (succeed) klappen **3.** vt (machine) bedienen; **work out 1.** vi (plan) klappen; (sum) aufgehen; (person) trainieren **2.** vt (price, speed etc) ausrechnen; (plan) ausarbeiten; **work up** vt **get worked up** sich aufregen; **workaholic** n Arbeitstier nt; **worker** n Arbeiter(in) m(f); **workman** n Handwerker m; **workout** n

SPORT Fitnesstraining *nt*, Konditionstraining *nt*; **work permit** *n* Arbeitserlaubnis *f*; **workplace** *n* Arbeitsplatz *m*; **workshop** *n* Werkstatt *f*; (*meeting*) Workshop *m*

world *n* Welt *f*; **world championship** *n* Weltmeisterschaft *f*; **World War** *n* ~ **I/II, the First/Second ~** der Erste/Zweite Weltkrieg; **world-wide** *adj, adv* weltweit; **World Wide Web** *n* World Wide Web *m*

worm *n* Wurm *m*

worn 1. *pp of* **wear** 2. *adj* (*clothes*) abgetragen; (*tyre*) abgefahren; **worn-out** *adj* abgenutzt; (*person*) erschöpft

worried *adj* besorgt; **worry** 1. *n* Sorge *f* 2. *vt* Sorgen machen + *dat* 3. *vi* sich Sorgen machen (*about* um); **don't** ~ keine Sorge!; **worrying** *adj* beunruhigend

worse 1. *adj comparative of* **bad**; schlechter; (*pain, mistake etc*) schlimmer 2. *adv comparative of* **badly**; schlechter; **worsen** 1. *vt* verschlechtern 2. *vi* sich verschlechtern

worship *vt* anbeten, anhimmeln

worst 1. *adj superlative of* **bad**; schlechteste(r, s); (*pain, mistake etc*) schlimmste(r, s) 2. *adv superlative of* **badly**; am schlechtesten 3. *n* **the ~**

is over das Schlimmste ist vorbei; **at** (**the**) ~ schlimmstenfalls

worth 1. *n* Wert *m* 2. *adj* **it is ~ £50** es ist 50 Pfund wert; ~ **seeing** sehenswert; **it's ~ it** (*rewarding*) es lohnt sich; **worthless** *adj* wertlos; **worthwhile** *adj* lohnend, lohnenswert; **worthy** *adj* (*deserving respect*) würdig; **be ~ of sth** etw verdienen

would *vaux* **if you asked he I ~ come** wenn Sie ihn fragten, würde er kommen; **I ~ have told you, but ...** ich hätte es dir gesagt, aber ...; ~ **you like a drink?** möchten Sie etwas trinken?; **he ~n't help me** er wollte mir nicht helfen

wouldn't *contr of* **would not**

would've *contr of* **would have**

wound 1. *n* Wunde *f* 2. *vt* verwunden, verletzen 3. *pt, pp of* **wind**

wove *pt of* **weave**

woven *pp of* **weave**

wrap *vt* (*parcel, present*) einwickeln; **wrap up** 1. *vt* (*parcel, present*) einwickeln 2. *vi* (*dress warmly*) sich warm anziehen; **wrapping paper** *n* Packpapier *nt*; (*giftwrap*) Geschenkpapier *nt*

wreath *n* Kranz *m*

wreck 1. *n* (*ship, plane, car*) Wrack *nt*; **a nervous ~** ein Nervenbündel *nt* 2. *vt* (*car*) zu Schrott fahren; *fig* zerstö-

ren; **wreckage** n Trümmer pl
wrench n (tool) Schraubenschlüssel m
wrestling n Ringen nt
wring out vt auswringen
wrinkle n Falte f
wrist n Handgelenk nt; **wrist-
watch** n Armbanduhr f
write 1. vt schreiben; (cheque)
ausstellen **2.** vi schreiben; ~
to sb jdm schreiben; **write
down** vt aufschreiben; **write
off** vt (debt, person) abschreiben; (car) zu Schrott fahren;
write out vt (name etc) ausschreiben; (cheque) ausstellen; **write-protected** adj IT
schreibgeschützt; **writer** n
Verfasser(in) m(f); (author)

Schriftsteller(in) m(f); **writing** n Schrift f; (profession)
Schreiben nt; **writing paper**
n Schreibpapier nt
written pp of **write**
wrong adj (incorrect) falsch;
(morally) unrecht; **you're ~**
du hast Unrecht; **what's ~
with your leg?** was ist mit
deinem Bein los?; **I dialled
the ~ number** ich habe mich
verwählt; **don't get me ~** versteh mich nicht falsch; **go ~**
(plan) schief gehen; **wrongly**
adv falsch; (unjustly) zu Unrecht
wrote pt of **write**
WWW abbr = **World Wide
Web**; WWW

X

xenophobia n Ausländer-
feindlichkeit f
XL abbr = **extra large**; XL,
übergroß

Xmas n Weihnachten nt
X-ray 1. n (picture) Röntgenaufnahme f **2.** vt röntgen
xylophone n Xylophon nt

Y

yacht n Jacht f; **yachting** n
Segeln nt
yard n Hof m; (US, garden)
Garten m; (measure) Yard
nt (0,91 m)
yawn vi gähnen
yd abbr = **yard**(s)
year n Jahr nt; **~s ago** vor Jahren; **a five-year-old** ein(e)

Fünfjährige(r); **yearly** adj,
adv jährlich
yearn vi sich sehnen (for nach
+ dat)
yeast n Hefe f
yell vi, vt schreien; **~ at sb** jdn
anschreien
yellow adj gelb; **~ fever** Gelb-
fieber nt; **the Yellow Pages**®

pl die Gelben Seiten *pl*

yes 1. *adv* ja; *(answering negative question)* doch; **say ~ to sth** ja zu etw sagen **2.** *n* Ja *nt*

yesterday *adv* gestern; **the day before ~** vorgestern; **~'s newspaper** die Zeitung von gestern

yet 1. *adv (still)* noch; *(up to now)* bis jetzt; *(in a question: already)* schon; **he hasn't arrived ~** er ist noch nicht gekommen; **have you finished ~?** bist du schon fertig?; **~ again** schon wieder; **as ~** bis jetzt **2.** *conj* doch

yield 1. *n* Ertrag *m* **2.** *vt (result, crop)* hervorbringen; *(profit, interest)* bringen **3.** *vi* nachgeben *(to + dat)*; MIL sich ergeben *(to + dat)*; **"~"** *(US)* AUTO „Vorfahrt beachten"

yoga *n* Joga *nt*

yog(h)urt *n* Jog(h)urt *m*

yolk *n* Eigelb *nt*

Yorkshire pudding *n* gebackener Eierteig, der meist zum Roastbeef gegessen wird

you 1. *pron (as subject)* du / Sie / ihr; *(as direct object)* dich / Sie / euch; *(as indirect object)* dir / Ihnen / ihnen; **~ never can tell** man weiß nie

you'd *contr of* **you had; you would; ~ better leave** du solltest gehen

you'll *contr of* **you will; you shall**

young *adj* jung; **youngster** *n* Jugendliche(r) *mf*

your *adj (sg)* dein; *(polite form)* Ihr; *(pl)* euer; *(polite form)* Ihr; **have you hurt ~ leg?** hast du dir das Bein verletzt?

you're *contr of* **you are**

yours *pron (sg)* deine(r, s); *(polite form)* Ihre(r, s); *(pl)* eure(r, s); *(polite form)* Ihre(r, s); **is this ~?** gehört das dir / Ihnen?; **a friend of ~** ein Freund von dir / Ihnen; **~ ...,** dein / deine ..., Ihr / Ihre ...

yourself *pron sg* dich; *(polite form)* sich; **have you hurt ~?** hast du dich / haben Sie sich verletzt?; **did you do it ~?** hast du es selbst gemacht?; **(all) by ~** allein; **yourselves** *pron sg* euch; *(polite form)* sich; **have you hurt ~?** habt ihr euch / haben Sie sich verletzt?

youth *n (period)* Jugend *f*; **youth hostel** *n* Jugendherberge *f*

you've *contr of* **you have**

yucky *adj fam* eklig

Yugoslavia *n hist* Jugoslawien *nt*

yummy *adj* lecker

Z

zap 1. *vt* IT löschen; (*in computer game*) abknallen **2.** *vi* TV zappen; **zapper** *n* TV Fernbedienung *f*

zebra (*US*) *n* Zebra *nt*; **zebra crossing** *n* (*Brit*) Zebrastreifen *m*

zero *n* Null *f*

zest *n* (*enthusiasm*) Begeisterung *f*

zigzag 1. *n* Zickzack *m* **2.** *vi* (*person, vehicle*) im Zickzack gehen / fahren

zinc *n* Zink *nt*

zip 1. *n* (*Brit*) Reißverschluss *m* **2.** *vt* ~ (**up**) den Reißverschluss zumachen; IT zippen;

zip code *n* (*US*) Postleitzahl *f*; **Zip disk®** *n* IT ZIP-Diskette® *f*; **Zip drive®** *n* IT ZIP-Laufwerk® *nt*; **Zip file®** *n* IT ZIP-Datei® *f*; **zipper** *n* (*US*) Reißverschluss *m*

zodiac *n* Tierkreis *m*; **sign of the ~** Tierkreiszeichen *nt*

zone *n* Zone *f*; (*area*) Gebiet *nt*; (*in town*) Bezirk *m*

zoo *n* Zoo *m*

zoom 1. *vi* (*move fast*) brausen, sausen **2.** *n* ~ (**lens**) Zoomobjektiv *nt*; **zoom in** *vi* PHOT heranzoomen (*on* an + *acc*)

zucchini *n* (*US*) Zucchini *f*

Anhang

German irregular verbs

backen	backte	hat gebacken
befehlen	befahl	hat befohlen
beginnen	begann	hat begonnen
beißen	biss	hat gebissen
bergen	barg	hat geborgen
betrügen	betrog	hat betrogen
biegen	bog	hat/ist gebogen
bieten	bot	hat geboten
binden	band	hat gebunden
bitten	bat	hat gebeten
blasen	blies	hat geblasen
bleiben	blieb	ist geblieben
braten	briet	hat gebraten
brechen	brach	hat/ist gebrochen
brennen	brannte	hat gebrannt
bringen	brachte	hat gebracht
denken	dachte	hat gedacht
dringen	drang	ist gedrungen
dürfen	durfte	hat gedurft
empfangen	empfing	hat empfangen
empfehlen	empfahl	hat empfohlen
empfinden	empfand	hat empfunden
erschrecken	erschrak	ist erschrocken
essen	aß	hat gegessen
fahren	fuhr	hat/ist gefahren
fallen	fiel	ist gefallen
fangen	fing	hat gefangen
finden	fand	hat gefunden
flechten	flocht	hat geflochten
fliegen	flog	hat/ist geflogen
fließen	floss	ist geflossen
fressen	fraß	hat gefressen
frieren	fror	hat gefroren
geben	gab	hat gegeben
gehen	ging	ist gegangen
gelingen	gelang	ist gelungen
gelten	galt	hat gegolten

genießen	genoss	hat genossen
geschehen	geschah	ist geschehen
gewinnen	gewann	hat gewonnen
gießen	goss	hat gegossen
gleichen	glich	hat geglichen
gleiten	glitt	ist geglitten
graben	grub	hat gegraben
greifen	griff	hat gegriffen
haben	hatte	hat gehabt
halten	hielt	hat gehalten
hängen	hing	hat gehangen
hauen	haute	hat gehauen
heißen	hieß	hat geheißen
helfen	half	hat geholfen
kennen	kannte	hat gekannt
klingen	klang	hat geklungen
kneifen	kniff	hat gekniffen
kommen	kam	ist gekommen
können	konnte	hat gekonnt
kriechen	kroch	ist gekrochen
laden	lud	hat geladen
lassen	ließ	hat gelassen
laufen	lief	ist gelaufen
leiden	litt	hat gelitten
leihen	lieh	hat geliehen
lesen	las	hat gelesen
liegen	lag	hat gelegen
lügen	log	hat gelogen
mahlen	mahlte	hat gemahlen
meiden	mied	hat gemieden
messen	maß	hat gemessen
misslingen	misslang	ist misslungen
mögen	mochte	hat gemocht
müssen	musste	hat gemusst
nehmen	nahm	hat genommen
nennen	nannte	hat genannt
pfeifen	pfiff	hat gepfiffen
raten	riet	hat geraten
reiben	rieb	hat gerieben
reißen	riss	hat/ist gerissen

reiten	ritt	hat/ist geritten
rennen	rannte	ist gerannt
riechen	roch	hat gerochen
ringen	rang	hat gerungen
rufen	rief	hat gerufen
salzen	salzte	hat gesalzen
saufen	soff	hat gesoffen
saugen	sog/saugte	hat gesogen/gesaugt
schaffen	schuf	hat geschaffen
scheiden	schied	hat/ist geschieden
scheinen	schien	hat geschienen
scheißen	schiss	hat geschissen
schieben	schob	hat geschoben
schießen	schoss	hat/ist geschossen
schlafen	schlief	hat geschlafen
schlagen	schlug	hat geschlagen
schleichen	schlich	ist geschlichen
schleifen	schliff	hat geschliffen
schließen	schloss	hat geschlossen
schmeißen	schmiss	hat geschmissen
schmelzen	schmolz	ist geschmolzen
schneiden	schnitt	hat geschnitten
schreiben	schrieb	hat geschrieben
schreien	schrie	hat geschrie(e)n
schweigen	schwieg	hat geschwiegen
schwimmen	schwamm	hat/ist geschwommen
schwören	schwor	hat geschworen
sehen	sah	hat gesehen
sein	war	ist gewesen
senden	sandte	hat gesandt
singen	sang	hat gesungen
sinken	sank	ist gesunken
sitzen	saß	hat gesessen
spinnen	spann	hat gesponnen
sprechen	sprach	hat gesprochen
springen	sprang	ist gesprungen
stechen	stach	hat gestochen
stehen	stand	hat gestanden
stehlen	stahl	hat gestohlen
steigen	stieg	ist gestiegen

sterben	starb	ist gestorben
stinken	stank	hat gestunken
stoßen	stieß	hat/ist gestoßen
streichen	strich	hat gestrichen
streiten	stritt	hat gestritten
tragen	trug	hat getragen
treffen	traf	hat getroffen
treiben	trieb	hat getrieben
treten	trat	hat/ist getreten
trinken	trank	hat getrunken
tun	tat	hat getan
überwinden	überwand	hat überwunden
verderben	verdarb	hat/ist verdorben
vergessen	vergaß	hat vergessen
verlieren	verlor	hat verloren
verschwinden	verschwand	ist verschwunden
verzeihen	verzieh	hat verziehen
wachsen	wuchs	ist gewachsen
waschen	wusch	hat gewaschen
weisen	wies	hat gewiesen
wenden	wendete/wandte	hat gewandt/gewendet
werben	warb	hat geworben
werden	wurde	ist geworden
werfen	warf	hat geworfen
wiegen	wog	hat gewogen
wissen	wusste	hat gewusst
ziehen	zog	hat/ist gezogen
zwingen	zwang	hat gezwungen

Numbers

Cardinal Numbers

0	null *zero, nought*	**30**	dreißig *thirty*
1	eins *one*	**40**	vierzig *forty*
2	zwei *two*	**50**	fünfzig *fifty*
3	drei *three*	**60**	sechzig *sixty*
4	vier *four*	**70**	siebzig *seventy*
5	fünf *five*	**80**	achtzig *eighty*
6	sechs *six*	**90**	neunzig *ninety*
7	sieben *seven*	**100**	(ein)hundert *a/one hundred*
8	acht *eight*	**101**	hundert(und)eins *a hundred and one*
9	neun *nine*	**200**	zweihundert *two hundred*
10	zehn *ten*	**572**	fünfhundert(und)zweiundsiebzig *five hundred and seventy-two*
11	elf *eleven*		
12	zwölf *twelve*	**1000**	(ein)tausend *a/one thousand*
13	dreizehn *thirteen*	**1998**	*as year:* neunzehnhundertachtundneunzig *nineteen (hundred and) ninety-eight*
14	vierzehn *fourteen*		
15	fünfzehn *fifteen*		
16	sechzehn *sixteen*		
17	siebzehn *seventeen*		
18	achtzehn *eighteen*	**2000**	zweitausend *two thousand*
19	neunzehn *nineteen*	**2010**	*as year:* zweitausendzehn *two thousand (and) ten*
20	zwanzig *twenty*		
21	einundzwanzig *twenty-one*	**61 48 25**	*as phone number:* einundsechzig achtundvierzig fünfundzwanzig *six one four eight two five*
22	zweiundzwanzig *twenty-two*		
23	dreiundzwanzig *twenty-three*		
24	vierundzwanzig *twenty-four*		
25	fünfundzwanzig *twenty-five*		
26	sechsundzwanzig *twenty-six*		
27	siebenundzwanzig *twenty-seven*	**1,000,000**	eine Million *a/one million*
28	achtundzwanzig *twenty-eight*	**2,000,000**	zwei Millionen *two million*
29	neunundzwanzig *twenty-nine*	**1,000,000,000**	eine Milliarde *a/one billion*

Ordinal numbers

1.	erste *first*	**29.**	neunundzwanzigste *twenty-ninth*
2.	zweite *second*	**30.**	dreißigste *thirtieth*
3.	dritte *third*	**40.**	vierzigste *fortieth*
4.	vierte *fourth*	**50.**	fünfzigste *fiftieth*
5.	fünfte *fifth*	**60.**	sechzigste *sixtieth*
6.	sechste *sixth*	**70.**	siebzigste *seventieth*
7.	siebte *seventh*	**80.**	achtzigste *eightieth*
8.	achte *eighth*	**90.**	neunzigste *ninetieth*
9.	neunte *ninth*	**100.**	(ein)hundertste *(one) hundredth*
10.	zehnte *tenth*	**101.**	hundert(und)erste *(one) hundred and first*
11.	elfte *eleventh*	**200.**	zweihundertste *two hundredth*
12.	zwölfte *twelfth*	**572.**	fünfhundert(und)zweiundsiebzigste *five hundred and seventy-second*
13.	dreizehnte *thirteenth*	**1000.**	tausendste *(one) thousandth*
14.	vierzehnte *fourteenth*	**1998.**	neunzehnhundert(und)achtundneunzigste *nineteen hundred and ninety-ninth*
15.	fünfzehnte *fifteenth*	**2000.**	zweitausendste *two thousandth*
16.	sechzehnte *sixteenth*	**500 000.**	fünfhunderttausendste *five hundred thousandth*
17.	siebzehnte *seventeenth*	**1 000 000.**	millionste *(one) millionth*
18.	achtzehnte *eighteenth*	**2 000 000.**	zweimillionste *two millionth*
19.	neunzehnte *nineteenth*		
20.	zwanzigste *twentieth*		
21.	einundzwanzigste *twenty-first*		
22.	zweiundzwanzigste *twenty-second*		
23.	dreiundzwanzigste *twenty-third*		
24.	vierundzwanzigste *twenty-fourth*		
25.	fünfundzwanzigste *twenty-fifth*		
26.	sechsundzwanzigste *twenty-sixth*		
27.	siebenundzwanzigste *twenty-seventh*		
28.	achtundzwanzigste *twenty-eighth*		

Fractions, decimals and
mathematical calculation methods

½	ein halb *one/a half*
½ m	eine halbe Meile *half a mile*
1 ½	anderthalb/eineinhalb *one and a half*
2 ½	zweieinhalb *two and a half*
⅓	ein Drittel *one/a third*
⅔	zwei Drittel *two thirds*
¼	ein Viertel *one fourth, one/a quarter*
¾	drei Viertel *three fourths, three quarters*
⅕	ein Fünftel *one/a fifth*
3 ⅘	drei vier Fünftel *three and four fifths*
0,4	null Komma vier *point four (.4)*
2,5	zwei Komma fünf *two point five (2.5)*
1x	ein mal *once*
2x	zwei mal *twice*
3x	drei mal *three times*
4x	vier mal *four times*
7 + 8 = 15	sieben plus acht ist fünfzehn *seven plus eight is fifteen*
10 − 3 = 7	zehn minus drei ist sieben *ten minus three is seven*
2 x 3 = 6	zwei mal drei ist sechs/zwei multipliziert mit drei ist sechs *two times three is six/two multiplied by three is six*
20 : 5 = 4	zwanzig (dividiert) durch fünf ist vier *twenty divided by five is four*

European currency

Germany and Austria

1 euro (€) = 100 cent (ct)

coins	banknotes
1 ct	€ 5
2 ct	€ 10
5 ct	€ 20
10 ct	€ 50
20 ct	€ 100
50 ct	€ 200
€ 1	€ 500
€ 2	

Switzerland

1 Swiss franc (Sfr) = 100 Rappen (Rp) / centimes (c)

coins	banknotes
1 Rp	10 Sfr
5 Rp	20 Sfr
10 Rp	50 Sfr
20 Rp	100 Sfr
½ Sfr (50 Rp)	200 Sfr
1 Sfr	1,000 Sfr
2 Sfr	
5 Sfr	

States of the Federal Republic of Germany

Baden-Württemberg	Baden-Württemberg
Bayern	Bavaria
Berlin	Berlin
Brandenburg	Brandenburg
Bremen	Bremen
Hamburg	Hamburg
Hessen	Hesse
Mecklenburg-Vorpommern	Mecklenburg-Western Pomerania
Niedersachsen	Lower Saxony
Nordrhein-Westfalen	North Rhine-Westphalia
Rheinland-Pfalz	Rhineland-Palatinate
Saarland	*das Saarland* the Saarland
Sachsen	Saxony
Sachsen-Anhalt	Saxony-Anhalt
Schleswig-Holstein	Schleswig-Holstein
Thüringen	Thuringia

States of the Republic of Austria

Burgenland	*das Burgenland* the Burgenland
Kärnten	Carinthia
Niederösterreich	Lower Austria
Oberösterreich	Upper Austria
Salzburg	Salzburg
Steiermark	*die Steiermark* Styria
Tirol	Tyrol
Voralrberg	Vorarlberg
Wien	Vienna

Cantons of the Swiss Confederation

Aargau	*der Aargau* the Aargau
Appenzell	Appenzell
Basel	Basel, Basle
Bern	Bern(e)
Freiburg	*French* Fribourg Fribourg
Genf	*French* Genève Geneva
Glarus	Glarus
Graubünden	Graubünden, Grisons
Jura	*der Jura* the Jura
Luzern	Lucerne

Neuenburg	*French* Neuchâtel Neuchâtel
Nidwalden	Nidwalden
Obwalden	Obwalden
Schaffhausen	Schaffhausen
Schwyz	Schwyz
Solothurn	Solothurn
St. Gallen	St Gallen, St Gall
Tessin	*Italian* Ticino **das Tessin** the Ticino
Thurgau	**der Thurgau** the Thurgau
Unterwalden	Unterwalden
Uri	Uri
Waadt	*French* Vaud Vaud
Wallis	*French* Valais **das Wallis**
	the Valais, Wallis
Zug	Zug
Zürich	Zurich

Temperatures

	°F (Fahrenheit)	°C (Celsius)
	400°	204°
	350°	177°
	300°	149°
boiling point	212°	100°
	100°	38°
	80°	27°
	60°	16°
	40°	4°
freezing point	32°	0°
	20°	− 7°
	0°	−18°

How to convert Celsius into Fahrenheit and vice versa

To convert Celsius into Fahrenheit

multiply by 9, divide by 5 and add 32.

To convert Fahrenheit into Celsius

subtract 32, multiply by 5 and divide by 9.

Weights and measures

Length

1 mm	(*Millimeter* millimeter/millimetre)
	= 0.039 inches
1 cm	(*Zentimeter* centimeter/centimetre)
	= 10 mm = 0.39 inches
1 m	(*Meter* meter/metre)
	=100 cm = 1.094 yards
	= 3.28 feet = 39.37 inches
1 km	(*Kilometer* kilometer/kilometre)
	= 1000 m 1094 yards = 0.62 miles

1 in (inch)	= 2.54 cm	
1 ft (foot)	= 12 inches	= 30.48 cm
1 yd (yard)	= 3 feet	= 91.4 cm
1 m (mile)	= 1760 yards	= 1.61 km

Volume capacity

1 l (*Liter* liter/litre)	= 2.11 pints (*US*)
	= 1.06 quarts (*US*)
	= 0.26 gallons (*US*)
	= 1.76 pints (*Brit*)
	= 0.88 quarts (*Brit*)
	= 0.22 gallons (*Brit*)
1 pint (*US*)	= 0.472 l
1 pint (*Brit*)	= 0.567 l
1 quart (*US*)	= 0.945 l
1 quart (*Brit*)	= 1.136 l
1 gallon (*US*)	= 3.785 l
1 gallon (*Brit*)	= 4.54 l

Weight

1 g (*Gramm* gram/gramme)
  = 15.432 grains

1 Pfd (*Pfund* (German) pound)
  = 500 g
  = 1.102 pounds avoirdupois
  = 1.34 pounds troy

1 kg (*Kilogramm, Kilo* kilogram/kilogramme)
  = 1000 g
  = 2.204 pounds avoirdupois

1 Ztr (*Zentner* centner)
  = 100 Pfd
  = 50 kg
  = 110.23 pounds avoirdupois
  = 1.102 US hundredweights
  = 0.98 British hundredweights

1 t (*Tonne* ton)
  = 1000 kg
  = 1.102 US tons
  = 0.984 British tons

1 ton (of 2240 pounds)
  = 1.01605 metric tonnes
  = 1016.05 kilograms/kilogrammes

1 pound
  = 0.4536 kilograms/kilogrammes
  = 453.6 grams/grammes

1 ounce avoirdupois
  = 28.3495 grams/grammes

1 ounce troy
  = 31.1035 grams/grammes

1 grain
  = 0.0648 grams/grammes